TO
BESIEGE
A CITY

OSPREY
PUBLISHING

DEDICATION
For Debbie

TO
BESIEGE
A CITY

LENINGRAD 1941–42

PRIT
BUTTAR

OSPREY PUBLISHING
Bloomsbury Publishing Plc
Kemp House, Chawley Park, Cumnor Hill, Oxford OX2 9PH, UK
29 Earlsfort Terrace, Dublin 2, Ireland
1385 Broadway, 5th Floor, New York, NY 10018, USA
E-mail: info@ospreypublishing.com
www.ospreypublishing.com

OSPREY is a trademark of Osprey Publishing Ltd

First published in Great Britain in 2023

A catalogue record for this book is available from the British Library.

ISBN: HB 978 1 4728 5655 5; PB 978 1 4728 5656 2; eBook 978 1 4728 5654 8;
ePDF 978 1 4728 5653 1; XML 978 1 4728 5657 9

23 24 25 26 27 10 9 8 7 6 5 4 3 2 1

Plate section image credits are given in full in the List of Illustrations (pp. 7–9).
Maps by Prit Buttar
Index by Alan Rutter
Typeset by Deanta Global Publishing Services, Chennai, India
Printed and bound in Great Britain by CPI (Group) UK Ltd, Croydon CR0 4YY

Editor's note
For ease of comparison please refer to the following conversion table:
1 mile = 1.6km
1 yd = 0.9m
1 ft = 0.3m
1 in = 2.54cm/25.4mm
1 lb = 0.45kg

Osprey Publishing supports the Woodland Trust, the UK's leading woodland conservation charity.

To find out more about our authors and books visit www .ospreypublishing .com. Here you will find extracts, author interviews, details of forthcoming events and the option to sign up for our newsletter.

CONTENTS

LIST OF ILLUSTRATIONS

Hands off Leningrad! The illustrations and rhymed captions in this Soviet propaganda poster from 1941 present various failed attempts of aggression against Leningrad. (Photo by Fine Art Images/Heritage Images/Getty Images)

A view of Leningrad as seen from two and a half miles away at the front line near Uritz, September 1941. To the left can be seen St Isaac's Cathedral. (Photo by Hanns Hubmann/ullstein bild via Getty Images)

Soviet militia divisions were created using volunteers who came forward in large numbers to defeat the Germans, such as these men from the Kirov Factory. (Photo by: Universal History Archive/Universal Images Group via Getty Images)

The Germans captured Shlisselburg (seen here) and Sinyavino on Lake Lagoda on 7 September 1941, cutting all land connections between Leningrad and the rest of the USSR. (Photo by Roger Viollet via Getty Images)

Occupation of a suburb of Leningrad by German infantrymen, September 1941. Residents try to save their belongings from the burning town. (Photo by ullstein bild via Getty Images)

Hooded and camouflaged spotters of a Soviet anti-aircraft gun detachment keep watch for enemy planes in a sunken look-out post at the approach to Leningrad. (Photo by Keystone/Getty Images)

The warship *Marat* (previously *Petropavlovsk*) provided valuable fire support for Red Army troops, but was sunk by Hans-Ulrich Rudel and Erwin Hentschel and another Ju 87 crew in September 1941. (Nik Cornish www.stavka.photos)

German soldiers occupying Soviet defence positions ahead of Leningrad, October 1941. (Photo by Heinrich Hoffmann/ullstein bild via Getty Images)

Leningrad inhabitants, including women of all ages, take shovels and picks to help defend their city to the last, October 1941. (Bettmann/Getty Images)

German troops fire heavy artillery, October 1941. Most of the shelling during the winter of 1941–42 deliberately targeted civilian targets and essential infrastructure such as water pumping stations. (Photo by ullstein bild via Getty Images)

German long range artillery shelling Kronstadt, the home of the Soviet Baltic Fleet, in October 1941. (Photo by Hanns Hubmann/ullstein bild via Getty Images)

This tram marked the deepest German penetration into Leningrad. The date given on the original caption sheet is 16 October 1941. (Nik Cornish www .stavka.photos)

Barrage balloons on Nevsky Prospekt, Leningrad, late 1941. The city's defences gave it a 'special, hard beauty' according to Major General Fedyuninsky. (From the fonds of the RGAKFD in Krasnogorsk via Stavka)

A ZPU 4M quadruple-barrelled anti-aircraft machine gun in front of St Isaac's Cathedral, Leningrad, winter 1941–42. The shortage of ammunition was problematic for such weapons. (Courtesy of TASS)

German infantry advance on Leningrad. The region over which the war would be fought was heavily forested and crisscrossed by waterways, small lakes and swamps. (Photo by Hulton Archive/Getty Images)

Soviet militia during the siege. Some of the volunteer formations would be transformed into regular army units. (Photo by D. Trakhtenberg/Slava Katamidze Collection/Getty Images)

Members of the Komsomol fire brigade Erna Kivi (right) and Galina Kuritsyna at a post organized on one of the roofs of Leningrad. (Nik Cornish www .stavka.photos)

A truck crossing the Road of Life over Lake Ladoga in 1942; the door is open to allow the driver to jump out if it starts to sink. The Germans did not anticipate the extraordinary achievements of the Road of Life and the indomitable spirit of ordinary Leningraders. (Photo by Slava Katamidze Collection/Getty Images)

Entering the Road of Life. The female guard is well dressed for the conditions. The sign reads, 'Lenfront. The Ice Mainline. Distance 30km'. (From the fonds of the RGAKFD in Krasnogorsk via Stavka)

A woman carries away a corpse on a sledge down Nevsky Prospekt. Many died of starvation during the terrible winter of 1941–42. (Photo by D. Trakhtenberg/Slava Katamidze Collection/Getty Images)

Two women sitting among the debris in the aftermath of the German bombardment of Leningrad in 1942. Trying to compel the Russian defenders to surrender, the Germans indiscriminately bombarded the city, resulting in enormous losses among civilians. (Photo by D. Trakhtenberg/ Slava Katamidze Collection/Getty Images)

Composer Dmitry Shostakovich (1906–75) opted to remain in Leningrad when the siege began in September 1941, continuing work on his Seventh Symphony. (Photo by Fine Art Images/Heritage Images/Getty Images)

The Leningrad première of Shostakovich's Seventh Symphony with the Leningrad Radio Orchestra on 9 August 1942. This photo is held in the Moscow Photo Museum (House of Photography). (Album / Alamy Stock Photo)

A German Tiger in combat south of Lake Ladoga, September 1942. The difficulties of the terrain are evident. Destroyed Soviet tanks can be seen in the background. (Photo by ullstein bild via Getty Images)

Soviet troops launch a counter-attack during the siege. The heaviest fighting was in the attempts to break the siege ring to the east and southeast, but there were constant raids by both sides along the rest of the siege perimeter. (Photo © Hulton-Deutsch Collection/Corbis via Getty Images)

A soldier of the Red Army takes cover behind the rubble of a building. Many of the villages and small towns around Leningrad were reduced to heaps of ruins, often with just the chimneys of wrecked buildings surviving the constant shelling. (Photo © Hulton-Deutsch Collection/Corbis via Getty Images)

Leningrad children racing on their scooters. Having seen so much in their young lives, they are not fazed by the notice behind them: 'Drive slowly! Unexploded bomb! Danger!' (Photo by: Sovfoto/Universal Images Group via Getty Images)

Leningraders were so weak from hunger that they had no strength to bury their dead during the siege. Bodies were taken to the edge of the city, and people were given extra rations to bury them. (Photo by: Sovfoto/Universal Images Group via Getty Images)

LIST OF MAPS

DRAMATIS PERSONAE

GERMANY

Bidermann, Gottlob – infantryman, 132nd Infantry Division

Böckmann, Herbert von – Generalleutnant, commander 11th Infantry Division

Both, Kuno von – General, commander I Corps

Brandenberger, Erich – Generalmajor (later General), commander 8th Panzer Division

Brauchitsch, Walther von – Generaloberst, commander-in-chief of the army until December 1941

Brockdorff-Ahlefeldt, Walter Graf von – General, commander II Corps

Busch, Ernst – Generaloberst, commander Sixteenth Army

Carius, Otto – Leutnant, company commander in *Schwere Panzer Abteilung 502*

Chappuis, Friedrich-Wilhelm – General, commander XXXVIII Corps

Förster, Helmuth – General, commander *Fliegerkorps I*

Fretter-Pico, Maximilian – General, commander XXX Corps

Haenicke, Siegfried – Generalleutnant, commander 61st Infantry Division

Halder, Franz – General (later Generaloberst), chief of the general staff 1938–42

Hamann, Joachim – Obersturmführer (later Sturmbannführer), SS officer in *Einsatzgruppe A*

Hansen, Christian – General, commander X Corps

Hoepner, Erich – Generaloberst, commander Fourth Panzer Group

Jäger, Karl – Standartenführer, commander *Einsatzkommando C*

Kinzel, Eberhard – Oberst (later General), chief of *FHO* until 1942

Küchler, Georg von – Generaloberst, commander Eighteenth Army, later commander Army Group North

Leeb, Wilhelm Ritter von – Generalfeldmarschall, commander Army Group North until January 1942

Lindemann, Georg – Generaloberst, commander L Corps, later commander Eighteenth Army

Lubbeck, Wilhelm – infantryman, 58th Infantry Division

Manstein, Erich von – General (later Generalfeldmarschall), commander LVI Motorised Corps

Paulus, Friedrich, Generalleutnant (later Generalfeldmarschall), Quartermaster General, later commander Sixth Army

Reichenau, Walter von – Generalfeldmarschall, commander Sixth Army, later commander Army Group South

Reinhardt, Georg-Hans – General (later Generaloberst), commander XLI Motorised Corps

Rudel, Hans-Ulrich – Oberleutnant (later Oberst), Stuka pilot

Schmidt, Rudolf – General, commander XXXIX Corps

Schulenberg, Friedrich-Werner Graf von der – German ambassador to Moscow prior to the war

Stahlberg, Alexander – Leutnant (later Hauptmann), officer 12th Panzer Division

Stahlecker, Franz Walter – Brigadeführer, commander *Einsatzgruppe A*

Wagner, Eduard – General, Quartermaster General of the German Army

Wengler, Maximilian – Oberst, commander 336th Infantry Regiment

Wodrig, Albert – General, commander XXVI Corps

SOVIET UNION AND IMPERIAL RUSSIA

Afanasyev, Nikolai Ivanovich – partisan officer

Akimov, Stepan Dmitriyevich – Lieutenant General, commander Forty-Eighth Army

Alferyev, Petr Fedorovich – Major General, deputy commander Second Shock Army

Andreyev, Andrei Matveyevich – Colonel, commander 86th Rifle Division

Astanin, Andrei Nikitovich – Major General, commander Primorsky Front Operational Group

Bardin, Stepan Mikhailovich – volunteer, 2nd Leningrad Militia Division

Berggolts, Olga – Leningrad poet

Beriya, Lavrenty Pavlovich – head of the NKVD

Berzarin, Nikolai Erastovich – Major General (later Colonel General), commander Twenty-Seventh Army

Bondarev, Andrei Leontyevich – Major General, commander Eighth Army

Budennyi, Semen Mikhailovich – Red Army Marshal, close associate of Stalin

Bukharin, Nikolai Ivanovich – Bolshevik revolutionary

Cherokov, Viktor Sergeyevich – Captain, commander Lake Ladoga Flotilla

Degtyarev, Georgy Yermolayevich – Major General, commander of artillery, Volkhov Front

Eliasberg, Karl Ilyich – conductor, Leningrad Radio Orchestra

Fedyuninsky, Ivan Ivanovich – Major General (later General), deputy commander Northern Front, later commander Fifty-Second Army, Leningrad Front, Fifty-Fourth Army, Fifth Army

Galanin, Ivan Vasilyevich – Major General, commander Fifty-Ninth Army

Gerodnik, Gennady Iosifovich – rifleman in a ski battalion

Govorov, Leonid Aleksandrovich – Lieutenant General, commander Leningrad Front

Gusev, Ivan Konstantinovich – platoon commander, Sukho garrison

Gusev, Nikolai Ivanovich – Major General, commander XIII Cavalry Corps, later commander Fourth Army

Kabanov, Sergei Ivanovich – Lieutenant General, commander Leningrad garrison

Kachanov, Kusma Maksimovich – Major General, commander Thirty-Fourth Army

Kamenev, Lev Borisovich – Bolshevik revolutionary

Khozin, Mikhail Semenovich – Major General (later Colonel General), commander Leningrad Front, later commander Fifty-Fourth Army, Volkhov Group

Khrulev, Andrei Vasilyevich – Lieutenant General, Deputy People's Commissar for Defence

Khuze, Olga Fedorovna – Leningrad schoolteacher

Kirov, Sergei Mironovich – Bolshevik revolutionary

Klykov, Nikolai Kuzmich – Lieutenant General, commander Fifty-Second Army, later commander Second Shock Army, deputy commander Volkhov Front

Konkov, Vasily Fomich – Major General, commander 115th Rifle Division

Konstantinov, Dmitry Vasilyevich – junior officer in a rifle regiment

Krestinsky, Nikolai Nikolayevich – Bolshevik revolutionary

Kudryavtsev, Grigory Konstantinovich – volunteer, 2nd Leningrad Militia Division

Kulik, Grigory Ivanovich – Marshal, commander Fifty-Fourth Army

Kuznetsov, Fedor Isidorovich – Colonel General, commander Baltic Special Military District and Northwest Front, later commander Twenty-First Army, Central Front, Fifty-First Army, Sixty-First Army

Larichev, Andrei Nikolayevich – Colonel, commander 92nd Rifle Division

Lazarev, Ivan Gavrilovich – Major General, commander Fifty-Fifth Army

Lelyushenko, Dmitry Danilovich – Major General (later General), commander XXI Mechanised Corps, later commander Fifth Army, Thirtieth Army

Lyapin, Petr Ivanovich – Major General, commander Fourth Army

Makianova Matus, Kseniya – oboist

Mekhlis, Lev Zakharovich – Deputy People's Commissar for Defence

Melnikov, Petr Yegorovich – naval officer

Meretskov, Kirill Afanasyevich – General (later Marshal), commander Leningrad Military District, later commander Seventh Army, Fourth Army, Volkhov Front

Mokhov, Rodion Mikhailovich – Sergeant, mechanic 98th Tank Brigade

Molotov, Vyacheslav Mikhailovich – Soviet foreign minister

Moniushko, Yevgeny Danilovich – young Leningrader

Morozov, Vasily Ivanovich – Lieutenant General, commander Eleventh Army

Murov, Mikhail Sergeyevich – Captain, 13th Rifle Division

Okhapina, Lidiya Georgiyevna – Leningrad resident

Ozarovsky, Nikolai Yurevich – Captain, commander Lake Ladoga Gunboats

Palkin, Yevgeny Yefremovich – medic, 22nd Rifle Brigade

Pavlov, Dmitry Vasilyevich – senior official, Soviet Food Commissariat

Pyadyshev, Konstantin Pavlovich – Lieutenant General, commander Luga Operational Group

Popov, Markian Mikhailovich – commander Leningrad Military District 1940

Riabinkin, Yura – schoolboy in Leningrad

Romanovsky, Vladimir Zakharovich – Lieutenant General, commander Second Shock Army

Ryutin, Martemyan Nikitich – Bolshevik revolutionary

Seitenov, Sergei Sergeyevich – machine-gunner, 33rd Rifle Brigade

Shaposhnikov, Boris Mikhailovich – Marshal, chief of the general staff

Shcheglov, Dmitry Alekseyevich – militia volunteer

Shcherbakov, Vladimir Ivanovicb – Major General, commander Eighth Army

Shevaldin, Trifon Ivanovich – Lieutenant General, commander Eighth Army

Shostakovich, Dmitry Dmitriyevich – composer

Sobennikov, Petr Petrovich – Major General (later Lieutenant General), commander Northwest Front, later commander Forty-Third Army

Sokolov, Grigory Grigoryevich – Lieutenant General, commander Second Shock Army

Sviridov, Vladimir Petrovich – Major General, commander Fifty-Fourth Army

Timoshenko, Semen Konstantinovich – Marshal, close associate of Stalin

Trotsky, Leon – formerly Lev Davidovich Bronstein, Bolshevik revolutionary

Tukhachevsky, Mikhail Nikolayevich – Marshal and military theorist

Vasilyev, Nikolai Grigoryevich – partisan officer

Vatutin, Nikolai Fedorovich – Lieutenant General (later General), chief of staff Northwest Front

Vishnevsky, Aleksandr Aleksandrovich – Colonel, senior medical officer Volkhov Front

Vlasov, Andrei Andreyevich – Lieutenant General, commander Second Shock Army

Voronov, Nikolai Nikolayevich – Colonel General, commander-in-chief Red Army artillery

Voroshilov, Kliment Yefremovich – Marshal, close associate of Stalin

Yudenich, Nikolai Nikolayevich – Tsarist general

Zhdanov, Andrei Aleksandrovich – First Secretary of Communist Party in Leningrad

Zhukov, Georgy Konstantinovich – Marshal

Zinovyev, Grigory Yevseyevich – formerly Hirsch Apfelbaum, Bolshevik revolutionary

INTRODUCTION

Leo Tolstoy's novel *Anna Karenina* commences with one of the best-known opening sentences of literature in any language: 'Happy families are all alike; every unhappy family is unhappy in its own way.'[1] In a similar manner, the relatively few nations that enter conflicts in a state of good preparation for what lies ahead have many factors in common: a good understanding of where threats will emerge; the likely means available to potential enemies; the probable enemy plans for war; the resources available for opposing these threats and hostile intentions; and the best way to use these resources. But on far more occasions, nations enter wars either in a state of poor preparation, or with preparations that are unsuited to what lies ahead. The reasons for such an unhappy state of affairs are as varied as the number of nations to which this applies – whilst many of these reasons are shared, others are unique. In the case of the Soviet Union in the Second World War, the weaknesses in preparations for war brought the nation to the brink of defeat. The poor state of the Red Army through the 1930s and into the early 1940s to defend the nation against attack included many factors in common with other countries – flawed doctrine, planning assumptions that were either outdated or simply incorrect, and equipment that was already obsolete by the time that hostilities commenced. However, like Tolstoy's unhappy families, the Soviet Union had its own unique contribution to its unhappiness and lack of preparation, and the city of Leningrad and its inhabitants were to pay a huge price for this. By the end of the Second World War, more Soviet citizens, civilian and military, died in and around Leningrad than British Empire war dead from both world wars combined. It was a horrific price to pay for victory, made even worse by the manner in which Leningrad and other parts of the Soviet Union suffered in the years before the conflict. That pre-war suffering was a critical and tragic component in the constellation of factors that brought the Soviet Union to the brink of defeat in 1941.

Since its inception, the Soviet state had faced a variety of threats, real and imagined, external and internal. The turmoil of its birth saw the Bolsheviks seize power, and the attempts by Western Powers to influence the outcome of the Russian Civil War that followed this ranged from supporting anti-Bolshevik 'White Russian' movements to active military intervention. From March 1918 to October 1919, an international force made up predominantly of a little over 14,000 British soldiers but including American, Italian, Serbian, Canadian, and French contingents seized the northern ports of Archangelsk and Murmansk and attempted to apply pressure on the struggling Bolshevik regime; at one stage, the expeditionary force advanced far down the valley of the Northern Dvina River before being driven back by growing pressure from the Red Army. Ultimately, with support in Britain and elsewhere for the intervention rapidly evaporating, the expeditionary force was evacuated. The operation achieved nothing militarily, but it left a strong impression upon the new Bolshevik government: the Russian Soviet Republic faced serious external threats. Preparing to face such threats was a military necessity.

Rapidly, Lenin and his contemporaries realised the political advantages that could be gained from the perception of an external threat. Throughout history, political movements have attempted to use external enemies – both real and imagined – as a means of engendering a sense of peril, which they have then used for a variety of internal purposes. There are few things that can unify a nation as much as a generally shared view that the nation is in danger from external enemies. In the case of the Soviet Union, the increasing literacy that was achieved in the years that followed the end of the Civil War gave the Soviet rulers an opportunity to use centrally produced literature to portray the governments of capitalist nations as implacable foes of the Bolshevik Revolution and therefore enemies of ordinary working class people. This sense of external threat served an important internal purpose: it provided an excuse for widespread repression of those who were thought to be actual, potential, or imagined confederates of hostile foreign powers.

Officially created in 1922 as the Civil War came to an end, the Union of Soviet Socialist Republics or Soviet Union was a traumatised nation. There was widespread lawlessness, the inevitable consequence of the turmoil of preceding years, and there was also considerable opposition to the ongoing dictatorial rule of the Bolsheviks. The assumption of almost complete power by Lenin – and then by Stalin as his successor shortly after the end of the Civil War – was a justifiable expedient during years of strife and at a time when the final victory of the Bolsheviks was uncertain, but by the mid-1920s there were calls both from within the Communist Party and from society as a whole for a more democratic system to be installed. After all, the revolutions and subsequent war had been ostensibly first to overthrow autocratic rule, and then to prevent its re-imposition. It was easy for opponents of Stalin to portray him and his inner circle as little more than replacements for the previous rulers of Russia, particularly as there were widespread and justified allegations of cronyism and corruption. As such opposition became more outspoken, Stalin embarked on a series of countermeasures that did huge damage to almost every institution in the Soviet Union. This damage would be a major factor in the weakness of Soviet preparations for war. One city in the north of the country, the cradle of the Bolshevik Revolution, would pay a particularly cruel price for the miscalculations of the pre-war years and deliberate vandalism of Stalin's purges. The history of this unique city shaped the manner in which Stalin would treat its inhabitants both before and during the Second World War.

Moreover, the lasting legacy and fear that continued into the years of war continued to have a malign influence on the functioning of almost every part of the Soviet state, but most significantly within the military. To fight effectively in a modern war, the Red Army needed to have a leadership structure that permitted officers a degree of freedom and initiative rather than relying on top-down, rigid command structures. By continuing such rigidity, the Soviet Union was doomed to pay a huge price in human life for its ultimate victory, and this legacy persists today.

CHAPTER 1

THE WINDOW TO THE WEST

A swamp in the desolate, barely populated northeast corner of the Baltic Sea was an unusual and curious choice for the location of a new city. But Peter the Great, 'by the grace of God the most excellent and great sovereign emperor and ruler of all the Russias', was an unusual and curious man.

Born in June 1672 to Tsar Alexis of Russia and his wife Natalya Naryshkina, Peter became tsar at the age of just ten. His father died in 1676 and was succeeded by Peter's half-brother Feodor, who was plagued by lifelong poor health. Feodor died in 1682 and immediately there was a dispute about the succession. Although Feodor had no offspring, Alexis had no fewer than 13 children by his first wife Mariya Milovskaya and three by his second wife, Peter's mother Natalya. The next in line of succession was Feodor's 16-year-old brother Ivan, who now became Tsar Ivan V, but concerned about his poor health and alleged 'infirmness of mind', the Russian boyars – the aristocracy immediately below the royal family – proposed that Peter, with his mother as regent, should become tsar. The result was a revolt led by Sophia, sister of Feodor and Ivan, who favoured the latter, and a compromise was reached: Peter and Ivan would be co-tsars, and Sophia would rule as regent. In 1689, Peter attempted to take power in his own name, resulting once more in conflict with Sophia and her supporters; eventually, Peter prevailed with the help of his mother's family. After Peter's mother died in 1694 – followed two years later by Peter's co-ruler, Ivan V – Peter became the undisputed ruler of Russia.

Peter the Great was a striking figure, about six feet eight inches tall, though he had narrow shoulders and small hands and feet. From the outset, he wished to modernise his realm and tried to sweep away much of traditional Russia. The greatest military threat to Russia lay in the south and he was involved in a protracted struggle against the Ottoman Empire for control of the Black Sea coast for many years. In an ultimately unsuccessful attempt to find foreign allies who would join him in his war against Turkey, he departed Moscow for Western Europe in 1697 on what would become a journey lasting 18 months; although he was officially travelling incognito under the name of Peter Mikhailov as part of a substantial official 'embassy', it was impossible for him to hide his great height and most of the officials and nobles he encountered had no difficulty in knowing who he was. The embassy was a remarkable group. In addition to the diplomats, courtiers and nobles who formed its core, it included six trumpeters, several singers, 70 soldiers, and even four dwarfs.[1] These travels took Peter to Amsterdam, where he displayed an astonishing range of interest in practical matters. He spent four months working – often physically labouring – in the dockyards of the Dutch East India Company; in his honour, the company ordered the construction of a new frigate, *The Apostles Peter and Paul*, with the explicit intention of permitting the young tsar to experience every aspect of shipbuilding, and Peter took part in almost every phase of its construction.

Shipbuilding was not the only field that interested Peter. Wherever he went, he would stop and ask workers about what they were doing and how their equipment worked. He spent several hours with Fredrik Ruysch, a professor of anatomy. This left him with the belief that he had sufficient knowledge of surgery to be able to perform operations, and many of those who were with him on the embassy tried to conceal their illnesses from him out of fear that he would insist on offering them his service.[2] He learned how to remove diseased teeth; he studied how to paint with watercolours; and he even showed great interest in the use of fire hoses and other modern equipment that was almost unknown in Russia. Wherever he travelled, he drew sketches of buildings and fortifications, determined to learn as much as possible about the world.

In 1698, Peter's travels were cut short by a rebellion in Russia. The *Streltsy* – infantry regiments armed with firearms and recruited from a distinct social class – were strongly disliked by Peter, and immediately before his departure for the west he had been made aware of three potential rebels in the ranks of their officers. Although the evidence against the three was weak, Peter had them arrested and bloodily slaughtered in Red Square – their limbs were hewn off with axes before they were beheaded. Perhaps provoked by these killings, in Peter's absence other members of the *Streltsy* made contact with the former regent Sophia, who was now confined to a monastery, and asked for her support in grievances about poor supplies that had left many starving. Sophia declined to help them, but the mutineers were now fearful that they had no alternative but to press on; the soldiers arrested their officers and marched on Moscow. The uprising was short-lived and was crushed by a loyalist force less than two weeks after the men rebelled – indeed, the rebellion was actually put down before news of it reached Peter – but as soon as he returned to Moscow, the tsar set about a brutal repression. Many of those who surrendered endured terrible tortures at Peter's instigation, and they and their families – and those who were denounced during the tortures – were exiled. It was an ominous precedent for future repressions in Russia.

The visit to Western Europe had a profound effect on Peter. In almost every respect, he felt that his country was lagging far behind other nations – Holland, with a fraction of the natural resources of Russia, was immeasurably wealthier. He set about modernising Russia with characteristic determination. When a group of nobles greeted him on his return to Moscow, he astonished everyone present by producing a razor and set about shaving off the beards of the boyars. This immediately put him at odds with the traditionalist clergy, who often refused to bless those who had shaved off their beards – Ivan the Terrible had proclaimed that it was a sin to shave men's faces as it defaced the image of man created by God. But Peter was not to be swayed and anyone who attended a meeting with him, or one of the frequent banquets organised by the tsar or his inner circle, could expect to have their beard shaved off before they departed. Orders were issued requiring state officials to insist that anyone who visited them was clean shaven and an annual tax was imposed on those who refused to shave. This was followed by a decree that traditional Russian dress was to be replaced by western clothing, on the grounds that the traditional garments were far less practical. Changes were made to the calendar, moving the start of the year from 1 September to 1 January, and the numbering of years was brought in line with the west, though the continuation of the use of the Julian calendar resulted in discrepancies slowly accumulating in the years that followed.

In the midst of the reforms, which included a radical reorganisation of Russian currency, Peter found himself at war with Sweden. Even before his embassy to the west, he had been fascinated by maritime matters and he was determined to seize control of the Baltic coast – the northern region of what is now known as the Baltic States was at the time the Swedish province of Livonia, and in 1700 Peter attempted an invasion, only to be badly defeated at Narva. But while the Swedes turned south to attack the Polish-Lithuanian Commonwealth, Peter found himself on the shores of the Baltic at its most eastern point where the Neva River flowed through swampy terrain to the sea, in what had been the Swedish province of Ingermanland or Ingria but had been captured by his troops.

Still obsessed by the wealth of Amsterdam and other western coastal cities, he dreamed of a new Russian capital with access to the sea, from which Russian ships would sail forth to trade with the world. Despite the bad weather that came from such a northern location, barely 500 miles from the Arctic Circle, and ignoring the huge swamps and endless forests, the lack of local resources such as stone quarries that would normally be regarded as essential for the construction of a major town, and the considerable distance to other Russian cities – with no all-weather roads existing between those towns and the Neva estuary – Peter proceeded with the same single-minded determination that he had repeatedly shown. The new city would be named Sankt Pieter Burkh (a Russified version of 'Saint Petersburg'), and would be a deliberately west-facing window for Russia, modelled on the European cities that Peter had visited during his travels. This would become the great city that played such an important part in the politics of the nation in the following centuries.

Lake Ladoga is the largest lake in Europe, about 136 miles from north to south and 86 miles from east to west at its widest point. The Neva River flows from its southwest corner to wind its way some 46 miles to the Baltic. As it approaches the sea, it breaks into numerous channels, creating an array of islands. When Peter started his project, there were more than 100 such islands, but now only 44 are left. When the tsar travelled to the estuary, he found that soldiers under the command of Aleksandr Danilovich Menshikov had established a fort of wooden palisades on one of these islands. In the months and years that followed, this first semi-permanent habitation to be built on the site would become the Peter and Paul Fortress. It seems that although he intended his city to be in this general area, Peter was uncertain about where the heart of St Petersburg should lie. At one stage, he preferred the island of Kotlin, about 12 miles to the west and the future site of the Kronstadt naval base; at others, he favoured Vasilyevsky Island, in the western parts of the modern city. For a variety of reasons, not least because these islands were so exposed to the elements, St Petersburg grew up on both shores of the Neva opposite the Peter and Paul Fortress.

The challenges that faced Peter and his workers were immense. There was no consistently reliable source of fresh water, with the salty Baltic often flowing into the lower reaches of the Neva; the ground was swampy with little by way of rocks and certainly no easily accessible quarries; and the local landscape was unsuitable for farming, making it difficult to supply the city with adequate food. Huge quantities of timber would be needed in order to create firm foundations for buildings, but although the hinterland was a huge forest, the region immediately around the Neva estuary was comparatively denuded of trees, largely because of the constant incursion of salt water. Consequently, every tree used in construction had to be felled far upstream near Lake Ladoga and then floated to the city. Thousands of workers – serfs, convicted criminals, and Swedish prisoners of war – perished in the early years of the project, as a writer described nearly 200 years later:

> It would be difficult to find in the annals of military history any battle that claimed more lives than the number of workers who died in St Petersburg. For those who built it, it turned out to be nothing but a huge graveyard.[3]

In the face of repeated floods, constant outbreaks of disease, and innumerable supply difficulties, the men and women who struggled to turn Peter's vision into reality slowly created new buildings and roads. At first, the buildings were wooden, but stone was brought to the area by barges and in 1712 sufficient progress had been made for Peter to move Russia's capital from Moscow to St Petersburg. By this date, he had been living in the city almost continuously for the preceding two years, repeatedly taking a small boat to the Peter and Paul Fortress where he would climb the tower in the heart of the fortress to survey the widespread construction projects. As the buildings began to rise, he ordered people to move to the new city – thousands of traders and artisans, as well as entire families of courtiers. General Aleksandr Danilovich Menshikov was one of the first to have a grandiose palace built, and a series of celebrated Western European architects were summoned to design and oversee construction of all manner of buildings. When Peter died in 1725, his new city had 19 churches and cathedrals and more than a dozen imperial palaces and aristocratic residences.[4]

Although the pace and energy of the construction project were nothing short of astonishing, the city on the Neva faced ongoing problems – indeed, the sheer speed of its growth created constant shortages of all kinds. Its isolation resulted in a high cost of living, making it unpopular with many of those who had been forced to relocate to this northern climate. Flooding and fires were constantly recurring problems and after the death of Catherine, Peter's wife and successor, just two years after Peter the Great, the new tsar – the 13-year-old Peter II, grandson of the founder of the city – moved the capital back to Moscow. But by this time, St Petersburg was firmly established as Russia's main maritime port to the west, and the steady flow of expensive items from other parts of Europe guaranteed its survival. Peter II died of smallpox in 1730, and his successor Anna moved the capital back to the north. The building projects that had languished or been abandoned in the preceding years were once more instigated and the city continued to grow as the century passed; by 1760, its population exceeded 100,000 and under the rule of Catherine the Great St Petersburg enjoyed a great boom of construction and enrichment. As the century approached its end, the population had grown to over 200,000, less than 100 years after Peter decreed the creation of his new city.[5]

Despite the attempts by Peter the Great and many – but not all – of his successors, Russia continued to lag behind other European nations in many respects, not least because the tsars were constantly worried that liberal ideas from the west would undermine their autocratic rule. There was little recognition that substantial progress would inevitably result in pressure for greater individual freedoms and rights, and the unremitting demands placed upon the peasants, artisans, and merchants of Russia resulted in frequent episodes of unrest across the nation. In 1825, about 3,000 soldiers attempted to stop Nicholas I from becoming tsar, resulting in fighting in St Petersburg in what became known as the Decembrist Revolt. However, when much of Europe was convulsed by revolutions in 1848, Russia was a notable exception, with Russian soldiers being sent to the aid of the Austrian emperor to crush an uprising in Hungary. In a belated attempt to modernise the country, Tsar Aleksandr II ordered the emancipation of Russia's serfs in 1861 as part of a major set of reforms but many remained restless and demanded faster change. The tsar survived attempts to assassinate him in 1866, 1867, 1879, and 1880, but his carriage was attacked in 1881 by Nikolai Ivanovich Rysakov and Ignati Ioakhimovich Grinevitsky, members of the *Narodnaya Volya* ('People's Will') movement. Rysakov threw a bomb that killed one of Aleksandr's Cossack guards and wounded the driver of the imperial carriage, and Grinevitsky took advantage of the resulting confusion to throw a second bomb, which fatally wounded the tsar. By this time, St Petersburg was a city struggling with the Industrial Revolution and the social problems that it brought. The workshops and factories that grew up around the elegant heart of the city were in areas that were home to about half a million people, most of whom lived in poverty and in overcrowded and unsanitary conditions. The first big cotton mills had appeared in the 1830s and 1840s, followed by foundries, railway enterprises, and armaments factories. The emancipation of the serfs left many in the countryside without any means of supporting themselves, and freed of their ties to rural estates, people were driven to seek employment in the cities, further boosting the population of St Petersburg, Moscow, and other large centres. But this search for better paid work in urban centres exacerbated the already terrible conditions in which most people lived;

the historical problems of an adequate clean water supply, for example, worsened hugely, adding to problems of overcrowding and ill health.

Despite the terrible conditions in which most ordinary people lived, St Petersburg and other large cities in Russia continued to draw in people from rural areas – at the end of the 19th century, more than two thirds of St Petersburg's residents had been born elsewhere. The contrast between the opulence of the palaces of the aristocracy and the salons of world-famous craftsmen like Peter Carl Fabergé and the surrounding slums was made all the more striking by their proximity – it was just a matter of a few minutes of walking from areas of affluence to the squalid areas inhabited by ordinary people. Whilst a great deal of light industry developed around Moscow, St Petersburg was the centre of Russia's heavy industry, and in 1905 many workers turned out to protest at restrictions on trade unions and industrial action. In January, large crowds gathered in six different industrial districts; singing hymns and patriotic songs, they moved slowly to the Winter Palace in the centre of the city where they were confronted by large numbers of soldiers. It was part of Russian culture that the tsar, the 'little father', was the representative on Earth of God, the 'great father', and the people hoped that they could secure the support of the tsar in improving their lives. In the absence of clear orders and control, some officers ordered the workers to disperse while others permitted them to proceed towards the palace in small groups. But a few officers ordered their troops to open fire, usually without warning, and there were numerous cavalry charges by Cossacks. The number of dead was officially estimated to be 96, with another 333 injured; more realistic estimates are at least an order of magnitude higher.

The massacre of protesters in St Petersburg in what became known as Bloody Sunday was the start of the 1905 Revolution. In addition to industrial workers who took to the streets of Russia's cities, the army and navy were also unsettled following the humiliating defeat of Russia at the hands of Japan in the Russo-Japanese War, and there were several mutinies, most notably aboard the battleship *Potemkin*. Eventually, the unrest that swept Russia in 1905 was suppressed, largely because, despite the mutinies aboard *Potemkin* and elsewhere, most of the military remained loyal to the tsar, and a limited form of representation was instigated with the creation of the Duma. But perhaps the biggest consequence was the change in attitude of ordinary Russians. Regardless of his status as 'little father', many of Russia's urban and rural poor now blamed Nicholas II for the bloodshed of Bloody Sunday, or for the widespread killings and exiles that followed. With so many workers in the industrial suburbs of St Petersburg, it was inevitable that these areas became hotbeds of dissent.

Unrest was never far below the surface in the Russian capital. On the eve of the First World War, while a military band played the *Marseillaise* to welcome a state visit by the French president, Cossacks were brutally charging protesters in the suburbs who were marching to demand just a small fraction of the rights that the French had demanded when they overthrew their monarch. But when war came in 1914, there was a huge surge of patriotism. A few challenged the right of Russia's ruler to send hundreds of thousands of men off to fight and die, but most put aside their grievances in what was felt to be a moment of national unity. The German embassy was stormed and looted by a crowd, and just a few weeks into the war the government announced that the city would now be known as Petrograd in place of its more German-sounding name.

The moment of unity and patriotic fervour soon passed. The first advances into East Prussia in August 1914 ended in disaster when Aleksandr Vasilyevich Samsonov's Second Army was completely destroyed at the Battle of Tannenberg; Samsonov committed suicide rather than surrender to the Germans, and the campaigns that followed saw the Russians driven back to and beyond their pre-war borders. Whilst Russia's armies fared better further south against the forces of the Austro-Hungarian Empire, this phase of the war petered out into a bloody stalemate in the Carpathians before a German counteroffensive in 1915 drove the tsar's forces first out of Austrian Galicia and then from the eastern parts of Poland. Maimed and wounded men returned to the cities of Russia with tales of incompetence and muddle, and there was a stark contrast between the dogged, stoic courage of ordinary soldiers on the one hand and officers from aristocratic families who successfully evaded being sent to the front line. Workers labouring in the suburbs to manufacture the immense quantities of materiel needed for modern warfare lived in wretched conditions and the Russian railway system, which barely coped with feeding urban populations before the war, found the task of doing so in wartime – when so many trains were committed to the war effort – an impossible one. The first food shortages developed before the end of 1914 and steadily worsened as the war progressed; the first anti-government leaflets began to circulate before the first anniversary of the start of the conflict.

When the final collapse of tsarist rule came in early 1917, the crucible of revolution was Petrograd. About 150,000 workers marched in protest at food shortages on 22 January*, carrying banners that often bore just single words –

---

* Dates are given in the old Russian calendar, which was 13 days behind the Gregorian calendar used elsewhere; in January 1918, Russia adopted the Gregorian calendar. All dates are given according to the calendar in use at that time.

'Bread' or 'Food'. But there were also many banners proclaiming 'Down with the Tsar!' and there were similar protests in other cities across Russia as people marked the anniversary of the failed 1905 Revolution. For once, the police and military didn't intervene and further protests and strikes followed. Historically, the tsars had used the army – particularly the Cossack cavalry regiments – to suppress any unrest, and on 27 January a group of Cossacks was ordered by General Sergei Semenovich Khabalov, the governor of Petrograd Military District, to intervene in protests in the Kolpino suburb of Petrograd. There must have been alarm in government circles when the police reported that the soldiers showed little enthusiasm for their task.[6]

The critical moment came a few days later when women from fabric factories in the Viborg district went on strike demanding bread. As was increasingly the case, this protest rapidly flared into general condemnation of the government and Khabalov ordered his Cossack regiments to deploy against the protesters. The following day, 23 February, the two sides confronted each other at the Aleksandrovsky Bridge across the Neva as the protesters attempted to cross from the northern bank. There was an uneasy stand-off until a group of women workers approached the soldiers. They pleaded with them not to use violence, reminding them that they too had sisters, wives, and mothers, and all the workers wanted was an end to the war that had taken over 2 million Russian lives and had left the population starving.[7] The soldiers glanced at each other, and then many of them grinned at the workers and winked at them. Some told the civilians that they had nothing to fear, and they sat at attention on their horses as the workers surged past. It was the moment that sent a tremor through the foundations of Romanov rule.

Other security forces, particularly the civilian police, showed less sympathy. Mounted officers attacked protesters without mercy but by the end of the day there were over 160,000 people on strike, many of them thronging through the streets. The day after the Cossacks refused to attack the workers on Aleksandrovsky Bridge, there was a further stand-off as a huge crowd surged north along Nevsky Prospekt and encountered a line of Cossacks outside Kazan Cathedral, about half a mile from the Winter Palace, the Admiralty, and the other key government buildings of the city centre. The workers raised a loud cheer; the Cossacks bowed in response. On Aleksandrovsky Bridge, mounted police under the command of Mikhail Shalfeev, chief of police of the 5th District of Petrograd, charged the protesters attempting to cross from Viborg. He and his men immediately found themselves caught in a dense crowd of workers who pulled Shalfeev from his horse; he was beaten with fists and iron rods, and then one of the protesters seized Shalfeev's revolver and shot him. On Nevsky Prospekt, mounted police attempted to disperse the crowds by charging in and wielding whips, but a nearby contingent of Cossacks immediately intervened. The accounts of the precise details of what followed vary, but one witness described how a police officer struck a Cossack and the soldiers then retaliated. In any event, the leader of the police detachment was killed and the other police officers forced to flee. The Cossacks, who had repeatedly propped up Tsar Nicholas' regime, had sided with the ordinary people. The tremor of the previous day was turning into an earthquake. Soldiers of the Guards regiments in the city varied in their reaction. Many refused to fire on the workers and joined the protesting crowds, while others followed orders and opened fire.

As the day drew to a close, there was growing concern in government ranks, particularly about a mutiny by soldiers of the Pavlovsky Guards Regiment; many of the leaders of the mutiny were arrested and, like dissidents ever since the founding of the city, they were confined in the Peter and Paul Fortress. A report by an agent of *Okhrana* – the tsar's secret police – presented a neat, if somewhat obvious, summary of the situation:

> At the moment, everything depends on the conduct of the military units. If they do not go over to the side of the proletariat, then the disorders will recede rapidly. If the troops turn against the government, then nothing can be done to save the country from revolutionary upheavals.[8]

Despite increasingly alarming reports from his capital, Tsar Nicholas remained astonishingly complacent. When Mikhail Vladimirovich Rodzyanko, the chair of the Duma, sent him an urgent message urging him to take decisive action, Nicholas demonstrated the gulf that separated his personal world from the reality of life in his capital. He turned to Count Vladimir Borisovich Frederiks, the Minister of the Imperial Household, and irritably commented, 'Again, this fat Rodzyanko has written to me lots of nonsense, to which I shall not even deign to reply.'[9]

It was probably already too late for any decisive action to be effective. A sergeant of the Volynsky Guards Regiment urged his fellow soldiers in their barracks to refuse to open fire on the people of the city:

> It would be better to die with honour than to obey any further orders to shoot into the crowds. Fathers, mothers, sisters, brothers, even brides, are begging for bread. Should we strike them down? Have you seen the blood running in the streets? I propose that we not march against them again tomorrow.[10]

Officers rapidly slipped away from the barracks; a few were caught and shot by the soldiers and the mutiny spread to other regiments. The seizure of a nearby arsenal released tens of thousands of weapons into the hands of the mutineers and the protesters. There were exchanges of fire with the few remaining loyalist troops as the growing revolution spread across the city, with other armaments depots and prisons swiftly overrun. The pace of revolution accelerated and within days the tsar and his family were under arrest. The long rule of the Romanovs was at an end.

The February Revolution was merely a forerunner of the far more significant October Revolution later in the year when the Bolsheviks seized control of Russia. In the intervening months, the city on the Neva became a centre of political activity. The new Provisional Government struggled to assert its authority, while the Bolsheviks – who refused to be part of the new government and through their Soviet of Soldiers' and Workers' Deputies exerted almost complete control over munitions factories, railways, the postal service, and an increasing part of the military – plotted and increased their support. All sides attempted to increase support for their factions in the army, and political activists journeyed to the units on the long front line to harangue the soldiers and seek their support. The likelihood of army units being supportive of the Bolsheviks was directly linked to their proximity to Petrograd – the closer they were to the capital, the more likely they were to be visited by Bolshevik agitators and persuaded that their best interests lay in opposing both the old tsarist order and the new Provisional Government. In the summer of 1917, Aleksandr Fedorovich Kerensky, the head of the Provisional Government, launched a new offensive against the German and Austro-Hungarian forces, which had largely been in a defensive posture since the February Revolution. The operation, which bore Kerensky's name, enjoyed limited success before it was overcome by a German counteroffensive. Confidence in Kerensky dwindled rapidly.

In Petrograd and other cities, the food shortages and appalling living conditions for ordinary people continued to deteriorate, further undermining the Provisional Government. There were fears that the coming winter would be even worse than the one that had brought about the collapse of the Romanovs. Inflation was rampant, with even the rich reduced to bartering jewellery and other valuables for food and other essential items. Vladimir Ilyich Lenin, leader of the Bolsheviks, returned to Petrograd via Finland and personally oversaw preparations for a new revolution; this was given new urgency by an attempt by Lavr Georgiyevich Kornilov, commander-in-chief of the army, to seize control of Russia by sending troops to Petrograd. The attempted coup failed, largely because Bolsheviks hindered rail travel for the units dispatched by Kornilov, and because political workers from the capital, representing all of the anti-tsarist groups, persuaded the soldiers to abandon their loyalty to Kornilov. In an attempt to prevent any recurrence, Kerensky's government formally abolished the monarchy, announcing the creation of a Russian Republic, but fears remained that right-wing forces would make a renewed attempt to seize power. Many of the workers of the capital had been armed in preparation for resistance against Kornilov's men and had been organised into formations known as the Red Guards; these units became increasingly visible around Petrograd in the weeks that followed.[11]

Whilst the February Revolution took place against a backdrop of unrest across much of the Russian Empire, it was nonetheless centred on Petrograd. By the last weeks of 1917, unrest was almost universal in Russia, both in the cities and the countryside. Many army units on what remained of the front line had simply disintegrated, with soldiers deciding to head for their homes rather than continue fighting. Lenin – living in hiding and moving around Petrograd in disguise – met his fellow Bolsheviks and argued strongly for immediate action, but not all supported him. Some were anxious that large parts of the military would side with Kerensky, but matters came to a head when Kerensky tried to pre-empt the Bolsheviks. After failing to secure approval from the government for a move against Lenin and his supporters, Kerensky issued orders on his personal authority for legal action to commence against the Bolsheviks' Military Revolutionary Committee, which was responsible for organising the Red Guards, and ordered the suppression of pro-Bolshevik newspapers. On 25 October the Bolsheviks went into action. The Russian Baltic Fleet's sailors issued a proclamation supporting the Bolsheviks while groups of Red Guards took control of key locations around the city. With rail transport and all communications – by post or telegraph – already under Bolshevik control, there was little that Kerensky could do. Unable to secure any military support within the city or to contact potential supporters elsewhere in Russia, the head of the Provisional Government managed to escape in a Renault car that he was given by diplomats in the American Embassy.[12]

The Bolsheviks later portrayed the seizure of the Winter Palace on the banks of the Neva as a crowning moment of the October Revolution, with film footage showing columns of Red Guards storming the imposing building, but these films were re-enactments after the event and the capture of the highly symbolic building was a more prosaic affair. About 3,000 defenders including a battalion of women volunteers had been assembled, and after they refused to surrender the Russian warship *Aurora* fired a blank round to signal the commencement of the attack and Bolshevik gunners in the Peter and Paul Fortress made a desultory and largely ineffective bombardment. The officers in the fortress were reluctant to inflict serious damage on the palace and offered a variety of excuses for not firing their weapons: most of the guns were unfit for use as they hadn't been cleaned; and there was no ammunition of the right calibre for the training guns that were available. It was only when the ordinary rank and file took control of the guns that any firing took place, and a total of fewer than 40 rounds were fired. At a range of less than 900m, the gunners succeed in hitting the palace with just two of their shots. Leon Trotsky, leader of the Red Guards, later attempted to explain this as being due to the unwillingness of the soldiers to be responsible for unnecessary destruction and loss of life.[13] Nor was this the only moment of difficulty at the Peter and Paul Fortress. Georgy Ivanovich Blagonravov, the fortress commissar, was meant to signal to the *Aurora* and to Bolshevik forces on the shore that he was ready to commence his bombardment by hoisting a red lantern onto the fortress' flagpole. At the very last moment, he realised that no such lantern was available, and he frantically set off in search of one. After briefly becoming stuck in a mud bank on the shore of the island, he managed to find a lantern, but it wasn't red, and in any case it was impossible to attach it to the flagpole.

Alfred Knox, the British military attaché in Petrograd, wrote a description of events at the Winter Palace that is probably more accurate than most, and was in stark contrast to the heroic legend that was created by the Bolsheviks:

> The garrison had dwindled owing to desertions, for there were no provisions and it had been practically starved for two days. There was no strong man to take command and to enforce discipline. No one had the stomach for fighting; and some of the ensigns even borrowed greatcoats of soldier pattern from the women to enable them to escape unobserved.
>
> The greater part of the Junkers of the Mikhail Artillery School returned to their school, taking with them four out of their six guns. Then the Cossacks left, declaring themselves opposed to bloodshed! At 10pm a large part of the ensigns left, leaving few defenders except the ensigns of the Engineering School and the company of women.
>
> The government was the whole time in communication with the front, and at midnight was elated by a message that troops were on the march for their relief. Then a report came that the Fleet Committee was coming to the palace with provisions.

During the bombardment the ministers moved about from room to room. Ragosin [aide de camp to the commander of the Petrograd Military District] afterwards related that when he had to report on some subject he found 'the Minister of Marine sitting in a window smoking a pipe and spitting. Other ministers were seated at a table. [Mikhail Ivanovich] Tereshchenko [the foreign minister] walked up and down like a caged tiger. [Aleksandr Ivanovich] Konovalov [minister for trade and industry] sat on a sofa nervously pulling up his trousers until they were finally above his knees' … In reality the plight of this handful of men must have been terrible. Deserted by their leader and surrounded from 6pm on the 7th, refusing to leave their post, though powerless to effect anything, they awaited their fate at the hands of the rabble.

The defence was unorganised and only three of the many entrances were guarded. Parties of the attackers penetrated by side entrances in search of loot. At first these parties were small and were disarmed by the garrison, but they were succeeded by larger bands of sailors and of the Pavlovsky Regiment, in addition to armed workmen, and these turned the tables by disarming the garrison. This was, however, carried out, as an office of the garrison afterwards stated, 'in a domestic manner,' with little bloodshed. The garrison fired little and is said to have only lost three Junkers wounded.

… At 2.30am on the 8th the palace was 'taken'. The ministers were arrested and marched through execrating crowds across the Troitsky Bridge to the Fortress of Peter and Paul …

According to Bolshevik accounts the company of women offered the most serious resistance, and a report stated that three of them were stripped and thrown into the Neva. The remainder, 137 in all, were marched to the Pavlovsky barracks, where they were 'searched for bombs in an unnecessary manner'. They were then passed on to the barracks of the Grenadiersky Regiment. These women were volunteers from all classes, but mostly from the intelligentsia.[14]

One of the biggest problems that the Bolsheviks encountered immediately after the capture of the Winter Palace was as a result of Red Guards and others breaking into the extensive wine cellars. Vladimir Aleksandrovich Antonov-Ovseyenko, the commissar who personally arrested the Provisional Government officials in the palace, later wrote a report full of unintended comedy. Troops from two different Guards regiments, he wrote, were ordered to secure the cellars but were unable to resist temptation. A special guard group was formed from trusted Bolsheviks on regimental committees, but they too became drunk. Antonov-Ovseyenko then ordered armoured cars to clear the large square outside the

Winter Palace in an attempt to stop ever greater numbers from breaking into the palace in search of loot but after a brief period, these vehicles 'began to weave suspiciously'. Attempts to block the entrance to the cellars also failed, and in desperation the local fire service was ordered to flood the cellars. Instead, the firemen joined the revellers. When Antonov-Ovseyenko and his fellow commissars nominated a special deputy and sent him to the cellars with a strong detachment of Red Guards, they discovered to their chagrin that their selected deputy 'also turned out not to be very reliable'.[15] The drunken celebrations of the fall of the Winter Palace continued for several days until the authorities announced that they intended to blow up the cellars with dynamite without any further warning unless the drinkers dispersed.

The Bolshevik seizure of power in Petrograd was relatively straightforward; most of those killed were military officers who were murdered by their rebellious soldiers. Knox, the British military attaché, bitingly commented that the sailors of the Baltic Fleet killed significantly more of their own officers than they had killed German officers during the entire war. But elsewhere in Russia, there was greater resistance to the Bolsheviks. There was heavy fighting in parts of Moscow; the Bolsheviks took control of the Kremlin, only to lose it to a strong counterattack by forces loyal to Kerensky's government. But neither side was able to secure a decisive advantage in the city and the Bolsheviks managed to negotiate a ceasefire while they awaited the definitive outcome of the revolution elsewhere. It seemed that such a moment was close when Kerensky attempted to return to Petrograd at the head of a column of troops made up largely of a Cossack division and several hundred officer cadets. As his force approached the capital, men began to slip away and it was a depleted group that formed up along the Pulkovo Heights at the southern outskirts of the city. Facing them were several thousand Red Guards, men of the Petrograd garrison who had gone over to the Bolsheviks, and sailors from the Baltic Fleet. Kerensky's forces attempted to break through the superior numbers of the Bolsheviks but were rapidly driven back to Tsarskoye Selo. With growing numbers of Cossacks deserting or refusing to fight, a ceasefire was negotiated, but the Bolsheviks moved into the town without warning and arrested the remaining officers of Kerensky's troops. Kerensky fled, eventually finding refuge in Paris and then New York where he died in 1970.

The collapse of Kerensky's attempt to recapture Petrograd resulted in a resumption of fighting in Moscow, where the Bolsheviks rapidly re-established their authority. But if the events in Petrograd had confirmed at least the initial success of the revolution, major problems remained. The fighting against forces loyal to either Kerensky or the tsar would eventually result in a civil war that raged for several years, but an even more pressing issue was the ongoing war against Germany. A peace treaty between the two sides was mutually desirable: the Germans were keen to take advantage of the rapidly diminishing time before the arrival of American forces in Europe to win the war in the west, and in order to do so they needed to transfer as many troops as they could from the east; the Bolsheviks faced the reality that Russia's armies were in no state to fight Germany and with a civil war rapidly developing, the situation would only worsen. In the negotiations that followed in the city of Brest-Litovsk, the Germans attempted to impose harsh terms on the Russians. Talks dragged on through the winter before collapsing in February 1918, and the Germans resumed hostilities.

As Lenin and Trotsky had feared, the Russian armies in their path were too weak and disorganised to put up any resistance. Generalmajor Max Hoffmann, chief of staff at *Ober Ost*, the German high command on the Eastern Front, had drawn up plans under the codename *Faustschlag* ('Punch'). These divided the available forces along three axes: 16 divisions were to move forward from positions in northern Latvia into Estonia, from where they could threaten Petrograd; the reinforced Tenth Army was to advance towards Smolensk; while the greatest concentration of forces would be in the south, to take control of Ukraine. The German divisions in the east were far from the first-class units with which Germany had started the war, but they were rested and well armed, and swiftly overcame the token resistance offered by their opponents. Hoffmann recorded the manner in which events unfolded in his diary:

> Our movements continue according to plan. It is the most comical war that I have ever experienced – it is conducted almost entirely on railways and with trucks. One puts a handful of infantry with machine-guns and a field gun on a train and drives to the next station, secures it, rounds up the Bolsheviks, brings up more troops by train, and drives on. In any event the experience has the attraction of novelty.[16]

After bitter debate, the Bolsheviks concluded that they had no option other than to accept German terms. At the beginning of March, the two delegations met once more in Brest-Litovsk and signed a treaty that was actually more severe on Russia than the terms rejected by Trotsky and other Bolshevik negotiators a few weeks earlier. One consequence of the treaty was that the entire Baltic region was to come under German control. This would put German soldiers on the Narva River, less than 80 miles from Petrograd.

Recognising the vulnerability of the city – especially given the parlous state of Russia's army – Lenin ordered that the government was to relocate to Moscow.

For the ordinary workers who had endured so much hardship in the capital city that Peter the Great had founded in the midst of a swampy, unpopulated province, the transfer of the capital to Moscow was just another in a series of blows. As predicted, there were major shortages of food throughout the winter of 1917–18, resulting in average daily calorie intake falling first to less than 1,400 at the beginning of the winter and then to half that in early 1918.[17] Nearly half of Russia's inadequate railway locomotives had ceased to function and a series of bitterly cold blizzards added to the misery of people huddling in overcrowded, inadequate housing. The loss of the status of capital city added to the woes of Petrograd, and throughout 1918 the situation deteriorated. Most factories were now closed through shortages of fuel and raw materials and people queued endlessly for meagre amounts of food; one academic calculated that the effort of waiting in line for hours on end and shuffling forward small distances often consumed more calories than were contained in the pitiful amount of food awaiting the recipient. Malnutrition and poor sanitation resulted in frequent outbreaks of typhus and other diseases, and the glittering city built by the tsars as their window to the west became an increasingly desolate and grim place.

The collapse of Kaiser Wilhelm's Germany resulted in Lenin and his Bolsheviks renouncing the terms of the Treaty of Brest-Litovsk. For the Bolsheviks, the revolution in Russia was always just the first step of their overall plan: Bolshevism could only succeed if it spread to all countries of the world. Exporting the revolution was therefore a high priority, and predictably the first places to experience this were the 'lost' parts of the Russian Empire. Large parts of Ukraine rapidly came back under Bolshevik control, though the area was repeatedly contested by armies supporting the 'White' Russian cause in the Civil War. Reoccupation of the Baltic coast was also a high priority for the Bolsheviks, not least because of the potential threat of invasion of Russia from that direction. Lenin foresaw little or no difficulty in mounting such an operation and anticipated that anti-Bolshevik resistance would rapidly collapse when he issued orders for an invasion: 'Cross the frontier somewhere, even if only to the depth of a kilometre, and hang 100–1000 of their civil servants and rich people.'[18]

The units of the Red Army that crossed into Estonia, Latvia, and Lithuania enjoyed varying degrees of success. From the perspective of defending Petrograd, the attack against Estonia was the most significant. At first, the

Bolshevik troops moved swiftly west along the flat coastal region, the traditional route via which armies had marched east and west through the centuries, and as 1918 drew to a close the leading elements of the Red Army were 21 miles from Tallinn, the Estonian capital. But it was the high tide mark and they would go no further on this occasion. Aided by Finnish volunteers and a British light cruiser squadron, the Estonians were rapidly organising themselves for defence and started to drive back the Bolsheviks. An attempt by the Baltic Fleet to lure the British light cruisers into an ambush ended disastrously with two Russian destroyers being captured and handed over to the Estonians, and a further attempt by the Red Army to renew its offensive in the early spring of 1919 was repulsed.

The fears of the Bolsheviks about the vulnerability of the Petrograd region to foreign invasion were about to be realised. In addition to the Estonian, Finnish, and British forces fighting the Red Army in Estonia, there was also a body of about 3,000 anti-Bolshevik White Russian soldiers under the command of Nikolai Nikolayevich Yudenich, who had been one of the tsar's generals. He was a physically uninspiring figure – slightly below average height, considerably overweight, and almost bald with a substantial moustache. Combined with a disdainful attitude to ordinary people, his physical appearance and dress habits showed quite clearly that he was an unreconstructed member of the old order, intent on restoring Russia's old ruling classes to their positions of privilege and power. Accompanied by small numbers of Estonian and even British volunteers, this force launched an operation codenamed *Belyy Mech* ('White Sword') on 13 May 1919, crossing into Russia near Narva. The Bolshevik 6th Rifle Division was swiftly routed and as Yudenich marched towards Petrograd, the Russian naval garrison in the fortress of Krasnaya Gorka mutinied against their Bolshevik commanders.

It was an important development. Krasnaya Gorka was less than 30 miles from the southwest suburbs of Petrograd, but internal divisions within the anti-Bolshevik groups prevented Yudenich from taking maximum advantage of the development. Although the Estonian authorities were aware of the mutiny, they took two days to inform Yudenich. The Estonians had been lukewarm about the entire operation from the outset with many Estonian politicians favouring an early peace treaty with Bolshevik Russia, and at first the Estonians attempted to take advantage of the mutiny by ordering their own contingent of Yudenich's army to march to the aid of the Krasnaya Gorka mutineers. This force proved to be too small to reach the fortress and before Yudenich could react, the Bolsheviks took their own measures.

Josef Stalin had been in exile in Siberia when the February Revolution overthrew Tsar Nicholas' government and after supporting Kerensky's government for much of 1917, he soon sided with the Bolsheviks and was heavily involved in the work of the committee that organised the October Revolution. Lenin now ordered him to take control of the defence of Petrograd and issued a defiant proclamation: 'Soviet Russia cannot give up Petrograd even for the briefest moment. The significance of this city, which first raised the banner of rebellion against the bourgeoisie, is too great.'[19]

In addition to improving the training and readiness of the Red Guards in the city, Stalin needed to move swiftly to suppress the mutiny and dispatched two of the large warships of the Baltic Fleet to bombard Krasnaya Gorka. An infantry unit was improvised using naval volunteers and stormed the ruins of the fortress, swiftly recapturing it. Many of those who had mutinied and then surrendered to the Bolsheviks were killed without any legal process or even presentation of evidence; Stalin also ordered the execution of several dozen naval officers in the Kronstadt base alleging that they were involved in a British-funded plot for a second mutiny.

As was frequently the case during the Russian Civil War, the conduct of both sides towards civilians was arbitrary and brutal, and many local people who might have joined Yudenich voluntarily grew resentful of the manner in which his men behaved. One of the senior officers in Yudenich's army was Stanisław Bułak-Bałachowicz, who had served as an officer in the Russian cavalry during the First World War and had commanded a special partisan regiment near Riga, fighting an effective campaign behind German lines for much of the war. He was wounded in the last days of fighting against the Germans – the incident actually took place two days after the Treaty of Brest-Litovsk came into effect – and after he joined the White Russian cause, he contributed significantly to the defeat of Bolshevik forces in Estonia. Operating on the southern flank of Yudenich's advance towards Petrograd, he and his cavalry terrorised the civilians in a manner that would become familiar during the German occupation of the same area: anyone suspected of pro-Bolshevik tendencies was at risk of summary execution, and Jews were singled out for punishment and death regardless of their political sympathies. The only way that the Jews could escape such risks was by paying huge ransoms, which Bułak-Bałachowicz allegedly used to settle his gambling debts. He repeatedly called on Bolshevik soldiers to defect, and then ordered his men to kill them when they did so, proudly proclaiming: 'You know me. I am the servant of the people. I am the sword of the people's justice.'[20]

When he took control of Pskov, Bułak-Bałachowicz arrested the members of the *Cheka*, the secret police precursors of the NKVD* and later the KGB. He then ordered the prisoners to execute themselves: 'I have no bullets to spare. And I have no one to hang you because all my men are busy with other things. I'll give you half an hour, you'll have to hang yourselves.'[21]

Perhaps fearing even worse mistreatment, the Chekists followed his instructions. The rope used by one of them broke and the man tried to flee; one of the White Russian officers caught him, dragged him to the river using the broken rope around his neck, and drowned him.

In many respects, Yudenich and others attempting to oppose the Bolsheviks were fighting the wrong war – conditioned by their experiences in the First World War, they continued to think in terms of huge quantities of artillery ammunition and other supplies instead of seizing the opportunities before them with speed and mobility. Weeks were wasted while Yudenich argued with the Western Powers for more aid but support was lukewarm at best, with little unity of purpose amongst the British, French and Americans. It took time for the supplies that were provided to be brought forward. It wasn't until the last quarter of 1919 that Yudenich's little army was ready to launch a decisive thrust at Petrograd.

At this stage, Yudenich enjoyed a stroke of good fortune. He was aware that the growing opposition to the Bolsheviks elsewhere in Russia had resulted in parts of the Petrograd garrison being transferred to the south, but he was unsure of the exact disposition of the troops facing him. As he prepared his invasion force, Colonel Lundkvist, who was chief of staff of the Bolshevik Seventh Army that was guarding the former Russian capital, made contact with the White Russian forces. He was willing to reveal the dispositions of all the city defences.[22] With 18,000 men now under his control and fully briefed on Bolshevik defensive positions and supported by a small force of British-operated tanks, Yudenich was confident that his numerically inferior force would prevail against the Bolsheviks. Stalin had spent the summer purging real, suspected and imagined anti-Bolsheviks from the Petrograd area, an experience that probably contributed to his lifelong distrust of the city – he would always regard it as too westward-looking, with an intellectual class that showed far too much independence of thought. By the time that Yudenich advanced, Stalin had been replaced in the city by Trotsky, the great orator who – with no military experience whatever –

---

* *Narodny Komissariat Vnutrennikh Del* or 'People's Commissariat for Internal Affairs', the Soviet Union's internal security force and forerunner of the KGB.

had played a leading role in arming and organising the Red Guards of the October Revolution. Trotsky once more called on the workers of the former capital to take up arms in defence of their revolution. As the White Russian force moved ever closer to Petrograd, many of its soldiers slipped away; some joined the Bolsheviks, while others merely took advantage of being in Russia to throw away their uniforms and set off for their homes, wherever they might be.

It was a critical time for the Bolsheviks. Advancing through almost constant rain and in appallingly muddy conditions, Yudenich began to move towards Petrograd. At the same time, other White Russian forces seemed to be gaining the upper hand in southern Russia, and the complete collapse of the Bolsheviks seemed to be a distinct possibility. All of the factors that had made the Neva estuary an unsuitable location for a new city in the time of Peter the Great, particularly its isolation from the rest of Russia, led many to question whether it would be possible to mount a meaningful defence. During the days of tsarist rule, Finland and Estonia had been part of the Russian Empire – now, both of them were independent and had fought against the Bolsheviks to secure their freedom. Although Yudenich's army had suffered from desertions and was actually outnumbered by Trotsky's forces in the city, it remained far better organised and was a formidable threat. Despite his previous assertions that Petrograd had to be held at all costs, Lenin and others in Moscow doubted that it would be possible to prevent the fall of the city, but Yudenich too was assailed by doubts. On his southern flank, the Red Army had retaken Pskov and it was only constant British pressure that prevented the Estonians from accepting repeated Bolshevik offers of peace – if a peace treaty were declared, Yudenich would find himself without any support or supply lines. He was also aware that the population of Petrograd faced a grim winter of food and fuel shortages and if he were to succeed in capturing the city, responsibility for rectifying this would lie with him. His staff suggested that he would need to ensure delivery of about 4,000 tons of food per week as an absolute minimum, which would require the cooperation of Estonia and the Western Powers.

Nevertheless, the initial advance of the White Russian forces towards the former capital made impressive progress. The railway line from Pskov to Petrograd was reached and cut at Luga, and the main thrust carried Yudenich's troops through the town of Gatchina. From here, they moved on, reaching and taking the Pulkovo Heights where Kerensky's advance in the aftermath of the October Revolution had come to a halt. Victory seemed very close, and the likelihood of success was so great that it even led to some disarray in White Russian ranks: Yudenich had ordered his 3rd Infantry Division to advance and cut the railway line running directly south from Petrograd, but instead the division commander turned north in the hope of being the first to enter the city.

Whilst Lenin might have been thinking about abandoning the city and adopting a shorter front line, Trotsky had other ideas. Even as the White Russian forces took Gatchina, he travelled north along the railway line that should have been severed by 3rd Infantry Division to reach Petrograd, insisting that the city – the cradle of the Bolshevik Revolution – had to be held. During his journey to the threatened city, his thoughts raced to formulate a proclamation that would inspire the city's defenders and fill them with confidence. In many respects, the thinking of this amateur soldier was far closer to the realities of urban warfare than that of the professional officers opposing him:

Our task is not only to defend Petrograd but to finish once and for all with the enemy's Northwest Army.

From this standpoint it would be militarily most to our advantage to let Yudenich's band get within the walls of the city itself, for Petrograd could without difficulty be turned into a trap for the White Guards.

Petrograd is not ... Luga ... In Petrograd there are nearly two-score thousand Communists, a substantial garrison, and immense, almost inexhaustible means of defence for use by the engineers and gunners.

If they broke into this gigantic city, the White Guards would find they had fallen into a stone labyrinth in which every building would be for them either a riddle, or a threat, or a mortal danger. From which direction should they expect the shot to come? From the window? From the attic? From the basement? From around the corner? From everywhere! We have machine-guns, rifles, revolvers, hand grenades ... We can block some streets with barbed-wire entanglements, while leaving others open and turning them into traps. For this purpose all that is needed is for a few thousand men to decide firmly that they will not surrender Petrograd.

What forces does the enemy have? Let us suppose that he has 5,000 men, or even 10,000. In the city streets they will be unable to manoeuvre either in compact masses or in extended lines. They will have to break up into small groups and detachments which will lose themselves in the streets and alleyways of Petrograd, without any proper communications and surrounded by danger at every corner.

The entire apparatus of communication within the city would be completely in our hands. Occupying a central position, we should operate along radial lines running from the centre to the periphery, aiming each of our blows in the direction of greatest importance for us. The possibility of uninterrupted transfer of troops and the abundance of means of transport would multiply our strength tenfold. Every fighter would feel that behind him was a well organised base and plentiful mobile reserves.

If the White Guards managed even to get sufficiently close to use their artillery before the arrival of our reinforcements, in that case too they would have gained nothing. An artillery bombardment of Petrograd would, of course, do damage to odd buildings here and there, and kill a certain number of the inhabitants, women and children. But the few thousand Red Guards, stationed behind barbed-wire entanglements and barricades, in basements or in attics would be subjected to very little risk in proportion to the total numbers of the population and to the number of shells fired.

In contrast, every White Guard who entered the city would be subjected to personal danger, for the defenders of Petrograd would shoot him as he advanced, from behind the barricades, from windows, and from around corners.

It would be most difficult of all for the White Guard cavalry since for each of them his horse would soon become a heavy burden.

Two or three days of street fighting like this would suffice for the invading bands to be transformed into a terrified, hunted herd of cowards who would surrender in groups or as individuals to unarmed passers-by or to women.

The whole heart of the matter lies in not giving up at the first moment. It was said long ago that a great city is a great panic, and there are undoubtedly in Petrograd not a few petty-bourgeois lackey remnants of the old regime, who are without willpower, energy, ideas or courage. This human pulp is, in itself, capable of nothing. But at a critical moment it often swells up strongly, absorbing the fumes of selfish fear and herd-like panic.

Fortunately for the revolution there are in Petrograd people of a different spirit, a different stamp: the advanced proletarians, and in the first place the conscious youth of the working class. Upon these elements rests the internal defence of Petrograd or, more precisely, the task of exterminating the White Russian bands if they should break into the proletarian capital.

Street battles do, of course, entail the risk of accidental victims and the destruction of cultural treasures. This is one of the reasons why the command in the field has to take all possible measures to prevent the enemy from entering Petrograd. But if the field units do not prove capable of doing this, and leave the way open for the enemy to get into Petrograd itself, this would not in the least mean that the struggle on the Petrograd front was over. On the contrary, the struggle would become more concentrated, more embittered and more resolute.

Responsibility for the innocent victims and the senseless destruction would lie wholly with the White bandits. But at the price of resolute, bold, fierce struggle in the streets of Petrograd we should achieve the complete extermination of the Northwest Army.

Petrograd, prepare!

More than once have October days been great days in your history. Destiny summons you to write during this October a fresh and perhaps even more glorious page in the history of the proletarian struggle.[23]

In short, Trotsky was prepared to draw the White Russian force into destructive urban warfare, but his preference was to defeat it before it could penetrate into the streets of Petrograd. Sensing a growing feeling of panic and despondency amongst his fellow Bolsheviks in the city – Grigory Yevseyevich Zinovyev, who was at that time chairman of the Petrograd Soviet, could barely gather enough energy to rise from a sofa in the Smolny Institute, which had been the headquarters of the Bolsheviks since the February Revolution – Trotsky used his instinctive feel for the morale of the people to superb effect. Many of the Red Guards had fled in terror from the small group of British tanks; Trotsky personally rallied them, riding out on horseback. He ridiculed the British war machines, telling the defenders that they were largely made of wood and could easily be disabled. He undoubtedly knew that this was untrue, but he had to harden the resolve of the city's defenders. He ordered the workers in the Putilov steel works in Petrograd to design and build a small force of armoured cars so that the Red Guards too could deploy such vehicles. Civilians were recruited into labour battalions to build barricades and dig trenches and arms were distributed to all who were capable of using them, but Trotsky covered all options. At the same time as active measures were taken to defend the city, a small fleet of motor vehicles was kept in the Smolny Institute in case a rapid evacuation of senior Bolsheviks became necessary. At first, the faces of the workers that Trotsky addressed were marked by fear and malnutrition, but with each passing day the determination of the workers hardened. The failure of Yudenich's subordinate to follow orders and cut the main railway line running south from the city proved to be disastrous: several trains carrying additional armaments managed to reach Petrograd, further boosting both morale and fighting power. Crucially, they also brought a brigade of battle-hardened Bolshevik troops from the south. But the centre of the defensive effort was Leon Trotsky. Even those like Zinovyev, who were resentful of Trotsky's personal ambitions, had to acknowledge the crucial role that he played:

Like fresh reinforcements arriving ... Trotsky's presence on the spot at once showed itself: proper discipline was restored and the military and administrative agencies rose to their task. Whoever was inefficient was demoted. The higher and the middle commanding personnel were changed. Trotsky's orders, clear and precise, sparing nobody and exacting from everybody the utmost exertion and accurate, rapid execution of combat orders, at once showed that there was a firm directing hand ... The inward rallying had begun. The staffs got into working order. Liaison, hitherto defective, became satisfactory. The supply departments began to function without a hitch. Desertion from the front was radically reduced. In all detachments field tribunals were in session ... Everybody began to realise that only one road was left: forward ... Trotsky penetrated into every detail, applying to every item of business his seething, restless energy and his amazing perseverance.[24]

For many of the inhabitants of the city, the change of name in 1914 from St Petersburg to Petrograd – and later, to Leningrad in January 1924 – made little difference. To them, their city was and always would be 'Piter', and they were determined to defend it. As a consequence of Trotsky's efforts, they now believed that they could prevail. A White Russian spy in the city sent a report to his superiors, describing the mood of the ordinary people:

The worker elements, at least a large section of them, are still Bolshevik inclined. Like some other democratic elements, they see the regime, although bad, as their own. Propaganda about the cruelty of the Whites has a strong effect on them ... Psychologically, they identify the present with equality and Soviet power, and the Whites with the old regime and its scorn for the masses.[25]

On 21 October, fighting erupted along the front line. Armed at first with nothing more than the rifles that they carried, the Red Guards fended off several White Russian attacks, including some that were led by the British tanks. The deployment of the experienced reinforcements who had just arrived by train swung the battle in favour of the Bolsheviks and Yudenich's army was levered out of its position along the Pulkovo Heights. Tsarskoye Selo – renamed Detskoye Selo to remove any association with the fallen Romanovs – and the Catherine and Alexandra Palaces were stormed in a battle that continued for three days. It was the second time that the Bolsheviks had successfully defended their city by defeating an enemy in this area.

Yudenich's retreat from Petrograd proved to be as swift as his advance to the outskirts of the city. With his army melting away as a result of desertion and battle losses, he had no choice but to order a withdrawal to Estonia. Gatchina was abandoned without a fight, and on 7 November – the anniversary of the October Revolution and coincidentally Trotsky's birthday – the man who had galvanised the defence of Petrograd was able to inform Moscow that victory was complete: 'In the Battle for Petrograd, Soviet power showed that it stands on its feet firmly and indestructibly. For that reason the Petrograd battle will have great significance in the weeks and months ahead.'[26]

Further humiliation awaited Yudenich when his beaten army reached the line of the Narva River: the Estonians would only permit him to cross the frontier if his army disarmed. It made little difference to Yudenich, whose ambitions were at an end. He resigned his command. Trotsky was inclined to pursue the White Russian forces across the frontier and issued a stern warning to the Estonians: they could not expect to function as an independent nation if they permitted their country 'to serve as a kennel for the pet dogs of counter-revolution'.[27] Determined to pursue an independent path into the future, the Estonians accepted the longstanding offer of the Bolsheviks for a ceasefire. This was followed by a peace treaty, establishing Bolshevik Russia's first formally agreed external border. Yudenich attempted to escape into exile in the west, but Bułak-Bałachowicz had him placed under arrest. He was briefly imprisoned, but with the general collapse of the White Russian cause, he was released and permitted to travel to France. He lived quietly near Nice until he died in 1933.

Yudenich left behind him the wreckage of his army. Thousands of men took shelter from the winter blizzards in the towns and villages of northwest Russia and didn't succeed in reaching Estonia; many were killed by the Bolsheviks, others were imprisoned or conscripted into the Red Army, or simply allowed to return to their homes. Disease swept through the ranks of those who did cross into Estonia, and the handful of men who managed to make their way south to join other White Russian forces took with them bitter memories of their failed campaign. The reversal of the fortunes of Yudenich's army was reflected by a similar series of setbacks elsewhere. Anton Ivanovich Denikin, who had seemed to be about to threaten Moscow, was driven back from the city of Orel, and Aleksandr Vasilyevich Kolchak, the nominal head of all White Russian forces, was defeated in Siberia and forced to retreat from Omsk. Trotsky was lauded as the hero who had saved Petrograd, cradle of the revolution. He became the first person to be awarded the Order of the Red Banner and the town of Gatchina was renamed Trotsk, but even before the Bolsheviks had completed their victory there were signs of internal division; Stalin was one of those who warned darkly of the risks of the cult of personality and 'Bonapartism' that was rising around Trotsky.

For the ordinary people who regarded 'Piter' as their home, the euphoria of victory over the White Russian forces was rapidly replaced by the reality of surviving another winter. Food and fuel remained in short supply and there was widespread malnutrition for several more months before the situation finally began to improve a little in the second half of 1920. Despite this, the following winter also saw widespread shortages and privations and it took a further two years for some semblance of normality to return to the region. To mark the third anniversary of the October Revolution in 1920, the Bolsheviks began what became a comprehensive series of attempts to redefine the events of the recent past. The most ambitious of them all was a huge spectacle in the centre of Petrograd entitled *The Storming of the Winter Palace*. Perhaps 100,000 people gathered in and around Admiralty Square as searchlights swung through the darkness, illuminating first one part of the great palace, then another. Soldiers drove into the square in trucks and formed up with fixed bayonets, machine-guns rattled, and out on the Neva the armoured cruiser *Aurora* fired a blank round as it had done three years before. Then columns of Red Guards entered the square and 'attacked' the Winter Palace. Silhouettes of figures in hand-to-hand combat were projected onto the walls; Kerensky was portrayed fleeing the scene disguised as a woman; and as a red banner was unfurled from the rooftops, the crowd gave a stirring chorus of the *Internationale*. But as the shortages and rampant inflation continued to bite, many workers once more took to the streets in February 1921 to protest at the lack of basic progress. Even the sailors stationed at Kronstadt, who had been staunch supporters of the Bolsheviks, showed increasing signs of discontent. They and many others in Bolshevik Russia began to wonder whether they had merely replaced one oppressive government with another, as a sailor later recalled after a visit to his home village: 'When we returned home, our parents asked why we fought for the oppressors. That set us thinking.'[28]

Dissent erupted into open revolt in March 1921 as the sailors in Kronstadt demanded an end to what they described as Lenin's 'Commissarocracy'. After a standoff that lasted a week, the Bolsheviks brought up artillery and commenced a bombardment of the island. On 17 March, fearing that the winter ice around the island was about to break up and make an assault much more difficult, Mikhail Nikolayevich Tukhachevsky, the prominent commander and theoretician of the Red Army, ordered his men to attack. Bitter fighting lasted all day before the last strongholds of the rebellious sailors were crushed.

The transfer of the government from Petrograd to Moscow had added to the problems caused by food and fuel shortages, as the Bolsheviks ensured that the new capital took top priority in getting what supplies were available. The aftermath of the Kronstadt Revolt saw a wave of arrests as Lenin and his colleagues moved to stamp out any faint embers of opposition, and faced by the impossibility of continuing to survive in a city with no jobs, no food and no firewood, people began to move away from Petrograd. In the last days of the rule of Tsar Nicholas, Petrograd had been home to about 2.3 million people, albeit most of them living in squalid and overcrowded conditions; as the guns fell silent on and around Kronstadt, the population had fallen to about 720,000.[29] In some respects, the remaining inhabitants were living through the death of the city known as Petrograd and its transformation into a new city. On 21 January 1924, Lenin – who had been ailing for some time and had suffered several strokes – lost consciousness and died. Five days later, the Bolsheviks renamed the city created by Peter the Great in honour of their dead leader. The change of name from Petrograd to Leningrad (and the renaming of many streets and buildings in honour of Lenin and other Bolsheviks) was more than symbolic. It marked the beginning of the development of the city in a new form. The desperate need for housing – even despite the huge fall in the city's population – led to many of the suburbs, particularly in the southern part of the city, being reorganised and redeveloped. The new apartment buildings that arose were austere and simple, but they were a huge improvement on the wooden shanties that had preceded them. When he came to power, Stalin deliberately set about moving the centre of the city from the grand buildings of the tsarist era on the southern banks of the Neva to the new areas of the south. Moskovsky Prospekt, a highway that ran due south from the central district, was to become the new main thoroughfare of Leningrad, with a new city hall built on the street.

Even as Leningrad's identity was changing, the portrayal of recent history continued to evolve. In 1927, Sergei Mikhailovich Eisenstein, the great Soviet filmmaker, commenced work on a new work entitled *October*. Ultimately, the film would go around the world with the title *Ten Days that Shook the World*, and it cemented the legend of the storming of the Winter Palace. Even though the fall and exile of Trotsky resulted in a downplaying of the significance of his defence of the city against Yudenich – the town that had been renamed Trotsk in his honour now became Krasnogvardeisk – the central role of Leningrad in the mythology of Bolshevism was firmly established.

As the 1920s and 1930s passed, the population gradually recovered and new industries replaced those that had died in the aftermath of the year of revolutions. By 1932, the manufacture of iron and steel products was five times that of 1913, and in addition to producing tens of thousands of tractors in factories that had been consciously designed for easy conversion to tank production, Leningrad manufactured 90 per cent of the Soviet Union's hydroelectric turbines and 80 per cent of its telephones. These figures grew steadily through the 1930s – even at the beginning of the decade, the city's factories accounted for a quarter of the Soviet Union's iron and steel products and over 30 per cent of its industrial chemicals. In addition to its symbolic importance as the cradle of the revolution, Leningrad was increasingly an irreplaceable industrial asset of the Soviet Union.

What the Soviet Union needed was a period of stability. It had emerged from the Civil War bearing the scars and divisions of the conflict, and the Bolsheviks inherited a country with a very limited industrial base. It would take time and a spell of peace to remedy these problems, and with Germany weakened by the terms of the Treaty of Versailles, there was at least the possibility of such a respite. But if there were few serious external threats to peace and stability, Stalin was quite capable of imagining such threats from within the country.

CHAPTER 2

STALIN'S PURGES

Leon Trotsky, the saviour of Petrograd, was born Lev Davidovich Bronstein in 1879, the fifth child of wealthy Jewish parents who lived in a small village in southern Ukraine. He was encouraged to embrace Marxism by his future first wife, Aleksandra Sokolovskaya, when he went to university to study mathematics; he abandoned his studies and became a political activist, but was arrested in 1898. He languished in prison for two years, during which time he adopted the name of Trotsky, allegedly copying the name of one of his jailors. He and his new wife were banished to Siberia for four years, but Trotsky escaped halfway through his exile and travelled to London. Here, he came into contact with Lenin and other prominent revolutionaries; it is perhaps unsurprising that the strong personalities of Lenin and Trotsky resulted in disagreement over many issues. Although Trotsky later expressed regret for his opposition to Lenin, the latter never forgave him, referring to him as a scoundrel and 'Little Judas'.

Trotsky returned to Russia in 1905 and took part in the uprisings that followed Bloody Sunday in 1905. He was arrested once more and as had been the case following his previous arrest, he was dispatched to Siberia after a lengthy spell awaiting trial. On this occasion, he escaped en route to exile. Like many Marxists he was strongly opposed to the First World War, seeing it as a war fought by and for the benefit of capitalists and rich aristocrats, but paid for with the blood of ordinary people. He was in Canada when the February Revolution overthrew the tsar and promptly tried to return to Russia. His ship was intercepted by the British and he was briefly detained before finally returning to his homeland in May. He played a prominent part in organising the October Revolution, something for which he was initially praised by Stalin, and rapidly became second only to Lenin in importance amongst the Bolsheviks. As People's Commissar for

Foreign Affairs (effectively the foreign minister), he led the Russian delegation in peace talks with the Germans at Brest-Litovsk. He was a prominent voice against accepting the punitive terms offered by the Germans but ultimately abstained in a critical vote, allowing Lenin to secure peace, albeit a humiliating one. Trotsky then resigned as foreign minister.

Immediately, he took up a new role as People's Commissar for Army and Naval Affairs (effectively defence minister). Despite no military experience he proved highly effective in organising the defence of Petrograd against Yudenich's army and showed no hesitation in taking severe measures against any who opposed the Bolsheviks. He was a proponent of harsh punishment for desertion and indiscipline, but also recognised the need for experienced soldiers and overruled many of his fellow Bolsheviks who wished to exclude all officers who had any connection with the old tsarist armies. It was inevitable that in the often chaotic world of Bolshevik plotting and manoeuvring for power, he would make enemies. Stalin was one such opponent, openly critical of Trotsky's policies, and during the war with Poland in 1920 the two men clashed again. Stalin and Trotsky had both cautioned Lenin against the war, but once the conflict began Stalin was one of the commanders of the Bolshevik Cavalry Army who ignored instructions from Trotsky to support the main attack towards Warsaw, choosing instead to try to capture Lviv. Thenceforth, the two men increasingly found themselves in opposing camps. When Lenin's health declined, Trotsky paid a heavy price for making enemies of other Bolsheviks like Zinovyev, who allied themselves with Stalin.

In early 1928, after several clashes that left him increasingly marginalised, Trotsky and his second wife were exiled to Alma Ata in Kazakhstan. A year later, they were expelled from the Soviet Union and travelled first to Turkey and after staying in a number of countries the couple finally reached Mexico in 1937. In March 1939 Soviet agents made an unsuccessful attempt to kill him, but a year later an agent of the NKVD, Ramón Mercader, fatally wounded him with an ice axe.

After exiling Trotsky, Stalin was not slow in moving against other opponents. Nikolai Ivanovich Bukharin, another prominent figure in the years of struggle, was at first a political opponent of Trotsky and allied himself with Stalin; a charismatic man with an infectious sense of mischief and humour, he was seen by Stalin as a friend, but the Soviet head of state also feared and envied him. Working together, the two men steadily eroded the support for Trotsky's wing of the Communist Party and at the time of Trotsky's exile Bukharin was widely seen as the leader of the right wing of the Bolsheviks. However, despite this period of close cooperation, differences soon emerged between Stalin and Bukharin; the former wished to press forward with rapid collectivisation of farming, whereas Bukharin feared that this amounted to almost feudal exploitation of rural communities, particularly in connection with Stalin's plans for forcible grain requisition.

Bukharin wanted the Soviet government to reward farmers for being more productive and called for financial benefits for those who worked more efficiently. Perhaps fearing Bukharin as a potential challenger, Stalin systematically sidelined Party members who supported Bukharin. In 1929, Bukharin was expelled from the Politburo and dismissed as editor of the newspaper *Pravda*. Amongst those who fell from high office with Bukharin was Martemyan Nikitich Ryutin, another opponent of agricultural collectivisation, who was temporarily expelled from the Communist Party in 1930. Working in secret, he attempted to build an opposition bloc within the Communist Party known as *Soyuz Marksistov-Lenintsev* ('Union of Marxist-Leninists'). This group published a number of pamphlets, including one that attempted to blame Stalin for the problems faced by the Soviet Union:

> The Party and the dictatorship of the proletariat have been led into an uncharted blind alley by Stalin and his associates and are now experiencing a mortally dangerous crisis. Using deception and slander, and aided by unimaginable pressures and terror tactics, Stalin has filtered out and removed from the leadership all the best, truly Bolshevik party groups over the past five years, has established in the Communist Party and the entire country his personal dictatorship, has broken with Leninism, and has embarked on a path of the most unregulated adventurism and unchecked personal arbitrariness.[1]

The group created by Ryutin was small, perhaps fewer than 20, but it provided Stalin with an opportunity to crush opposition to his personal vision of how the state should be governed. For many years Stalin and others had told the Soviet people that their nation faced real and existential enemies beyond its borders; it was an easy step to transition from this to dealing with internal enemies who might aid and abet the foreign threats. The opposition from Trotsky had already stimulated Stalin's sense of paranoia, and although the *Soyuz Marksistov-Lenintsev* was almost insignificant in terms of its size, it contributed to Stalin's growing fear of internal opposition. In late 1932 several leading figures were expelled from the Communist Party and exiled from

Moscow. Ryutin was arrested and interrogated; he was then sentenced to ten years' imprisonment.

In order to fund industrial expansion and to purchase heavy machinery from other countries, the Bolshevik government appropriated large quantities of grain from farmers in Ukraine, creating widespread shortages that rapidly escalated into a famine, resulting in millions of deaths through starvation. Any dissent was violently crushed, with those who complained of the devastation caused by grain appropriation and collectivisation of farming being condemned as reactionaries. Even in the nation's industrial cities, there was no escape from Stalin's increasing paranoia, and he watched the resurrection of Leningrad with mixed feelings. In particular, he was concerned by the popularity of Sergei Mironovich Kirov, who impressed Leningraders with his honesty and openness in his role as First Secretary of the Leningrad City Committee of the Communist Party. He deliberately adopted a manner that contrasted strongly with Stalin – instead of living in a fortress surrounded by guards and his inner entourage, he shared a large house with other residents of the city (many of the palaces and mansions of the tsarist era had been converted into communal housing for several families to share) and walked to work, greeting his fellow citizens openly, though he was usually accompanied by bodyguards who kept a discreet distance. At the Communist Party's Seventeenth Congress in 1934 Kirov allegedly topped the poll in elections, resulting in some of Stalin's supporters deliberately destroying sufficient ballot papers to ensure that Kirov shared the top spot with Stalin. Later that year, Stalin moved against his rival. Leonid Vasilyevich Nikolayev, who allegedly feared that his wife was having an affair with Kirov, went to the Smolny Institute on 1 December where the usual guards were inexplicably absent. He waited in a hallway and shot Kirov in the back of the neck as he passed.

Nikolayev was arrested, tried, and executed before the end of the month before any serious investigation could be carried out. Stalin used the murder of Kirov as a pretext for unleashing his wave of terror across the Soviet Union, and Andrei Aleksandrovich Zhdanov, a Stalinist loyalist who replaced Kirov at the head of the Party administration in Leningrad, showed particular ruthlessness in purging those he and Stalin regarded as less than completely loyal. As the pursuit of 'enemies of the state' spread through the Soviet Union, almost everyone faced the risk of arrest. Confessions were beaten out of those who were dragged from their homes, and most victims were forced to provide a list of other 'conspirators' in return for a modicum of leniency. The number of suspects thus soared, and extended into all walks of life. Osip Emilyevich Mandelshtam, a widely respected poet who lived in Moscow, quipped to his friends that the Soviet Union took poetry more seriously than any other nation in the world, adding that there was no country where more people were killed for it. In the prevailing atmosphere of suspicion and betrayal, it was a dangerous thing to say. Even more dangerous was a short poem that Mandelshtam composed – he was careful not to write it down, merely reciting it to close friends – that described Stalin in the most unflattering terms and accusing him of delighting in mass killings. He was denounced and arrested and sentenced to internal exile. He was later given a partial reprieve, only to be arrested again almost immediately. He died in a transit camp in 1938.

The period of terror that spread throughout the Soviet Union in 1934 became known as the Great Purge, with hundreds of thousands of people being detained. One of the striking features of this wave of repression was the manner in which belonging to the Communist Party was of little significance. What was at issue was not whether an individual was against Communism: it was unmistakably repression of any and all individuals and groups that might attempt to oppose Stalin. Another victim of these arrests was Aleksandra, the first wife of Leon Trotsky. She disappeared into the prison system in 1935 and was executed a few years later. Orders to arrest individuals were carried out with little regard for circumstances. One man was undergoing surgery for a stomach ulcer when officers arrived to take him into custody and he was dragged away to the cells with his abdomen unsutured.[2]

Commencing in 1936, there were several major show trials in Moscow. The first was held in August and featured the prosecution of 16 former Communist Party members, notably Zinovyev and Lev Borisovich Kamenev, both of whom had been prominent Bolshevik figures in the previous decade; ironically, Stalin had relied heavily on both these men to secure his position as Lenin's successor and to oppose Trotsky. All those charged were found guilty, sentenced to death, and executed. A year later, 17 more former Party members were charged. Of these, 13 were executed, and the other four dispatched to labour camps where they died within months. At the same time, tens of thousands of ordinary people were arrested and dispatched to labour camps in Siberia or shot. The families of those who disappeared often received little or no news. Some were told that those who had been arrested had been sentenced to ten years' imprisonment 'without the right to correspondence'. This was almost always untrue – the prisoners were usually already dead before their families were informed. When the end of the ten-year period came, families who anxiously enquired if they could now send letters were curtly told that their family members had died during their imprisonment.

The scale of the repression was huge. Spies and saboteurs were identified everywhere, not least because people under arrest were put under huge pressure to denounce others in return for marginally more lenient treatment. After a coalmine disaster in November 1936, instructions were issued effectively declaring any railway and industrial accidents, fires etc. as acts of sabotage, with a requirement for those responsible to be identified and punished. At the beginning of 1937 the level of suspicion about sabotage reached surreal levels: when a census of the Soviet population was completed, it was found that there were fewer Soviet citizens than the Party hierarchy had believed existed. The census report was promptly classified as secret and its authors imprisoned.

The repression gathered pace through 1937. The NKVD was one of the main instruments of repression and its ranks were also extensively purged before it was strengthened and enlarged. This became an area of repeated attention – in 1938 and 1939, the NKVD was restructured three times. During the summer of 1937, Stalin ordered the NKVD and local Party officials to produce estimates of the numbers of those liable for arrest – suspected 'criminals' and 'kulaks' (peasants who owned even modest parcels of land and livestock), former officials of Imperial Russia, and those suspected of having been members of political parties other than the Communist Party. A few weeks later, a huge roundup commenced. The detainees were mostly sent to Siberia or executed with no legal process. Such was the scale of work that despite deploying 25,000 personnel for the task, the NKVD couldn't cope and had to draft in reinforcements from the ordinary police. When this proved to be inadequate, Party officials were ordered to serve alongside the NKVD. Those interrogated were often forced to sign blank confessions in order to speed up the process; details could be added at a later stage if required.[3]

The show trials in Moscow for more prominent figures continued throughout this period. In March 1938, more well-known Bolsheviks were brought before the court. One, Nikolai Nikolayevich Krestinsky, immediately declared that he disowned the written confession that had been shown to the court and pleaded not guilty; the following day, nursing a freshly dislocated left shoulder and other injuries, a subdued Krestinsky admitted his guilt.[4] Bukharin, another of the defendants, was in many respects the 'star defendant' and despite frequent denials of mistreatment by senior Soviet figures, he was repeatedly beaten and tortured; after three months of such treatment, he finally gave in when his captors threatened to inflict the same violence on his wife and children. The outcome was a lengthy confession that was in part a repudiation of the entire process, largely demonstrating that he could disprove most or all of the allegations made against him. Nonetheless, he was executed. The promise made by his interrogators to spare his family was ignored – his wife was sent to a labour camp.

The damage to Soviet society was huge, but the repression had acquired a momentum of its own and continued into all parts of the Soviet system. Through 1937 and 1938, various nationalities within the Soviet Union were identified as 'enemies' and systematically persecuted. Tens of thousands of ethnic Poles, Lithuanians, Latvians, Estonians, Finns, and Chinese were rounded up; in many cases, local NKVD officials were ordered to arrest a specific number of people and simply fulfilled these quotas with no regard for any legal process. A woman went to the local offices of the NKVD in a city near Rostov to complain that an earlier arrest had left a small baby without anyone to care for it; in an attempt to fulfil their quota, the NKVD personnel took her to the cells. Between half and three quarters of those arrested were executed. Wives of those arrested were sentenced to hard labour for five to ten years and their children were placed in orphanages. But in terms of its impact upon the nation's readiness to deal with a foreign military threat, the greatest damage was done when the purges reached the ranks of the army.

Mikhail Nikolayevich Tukhachevsky was one of the great figures of the early Red Army. He joined the Imperial Russian Army in 1912 and graduated from a military school two years later with high marks. After serving as a junior officer in the Life Guards Semenovsky Regiment, he was taken prisoner by the Germans in 1915. He made several attempts to escape, succeeding in reaching Switzerland in 1917 after his fifth attempt. He volunteered to join the Red Army the following year, becoming military commissar of the Moscow Defence District and then commander of First Army, which he led with distinction; this was his first opportunity to put into practice his ideas of deep penetration of the enemy front and rapid, flexible operations as the battle unfolded.

Despite being in overall command of the Red Army's forces that invaded Poland in 1920 and were then resoundingly defeated, Tukhachevsky remained a prominent personality in the military. He commanded Seventh Army in the suppression of the Kronstadt uprising in 1921, working closely with Trotsky; this was followed by the brutal repression of a peasant uprising in the Tambov area in which he showed no compunction to use whatever means were necessary. His orders of June 1921 made this clear:

The forests where the bandits are hiding should be cleared with poison gas, precisely calculated so that a cloud of suffocating gas spreads through the forest, destroying everything that is hiding in it.

The Inspector of Artillery is to deliver the required number of poison gas cylinders and the necessary specialists to the field immediately …

Upon arrival [of the Bolshevik forces] the rural district is to be cordoned off, up to 100 of the most prominent locals seized as hostages, and a state of siege established … Residents are given two hours to hand over bandits and weapons, as well as the families of bandits … If the population does not identify the bandits and hand over weapons within two hours, they are to be gathered a second time, and the hostages are to be shot before the eyes of the population, after which new hostages are taken and those at the gathering are again ordered to hand over bandits and weapons.[5]

After the anti-Bolshevik turmoil across the country had been eliminated, Tukhachevsky continued to rise, first to command of Western Front and then Leningrad Military District. During this time he was also head of the Red Army's Military Academy and began to write extensively about future military operations. His criticism of the unpreparedness of the Red Army for a major conflict – based partly on his personal experiences in Poland – resulted in harsh criticism from Stalin and others, particularly because some of Tukhachevsky's analysis was implicitly or explicitly directed against senior figures in the military who were close friends and associates of Stalin. But despite the hostility from Stalin, Tukhachevsky was promoted to marshal in 1935 with responsibility for preparing the Red Army for future wars. He wrote extensively about the concept of 'deep battle', in which infantry, artillery, motorised units, and aircraft would cooperate closely to conduct an operation that extended through the full depth of enemy positions. He specifically recognised that the traditional Red Army practice of top-down control was inappropriate for modern warfare; officers should not have to wait for orders from above, but should be trained to think for themselves and to respond rapidly to new developments on the battlefield.

The armies of all the major military powers of the world had been struggling with issues of command and control for at least a century. Even during the Napoleonic Wars, it had become clear that it was almost impossible for generals to direct operations successfully if unexpected circumstances arose. The solution for this was the adoption of increasingly detailed and lengthy sets of orders that attempted to cover all possibilities, but such a policy was unwieldy and doomed to failure – the orders took too long to draft and in any case couldn't possibly provide instructions that dealt with all eventualities. Seeking a solution to this, Helmuth von Moltke, chief of the general staff of first the Prussian Army and then the German Army, formulated a different approach. The solution to the increasing complexity of warfare was independent thinking and initiative by subordinate commanders. He summarised this in a single sentence:

> Diverse are the situations under which an officer has to act on the basis of his own view of the situation. It would be wrong if he had to wait for orders at times when no orders can be given. But productive are his actions when he acts within the framework of his senior commander's intent.[6]

Many of the successes of the armies of Germany can be attributed to this devolved form of command: subordinates were routinely trained to show initiative and to act as their judgement dictated, whilst always staying within the overall intention of their superiors. But such an approach required a highly educated officer corps with trust working in both directions: superior officers had to trust the judgement and decision-making of their subordinates, while those subordinates had to understand and approve of the overall objectives of their superiors. Few armies succeeded in achieving such flexibility, and although Tukhachevsky recognised the need for commanders involved in 'deep battle' to think for themselves, he must have been aware that he faced serious obstacles in implementing such policies in the Red Army. Despite rising levels of literacy since the Russian Revolution, the education of many officers remained far below the standard that was normal in other armies, and their military training placed no emphasis on the freedom of thought and flexibility that men like Moltke regarded as essential. Moreover, there were many within the Soviet hierarchy who regarded such independence of thought amongst military figures as an unacceptable threat to the state.

Tukhachevsky was criticised for more than just his overall approach to decision-making and the conduct of operations. His views on the use of modern weapons were in stark contrast to some of the veterans of the Russian Civil War who formed Stalin's inner circle, particularly Kliment Yefremovich Voroshilov, Semen Mikhailovich Budennyi, and Semen Konstantinovich Timoshenko. Budennyi, the former commander of the Bolshevik First Cavalry Army, was particularly critical of Tukhachevsky and complained that resources were being wasted on tanks that could be better used in training more cavalry. Tukhachevsky was frequently outspoken in his responses as Georgy Konstantinovich Zhukov, who would play such a major role in the Second World War, later recalled:

> Voroshilov ... was a man of little competence. He remained an amateur in military matters to the end and never understood them deeply and seriously ...

In practical terms, a significant part of the work in the People's Commissariat [for defence, i.e. the Soviet defence ministry] lay at that time with Tukhachevsky, who was a real military specialist. He often clashed with Voroshilov and they had a mutually hostile relationship … [On one occasion] Voroshilov began to express dissatisfaction [with a report from Tukhachevsky] and made a rambling speech. After listening to him, Tukhachevsky said in his usual calm voice, 'Comrade People's Commissar, the commission cannot accept your recommendations.'

'Why not?' asked Voroshilov.

'Because your recommendations are incompetent.'[7]

As Stalin's purges tore through all parts of society, his paranoia was fuelled by the huge numbers of confessions and denunciations, even though most had been extracted under huge duress and had often been drawn up by the interrogators in advance. Inevitably, he became increasingly reliant on his old comrades and suspicious of all those outside this circle. After the May Day parade of 1937, he told Budennyi and other close associates that the time was ripe for the elimination of enemies throughout the Soviet Union, including those within the army. Budennyi and Voroshilov had been urging Stalin to move against those they saw as opponents within the army for some considerable time; the latter repeatedly drew Stalin's attention to Tukhachevsky's alleged contacts with French and German military figures. These were claimed to have arisen during Tukhachevsky's period of imprisonment in the First World War, when he was a lowly NCO – even if he had made contact with foreign officers at that time, it was surely wildly unlikely that these would later mature into some sort of anti-Soviet conspiracy. In later years, the Germans would claim that they manipulated the course of events, laying false evidence that Tukhachevsky was plotting Stalin's overthrow, but this too seems unlikely. Indeed, a later study suggested that Nikolai Ivanovich Yezhov, head of the NKVD, acted on Stalin's instructions to leak information to the Germans via a double agent about a potential plot led by Tukhachevsky to overthrow Stalin. When the Germans then used this information to undermine Tukhachevsky, they were unwittingly furthering Stalin's aims.

On 11 May, Stalin made his move. Tukhachevsky was dismissed as Deputy Defence Commissar and dispatched to the Volga region. Eleven days later he was arrested and brought back to the capital and subjected to brutal interrogation. This was a recurring feature of Stalin's purges – when officials were dismissed, they were first transferred to another post, perhaps in an attempt to encourage them to believe that this was the full extent of their fall from grace, before they were placed under arrest. As a result of his interrogation, Tukhachevsky pleaded guilty to charges that he was preparing a military conspiracy. The document recording his confession and bearing his signature has survived; it includes bloodstains that were probably splashed across it when Tukhachevsky was being beaten. In June 1937 there was a brief, closed trial. Tukhachevsky and six others were found guilty and sentenced to death; they were shot within a day. Almost immediately, members of Tukhachevsky's family were placed under arrest. His wife Nina and his two brothers – both were instructors in Soviet military academies – were executed within a few weeks. Three of Tukhachevsky's sisters were arrested and sent to prison camps in Siberia. His daughter Svetlana, who was aged 15, was also arrested and imprisoned in Siberia and remained there until 1956 when Nikita Khrushchev came to power.

It was the beginning of a widespread and hugely damaging purge that tore through the ranks of the Red Army. At the time, the Red Army had four men holding the rank of marshal in addition to Tukhachevsky. In the months that followed, two further marshals – Vasily Konstantinovich Blyukher and Aleksandr Ilyich Yegorov – were arrested, charged, and executed. Both men had been part of the eight-man tribunal that had sat in judgement in Tukhachevsky's trial, and three other generals from the tribunal were also arrested. Two – Yakov Ivanovich Alksnis and Nikolai Dmitriyevich Kashirin – were executed. The third – Yelisei Ivanovich Goryachev – committed suicide. The Red Army had 15 army commanders, and 13 of them were removed from their posts together with eight of the nine admirals in the navy, 50 out of 57 corps commanders, all 16 army commissars, and 25 out of 28 corps commissars.[8] Over the next two years, over 33,000 officers in the army, navy and air force were either dismissed from their posts or arrested; many of the latter were then executed.[9] The result was devastation to the ranks of the military. In many cases, the men appointed as replacements barely had time to take up their new posts before they too were arrested. The influence of the Communist Party was greatly increased at every level. Although political commissars had been in place before the purges, they were now regarded with fear by army officers, who lived under the constant danger of being denounced or reported for the slightest deviation from official instructions or doctrine. The consequence was the almost complete elimination of the sense of initiative and local decision-making that Tukhachevsky had rightly identified as an essential part of modern warfare.

The arrest of Tukhachevsky resulted in a ripple of arrests into groups that had already been purged, such as the Soviet intelligentsia. Some had lucky escapes, sometimes because the purges were extended into the ranks of the security forces that were responsible for the arrests. Dmitry Dmitriyevich

Shostakovich, the famous composer, fell from favour when his Fourth Symphony was criticised – almost certainly on the instructions of Stalin – for being too 'formalist'. Although 'formalism' was a term widely used in criticism of Shostakovich and other artists, it was a dangerous word with no real meaning – Stalin and others could interpret it in almost any manner they wished. At the height of the purges, Shostakovich was summoned to the headquarters of the NKVD in Leningrad and questioned about meetings that he had had with Tukhachevsky. The two men had been close friends, and Shostakovich protested in vain that their conversations had been apolitical. He was sent home and told to return two days later, having thought carefully about what he intended to say. Shostakovich spent the weekend saying farewell to his family, believing that he was certain to be arrested and would then disappear. But when he returned to the NKVD building, he waited in vain to be called in for further interrogation, and learned late in the day that he was free to go: the NKVD officer who had seen him two days previously had himself been arrested and charged with treason, and all of his appointments had been cancelled.[10]

Even as the purges began, the NKVD was already divided into mutually suspicious factions either centred around key personalities like Yezhov and Genrikh Grigoryevich Yagoda, or based on regionality – there were thus groups of officers from Ukraine, the Caucasus, etc. As soon as he was appointed as head of the NKVD in September 1936, Yezhov used the investigations into the killing of Kirov as an opportunity to remove large numbers of personnel who had been employed by (and therefore might owe allegiance to) his predecessor Yagoda. In conducting this purge, Yezhov relied heavily on personnel that he brought to Moscow, Leningrad and other major cities from the Caucasus. Yagoda had been transferred from his post as head of the NKVD and appointed People's Commissar for Communications, but he was arrested in March 1937 and charged with 'crimes against the state' during his time as head of the NKVD. There is some evidence that he was involved in a scheme to export timber felled by labourers from prison camps in Siberia and that the proceeds of this were placed in a Swiss bank account. The money placed in this account was still unclaimed in 2014.[11] But as was the case with so many of those arrested, the charges against him centred on his involvement in conspiracies to overthrow Stalin on the basis of his denunciation by several other senior figures. He was tried in March 1938, found guilty of treason, and executed.

In August 1938, Lavrenty Pavlovich Beriya, a Georgian who had been active in purging suspected conspirators throughout the Caucasus region, was appointed as Yezhov's deputy. Almost immediately, power began to slip away from Yezhov.

Several senior NKVD officers fled the country in order to escape arbitrary arrest and punishment and Yezhov found himself facing charges of permitting enemies of the people to infiltrate the ranks of the NKVD. Aware that his arrest was probably imminent, Yezhov wrote to Stalin in late 1938, begging the Soviet leader not to take any action against Yezhov's elderly mother. He was removed from his post in the NKVD in November 1938 and arrested the following April. In addition to aiding enemies of the state, he was prosecuted for homosexuality and was executed in 1940. All of those accused of having homosexual affairs with him were also executed.

The pace of the purges slackened after Beriya took charge of the NKVD, not least because the widespread arrests and executions had eliminated so many people in high positions and they had been replaced with personnel deemed to be 'clean' – in reality, this meant that they had almost no experience whatever in their roles but were regarded as being rigidly loyal to Stalin. Nonetheless, there was another huge reorganisation of the NKVD with some of those thought to have been too closely associated with Yezhov being moved to lesser positions within the state structure, usually outside the security apparatus. Over 300,000 of those arrested from all walks of life who had escaped execution or death during imprisonment were released in the two years immediately before the onset of hostilities with Germany, but many found themselves severely constrained and were unable to return to their previous work. Those who did manage to be reappointed were understandably exceedingly cautious about any activity that might draw attention to themselves.

The damage to almost every part of Soviet life, with academics, political figures, army officers, artists, and industrialists dispatched to Siberia or executed after minimal legal process, was huge. The shadow of the purges was still hanging heavily over the nation as war clouds began to gather in the late 1930s. But regardless of the change of status of the city, or the change of its name, or the fall of its saviour Trotsky, or even the terrible purges of the 1930s, the people of Leningrad had no doubt about the central place of their city in the Soviet Union. There was almost a paradox at the heart of the city: on the one hand, a large proportion of its population had been born elsewhere and had moved to Leningrad; but on the other hand, regardless of whether they were relative newcomers to the city or had lived there all their lives, they shared an intense pride and sense of identity. Their numbers had increased again, now standing at 3.8 million. Leningrad, created by Peter the Great from nothing in an unpromising corner of his empire, was where the people had risen up to overthrow the tsar, and had then rebelled again to put the Bolsheviks in power. The Red Guards –

recruited from the ordinary workers of the city – had defended it, first against Kerensky's forces and then against the White Russian army of Yudenich. On both occasions, they had halted the enemy along the Pulkovo Heights at the southern outskirts of the city. However much Stalin might try to downplay those events in order to detract from Trotsky's memory, the ordinary people remembered. If the need arose, they would fight again for the cradle of the revolution, for the industrial powerhouse of the Soviet Union, but particularly for 'Piter', their home. Even the suffering inflicted by Stalin's purges couldn't eliminate the defiantly independent mindset of Leningraders. They might be more careful how they showed this mindset, but their spirit remained strong.

CHAPTER 3

FLAWED PLANS FOR WAR

When the tsar's military advisers prepared for war prior to 1914, they did so with a mixture of expectation and trepidation. They were in the midst of a long programme of modernisation, which combined with Russia's traditional strength in numbers would give the army a decisive advantage over the forces of the Central Powers; but at the same time, they were deeply fearful of the capabilities of the opposing armies, particularly the Germans. Nor was it purely the land forces that caused them concern. In his attempt to build a fleet capable of challenging the British, Kaiser Wilhelm had created a navy that was far stronger than that of Russia, and the Russians worried that, backed by the guns of their battleships, the Germans would attempt a naval landing close to their capital. Consequently, substantial forces were held in the area around Petrograd throughout the war to prevent such an eventuality, and when hostilities began, large minefields were laid off the coastline of Latvia and Estonia, and in the Gulf of Finland.

Eventually, the Germans did send an amphibious expedition into the Baltic Sea but its objectives were modest and directed at the large islands off the Estonian coast. The success of the German operation merely confirmed Russian fears that Petrograd was vulnerable – Peter the Great's decision to build a city with easy access to the west was proving to have its disadvantages. As the tsar's empire crumbled and first Finland, then the Baltic States gained their independence, there was another threat. In addition to the danger of assault from the sea, there were now potential foes just a short march across dry land. The ultimately unsuccessful attack by Yudenich highlighted the vulnerability of Petrograd, and even though it was no longer the capital of the nation, it remained of paramount importance for both political and industrial reasons. As the Russian Civil War drew to a close, Soviet military planners gave serious thought to how they could defend this potentially exposed city in the north.

During peacetime, Soviet military forces were organised into military districts; once mobilisation began, each district would be transformed into a 'Front' consisting of several armies. Throughout the 1920s and 1930, Leningrad Military District enjoyed a series of illustrious commanders and was the centre of much of the Soviet Union's experimentation and innovation in military matters. In 1926, Boris Mikhailovich Shaposhnikov oversaw field tests of coordinated air defence and measures to be taken in the event of chemical warfare; his successor, Avgust Ivanovich Kork, rehearsed amphibious and parachute landings in the region for both defensive and offensive warfare; and Tukhachevsky used his period as commander of the district to elaborate on his concepts of deep battle and deep operations.

The first full test of the Red Army in the Leningrad region since the Civil War came in late 1939. Finland, part of the tsar's empire, had broken away in the aftermath of the 1917 revolutions. But despite slow improvements in diplomatic relations between the two countries, Stalin remained deeply suspicious of his neighbour to the north and referred to the Mannerheim government as Fascists who could not be trusted. Once he had secured his grip on the Soviet Union by purging real and imagined opponents during the 1930s, Stalin felt ready to deal with the threat that he perceived as lying to the northwest of Leningrad: the frontier with Finland was only 20 miles from the city. Negotiations with Finland with a view to changing the border began in April 1938 and continued in a desultory fashion in the months that followed. In August 1939, the world was stunned by the announcement of a non-aggression pact between Germany and the Soviet Union, and this led to the partition of Poland by the Soviet Union and Germany in September and the deployment of Soviet forces in the Baltic States; formal annexation would follow in 1940. Stalin made further demands that the frontier with Finland should be moved away from Leningrad. He proposed that the new border between the states would run close to the Finnish city of Viipuri – known to the Soviets as Viborg – and that the Finns should dismantle their fortifications in the region. Islands in the Gulf of Finland were also to be handed over to the Soviet Union, as was the Rybachy Peninsula in the far north. In exchange, Finland would gain some territory from the Soviet Union, but in areas that were of little strategic importance.

The Finnish government knew that militarily it was heavily outgunned by the Soviet Union, but nonetheless rejected Stalin's demands. At the end of November

1939, the Soviet Union reported that one of its border posts had been shelled by Finnish forces – in reality, the shelling was carried out by an NKVD unit. Vyacheslav Mikhailovich Molotov, the Soviet foreign minister, demanded that Finnish forces pull back from the border region. The Finns refused, and the countries found themselves at war.

The Soviet general staff had drawn up plans for a war against Finland under the overall control of Shaposhnikov, who was now chief of the Soviet general staff. This plan correctly judged that a conflict with Finland would be far from straightforward and the Red Army would only prevail after several months of intense, difficult fighting.[1] When the plan was presented to Stalin, he rejected it on the grounds that it overestimated the capabilities of the Finnish Army. Instead, he ordered Kirill Afanasyevich Meretskov, the commander of the Leningrad Military District, to draw up plans for a faster victory. From the point of view of Stalin and the Bolshevik establishment, Meretskov was in many respects a model senior officer. His ancestry was impeccably from peasant stock and he became involved in industrial politics in Moscow in 1915, at the age of just 18. He helped the Bolsheviks secure control of the city of Sudogda, to the east of Moscow, in the aftermath of the October Revolution and served in the Red Army during the Russian Civil War, being wounded several times. Rising steadily through the ranks, he spent several months in Spain during the Spanish Civil War (during which he was wounded again) and managed to avoid arrest during Stalin's purges, serving as deputy chief of the general staff, then commander of the Volga Military District, before moving to Leningrad at the beginning of 1939.

Given Stalin's likely reaction if he weren't presented with a plan that met with his approval, it was unsurprising that Meretskov devised a new plan that was far more optimistic. It also took little or no account of the difficult terrain, the lack of roads, and the likely determination of the Finns to resist. Furthermore, the new plan was at odds with almost all accepted military thinking – Meretskov intended to attack on a large number of axes in the belief that by doing so, he would force the Finns to disperse their forces, permitting the Red Army to crush them in detail. The reality was that his strategy would expose the Red Army's attacking groups to piecemeal defeat. The Finns would be able to concentrate their limited resources against the most dangerous Soviet axes of advance, covering the others with the minimum numbers of troops required to delay the Red Army's advance through difficult terrain.

The true scale of Soviet intentions remains a subject of dispute. Stalin ordered the creation of a puppet Finnish government, but there is no documentary evidence to suggest that there were ever any serious plans for complete conquest.[2] It is perhaps likely that whilst the intention was to improve the frontier close to Leningrad, Stalin was preparing for a wider success should this arise. In the recent Manchurian campaign against the Japanese, the Red Army had achieved an impressive victory at Khalkin Gol and many in the Soviet Union – particularly those like Stalin who were not familiar with the terrain – were confident of a quick victory against Finland. Others had reservations; despite his optimistic plan, Meretskov had visited much of the long Soviet–Finnish frontier during 1939 and had few illusions of how difficult an offensive operation would be. The region over which the war would be fought was heavily forested and crisscrossed by waterways, small lakes and swamps. Nonetheless, Meretskov's public statements were completely in keeping with the overall confident mood.

The campaign began on 30 November with nearly half a million Soviet soldiers being committed. The main Finnish defences in the Karelian Isthmus to the northwest of Leningrad, organised into the Mannerheim Line, lay about 20 miles behind the frontier, and over the first week of the conflict the Finns fell back slowly to these positions. In bitterly cold weather, the Red Army followed cautiously and then attempted to force its way forward through the Mannerheim Line; at first, every assault was beaten off with heavy losses. Almost every aspect of Red Army organisation and equipment was found to be badly deficient. Many Soviet units had inadequate winter clothing; tanks were often committed to battle in completely unsuitable terrain and the engineering and vehicle recovery teams were too few and poorly equipped to prevent large numbers of vehicles becoming stuck or simply breaking down; coordination between different arms was poor, with the few tanks that reached the front line lacking adequate infantry and artillery support; despite almost complete air superiority, Soviet aircraft failed to make much impression on the ground fighting and suffered considerable losses; and morale almost collapsed as Soviet officers, hamstrung by political commissars who oversaw their decision-making, resorted to repetitive and increasingly bloody frontal attacks to try to overcome their opponents rather than showing any flexibility and improvisation.

As the predicted swift advance of the Red Army turned into a bloody stalemate, Stalin made major changes. Shaposhnikov was given full authority over the stalled campaign. Marshal Voroshilov, who had been commander-in-chief of the Red Army and was a close associate of Stalin and owed his position more to his friendship with the Soviet leader than to any inherent abilities, was replaced by Timoshenko. The armies were regrouped and reorganised and attacked once more after a heavy bombardment in February 1940. On this occasion, despite continuing to move their infantry forward in formations that were too dense and resulted in heavy losses, the Soviet units were able to penetrate the Finnish defences at the western end of the Karelian Isthmus. In early March, the leading elements of the Red Army moved closer to Viipuri while naval forces landed troops on the coast to the west. With their stubborn defences collapsing, the Finns had no choice but to sue for peace. The terms were severe: in addition to moving the frontier a significant distance from Leningrad, the Soviet Union also gained control of Viipuri, now renamed Viborg. This alone cost Finland its fourth largest city and much of its industrial base. Casualties in the war had been heavy for the Finnish Army, with about 70,000 killed, wounded or missing.[3] The losses of the Red Army were far worse, with figures varying between a lower estimate of 207,000 and a higher total of 392,000.[4]

On the scale of the huge conflict that was to follow, the Finnish-Soviet War – often known as the Winter War – was a relatively small-scale operation, but its impact was considerable. Just a few weeks after the end of the fighting, Stalin and his senior commanders held a series of meetings to analyse the conflict. The assessment of why the campaign had gone so badly was generally accurate. There were problems with almost every aspect of the Red Army's performance. Mobilisation for war had been slow and incomplete, and a historical trend to favour combat formations at the expense of logistic and support elements meant that soldiers were often 'mobilised' only to find that there wasn't adequate transportation available for them to move to the front line. The presence of political commissars and their ability to oversee and potentially veto almost every decision made by unit commanders, combined with the consequences of the purges of the Red Army's officers in preceding years, resulted in an almost complete absence of local initiative; with the ever-present threat of arrest and imprisonment or summary execution for any imagined offence and working under the watchful supervision of the commissars, few officers were prepared to take the risk of questioning, let alone opposing the views of their superiors. At a tactical and operational level, the choices made by Soviet commanders were often unsuited to the terrain on which the battles were then fought, resulting in heavy losses when attempting to storm well-prepared defences. There was poor intelligence of the capabilities and disposition of Finnish forces, and coordination between different elements of the Red Army fell far short of the required standard.

Timoshenko was rewarded for achieving victory by promotion to marshal and as People's Commissar for Defence he was tasked with overseeing the improvements that would be needed to the Red Army in order to correct the problems that had been identified. Meretskov remained in post as commander of Leningrad Military District until the summer of 1940, when he was replaced by Lieutenant General Markian Mikhailovich Popov. An early area of attention for Timoshenko was the role of political commissars, and after close discussions with Stalin he issued instructions that the influence of the commissars was to be diluted in an attempt to give field officers greater ability to control their units without having to defer to the judgement of the commissars. In addition, the organisation of field units was to be changed. All military districts were to reorganise their units to create mechanised corps in an attempt to improve all-arms cooperation – it was expected that by having infantry units incorporated into the same formations as tanks, the poor cooperation between different arms that had caused such problems in the Winter War could be overcome.

The armoured forces of the Red Army had not been as effective as Soviet commanders had expected. Despite facing an enemy with few anti-tank weapons, Soviet units lost over 3,500 tanks, roughly half of all those that were committed. Crucially, only 316 of these were actually destroyed in combat – the rest were lost due to terrain difficulties or breakdowns.[5] Aircraft losses were also very high, with about 1,000 planes being lost, though fewer than half were due to Finnish action. As was the case with tanks, mechanical problems proved to be a major contributor to losses.

New improved tanks were already being designed, but there was disagreement on how to proceed with these. Some in the army had not been enthusiastic about adopting the new T-34, which was seen as an expensive and far heavier vehicle than the tanks that it was intended to replace. Others preferred the even heavier KV-1, which was seen as a safer, more conservative design and a direct replacement for the multi-turreted T-35. Moreover, the KV-1 was already in production whereas few T-34s had been produced to date. The KV-1 had been deployed against Finland in small numbers, largely to test its performance, and was regarded as an effective combat vehicle. However, there were significant issues with the KV-1. Its weight – 45 tons – made it unsuitable for use in much of the Soviet Union, where bridges were likely to collapse under such a load, and it was a difficult vehicle for its crew, with the driver in particular having to deal with heavy steering and transmission. All Soviet tanks had struggled against the heavily fortified bunkers of the Mannerheim Line and given that the role of the KV-1 was as a 'breakthrough tank', a new version was produced specifically for such a task.

In its huge slab-sided turret, the KV-2 carried a 152mm howitzer, but the result was that the overall weight increased to 52 tons with a maximum speed of only 17 miles per hour. Consequently, it was of very limited use in anything other than a deliberate attack on a heavily fortified position. Changes to address some of the problems with the initial design of the T-34 were still awaiting final confirmation when the tank entered mass production in the summer of 1940; in particular, the original gun of the T-34 was regarded as giving poor performance and an upgraded 76.2mm gun was recommended. In the absence of official approval from Timoshenko's ministry, the armaments factory in Gorky decided to proceed with the new weapon, and official permission was only given several months after it had entered service.[6]

The new mechanised corps might have been a response to perceived shortcomings in the war against Finland, but they were far from what was required. Each mechanised corps consisted of two tank divisions and a motorised rifle division. The tank divisions fielded about 375 tanks each and the corps as a whole had an establishment strength of about 36,000 men and 1,000 tanks, but there were few field exercises where all elements of the corps were present – in the absence of such exercises, it was impossible for officers to learn how to coordinate such a concentration of forces. To make matters worse, only command tanks were equipped with radios. It was expected that unit commanders would communicate with their subordinate tanks by waving flags from their turret hatch. The reality was that in the heat of combat, few if any of the subordinates were able to see these flags and respond to them. The result was that Soviet armoured forces would go into action according to the orders that had been issued before the battle, and would have little or no ability to respond to unexpected events.

Although the tank fleet of the Red Army was vast, many of its tanks were unusable. This was at least partly due to a deliberate decision by local commanders – there was little to be gained by expending huge efforts to locate spare parts for tanks that were in any case obsolescent and were meant to be replaced by newer models. But when these newer models proved to be slow to appear, the consequences were serious. Even when new tanks were provided, there were significant problems. By the beginning of the German invasion, many tank crews had barely any experience of using the new KV tanks and T-34s; drivers often had just a few hours' training, and some units would go into action in brand-new tanks that had not been prepared properly for combat.

Whilst much of the tank fleet of the Red Army was obsolete, the same could be said of almost any army of the period. The BT series of tanks –

Bystrokhodnyy Tank or 'high speed tank' – evolved steadily in the 1930s. The BT-2 dated from 1932 and appeared with three different turrets over its years of service, carrying either a single 37mm gun, an additional machine-gun to the main armament, or twin machine-guns in place of the 37mm gun. A few years later, the BT-5 appeared, armed with a 45mm gun; nearly 1,900 were built before the onset of hostilities with Germany. The last version of the series was the BT-7 with a more powerful engine and partly sloping armour but the same main armament as the BT-5, and about 5,500 were built. These fast 'cavalry tanks' were intended for exploitation operations and their excellent power-to-weight ratio – the result of a 400hp engine and a weight of just 12 tons – gave them good manoeuvrability. They formed a substantial part of Zhukov's force in the fighting against the Japanese in the Battle of Khalkin Gol where they proved to be vulnerable in hot conditions – unlike later Soviet tanks, they had gasoline engines and fuel vapour escaping from the engines was easily ignited by simple weapons such as Molotov cocktails. Both BT-5s and BT-7s took part in the Soviet occupation of eastern Poland and the Baltic States; during these operations, the line of march of Red Army tank units was marked by broken-down tanks and any questions about the efficacy of these light vehicles were settled by their dismal performance in the war against Finland.

In addition to the BT-5s and BT-7s, the Red Army also had a huge fleet of T-26 tanks. These were based upon the British Vickers six-ton tank of 1928, though the Soviet versions were nearly twice as heavy as the original. The T-26 first entered service in the Red Army in 1931 and underwent a number of modifications, but most models were equipped with a 45mm gun. They first saw combat in the Spanish Civil War where they proved to be superior to the German Pz.I, and because many of the Red Army officers involved in the Spanish Civil War came to dominate military thinking in the Soviet Union in the years that followed, this was used as an argument against developing newer and more expensive tanks. Like the BT series, the T-26 performed badly in the war against Finland and poor maintenance resulted in large numbers of tanks being unusable – on 1 June 1941, the Red Army had over 10,000 T-26s, but at least half couldn't be deployed due to mechanical problems.

In addition to these relatively light tanks, the Red Army also had heavier machines prior to the appearance of the KV-1 and T-34. The T-28 entered production in 1933, with about 500 being built. At 28 tons, it was a far bigger and better-armoured vehicle than the BT tanks or the T-26 and it carried a 76mm gun. Unlike most Soviet tanks, it was equipped with a radio and its firepower, protection, and mobility was not dissimilar to the German Pz.IV, but the design of its suspension was outdated by 1941 and it performed poorly in combat. Even larger was the remarkable T-35, which was produced in small numbers – only about 60 were built – from 1934 to 1939. Weighing 45 tons, the T-35 was unusual in having multiple turrets that carried a 76mm gun, two 45mm guns, and several machine-guns. Even by 1940, it was regarded as obsolete and once fighting began it proved to be susceptible to mechanical breakdown. Its striking appearance made it popular with German soldiers, who frequently posed for photographs on destroyed T-35s.

The development of Soviet armoured and mechanised units suffered from a further problem. Stalin, Budennyi, Voroshilov and Timoshenko – the dominant figures in the continuing evolution of the army, especially after the fall of Tukhachevsky – were all cavalry veterans. In a relatively underdeveloped country with poor quality roads, horses remained a vital means of transport long after motorisation had effectively replaced them in other countries; men recruited into the Red Army from rural or semi-rural settings were likely to be competent riders, and the creation of mobile cavalry units was therefore simpler than creating, equipping and training modern mechanised units. The powerful influence of these old cavalry commanders together with the relative ease of creating cavalry formations ensured that cavalry divisions and corps remained part of the Red Army until the end of the Second World War, but in the years immediately before the war the cavalry 'establishment' often raised objections to the expenditure required for mechanisation. Cavalry had proved to be of little use in the First World War, and in many respects had been a negative asset: during much of the war, Russia's military had to commit more rail transport to moving fodder for horses than it used to move food for soldiers. And on the few occasions that it was possible to deploy cavalry in its traditional role of exploiting success, for example in the German conquest of Romania in 1916, the result was a crippling attrition rate – the German generals realised that they could call upon tired infantrymen to press on in pursuit of the defeated enemy with minimal supplies in order to complete the campaign, but if they attempted the same with cavalry, the horses weakened rapidly and died. However, the ratio of space to manpower was markedly different during the Russian Civil War, and the only effective way of covering the huge spaces involved was either on horseback or by train. Consequently, the Red Army either ignored the lessons about the relative weakness of cavalry or forgot them entirely. The result was perhaps less attention to the use of mechanised units than was the case in other nations.

The artillery of the Red Army also faced huge difficulties. In many respects, its equipment was fairly modern, but there were shortages of tractors – in most cases, artillery regiments had less than 20 per cent of the towing equipment that they needed for full mobility, and although this improved through the first half of 1941 the average figure was less than 38 per cent on the eve of war.[7] There were also critical shortages of radios and other communication equipment and target acquisition and fire control systems. Spotter aircraft were on the establishment strength of every corps, but few actually had them and there had been very little training in using them to direct and correct artillery fire. Even where gunners had received a barely adequate level of training, their officers had little or no experience in coordinating their fire with that of other units to conduct concentrated bombardments. The rapid direction of fire against enemy armour was an area where there had been almost no training at all; this would prove disastrous once fighting began.

The creation of divisions and armies, and equipping them with enough weapons, was a huge challenge for the Soviet Union at a time when its industrial base was still comparatively undeveloped compared with that of Germany and other nations. But even if the intended forces could be created, they would achieve nothing without ammunition. There were shortages of all types of ammunition, ranging from infantry weapons to heavy artillery. The Soviet general staff had drawn up estimates of how much ammunition would be needed during a war, but in almost every case the actual quantities available fell short of these requirements. In some cases, particularly with weapons like 85mm anti-aircraft guns, ammunition was in such short supply that training was almost impossible.

To make matters worse, there had been little attention to the need for transport to bring ammunition from depots to front-line units. In the Wehrmacht, there were division-level units for ammunition transport as well as at higher levels, but in the case of the Red Army these barely existed at all. A report that was produced shortly after the beginning of the war with Germany highlighted this weakness:

> From the commencement of combat operations, most units in the border regions, lacking adequate motorised transport for ammunition resupply, were forced to leave more than half their ammunition at their barracks, and given the rapid development of combat operations the artillery ammunition left by these units at their bases was blown up or left to be captured by the enemy.[8]

There were other problems in the organisation of the Red Army that were either not identified or simply not addressed. This was at least partly due to the limitations of the campaign that had been fought. The scale of the fighting and the distances covered were not great enough to expose the major weaknesses of all Soviet logistic and support services, and even where issues had been identified, it remained to be seen whether the solutions would be adequate. In the meantime, Red Army officers at every level laboured to implement the stream of new directives issued by Timoshenko. The continuing fear of further purges hung over everyone: if they carried out changes that were later rescinded, they faced the threat of being punished; but if they failed to follow the directives, that too could result in punishment. This sense of threat extended throughout military thinking, stifling any independence of thought and any consideration of local initiative. It was far safer to proceed cautiously, ensuring that written orders from higher authorities could be used to justify any decisions.

The hugely damaging effect of Stalin's purges of the Red Army was exacerbated by the steady expansion of the Red Army in the years before the Second World War. This expansion could only have been implemented successfully had there been sufficient high-calibre officers and NCOs available, and if there had been adequate equipment for training. Instead, there were huge shortages of both, with men often promoted several steps above their level of training and competence in order to fill the gaps – it was commonplace for men commanding regiments to have completed the relatively limited training of officers who would normally command platoons or companies. Lacking the training and experience needed for their new posts, these officers often resorted to harsh discipline and a dictatorial attitude, insisting that orders (which they had often received from above and were merely passing on to their subordinates) be followed rigidly. The constant fear of criticism or arrest further strengthened this tendency. Persistent shortages of equipment, fuel and ammunition made it almost impossible for the enlarged army to receive the training that it needed, and there was a longstanding practice for the Red Army to release men during the harvest season so that they could help on farms. As a result, whilst the Red Army undoubtedly grew in size, its overall skill level actually declined.

The Winter War had been fought to improve protection for Leningrad, and one of the many tasks of the Leningrad Military District was to put in place new defences that took account of the changed circumstances. The region for which the district had overall responsibility was huge, stretching along the entire Finnish border to the Barents Sea in the north. The last order before the German invasion from Timoshenko to Popov about the defences of the district, in May 1941, gave an indication of the scale of the task that had to be undertaken. Within just one week, Leningrad Military District was to produce two pieces of work:

a. A detailed plan for defence of the coast from the Barents Sea … including the state border from the Barents Sea to the Gulf of Finland and the coast of the Estonian SSR from the Gulf of Narva to the Gulf of Matsala.
b. A detailed plan for air defence with primary attention to a reliable defence of the city of Leningrad.[9]

By this stage, after heavily rigged elections, the three Baltic States had been annexed by the Soviet Union, which created a new set of problems.[10] On the one hand, the frontier from which an attack towards Leningrad from the southwest was now several hundred miles further away; but on the other hand, the defences that had been prepared along the old Soviet frontier prior to the annexation of the Baltic States were of less value. Using plans that had already been prepared, Popov and Nikandr Yevlampiyevich Chibisov, his chief of staff, duly drew up the required documentation, but this was based on assumptions that were critically flawed. Firstly, the Soviet planners at all levels based their plans on the belief that if Germany decided to attack, preparations for such an attack would be clearly visible for at least ten days prior to the onset of hostilities. This would allow border forces to mobilise fully and to be ready for the German attack. In the case of the Leningrad Military District, it was assumed that the Baltic Special Military District would be able to stop any German advance, and the forces from the Leningrad area would face little serious defensive fighting against the Germans. Given the timescale dictated by Timoshenko, it was inevitable that the plans drawn up by Popov and Chibisov were not as detailed as they needed to be, and even by the time of the German invasion they were far from complete. The plan defined the mission of Leningrad Military District in several steps:

1. To prevent both enemy ground and air invasion of the district's territory.
2. A firm defence of fortified regions and field fortifications along the line of the state borders …
3. Beginning on the ninth day of mobilisation, accept transfer of the Estonian SSR coast …
4. Assist the Red Banner Baltic Fleet in closing off the entrance of the Gulf of Finland to enemy naval forces …
5. Determine in timely fashion the nature of enemy forces, concentrations and groupings by all types of intelligence means available to the district.

6. Gain air superiority by active air operations, and destroy and disrupt the concentration and deployment of enemy forces by powerful strikes, primarily against railroad centres, staging areas, and force groupings.

7. Prevent enemy airborne assaults and diversionary activity on the district's territory.

8. If conditions are favourable, all defending forces and army and district reserves will be prepared to deliver decisive blows against the enemy in accordance with *Stavka* [the Soviet high command] orders.[11]

In order to deliver this ambitious outline, Popov intended to deploy his forces in a series of distinct sectors. One army (Fourteenth) was to protect Murmansk in the north and the frontier with Finland to roughly half the distance from the northern coast to Lake Onega. A second army (Seventh) would defend the line to Lake Onega and the region between Lake Onega and Lake Ladoga. Although the two areas covered by Fourteenth and Seventh Armies were considerable – the distance from the Barents Sea to Lake Ladoga is over 550 miles in a straight line – it was not unreasonable to expect two armies to be able to hold this extended front. There were few roads in the heavily forested region and any invasion from Finland or German-occupied Norway faced huge logistic difficulties in concentrating sufficient men and materiel for a sustained campaign. The third area that Popov and Chibisov described was in many respects more important, covering the frontier around Viborg, and this was assigned to Twenty-Third Army, which was to prevent the Finns from reversing the Soviet gains of the Winter War.

Further south, the Baltic coast as far as Tallinn would come under the control of LXV Rifle Corps, which was handed over to Baltic Special Military district on the eve of the German invasion. In addition to these forces, Popov held back three rifle divisions and the two divisions of I Mechanised Corps under his personal control. It was hoped that once the forces of Baltic Special Military District had blunted any initial German attack, these and other units could be deployed to launch successful counteroffensives to drive back the Wehrmacht. But the main emphasis of Popov's planning was to defend against an attack from Finland. His plans made little or no use of Leningrad Military District's resources to oppose a German advance from the southwest. Accordingly, field defences were prepared mainly in the Karelian Isthmus and further north, with little attention being given to defences facing the southwest – defence from that direction was effectively subordinated to the Baltic Special Military District.

In order to defend the region from air attack, Popov had substantial resources, at least on paper. The total of aircraft available – a little over 1,300 – was impressive, but included many obsolete models. The great purges that tore through the Soviet Union in the 1930s affected all walks of life, not just military and political circles, and this had a profound effect on technological development. For example, the Ilyushin Il-2 ground attack aircraft was in development throughout 1940 and was originally armed with two 23mm guns that were fed ammunition in clips. This weapon system was the invention of Yakov Grigoryevich Taubin, but when it was decided instead to adopt a single belt-fed 23mm gun, Taubin was suddenly accused of deliberately designing a substandard weapon system in order to weaken the overall aircraft. He was arrested and imprisoned, and was executed shortly before the German invasion commenced in 1941. Newer aircraft like the Il-2 were available in only very limited numbers and few aircrew had received anything more than the most rudimentary training on their use; training programmes were hampered by fears that if aircraft were damaged or lost due to training accidents, those involved would find themselves charged with sabotage. Such fears were well founded. In April 1941, Timoshenko submitted a report to Stalin complaining that training accidents were resulting in the daily loss of two or three aircraft and demanded the removal of several senior air force officers.[12] Nonetheless, the ease with which Soviet air units dominated the skies over Poland in 1939 and Finland shortly after left senior air force officers with an unjustified sense of confidence, and rigid adherence to pre-war plans for the massed use of airpower took little account of the skill that the Luftwaffe had demonstrated in preceding campaigns. Astonishingly, many Soviet aircraft – particularly the large numbers of older planes – lacked radios. Moreover, many of the planes that were equipped with radios only had receivers; Soviet theorists had judged that this would be sufficient, allowing ground controllers to direct the aircraft to their objectives. It had been assumed that there would be little or no benefit in having two-way conversations between pilots and their controllers, or between pilots on the same mission.

The Red Banner Baltic Fleet was, like all parts of the Soviet armed forces, a numerically powerful force with over 300 ships, including two battleships, two cruisers, 20 destroyers, and 68 submarines. In addition, it had over 650 aircraft and substantial coastal defence artillery units. Ships operating out of the ports of the former Baltic States – particularly Tallinn and Liepāja – were to act in support of the Baltic Special Military District, while the forces based in Kronstadt and Hanko would come under the control of the Leningrad Military District. But many of these warships were poorly maintained and not ready for combat and throughout the Second World War the Baltic Fleet operated with a considerable degree of caution, carefully avoiding any surface clash with German warships. Its performance in the Leningrad area was further compromised by the status of the base at Kronstadt. In the aftermath of the suppression of the naval mutiny in the 1920s the base had been closed, but was re-established immediately before the beginning of the war with Finland. In June 1940 the base was shut down again and remained inactive until October 1941 when it was hastily reactivated as Soviet warships withdrew from their bases further west. As a consequence, Kronstadt lacked the heavy machinery needed for major ship repairs, and stockpiles of ammunition and other materiel were very limited.

Divisions in the Red Army were classified according to their readiness for action, with first-line units being the strongest and third-line formations, held in reserve, the weakest. By June 1941, the establishment strength of a Soviet rifle division was a little under 14,500 men. Units classified as first-line divisions, generally those in the border districts, usually had barely half this strength with the rest expected to arrive once mobilisation began. Second-line divisions were weaker, with just 5,200 men, and third-line divisions often lacked anything more than the most rudimentary cadre of trained personnel. The scale of mobilisation that would take place in the event of war was immense. About 5 million reservists, including 600,000 officers and 885,000 NCOs, would return to the ranks, though in many cases these men would have no knowledge or experience of the newer weapons with which they were expected to fight. Huge numbers of vehicles – about 248,000 trucks and cars and 36,000 tractors – would be requisitioned from civilian use for the military, together with 730,000 horses. However, these plans failed to take any account of how many of these civilian vehicles were likely to be operational. Many collective farms and factories completed their reports of what equipment they had more to avoid criticism and punishment than to provide a realistic picture of what they actually possessed. Consequently, many of these tractors and trucks were either unusable due to breakdowns and spare parts shortages, or simply didn't exist at all.

In April 1941, as the danger of war grew, the Soviet defence ministry ordered 99 rifle divisions on the borders of the Soviet Union to be brought up to full strength. Two months later, when war broke out, only 21 divisions had achieved the required numerical strength, and in most cases they lacked their full complement of weapons and other equipment. The divisions were meant to have two artillery regiments; most had just one, and there were shortages of machine-guns of every sort. Although each division was intended to have a tank battalion and integral anti-tank forces, these had been badly neglected owing to the emphasis on creating the new mechanised brigades and corps. Consequently, the few tanks that the rifle divisions possessed were obsolete and poorly maintained, and their anti-tank establishment was also deficient, made up largely of the far less effective anti-tank rifles than the more modern anti-tank guns that were being diverted into dedicated anti-tank brigades. Even these anti-tank rifles – which were quite capable of taking on German Pz.II and Pz.35(t) vehicles – were of limited use due to lack of training. The Red Army's gunners would simply have to learn how to use their weapons once fighting began.

The huge mobilisation plan would be highly dependent upon the Soviet Union's railway system. On the eve of war, Stalin ordered significant forces to be moved from the Soviet interior to the Moscow region where they would be grouped into seven armies as a central reserve. In order to implement this, it was estimated that 939 trains would be required, but by 22 June 1941 only 538 had actually been loaded. Of these, only 83 had actually reached their destinations and been unloaded.[13]

*　*　*

The performance of the Red Army during the Winter War against Finland led to a major effort by the Soviet Union to improve its armed forces, but the brief conflict also had a profound effect on German thinking. Hitler had made no secret of his ultimate aim of securing a land empire for Germany at the expense of the Soviet Union and repeatedly stated his view that Bolshevism – portrayed repeatedly by the Nazis as 'Jewish-Bolshevism' – had to be eliminated to safeguard Germany, but the sheer size of the Soviet Union and its armed forces meant that for many years his rhetoric was somewhat at odds with the political policies that he followed. These policies culminated in 1939, on the eve of the German invasion of Poland, in the Molotov–Ribbentrop Non-Aggression Pact. In addition to agreeing not to attack each other, Germany and the Soviet Union also agreed – in a secret protocol of the pact, which the Soviet Union continued to deny for decades after the war – to divide Eastern Europe into spheres of influence. Under these terms, the Baltic States were deemed to lie within the Soviet sphere; originally, much of Lithuania was to be German territory, but as the Wehrmacht had advanced further east in parts of Poland than originally anticipated, there was an adjustment in arrangements so that all three Baltic States came under Soviet control. However, neither Hitler nor Stalin had any intention of sticking to the terms of the Non-Aggression Pact, telling their associates that it was nothing more than a temporary arrangement.

The Germans were of course aware of the chaos that had ensued in the Red Army as a result of Stalin's purges. Nonetheless, the practical considerations of a war of conquest in the east were daunting. The scale of the war would be far greater than anything that had preceded it and would require a huge advance across terrain that had a poor network of roads and railways. Matters were further hindered by the fact that the Soviet Union's railways were of a wider gauge than railways in the rest of Europe – a deliberate decision made during tsarist times to hinder the advance of any invasion from the west. The Germans could regard the Soviet armed forces as being inferior to the Wehrmacht in terms of training, organisation, doctrine, and in some respects equipment, but the sheer scale of the Red Army and the vastness of the terrain meant that achieving victory was a huge challenge. But the poor performance of the Soviet forces against Finland shifted perceptions considerably. The Red Army was weaker than the Germans had feared and its performance was poor in almost every area. In these circumstances, it seemed that a military success was possible, despite all the obstacles.

As part of the preparations for a possible war with the Soviet Union, the Germans conducted a detailed wargame under the control of Generalleutnant Friedrich Paulus. Accustomed to working late into the night, Paulus often took large quantities of material home for further study and although he ensured that all secret documents remained secure, the maps of Eastern Europe and the Soviet Union left no doubt in his family that plans were being drawn up for an invasion of the Soviet Union. Paulus' wife Constance was opposed to any such war, not least because both of her sons, who were serving in the army at the time as junior officers, might find themselves in mortal danger. She pointedly gave her husband books to read on the French invasion of Russia of 1812, particularly the memoirs of Armand-Augustin-Louis de Caulaincourt, who had tried unsuccessfully to persuade Napoleon not to carry out the invasion.[14] Regardless of his wife's views, Paulus continued his work, contributing to the increasing preparations at the highest levels of the German military.

Practical discussions about a possible invasion of the Soviet Union began in earnest in the closing weeks of 1940, originally under the codename Operation *Otto*. Writing in his diary on 5 December, General Franz Halder, the chief of staff of *Oberkommando des Heeres* ('Army High Command' or *OKH*), outlined the main objectives discussed in Hitler's latest conference – sufficient territory was to be gained to prevent any future air attacks on Germany, and Soviet forces were to be crushed as close to the western frontier of the Soviet Union as possible. It is worth noting that Halder specifically stated that Moscow was 'of no great importance':

The Russian is inferior. The army lacks leadership. It is questionable if the military leadership has exploited the most important recent experiences. The new inner orientation of the Russian Army will be no better in the spring [of 1941].

We will have in the spring a perceptibly better position in leadership, material, troops, while the Russians will be at an unmistakeable low point. When the Russian Army is battered once, the final disaster is unavoidable.

By any attack against the Russian Army, one must avoid the danger of simply pushing the Russians back. We must use attack methods which cut up the Russian Army and allow its destruction in pockets. A starting position must be created which allows the use of major envelopment operations. When the Russians are hard hit by these desperate blows, a moment will come when, as in Poland, the travel and communications networks will collapse and create total disorganisation.[15]

On 18 December 1940, with Britain showing no signs of conceding defeat in the west, Hitler issued Directive 21. This document outlined how the Germans were to proceed against the Soviet Union, confirming many of the points that he had discussed with Halder and others in the preceding days:

The German Wehrmacht must be prepared to crush Soviet Russia in a rapid campaign even before the conclusion of the war against England ...

I shall order the concentration against Soviet Russia possibly eight weeks before the intended start of operations.

Preparations requiring more time to be completed are to start now – if this has not already been done – and are to be completed by 15 May 1941 ...

The mass of the Russian Army in western Russia is to be destroyed by bold operations, by driving forward deep armoured wedges, and the retreat of units capable of combat into the vastness of Russian territory is to be prevented.

In quick pursuit, a line is then to be reached from which the Russian Air Force will no longer be able to attack the territory of the German Reich. The ultimate objective of the operation is to establish protection against Asiatic Russia from the general line Volga-Archangelsk. Then, if necessary, the last industrial area left to Russia in the Urals can be eliminated by the Luftwaffe ...

The area of operations is divided into southern and northern halves by the Pripet Marshes. The point of main effort will be made in the northern half. Here two army groups will be deployed.

The southern of these two army groups – in the centre of the entire front – will have the task of breaking out of the area around and to the north of

Warsaw with exceptionally strong armoured and motorised formations and of destroying the enemy forces in Belarus. This will create a situation that will enable strong formations of mobile troops to swing north; such formations will then cooperate with the northern army group – advancing from East Prussia in the general direction of Leningrad – in destroying the enemy forces in the area of the Baltic States. Only after the accomplishment of these offensive operations, which must be followed by the capture of Leningrad and Kronstadt, are further offensive operations to be initiated with the objective of occupying Moscow, the important centre of communications and of armament production.

Only a surprisingly rapid collapse of the Russian ability to resist could justify an attempt to achieve both objectives simultaneously.[16]

There are several key points in this early directive. Firstly, Hitler correctly recognised the need to trap and destroy Red Army units before they could withdraw into the Russian interior – at the very least, such a withdrawal would lead to a protracted war and place potentially unsustainable pressure upon Germany's resources. Secondly, the plan required an advance that would exceed 1,000 miles over an area that was sparsely populated – particularly so the further the Germans moved from the Soviet Union's western frontiers – and consequently had few good roads and railway lines. Thirdly, the directive recognised the importance of the main German axis to the north of the Pripet Marshes. Even within this axis, Hitler explicitly specified that the intention was a swift advance to capture Leningrad and Kronstadt, thus eliminating the bases from which Soviet warships could threaten German forces, before any attack towards Moscow – this latter objective could only be pursued simultaneously if the Red Army collapsed faster than expected. And even this early advance on Leningrad was to follow the defeat of the Red Army in the field: the destruction of the Soviet Union's armed forces had to occur first.

A glance at a map of Eastern Europe reveals another essential factor. As soon as the Wehrmacht and its allies crossed into the Soviet Union from the west, they would face an expanding front line, requiring either the commitment of substantial reserves to ensure a continuous front or a dilution of front-line strength, with the possibility of areas being left weakly covered or with no cover at all. In these circumstances, the ability of the Soviet Union to bring more forces to the west might prove critical. It was therefore essential for the Germans to have an accurate understanding of the strength of the Red Army both at the start of the conflict and after full mobilisation.

Responsibility for assessing the strength of the Soviet Union lay with *Fremde Heere Ost* ('Foreign Armies East' or *FHO*), a branch of *OKH*.[17] A consistent failing of Nazi Germany was an amateur approach to intelligence matters. The head of *FHO* during the critical months of planning for an invasion of the Soviet Union was Oberst Eberhard Kinzel, who had served in the First World War as an infantry officer. He was part of Germany's small army between the end of that war and Hitler's accession to power and during this period he escorted Soviet officers who were visiting Berlin in 1929 and spent the first three years of Hitler's reign as military attaché in Warsaw. But he had no formal training in intelligence matters and didn't speak Russian; his credentials for the task of assessing intelligence on potential enemies to the east of Germany were therefore very limited. Drawing on information gained from radio intercepts, reports written by German agents and commercial travellers (particularly in the former Baltic States), information furnished by the intelligence services of Germany's allies, reports from German military attachés in foreign capitals, and information provided by Soviet defectors, Kinzel produced a series of documents that were often little more than semi-educated guesses. A further hindrance was that whilst the German intelligence agencies were decidedly amateur in their approach, their Soviet equivalents were far better organised and repeatedly succeeded in discovering German spies and arresting them, or gave them false information to pass on to Berlin. In other cases, the Soviet intelligence services 'turned' German spies; in some cases, it later turned out that from the very outset, the German spy networks had been compromised and had actually been working for Moscow.

Some senior German officers, such as Alfred Jodl, chief of the operations staff of *Oberkommando der Wehrmacht* ('Armed Forces High Command' or *OKW*), regarded the intelligence material provided by Kinzel as satisfactory, but others – including some of Kinzel's subordinates – were aware from the outset that the data was not based on accurate information.[18] The initial estimates provided by *FHO* informed Hitler and the high command that the Red Army would be able to deploy 20 field armies which consisted of 150 rifle divisions, between 32 and 36 cavalry divisions, and 36 motorised or mechanised brigades. Like others in Germany, Kinzel was convinced that the poor performance of the Red Army in the war against Finland demonstrated that even this substantial force was unlikely to put up prolonged resistance. In January 1941, he wrote in one of his regular reports:

The clumsiness, schematism, [and] avoidance of decisions and responsibility has not changed ... The weaknesses of the Red Army reside in the clumsiness of officers of all ranks, the clinging to formulae, insufficient training according to modern standards, the aversion to responsibility, and the marked insufficiency of organisation in all aspects.[19]

Throughout this period, the map-based wargame that Paulus oversaw continued to evolve in distinct phases. As a result of the first phase, which simulated the initial attack and destruction of the Red Army to the west of the Dnepr and Dvina Rivers, Paulus became increasingly convinced that a military success against the Soviet Union was achievable, despite the reading material helpfully furnished by his wife. However, in his report on the first wargame, Paulus recommended that the southern group of Axis forces – which would include a substantial Romanian contingent operating on their southern flank – should originate mainly from Poland rather than Romanian territory, because of the difficulties of setting up adequate supply lines across the Balkan region. This resulted in the entire operation shifting its centre of gravity more to the central region of the long front. Further wargames followed, demonstrating the need for a substantial pause in operations after the initial advance to the Dnepr and Dvina was completed – the Soviet railways would need to be modified to allow trains to run to the new front line, and supplies and replenishment drafts would have to be brought forward prior to a second advance.

Even at this early stage in planning, differences of emphasis were developing and the failure of the Germans to recognise these different views and to select which was to prevail contributed greatly to the ultimate failure of the Wehrmacht in 1941. Hitler remained certain in his mind that the strategic objectives of the coming conflict were to secure industrial and agricultural resources in the north – around Leningrad in particular – and the south, in Ukraine. Halder and other senior generals tended to the view that ultimately, the campaign would be decided by a major battle for Moscow. But as both views were predicated upon the complete destruction of the Red Army to the west of the Dvina–Dnepr line, these differences of opinion seemed not to matter. Hitler remained confident that in his supreme role, his opinion would prevail; Halder and others quietly believed that operational realities would impose themselves and ensure that their preferred option became reality.[20] In any event, even Hitler had acknowledged that simultaneous pursuit of all objectives was quite possible if the Red Army collapsed entirely, and there was growing confidence that this could be achieved.

Towards the end of January, senior German figures began to quantify the resources they intended to commit for the coming conflict. Halder noted in his diary on 28 January:

Around 110 infantry divisions, 20 panzer divisions, 13 motorised divisions, one cavalry division; total 144 divisional units ...

Execution should evidence the following characteristics:

a. Great space to the Dnepr [the equivalent of] Luxembourg to the mouth of the Loire.

b. *Speed* [emphasis in original]. No stop! No waiting for the railroad. Depend on motor transport.

c. *Increased motorisation* (as opposed to 1940): 33 mobile units, motorised artillery, engineers, signals, etc.

Since the railroad (destruction, water courses, gauge) cannot be counted on for the desired tempo, the continuous operation depends on motor transport ...

Satisfactory progress is possible only when the point of main effort is prepared through the collaboration of all forces in order to solve the most significant supply issues concerning transportation, tyres, fuel, and storage.[21]

Whilst Halder might have wished to substitute motor transport for railways, this was dependent upon three factors. Firstly, any such plan would need adequate roads. Secondly, it would require a huge fleet of motor vehicles; and thirdly, the supplies to keep them operational had to be available. Trucks of all shapes and sizes, representing over 2,000 different models, were requisitioned across Europe for the forthcoming campaign, with the result that an impressive capacity was gathered – the truck fleet could carry an estimated 60,000 tons of cargo. But this apparently impressive figure is put into perspective by the resources that the Western Allies deployed following the Normandy Landings of 1944: the cargo capacity of allied transport in northern France amounted to 67,000 tons, and moreover benefited from reliance on just a few different types of truck. The consequence of relying on so many different types of vehicles was that the attrition rate due to breakdown and enemy action – worsened greatly by the poor state of roads in the Soviet Union – would result in a rapid decline in German transport capability as the campaign developed. The availability of sufficient fuel was a matter that was never addressed in sufficient detail, despite Halder's recognition that 'satisfactory progress' required the collaboration of all agencies. If the Germans recognised that these potential problems remained partly or completely unresolved, they generally dismissed them on the grounds that the war against the Soviet Union was expected to be brief. Once the Red Army had been trapped and destroyed close to the western frontiers, further exploitation could unfold at a more leisurely rate. But Halder's diary entry fails to highlight an additional fact. Even if the Wehrmacht enjoyed a greater degree of motorisation than in 1940, it was still heavily dependent on non-motorised transport. Every infantry division included an establishment of several thousand horses, which were used for scouting, messengers, and for pulling the heavy equipment of the divisions, such as artillery and supply wagons. The task of providing sufficient fodder for these horses was itself a huge logistic challenge.

One of the enduring myths of the Second World War is the efficiency of German planning and organisation. When it came to logistics, the Wehrmacht was remarkably weak in its capabilities and approach. The logistics branch of the German general staff was widely regarded as a second-rate part of the army and officers from this department were rarely if ever asked to contribute to planning decisions. Instead, operational and strategic objectives were discussed and drawn up by senior figures and the logistics branch was then simply tasked with making these plans workable. Even after the war, Halder insisted that the task of logistics officers was merely to provide the means for operations rather than to contribute to planning decisions: 'According to our opinion the material has to serve the spiritual. Accordingly, our quartermaster service may never hamper the operational concept.'[22]

An almost circular thought process began to prevail in German circles. The Red Army had to be destroyed quickly before it could retreat into the Soviet interior, and before the Wehrmacht became constrained by supply difficulties. In order for this to become a reality, estimates of the timescale required for this first phase steadily shortened in order to minimise the possible effect of supply problems.[23] This led to a growing sense of confidence in the early destruction of the Red Army, and so the process continued. The original thinking for the coming war had been that it would take up to five months for complete success, but by the end of 1940 this had shrunk to just two months plus a lengthy pause for regrouping. In early 1941, the estimate was that the entire operation, including the pause, would be complete in less than ten weeks, and finally in April 1941 it was widely believed that there would be perhaps a month of tough fighting, followed by a relatively leisurely advance into the Soviet interior against an utterly defeated foe. This is all the more remarkable given that everyone within German upper echelons was aware that fuel reserves were modest and the scale of the operations would devour stocks at an unsustainable rate. Any objections from logistics officers were brusquely pushed to one side. The supply officer of the German Twelfth Army, which was to be deployed in the Balkan region prior to the onset of *Barbarossa*, informed Halder and Paulus that he had inadequate resources for the tasks assigned to his army; Halder noted that he and Paulus agreed that the man was 'not equal to his job'.[24]

The coming conflict was to be different from any war that Germany had fought in the past. Whilst Hitler outlined his intentions in Directive 21 in purely strategic terms, there were always additional dimensions to his plans. There was no place in the world for both National Socialism and Bolshevism; one would have to perish. This was a war that was essential to the survival and success of Nazi Germany, and Bolshevism was defined as the mortal enemy of Germany. Consequently, anything associated with Bolshevism had to be destroyed without mercy. From the early 1930s, senior members of the Nazi Party had portrayed Bolshevism as 'Jewish-Bolshevism', and it was therefore essential that, if Bolshevism was to be destroyed, the Jews would also face destruction, as would political commissars and anyone else identified with the Bolshevik regime. The intention was explicitly not to seize territory and establish pro-German regimes – it was to create the conditions for the wholesale destruction of the population of the European parts of the Soviet Union in order to make space for German settlers.

Hitler's intention to capture Leningrad as an early priority was based partly on his recognition of its importance as an industrial centre, but the role that the city had played in the rise of the Bolsheviks also ensured that it was seen as an ideological target. As planning for the coming campaign gathered pace, Hitler visited the headquarters of Army Group North, which would be responsible for the advance through the Baltic States and beyond. He told the senior officers:

> The fall of Leningrad will deprive the Soviet state of the symbol of its revolution,
> a symbol which for the last 24 years has deeply sustained the Russian people.
> Reverses in battle will undermine the Slavic race, but the loss of Leningrad will
> cause a complete and utter collapse.[25]

In an attempt to get clearer information about Soviet troop dispositions, the Luftwaffe carried out wide-ranging high-altitude photo-reconnaissance flights over the western parts of the Soviet Union; in the northern sector, these extended as far east as Lake Ilmen. Information from Kinzel's *FHO* continued to give updates on estimates of the strength of the Red Army, and on 29 March Halder noted that the latest report increased the strength of Soviet forces in European Russia by 15 divisions above previous estimates. In addition, the Germans were now aware of the creation of the new mechanised corps.[26] Further updates followed – just a few days later, Kinzel put the overall strength of the Red Army in the western Soviet Union at 171 infantry divisions, 36 cavalry divisions, and 40 mechanised brigades. Halder even noted that Finnish and Japanese sources had always questioned the previously low estimate provided by *FHO*, but despite this clear evidence of inaccuracies he continued to accept reports from *FHO* without question.

The actual strength of the Red Army was so much greater than Kinzel's figures that it is difficult to understand how *FHO* could have arrived at such a modest figure. On the eve of war, the Red Army planned to deploy 20 armies with a total of 196 rifle divisions, 31 mechanised and motorised rifle divisions, 13 cavalry divisions, 61 tank divisions, and five airborne corps. In addition, there were 120 'fortified regions', a unique Red Army formation of relatively immobile troops that were intended to defend a fixed defence line, thus freeing other units for more mobile operations.[27] On full mobilisation, these numbers would grow still further. Kinzel confidently asserted – without providing any evidence – that it would be impossible for the Red Army to transfer significant forces from Asia to the west. This proved to be a terrible miscalculation.

There were also growing indications that *Barbarossa* would stretch German resources to the limit. In the northern sector, there were concerns that there would be insufficient motorised formations to achieve the depth of penetration required to trap and destroy Red Army units close to the border. Halder could do no more than urge Army Group North not to dilute its main armoured concentrations, but to 'improvise' as best it could to deal with what were deemed to be secondary objectives. But even though the huge challenges posed by *Barbarossa* were becoming more and more clear, the extreme nature of the coming conflict remained dominant in German thinking, and thoughts even turned to the future beyond the anticipated defeat of the Soviet Union. At the end of March, Hitler addressed his inner circle at length, as Halder described in his diary:

> With our goals in the east achieved, we shall need no more than 50 to 60 divisions (armour). One part of the ground forces will be discharged into armament production for the Luftwaffe and navy; the others will be required for other missions, e.g. Spain.
>
> [This will be a] clash of two ideologies. Crushing denunciation of Bolshevism, identified with a social criminality. Communism is an enormous danger for our future. We must forget the concept of comradeship between soldiers. A Communist is no comrade before or after the battle. This is a war of extermination.

If we do not grasp this, we shall still beat the enemy, but 30 years later we shall again have to fight the Communist foe. We do not wage war to preserve the enemy ...

Extermination of the Bolshevist commissars and of the Communist intelligentsia. The new states must be [National] Socialist, but without intellectual classes of their own. Formation of a new intellectual class must be prevented. A primitive Socialist intelligentsia is all that is needed ... The troops must fight back with the methods with which they are attacked. Commissars and GPU men are criminals and must be dealt with as such ...

This war will be very different from the war in the west. In the east, harshness today means lenience in the future. Commanders must make the sacrifice of overcoming their personal scruples.[28]

The first part of this entry highlights another aspect of *Barbarossa*. In order to create an army large enough for the task ahead, Germany had mobilised large numbers of men who would otherwise have been classified as working in essential industries. This was unsustainable in anything other than the short term, adding still further to the necessity for a rapid, successful conclusion to the war against the Soviet Union.

Army Group North, which was to control the German forces attacking towards Leningrad, was under the command of Generalfeldmarschall Wilhelm Ritter von Leeb. Like almost every senior officer of his generation, he had served in the First World War, ending the conflict with the rank of major. He was a conservative Catholic from Bavaria and had retired from the army in early 1938 but returned to the ranks first during the Sudetenland Crisis of the following summer and again a year later. He was the second oldest serving officer in the Wehrmacht – only Gerd von Runstedt was older – and deeply sceptical about Hitler's regime; when France and Britain declared war on Germany, he wrote in his diary: 'Hitler is a deluded fool, a criminal!'[29]

Despite these reservations, he commanded Army Group C in the advance into France in 1940. His headquarters was then transferred to the east to start preparing for *Barbarossa*. His command would encompass two infantry armies and a panzer group (these would be renamed panzer armies at the end of 1941). On the western side of the group, closest to the Baltic coast, was Eighteenth Army commanded by Generaloberst Georg von Küchler; to its right was Fourth Panzer Group, led by Generaloberst Erich Hoepner; and Generaloberst Ernst Busch's Sixteenth Army was deployed on the eastern flank.

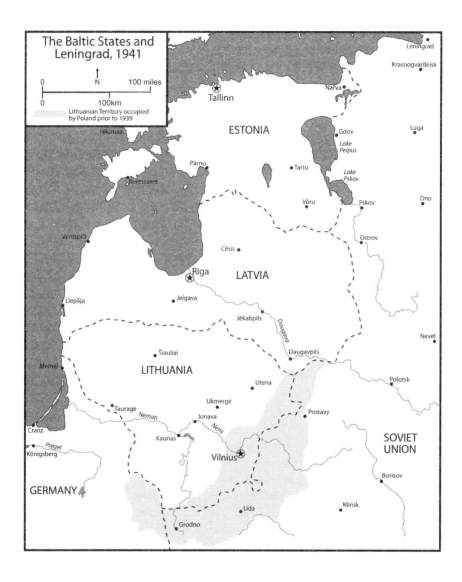

The Baltic States and
Leningrad, 1941

0   N   100 miles

0   100km

Lithuanian Territory occupied
by Poland prior to 1939

Leningrad

Krasnogvardeisk

Narva

Tallinn

ESTONIA

Gdov

Lake
Peipus

Luga

Hiiumaa

Pärnu

Tartu

Lake
Pskov

Võru

Pskov

Dno

Kuressaare

Ostrov

Ventspils

Cēsis

Riga   LATVIA

Liepāja   Jelgava

Jēkabpils

Daugava

Nevel

Šiauliai

Daugavpils

Polotsk

Memel   LITHUANIA

Utena

Ukmergė

Postavy

SOVIET
UNION

Tauragė   Neman

Jonava

Neris

Cranz

Kaunas

Pregel

Königsberg   Vilnius

Borisov

GERMANY

Lida

Minsk

Grodno

Küchler had been dismissed from command of Third Army at the beginning of the war when he attended the funeral of the former commander-in-chief of the German Army, Generaloberst Werner Freiherr von Fritsch and made remarks that were critical of Hitler and the high command in their treatment of Fritsch. Despite this he was then given command of Eighteenth Army after the intervention of Generaloberst Walther von Brauchitsch, who had replaced Fritsch as commander-in-chief. Although he missed the Polish campaign, Küchler was made aware of the war crimes that were committed by German troops in Poland, but in August 1940 he wrote in his diary:

> I emphasise the need to ensure that all soldiers in the army, particularly the officers, reject any criticism of the struggle against the population of the *Generalgouvernement* [the German administration for the remnants of Poland that hadn't been formally annexed by Germany or the Soviet Union], e.g. the treatment of Polish minorities, the Jews and ecclesiastical individuals. The final population solution to these conflicts of nationalities, which have raged on the eastern frontiers for centuries, requires particularly strong measures.[30]

It seems that his criticism of the Nazi government with regard to Fritsch was more concerned with the unfair treatment of a fellow officer than any concerns about Nazi ideology.

Hoepner, commander of Fourth Panzer Group, had been a cavalry officer in the First World War. He commanded XVI Motorised Corps during the invasion of Poland, urging his men forward with the words that they were to conduct the 'merciless annihilation of the enemy'.[31] He too had no doubt about the nature of the war on Germany's eastern frontiers, as he told his staff in May 1941:

> The war against Russia is an essential phase in the struggle for existence of the German people. It is the old struggle of the Teutons against Slavs, the defence of European culture against the Muscovite-Asiatic inundation, the defence against Jewish-Bolshevism. The aim of this struggle must be the destruction of today's Russia and must therefore be waged with unprecedented severity. Every combat action must be guided in its conception and implementation by the iron will to achieve the merciless, complete annihilation of the enemy. In particular, the proponents of today's Russian-Bolshevik system must not be spared.[32]

Given his clear acceptance of correlation between Jews and Bolsheviks, these were ominous words for the substantial Jewish population that lay in the path of his troops.

Ernst Busch was wounded three times while serving as an infantry officer on the Western Front in the First World War. In 1938, Generalleutnant Ludwig Beck, chief of the general staff, was critical of Hitler's intentions towards Czechoslovakia; Busch was one of the senior officers who spoke out against him and expressed their full support for the Führer. At the beginning of the war in

1939 he was sceptical of the value of armoured forces, believing in the primacy of infantry though he accepted a supporting role for tanks, and he led VIII Corps across Poland to the city of Lviv in 1939. He too had few doubts about the nature of the conflict ahead and showed every intention of prosecuting the war completely in keeping with Hitler's instructions.

In May 1941, shortly before the beginning of *Barbarossa*, Hitler issued the infamous 'Commissar Order', officially known as *Richtlinien für die Behandlung Politischer Kommissare* ('Guidelines for the treatment of political commissars'). This stated that any Germans who were taken prisoner could expect to be treated with 'hatred, cruelty and inhumanity' by political commissars. International law had no place in this conflict and as commissars were the originators and instigators of 'barbaric, Asiatic methods of warfare', they should be separated from other prisoners as soon as they fell into German hands. If they were suspected of being active against the Germans – which was inevitably going to be the case, given their political role and the manner in which the Germans had defined Bolshevism as the mortal enemy of the German people – they faced summary execution. Aware that this directive was incompatible with international law, Hitler ensured that it was passed down verbally and commanders were expected to issue it in their own name. The three senior commanders in Army Group North showed no hesitation in complying. Hoepner ordered his men to execute both military and civilian commissars, and Küchler declared that the arrest and punishment of commissars would result in the Russian people being freed from bondage to the Bolsheviks.

Between them, Küchler, Hoepner, and Busch commanded 29 divisions; of these, three were panzer divisions, two were motorised divisions, and one was the *SS-Totenkopf* Division, organised at that time as an infantry division but with a larger degree of motorised transport than regular Wehrmacht infantry divisions. In addition, Army Group North would be accompanied in its advance by a group of SS personnel who formed *Einsatzgruppe A*, under the command of Brigadeführer Franz Walter Stahlecker. The role of *Einsatzgruppe A* was to ensure security immediately behind the front line, but the manner in which this concept was interpreted meant that its personnel would be responsible for some of the worst war crimes in history. As Jews were regarded as practically synonymous with Bolsheviks, the task of the *Einsatzgruppen* all along the Eastern Front was to ensure the early instigation of local attacks on Jews and the rapid incarceration of Jewish survivors in ghettos, from where they could be taken and killed in stages. All others who were regarded as enemies of Germany, such as known or suspected Communists, and those seen as 'undesirable' populations, such as Roma and the physically and mentally ill, were to be exterminated by the *Einsatzgruppen*. In terms of its numerical strength, *Einsatzgruppe A* was approximately the size of a reinforced battalion, and it would require the cooperation of pro-German elements of the population and of the Wehrmacht to carry out its tasks. Before the invasion began, Stahlecker and other SS officers held meetings with anti-Bolshevik émigrés from the Baltic region in order to ensure their support.

The early successes of the Wehrmacht against Poland in 1939 and the Western Powers in 1940 hid many structural weaknesses. In 1941 much of the tank fleet was made up of vehicles that had already been shown to be obsolescent, such as the Pz.II, the Pz.35(t) and the Pz.38(t). Despite being shown to have inadequate armour and firepower to engage enemy tanks in the campaign in Belgium and France, production of the Pz.II actually increased in 1941 and finally peaked in 1942; thereafter the chassis remained in production mainly for mounting anti-tank guns and howitzers. Only a limited number of Pz.35(t) tanks were deployed, not least because production in the factories of the former Czechoslovakia had ceased and there were no spare parts available, but nonetheless 6th Panzer Division – which would form part of Army Group North – was heavily dependent upon these tanks. The Pz.38(t) had a larger gun than the Pz.II – 37mm in place of 20mm – and better armour. Like the Pz.35(t), it was a Czech design produced by Skoda before the war for the Czechoslovak Army and then adopted and modified by Germany. Modified versions of the tank remained in production until June 1942, and like the Pz.II chassis production thereafter was used to produce self-propelled guns.

The Pz.III was intended as a medium tank and entered production in 1937. Like the Pz.38(t), it was originally armed with a 37mm gun but from mid-1940 this was replaced with a 50mm gun; although this was still inferior to the 76mm guns of the T-34s and KV-1s that it would face on the Eastern Front, it was a substantial improvement on the older 37mm weapon. From its first encounters with the newer Soviet tanks, it was clear to the Germans that it was unable to engage them on equal terms. Later versions had improved armour and a longer-barrelled 50mm gun, remaining in production into 1943 by which time it was generally recognised as being obsolete. Later versions were armed with short-barrelled 75mm guns – these were primarily intended as infantry support weapons firing high explosive rounds but they could fire a shaped charge projectile for engaging enemy tanks at short range.

Despite its rapid obsolescence as a tank, production of the Pz.III chassis continued for most of the war. During the 1930s, there were proposals for all

German infantry divisions to have a battalion of armoured artillery and this led to the development of the Sturmgeschütz III assault gun, a Pz.III chassis with a 75mm gun with limited lateral traverse. The first versions entered service in time to be deployed against France and Britain in 1940 and from early 1942 it was armed with a long-barrelled 75mm gun that turned it into a highly effective tank hunter. Production was never high enough to achieve the original intention of equipping every division with a battalion of these assault guns, and most were deployed in independent brigades or battalions assigned to army corps, which would in turn use them to support divisions in the field.

The beginning of *Barbarossa* was delayed through a combination of unfavourable weather and the need to divert forces to the Balkan region; originally intended to commence in May, the invasion would now start on 22 June, with Halder noting that greater speed in redeploying the forces sent into Yugoslavia and Greece was impossible due to a combination of transport limitations and the need for the units involved to be replenished. The reports regarding the state of the Red Army gave no cause for concern; although substantial troop movements had been detected in the late spring, these were seen as merely bringing existing units closer to their establishment strength. Oberst Hans Krebs, who would end the war as chief of the general staff, returned to Berlin in May from a visit to Moscow with further reassuring information:

> He found the Russians very conciliatory. Russia will do anything to avoid war and yield on every issue short of making territorial concessions. Russian higher officers' corps decidedly bad (depressing impression). Compared with 1933, picture is strikingly negative. It will take Russia 20 years to reach her old level.[33]

In addition to Army Group North, the Soviet defenders would have to deal with the Finnish Army, which was steadily mobilising in preparation for *Barbarossa*, though it was unlikely that this process would be completed in time for 22 June. About four Finnish divisions would strike across the Karelian Isthmus to recapture Viborg before pushing on towards Leningrad. This was the direction from which Leningrad Military District had anticipated the greatest threat against the city, yet the total strength of the attack was a small fraction of the force that would advance across the Baltic States. Moreover, the Finns had little intention to advance deep into the Soviet Union – their priority was purely to recover their lost territory.

As the days lengthened through May and June, it was impossible to hide the German preparations for war. Soviet mobilisation plans were based upon an expectation that an imminent German attack would become obvious at least ten days before it took place. Reports of German preparations did reach Moscow in plenty of time to comply with this plan, from a number of different sources, but Stalin refused to believe them for a variety of reasons. Perhaps the biggest factor was that he believed that he understood Hitler's mindset and had concluded that there would be no war until Germany had either defeated Britain or secured peace in the west – Hitler would not risk a two-front conflict. Furthermore, the task of defeating Britain or forcing the British to come to terms would be very costly for the Wehrmacht and it would then require a substantial period to recover its strength before it could turn against the Soviet Union. By then, the construction of new fortifications along the frontier would be complete and Timoshenko's reforms would have improved the state of the Red Army to such a level that Hitler wouldn't dare go to war. Stalin also had an abiding mistrust of the Western Powers, influenced perhaps by their abortive interventions during the Russian Civil War. Zhukov later described how this mistrust influenced Stalin's thinking:

> In 1940 [prior to the defeat of France], rumours began to circulate in the international press that British and French military forces were themselves preparing to launch an attack on the northern Caucasus region to bomb Baku, Grozny, and Maikop [the key cities for Soviet oil production]. Documents then appeared to confirm this. In short, not only the general anti-Soviet and anti-Communist attitudes and statements that Churchill made no attempt to conceal but also the specific facts of diplomatic life at that time may have encouraged Stalin to be wary of information from Western imperialist circles.[34]

The Germans were aware of Stalin's mistrust of Britain and when British newspaper articles about the growth of the Red Army appeared in 1941, the German press responded by claiming that this was a deliberate attempt to drive a wedge between Germany and the Soviet Union. Zhukov described Stalin's response: 'You see? They scare us with the Germans, and they scare the Germans with the Soviet Union, and set us against each other. This is a subtle political game.'[35]

When Zhukov and others persisted in trying to draw Stalin's attention to the German build-up in Poland, the Soviet leader dismissed their concerns:

> I remember how once, in response to my report that the Germans had strengthened their aerial and ground reconnaissance and intelligence gathering, Stalin said,

'They're afraid of us. I'll tell you a secret. Our ambassador had a serious conversation with Hitler himself and was told in confidence: "Please don't worry when you receive information about the concentration of our troops in Poland. Our troops are undergoing extensive retraining for particularly important missions in the West."'[36]

It seemed that the closest Stalin was prepared to come to accepting the reality of impending war was when he told Red Army officers at a dinner in early May 1941 that if Molotov could delay the start of a war by a further two or three months, the Red Army would be in a far stronger position.

Friedrich-Werner Graf von der Schulenberg was the German ambassador to Moscow. He had been instrumental in securing the Molotov–Ribbentrop Pact but used his position to organise the escape of Polish diplomats from Moscow before they could be arrested by the Soviet authorities. His intention had been to secure peace for Germany but he rapidly realised that the Pact gave Hitler a free hand to start a wider war; in a private letter he wrote 'Hitler now has the opportunity to start a war and we will lose it.' Although he was not notified of German preparations, he was deeply suspicious that an invasion was planned and tried to dissuade Hitler from war with the Soviet Union. At the same time he attempted to drop hints about his fears to Soviet diplomats. When reports of these conversations were passed to Stalin, he rejected them with a contemptuous comment that 'disinformation has now reached ambassadorial level'.[37] Pressed by Zhukov and others, Stalin grudgingly gave permission for a partial mobilisation with 500,000 reservists being summoned to the ranks, but refused to authorise any action against reported Luftwaffe reconnaissance flights.

Another source of information for the Soviet Union was Richard Sorge, a German journalist who had been recruited by the Bolsheviks as an agent in 1920 and was then sent on a number of assignments. He joined the Nazi Party in 1929 and distanced himself from left-wing groups to ensure he came under no suspicion, and was sent to Japan as a reporter for several German publications. As he appeared outwardly to be an ardent National Socialist, he often attended functions in the German embassy in Tokyo and he became a close associate of Eugen Ott, the German military attaché. When Ott became the German ambassador to Japan in 1938, this friendship – at various points during the 1930s, Sorge was having an affair with Ott's wife Helma, apparently with Ott's knowledge – gave Sorge access to large amounts of sensitive information. Helma often copied documents for him and at the end of May 1941 Sorge sent a message to Moscow: 'Berlin informed Ott that German attack will commence in the latter part of June. Ott 95 per cent certain war will commence.'[38]

Still, Stalin remained unwilling to take any steps. On 13 June Timoshenko and Zhukov jointly urged Stalin to take reports of German activity on the frontier more seriously; three days later, Harro Schulze-Boysen, a Luftwaffe staff officer who worked for the Soviets under the codename *Starshina*, confirmed reports that he had already sent about German preparations and advised that a final decision to attack the Soviet Union had been made. When Vsevolod Nikolayevich Merkulov, head of Soviet intelligence and counter-intelligence, passed this report to Stalin, the Soviet dictator scrawled a reply on the report: 'Tell the "source" in the staff of the Luftwaffe to fuck his mother! This is no source, but a disinformer.'[39]

Further information was furnished by spies, frontier patrols, and from overseas – Britain sent Moscow a warning based upon decoded German signals – but Stalin refused to acknowledge reality and the precious days needed for the Red Army to mobilise slipped away steadily. Finally, late on 20 June, reports reached Moscow that 25 German merchant vessels in Riga harbour were leaving without completing loading of cargo. The following day, the Moscow fire brigade reported that the German embassy was burning large quantities of documents. That evening, Stalin ordered Molotov to protest to Schulenberg about German reconnaissance flights and further information arrived from the frontier. Timoshenko informed Stalin that a German deserter had told Soviet border units that the Germans would invade at dawn. When a second deserter gave the same information, Stalin gathered an inner circle around him. Timoshenko and Zhukov urged Stalin to place all frontier districts on full battle alert but Stalin continued to prevaricate, suggesting that the deserters had been sent by the Germans to provoke the Soviet Union. Finally, Stalin agreed to a watered-down announcement to all military districts: 'A surprise attack by the Germans is possible during 22–23 June … The task of our forces is to refrain from any kind of provocative action.'[40]

Throughout the night of 21–22 June, German troops were moving forward into their final positions. The army that would cross the frontier was a formidable one. Most of the troops were experienced soldiers, having fought in the battles against Poland, France, Britain, and in the Balkans. In 1930, Hitler had told his followers: 'Armies for the preparation of peace do not exist. They exist for triumphant exertion in war.'[41]

The coming conflict would be the ultimate test for the Wehrmacht to exert itself in order to deliver triumph through a gargantuan effort. Given the overall situation in the war and the scale of the task, German forces would have to succeed on a scale that surpassed any of their previous achievements. Even this was predicated upon the belief that the information from Kinzel's *FHO* about the strength of the Red Army was correct. Derailment of the ambitious plan to dismember and destroy the Red Army close to the frontier would create unsustainable stresses. Only a swift victory on a huge scale would suffice: such was the gamble that was *Barbarossa*.

CHAPTER 4

BARBAROSSA UNLEASHED

Before first light on 22 June, German aircraft crossed the frontier with the Soviet Union in large numbers. On the ground, gunners commenced bombardment of Soviet border positions as infantry and armour prepared to advance. *Barbarossa*, Hitler's invasion of the Soviet Union, had begun.

A large proportion of the Soviet troops deployed on the frontier were from the NKVD – in some respects, their task was to protect the western border of the Soviet Union from those who might seek to cross it in either direction. Despite the last-minute alerts from Moscow, many were taken by surprise by the German attack and overwhelmed by artillery fire and the advance that followed. In the northern sector, the sky was never completely dark in midsummer and German troops crossed into Soviet-occupied Lithuania before dawn, encountering varying degrees of resistance.

The main striking power of Leeb's Army Group North was Hoepner's Fourth Panzer Group, which was made up of XLI and LXVI Motorised Corps, commanded by two men who would rise to high office in the years that followed. General Georg-Hans Reinhardt had led his XLI Corps in a swift advance to the Meuse crossings in the summer of 1940 and then took part in the planning for Operation *Seelöwe* ('Sea Lion'), the invasion of Britain. He impressed his superiors with the speed with which he adapted to modern conditions, as General Johannes Blaskowitz, commander of First Army, wrote in early 1941:

[He is] clear-thinking, astute, courageous in front of the enemy and decisive, particularly in his understanding of armoured formations. [My] evaluation: He fulfils [his tasks] very well. Recommendation: command of a panzer formation.[1]

Reinhardt's corps was on the western flank of Hoepner's panzer group, and consisted of 1st and 6th Panzer Divisions, 36th Motorised Infantry Division, and 269th Infantry Division. To Reinhardt's right was Erich von Manstein with LVI Motorised Corps, consisting of 8th Panzer Division, 3rd Motorised Infantry Division, and 290th Infantry Division.

Born Fritz Erich Georg Eduard von Lewinski, Manstein was the tenth child of a military family. As was fairly common practice at the time, he was adopted by his childless maternal aunt who was married to Georg von Manstein, together with another cousin; Manstein, who was aware of the arrangement, nonetheless always referred to his adoptive parents as 'Mother' and 'Father' and adopted the family name. During the 1930s he was instrumental in Germany adopting the turretless *Sturmgeschütz* or assault gun as infantry support weapons. He was chief of staff of Army Group South during the invasion of Poland in 1939 and demonstrated what was to become his hallmark of quick, decisive decision-making when he dealt with a surprise counterattack by the Polish Army, turning an awkward moment into a considerable German success.

After the Polish campaign, German attention turned to the west where the original intention of the Germans was to mount a repeat performance of the 1914 drive to turn the northern flank of Anglo-French forces – on this occasion, the sweep would also encompass the Netherlands. Manstein proposed a radical alternative: a powerful thrust through the Ardennes and Sedan to isolate and then destroy French and British forces in Belgium, opening the way for the complete defeat of France. Despite initial resistance from more conservative figures in *OKH*, the plan was adopted with dazzling success. Manstein's part in the operation was modest; he commanded XXXVIII Corps on the southern flank of the great drive to the English Channel to guard against possible French counterattacks and he then improvised motorised columns from his units and led them during the swift advance across France that followed the British withdrawal from Dunkirk. He was rewarded with the Knight's Cross and given command of LVI Motorised Corps in 1941. For the first time, he would have panzer formations under his personal command.

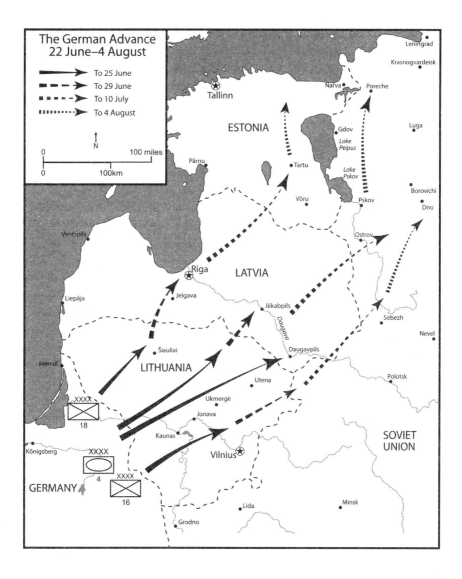

In the planned march to Leningrad, the forces of Army Group North faced two physical obstacles. The first of these was the valley of the Daugava or Western Dvina River, flowing through southern Latvia to Riga. Seizure of crossings over this river was essential if the tempo of the proposed operation was to be maintained and the intention of *Barbarossa* in this sector was explicitly to destroy the Red Army west of the river. Thereafter, the Germans would have to deal with a line of fortifications that had been built along the old frontier of the Soviet Union prior to the annexation of the Baltic States, the so-called Stalin Line. This was not a continuous series of defences – such a line would have been almost impossible given the huge length of the frontier – but consisted of a series of fortified districts with entrenchments and concrete bunkers, positioned in a manner intended to channel invading forces into distinct regions where they could be counterattacked. When the Baltic States were occupied in 1940, a decision was made to construct a new line along the new western frontier resulting in many of the guns in the Stalin Line being removed. By the summer of 1941 the trenches and some of the other fortifications were in a poor state, but if the Red Army succeeded in falling back to this line relatively intact there was at least a possibility of mounting serious resistance to the German advance. It was therefore important that even if the bulk of the Soviet forces in the Baltic region were destroyed to the west of the Daugava, the survivors had to be pursued rapidly to prevent them from establishing a rallying line that could be used to hold up the German advance until the arrival of fresh Red Army reserves.

In order to overcome these obstacles, Hoepner intended to give the main role to Manstein's LVI Motorised Corps with instructions to seize crossings over the Daugava as quickly as possible. The commander of 8th Panzer Division, Generalmajor Erich Brandenberger, was to lead the way and he and his staff carefully planned their advance. They identified 37 different rivers and streams between their start line and the Daugava, of which seven constituted substantial barriers. In order to deal with these obstacles, Brandenberger ensured that additional bridging resources would be available to the division. When the attack began, he divided his division into three battlegroups, two leading the attack and one positioned to support whichever attack made the best progress, with the most powerful battlegroup being on the left. When *Kampfgruppe Crisolli* on the right flank made unexpectedly rapid progress and swiftly broke into open country, Brandenberger showed all of the flair associated with panzer divisions, switching the emphasis of his attack to take advantage of this success. He moved to join Crisolli's battlegroup and ordered the rest of the division to follow.[2]

What followed was the essence of the German way of war. Within hours of the commencement of *Barbarossa*, 8th Panzer Division had effectively disappeared from sight as far as the Red Army was concerned. Confident that their corps commander would protect their flanks and rear, Brandenberger and Crisolli moved forward swiftly to secure Manstein's objective of capturing the Daugava bridge at Daugavpils before it could be destroyed. Elsewhere on the Eastern

Front, there were similar moments as the Soviet forces struggled desperately to keep up with events.

Whilst Stalin might have been refusing to accept any evidence of the imminent attack, others were aware of what was about to happen. Zhukov spent most of the night in his office, awaiting reports. They weren't long in coming:

> At 0300 I received a radio call from the commander of the Black Sea Fleet, Admiral [Filip Sergeyevich] Oktyabrsky, who said, 'The radio systems of the fleet report the approach from the sea of a large number of unidentified aircraft; the fleet is on full combat readiness. I ask for instructions.'
>
> I asked the admiral: 'What is your preference?'
>
> 'There's only one option: to meet the aircraft with defensive fire.'
>
> After speaking to Timoshenko, I replied to Oktyabrsky, 'Take action and report to your commissar.'
>
> At 0330 the chief of staff of the Western District, General [Vladimir Efimovich] Klimovskikh, reported German air raids on cities in Belarus. Three minutes later, the chief of staff of the Kiev District, General [Maksim Alekseyevich] Purkayev, reported air raids on cities in Ukraine. At 0340, the commander of the Baltic Military District, [Colonel-] General [Fedor Isidorovich] Kuznetsov, reported on enemy air raids on Kaunas and other cities.[3]

Zhukov tried to phone Stalin. After what seemed an interminable delay, Major General Nikolai Sidorovich Vlasik, the chief of Section 1 of the NKVD, came to the phone and sleepily asked who was calling.

> 'Chief of the General Staff Zhukov. I ask you to connect me urgently to Comrade Stalin.'
>
> 'What? Now?' The head of security was amazed. 'Comrade Stalin is sleeping.'
>
> 'Wake him immediately. The Germans are bombing our cities, the war has begun.'
>
> There was silence for a few moments. Finally, he answered dully, 'Wait.'
>
> About three minutes later, Stalin came to the phone. I reported the situation and asked for permission to commence retaliatory action. Stalin was silent. I could hear his heavy breathing. 'Do you understand me?' Silence again. 'What are your instructions?' I asked insistently.
>
> Finally, as if waking up, Stalin asked, 'Where is your commissar?'
>
> 'Speaking by radio to the Kiev District.'

'Come to the Kremlin with Timoshenko. Tell [Aleksandr Nikolayevich] Poskrebyshev [chief of the 'Special Section' of the Central Committee of the Communist Party] to summon all the members of the Politburo.'[4]

It should be borne in mind that Zhukov wrote this account after Stalin's death, and of course we only have his version of what was said. Nonetheless, it seems that despite the numerous warnings of the preceding days, Stalin still struggled to accept that Hitler had attacked. When Timoshenko and Zhukov went to the Kremlin, they informed Stalin and the Politburo that German ground forces were also reported to be attacking. Stalin mused whether this was some sort of provocation, and suggested that perhaps the German military had started the attacks without Hitler's knowledge. All doubt was removed when Schulenberg – who had only received formal notification of the invasion a few hours earlier – requested a meeting with Molotov and informed him that Germany had declared war. Stalin finally authorised countermeasures but added that even now, Soviet forces were not to cross the western frontiers of the Soviet Union.

Slowly, the Soviet high command began to react. On the ground, local Red Army and NKVD commanders tried to make sense of what was happening but remained hamstrung by the atmosphere of caution and fear that was the legacy of the purges of preceding years. In almost every sector, the fortifications that had been constructed were both incomplete and not fully manned. Wherever they encountered resistance, German units were able to bypass it and continue their advance. In the Baltic Special Military District, the Soviet Eighth and Eleventh Armies had only a single regiment each in the forward defences, with most of their troops still in peacetime barracks; as they hastily moved forward, they encountered the debris of the front-line units streaming back in defeat followed by the German ground forces. Overhead, the Luftwaffe controlled the skies and rained down bombs on the struggling Soviet columns.

The forces of the Baltic Special Military District were under the command of Colonel General Fedor Isidorovich Kuznetsov. He served as a junior officer in the Red Army in the Civil War and was repeatedly wounded; he was decorated twice with the Order of the Red Banner, one of only about 100 soldiers to receive the award twice. During the late 1930s he was a senior instructor and involved in organising tactical training in the Red Army. He was remembered by some of his pupils as being an enthusiastic teacher of theory, using maps and sand tables in his lessons, but rarely demonstrating his lessons in field exercises. Throughout 22 June, Kuznetsov and his staff tried to implement the defensive plans that they had drawn up in advance, either unaware that events were proceeding far faster than they could have expected or ignoring the few reports that reached them from the front line. During the evening, instructions arrived from above:

> While holding on firmly to the coast of the Baltic Sea, deliver a powerful blow from the Kaunas region into the flank and rear of the enemy Suvalki grouping, destroy it on cooperation with Western Front, and capture the Suvalki region by day's end on 24 June.[5]

The 'Suvalki grouping' was Hoepner's Fourth Panzer Group, which had no intention of waiting passively for the Red Army to mount a pincer attack against it. Brandenberger's 8th Panzer Division was pushing on towards the Daugava and when Kuznetsov sent his XII Mechanised Corps, with two tank divisions, into action against the German forces immediately to the west of Fourth Panzer Group, the Soviet tanks found themselves operating with little or no infantry support. All of the shortcomings of Red Army doctrine – the lack of radios and the rigid implementation of orders – resulted in the two tank divisions floundering forward in uncoordinated advances. German anti-tank gunners and soldiers armed with demolition charges destroyed hundreds of Red Army tanks while others were lost to mechanical breakdown or became immobilised when attempting to cross unsuitable ground. Over three days of confused fighting, the two divisions lost all but 45 of their original 749 tanks.[6] Immediately to the east of this 'counterattack', the Soviet 48th Rifle Division attempted to push forward as ordered into the flank of Hoepner's forces but was cut to pieces by the German 6th Panzer Division.

The southern 'pincer' of the ordered counterattack was also a disastrous failure. Running into powerful German units moving in the opposite direction, the Soviet forces rapidly broke up in disorder, but the Soviet 2nd Tank Division succeeded in moving forward towards Raseinai. Almost immediately, German aircraft spotted the Soviet column and reported to 6th Panzer Division that about 180 Soviet tanks were approaching. The Red Army division included about 50 new KV-1 tanks and to the alarm of the Germans, these proved to be almost invulnerable to German anti-tank fire. Within a few minutes, 6th Panzer Division's reconnaissance battalion was driven off in disarray:

> The battalion might have held out longer had it not been for the monster tanks, whose 70cm tracks literally ground everything in their path into the earth – guns, motorcycles, and men. There wasn't a single weapon in the bridgehead that could

stop them. After the massacre, the tanks waded through the Dubysa, easily crawling up the 45-degree banks.[7]

The staff of 6th Panzer Division scrambled to organise their forces to counter this Soviet thrust:

> The division now strove to move strong forces, in particular tanks, to the Raseinai area in order to prevent the enemy from crossing the Dubysa. However there was serious traffic congestion and consequently the attempts had little success. The Russians succeeded in capturing the Dubysa crossing at Kybarteliai. But they were unable to advance further due to our hastily deployed defences on the high ground to the east of Raseinai. There were particular concerns about our right flank in the area around Betygala. There was still no sign of 269th Infantry Division, which was deployed immediately on our right. It was still stuck to the northeast of Erzwilkas, and 1st Panzer Division was meant to be advancing along the main road to Kelme. It was clear that 6th Panzer Division would have to deal with the enemy thrust on its own for the moment. The division command sensed that the enemy was growing stronger and planned to attack him at dawn on 24 June with its massed strength from the Raseinai area, pushing him back over the Dubysa and towards the east.[8]

The planned counterattack ran into a renewed thrust by the Soviet armoured division, and its obsolescent Pz.35(t) tanks proved to be almost useless against the slow but implacable KV-1s. Major Johann Graf von Kielmansegg was 6th Panzer Division's chief of operations, and later described the battle:

> Before our own attack could begin, the Russians attacked with strong tank and infantry forces from their bridgehead over the Dubysa towards Raseinai. Despite achieving surprise their infantry failed to make progress despite repeated attempts. Nonetheless a serious crisis developed during the day. This was due to the appearance of hitherto completely unknown super-heavy tanks of up to 52 tons
> ...
> In total six or seven of these tanks drove behind our lines completely undisturbed. When they approached 11th Panzer Regiment, our tanks fired with all guns but without any success. Whilst the troops generally dealt with this unpleasant surprise rather well, there began to be the risk of general panic as it became clear that none of our weapons, even on our heavy tanks, could achieve anything against these tanks.[9]

The arrival of German artillery – in particular, the famed 88mm guns of the division's anti-aircraft battalion – proved decisive. Without infantry support, the Soviet KV-1s and a small number of KV-2s were unable to drive the Germans back and were knocked out one by one through a mixture of fire from the 88mm guns and the efforts of infantry using demolition charges. Having gone into battle short of ammunition and fuel, the heavy tanks had limited stamina and gradually the attack came to a halt; interrogation of captured tank crewmen revealed that they had been ordered simply to advance and crush the German vehicles under their tracks, and that in many cases the tanks had arrived from factories on the very eve of the attack – as a result, the crews had no opportunity to learn how to use them properly, and their guns hadn't even been bore-sighted. But it was a chastening shock for the Germans: their enemies were better armed than they had expected, and had they been used in better coordinated attacks, the outcome would have been very different. However, such coordination would have required better training, different tactical doctrine, and above all radios in every tank. Such developments would take several painful years to emerge in the Red Army.

Nevertheless, in a manner that was to prove characteristic of the Red Army throughout the years of war, there were attempts to learn lessons from what had happened. Major General Nikolai Mikhailovich Shestapalov, the commander of XII Mechanised Corps, struggled to extract the remnants of his divisions from the defeat and was badly wounded on 27 June. He died in hospital in August, but he still managed to draft a report for Kuznetsov and other senior commanders, accurately identifying many of the factors that had led to the poor outcome of the attack:

> The combat equipment in the formations was old and worn out, in particular the BT tanks that had participated in the march to liberate western Belarus [i.e. the invasion of eastern Poland as part of the Molotov–Ribbentrop Pact in 1939], in the march into Lithuania, etc.
>
> After the first day's march, and especially after the first day of fighting, dozens of tanks rapidly broke down. Because of the absence of reserve units, these vehicles couldn't be recovered both on the march to contact and during combat and, if they were repaired, it had to be on the field of battle as the lack of tractors did not permit their recovery to the collection points for damaged vehicles. As a result, much of the equipment was abandoned on enemy-controlled ground.
>
> The anti-aircraft battalions were poorly supplied with ammunition. For example, the batteries had only 600 37mm rounds (this insignificant quantity

was expended during the first two days of operations) and the complete absence of 85mm anti-aircraft ammunition at the moment when units were placed on full alert shows a clear picture of the state of the anti-aircraft defences of the corps ... This situation, as well as the absence of our fighters in this sector, permitted the enemy to achieve complete air superiority. Enemy bombers thus did whatever they wished. They smashed units on the march, in crossings and while stationary, and through the destruction of equipment and the killing and wounding of men, they reduced the combat readiness of these units. While on the march in just one day, enemy aircraft bombed units two or three times. On 26 June enemy planes destroyed 17 combat vehicles and about 20 transports ...

The divisions had no 152mm shells despite repeated demands for them before the beginning of hostilities ...

Command staff showed exceptionally poor attention to detail during combat operations and there were instances of cowardice ... [but] command staff personnel suffered heavy losses. For example, in the course of one battle, one of 28th Tank Division's regiments lost the deputy commander, two battalion commanders, and one commissar killed or wounded ...

Command and control of forces was poor because of the lack of radios. Wire communications were frequently interrupted. As the divisions were scattered, the establishment of wire communications was inadequate. Radio communications failed almost completely. The only means of communication during the course of the operation was the use of liaison officers.[10]

Further details were provided by Shestapalov's successor, Colonel Vili Yanovich Grinberg. He had been commander of 28th Tank Division during the attack and he described how his motorised rifle regiment was absent, presumably misdirected elsewhere in the confusion. He had no reconnaissance information and radio communications failed completely.

All of these reports contributed to the slow and painful evolution of the Red Army into a war-winning machine, but the process would take several years and many false starts. Just as the analysis of such failures was commonplace, it was also commonplace for almost no practical steps to be taken to remedy the problems that were identified. Even when such steps were taken, it was only when one problem was resolved that other problems were revealed. For example, the shortage of tractors to tow disabled tanks and other vehicles to repair teams was highlighted as a reason why so many had to be abandoned on the field of battle but as the number of recovery vehicles increased, this merely showed that the vehicle repair teams lacked the capacity to handle the large numbers of vehicles that were brought back to them. In early 1943, when the Red Army briefly recaptured Kharkov, the Soviet XV Tank Corps was reduced to just a handful of tanks and the repair teams were overwhelmed and unable to cope with the sheer volume of work. Fortunately, help was at hand. Local factory workers who had previously worked in the Kharkov tank factory before it was evacuated further east volunteered to help and worked alongside the men of 96th Mobile Tank Workshop. Within a few days, their collective efforts returned 34 T-34s and several T-70s to the front-line units.[11] As a result of this experience and other similar incidents the capabilities of the repair teams was increased, but this in turn revealed a further weakness: the repair teams had to be provided with adequate supplies of spare parts. In the absence of this, the best that they could do was cannibalise the vehicles that were most severely damaged. Slowly, matters improved with the result that the Red Army was then able to mount sustained operations in the second half of 1943 and into 1944, forcing the Wehrmacht out of central and western Ukraine. But it wasn't just the Red Army that was forced to salvage spare parts from wrecked vehicles to fix other tanks. With no further production of the Pz.35(t), only a small number of damaged vehicles could be repaired by the mechanics of 6th Panzer Division, almost always by stripping other wrecks for replacement parts.

Meanwhile, Brandenberger was racing on into the depths of Lithuania and into Latvia. There were two crossings over the Daugava River at Daugavpils – a road bridge in the town itself, and a rail bridge about a mile to the west. Most of the town lies on the northern bank of the river, so the Germans had a relatively open area over which to advance until they reached the valley. *Kampfgruppe Crisolli* was still leading the way with a company of soldiers from the Brandenburg Regiment, a unit that functioned a little like 'special forces' in other armies. Wearing Russian uniforms and riding in captured Red Army trucks, the company – led by Oberleutnant Knaak, who like his men spoke fluent Russian – was meant to secure the road bridge before Soviet soldiers could trigger the demolition charges that were known to be in place. The war diary of 8th Panzer Division described the events that unfolded when the Germans reached Daugavpils early on 26 June, just four days after crossing the frontier:

10th Panzer Regiment set off in the early morning hours towards Daugavpils. After a brief but fierce fight, it succeeded in seizing the bridge at Zarasai [14 miles to the southwest of Daugavpils] in a surprise attack, breaking through the Russian defences there and pushing on to the Daugava bridges without a pause.

With them was [the Brandenburg Regiment detachment] under the command of Oberleutnant Knaak, who had received a gunshot wound in a similar operation in Kėdainiai but had stayed with his men. The left group … which was sent to the railway bridge drove past five enemy armoured cars and reached the bridge, where it encountered more enemy armoured cars, and couldn't attack with its machine-guns. Consequently, it pulled back to the main road to the south and took up positions near the road bridge. There, Feldwebel Krückeberg was able to cut through a cable, which he guessed had been laid in preparation for demolition of the bridge.

The second group [of men from the Brandenburg Regiment] was deployed against the road bridge with Oberleutnant Knaak in the leading vehicle. The Russian guards on the west side of the bridge, who were chatting to civilians, were taken completely by surprise and gunned down, and the group drove over the Daugava bridge to the other bank. Meanwhile, an anti-tank gun had been spotted there and it fired on the leading vehicle, knocking it out and mortally wounding Oberleutnant Knaak. At the same time, a deadly fire erupted from the Daugava bank, which was strongly occupied, and from all the houses on the other side of the bridge.[12]

Soviet artillery succeeded in punching a hole in the rail bridge, but tanks from 8th Panzer Division now joined the Brandenburgers on the northern bank of the Daugava. Both sides rushed to get more troops into the battle but through a combination of speed and greater firepower, the Germans were able to gain the upper hand in heavy fighting. A number of Soviet light tanks attempted to mount a counterattack in the afternoon but although a small group almost reached the vital road bridge, all of the vehicles were destroyed. The first critical obstacle in the path of Army Group North had been crossed; moreover, a key escape route for Kuznetsov's armies operating south and west of the Daugava was now in German hands. Manstein's LVI Motorised Corps had advanced a remarkable 185 miles in just four days, completely dislocating the defences of Northwest Front, as Kuznetsov's Baltic Special Military District was now known. In an attempt to restore the situation, *Stavka* – the Soviet high command – ordered Twenty-Seventh Army, commanded by Major General Nikolai Erastovich Berzarin, to move from reserve to Kuznetsov's command, where it was to fill the gap that had opened in the centre of Northwest Front. In addition, Twenty-Second Army was to move to reinforce Kuznetsov's western flank and Major General Dmitry Danilovich Lelyushenko's XXI Mechanised Corps was ordered to reinforce Twenty-Second Army.

Lelyushenko's corps was a new formation and was being assembled as the German invasion unfolded. It had received 95 anti-tank guns a day after the German invasion commenced and two battalions of light BT-7 tanks arrived on 24 June. Lelyushenko and his staff had to organise these new units into their divisions on an ad hoc basis, improvising the best combination that they could. As they moved forward, the men of XXI Mechanised Corps came under air attack in Idritsa even before reaching the old frontier with Latvia, as Lelyushenko described:

> On 25 June, the enemy launched two major air attacks on the Idritsa rail station and the corps barracks. At the station there were three military formations: two with wounded from the front, and one with the families of officers. It was a dreadful scene: frightened people rushed about, one woman had a child in her arms and another, clutching her belongings, was running somewhere. Another stood as if petrified, and one lay motionless on the ground. There was nobody to help these people and the Fascist pilots made a second pass, finishing off the wounded with machine-guns.[13]

During the afternoon, a number of anti-aircraft guns reached Lelyushenko's divisions, giving them a degree of protection, but air attacks continued as the formations struggled forward through the columns of refugees fleeing in the opposite direction:

> Not far from the small town of Dagda [40 miles northeast of Daugavpils] the chief of staff and I got out of the car to inspect the area. On the side of the road, Aseychev saw a girl of 11 or 12 with a leg broken by shrapnel from a bomb. The girl was screaming, calling for her mother with all her strength. And next to her lay a mutilated female corpse: obviously her mother. I instructed my adjutant to drive the child immediately to the medical station.
>
> During the afternoon of 27 June, despite significant losses from enemy air attacks, our divisions nonetheless reached their assigned areas. The situation was extremely difficult: enemy aircraft dominated the air, so all regrouping, movement and attacks would have to be prepared at night as the enemy bombers and fighters would inflict huge losses during daylight and frustrate any plans.
>
> Before Corps Headquarters had established itself in a grove 20km northeast of Daugavpils, the deputy commander of Northwest Front, Lieutenant General Stepan Dmitriyevich Akimov, drove up to us. He looked tired. His eyelids were

puffy and reddened – he probably hadn't slept for days. In addition, he brought bad news.

'Matters are serious,' said Akimov. 'Yesterday morning the enemy crossed the Daugava and broke into Daugavpils. Attempts by Major General [Ivan Semenovich] Bezuglyi's V Airborne Corps, which hasn't completed its mobilisation, to dislodge the Nazis failed.' Akimov said that Berzarin's Twenty-Seventh Army was advancing to defend the line of the Daugava from Livany station to Kraslava, a front of about 80km. Our corps, apparently, would be part of it ...

I reported that we could start our counterattack on the morning of 28 June as the enemy, who had broken into the city, had probably had sufficient time to bring up substantial forces and gain a foothold. After driving the Nazis from Daugavpils, the corps would take up defensive positions on the northern bank of the river on a front of 15–20km.[14]

Lelyushenko had three divisions in his corps, and ordered 46th Tank Division to attack from the north while 42nd Tank Division advanced from the east. He held 185th Motorised Division in reserve. The attack began at first light on 28 June and clashed with German tanks about seven miles from Daugavpils; by working around to the west, Lelyushenko's armour was able to link up with the Soviet V Airborne Corps and penetrated into Daugavpils itself. Heavy fighting for the city followed and Lelyushenko described in his memoirs how his men left the streets littered with burning German tanks, but German infantry from Sixteenth Army had now reached the river and began to put pressure on the Red Army to the east of the town. After receiving further reinforcements the Germans went onto the offensive and drove the Soviet troops out of the northern parts of Daugavpils, forcing Lelyushenko to pull back. His tanks were almost out of ammunition and fuel and there was no prospect of destroying the German bridgehead.

Despite their failures, the counterattacks at Raseinai and Daugavpils served valuable purposes. It was the beginning of a long, painful but ultimately successful learning process in which the Red Army found a way to win. Almost everything would have to change – the equipment, the training and doctrine, the organisation of units, the skill-sets of officers at all levels – and the lessons would have to be learned by the soldiers in the most testing of circumstances whilst quite literally fighting for their lives. The battles also served as a series of checks for the German advance. The entire concept of *Barbarossa* was predicated upon rapidly advancing armoured forces cutting up the Red Army and preventing its retreat and each of these counterattacks inflicted serious casualties on those armoured forces, reducing their capability. The panzer forces had suffered heavy losses in earlier campaigns too, but the scale of the demands placed upon them in *Barbarossa* was completely different. Even modest losses threatened to derail the huge ambitions with which the operation had been mounted.

The battles also highlighted another weakness of the Wehrmacht that had been present in earlier campaigns, but had largely been overlooked because of the rapidity of German victories. Even at this early stage of the campaign, the panzer divisions were often forced to deal with Soviet counterattacks with little or no support from the infantry divisions that were struggling to keep up with their advance. The comparative lack of mobility of most of the army when compared to the relatively few motorised formations would become ever more obvious and problematic as the campaign unfolded across the vast landscape of the Soviet Union. In many respects, the German predictions that their motorised forces would be able to get behind the Soviet armies and cut them off would prove to be correct with a series of great encirclements unfolding in the first few weeks of the drive into the Soviet Union in the central sector, but the panzer divisions lacked the infantry strength to seal off these encirclements and the motorised divisions that accompanied them were too few to make up for the infantry that toiled along the dusty roads of the Baltic States, Belarus, and Ukraine. The consequence was that thousands of Red Army soldiers slipped away from the encirclements, either escaping to the east where they were able to link up with other Soviet troops or disappearing into the forests and countryside to join a partisan movement that would grow in strength with almost every week that passed.

Like Shestapalov, Lelyushenko wrote a detailed report of the setbacks of his mechanised corps. He wrote that his corps started the war with between 80 per cent and 90 per cent of its establishment manpower, but the great majority had been in the army no more than two months and therefore had barely completed basic training; the situation was so bad that Lelyushenko had to leave several thousand men behind when he deployed so that they could complete their training. When these men moved forward to try to rejoin his corps, the military authorities that controlled the regions through which they were moving refused to provide supplies for them and attempted to 'requisition' both the men and their equipment in order to bring other formations up to strength. The transport component of his corps – inadequate even if fully present by the standards of the Wehrmacht, and far behind the level of transport used by the British and Americans – had only 15 per cent of the wheeled vehicles intended and there were widespread shortages of artillery, machine-guns, and mortars. Most of the excellent 76mm guns had no gunsights, and range-finders for small-calibre anti-aircraft guns appeared only as the conflict was commencing with the result that none of the gun-crews had a chance to familiarise themselves with them. But he added that despite losing about 60 per cent of its combat strength, the combat spirit of his corps remained high, though he doubted that the corps could survive for long given the lack of replacements and the ongoing casualties that it was suffering.[15]

Despite the hard fighting they endured in Daugavpils, the men of Brandenberger's 8th Panzer Division were understandably proud of their achievements and as they regrouped and rearmed, they confidently expected to resume their swift advance towards Leningrad. In less than a week, they had covered perhaps a third of the distance to their ultimate objective and had every expectation of continuing at a similar pace. But permission for a further rapid advance was not granted. Concerned by the slowness of the infantry, Leeb ordered the motorised units gathering along the line of the Daugava to hold their positions until the rest of the army group arrived. Hoepner, who at first was swept up with the infectious enthusiasm of Brandenberger and the other panzer commanders, was also growing more cautious as became clear in his new orders to Reinhardt and Manstein:

> The Commander-in-Chief of the Army Group is strongly influenced by the idea that given the existing situation, the Panzer Group alone cannot break enemy resistance between the Daugava and Leningrad and is taking measures to bring up the infantry armies closer yet to the Panzer Group.[16]

Despite these instructions, Brandenberger permitted his division to probe to the north, encountering little or no resistance. Manstein, his immediate superior, was also impatient at the delay, as he later described:

> Whilst [the order from Leeb via Hoepner] was certainly the 'safe' staff college solution, we had had other ideas. As we saw it, our sudden appearance so far behind the front must have caused considerable confusion among the enemy. He would obviously make every attempt to throw us back across the river, fetching in troops from any quarter to do so. The sooner we pushed on, therefore, the less chance he would have of offering us any systematic opposition with superior forces. If we drove on towards Pskov – while, of course, continuing to safeguard the Daugava crossings – and if, at the same time, Panzer Group Headquarters pushed the other panzer corps straight through Daugavpils behind us, it seemed

likely that the enemy would have to keep on opposing us with whatever forces he happened to have on hand at the moment, and be incapable for the time being of fighting a set battle. As for the beaten enemy forces south of the Daugava, these could be left to the infantry armies coming up behind.

It goes without saying that the further a single panzer corps – or indeed the entire panzer group – ventured into the depths of the Russian hinterland, the greater the hazards became. Against this it may be said that the safety of a tank formation operating in the enemy's rear largely depends on its ability to keep moving. Once it comes to a halt it will immediately be assailed from all sides by the enemy's reserves.[17]

Finally, Manstein and his subordinates were given permission to resume their advance on 2 July. They were to advance first to Rēzekne, and then on to Ostrov and Pskov, an overall distance of 150 miles. Once this was accomplished, they would have covered two thirds of the distance from East Prussia to Leningrad and in the process would, it was assumed, have inflicted sufficient damage upon the Red Army that further resistance would be impossible.

Lelyushenko's divisions were licking their wounds after their failed attack on Daugavpils and received orders from Berzarin to start a sequential withdrawal if the Germans attacked. Almost immediately, this was rescinded by new instructions: the entire Twenty-Seventh Army was to attack the German forces north of the Daugava and destroy them. This revised order came from Kuznetsov, who in Lelyushenko's opinion had a poor understanding of the reality on the ground. In many respects, this reflected the manner in which his tactical lessons in the 1930s had concentrated on paper exercises rather than the reality of operations on the ground. In any case, the Germans struck first and Lelyushenko began a slow withdrawal. His formations had lost half their personnel and equipment in the preceding days, but nonetheless took advantage of an opportunity to surprise the reconnaissance battalion of *SS-Totenkopf* and make a stinging counterattack. But despite the welcome boost to morale from such local successes, the Soviet forces were driven out of Rēzekne on 3 July and a day later Berzarin gave up all pretence of following Kuznetsov's instructions for a counterattack and ordered his army to withdraw to the old Soviet frontier. Even this was too late: Reinhardt's XLI Motorised Corps reached and captured Ostrov on 4 July. The panzer troops had covered more than half the distance to Leningrad in just 12 days.

Within days, the losses suffered by the Red Army resulted in a new organisational change. The mechanised corps were to be disbanded and their divisions subordinated directly to the field armies. Lelyushenko was ordered back to Moscow for a new post as deputy head of the Main Armoured Directorate. He was told that he was to organise 22 tank brigades as quickly as possible. Meanwhile, the hapless Kuznetsov was dismissed from command of Northwest Front. In his place, Major General Petr Petrovich Sobennikov, who had been in command of Eighth Army, took control, with Lieutenant General Nikolai Fedorovich Vatutin, who had been deputy chief of the general staff, as his chief of staff.

The mood in the German high command was generally optimistic, as Halder noted in his diary on 3 July:

> On the whole … it may be said even now that the objective to shatter the bulk of the Russian army this side of the Daugava and Dnepr has been accomplished … It is thus probably no overstatement to say that the Russian Campaign has been won in the space of two weeks. Of course, this does not yet mean that it is closed. The sheer geographical vastness of the country and the stubbornness of the resistance, which is carried on with all means, will claim our efforts for many more weeks to come.[18]

Such an assessment seems astonishingly complacent with the benefit of hindsight, but at this point Halder still believed that the estimates of Red Army strength provided by *FHO* were correct. Given the numbers of prisoners taken and Soviet units destroyed, it seemed reasonable to assume that the bulk of the work had been done. Halder felt sufficiently confident to indulge in speculation: there would no longer be any major battles to destroy Soviet armies, rather there would be a concentration on seizing Soviet industrial centres to prevent the creation of new forces; once a firm base had been established 'around Leningrad', forces could mount operations against Moscow; and preparations could commence for an offensive operation to open a land route across the Nile to the Euphrates with additional German forces deploying through Turkey.

Army Group North was now approaching the second barrier that had been anticipated, the old fortifications of the Stalin Line. It is a measure of the weakness of German intelligence gathering that they were unaware of how badly neglected these defences were. From Manstein's memoirs, it seems that the poor roads of the area were at least as much an obstacle as Red Army resistance. As they approached the old frontier, the two corps of Hoepner's group received new orders. Manstein's LVI Motorised Corps was to deviate due east in order to outflank the Soviet defensive forces that were thought to be gathering around Pskov, much to Manstein's irritation – he doubted the accuracy of the reports about Soviet troops concentrating in Pskov, and in any case the new orders sent his divisions into swampy terrain where their ability to manoeuvre would be severely restricted, as 8th Panzer Division rapidly discovered:

> Early on 4 July the battlegroups set off once more. The enemy had withdrawn during the night so that at first the advance proceeded quickly. There was almost no fighting as the remnants of the enemy forces fled as fast as they could before the advancing half-tracks, and consequently the Russian frontier was reached at Goliseva between 1600 and 1700. Here, the division was prevented from advancing further down the road at first by about 50 vehicles that had been destroyed by the enemy. The wrecks could only be pushed aside by tanks …
>
> The division's road was only usable for about 800m to the Ludza River, thereafter were 400m of bottomless swamp.[19]

Other units were also unable to advance; 3rd Motorised Division had to be pulled back to its start line and sent directly towards Ostrov in the wake of the neighbouring XLI Motorised Corps. *SS-Totenkopf*, now assigned to Manstein's corps, enjoyed better luck in terms of roads and terrain as it advanced on Sebezh on the southern flank of the advance towards the east. But there were numerous concrete fortifications for Soviet troops to use to defend against any advance along the good road that ran in this direction. Matters were worsened by the relative inexperience of SS officers and NCOs, many of whom owed their posts more to seniority within the SS and the patronage of figures like Heinrich Himmler than to any military experience or aptitude. As a result, the division suffered disproportionately heavy losses and was soon forced to reorganise its three regiments into two new formations.

Manstein's march to outflank the presumed Soviet defences around Pskov made almost no progress and on 9 July Hoepner ordered him to abandon the attempt. Infantry divisions from Sixteenth Army were slowly arriving from the southwest to replace the motorised units and Manstein's corps was ordered to move up to Ostrov, where it was to gather its strength. Thereafter, Reinhardt's XLI Motorised Corps was to advance directly on Leningrad while LXVI Motorised Corps operated on its eastern flank, aiming to cut road and rail links between Leningrad and Moscow. In Hitler's headquarters, there was general satisfaction that the serious fighting was as good as over. The number of Red Army units destroyed in the initial phase of the operation suggested that – assuming Kinzel's estimates of Red Army strength were correct – the task of destroying Soviet forces before they could retreat into the interior had been achieved. Hitler reaffirmed his orders for Leningrad to be taken before any advance on Moscow, and now made explicit his intentions regarding both cities:

> It is the Führer's aim to level Moscow and Leningrad, and make them uninhabitable, so as to relieve us of the necessity of having to feed the populations through the winter. The cities will be razed by the Luftwaffe. Tanks must not be used for the purpose. 'A national catastrophe which will deprive not only Bolshevism, but also Muscovite nationalism, of their centres.'[20]

The details of the plans that were drawn up for what was to follow *Barbarossa* reveal just how different this conflict was intended to be. There was no intention to create client governments in the conquered areas; instead, Hitler intended to settle European Russia with ethnic Germans and to use the agricultural resources of Ukraine to provide Germany with food supplies. Since the revolutions of 1917, the population of the Soviet Union had grown by about 20 million people, mainly in urban areas – indeed, the deliberate famine created by Stalin in Ukraine, in an area that was by far the richest farming land in the Soviet Union, had reduced the rural population significantly. If the Germans followed through with their intentions of appropriating Ukrainian grain surpluses for their own use, the inevitable consequence would be the death through starvation of millions of Soviet citizens, mainly in the larger cities. This was both recognised and accepted as a desirable consequence. In this context, once Leningrad had ceased to function as an industrial centre and its capture had dealt a blow to Bolshevik ideology, its value to the Germans was minimal. Its citizens had no value whatever. They would either starve in the first winter, or were to be driven away into Siberia to fend for themselves.

There is another aspect of Halder's diary entry that is worth noting. It was now several weeks since German troops had invaded the Soviet Union, and planning for the invasion had been developed over many months before the fighting began – but this is the first entry in Halder's diary that explicitly records what was to happen when German forces reached Leningrad and Moscow. If there had been any discussion about how the Wehrmacht was to conduct operations in or near these large urban areas, Halder made no note, which would be astonishing in itself. It seems that critical decisions such as this had been left for later on the assumption that by the time the Wehrmacht reached Leningrad and Moscow, the campaign would be as good as over and there would be little or no pressure upon military resources.

The capability of the Luftwaffe to carry out destruction on such a scale was also greatly overstated. From the outset, the aircraft and organisation of the Luftwaffe were intended to fulfil its main role as tactical support for ground operations. The main 'heavy' bomber of the Luftwaffe was the Heinkel He-III, which could deliver a bombload of 4,400 pounds. This was similar to the British Handley Page Hampden and Vickers Wellington but barely half the bombload of the Armstrong Whitworth Whitley; the larger Handley Page Halifax and Avro Manchester, which entered service in 1940, could carry nearly 10,000 pounds and 13,000 pounds and the later Avro Lancaster managed to deliver up to 14,000 pounds. The ability of the He-III and other German bombers that were currently available to carry out the large-scale destruction required to destroy cities the size of Moscow and Leningrad was therefore highly questionable. However, they were capable of inflicting considerable damage, and the expectation was that if sufficient houses were destroyed or damaged, by either high explosive or incendiary bombs, the population would succumb to starvation and the weather faster than would otherwise be the case.

For many of the soldiers of the Wehrmacht, particularly those following in the wake of the swiftly advancing panzer divisions, the war consisted of occasional sharp fighting and long tiring marches under the blazing sun. Wilhelm Lubbeck, a private in 58th Infantry Division, crossed the frontier on 23 June as part of Sixteenth Army's second echelon. His account of what became known to many German soldiers as the *Blumenkrieg* ('flowers war') was repeated all along the long front line as the people of the western Soviet Union celebrated the departure of Communist authorities; the entire region, from the Baltic states in the north, through what had been eastern Poland prior to 1939, and into Ukraine, had large populations that were hostile to Bolshevism:

Battling both stifling heat and thick clouds of dust, we plodded countless miles. There were few breaks from our march, except for the occasional chance to hitch a lift on one of our company's horse-drawn vehicles. After a while, a kind of hypnosis would set in you as you watched the steady rhythm of the man's boots in front of you. Utterly exhausted, I sometimes fell into a quasi-sleepwalk …

On our march northeast, we covered the roughly 70 miles from the Lithuanian city of Siauliai to the Latvian capital of Riga within a week. Upon entering the city on 5 July, small crowds along the streets greeted us with shouts of '*Befreier!*' ('Liberator!') and presented us with flowers or chocolate in gratitude for their rescue from the Russian occupation. Whilst some of the population remained fearful and hid in their basements, the generally positive reception we received here and throughout the Baltic States ... reinforced our conviction that our cause was just.[21]

Most of those who sheltered fearfully in their basements were Jews, and the recollections of other soldiers – particularly those who passed through towns and cities a little behind the combat troops – paint a very different picture. A military bakery company passed through Kaunas on 27 June and its personnel witnessed a horrific scene:

I saw how Lithuanians armed with a variety of striking implements were raining down blows on other civilians until they showed no more signs of life. As I didn't know why these people were being killed in such a gruesome manner, I asked a nearby medical Feldwebel (sergeant) whom I didn't know personally. He told me that the people who were being killed were all Jews who had been seized by Lithuanians in the city and were being brought to this square. I didn't find out why these Jews were being killed. At that time I had no personal experience of the persecution of Jews, and had heard nothing about it. Almost all of those watching were German soldiers, who stared at the grim scenes with fascination.

When I reached the square where the Jews were being killed about 15 corpses or badly wounded were laid out on the square. There were about five Lithuanian convicts nearby who had been released and were ready to kill more Jews ... As I was an amateur photographer, I took two photographs of this singular scene that I could see by standing on my vehicle. As the film was then finished I took it from the camera in order to load a fresh roll. At that moment a Wehrmacht officer, probably a paymaster, approached me and told me that we weren't to take any photographs of such events. I had to give him my personal and unit details and he confiscated my camera. I could only save the photographs that were on the film that I had already removed ... [In these photos] five Lithuanian convicts can be seen clearly, holding implements in their hands and striking right at the bodies of the Jews lying before them. Members of the Lithuanian 'freedom fighters' can also be seen, with armbands on their left arms. They constantly brought more Jews to the square where they too were killed by the convicts. The Jews lying in the square weren't all killed at once. After they were brought to the square, they were struck quite indiscriminately on the head or face until they were stunned and collapsed on the ground. Then they were struck by the convicts until there were no more signs of life. Then more Jews were brought into the square and killed in the same manner. I remained on the spot where this grim scene took place for about ten minutes. While I was watching the square, I witnessed between ten and fifteen Jews being killed ...

Before they were killed, the Jews prayed and muttered to themselves. Some of the badly wounded Jews lying on the ground also murmured amongst themselves.[22]

These killings were carried out by Lithuanians who had armed themselves as the Red Army fled. Many were part of anti-Bolshevik groups that had been encouraged by the Germans, and they were swift to take their revenge on those they regarded as collaborators with the Soviet occupation. The ease with which they associated Jews with Bolshevism was deliberately encouraged by the Germans, and whilst some of the pogroms that broke out were spontaneous, many were actively instigated by the Germans; the personnel of the *Einsatzgruppen* had been ordered to encourage such acts, but to take measures to conceal their involvement. The intention was to portray such attacks as spontaneous 'self-cleaning' by the local population.

The units of *Einsatzgruppe A*, Stahlecker's SS formation, deployed swiftly. Lithuania was overrun so quickly that its substantial Jewish population had almost no opportunity to flee and those who escaped the violence of the first few days soon realised that their ordeal was far from over. The 'spontaneous' pogroms rapidly died away, not least because the German occupation forces wished to avoid any impression of ongoing lawlessness, but the Jews were first herded into ghettos and then systematically killed, mainly by shooting. Given the limited size of the *Einsatzgruppen*, they were dependent upon help from other agencies to carry out the killings. Many of the anti-Bolshevik partisans who took part in the early pogroms were enrolled into paramilitary units that then provided most of the manpower for the mass killings but there was also widespread support and aid from Wehrmacht units, which often provided transport and ammunition for the killings. In his reports to Berlin, Stahlecker explicitly praised local Wehrmacht commanders and expressed his gratitude for their assistance. Relations with higher commands, he wrote, were satisfactory; in the case of Fourth Panzer Group, he described them as 'cordial'.

Some German soldiers were dismayed by what they saw of the activities of the SS. A few complained; a staff officer from the headquarters of Sixteenth Army who also witnessed the pogrom in Kaunas reported the event to his superiors but was told that orders 'from above' dictated that the Wehrmacht was not to intervene in such local matters. The following day, the staff officer ventured out onto the streets once again:

I didn't see any more executions taking place in the streets as I had the previous day. Instead though there were long columns of 40 to 50 men, women and children who had been driven from their homes and were being herded through the streets by armed men. From one of these columns a woman broke away and fell to her knees before me, and pleaded with me with her hands raised for mercy and to help her, before she was thrust back in the roughest of manners. I was told that these people were being taken to the city prison. But I suspect that they were taken directly to a place of execution.[23]

Whilst security matters were under the control of *Einsatzgruppe A*, responsibility for military rear area units behind the front line lay with General Franz von Roques, and an indication of the overlap between the Wehrmacht and SS is that the creation of ghettoes in areas with substantial Jewish populations was his responsibility. When he took control of the occupied parts of Lithuania, Roques gave the matter little priority but not out of any sense of leniency towards the Jews – rather, he preferred to use his limited resources on other matters. After the war he would claim that he had refused to implement the Commissar Order but this was contradicted by some of his subordinates; for example, his intelligence officer recorded in his diary as early as the end of June that the task of identifying commissars was proceeding with little difficulty and they were then 'rendered harmless'. *Einsatzkommando 3*, a subunit of *Einsatzgruppe A*, was commanded by Karl Jäger and had responsibility for activities in Lithuania. When he arrived in Kaunas, he was dismayed by the lack of any progress towards creating a ghetto and took the matter in hand immediately. He also discussed with Roques the location of suitable places for mass detention. Roques must have been aware that such detention would be followed immediately by mass execution; he informed Jäger that the network of old fortifications around the city, dating from the 19th century, would be ideal. One such fort was already being used as a killing ground, and tens of thousands of Jews would perish in these locations in the weeks that followed.

When the German invasion commenced, the first tremors of what was to come were felt in Leningrad as the military district transformed itself into Northern Front. Just a day after *Barbarossa* commenced, anti-aircraft gunners in the northern part of the city shot down a German Ju-88 bomber and a fighter pilot claimed the destruction of a He-111 bomber, but there were already concerns about the state of readiness of Soviet forces – many of the units that were mobilising reported inadequate ammunition and fuel stocks and large numbers of tanks and aircraft were unusable due to shortages of spare parts.[24] The primary role of the

Front was to defend Leningrad from attacks from Finland and to a large extent this seemed to have been fulfilled, with Finnish troops making only modest progress through the forests of the Karelian Isthmus and further north as German troops crossed into Soviet territory from Norway; but there were few illusions about this, and there was an awareness that as German forces moved closer to Leningrad in their drive across the Baltic States, these northern attacks would resume with greater energy. The original strategic plan – that Leningrad Military District would be responsible for defending the Soviet frontier to the northwest while the Baltic Special Military District defended the Baltic region – was clearly in ruins and on 4 July Popov was ordered to make preparations to take up defensive positions facing Estonia. He had already sent his deputy, Lieutenant General Konstantin Pavlovich Pyadyshev, to the region. Pyadyshev's recommendation was to construct a main defensive line running broadly along the Luga River from Kingisepp in the northwest to Lake Ilmen in the southeast. He suggested that in addition, there should be further defences closer to the city and Popov promptly adopted these proposals. The civilian population was mobilised and organised into work battalions that were taken by train to the new defence lines; in some cases they were brought back to the city at dusk, but on other occasions they camped by their work areas in the balmy summer weather.

Yevgeny Danilovich Moniushko was aged 15 when the war with Germany began. He was working for the summer as a laboratory assistant in Vyritsa, about 30 miles south of Leningrad and helped pack away the laboratory's equipment for evacuation to the east. Together with many others from his school he was put in one of the work battalions deployed to build the new defensive lines. They were taken by train to the Luga River near Kingisepp:

> Our job was to dig an anti-tank ditch. The work schedule involved digging for eight hours and then resting for four hours right there on the ground. We ate some food, primarily bread and tinned meat, and then worked for eight hours again, and so on.
>
> The ditch we dug was approximately 6m wide and 3m deep and was triangular in cross-section. Templates had been made from boards for us to check its exact dimensions. Even though they assembled a large group of people to do this work, it progressed very slowly since no one had any experience in such matters. Apparently, one of the teachers who served as the escort for our group had served in the army sometime in the past, since he was dressed in a semi-military uniform but without any insignia. Therefore, people constantly asked him various questions, seeking his expert advice.[25]

But whilst construction of defensive positions posed considerable difficulties, these fortifications would be worthless unless troops could be provided to man them. The Luga Operational Group was created and given two rifle divisions, with a further two divisions raised from the Leningrad People's Militia and various ad hoc units assembled from the personnel of the Leningrad Infantry and Machine-Gun Schools together with a separate mountain rifle brigade. In addition, XLI Rifle Corps of Eleventh Army was assigned to the group but was already in action against the Germans and would have to withdraw to the new line. Pyadyshev was placed in command of the new group with orders to hold the Luga Line, as it became known, at all costs. Further reinforcements were promised to give his forces sufficient strength to carry out their task. Meanwhile, the forces of Northwest Front continued their withdrawal through the Baltic region. The divisions of Eighth Army, now pulling back into Estonia, had been reduced to about 2,000 men per division.[26] In an attempt to improve coordination between the disparate Fronts, Stalin ordered the creation of a new command group designated the Main Command of the Northwest Direction, with Voroshilov in overall command; he immediately assigned Eighth Army and part of Eleventh Army from Northwest Front to Northern Front. Any complacency about the situation on the front line facing the Finns was dispelled when Finnish troops attacked again on 10 July and moved closer to Leningrad.

The militia divisions were created using volunteers who came forward in large numbers to fight against the Germans. As early as the second week of July, over 100,000 people had volunteered in Leningrad and they were first organised into machine-gun and artillery battalions, then into divisions. The first full division – 1st Leningrad Rifle Division of the People's Militia – was raised in the Kirov district of the city but from the outset it was short of weapons – compared to the requirements that had been drawn up, it had barely a third of the pistols, none of the submachine-guns, heavy machine-guns or anti-aircraft weapons, and very few mortars. Its artillery regiment had a mixture of guns of different calibres, creating serious supply problems; it even received 300 rounds of artillery ammunition that couldn't be used by any of the weapons that it possessed. Other equipment – shovels, binoculars, compasses etc – also fell far short of what was required but the division was nonetheless sent to the front on 10 July, taking up positions the following day between Luga and Lake Ilmen. Almost immediately, it came under air attack and suffered its first casualties.[27]

Stepan Mikhailovich Bardin was one of the many volunteers who came forward. He would eventually serve with 2nd Militia Division and he described how he and his fellow workers gathered around a local Communist Party official in their factory:

Frankly, I listened to the speakers with half an ear, absorbed in thoughts about what lay ahead for us, what the war would be like. Would it be like in the movies – the smoke of guns smashing the enemy, the roar of advancing tanks, victorious infantry marches to the sound of military bands – or something different?

Of all that was said at the rally, I only remember the words of Party Committee Secretary Smirnova: 'In the entire history of our glorious city, the enemy's boot has never stepped on its streets and squares. He won't step there now. The Nazis will be defeated.' She turned to us. 'We believe that you will show courage and resolution, and stop the enemy troops on the distant approaches to Leningrad!'

Her words were drowned in applause, showing the emotions and mood of both those who were to go to the front and those who remained in the factory. Nikolai Chistyakov couldn't resist and shouted out passionately, 'We assure you that we will not spare our lives to protect our beloved city, our native country! The enemy will not pass!'

And then everything became muddled. We were surrounded by a dense crowd of workers, and all factory work stopped. The factory waved farewell to its sons. They hugged us and gave us flowers. Ivan Melekhov, my former acquaintance in the sheet metal cutting team, thrust a cigarette case at me although he knew that I was a non-smoker: 'Put it in the left pocket of your tunic. At least it'll be a barrier to bullets.'[28]

The new preparations for defending Leningrad were badly needed. The battered armies of Northwest Front could do little to stop the onward advance of the Wehrmacht. On 11 July, Reinhardt advanced beyond Pskov and issued orders for a thrust to the Luga River at Poreche, about ten miles to the southeast of Kingisepp – if this town could be captured rapidly, the Soviet defences on the Luga Line would be compromised even before they were in place. As they moved forwards the German tanks were spotted by Soviet aircraft, but the presence of an armoured column at this location was so unexpected that the pilots assumed they had to be Red Army units withdrawing towards the new defensive line. Later in the day, the planes returned and dropped leaflets on the armoured column calling on it to identify itself. Ignoring the aircraft, the tanks motored on. As darkness fell, they reached the Luga and stormed over the bridge in Poreche, taking the small Soviet unit in the town completely by surprise.

It was a dramatic moment, with the leading German troops now barely 70 miles from the centre of Leningrad and almost no substantial body of Soviet troops in their path, but there was no prospect of the Germans being able to exploit their success. Manstein's LVI Motorised Corps was meant to be advancing to protect the southeast flank of the drive towards Leningrad, but Brandenberger's 8th Panzer Division encountered unexpected resistance. It had been ordered to lead a drive from Ostrov through the town of Porkhov towards Lake Ilmen, but from the outset it faced the problems created by the speed of the German advance – there were large groups of Soviet soldiers trying to escape from the region to the north and east, and Brandenberger was forced to deploy his units to cover the possibility of clashes with the enemy from any direction. Almost immediately the leading battlegroup encountered Soviet troops backed by KV-1 and KV-2 tanks, and it was only when the redoubtable 88mm guns of the anti-aircraft battalion were brought forward that the Soviet armour was driven off. Still guarding against attacks, particularly against the open southern flank, 8th Panzer Division tried to move forward again the following day, 12 July. Promptly, it encountered resolute Soviet defences at the town of Borovichi on the Shelon River, roughly midway between Pskov and Lake Ilmen. Several German tanks were lost in fighting against the heavy Soviet tanks and for the next two days the German division tried to move along the line of the Shelon towards Lake Ilmen, constantly clashing with Red Army tanks. The promised support of infantry divisions from Sixteenth Army on its southern flank failed to appear, forcing Brandenberger to deploy more and more of his units to shield against possible counterattacks – by 14 July this open flank stretched for 42 miles, with the situation on the northern flank not much better.

This was the moment that Voroshilov and Vatutin threw their forces into a counterattack. Lieutenant General Vasily Ivanovich Morozov's Eleventh Army was to strike against the exposed German forces with two groups – from the north, 21st Tank Division would continue the attacks it had been making in preceding days with support from two rifle divisions, while three rifle divisions attacked from the south. In addition, three further rifle divisions were variously to try to pin down 8th Panzer Division's leading and trailing elements, while Berzarin's Twenty-Seventh Army was to drive away the German Sixteenth Army, struggling up from the south. Whilst this might sound like an impressive concentration of forces, it should be remembered that none of these Soviet divisions was remotely near full strength. Nevertheless, the attack came as an unwelcome surprise for the Germans, as the division war diary recorded:

> Aerial reconnaissance reports that enemy forces have marched up from the north and deployed [against the division]. Well-camouflaged tanks are already in position. More tanks are on the march from the north and villages are strongly held by enemy troops. Riflemen and horses can be seen moving through woodland …

Road conditions are bad … But aside from the degraded roads and sandy tracks, much of the problem lies with difficulties created by the disorderly, chaotic influx of units that are not part of the division into the marching columns. [There are] numerous reports from all sources about the often-unrestrained behaviour of units, particularly corps-level troops.[29]

The congestion was inevitable, given the few roads that could be used. As Soviet forces began to gather on the flanks of 8th Panzer Division, Brandenberger had his hands full just fending off the attacks on his exposed forces without being able to consider further advances of his own. On 15 and 16 July Red Army counterattacks took control of a ten-mile stretch of the road being used by 8th Panzer Division and numerous corps-level units. Rear area personnel found themselves pressed into action as makeshift infantry as the Soviet Eleventh Army applied ever greater pressure; by 16 July, Manstein's entire corps was fighting on three fronts facing north, east, and south. But Berzarin's attack on Sixteenth Army proved to be a failure with the Germans turning the tables on their opponents, encircling and destroying much of Twenty-Seventh Army, and the German infantry finally began to arrive on Manstein's southern flank. It was now possible for 8th Panzer Division to hand over its sector to *SS-Totenkopf* and regroup; it was to take part in a renewed attack towards the east and Lake Ilmen, starting from a position slightly further to the north. But the diversion of *SS-Totenkopf* to this sector from the Kingisepp–Luga sector meant that German efforts elsewhere were weakened. Moreover, the battle had cost 8th Panzer Division and the nearby 3rd Motorised Division substantial casualties. These were the fast-moving mobile German forces that were meant to cut up the Red Army and prevent it from retreating, but 8th Panzer Division had now lost about half its remaining tanks. It was a chastening moment for Brandenberger, Manstein, Hoepner, and Leeb. For all their successes and belief that they had destroyed the bulk of the forces opposing them, it was clear that the Red Army remained strong enough to oppose them and drive them back, and it was only due to the relative clumsiness and uncoordinated nature of the Soviet attack that the Germans escaped without heavier losses. The casualties suffered by the Red Army in this operation are unknown, but were unquestionably heavy. However, the overall result was that the German thrust towards Leningrad was derailed for a week, precious time for the defences to be prepared.

The failure of the attempt by the Red Army to seize the initiative with its counterattack against Manstein's corps meant that defending the Luga Line assumed even greater importance than before. Voroshilov tried to assemble a reserve of four rifle divisions and a tank division with which he would be able to counter any thrust by the Germans through the defensive line, but the continuing advance of Finnish troops from the northwest and the successful advance of the German Eighteenth Army into Estonia forced Voroshilov to acquiesce to the rifle divisions being sent elsewhere. As a result, his local operational reserve was reduced to the single tank division, which he positioned in Krasnogvardeisk, the town that had variously been known as Gatchina and Trotsk in the past.

Even at this stage of the war, the Red Army was implementing changes in its structure as a result of lessons learned, and to take account of reality. On 15 July, *Stavka* issued instructions that henceforth field armies were to consist of just five or six divisions, with no intermediate corps headquarters. This was partly to improve flexibility and speed of response, but partly dictated by the losses of staff officers and the problems caused through a combination of inexperience and fear of punishment. The changes were to be introduced as circumstances permitted, without any disruption of existing operations.[30] A week later, Voroshilov used these instructions for reorganising the Red Army to remove Pyadyshev from his post as commander of the Luga Group. To date, Pyadyshev had carried out his assignments to the best of his ability, given the poor resources at his disposal – it should be remembered that four rifle divisions that he had expected to receive had been assigned elsewhere – but not long after his dismissal he was arrested and charged with dereliction of duty. In October, he was sentenced to ten years' imprisonment; he died in prison in the summer of 1944.

The Luga Group was now divided into three sectors. The Kingisepp Defence Sector was to defend a line from the Baltic coast through Kingisepp along the Luga, with elements of the Baltic Fleet, two rifle divisions, two militia divisions, and a number of improvised units; it was commanded by Major General Valentin Vladislavovich Semashko. Next in line was the Luga Defence Sector under Major General Andrei Nikitovich Astanin with three rifle divisions, a tank division, and some militia formations. The Eastern Defence Sector, where 1st Militia Division had been deployed with a number of other militia units, was commanded by Major General Filipp Nikanorovich Starikov. The reality was that these new commands inherited the same weak formations that had been available to Pyadyshev. Their ability to withstand a serious German attack was very doubtful.

To date, all construction of defensive positions had concentrated on the Luga Line, and although Voroshilov had sketched out defences closer to Leningrad almost no work had been done on them. Towards the end of July, Stalin and *Stavka* moved to address the numerical weakness of Leningrad's defenders. A new Forty-Eighth Army was formed under the command of Lieutenant General

Stepan Dmitriyevich Akimov consisting of 1st Militia Division, three regular rifle divisions, and 21st Tank Division. However, the greatest respite to the Red Army came not from reinforcements but German inaction. After seizing its small bridgehead over the Luga, Reinhardt's corps had made no further threat towards Leningrad, fearing that its flanks would be too exposed. The infantry divisions of Eighteenth Army were moving up through Estonia, hopefully eliminating any threat from the northwest, but Hitler and Halder continued to fret over Leeb's deployment of his forces. Hitler was critical of Leeb's failure to identify a major focus of concentration, but took little account for the diverging axes on which he was obliged to operate. There were also signs that Hitler was deviating from his original plans, as Halder noted on 26 July:

> The Führer's analysis, which at many points is unjustly critical of the field commands, indicates a complete break with the strategy of large operational conceptions. You cannot beat the Russians with operational successes, he argues, because they simply do not know when they are defeated. On that account it will be necessary to destroy them bit by bit, in small encircling actions of a purely tactical nature.
>
> Of course, there is something in these ideas ... But following such a course ... reduces our operations to a tempo which will not permit us to reach our goal, the Volga. We must remember that the Russians have plenty of manpower, and it is very unlikely that we could pursue the new policy to the point where the enemy cracks and the way is clear again for operations on a big scale ...
>
> General Paulus reports on his visit to Army Group North. Hoepner, Manstein and Reinhardt concur that the area between Lake Ilmen and Lake Peipus is unsuited to operations of armoured units. All we can do at Lake Ilmen is to attack with infantry while keeping in readiness the armour not yet committed [mainly 8th Panzer Division, which had been pulled back from the front line] for a follow-up where infantry has cleared the path. As a consequence, development of the battle will be very slow.[31]

Both Hitler's view and Halder's comments are at odds with the original concept of *Barbarossa*. The intention had been to crush the Red Army as close to the frontier as possible, thus permitting large-scale advances, but Hitler was now turning away from this; at the same time, Halder seemed to acknowledge that Soviet manpower resources had been seriously underestimated. And the recognition that the terrain where Fourth Panzer Group was operating was unsuitable for armour was a remarkable admission of failure: reconnaissance should have identified the problems that motorised units would face in this area, but it seems that the plans had been drawn up without any proper attempt to correlate the appearance of large-scale maps with the actual terrain. Halder's diary also showed the development of another issue that had been permitted to remain unresolved throughout the planning of *Barbarossa*. He and many other army commanders had always favoured an attack to capture Moscow, hence his reference to the Volga – he meant the upper Volga, rather than further south where the river flowed past Stalingrad to Astrakhan and the Caspian Sea. By contrast, Hitler had insisted from the outset that an attack on Moscow could only develop when all strategic objectives in the northern and southern sectors had been secured. The failure to reach a definitive solution to this discrepancy would play an increasing part in German decisions and arguments in the coming days.

CHAPTER 5

THE APPROACH TO LENINGRAD

By the end of July, the work of *Einsatzgruppe A* was in full swing across Lithuania and Latvia; being the most northerly of the former Baltic States, Estonia was the last to come under German control and had a smaller Jewish population, with the result that most Estonian Jews were able to escape before the arrival of the Wehrmacht. Those further south were less fortunate. In Kaunas, Karl Jäger – increasingly haunted by nightmares of dead women and children, but still resolutely implementing the orders that he had been given – meticulously recorded the daily total of victims. By the beginning of August, his men and their Lithuanian auxiliaries had killed 4,400 people. With characteristic attention to detail, Jäger listed these by category: 4,102 male Jews, 135 female Jews, 157 Communists (a mixture of Lithuanians, Russians, and even one German), and six others. The concentration on male Jews was deliberate – the intention was to start by eliminating those who might be able to organise resistance to the Germans. As August passed, the toll grew at a horrific rate; Jäger's unit was responsible for the deaths of a further 38,324 victims during the month, most of them Jews.[1] There were further killings in Latvia, particularly in and near Riga.

While his subordinates were busy with their tasks of mass murder, Stahlecker was turning his attention to Leningrad. The *Einsatzgruppen* submitted regular reports to Berlin where they were collated and redistributed to senior officials, and as early as 18 July, Stahlecker – now in Pskov – described preparations for what he and others thought lay ahead:

> The fall of Petersburg can be expected in three to five days at the earliest. The operation of the *Sicherheitspolizei* ['security police', in this case *Einsatzgruppe A*] with Hoepner's Panzer Group, which has been directed to Petersburg, has been agreed after discussions with the Ic [military intelligence officer], chief of staff and

Generaloberst Hoepner. Following this, plans drawn up by the *Sicherheitspolizei* command will be passed to the advancing divisions. As the advance parties of *Einsatzkommando 1a* and *Einsatzkommando 1b* cannot be released by Eighteenth and Sixteenth Armies, the *Einsatzgruppe* is ordering all forces of *Einsatzkommando 2* and *Einsatzkommando 3* that are not essentially required in Kaunas and Riga to proceed to Pskov. From here they will move forward to the divisions [of the Wehrmacht].[2]

A further report on 23 July reiterated the close working between Hoepner and Stahlecker, with arrangements for 'security' in Leningrad being agreed in detail. Such arrangements had been seen before when the Germans marched into Warsaw and other cities: the *Einsatzgruppe* would prepare lists of known actual and potential opponents of the Germans so that they could be arrested as quickly as possible. In most cases, this detention would be followed by execution with minimal or no legal process. Although many Wehrmacht officers went to great lengths after the war to portray their own activities in the best possible light, placing blame for all atrocities on the SS, there was clearly a very close working relationship between military units like Fourth Panzer Group and SS formations involved in mass murder. It seems that there were discussions at high level about moving Stahlecker to a new post, but on 24 July a senior officer wrote to Reinhard Heydrich, head of the *Reichssicherheitshauptamt* ('Reich Security Head Office' or *RSHA*, the body that controlled the *Sicherheitspolizei* and the *Sicherheitsdienst*, the intelligence agency of the SS):

> After discussion with [Gruppenführer Hans-Adolf] Prützmann [SS officer with overall responsibility for police and SS units in the Baltic States and northern Russia] I request that Brigadeführer Stahlecker is left in post, at least until Petersburg has been occupied and secured. The relationship between Stahlecker and the Wehrmacht is so good that his transfer will definitely be disadvantageous.[3]

It is beyond question that the senior officers of Army Group North knew of the activities of *Einsatzgruppe A*. The good relationship that they had with Stahlecker further emphasises that their later protestations of innocence and ignorance are highly questionable.

Despite the attempts by Halder and others to keep up momentum towards Moscow, Hitler continued to insist on giving Leningrad a greater priority. Before the end of July, he ordered Third Panzer Group to be transferred from Army Group Centre to Army Group North in order to expedite the attack on Leningrad; once the city was taken, the panzer group would be reassigned to Army Group Centre.

At the same time Fourth Panzer Group, together with what infantry units were deemed to be surplus to requirements, would return to Germany. As the attempts to advance in late July foundered, he issued fresh instructions at the end of the month. Army Group North was to advance in the broad region between Lake Ilmen and Narva towards Leningrad, linking up with Finnish forces advancing from the northwest. The divisions of Third Panzer Group were to thrust towards the northeast beyond Lake Ilmen in order to secure both the southern flank of Army Group North and the northern flank of Army Group Centre.

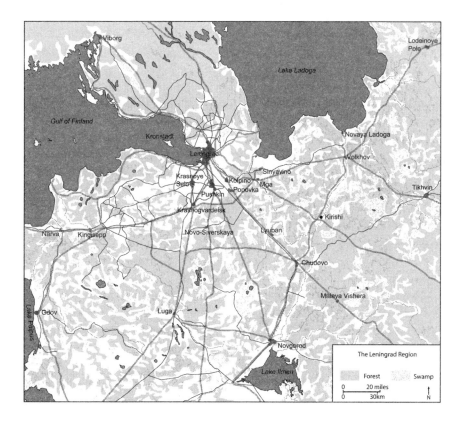

Leeb accordingly drew up his orders. He organised three powerful groups for the new offensive. Advancing from the bridgeheads secured in and near Poreche, the Northern Group was to strike north towards Kingisepp with XLI Motorised Corps and XXXVIII Corps; after taking Kingisepp, the group would turn east towards Leningrad. On its right flank, the Luga Group – Manstein's LVI Motorised Corps, with 8th Panzer Division in reserve, still recovering from its

135

mauling – would attack to capture Luga and was then to advance along the main road to Krasnogvardeisk and thence the southern outskirts of Leningrad. Finally, a Southern Group from Sixteenth Army was to attack along the northern shore of Lake Ilmen to capture Novgorod and then advance northeast to Chudovo, cutting the road and rail link between Leningrad and Moscow.[4] At the same time, Eighteenth Army was to complete its conquest of Estonia and would attack towards Narva while Sixteenth Army cooperated with Third Panzer Group on Hoepner's southern flank. Almost all of the troops available to Army Group North would be used in the assault, with only three security divisions – intended mainly for rear area tasks such as guarding bridges and railways and assisting the *Einsatzgruppen* in their tasks – in reserve.

A glance at the map of the region shows the daunting task that lay ahead for Leeb's armies. The entire area is heavily forested and has widespread swamps, with little high ground. There were few good roads across the area in 1941 and many towns were accessible in the winter almost exclusively by railway. Furthermore, the Wehrmacht was beginning to suffer the consequences of its advance. When *Barbarossa* commenced, the front line ran for a daunting 1,160 miles. As the Germans advanced into the Soviet Union, the front line grew through a combination of the development of deep salients and the manner in which the Baltic coast ran northwards and by early August the Wehrmacht was spread out over a front line that was nearly 690 miles longer. The operation had begun with relatively modest high-level reserves, and these were now fully committed. The expectation had been that the Red Army would be destroyed to the west of the Daugava–Dnepr line, with the consequence that the expanding front line would not have been so important, but despite the undoubted casualties suffered by the Soviet forces, they showed little sign of the collapse that had been predicted so confidently. By 1 August, the Germans had destroyed 46 Red Army divisions and severely damaged many more, but despite this the scale of Soviet mobilisation was such that the Red Army now fielded a staggering 401 divisions.[5] Kinzel's most pessimistic forecast had been that the Red Army could raise a total of about 300 divisions, of which he confidently predicted that about 80 would remain on the eastern frontiers of the Soviet Union, leaving the Wehrmacht to deal with no more than 220 divisions. Even if his unfounded expectations of Stalin being unable to move the eastern armies had been true, the Germans were still facing over 320 divisions in the west, more than the *FHO* estimate of the entire strength of the Red Army.

When he conducted his wargames prior to *Barbarossa*, Paulus anticipated much of what later transpired during the campaign. The ever-widening front line would result in a need to divert mobile forces from the central axis towards the north and south in order to establish continuity of front line, but the conclusions of the wargame cautioned that such a policy would take both time and resources that might be better used to continue the destruction of the Red Army, without which it would be impossible to achieve a lasting victory. Hitler now chose to ignore the recommendations arising from the wargame, largely because the damage inflicted upon the Red Army was thought to be so great that such a diversion of effort was justifiable.

The use of all available Wehrmacht forces in the front line for a further offensive, with only minimal reserves at every level, carried a risk. If it succeeded, all would be well; if it failed, and particularly if the Red Army was able to mount a counterattack, the Wehrmacht would be left struggling to cope. Such a counterattack was being planned even as Leeb moved his forces into position. *Stavka* had issued orders to Northwest Front to mount a further counteroffensive against the southern flank of the German forces threatening Leningrad and with characteristic aggression Vatutin drew up plans for a major assault with all available forces. Almost immediately *Stavka* intervened, ordering him to reduce his ambitions to a more realistic scale and turning down his request for additional reinforcements. Using three armies, he was to attack on 12 August towards Dno. The instructions from *Stavka* showed that the Soviet forces were already learning from their previous setbacks:

> Experience indicates that during our offensive, the enemy will deliberately withdraw in front of our assault group. Then, while giving the appearance of a rapid and easy advance, he will immediately regroup his forces on the flanks of our assault group with the intention of subsequently encircling it and isolating it from the main front line. I therefore order you not to go too far forward during the assault ... Pay attention to reconnaissance and protect the flanks and rear, and consolidate the territory you seize ...
>
> Prepare the operation with the utmost secrecy, and avoid telephone conversations and unnecessary correspondence so that as has often been the case, the enemy does not discover our plan and the start date of the operation and does not disrupt the offensive.[6]

The target of the Soviet operation would be the German X Corps, part of Busch's Sixteenth Army. General Christian Hansen, the corps commander, had just two divisions at his disposal – 30th and 290th Infantry Divisions – immediately around Staraya Russa, south of Lake Ilmen. His southern neighbour was General

Walter Graf von Brockdorff-Ahlefeldt's II Corps, but its forces were mainly concentrated around Kholm, 59 miles to the south. When Vatutin began his attack, II Corps rapidly took up defensive positions and fought off every attempt to drive it west, even though its lines of communication became increasingly tenuous. But a little to the north the main Soviet assault, made by Major General Kuzma Maksimovich Kachanov's Thirty-Fourth Army, burst through the gap between the two German corps. Led by two motorised divisions and a cavalry division, the Soviet force thrust forward 28 miles in two days, paying little attention to the instructions from *Stavka* to exercise caution and to monitor potential threats from the flanks.

On 15 August Manstein was ordered to move his corps headquarters and 3rd Motorised Division to an area southeast of Narva. The redeployment was slow and difficult due to the limited number of good roads through the swampy and forested terrain, but as soon as Manstein arrived near Lake Samro he was given new orders. The new attack by the Red Army was forcing a change in German plans: with 3rd Motorised Division and *SS-Totenkopf*, he was to move south to deal with Vatutin's assault. When he reached Busch's headquarters, Manstein was brought up to date on developments; having driven west, the Soviet forces were now pushing X Corps back into Staraya Russa and attempting to isolate it completely.

Halder was critical of this decision to redeploy Manstein's forces, judging Vatutin's attack as inconsequential and deploring the diversion of German forces away from the main axis of advance. Just a few days later, as the plight of X Corps worsened, he became less critical of this redeployment and recognised a little belatedly that his previous impatience had been incorrect – if Vatutin and Kachanov had been permitted to continue their attack and had succeeded in driving back X Corps, a dangerous breach would have appeared in the German front line, potentially threatening the formations further north. It was an inevitable consequence of overstretch – there were no reserves available to react to this crisis, and therefore a delay in the planned strike towards Leningrad was unavoidable.

Much as *Stavka* had anticipated, Manstein was ordered to deploy his corps to counterattack into the exposed flank of Vatutin's drive. After two days of preparation, the two German divisions began their thrust. Rapidly gaining pace, the German units proved to be too nimble for their opponents and in a week drove the Soviet forces back to their start line along the Lovat River to the east of Staraya Russa. Losses amongst the Red Army units were heavy, with Thirty-Fourth Army losing over half its personnel and equipment.

But whilst Vatutin's operation failed the result was the diversion of LVI Motorised Corps from the Leningrad axis to the south, forcing a further delay in the planned advance towards Leningrad. Not for the last time, Vatutin was censured for his headlong advance and the manner in which he lost control of his formations, though to a large extent this was due to factors beyond his control, e.g. the poor standard of radio equipment and communication, and the poor roads in the region. Others too were punished, in many cases more severely. Kachanov was arrested shortly after and charged with deliberately sabotaging the operation. He was condemned to death and executed on 29 September.

Elsewhere, the workers' militia divisions that had been deployed to defend the Luga Line were learning how to be soldiers. Having dug in and constructed trenches, the men of 2nd Division moved their modest number of mortars and guns forward so that they could bombard the German-held village of Ivanovskoye. The following day German reconnaissance aircraft appeared, seeking out the positions of the mortars, and were followed by bombers. After the bombers departed the Germans struck with several brief but powerful artillery bombardments, but the Soviet gunners had dispersed their weapons carefully to minimise losses. The militia were then ordered to try to capture Germans for interrogation – such prisoners were widely known as 'tongues'. Bardin, who had left his factory in Leningrad with such patriotic fervour a few weeks before, crept forward with his friend Apollon Mikhailovich Shubin. They ambushed a solitary car but were unable to capture a prisoner; the three occupants of the car were killed when it crashed. Meanwhile, the Germans dropped leaflets on the Soviet positions, urging the militiamen to desert. Some of the leaflets were signed by Yakov Dzhugashvili, Stalin's illegitimate son. The militiamen assumed that the signature was a forgery, refusing to believe that the Soviet leader's son could have been taken prisoner, but he had in fact been captured on 16 July in fighting near Smolensk. A small number of militiamen slipped away from time to time, either deserting or trying to return to their homes, but the majority remained steadfast. Most shared the views of Bardin, which he expressed strongly in a discussion with his comrades:

> 'We? We are Leningraders!' And Leningraders – how could I say this? 'People of a special temperament, of a special mood, Soviet power was born in our city,' I thought aloud. 'The Socialist Revolution began its march from here. Is it possible to surrender such a city? No. This won't happen. We will not surrender Leningrad!' ...

In those days, like many Soviet people, I was convinced that our army was about to go on the offensive and crush the Fascist hordes. There must be reserves somewhere! After all, our country surpassed Germany both in territory and population. I was also sure that reinforcements would soon arrive from Leningrad. Although we, the militia, were playing a large role in the defence of Leningrad, we were nonetheless an auxiliary force. The militia divisions would do their job and gain time. But in order to defeat the Nazis, well-trained and well-armed troops were needed. And they would finish what we started.[7]

It is tempting to dismiss this as a piece of writing that is inspired more by official Soviet ideology than actual reality, but it is consistent with many other accounts, such as those from veterans recalling those days decades later. They were proud citizens of a singular city and recognised both its unique character and as a result their own status, and were determined to protect their homes and their heritage.

Another volunteer in 2nd Militia Division, Grigory Konstantinovich Kudryavtsev, described how he and his comrades were thrown into action with almost no training:

During the evening we reached Sredne Selo [just to the east of Kingisepp] and formed a line. We lay on the ground all night and then came a command: 'Forward!' We walked across a field where we came across corpses of our soldiers. It was a hot day and the dead were swollen, flies swarming over them. When they ordered us to attack, some shouted 'Urrah! Forward, for the Motherland, for Stalin!' We were like children. We ran forward in short bursts. We didn't see anyone but started to shoot, shouting 'Urrah!' It seems to me that our officers didn't know how to fight and we generally had almost no training. I saw shots fired at me but didn't understand what was happening. The ground in front of me rose a little. I fell and rolled over ... I ended up on the road. From beyond the road, a German with a submachine-gun fired a burst, wounding one of our soldiers. Others bandaged him. Then a motorcyclist drove along the road. I set up the machine-gun and fired a burst. I don't know if I hit anything or not, but the motorcyclist disappeared. I ran out of ammunition, I had nothing to fight with. I saw the company commander and ran over. He said, 'Go over there, into the forest.' A lot of us gathered there. It turned out that without seeing the enemy, they had fired off all their ammunition and now had nothing left. If the Germans had attacked at that moment, they could have caught us with their bare hands.[8]

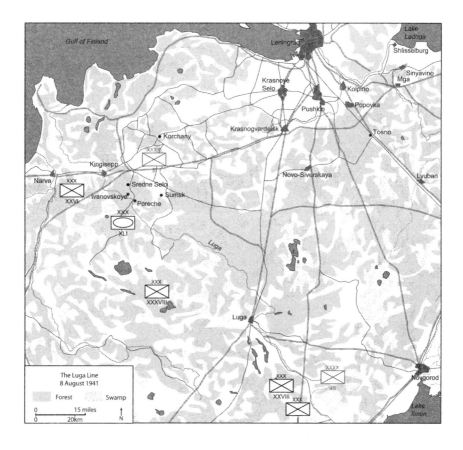

While Manstein was defeating Vatutin's counterattack, Reinhardt's XLI Motorised Corps attempted to advance from the small bridgeheads it had secured over the Luga. On 8 August, 1st and 6th Panzer Divisions commenced their attack in heavy rain and the weather remained bad for three days – this had an adverse effect both on the mobility of ground forces and on the ability of the Luftwaffe to provide support, either by reconnaissance or by dive-bombing. Although a battlegroup from 1st Panzer Division made some progress, the attacks on either flank – by 6th Panzer Division and 36th Motorised Division – foundered in the face of determined resistance and difficult terrain. Reinhardt ordered the isolated battlegroup to return to its start line. Having suffered substantial casualties in achieving this modest advance, Oberstleutnant Wend von Wietersheim, commander of the battlegroup, was reluctant to pull back and after lengthy exchanges with higher commands was given permission to remain in position.

After a day of defensive fighting, 1st Panzer Division attempted to resume its advance on 10 August, seeking to cut the railway line running from Leningrad through Krasnogvardeisk to Kingisepp and Narva. The leading elements reached the small village of Sumsk, nine miles to the east of the Luga River. In heavy fighting, 1st Panzer Division ground forward perhaps another five or six miles, but the combination of unsuitable terrain, escalating losses, supply difficulties, the weather, and fierce resistance prevented a decisive breakthrough. To add to its difficulties, Soviet aircraft repeatedly attacked the division's artillery regiment and inflicted significant casualties. This was not a sign of resurgence in Soviet aerial capability; rather, it demonstrated that just like the ground forces, the Luftwaffe was severely overstretched and couldn't maintain a presence on all parts of the huge front line in sufficient numbers to maintain air superiority.[9]

Bardin's militia company was in the path of the German attack and pulled back after the initial German bombardment:

> Lupenkov [the battalion commander] tried the telephone and angrily hung up immediately: there was no connection. 'Let's go, men,' he said, 'there's nothing we can do here. It's better to return to the regiment.'
>
> The rural forest road from Yurki to Ivanovskoye, along which we walked with the battalion commander, was crossed by the defence line of 8th Company. Halfway along the road we began to meet first one, then another orderly with wounded soldiers. 'What's going on?' Lupenkov stopped an elderly orderly who was helping a wounded man with a bandage around his head; he was leaning heavily on the orderly, and apparently his wound was severe. His bandage was soaked through with blood.
>
> 'Comrade Captain, the Germans broke into our trenches.'
>
> There was complete confusion in the company. Where was the commander? Nobody knew. He was later found dead. The soldiers dispersed in the remaining trenches and acted according to their instincts as best they could. The situation was critical – a little further and the Fascists would drive a wedge into the battalion and break through to Yurki. We could eliminate this threat only by concentrating our soldiers for an immediate counterattack. Lupenkov and I managed to do this. At the same time we sent a runner to 9th Company with an order to strike the Fascists in their flank. As soon as we launched a counterattack, the Nazis resumed shelling. Now they weren't firing at Yurki, but at the positions of 8th Company. Like a giant tractor, the enemy artillery 'walked' through the company positions. Deep craters, uprooted trees, crushed and shattered firing points, mutilated corpses – that was how the positions of 8th Company looked now.[10]

Bardin described how he and his comrades repulsed the German attacks, but the militia were soon driven from their positions with heavy losses. They slowly retreated to the village of Korchany, astride the road between Kingisepp and Leningrad. Here, they made contact with what remained of the rest of the division. Other soldiers also made their way back from the Luga positions but some remained in the area, disappearing into the forests. The map above shows the nature of the terrain: for much of its length, the Luga River runs through dense forest, and the lack of good roads meant that the Germans were forced to channel their forces either north of this area into Reinhardt's bridgehead, or to the south, closer to Luga. In these forests, the stragglers of the Red Army mounted an increasingly effective partisan campaign against the Germans. As early as 10 August, the daily summary of reports from the *Einsatzgruppen* described some of the difficulties faced by the Germans:

> It is completely impossible to comb through the forests with the troops available. Effective countermeasures can only be taken by extensive intelligence work and sharp terror tactics against the population of the countryside in which the partisans operate, so that as a consequence of this terror the population will denounce the partisans.
>
> For Army Group North, the war against the partisans as well as overall tactical command is particularly difficult because of the pronounced double nature of the front line to the north in Estonia and east of Lake Peipus ... The deployment of the Security Police is very difficult due to being dispersed on a front from Pernau [on the Baltic coast just north of the Latvian–Estonian frontier] to Sebezh [just within the old frontier of Russia, to the east of southern Latvia].[11]

With 8th Panzer Division now deployed in support of its southern flank, Reinhardt's corps struggled onwards, reaching and crossing the railway line that had been its objective in earlier attacks. Despite the hard fighting and steadily rising casualties, the mood amongst the German units remained good, as 6th Panzer Division's operations officer recorded in his diary on 13 August:

> The mood of the division is optimistic. The corps chief of staff sent his congratulations that the division was the first to have reached the Kingisepp– Leningrad railway line. The corps commander sent his appreciation to the division. Fresh orders from corps headquarters by radio at 2330: it brings the welcome news that a new advance is to commence the following day at 0900.

We thus have limited time to resupply the troops who in many cases haven't had warm food for several days, or any opportunity to wash, and still haven't received clean, dry clothing.[12]

The casualties and difficult conditions were acceptable if victory could be achieved; as 6th Panzer Division's orders announced the following morning, the leading elements were less than 60 miles from Leningrad. But although the orders declared that a definitive breakthrough of the Soviet defensive line had been achieved, the advance effectively came to a halt: 1st and 8th Panzer Divisions were ordered to turn southeast in order to cut the road running south to Luga, thus isolating Red Army units in that area. In the meantime, 6th Panzer Division had to take up a defensive posture. The drive to the east reached the communication links between Krasnogvardeisk and Luga on 20 August and the leading tanks of 1st Panzer Division shot up a train carrying supplies south to Luga; these tanks were now just seven miles from the southern outskirts of Krasnogvardeisk and 25 miles from the southern edge of Leningrad but until other German units were able to assemble alongside, Reinhardt's forces could achieve no more. Whilst the advance had moved the front line closer to Leningrad, the substantial Soviet forces to the north, around Narva, Kingisepp, and Krasnogvardeisk, remained intact.

A little to the west, elements of Sixteenth Army that had advanced along the eastern shores of Lake Peipus were attempting to push north to cut the Red Army's lines of retreat from Narva. Wilhelm Lubbeck was now a forward observer for his division's artillery regiment and by the time he and his comrades reached Narva, struggling forward in the face of stiff resistance, the bulk of Red Army units further west had already withdrawn. His division moved up to Kingisepp, where it became involved in bitter fighting:

When our regiment arrived we briefly experienced our first street fighting with Red Army units, though it took place among widely spread houses rather than inside a built-up area.

Because our regimental infantry needed direct fire support ... our company brought its 75mm howitzers to within a few hundred yards of the front, much closer than their normal position at least half a mile in the rear. Unlike the much heavier 150mm gun, the 75mm howitzer could be manoeuvred a short distance by its five-man gun crew, making it practical for use in urban combat conditions ...

Reaching our gun crew on the outskirts of Kingisepp, I watched as they systematically destroyed enemy strongpoints ahead of us.

Even with the risks to our guns in such circumstances, it was the infantry companies that always suffered the worst of the fighting, especially in house-to-house combat. With relatively limited opportunities for support from our heavy guns, they advanced through a chaos of numerous large and small engagements in which enemy attacks might come from any direction. By the time we finished eliminating the last pockets of Russian resistance on 20 August, we had claimed a town in which many homes were only flattened rubble.[13]

There were heavy rain showers throughout mid-August. The result was further delays to German preparations as the inadequate roads, already damaged first by retreating Red Army traffic and then further chewed up by the advancing Wehrmacht, turned into muddy rivers that were almost as difficult to traverse as the swamps and woodland to either side. Finally on 22 August, the long-anticipated attack of Third Panzer Group from the south began. General Adolf Kuntzen was commander of LVII Motorised Corps with two panzer divisions at his disposal and supported by XL Corps to the south and II Corps to the north, rapidly advanced to capture Velikiye Luki and Toropets, effectively closing the gap in the German line between Army Group North and Army Group South. As soon as the thrust had dislocated the Soviet defences, ultimately leading to the destruction of much of Twenty-Second Army, 19th Panzer Division was withdrawn from the attack and moved northwest to Kholm from where it attacked on 31 August towards the northeast in conjunction with II Corps. In just a week, the panzer division covered 60 miles and captured its objective. These two thrusts removed the threats to the flanks of II Corps and any lingering threat to X Corps at Staraya Russa, from where Manstein's LVI Motorised Corps moved east. Convergent attacks from the south resulted in much of the Soviet Twenty-Seventh, Eleventh, and Thirty-Fourth Armies being encircled and destroyed. But whilst the elimination of three Soviet field armies sounds impressive, it should be remembered that each army consisted of at most four divisions, which were at half their establishment strength at best. Nevertheless, the destruction of these three armies added to the growing toll on the Red Army. In a further blow, the German I Corps pushed forward north of Lake Ilmen and captured Novgorod and Chudovo, cutting the direct road and rail link between Moscow and Leningrad.

The distance from Chudovo to Leningrad is no more than 67 miles, and the men of 12th Panzer Division were anxious to press on as fast as they could. The 'highway' that they had cut was far from what they might have expected, but it seemed as if the path to a quick, decisive victory lay before them. Alexander Stahlberg was an officer in the panzer division:

Now the road to the old capital of the Tsarist Empire lay before us, straight as a ruler. 'Wide as the Champs-Elysées,' commented Engelhardt [the division's orderly officer]. Down the middle of a far too wide break in the old forests ran a lonely causeway, gravelled, yes, but scarred with potholes.

Slowly we advanced, far too slowly it seemed to us, with our marching infantry setting the pace. What could have got into our military leadership? It seemed to us that if only we were allowed, we could be in Leningrad in two or three days. After all, we had the experience. The whole question of momentum of a well-run panzer offensive seemed suddenly to have been forgotten.[14]

Meanwhile, Hitler's thinking had evolved further. On the eve of the attack by LVII Motorised Corps, he issued a new directive. He reiterated his view that an attack on Moscow had to wait until matters had been resolved in the south and north, but the emphasis now changed – the directive referred to 'the encirclement of Leningrad and junction with the Finns' rather than the physical capture of the city or its immediate destruction by aerial bombing.[15] In a letter to his wife, General Eduard Wagner, the quartermaster general of the Wehrmacht, explained the situation. The city was to be isolated from the outside world:

First we will have to let them stew in Petersburg, what can we do with a city of 3.5 million who will just be a drain on our food resources? There is no room for sentimentality.[16]

Küchler, whose Eighteenth Army was to be responsible for the city once it was under German control, issued advance instructions that all the Jews in the city were to be registered and made available to Stahlecker's units; he explicitly stated that there was no need for any food to be supplied to the civilian population. It was the intention of the Germans to starve the Leningraders to death. This was of course entirely in keeping with the plans drawn up prior to the invasion of the Soviet Union. Herbert Backe, minister of food and agriculture in Germany, was a committed Nazi and held extensive talks with other senior officials prior to the invasion. In May 1941, recognising the difficulties of transporting sufficient food into the Soviet Union to feed the Wehrmacht, he and others concluded:

The war can only be continued if the entire Wehrmacht is fed from Russia in the third year of the war [counting from September 1939].

If we take what we need out of the country, there can be no doubt that tens of millions of people will die of starvation.[17]

Three weeks later, a report from another worker elaborated on this:

> Many tens of millions of people in this country will become superfluous and will die or must emigrate to Siberia. Attempts to rescue the population there from death through starvation by obtaining surpluses from the black earth zone [i.e. Ukraine] prevent the possibility of Germany holding out until the end of the war.[18]

The overarching plan to divert food from feeding people in the Soviet Union to satisfying German requirements became known as the Hunger Plan. Implementation began almost as soon as the Wehrmacht crossed the frontier. Daily rations for Jews in ghettoes usually amounted to no more than 420 calories per day, perhaps slightly more for those deemed to be in gainful employment, and food for Soviet prisoners of war was also strictly limited. It is estimated that by February 1942, about 2 million captured Red Army soldiers had starved to death in German compounds.[19]

In addition to the gap between Army Group North and Army Group Centre that was closed by Third Panzer Group, a similar gap existed between Army Group Centre and Army Group South, particularly as the latter's advance into Ukraine had deviated somewhat to the south. As a consequence, a large concentration of Red Army units under the command of Stalin's old comrade Budennyi was centred on Kiev, potentially able to threaten the flanks of both German army groups. Halder and others continued to demand a continuation of the advance towards Moscow in the central sector but just like Hitler, Halder was falling victim to operational greed. The positions of Army Group Centre and Army Group South meant that a swift convergent attack by the two groups might result in the destruction of the last major concentration of Red Army units. Thereafter, an advance to Moscow would surely be a formality. Many of the commanders on the battlefield believed – like Generaloberst Heinz Guderian, commander of Second Panzer Group – that the thrust towards Moscow should be given priority, while others wanted to strike against Budennyi's armies around Kiev. Halder wrote in his diary:

> I regard the situation created by the Führer's interference unendurable for *OKH*. No other than the Führer himself is to blame for the zigzag course caused by his successive orders …
>
> The afternoon discussions are interrupted by telephone talks with Generalfeldmarschall von Bock [commander of Army Group Centre] who again emphasises that he can maintain his front against Moscow in the long run only by remaining on the offensive.[20]

This was disingenuous at best. Hitler had persistently insisted on dealing with objectives to the north and south with Moscow, a secondary objective, having to wait until the flanking operations were completed – it was Halder, Bock, Guderian, and others who were constantly pressing for a change in priority so that they could push on to Moscow. Manstein described the contradictory rumours and orders circulating at the time but also noted a slow change in mood, despite the recent successes of his corps:

> We still failed to find any real satisfaction in these achievements however, for no one was clear any longer what the actual aim of our war strategy was or what higher purpose all these battles were supposed to serve. Whatever else might happen, the period of sensational advances of the kind we had made on Daugavpils was at an end.[21]

It was the end of Manstein's involvement in Army Group North. He was transferred to the far south of the Eastern Front to take command of Eleventh Army. His corps, too, was no longer involved in the drive on Leningrad. It was to be transferred to Third Panzer Group in preparation for operations towards Moscow.

On the other side of the front line, Voroshilov was attempting to reorganise his forces. As a result of the heavy fighting of August, his armies were badly depleted – for example, the remnants of Forty-Eighth Army, covering the southern approaches of Leningrad, had barely 6,200 men left.[22] Northern Front, which had been responsible for the defence of the long frontier with Finland, was now divided in two. Leningrad Front was formed to take control of the city's defences, while the far north came under Karelian Front. Voroshilov's Northwest Direction was abolished by *Stavka* on 27 August, with Karelian, Leningrad, and Northwest Fronts now directly subordinated to *Stavka*. It was recognition that Voroshilov's tenure had been largely ineffectual, though Stalin spared his old comrade from complete disgrace by appointing him commander of Leningrad Front.

If Leningrad was to be saved, further reinforcements were needed for the defenders. Accordingly, *Stavka* dispatched the new Fifty-Fourth and Fifty-Second Armies to prevent the Germans from advancing across the Volkhov River towards Tikhvin. They were later joined by Fourth Army; the original Fourth Army had been destroyed in the central sector in July, and the new army was created using reserve divisions. Even with these reinforcements, the defences were in poor shape. To the west of Leningrad, Eighth Army had been driven out of Estonia and abandoned Narva on 25 August. The Luga Operational Group had been driven back to Krasnogvardeisk; the remnants of XLI Rifle Corps were a little to the south, pinned down by German forces. To the east of these units was the remnant of Forty-Eighth Army, trying to cover a front line of 25 miles with its 6,200 men. The new forces were further to the east; whilst the German expectations of destroying the Red Army before they could retreat from the frontier zone had not been entirely successful, the Soviet forces were badly degraded and seemed close to the end of their strength. Surely one more effort would see the Wehrmacht reach its northern objective, allowing substantial forces to be released for a crowning triumph at Moscow.

The threadbare defensive line collapsed at the first blow on 25 August, when XXXIX Motorised Corps – transferred from Third Panzer Group – broke through Forty-Eighth Army's lines with help from XXVIII Corps on its left flank and captured the town of Lyuban on the Leningrad–Moscow highway, 45 miles from the southern edge of Leningrad. Without pausing, the German divisions pushed onwards towards Kirishi and Volkhov to the northeast and north along the highway towards Leningrad. Desperately, Popov – serving as chief of staff to Voroshilov – sent the only forces available, a rifle division from north of Lake Ladoga and another militia division raised from the city's workers – to plug the gap that had been torn open, but just four days later the German 20th Motorised Division reached and captured Tosno, nearly midway between Lyuban and Leningrad. The town of Mga became a keenly contested spot; the Germans took it on 26 August but Voroshilov ordered an immediate counterattack, which succeeded in expelling the Germans a day later. On the last day of August, the German 20th Motorised Division recaptured Mga and drove off the Soviet forces. Supported by elements of 12th Panzer Division, 20th Motorised Division pushed on northwards and reached the shore of Lake Ladoga on 7 September, capturing Sinyavino and Shlisselburg. It was a significant moment: all land connections between Leningrad and the rest of the Soviet Union were cut. The only contact was over the waters of Lake Ladoga.

Stahlberg and the units of 12th Panzer Division that had not been sent towards Shlisselburg were close to the southern outskirts of Leningrad. Together with his regiment commander, Stahlberg went forward to study the city they had approached over the preceding days:

> Reaching a height from which we could overlook large parts of Leningrad, we found one of our artillery observation posts, where they let us use the binocular periscope. We saw a factory with a smoking chimney. We saw people in the

streets. And then we saw another factory, whose gates suddenly opened and out rolled a tank, straight off the production line. Obviously they had not yet given a thought to camouflage over there.[23]

When the German drive to Shlisselburg began, Red Army units were still holding Luga, far to the south. The Wehrmacht commenced attacks on the town on 24 August with the relatively fresh *SS-Polizei* Division making the main assault. To the north of the town, 8th Panzer Division moved forward from the west to cut the Soviet line of retreat. Still recovering from the mauling inflicted in earlier fighting, the panzer division struggled to make any progress in difficult terrain and took up a defensive posture late on 25 August, beating off repeated Soviet attempts to break out towards the north. As August drew to a close, the Germans completed a tenuous encirclement of the Soviet forces pulling back from Luga, but their line was porous and although large numbers of Red Army soldiers were killed or captured, others slipped through to the north in confused fighting that continued for several days. Many stragglers remained in the forests and late on 4 September, 8th Panzer Division was ordered to make anti-partisan sweeps through the woodland in an attempt to clear the area.[24]

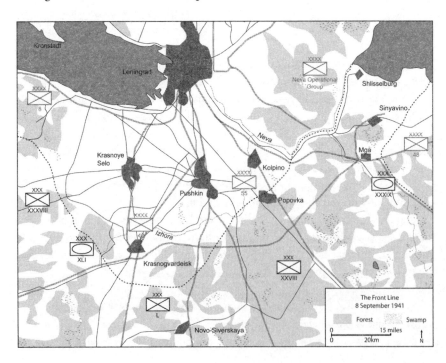

On the left flank of the thrust that reached Lake Ladoga, the German XXVII Corps drove back the Soviet Fifty-Fifth Army towards Krasnogvardeisk. As the Red Army pulled back, the German advance slowed and on 9 September was brought to a halt along the Izhora River, between Krasnogvardeisk and the Leningrad–Moscow highway, just 13 miles from the southern edge of Leningrad. In order to complete the isolation of Leningrad, Leeb ordered his forces to complete their seizure of the southern shore of Lake Ladoga. In particular, if Volkhov could be captured, it would be almost impossible for the Soviet Union to maintain any meaningful link to Leningrad even across the waters of the lake. But the resources with which he was to achieve this were rapidly diminishing. Concluding that Leningrad had been successfully isolated, Hitler ordered substantial forces – almost all of the remaining panzer units and a large part of the Luftwaffe support – to be transferred from Army Group North to Army Group Centre. It was time for the Wehrmacht to concentrate on the final task of capturing Moscow. After what had seemed like interminable arguments – at one stage Halder threatened to resign in protest unless priority was given to advancing on Moscow – Guderian's Second Panzer Group finally turned south on 23 August to strike into the rear of the Soviet force around Kiev. The result would be a huge encirclement in which the Red Army lost over 700,000 men, but the delays and losses suffered by the Germans would ultimately undermine their attack towards Moscow in the late autumn and winter. Aware that he was about to lose his main strike force, Leeb issued fresh orders. XXXIX Motorised Corps was to continue operations around Lake Ladoga and XLI Motorised Corps was to push forward from the southwest before its transfer to the south. At the same time, Eighteenth Army was to drive in from the south. Two shock groups were formed – one was to concentrate on taking Krasnogvardeisk, with XXXVIII and I Corps supporting XLI Motorised Corps, and the other was to widen the narrow corridor running to Lake Ladoga. The intention was to make the siege perimeter as tight and as solid as possible before the departure of forces to the coming battle to capture Moscow.

On 18 August, Joseph Goebbels, Hitler's propaganda minister, had written in his diary that Hitler did not wish to waste time occupying Soviet cities:

> He wants to avoid casualties among our soldiers. Therefore he no longer intends to take Petersburg by force of arms, but rather starve it into submission. Once it has been cut off, his plan is to bombard the city's means of supporting its population, using the Luftwaffe and artillery. Not much will be left of this place. No doubt there will be a degree of chaos among its millions of inhabitants – but

the Bolsheviks would not have it otherwise. The first Luftwaffe attacks will hit Petersburg's water, power and gas stations.[25]

With German plans having changed from capturing Leningrad to isolating the city and starving the population, senior Wehrmacht officers met Professor Wilhelm Ziegelmeyer, the head of the Munich Institute of Nutrition, on 8 September. Ziegelmeyer was given documents providing details of the population of Leningrad, the estimated food stocks within the city, and normal winter temperatures in the area; he was asked to calculate how long the Wehrmacht would have to blockade Leningrad before a significant proportion of the population starved to death. The following day, Ziegelmeyer informed the officers that rationing of food would have to be imposed rapidly and that provided the blockade was maintained through the winter, the majority of Leningraders would starve to death before the spring thaw. He added:

> It is not worth risking the lives of our troops. The Leningraders will die anyway. It is essential not to let a single person through our front line. The more of them that stay there, the sooner they will die, and then we will enter the city without trouble, without losing a single German soldier.[26]

German artillery began to bombard Leningrad on 1 September, shortly before the meeting with Ziegelmeyer, and the first scattered shelling was replaced by more intense, better targeted fire over the following days. Luftwaffe attacks had taken place sporadically for several weeks, and on 8 September a major raid struck the Badayev warehouses in the eastern part of the city. These were a sprawling mass of wooden buildings built by the industrialist Sergei Ivanovich Rasteryayev adjacent to railway yards, and were named after Aleksei Yegorovich Badayev, who had been Deputy People's Commissar for the Food Industry until 1938. The warehouses were used as a central stockpile of food and it is estimated that about 3,000 tons of flour and 2,500 tons of sugar were stored there when German bombers appeared overhead in the evening. The air raid dropped explosives and incendiaries on the wooden buildings, which rapidly caught fire. The blaze continued for several days resulting in the destruction of much of the food stored there. There are differing accounts of just how much of Leningrad's food supply was lost in the raid; for example, one account suggests that the total city stockpiles were sufficient for about 35 days, and the warehouses contained only a little over 4 per cent of this total.[27] Other accounts portrayed the destruction of the warehouses as a major disaster. Nonetheless, the destruction of this food store – and the loss of similar quantities when bombers sank barges carrying food across Lake Ladoga a few days later – exacerbated the problems faced by the city authorities. Two days after the air raid, Goebbels noted in his diary: 'We shall not trouble ourselves with demanding Leningrad's surrender. It can be destroyed by an almost scientific method.'[28]

Generalmajor Walter Warlimont, deputy chief of the operations staff at *OKW*, prepared a lengthy memorandum on how the siege of Leningrad was to be conducted. He described the preferred solution:

> Seal off Leningrad hermetically, then weaken it by terror and growing starvation. In the spring, we shall occupy the town … remove the survivors into captivity in the interior of Russia, and level Leningrad to the ground with high explosives.[29]

After the city had ceased to exist, the region would he handed over to the Finns. Jodl, Warlimont's superior, approved of this plan, adding that the policy was morally justified as the enemy would probably have rigged booby traps in the city and a military occupation would expose German soldiers to the risk of contagious diseases. He briefly speculated on an alternative policy: it might be expedient to expel the population of Leningrad to the east, in the expectation that this would spread panic and dismay amongst the citizens of the Soviet Union. Throughout the higher echelons of the German military, there seemed to be agreement that Army Group North had largely achieved its objectives – on 5 September, Halder noted in his diary: 'Our object has been achieved. [The Leningrad sector] will now become a subsidiary theatre of operations … [All that remains is] investment from the east, junction with the Finns.'[30]

Once the ring was tightly established, the population could be starved to death. Warlimont's plan was to use electrified fences to confine the Leningraders to their city in an attempt to spare German soldiers the ordeal of having to fire on women and children attempting to flee. But before such plans could be implemented, there was still heavy fighting ahead. The assault from the west, immediately to the north of Krasnogvardeisk, was led by 36th Motorised Division and fell on a sector of the front manned by one of the militia divisions; the unequal struggle resulted in a swift breakthrough for the motorised division, which pushed on to the Duderhof Heights, roughly between the edge of Leningrad and Krasnogvardeisk. Heavy Soviet artillery fire supplemented by the guns of the Baltic Fleet – several ships had had their guns dismounted and transferred to concrete emplacement – finally brought the Germans to a standstill.

Nikolai Matveyevich Karpenko was a signaller in 2nd Militia Division. His duties working for his regiment commander kept him out of the front line, but he watched in horror as a man named Ivanov, who had formerly taught him chemistry in school, was decapitated by shrapnel in an air raid. He and a group of others were caught up in the dogged retreat and witnessed the first big raid that devastated the Badayev warehouses:

> We started 140km from St Petersburg, but 20 days later we were pressed against the Gulf of Finland near Oranienbaum … Before our eyes, on 8 September, there was the most terrible raid on St. Petersburg. And then we watched as the Germans bombed Kronstadt. There, before my eyes, our battleship *Marat* was hit.[31]

The warship *Marat* had been built before the First World War and named *Petropavlovsk*. Her crew originally supported the Bolsheviks in the October Revolution but then took part in the mutiny of 1921, after which the ship was renamed *Marat*. As German forces closed in on Leningrad, her weapons – four 12-inch guns and 16 4.7-inch guns – provided valuable fire support for Red Army troops. The attack described by Karpenko actually took place on 16 September and was carried out by Stuka dive-bombers. Hans-Ulrich Rudel, who would end the war as one of the most highly decorated Luftwaffe pilots, was part of the squadron tasked with the attack and flew through thick, low cloud to the objective. He spotted the Soviet warship through a small gap in the cloud and followed Steen, his squadron commander, into the attack:

> The bombs from Steen's aircraft are already on their way down … near miss. I press the bomb switch … dead on. My bomb hits the after deck. A pity it is only a 1,000 pounder! All the same I see flames break out. I cannot afford to hang around to watch it, for the flak barks furiously.[32]

A few days later, Rudel took part in a second attack on the battleship. On this occasion, the Stukas carried 2,000-pound bombs and, together with another pilot, Rudel scored a hit on the bows. The resulting explosion detonated the forward magazine, wrecking the forward turret and causing extensive damage. *Marat* settled in the shallow water of Kronstadt harbour and was later refloated; many of her guns were dismounted for use in Leningrad's defences, but the remaining weapons continued to fire on the German lines around the city. The damage inflicted by Rudel and his comrades was never repaired and the ship – renamed *Petropavlovsk* in May 1943 and *Volkhov* in 1950 – served as a stationary vessel until she was scrapped in 1953.[33]

Even as the Soviet defences creaked and threatened to give way, *Stavka* sent a special fact-finding mission to Leningrad to ascertain what was happening. The result of the visit was a sudden change in command arrangements: Voroshilov was dismissed from his post. He had repeatedly shown that his military skills were distinctly limited and his prominence within the Soviet system was based almost entirely on his Civil War record and his personal relationship with Stalin; in his memoirs, Nikita Khrushchev, the post-war leader of the Soviet Union, was repeatedly disparaging in his recollections and made it clear that he thought Voroshilov had no real capability and was merely interested in appearances:

> When I worked in Kiev in 1928, huge military manoeuvres were held there. These were on a grandiose scale – the movement of the troops, followed by receptions, discussions, and reports. Everything was directed by Voroshilov ...
>
> The military had a very low opinion of Voroshilov at that time. They formally accepted him, but everyone considered himself as smarter than him. In 1928, he was only interested in show: when he later discovered that I had worked in a district in Kiev, he told me how they threw flowers at him there. Whilst this may of course be of great importance for the country's defence capability, it is nonetheless not the main thing.[34]

Although his brutal loyalty to Stalin and a shared history that stretched back to the bloody days of the Civil War was sufficient to ensure his survival and rise through the Soviet system in peacetime, the exigencies of an existential war were very different. His vanity was a source of constant, if discreet, ridicule amongst other figures. In his defence, the resources with which he had attempted to defend Leningrad were inadequate, but his conduct did not inspire confidence. He failed to inform Stalin that the Germans had captured Shlisselburg – the Soviet leadership first learned of this disastrous setback from German announcements. If the cradle of the revolution was to be saved, changes were necessary. Other senior figures might have faced arrest and imprisonment or even execution after a brief trial, but Stalin didn't turn his back on his old comrade. He dispatched him to a largely nominal post as commander of the partisan movement where he could do little further harm. His replacement was Zhukov, who now faced his sternest challenge.

On the southern flank of the German thrust from the southwest was 6th Panzer Division, which had just received a welcome draft of replacement personnel. Together with 36th Motorised Division, the panzer division attacked towards the north on 11 September, defeating a Soviet counterattack headed in the opposite direction. Fighting was escalating in intensity with both sides realising that a decisive moment was at hand, but neither could scrape together more than a few modest formations to reinforce the fighting. Reinhardt had intended to commit 6th Panzer Division alongside 1st Panzer Division but was unable to extract it from fighting on the edge of Krasnogvardeisk; the Red Army succeeded in holding this town until 13 September, disrupting German plans and preventing the concentration of forces as originally planned.

Yury Konstantinovich Smirnov was 18 when the war began, and worked in a factory in Leningrad that produced mine detectors. Like tens of thousands of others, he volunteered to join the militia in the opening days of the war; he and the other volunteers from his workshop ended up in the same platoon. They spent the next few weeks in Krasnoye Selo where they underwent rudimentary training, and in mid-August they moved to occupy a defensive line about seven miles to the west of Krasnogvardeisk. Three days later, they were pulled back and put in position on the Izhora River immediately to the northwest of Krasnogvardeisk. As they marched to their new positions, the militiamen had their first experience of war:

> We were walking along the highway towards Krasnogvardeisk. Right on the Izhora River, just to the right if I recall, planes appeared. There was nowhere to hide and we scattered in all directions along the road. The planes flew past on the right so I ran to the left to hide behind the road embankment, so that if bombs fell to the right of the road or even on the road, I would not be hurt. It was scary, very scary. The earth shook like a sprung mattress, up and down. That first bombing was terrible.[35]

The militia were then caught up in the fighting around the town as German forces closed in:

> On 8 September, a massive German assault began. First, a Focke-Wulf 189 spotter plane flew over, circled our positions, probably spotted everything, transmitted a report, and flew away. About 100 German planes then flew up and began to bombard us. In addition, lots of tanks appeared, trying to capture Novaya Pudost in order to break through to the Krasnogvardeisk–Taytsy road. On the first day, they failed to achieve anything, nor on the second day. But on 11 September they struck us very hard. In Novaya Pudost, almost half of the battalion was killed ...

On 11 September I was wounded. Our machine-gun was in a trench facing the direction from which the Germans were expected to advance. My number two was Kolya Kiselev. The day before, Nikolai Petrovich Egorov, ... then a private, brought us Molotov cocktails and matches. We had plenty of ammunition. We were protecting a highway along which troops retreating from the Germans would pass ...

Not far from us, our gunners knocked out a tank and the Germans began to crawl out of it through the upper hatch. I started shooting and wounded or killed one. I had struck a blow but half an hour later I too was hit. A tank shell exploded on the left, not far from me, and I was wounded in both legs and both arms. I could see the shrapnel sticking out of my boots and the orderly put a bandage right over them. Kolya Kiselev stayed with the machine-gun and he remained alive through the battle. After demobilisation I tried to find him. I found his mother, who told me that Kolya died on the Nevsky Pyatachok [Neva bridgehead].

Only remnants of the battalion were left. Our clerk and someone else, after leaving the encirclement, hid the battalion's banner in the forest near the Thais River. It still lies there somewhere. The battalion was then disbanded and the remaining soldiers were sent to an assembly point, from where they all went to the Neva Operational Group, to the Nevsky Pyatachok.

When the fighting subsided a little, we who were still alive and could be reached were gathered together. With three other wounded, I was sent in a cart to a medical battalion in the village of Romanovka. When we arrived there, we asked a senior lieutenant where our battalion was. He said, 'Guys, the battalion is gone.'[36]

Even if a few broken Red Army units were still fighting near Krasnogvardeisk, the battle was becoming increasingly irrelevant due to the advance of 36th Motorised Division. After its thrust directly towards Leningrad it now turned north, backed by 1st Panzer Division. A mixture of militia and a naval infantry brigade was brushed aside and as his tanks reached a low crest, the commander of one of 1st Panzer Division's panzer companies excitedly reported by radio: 'I can see Leningrad and the sea!'[37] It was almost the last act of the panzer division before it was transferred out of Army Group North; bitter fighting raged around the tip of the German salient as the Soviet Forty-Second Army, reinforced by a rifle division from Zhukov's minimal reserves, was thrown into counterattacks. On 15 September the Germans pushed north again, moving within about a mile of the coast. The Wehrmacht was close to the Pulkovo Heights, where White Russian forces had stood a little more than two decades earlier.

When he reached the city, Zhukov went directly to the Smolny Institute from where Lenin and Trotsky had directed the October Revolution. He brought with him two officers who had served with him in the successful fighting against the Japanese at Khalkin Gol in 1939, Major Generals Ivan Ivanovich Fedyuninsky and Mikhail Semenovich Khozin. Fearing the city's imminent fall, Voroshilov had ordered the destruction of military installations in Leningrad; Zhukov cancelled these orders and on his instructions the Leningrad Front Military Council sent an uncompromising instruction to Forty-Second and Fifty-Fifth Armies. There would be no further withdrawals, and anyone who disobeyed faced the severest sanction:

> All commanders, political workers and soldiers who abandon the indicated line without a written order from the Front or Army Military Council will be shot immediately.[38]

Fedyuninsky left a poetic description of the impression Leningrad made on him when he arrived with Zhukov:

> Leningrad was beautiful in that first autumn of the war. September was sunny and unusually warm. The usually short summer didn't want to leave here, to be replaced by an uncongenial, gloomy, and foggy autumn.
>
> The breath of war had already left its mark on the city. The usually busy streets and squares were comparatively sparsely populated. The gilded dome of St Isaac's Cathedral was covered with grey protective paint. In the gardens and squares, strewn with crimson leaves, one could see recently dug trenches and the positions of anti-aircraft gunners. There, in anticipation of the nightly service, silver barrage balloons, resembling large, clumsy fish, took refuge. All of this gave the city a special, hard beauty. Leningrad, like a mighty hero with its head proudly raised, was preparing for a fierce battle with the enemy.
>
> It was impossible not to admire this amazing city with its wide, clean, arrow-straight streets, its numerous palaces, light and airy, as if gazing thoughtfully into the calm waters of the Neva. The bright northern sky was reflected in windows, which were criss-crossed with paper tape.[39]

He was now ordered to the headquarters of Forty-Second Army to oversee the continuing defensive effort. He was dismayed by what he found at his destination:

> The headquarters of Forty-Second Army was located in reinforced concrete bunkers in the Pulkovo fortified line. From here it was so close to the front line

that when I walked along the trenches to the commander's dugout, I heard the familiar angry whistling of bullets overhead …

I knew Lieutenant General [Fedor Sergeyevich] Ivanov as a man distinguished by an enviable cheerfulness, very energetic and commanding, with a strong will. But now he sat in front of me, tired, unshaven and haggard, his spirits low. Ivanov expressed no surprise when he saw me, as if we had last met just a few days ago. He only asked, albeit disinterestedly, 'Why are you here? I heard you were given a corps in Southwest Front?'

I replied that I had come as deputy Front commander to get acquainted with the situation and asked Ivanov to show me on a map where the army's troops were located. 'I don't know,' Ivanov said irritably, 'I don't know anything.'

'Are you in contact with your units?'

'There is no contact. The fighting today was heavy. I had to pull back. Communications have been broken.' Ivanov didn't even try to justify himself.

I had to call the chief of staff, Major General [Georgy Andreyevich] Larionov, and the head of the operations department in order to get a general description of the situation. The more they told me, the better I understood that the defence of Forty-Second Army's zone was holding literally by a miracle. Fierce battles during the day were fought along the entire front line from Uritsk to the outskirts of Pulkovo. The enemy occupied Panovo and infiltrated in small groups into Uritsk. It was fortunate that he too was exhausted and stopped at nightfall. But his onslaught could resume at any moment and then – then it would become immediately clear that here, the gates of Leningrad were not firmly closed.

What was to be done? Mentally, I outlined some priority measures but I was then urgently summoned back to Smolny. I left the dugout accompanied by Ivanov.

On the front line, right in front of the army command post, machine-gun fire intensified. Every now and then, flares soared into the dark sky, froze for a moment, and then rapidly descended, scattering sparks. 'Perhaps we should move the command post again,' Ivanov said, 'it's painfully close to the front line here.'

'No, you can't move,' I objected. 'As deputy Front commander, I forbid moving the command post.'

'Very well, we'll try to hold on,' agreed Ivanov with a sigh.[40]

When he reached the Smolny Institute, Fedyuninsky learned that despite this exchange with Ivanov, the commander of Forty-Second Army had in fact withdrawn his headquarters. Zhukov ordered his immediate dismissal and that of his chief of staff, Larionov. Fedyuninsky was to return to the front line and take Ivanov's place. At first, it seemed that, somewhat improbably, Ivanov would survive his failure to hold back the Germans and particularly his withdrawal of his army headquarters despite clear orders to the contrary. After a few days kicking his heels in the Smolny Institute, he was appointed commander of the Leningrad Garrison and the city's internal defences, a post of little significance given that every available man had been sent to the front-line armies. But in February 1942, he was arrested and held on charges of dereliction of duty. He was released without further prosecution in 1946. Larionov was reported missing in action the day after he was dismissed. His body was never recovered.

There was a very real danger of the Soviet troops defending the approaches to Leningrad being split in two – if the Germans could complete their advance to the Baltic coast, Major General Vladimir Ivanovich Shcherbakov's Eighth Army would be left pinned to the coast to the west of Leningrad while the remnants of Forty-Second Army were driven into the southern outskirts. This development had to be prevented and Zhukov also believed that the Germans had exposed their spearhead to a counterattack by pressing forward with such a narrow thrust. He therefore ordered an immediate counterattack. Shcherbakov was given permission to withdraw a short distance on the western side of his positions in order to release sufficient troops for an attack against the German advance by 36th Motorised Division and 1st Panzer Division. Shcherbakov protested that his divisions were too badly weakened to carry out such an attack; Zhukov promptly dismissed him and ordered Lieutenant General Trifon Ivanovich Shevaldin to replace him. But a change in command made no difference to the depleted ranks of the divisions in the front line, and Shevaldin too could see that there was no prospect of success. In any event, the Germans beat the Red Army to the punch and attacked again even while Eighth Army was attempting to regroup. In heavy, costly fighting, the Germans drove Fedyuninsky's army back to the very edge of Leningrad; Fedyuninsky had barely enough time to organise new lines of defence before they were contested. A little to the west, 1st Panzer Division and 58th Infantry Division struck Shevaldin's Eighth Army on 16 September before it could organise itself for its counterattack and captured Petergof and Uritsk, reaching the Baltic. Here, the full weight of the Baltic Fleet's artillery made itself felt and the German advance was halted. As Zhukov had feared, the Soviet Eighth Army was left in a long, shallow stretch of the Baltic coast in what became known as the Oranienbaum pocket. At the end of September, the exhausted German troops came to a halt.

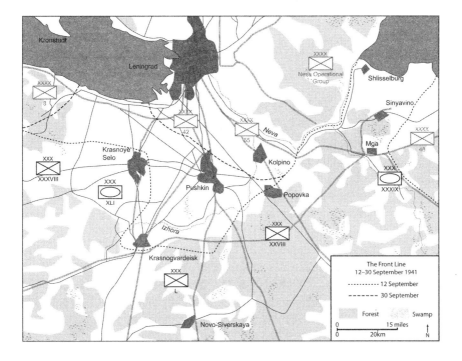

Bardin, who had been promoted to the post of political commissar for his regiment, witnessed the German attacks on the old imperial Petergof Palace:

> In order to avoid heavy losses and encirclement, Major Arsenov, the regiment commander, gave orders for us to withdraw under cover of night to Stariy Petergof, take up defensive positions on its outskirts and at the same time prepare for street-fighting. But we didn't get to stay in Stariy Petergof.
>
> Following this order, our regiment broke into small groups and began to move to the sea through the Petergof park, which was still tidy and well-trimmed, and then enemy bombers appeared. As methodically as ever, they dropped large, whistling bombs, one after the other. The attempts of our anti-aircraft gunners to repel the Fascist raiders were in vain. Bombs detonated throughout the parkland. Statues fell, and pavilions collapsed. Water fountained up from the Sea Canal. One of the bombs hit a corner of the palace and a fire broke out. We were powerless to stop this truly barbaric raid. To disperse and drive away the raiders, we needed fighter planes and anti-aircraft artillery.[41]

Unable to reach the rest of the division, Bardin and the remnants of his regiment held a position with their backs to the sea until they were evacuated by small boats.

The failed Soviet counterattack to prevent the isolation of Eighth Army was not the only offensive that Zhukov ordered; another battle had commenced a week earlier, to the southeast of Leningrad, as is described below. The Germans too had sufficient strength – and time before the onset of winter – to launch one more major attack and were making a determined attempt to secure the southern shore of Lake Ladoga. But everywhere around the siege perimeter itself, the Germans were making what would prove to be their last advances. Krasnogvardeisk was finally cleared of Red Army troops; stragglers continued to slip through the German lines for several weeks. After many delays, Hoepner's Fourth Panzer Group began to entrain for its move to what was expected to be the final battle of the conflict – Operation *Taifun* ('Typhoon'), the assault on Moscow. The diarist of XLI Motorised Corps was justifiably proud of what had been accomplished, but in his entry of 17 September he couldn't hide his disappointment that, regardless of the wishes of higher authorities to avoid costly urban fighting, Leningrad had not been taken:

> For weeks, Petersburg has been our objective, to which all of our efforts and all the strength of our operations had been directed. Many times in our advance we were the battering ram of the army group and were able to open the way for others, and the crowning moment was the penetration of the strong fortifications of Petersburg and the storming of the commanding heights in front of this city. I know how difficult the road to this point has been. The graves along our axes of advance speak a serious language. With these sacrifices, enduring great hardships and efforts, every member of the corps did his best to achieve every success, carrying us to the gates of Petersburg ... When we turn back today, without having been able to follow through to the end with the storming of Petersburg, we wish to do so in the proud knowledge that, when the capture of the city is announced later, the work commenced by us will have come to an end and we have played an outstanding part in this victory.[42]

With the departure of Fourth Panzer Group, Leeb was left with very limited motorised assets: 18th and 20th Motorised Divisions and 8th and 12th Panzer Divisions. With these, he was expected to complete the creation of a tight siege perimeter so that Leningrad could be starved to death.

CHAPTER 6

SINYAVINO AND TIKHVIN

The Neva River flows from the southwest corner of Lake Ladoga, near Shlisselburg, almost due south for about ten miles before angling to the southwest for a further eight miles; thereafter, it turns northwest to Leningrad. Near the first of these two points at which its direction changes was the village of Nevskaya Dubrovka, on a road running close to the river from Leningrad to Shlisselburg. The two sides faced each other across the river; if the Germans were to move north to link up with the Finns to the east and northeast of Leningrad, they would have to force a crossing. Similarly, if the Red Army was to break the siege perimeter by linking up with Fifty-Fourth Army, it too faced the formidable task of crossing the river.

Just to the north of Nevskaya Dubrovka, the Soviet-held bank was defended by a regiment of militia from Leningrad. Discipline was often enforced with ruthless inflexibility. Dmitry Alekseyevich Shcheglov was a volunteer serving in its ranks, and he described one such episode:

Gaidukov, a soldier from 1st Company, was charged because when he was sent as a runner with a report to the division headquarters, he met an unknown person en route, agreed to go to a nearby empty hut, and got drunk there. In the morning when he awoke, he couldn't find the report that he had placed in his earflaps.

Before the trial, Gaidukov looked quiet and pitiful. He made no insolent answers to the commander and explained that it was all because he had been drunk. The most serious part of his offence was that the document, marked 'urgent', was apparently stolen from him by the stranger. Gaidukov answered all questions as if the matter didn't concern him. Perhaps he didn't know about the serious consequences of such a crime or had resigned himself to the inevitable, but most likely he didn't think that his own people would sentence him to the 'severest sanction' for such an offence …

'Are you aware that the Germans are on the other side [of the river]?'

'I heard they were.' Gaidukov raised his eyebrows slightly and shrugged. 'But I didn't know.' When the verdict was read, Gaidukov was motionless, gazing without expression at the judges' table. Only when asked by the judge if he had any last words did he look up and said earnestly, 'Don't tell my parents I've been shot. Tell them I fell in battle.' …

Gaidukov was shot in front of the platoon.[1]

The widespread application of severe punishment and the relative resignation with which it was accepted are recurring features of accounts of life in the Red Army. Prior to the Soviet era, the authority of the state and the aristocracy was almost unquestioned across most of the Russian Empire, and perhaps this was why the revolutions of 1905 and 1917 were so striking in their intensity and violence – this unrest was in stark contrast to what passed as 'normal' life, and the pent-up frustrations and injustices overflowed into severe disturbances. Born out of the Civil War, the Soviet state was an institution where harsh authoritarianism was widespread. At first, this was justified as a means of repressing any lingering pro-tsarist sentiment; by the time of the purges of the 1930s, this authoritarianism had acquired a life of its own and was further intensified by the ever-present fear of denunciation.

The German thrust to the southern shores of Lake Ladoga had created a long salient with its northern edge running along the left bank of the Neva. For much of its length, the salient was only nine miles wide. It looked like a tempting target. Accordingly, Zhukov issued instructions for the creation of the Neva Operational Group, which was to cross the Neva and attack towards the southeast. At the same time, Marshal Grigory Ivanovich Kulik's Fifty-Fourth Army – which was directly under the control of *Stavka* rather than being assigned to a Front – would strike the German salient from the southeast. On paper, it looked like a straightforward exercise but the plans ignored the reality on the ground. The terrain was difficult, with few roads that could be used for the assembly of the strike forces, and the Neva Operational Group would first have to secure a bridgehead over the Neva. Nor was it clear that either attacking group actually had the strength and resources for such an operation.

Zhukov chose the Nevskaya Dubrovka sector for his counterattack on the grounds that this was the narrowest part of the river, intending then to expand the bridgehead towards Lake Ladoga. This ignored the fact that the current would also be strongest here. Recognising that the resources available within the encirclement were limited and almost fully committed against the German units that had pushed towards the Pulkovo Heights – and unaware that the German offensive efforts were largely over – Zhukov requested that *Stavka* assign the main effort for what was to become the First Sinyavino Offensive to Fifty-Fourth Army. The best that he could do was to scrape together sufficient forces to cross the river in the hope that he would be able to expand his bridgehead, though creating the bridgehead and holding it until Kulik's army arrived was probably a more realistic expectation.

Like all senior figures in the Red Army, Kulik was a Civil War veteran; he first met Stalin in the Battle of Tsaritsyn towards the end of 1918 and held a number of posts in the years that followed, mainly as an artillery commander. He acted as a military adviser to Republican forces in the Spanish Civil War under the pseudonym of 'General Cooper' and was deputy chief of the general staff until the eve of the German invasion, but many in the Red Army had a low opinion of his abilities. Nikolai Nikolayevich Voronov, who held various senior posts during the war and previously had been a subordinate of Kulik in Spain, later wrote:

Kulik was a man of little organisation, who thought a lot about himself and considered all his actions to be infallible. It was often difficult to understand what he wanted or what he was trying to achieve. He considered that the best method of work was to keep his subordinates in fear. His favourite saying when setting tasks and orders was 'Prison or obey orders'. Every morning he usually summoned several subordinates, set their tasks very vaguely, threateningly asked 'Do you understand?' and ordered them to leave his office. Everyone who received assignments usually came to me and asked for clarification and instructions.[2]

Kulik oversaw the shelling of a Russian village close to the Finnish border in 1939, which was subsequently blamed on the Finns and used as the pretext for the Winter War; he was rewarded for this by promotion to marshal. In the autumn of 1941 he was given command of the new Fifty-Fourth Army, When the Germans captured Shlisselburg, he claimed that he had been misled by his subordinates:

They reassured me that everything was going well in this area and as the army was concentrating, I could not go to that location and trusted the headquarters of Forty-Eighth Army and its commander that they would not permit the enemy to advance towards Shlisselburg. I was fully occupied with organising the regrouping to capture Mga. During this period, I could have sent a single rifle division, which would have prevented the capture of Shlisselburg.[3]

During the preparations for the new counterattack, Zhukov complained regularly that Kulik was not keeping him informed of preparations. On 9 September, Kulik's army began its offensive with an attack on Sinyavino, a short distance to the east of Shlisselburg and near the point where the Neva flows out of Lake Ladoga. This was a considerable distance from where the Neva Operational Group was planning to create its bridgehead; the attack rapidly bogged down and a sharp German counterattack threatened to destroy the leading units of Fifty-Fourth Army. The Soviet forces regrouped and tried again, this time attacking towards Mga, with only modest success. A soldier in 286th Rifle Division, one of the new formations created from reservists since the beginning of the war, described the fighting:

> We were told to attack through a swamp with fixed bayonets. The water was above our knees and there were just a few stunted trees – there was no cover. The Germans were sitting on high ground and dropped mortar bombs on us and sprayed us with machine-guns as we advanced. We exchanged fire, but we had just our rifles, and they had light and heavy machine-guns. The wounded fell, they couldn't even scream, as they were immediately swallowed by the swamp mud. My comrade was beheaded by a shell. I turned and he was standing there, but without a head. His overcoat was caught on a felled birch trunk, holding him upright. They wrote that he was 'missing' in the records. All the swamps from Voybokalo to Sinyavino were lined with these 'missing' men. But I avenged him. The German machine-gunner ran out of ammunition. He stood, yelling to his assistant who was behind him, dragging up a metal box of machine-gun belts. So I first shot the ammunition carrier, then turned to the machine-gunner. He threw aside his machine-gun and rushed at me with a knife, but I got him with my bayonet.
>
> Of our company in that battle, seven survived.[4]

One of the units of Fifty-Fourth Army, 310th Rifle Division, lost 4,700 men for almost no gain.[5] In some areas, there was rather more by way of cover, but it tended to favour the defenders. An artillery officer in 3rd Guards Division remembered the difficulties faced by his men:

> The area nearest Sinyavino was rugged, wooded, ideal for covert movement and the deployment of the enemy's artillery and mortar batteries. It was particularly

troublesome for the infantry, because when enemy shells struck the branches of the trees they exploded and their shrapnel killed everything over a large area. Unsurprisingly, we therefore attached great importance to observing the enemy guns. Importantly, our scouts, gunners, and signallers gained experience of combat every day. For example, gun crews began to work calmly and efficiently, trying to save their strength. After all, maintenance of a heavy artillery system like a 152mm howitzer is not easy and requires remarkable efforts from all the crew. After the first ten to fifteen minutes of action, the loader and his assistants discarded their quilted jackets and unbuttoned their tunics ... They had to wipe each 40kg projectile with a rag, pass it by hand to the loader, up to 45 times over 15 minutes – so during that time they each moved up to 1.5 tons of material.[6]

In Leningrad, Zhukov was growing ever more impatient with Kulik. On 15 September, the two men spoke by telephone, and Zhukov urged Kulik to show greater energy:

Zhukov: Grigory Ivanovich, thank you for the information. I request urgently – do not wait for the enemy to attack, immediately organise artillery preparation and go on the offensive in the general direction of Mga.

Kulik: Of course. I think [I can do so] on 16 or 17 September.

Zhukov: 16–17 is too late! The enemy is regrouping and we must pre-empt him. I am sure that if you attack, you will enjoy great success. If you still can't advance tomorrow, I ask that you use all your aviation to attack the enemy ... on the Izhora River, 4–5km southeast of Slutsk ... I beg you to attack the enemy and insert your cavalry through the enemy lines as soon as possible. That's all I have to say.

Kulik: I can't go on the offensive tomorrow because the artillery hasn't been brought forward, fire plans haven't been worked out, and not all the units have reached their starting positions. I have just been informed that the enemy went on the offensive in the area around Shlisselburg–Sinyavino. The attack was repulsed ...

Marshal Kulik was wrong: the actions of the enemy were nothing more than an attempt to reconnoitre our defences. Kulik clearly didn't imagine or did not want to understand the extremely serious situation near Leningrad.

No longer hiding my annoyance, I said, 'The enemy didn't go on the offensive, but just conducted reconnaissance in force! Some people, unfortunately, interpret every reconnaissance or minor action of the enemy as an offensive. It is clear that you care mainly about the well-being of Fifty-Fourth Army and apparently you aren't worried enough about the situation near Leningrad ... I realise that I can't count on an active manoeuvre on your part. I will solve the problem myself. I must say that I am struck by the lack of interaction between your unit and [Leningrad] Front.'[7]

Given that Kulik's forces had made no significant progress in their first attack, his protests about the artillery and other units not yet being in position to attack are incomprehensible. Whilst he may have been awaiting reinforcements to replace the losses his units had suffered, the artillery should at least have been deployed sufficiently far forward for a new assault.

The forces that Zhukov felt he could allocate to the Neva Operational Group were far too weak for the task ahead. A small reconnaissance group had crossed the Neva on 12 September and a week later, the main group – less than a division of NKVD border guards, a brigade of marines (in reality, largely composed of sailors withdrawn from their ships), and 115th Rifle Division – was ordered to establish a permanent bridgehead. An officer in the NKVD force described the attempt to cross the river:

> The preparations were terribly rushed. Our unit was force-marched nearly 60km to Nevskaya Dubrovka, where we halted to pick up supplies and equipment. Our orders were to cross the Neva – but to our astonishment we found that there were no boats! So we had to make rafts, each one taking a group of eight men and piled high with ammunition. It was dark, but as we approached the river German flare rockets suddenly lit up the sky and then their artillery opened up. It was absolute carnage. Because of the lack of supply boats, each raft was carrying double the regulation load of ammunition and mountains of grenades. As we approached the far back the enemy found his range and the water was rocked by explosions – our ammunition was blowing up all around us. Our guys on the rafts were sitting ducks – we lost an entire battalion during the crossing.[8]

Major General Vasily Fomich Konkov's 115th Rifle Division was meant to cross at the same time, but Konkov insisted on a short delay as many of his men and those of 4th Marine Brigade were still en route, and in any case he had no means with which to cross the river:

> For the remaining one night and one day at our disposal, it was necessary to collect and prepare the means of crossing, determine the exact landing sites, instruct the commanders of the first echelon, and organise cooperation with other parts of the division and the marines.

Before the start of the crossing, all of us – the division headquarters and subunit commanders – carefully studied the area on the opposite bank. Having assessed the situation, the commissar and I decided to force the Neva at night without artillery preparation, to strike suddenly. The first echelon was a battalion of 576th Rifle Regiment under the command of Captain Dubik, the second echelon was a battalion of 638th Rifle Regiment commanded by Captain Menkov. The rest of the division, and two destruction battalions of militia, would defend the right bank.

We only had a few fishing boats that we had collected from all along the right bank for transportation. A small number of pleasure boats were brought out to us from the city. We made several rafts from improvised material and assembled our entire 'fleet' at the mouth of the Dubrovka River …

The night of 20 September was rainy.

Captain Dubik's soldiers silently carried their boats to the water. The first wave silently boarded the boats. A brisk command of 'Forward!' – and the first landing party set off across the Neva to the enemy shore.

At the division command post, not far from the crossing, we all anxiously awaited the first report. I was haunted by questions. Had the enemy spotted the crossing attempt? Would the first wave succeed in disembarking in pitch darkness at the designated spot? Had the enemy prepared some sort of 'surprise' for our intrepid men? …

'The battalion commander is a brave and resolute man,' I told myself. 'Of course he will have thought of every little detail in order to succeed.'

Finally, the first report came in from the other side. Having crossed the river undetected, the soldiers silently climbed the steep left bank, broke into the enemy trenches using bayonets and hand grenades, and drove the Nazis from their trenches and dugouts. The sudden blow stunned and panicked the enemy …

During the night all of Captain Dubik's battalion crossed to the left bank of the Neva.[9]

The following day, the men who had crossed drove back elements of 20th Motorised Division, establishing a toehold a little more than a mile wide and a mile deep; it was what became known as the Neva Bridgehead. Soldiers often referred to it as the *Nevsky Pyatochok* – a reference to the popular name for a five-kopeck coin and an indication of the tiny size of the bridgehead. The Germans immediately launched counterattacks to eliminate the bridgehead, but the men who had managed to cross were able to cling to their positions. As more troops crossed it was even possible to widen the bridgehead, but a major

German assault rapidly reduced it to its original width and a depth of less than half a mile. Red Army losses, both in the crossing and subsequent fighting, were heavy; Konkov's division lost 865 men and 4th Marine Brigade was reduced to just 20 per cent of its starting strength. The bridgehead was too small to force the Germans back out of range of the river, with the result that crossing the Neva had to take place at night. Even moving along the bank attracted fire during the day, as Konkov described:

> During the day, the wide ribbon of the Neva was deserted. It looked cold and gloomy. In daylight, not a single boat dared to cross the 500m span from one coast to the other. It would certainly have been hit before it could reach the middle of the river. Both on the bridgehead and on our right bank, everything was visible to the enemy from the reinforced concrete mass of the hydroelectric power station. Every metre was swept by machine-gun fire and artillery.[10]

Shcheglov, who had witnessed the execution of a soldier for losing an important message while drunk, was on the Soviet shore opposite the bridgehead. His description of the desperate position on 27 September was equally bleak, as was the testimony of civilians who managed to reach Soviet lines:

> The dugout trembled – again a ferocious artillery attack.
>
> Some six days had passed since our men landed on the left bank but it seemed like weeks had gone by. An insignificantly small piece of land, a foothold that our troops managed to secure, was being combed up and down. Somewhere, in the direction of Mga, there was the rumble of new battles ...
>
> We had some difficult moments today. From the far shore, people were brought across in boats. According to their documents, they had been residents of Dubrovka [the village on the German-held bank, opposite Nevskaya Dubrovka] and Mga: a teacher, an agronomist, a frightened woman with three children, and two dozen more peasants and various village residents. Their stories, told calmly, were terrible, full of blood, violence and death. In the village of Ivanovo, the Nazis herded the women and children of Soviet [government] employees into a barn, then doused the walls with gasoline and set them on fire ... Near Mga, a German car ran over a mine. Who laid it? Nobody knew. All the inhabitants of the village were herded into the river, waist-deep in ice-cold water. 'You will stay there until you point out the guilty parties!' What could they say? Even if they knew, they wouldn't give them away. They stood silently for two hours, then three, then four. The children began to lose consciousness. Then an old man, Taras Morozov, came

forward and said that he had found a large mine in the forest and buried it on the road. But everyone knew that it was the partisans who laid the mine.[11]

Despite the desperate efforts of Soviet soldiers on either side of the German salient, the First Sinyavino Operation failed. Estimates of the casualties of both sides vary; one estimate puts Red Army losses as high as 55,000 killed, wounded, or taken prisoner, but this includes the Second Sinyavino Operation, described below. German losses in XXXIX Motorised Corps, which bore the brunt of the fighting, amounted to about 3,000 killed, wounded or missing.[12] As the fighting died down, the XXXIX Motorised Corps withdrew and handed over the sector to other units – it was to prepare for new offensive operations.

Kulik, who had attracted criticism from both Zhukov and Stalin, was dismissed from command of Fifty-Fourth Army in the last week of September. He was blamed for not mounting a more energetic attack, but regardless of his manifest shortcomings as a senior officer, such an attack was beyond the capabilities of Fifty-Fourth Army at that time. The army was assigned to Leningrad Front under the command of Khozin. As was often the case, Stalin took a gentler line with an old associate than he did with other officers and sent Kulik south to Crimea where he oversaw the Soviet evacuation of Kerch. A longer defence of Kerch with the forces available would merely have resulted in their complete destruction, but he was criticised again and charged with abandoning the city contrary to the orders of *Stavka*. He was stripped of his numerous medals and demoted to major general. He held numerous posts until the end of the war and had his rank restored, but did little to impress Stalin and others. In 1945 he was charged with looting and the use of military personnel to build him a dacha close to Moscow. He was once more demoted to major general and in 1947 he was once more arrested. He was brought before a closed court three years later and charged with conspiracy to overthrow Stalin. He told the court that his 'confession' had been extracted by illegal means, but he was found guilty and executed. His personal life was also marred by controversy and conflict with the Soviet authorities. In 1930, he met and married a woman who was the daughter of a tsarist nobleman who had been executed in 1919. She was constantly followed by security police and was arrested in 1939 and executed without trial shortly after. Kulik was not informed of the exact circumstances of her death, but a year later he remarried; this time, his wife was a school friend of his daughter aged just 18, 32 years younger than Kulik.

Konkov had succeeded in establishing the Neva bridgehead and was rewarded by being given control of the entire Neva Operational Group. It was to be a difficult command. On paper, the Neva bridgehead looked like a good position from which to make further attempts to break the siege, but it would prove to be a deadly battlefield where large numbers of men would die for little gain or loss.

There were some crumbs of comfort for the Red Army as a result of the failed offensive. Leeb transferred 8th Panzer Division and part of an infantry division to defend the salient running to Shlisselburg, reducing pressure elsewhere on the defences around Leningrad. In addition, the Spanish 250th 'Blue' Division and an additional infantry division were sent to the area from elsewhere, troops that otherwise might have been available for the Battle of Moscow. Zhukov claimed credit for preventing the fall of Leningrad, and it added to his steadily growing reputation; as fighting died down, he was summoned back to Moscow on 5 October to oversee the defence of the Soviet capital. The extent to which he made a decisive difference in Leningrad is open to question. His uncompromising determination and intolerance of weakness in his subordinates may well have stiffened resolve, but his tactical and operational interventions were perhaps less effective.

A pattern was emerging in the manner in which Zhukov conducted battles. His great victory against the Japanese at Khalkin Gol was due to his use of massed armour against the flanks of an earlier Japanese advance, and this justifiably became his preferred form of counterattack, as was demonstrated when he ordered offensives against the German salients at Shlisselburg and immediately to the southwest of Leningrad. But when such attacks failed, his instinct was to order repetitive assaults that were almost always doomed to failure, as the Germans were now aware of the danger and would have taken precautionary measures. The following year, he would repeat this with equally obstinate assaults against the German Army Group Centre when he launched repeated attempts to destroy the Rzhev salient. But in Stalin's eyes he was a successful commander who knew how to fight and how to stop the Germans. Given the failure of so many of Stalin's old associates – Voroshilov and Kulik at Leningrad, and Budennyi in Kiev – it is unsurprising that the Soviet ruler placed such high regard on the man who could claim, with at least some justification, that he had been successful.

Despite the diversion of substantial German military assets to the imminent Battle of Moscow, Hitler remained determined to complete operations in the north. All land contact between Leningrad and the rest of the Soviet Union had been cut, but there remained a link across Lake Ladoga. Once the winter set in, the lake would freeze and it would be possible for supplies and reinforcements to cross the ice. This would not have been possible if Army Group North had completed its close investment of Leningrad by advancing between the city and

Lake Ladoga and establishing contact with the Finns; consequently, Leeb was ordered to draw up plans for a further operation, even though he had been deprived of most of the units that had given his army group its striking power. After all, the Red Army was believed to be at the end of its strength. Even the modest resources that remained in the north should be sufficient to finish off the mission that had been assigned to Leeb.

Even though Army Group North still fielded an impressive 53 divisions and seven independent brigades, many of these were far from their establishment strength. Nevertheless, Leeb drew up two proposals for potential operations. The first was to eliminate the Oranienbaum bridgehead. This would have no immediate impact on the siege perimeter, but it would release units that were currently blockading the Red Army bridgehead and would remove an irritating thorn in the side of Army Group North. The second option was to attack across the Volkhov River from the Chudovo–Kirishi sector to reach Tikhvin and Volkhov, thus securing the last railway terminus from which relief supplies could be sent to Leningrad. After considering the resources that he had available, Leeb decided that Tikhvin – 53 miles to the east of Kirishi – would be too great a distance, particularly given the unfavourable terrain with few roads. Instead, he preferred an attack along the Volkhov River to Volkhov itself, a distance of 33 miles. This would achieve the same result, without creating such a long exposed flank.

This attack would also involve movement across unfavourable terrain, as Hitler was quick to point out. Instead, the Führer ordered Leeb to use XXXIX Motorised Corps with Army Group North's four mechanised divisions – 8th and 12th Panzer Divisions and 18th and 20th Motorised Divisions – to attack along the relatively good road from Chudovo to Tikhvin. From there, the armour would turn northwest to sweep up to encircle Volkhov, thus trapping and destroying the Soviet Fifty-Fourth Army. At the same time, Finnish forces to the north of Lake Ladoga were to attack and secure the eastern shore of the lake, linking up with the Germans to the north of Tikhvin. It was a far more ambitious operation than Leeb felt was possible, and Halder agreed with him, regarding such a grandiose advance with reduced assets in worsening weather as pure fantasy, but all objections were overruled.[13] Acting on Hitler's instructions, Halder told General Rudolf Schmidt, the commander of XXXIX Motorised Corps, to commence his advance on 16 October. Four infantry divisions under the control of I Corps would be on the northern flank, either to exploit any Soviet weakness and advance swiftly on Volkhov, or to hold the line of the planned encirclement.

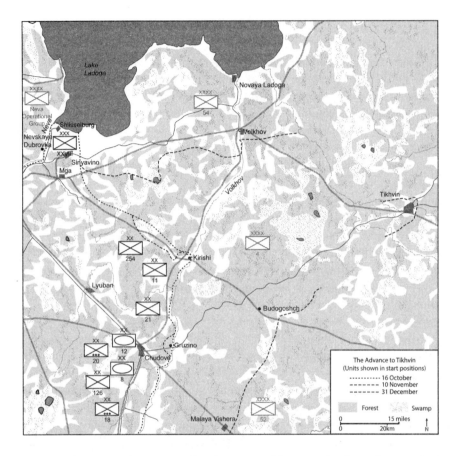

As orders were drawn up, the German soldiers in the front line studied their maps, aware that they were of poor quality and wouldn't give them a completely clear picture of what lay ahead. Stahlberg and his comrades in 12th Panzer Division also discussed the reasons that they had been given for the new advance:

At the same time as we were crossing the Volkhov, our Finnish allies would be attacking southward to the east of Lake Ladoga. In Tikhvin we would be shaking hands with the Finns. It sounded wonderful. Of course, we did not know where the Finns were at present, but we felt we had a reasonable and presumably important job to do.

The Tikhvin order contained yet another, apparently extremely weighty reason for our offensive: at Tikhvin, we read, there were considerable stocks of bauxite. The blue bauxite mined on the surface was the raw material for the manufacture of aluminium. Since Germany possessed little or no bauxite, possession of the bauxite mines at Tikhvin was of decisive significance to the war. This also sounded good, though we found it difficult to imagine how 12th Panzer Division was to quarry the bauxite of Tikhvin in the war zone, or protect the mining operations and arrange for the transport of the bauxite to Germany.[14]

Hitler often included such 'economic considerations' in justification of his orders, sometimes complaining that his generals tended to take a purely military view of matters and failed to understand economic nuances. As the war progressed, he would increasingly use such justifications to oppose abandonment of territory – in 1943 and 1944, the continued control of Nikopol in Ukraine was deemed essential because of the nearby molybdenum mines. Just how essential the seizure of such resources was for the German war effort is highly questionable and in an argument with Albert Speer, the armaments minister in the second half of the war, Hitler admitted that his real motivation for such thinking was that it forced the Wehrmacht to stand and fight rather than retreat.

The Germans were not alone in planning offensive operations. Stalin was keen for the Leningrad sector to tie down as much of the Wehrmacht as possible in order to improve the odds in the fighting around Moscow in favour of the Red Army. When Zhukov departed Leningrad on 5 October, he handed over control to Fedyuninsky, who was in command until the arrival of Voronov, the deputy defence minister. Fedyuninsky's instructions were to break the siege ring and thus force the Germans to commit more troops to the north while at the same time alleviating conditions within the city. The result would be the Second Sinyavino Offensive. As before, this would involve convergent attacks from both inside and outside the encirclement: Major General Ivan Gavrilovich Lazarev's Fifty-Fifth Army was to strike from the right bank of the Neva to seize the German-held bank as far as Lake Ladoga, while Fifty-Fourth Army – now commanded by Lieutenant General Mikhail Semenovich Khozin, formerly the chief of staff of Leningrad Front – made a fresh assault from the east to capture Sinyavino.

For the attack from within the siege perimeter, Fifty-Fifth Army created an Eastern Sector Operational Group consisting of five rifle divisions, two tank brigades, and an independent tank battalion. The initial assault would secure crossings over the Neva to the southwest of the existing Neva Bridgehead; the forces of the Neva Operational Group would protect the northern flank of this attack as it moved first east, then north in order to trap the German units defending the Sinyavino sector. From the east, Khozin would attack with three rifle divisions and two tank brigades. The timetable suggested that it would take just two days for the two groups to defeat their opponents and link up. On paper, the Red Army enjoyed a numerical advantage with about 71,000 troops facing 54,000 Germans; in addition, the attacking forces had nearly 100 tanks whereas the Germans had none. However, it is an indication of the degree to which the Soviet formations were under strength that these 100 tanks comprised the collective strength of four tank brigades and a separate tank battalion.

The Red Army was still getting its units into position when Leeb launched his attack towards Tikhvin. The best road for the advance crossed the Volkhov River to the east of Chudovo at Gruzino; indeed, it was one of the very few roads that could be used in this forested and swampy region. On 16 October, the German 21st and 126th Infantry Divisions attacked across the Volkhov to secure crossings, apparently taking the defenders by surprise and rapidly capturing a bridgehead; crucially, they were able to secure an intact railway bridge.

Two days later, Schmidt ordered 12th Panzer Division and 20th Motorised Division to launch the thrust towards Tikhvin. At the same time, 8th Panzer Division and 18th Motorised Division were to attack on the southern flank, thrusting southeast in order to roll up the Soviet line. By chance, the assault struck the Soviet lines at the junction of Fourth Army to the north and Fifty-Second Army to the south. Neither had any significant reserves and as they withdrew, the Soviet soldiers fell back on diverging axes, opening a gap in the line. *Stavka* ordered the two Soviet armies to launch convergent counterattacks to restore the situation, but without reserves this was impossible.

Despite the poor roads, worsened by a mixture of rain and snow showers, and constant aerial harassment by Soviet aircraft of the river crossings, the German offensive had got off to an encouraging start, but building up sufficient strength on the eastern bank of the Volkhov proved to be a slow business. The first elements of 8th Panzer Division set off on 19 October in difficult conditions, as the adjutant of one of its motorised rifle regiments recorded:

> *Kampfgruppe Crisolli* had to move forwards from the Volkhov along an isolated, single-track railway line. To right and left were impassable swamps. Whenever a vehicle was unable to continue – and a countless number of vehicles were left along the rail-tracks – it had to be pushed aside from the railway, whether it was a tank or a truck. Only in this manner was it possible for the advance to continue. An unbelievable scene: hundreds of vehicles lay to the right and left of the railway line, irretrievably lost.[15]

In order to gather together the required vehicles for *Barbarossa*, the Wehrmacht had requisitioned cars and trucks from much of Europe. Most had been designed for use on metalled roads and simply disintegrated on the roads and tracks of the Russian interior, and it was quite impossible for the repair teams to locate replacement parts for the vehicles that were recovered and returned to their workshops. Consequently, even the mechanised elements of the Wehrmacht were losing their mobility. The weather continued to be terrible, with alternating snow and rain – a settled period of cold weather would at least have frozen the ground hard enough for German vehicles to proceed relatively easily, but in the conditions that prevailed the few roads rapidly resembled the marshes to either side. To make matters worse, the maps available to the Germans were large-scale, 1:300,000, and based upon Soviet maps of the 1930s. They proved to be far from accurate and many of the roads that they showed turned out to be unmetalled tracks, or simply didn't exist at all. Nonetheless, both German thrusts laboured forward, engaging in occasional skirmishes with Red Army units in their path.

Alongside 8th Panzer Division, 12th Panzer Division was also moving forward. For many of the soldiers of the division, it was their first experience of Russian winter conditions, as Stahlberg described:

A column many kilometres in length crossed the wooden bridges built by our pioneers at Chudovo. Then it began to snow. In the car Becker [Stahlberg's driver] turned and looked at me, his face grave. Engelhardt, our 'local expert' [he was a Baltic German from Estonia], said that as a rule the first snow arrived 'up here' at the beginning of November. Did this mean an early winter, or even a particularly harsh one? None of our soldiers had any winter clothing.

The first snowflakes turned into a heavy snowfall. Our drivers could see the vehicle in front only from extremely close range. We advanced very slowly, anyone who needed to warm up jumping off and walking beside his vehicle so that at least his feet were warm.

During the column's frequent halts, we strained our ears for any sound in the white landscape, the drivers having been ordered to switch off their engines as soon as they stopped, to save petrol. The noise of battle came from far ahead. We were marching as what we called 'mixed troops'. As long as our troops could not deploy but were compelled to advance along a narrow road, the endless column had to be strong enough not only at its head but throughout its length to defend its flanks immediately.[16]

Progress along the road was slow. It ran along a raised causeway flanked by swamps, and there was barely enough room for vehicles going in opposite directions to pass each other. Stahlberg moved up to the head of the column aboard a motorcycle-sidecar combination and learned that the pace of the advance was hampered by mines laid by the retreating Soviet soldiers; these were now covered with snow, making the task of locating them more difficult. As Stahlberg watched, a tank attempted to turn on the road and slipped into the swamp, disappearing from view. Every attempt to locate it or to rescue the crew failed.

Despite the advance of the German panzer divisions, *Stavka* ordered the new attack on Sinyavino to go ahead as planned. Both pincers of the operation attacked on 20 October. The forces of Fifty-Fifth Army struggled to secure a foothold across the Neva and it was quite impossible for their tanks to cross; instead, they were withdrawn and ordered to cross the river closer to Leningrad before attempting to advance along the German-held shore. Such difficulties should have been anticipated, especially after the experiences of the First Sinyavino Offensive, but as was so often the case with Red Army operations at this stage of the war, too much planning was reliant upon maps rather than a proper understanding of the terrain. If army commanders regarded their orders as unrealistic, they were too inhibited by the threat of arrest and punishment to raise objections.

The bridgehead that had been won at such cost in the first attempt to break the encirclement was extended a little, but the Germans had anticipated attacks from the Red Army's toehold and their withering fire brought the Soviet advance to an abrupt halt with further heavy casualties. Colonel Andrei Matveyevich Andreyev, commander of 86th Rifle Division, was part of the assault group. He was on the right bank, waiting until dusk for the opportunity to cross to join the men of his division who had already reached the far bank:

All the departure points on the right bank of the Neva for the crossing were under enemy surveillance and consequently under well-directed artillery and mortar fire. The water was also swept by shells and machine-guns from Arbuzovo on the right and the hydroelectric station on the left ...

From the neighbouring departure points, the crossing began. Boats set off across the 500m distance every 10–12 minutes. The enemy brought almost every boat under fire. Shells and mines exploded behind, in front, to the right and left.

'It's time for us to cross too,' said the senior lieutenant. He called out to someone in the gathering darkness. An old soldier appeared. His tunic fitted poorly across his rounded shoulders. It was clear he hadn't worn a military uniform before. His spectacles flickered in their gilded frame as he said in a calm voice.

'Comrade Colonel, I ask you to wait for five or six minutes. The Hitlerites are tidy people. They fire on schedule. Right now, they're firing at the second crossing point, and we are in the fourth crossing point. They fire first on the even numbered crossings, then the odd ones.' In less than two or three minutes, the Nazis unleashed a flurry of fire on the area of our crossing. The river was completely covered. Our boat was already afloat and a few minutes later we reached the middle of the river. Having paused their firing briefly, the enemy spotted our boat and fired again. The same bespectacled soldier said, 'Listen and look! Their shells are falling on the second crossing. They'll fall closer to the right bank and much to the right of our boat.' The rowers had thoroughly studied the character and most likely lines of enemy fire. Manoeuvring the boat to the right, then to the left, we quickly passed the swept area.[17]

Andreyev was surprised at the perspicacity of the soldier until his senior lieutenant explained: he was a professor of music from the Leningrad Conservatory, a volunteer in one of the militia divisions.

The attack by Khozin's Fifty-Fourth Army also faltered and made little progress. Once more, the Soviet riflemen struggled forward through almost impossible terrain; by the end of the first day's assault, some of the rifle divisions could field barely 1,000 men. In any event, the success of the German attack across the Volkhov forced a reassessment and Khozin was ordered to dispatch three rifle divisions to help repair the breach that had opened up in Soviet lines. As the fighting bogged down, Fedyuninsky telephoned *Stavka* and spoke to Marshal Aleksandr Mikhailovich Vasilevsky, the acting chief of the general staff:

'Don't misunderstand me,' I said, 'I was awarded the rank of general only two months ago and I'm proud to hold such an important position. At the same time, the former chief of staff of the Front, Lieutenant General Khozin, who is certainly more experienced than me, commands Fifty-Fourth Army and is subordinated to me. It seems to me that this is not very expedient. Moreover, at one time he commanded a division in which I served as a battalion commander.'

Vasilevsky listened attentively to me. 'Well, perhaps you're right,' he said thoughtfully. 'I will report to the supreme commander.'

That night, an order was received, appointing me as commander of Fifty-Fourth Army.[18]

Khozin and Fedyuninsky swapped roles; it is certainly arguable that such a change of command should have been made prior to the offensive beginning, and both men would have to come to grips with their new roles in the midst of heavy fighting. For Khozin, the task was perhaps easier, as he was returning to the Front where he had previously been chief of staff, but Fedyuninsky would have to learn about his new command in difficult circumstances. Nonetheless, the new command arrangements made a great deal of sense. Fedyuninsky had demonstrated that he was an energetic, aggressive commander, whereas Khozin – though better than Kulik, his predecessor – had acted with great caution. The men were better suited to their new roles.

After its early success, the German thrust across the Volkhov had turned into a slow struggle along the terrible roads of the region. Unable to manoeuvre off the roads that ran on raised embankments through the swampy landscape, the panzer divisions had to deal with constant ambushes from enemies lurking in nearby clumps of trees. On 23 October, 12th Panzer Division reached and took Budogoshch, perhaps a third of the way from the Volkhov crossings to Tikhvin. Whilst XXXIX Motorised Corps was labouring towards the east, the German 11th Infantry Division, under the command of Generalleutnant Herbert von Böckmann, was pushing north from Kirishi along the Volkhov River towards Volkhov itself, driving back the remnants of three weak rifle divisions in its path. A combination of terrain difficulties, growing supply problems, and stiffening Soviet resistance brought this advance to a halt the day after the capture of Budogoshch. Throughout this period, the German threat to Moscow seemed to be ever greater, but *Stavka* continued to watch developments in the north. Fifty-Second Army had been driven southeast by the German attack from Chudovo and Stalin ordered it to hold firm, sending a trickle of reinforcements. Other troops were assigned to Fourth Army to the north, with a rifle division flown directly to Tikhvin while a second rifle division and a tank division were dispatched by land. Slowly, the retreat of Fifty-Second Army came to a halt. Nonetheless, the attack to the southeast had achieved the objectives set for it by Schmidt and Leeb and 8th Panzer Division was withdrawn; it would be used to strengthen the attack towards Tikhvin.

The diary of 8th Panzer Division during these days gives a graphic picture of the conditions faced by soldiers of all formations on either side of the front line:

> On average, as a result of the poor roads on which the division was operating, the tempo of movement of supply vehicles and heavy weapons was no more than 5km/h. *Gruppe Kütt* took up positions to attack Gryady. Here too the roads

delayed all preparations. Along the corduroy road [made by laying logs side by side] 1km north of Hill 55.9 there was a shell crater with a diameter of 20m. In their attempts to pass this through the bogs to right and left, seven tanks were left stranded. Recovering them was only possible with difficulty. There were no other routes available …

The health of the combat elements has become markedly unsatisfactory as a result of the exertions of the past weeks. The troops are unable to cope with the demands of further foot marches due to the weight of equipment they have to carry for subsequent redeployment. Foot problems and cold injuries are becoming numerous.[19]

It would take two days for 8th Panzer Division to commence its redeployment. Given the losses of the preceding months, Brandenberger ordered each of his rifle regiments to disband a company so that the personnel could be better concentrated; one of the division's four panzer battalions was also disbanded. It was a source of frustration to panzer commanders when their divisions were divided by higher commands to provide armoured reinforcements for other units, and Brandenberger was forced to parcel out his division, leaving some elements to defend the southern flank of the thrust east of the Volkhov River while other units took up positions close to Tikhvin. At the same time, another battlegroup from the division – together with much of 21st Infantry Division – was ordered to join 11th Infantry Division so that it could renew its attack along the river towards Volkhov. The new group formed by 11th Infantry Division and the additional reinforcements was given the title of *Gruppe Böckmann*. Despite this reshuffling of units, the balance of strength was steadily tilting in favour of the Red Army, but the commanders of both Fifty-Second Army and Fourth Army threw their reserves into action as they arrived rather than concentrating them for a single effort. The result was that they were frittered away in local counterattacks that achieved little.

It seems that both the Soviet high command and local army commanders were at fault, failing to recognise the need for adequate concentration of resources. Orders from *Stavka* often stated that the reinforcements they received were to be used for immediate attacks, but on other occasions the decision to deploy them prematurely was due to army commanders acting on their own initiative. Fourth Army was ordered to form two assault groups, which were to counterattack against 12th Panzer Division; the attack was meant to commence on 1 November but instead each assault group attacked individually, one on 2 November and the other two days later; the Germans smashed each one in turn. A few days later, the recently arrived 92nd Rifle Division was thrown into an attack as Major Kirill Yefimovich Kartsev, the division chief of staff, later recalled. His account includes a clue to the thinking that lay behind these hasty assaults:

> There was limited time to prepare for the attack. It was clear to everyone that we had to strike the enemy without delay before he was properly entrenched and had created a strong defensive line in the area. In addition to its three rifle regiments, 92nd Rifle Division included two artillery battalions, a tank battalion and a reconnaissance battalion …
>
> We were 25km from Budogoshch, which lay on the main line of communication for the enemy's Tikhvin group. It didn't look far on a map but it became increasingly difficult to advance. The enemy mounted increasingly stubborn resistance, bringing up reserves. They kept the roads under fire and if our units tried moving away from the roads they were hampered by deep snow. The division didn't have skis, so there was almost no possibility for the infantry units to manoeuvre on the battlefield. On 6 November, 203rd Rifle Regiment, reinforced by ten light T-26 tanks, tried to take a ridgeline with a quick attack. The assault was preceded by powerful artillery preparation. When the batteries moved their fire to the depths of the enemy position, two rifle battalions attacked together. But the quick attack failed. The men moved too slowly, floundering up to their waists in the snowdrifts. Worried about getting stranded in the snow or straying into minefields, the tanks rushed forward trying to break through along the road, but their path was blocked by enemy anti-tank guns firing from the village outskirts.
>
> The terrain was flat and open. No forests, no bushes – everything clearly visible at a glance. Watching the course of the battle, Colonel Larichev [the division commander] just shook his head in dismay.[20]

With the temperature plummeting on some nights to as low as -40°C, the terrain grew sufficiently firm to permit vehicles to achieve a degree of mobility and the advance on Tikhvin continued. On 8 November 12th Panzer Division succeeded in reaching the town, beating off several Soviet counterattacks. However, one of the objectives of the advance – to link up with the Finns to the east of Lake Ladoga – looked increasingly unlikely.

The German general staff, created by Helmuth von Moltke from the highly effective general staff of Prussia, was both renowned and feared for its capabilities. When it came to operational matters, there was no question that it was a highly effective system of skilled officers who knew precisely how to achieve their objectives; entry into the general staff was reserved for only the best officers and their training was rigorous, with many failing to complete the detailed and challenging course. Similarly, the tactical skill of lower officers and NCOs gave the German forces a considerable advantage over many of Germany's enemies. But at a strategic level, matters were more problematic. Whilst it is tempting to blame strategic errors in the Second World War on Hitler's leadership, the Germans had actually shown poor strategic judgement in the First World War too. Although the famous Schlieffen Plan of 1914 involved a powerful sweep through Belgium in order to outflank the French armies before attempting a huge encirclement somewhere to the east of Paris, the plan had actually been drawn up by Schlieffen purely as the best option he could devise given the resources available. In particular, he had stressed that the level of sustained mobility required for such an operation was beyond the capability of the German Army. Even worse, there had been no detailed discussions with the military authorities of the Austro-Hungarian Empire about coordination of effort in the east against Russia. There was an assumption in Berlin that the Austro-Hungarian forces would be able to tie down the bulk of the Russian Army, while ground would be conceded in East Prussia until the German Army could defeat the French and then turn east in strength. In Vienna, Franz Conrad von Hötzendorf, the chief of the general staff of the Austro-Hungarian Empire, assumed that the German forces in East Prussia would cooperate with his forces to attempt a pincer attack on Russian units in the Warsaw area. He had little justification for such a belief and had held no detailed discussions about such an operation with his German counterpart, but the result was confusion and disaster. In the invasion of the Soviet Union, Hitler made assumptions about the intentions of the Finns on the basis of his own needs and wishes rather than any concrete assurances from Helsinki. For the Finnish government of Carl Gustav Mannerheim, the purpose of the war was to recover the territory lost to the Soviet Union during the Winter War – there was little or no desire to advance to and beyond Leningrad. In October 1941, Hitler asked the Finns to advance along the northern and eastern shores of Lake Ladoga with the intention of achieving a link-up somewhere near Tikhvin, but the Finnish government studiously avoided giving a firm commitment. Hitler then ordered the advance over the Volkhov with nothing more than his personal assumption that the Finns would cooperate. But by the time that 12th Panzer Division reached Tikhvin, the Finnish Army had barely moved.

For the men of 12th Panzer Division, there was great dissatisfaction at how their division had been deployed. Stahlberg later recalled:

There had been little resistance in the town itself – what would have been the point? After all, in Tikhvin we were like rats in a trap. The small town had been evacuated, there was not a soul to be seen. The troops prepared themselves for the defence of this town in complete peace and quiet, an eerie silence filling the market-place, now under deep snow. The infantry dug themselves in, our guns disappeared in defilades, the tanks camouflaged themselves in barns and cowsheds, breaking openings in the walls for their gun muzzles. Tikhvin was now a 'fortress' and 12th Panzer Division, intended for mobile warfare, was now engaged in positional warfare.[21]

In an attempt to restore mobility to one of his few mechanised assets, Leeb dispatched 61st Infantry Division to Tikhvin and ordered Schmidt to pull 12th Panzer Division out of the town once the infantry had relieved him. After regrouping, the weakened motorised forces of Army Group North were to commence their attempt to envelop the Soviet Fifty-Fourth Army to the north. While they waited for relief, the soldiers of 12th Panzer Division searched the houses of Tikhvin for winter clothing – they were still wearing the uniforms that they had had when they crossed the frontier in June. Tank engines had to be run for extended periods merely to keep the crews warm, resulting in growing concerns about fuel – the road from the Volkhov crossings to Tikhvin was now under intermittent attack, meaning that supplies didn't arrive regularly. Within days, there were cases of frostbite. In addition to the fuel shortage, there were growing concerns about the limited quantities of ammunition and even food. It was a chastening state of affairs for men who had believed that the campaign against the Soviet Union was as good as finished.

Having received reinforcements in the shape of the reinforced battlegroup from 8th Panzer Division, *Gruppe Böckmann* was able to resume its advance towards Volkhov and reached the southern outskirts of the city on the same day that 12th Panzer Division took Tikhvin. The situation for the Red Army was now critical, with growing likelihood of Fedyuninsky's Fifty-Fourth Army being pinned to the shores of Lake Ladoga. Desperate to find a combination of commanders who could prevent catastrophe, Stalin ordered Meretskov, who had been involved in the attack on Finland in 1939 and was currently commanding Seventh Army, to take command of Fourth Army. As he took up his new appointment, *Stavka* also called off the Second Sinyavino Offensive. The situation created by Leeb's attacks towards Tikhvin and Volkhov took priority.

After the shambolic performance of the Red Army in the Winter War, Meretskov had held a number of posts, including chief of the general staff in the last months of 1940, but a few days after the German invasion commenced he was arrested on charges of treason on the basis of testimony from several men, many of whom had been arrested as part of Stalin's purges before the war and, as was so often the case, had offered the names of others to their interrogators in attempts to escape further physical suffering. During his period of captivity, Meretskov was badly mistreated and forced to witness the brutal beating of other prisoners, and signed a confession apparently on condition that his family was spared from punishment.[22] In August, he wrote to Stalin requesting that he be sent to the front line where he would have the chance to die with honour. When he was released from captivity, he could hardly walk; he attended a meeting with Zhukov, Stalin and several others, and was the only person present other than Stalin who was permitted to sit.[23] His first assignment was command of Seventh Army on the front against the Finns, where he managed to stop the Finnish advance on the Svir River.

Just as orders were being sent from Moscow to abandon the Second Sinyavino Offensive, the Soviet forces in the Neva bridgehead tried once more to break out. Sergei Nikolayevich Spitsin, a signaller, was a native of the Leningrad region and was part of a militia unit that was pulled out of the front line to the southwest of the city and sent into the bridgehead as reinforcements. He watched as some of his comrades crossed the river:

On 6 November, we were gathered together and paraded and told: 'There is only sufficient food in the city for a week. We need to break through and restore communications at all costs. At the same time, there will be an attack [from the outside] to link up with us.' On the night of 7 November we gathered and boarded the boats. They were fairly big, probably fishing boats, packed with about 30 men apiece. The sides were no more than the width of my palm above the water. The Neva was muddy and there were no waves or we would have been swamped. The Germans launched flares and opened fire but we crossed safely. We were told to take cover until the morning, when we were shown our positions. The left bank was about 3m above the water. Dugouts had been dug here and there were a few tents. I squeezed into one but was turned away with foul curses. I had to dig [a shelter]. It was frosty, but only the top layer of ground was frozen. I dug through the sand until I came across a rag. I tried in vain to pull it out – it turned out to be a corpse, and the rag was its overcoat. I tried a different spot and my shovel struck a helmet, with a head in it. The entire shore was littered with corpses barely covered in sand. I went up the bank a little to a gnarled tree with half-exposed roots. I crawled into a hole there and fell asleep. It was terribly cold.[24]

The following morning, Spitsin and the others crawled forward under shellfire to the front line. Soviet artillery on the right bank commenced a bombardment of the German positions and then the moment came to attack:

> Someone senior stood up with a pistol: 'Forward!' We arose and set off with fixed bayonets. The ground wasn't flat and we struggled over the ruts. It was silent for the first few metres. Then there was a shot from one side, then another, and a machine-gun began to fire, then a mortar. We had to run about 80m to the German trenches, and we covered about half of this. I looked at the next man and he fell, others too, bullets whistled past. I saw everyone lying down so I did too. The Germans flayed the ground, clods of mud were flying up and I prayed to God to spare me. Using a shovel, I began to scrape a hole in order to dig in. I hid behind a corpse and dug and dug, almost as deep as I was tall. I looked around and the others were digging too ... By morning my trench was quite good. The others and I had agreed to link our dugouts.[25]

The German defences were ready for the renewed attack and the result was a massacre. Amongst the units involved was 168th Rifle Division, which had just arrived in the bridgehead. It was already badly weakened by fighting to the north of Krasnogvardeisk, and within just two days it was reduced to just 200 men; the neighbouring 20th NKVD Rifle Division was also smashed, reporting that it had only 300 fighters left in its ranks.[26] *Stavka* was critical of the attempt, blaming it on infantry attacking without tanks in support. In response Zhdanov, the Communist Party chief in Leningrad, replied that it had proved impossible to move tanks into the bridgehead. Over the following days, it was possible to move 11 tanks across the Neva (out of a planned deployment of 40) and a fresh attempt was made on 9–11 November. Once again, the German defences were easily able to crush the attacks, leaving more dead to sink into the swampy ground.

Both sides constantly issued proclamations across the front line, calling on their opponents to lay down their arms. Most of these were ignored, but there were desertions from both the Red Army and the Wehrmacht. Post-war Soviet historiography attempted to play down the significance of Soviet defections, but on occasion these were more than just a couple of soldiers who tried to escape from the brutal conditions of the war. An officer in 294th Rifle Division, part of Fifty-Second Army, recalled one incident:

> In our division at the end of 1941 there was a case when a whole rifle company went over to the Germans without a shot being fired. At that time, companies had

been reduced to 20–30 men. As far as I recall, it was only the soldiers, without their officers. What can I say? It's obvious that there were problems and that there was some sort of conspiracy. The soldiers were from the Smolensk region, which was occupied at that time, and perhaps they hoped that the Germans would let them go home. Captain Sugrobov, the battalion commander, was put on trial. He was demoted and sent to the front line. However, he was later restored to his rank. The division commander, Colonel Martynchuk, was also punished. He was a competent commander and a good man. He was removed … But not a single political officer was punished. Weren't they to blame? Wasn't it their specific duty to work closely with the soldiers?[27]

Fedyuninsky had been ordered to prepare various installations in the city of Volkhov for destruction. He ordered demolition charges to be placed, but they were to be detonated only on his specific command. In the meantime, he was struggling with another problem:

As luck would have it, I developed terrible toothache. The pain didn't subside for a minute and made it difficult to concentrate. I tried to drown it out by smoking, holding a bottle of hot water against my cheek, rinsing my mouth with vodka – nothing helped. Completely exhausted by this misfortune, I said to the adjutant, 'Find me a dentist.'

'We probably won't find one anywhere. There are surgeons, also other paramedics, but no dentist. We'll have to go to the hospital or a medical battalion,' explained Lieutenant Rozhkov. But realising I wasn't disposed to listen to his arguments, he disappeared and returned two hours later with a military doctor, an elderly, plump and apparently very determined woman …

Having laid out on the table a set of various metal hooks and tongs, the very sight of which made me feel uneasy, the doctor came up to me and ordered in a low, almost masculine voice, 'Open your mouth, patient. Wider, please.'[28]

After the extraction of three teeth – the doctor declared them all damaged, and Fedyuninsky was too impatient to wait until she had determined which one was responsible for the pain – the toothache subsided and Fedyuninsky was able to resume preparations to save his army.

The German advance might have created a crisis for the Red Army, but it was also a huge strain on Army Group North's limited assets. As a result of the advance, the front line had grown by an additional 165 miles, on terrain where it was almost impossible to establish a continuous front line. After its earlier withdrawals, the Soviet Fifty-Second Army was now taking a more aggressive stance and threatened the German salient from the south, with the result that isolated German battlegroups, often reliant on intermittent supply drops from the Luftwaffe, were fighting increasingly difficult defensive actions. On 16 November, Leeb and Halder discussed the situation by telephone. For the moment, it seemed that there was little pressure on Tikhvin itself, but Leeb reported signs of a Soviet build-up in the area. He suggested abandoning the town and falling back to concentrate on Volkhov; this would shorten the front line considerably and concentrate resources on completing the encirclement of Fifty-Fourth Army, as well as reducing the strain on his overstretched logistic services. Halder overruled him, stressing that Tikhvin had to be held 'at all costs' – although not explicitly stated, this instruction almost certainly came from Hitler, who continued to hope that the Finns would finally move forward to link up with the Wehrmacht units in the town.

The Soviet concentration around Tikhvin that gave Leeb cause for concern was the beginning of a new regrouping of forces intended to drive the Germans back across the Volkhov River. Meretskov was to attack Tikhvin with three groups, each little more than a division in strength; Fedyuninsky was to strike at Böckmann's western flank and then advance on Kirishi, where it was hoped he would link up with Fourth Army advancing from Tikhvin; and Fifty-Second Army was to strike from the south. Numerically, the Red Army had a considerable advantage in infantry, but the Germans had more tanks. Whether they could be used effectively in the terrain, even now that it was frozen hard, remained to be seen.

Unsurprisingly, given the weather and the parlous situation in which the Red Army found itself, it proved impossible for the three attacks to commence on the same day. Fifty-Second Army had already been pressuring the southern flank of the salient since 12 November and its attacks intensified over the following days. On 19 November, the three strike groups of Fourth Army began their attacks on Tikhvin, but Fedyuninsky was unable to get his forces moving until 3 December. At the start of what developed into a major counteroffensive, the diary of 8th Panzer Division recorded its depleted state:

> With its currently weakened forces, including the supply formations, drivers and rear area troops who have been withdrawn, the division hopes ... it will be able to hold its positions for a limited time ... the state of personnel and equipment is at the extreme limit of functionality.[29]

The division reported that it had nine Pz.II tanks – obsolete and of little use other than for reconnaissance – and seven Pz.IV tanks, together with two command vehicles. Overall, it had lost about 70 per cent of its other vehicles. As was the case for much of the Wehrmacht, the division had received very little winter clothing – there simply wasn't sufficient railway capacity to transport the munitions and fuel needed for the various offensives still unfolding whilst simultaneously shipping bulky cold weather uniforms. Other equipment essential for working in such extreme conditions was also missing. Oberstleutnant Helmut von Scotti, an officer in the division's artillery regiment, later wrote in his memoirs:

> Small fires were lit under the guns to stop the lubricant in the recoil mechanism from freezing. The gunners carried the firing pins of the guns in their pockets next to their warm bodies. They also kept their meagre bread ration with them [to prevent it from freezing].[30]

Frostbite cases in all German divisions increased steadily; the senior doctor of 8th Panzer Division recorded that there had been 275 cases during November, 92 of them severe enough to require surgery. But for the moment, there was no possibility of relief from the harsh conditions – one of the consequences of moving into such a barren region was that there was little natural shelter from the winds sweeping from the north or east, and few villages where the men might find some protection. Furthermore, many of those villages had been badly damaged, either by the retreating Red Army or by the Germans themselves.

All along the Eastern Front, the Germans were about to learn a painful lesson. Armies configured for an offensive posture were poorly positioned to deal with a powerful enemy counteroffensive. According to Wehrmacht doctrine, the correct posture for defensive operations required a line held by infantry units, with mobile formations poised a short distance behind from where they could mount devastating counterattacks. But as a consequence of the recent offensive, nearly all German mobile units were in the front line, at the very tips of the salients that were now being threatened by Soviet attacks. In any case, the front line was so long that there were inadequate infantry resources to provide much more than a series of 'strongpoints' with substantial gaps between them.

A further problem was lack of mobility. The motorised formations had all suffered punishing attrition of their vehicles; the figures for 8th Panzer Division quoted above were similar to those of almost every similar unit. The infantry had lacked adequate motorised transport from the outset and the loss of tens of thousands of heavy draft horses in the preceding months had not been made good. In many cases, the infantry formations had seized horses from civilians or had attempted to use the stocky ponies captured from Soviet cavalry divisions, but these animals were not strong enough for pulling heavy guns and other equipment. Moreover, the loss rate for horses rose rapidly as temperatures plummeted. It had always been almost impossible to bring forward sufficient fodder for the horses, a recurring problem that stretched back to earlier wars. Without horses to pull them, many guns were simply abandoned.

The Wehrmacht's 250th Infantry Division was one of the reinforcements sent to Army Group North; it had an unusual history. When *Barbarossa* began, many pro-German states sought to be involved. Mussolini ordered a substantial Italian contingent to be sent to the Eastern Front so that Italy could claim a share of the spoils of victory, and in Spain too there was interest in sending troops. The reasons for this were complex. Some in Spain perceived involvement in a war against the Soviet Union as a continuation of the Spanish Civil War, in which the Soviet Union had sided with the opponents of Franco's Fascists. The Soviet Union (and Imperial Russia before 1917) was often seen in Spain as a source of malevolence – in earlier times, it represented a primitive oriental barbarism, and after the Russian Revolution the Soviet Union was the agency that sought to destroy western civilisation and traditional Christian culture. For many Spanish politicians and ordinary people, a war against this foe was therefore highly desirable. Some more traditionally minded Spaniards had reservations about the atheistic attitude of Nazi Germany but were prepared to put that to one side: once the Bolshevik antichrist had been destroyed, Germany could be encouraged to see the light and accept Christianity.

The suggestion of a Spanish contingent originated with the Spanish foreign minister, Ramón Serrano-Suñer, who wanted Spain to take part in what he saw as a great crusade against Bolshevism. Hitler responded positively to the Spanish offer, even though Spain declined his request to declare war on the Soviet Union – instead, involvement would be limited to a mission of revenge for Soviet support of the anti-Franco forces during the Civil War. Thousands of Spanish men responded to a call for volunteers for a variety of reasons. Many were veterans of the Civil War with deep-rooted enmity towards the Soviet Union – during the fighting in Spain, some of those on Franco's side routinely referred to all their enemies as 'Russians', even though the number of Soviets deployed in Spain was minimal. When he was refused on the grounds of his wounds from the Civil War, one veteran wrote to the local Falangist Party office to protest:

It is not in my thoroughly Falangist spirit to be left behind in the heart-rending conflagration of the entire world, where our heroic Blue Shirts are fighting in cooperation with noble Italo-Germanic comrades for the destruction and extermination of the corrupted barbaric Asiatic hordes, who with their disastrous ideals bloodied our homeland leaving a terrifying trail of blood in their wake, and who with their fierce Bolshevik doctrine threaten Christian civilisation.[31]

Others volunteered for career reasons – a sergeant from Madrid wished to serve with the contingent in the hope that it would improve his service record. In a generally poor country, the pay that was on offer was also a strong motivator: the volunteers would receive both German and Spanish pay, together with a supplement for front-line service. Inevitably, recruitment was lower in areas where the defeated Republicans had been dominant. There were even volunteers from Spanish territories in Morocco, but these were unacceptable to the Germans. The Spanish authorities permitted only a few African volunteers, mainly serving NCOs, to join the division and most of these were then weeded out and returned to Spain by the Germans.

The volunteers were given blue shirts – the traditional colour of the Spanish Falangist movement – resulting in its nickname of the *División Azul* ('Blue Division'). In the field, the division would be part of the Wehrmacht and would wear the usual German field grey uniform, though with a shoulder badge identifying its men as Spanish.[32] There was a considerable sense of urgency in organising the division, as a swift German victory was widely expected. The division left Spain for Bavaria in mid-July, where it underwent training for between five and six weeks – this was half the training normally undertaken by German units, but was truncated on two grounds. Firstly, a large proportion of the Spanish volunteers were either serving members of the Spanish Army or had combat experience from the Civil War; and secondly, there was widespread expectation that the war would soon be over, with the Wehrmacht having done all the serious fighting.

Relations between the Spanish soldiers and the Germans around them varied. Many Wehrmacht personnel were shocked by the apparent indiscipline of the Spaniards – they often didn't button up their tunics properly in the German fashion; they marched carrying their guns in whatever manner they chose; and there were occasions when they simply refused to obey orders or went to great lengths to evade them. Many of the local women around the barracks where they were being trained were happy to have a large group of young men with exotic behaviour and language, particularly as so many

German men were away on active service, and there were large numbers of liaisons of varying degrees of intimacy. A Spanish medical officer recorded in his diary:

> After work, coffee shops get full of *Mädchen*, Spanish guys and German ladies devote themselves in a joyful and open way to teaching each other their respective languages. We are accustomed to our beauteous Spanish morality, and are shocked by some of the liberties that German girls take with the Spaniards in the most natural way ... Almost every Spaniard has a German girlfriend. The boys say this is to learn German properly.[33]

Many soldiers did more than learn German – several had to be sent home after contracting sexually transmitted diseases. Many in Germany disapproved of such behaviour and one Spanish soldier wrote that he had noticed members of the Hitler Youth taking note of the names of women who flirted with Spanish soldiers. The Spanish authorities issued instructions in early 1942 that liaisons with German women were to be avoided; there is no evidence that these orders had any significant effect.

The Blue Division was formally adopted into the Wehrmacht at the end of the month. Its men were then taken by train to Suwałki, close to the frontier with Lithuania, from where they set off on foot to join Army Group Centre before they were diverted to the north. They had to cover most of the distance from eastern Poland to Vitebsk on foot, a long gruelling march that left over 2,000 needing medical treatment. Discipline during the march was poor. The Spanish soldiers had a very different attitude from the Germans towards tidiness and even fairly basic duties such as looking after weapons, equipment, and horses, but their morale remained good. By the time they crossed into the Soviet Union, most of the men had settled down into the routine of military life, though there continued to be disparaging comments from Germans about their general appearance. When they learned that they were not being sent to help capture Moscow but instead would join Army Group North, the men reacted in varying ways. A private wrote:

> They say that the general of the army corps we were assigned to doesn't want us, as in our marches we give the impression of being a useless force. Perhaps it is because we go unbuttoned, with our hats to one side and because some of our anti-tank pieces have names: Lola, Carmencita, etc, and the occasional chicken hanging from the tow.[34]

РУКИ ПРОЧЬ ОТ ЛЕНИНГРАДА!

ШЛИ ОТ КАЙЗЕРА К НАМ ГОСТИ — ДА ОТ НИХ ОСТАЛИСЬ КОСТИ...

ШЕЛ ЮДЕНИЧ — ГЕНЕРАЛ — ДА ЧУТЬ ЖИВ ОТ НАС УДРАЛ...

МАННЕРГЕЙМ К НАМ СУНУЛ НОС — ДА ЕДВА ЕГО УНЕС...

И С ФАШИСТОМ БУДЕТ ТО ЖЕ: В ЗЕМЛЮ ЛЕЧЬ ЕМУ ПОМОЖЕМ...

Hands off Leningrad! The illustrations and rhymed captions in this Soviet propaganda poster from 1941 present various failed attempts of aggression against Leningrad. (Getty Images)

A view of Leningrad as seen from two and a half miles away at the front line near Uritz, September 1941. To the left can be seen St Isaac's Cathedral. (Getty Images)

Soviet militia divisions were created using volunteers who came forward in large numbers to defeat the Germans, such as these men from the Kirov Factory. (Getty Images)

The Germans captured Shlisselburg (seen here) and Sinyavino on Lake Lagoda on 7 September 1941, cutting all land connections between Leningrad and the rest of the USSR. (Getty Images)

Occupation of a suburb of Leningrad by German infantrymen, September 1941. Residents try to save their belongings from the burning town. (Getty Images)

Hooded and camouflaged spotters of a Soviet anti-aircraft gun detachment keep watch for enemy planes in a sunken look-out post at the approach to Leningrad. (Getty Images)

The warship *Marat* (previously *Petropavlovsk*) provided valuable fire support for Red Army troops, but was sunk by Hans-Ulrich Rudel and Erwin Hentschel and another Ju 87 crew in September 1941. (Nik Cornish)

German soldiers occupying Soviet defence positions ahead of Leningrad, October 1941. (Getty Images)

Leningrad inhabitants, including women of all ages, take shovels and picks to help defend their city to the last, October 1941. (Getty Images)

German troops fire heavy artillery, October 1941. Most of the shelling during the winter of 1941–42 deliberately targeted civilian targets and essential infrastructure such as water pumping stations. (Getty Images)

German long range artillery shelling Kronstadt, the home of the Soviet Baltic Fleet, in October 1941. (Getty Images)

This tram marked the deepest German penetration into Leningrad. The date given on the original caption sheet is 16 October 1941. (Nik Cornish)

Barrage balloons on Nevsky Prospekt, Leningrad, late 1941. The city's defences gave it a 'special, hard beauty' according to Major General Fedyuninsky. (RGAKFD via Stavka)

A ZPU 4M quadruple-barrelled anti-aircraft machine gun in front of St Isaac's Cathedral, Leningrad, winter 1941–42. The shortage of ammunition was problematic for such weapons. (TASS)

German infantry advance on Leningrad. The region over which the war would be fought was heavily forested and crisscrossed by waterways, small lakes and swamps. (Getty Images)

Soviet militia during the siege. Some of the volunteer formations would be transformed into regular army units. (Getty Images)

Members of the Komsomol fire brigade Erna Kivi (right) and Galina Kuritsyna at a post organized on one of the roofs of Leningrad. (Nik Cornish)

A truck crossing the Road of Life over Lake Ladoga in 1942; the door is open to allow the driver to jump out if it starts to sink. (Getty Images)

Entering the Road of Life. The female guard is well dressed for the conditions. The sign reads, 'Lenfront. The Ice Mainline. Distance 30km'. (RGAKFD via Stavka)

A woman carries away a corpse on a sledge down Nevsky Prospekt. Many died of starvation during the terrible winter of 1941–42. (Getty Images)

Two women sitting among the debris in the aftermath of the German bombardment of Leningrad in 1942, which resulted in enormous losses among civilians. (Getty Images)

Composer Dmitry Shostakovich (1906–75) opted to remain in Leningrad when the siege began in September 1941, continuing work on his Seventh Symphony. (Getty Images)

The Leningrad première of Shostakovich's Seventh Symphony with the Leningrad Radio Orchestra on 9 August 1942. (Alamy)

A German Tiger in combat south of Lake Ladoga, September 1942. The difficulties of the terrain are evident. Destroyed Soviet tanks can be seen in the background. (Getty Images)

Soviet troops launch a counter-attack during the siege. The heaviest fighting was in the attempts to break the siege ring to the east and southeast. (Getty Images)

A soldier of the Red Army takes cover behind the rubble of a building. Many of the villages and small towns around Leningrad were reduced to heaps of ruins. (Getty Images)

Leningrad children racing on their scooters. Having seen so much in their young lives, they are not fazed by the notice behind them: 'Drive slowly! Unexploded bomb! Danger!' (Getty Images)

Leningraders were so weak from hunger that they had no strength to bury their dead during the siege. Bodies were taken to the edge of the city, and people were given extra rations to bury them. (Getty Images)

During their march through Poland and Belarus, the Spanish soldiers frequently encountered local people and traded clothing and tobacco for food; a few of the more perceptive soldiers wondered at how voluntary this trade really was, as the peasants were clearly short of food, and speculated whether they felt obliged to trade with men wearing the same uniforms as the German occupiers. There were also many occasions when the Spaniards simply appropriated food much as German soldiers did, but the Catholic soldiers felt an affinity with the Poles and rarely looked down on them in the same manner as the Germans.

Once they crossed the border into the Soviet Union, the attitude of many of the soldiers changed. Many wrote about the squalor and poverty that they saw everywhere. One letter back to Spain described a village through which the soldiers marched:

> The village couldn't possibly be constructed any worse. The houses are all made of wood, filled with a foul stench that I would not recommend, as the stables are in fact a room in the house. This is the Russian paradise the Reds dreamed of![35]

This conclusion – that the scenes they saw were the direct consequence of Bolshevism and consequently the war against Bolshevism was entirely justified – failed to take account of several factors. Firstly, in 1917 the Bolsheviks had inherited a country that was impoverished by the standards of much of Europe. Secondly, this poverty worsened considerably during the years of the Russian Civil War. Thirdly, the retreating Red Army deliberately destroyed infrastructure to hinder the Germans; and finally, there was widespread destruction due to the fighting, worsened by the manner in which the Germans seized anything that they wanted. The distaste expressed by the Spanish soldiers was perhaps predictably more pronounced amongst those from urban backgrounds; many wrote that their experiences in the Soviet Union confirmed the impressions they had gained from reading 19th-century Russian literature. Soldiers from Spain's rural hinterland were less critical, recognising the impossibility of constructing stone houses in a land where there was so little stone available. Some even acknowledged that the peasant houses were actually designed efficiently to keep their occupants warm, even if the smell from cohabiting with farm animals was unpleasant. Regardless of their distaste for the state of Soviet villages, the soldiers generally felt sympathy for local people, repeatedly writing that the Soviet state had betrayed them and failed to provide for their most basic needs.

Rapidly, the prevailing attitude amongst Spanish soldiers towards the civilians of the Soviet Union diverged from that held by their German counterparts. The overarching plans for *Barbarossa* explicitly described the death of most of the Slav population of the Soviet Union in order to create space for German settlement; by contrast, most Spanish soldiers came to see the local people in the same manner that they viewed the African inhabitants of European colonies. These were primitive people who needed guidance and education in order to better themselves. An article appeared in a journal that was published in the Blue Division, describing how the Russian people had lived in an environment of alcoholism, crime, and sexual degeneration prior to the 1917 revolutions – this was then exploited as fertile ground for the spread of Bolshevism. Some saw the only solution as the German one, namely the extermination of such a degenerate part of mankind, but this was a minority view. Most believed that Europeans in general and the Spanish in particular had a duty to bring civilisation and the word of God to these unfortunate, ignorant savages.

Under the command of Generalmajor Antonio Muñoz Grandes, the division boarded trains in Vitebsk for Pskov. The officers of Army Group North were as disappointed with the appearance of the Spanish troops as their colleagues in Army Group Centre and many were particularly unimpressed by the Spanish officers – they routinely expected better rations and accommodation than their men and lacked the rigorous training and professionalism of their German equivalents. The attitude of ordinary German and Spanish soldiers towards each other was more nuanced. Generally, German infantrymen regarded the Spanish as good comrades and tough fighters, but there were frequent clashes in rear areas, often over women or the seizure of supplies from the local population.

Regardless of the unfavourable impression that many German senior officers had, the need for reinforcements overrode any doubts and the Blue Division was dispatched to the Volkhov sector immediately north of Novgorod. Here, its men found themselves in a landscape that was utterly different from their homeland. As temperatures plummeted and food supplies became increasingly irregular, many of its volunteers must have wondered at the strange sequence of events that had led them from the southwest limits of Europe to the northeast edge, where they faced the prospect of a bitterly cold winter and combat against a determined foe.

The Spanish soldiers began to deploy in the front line on 7 October, with the entire division arriving over the following ten days. The previous units in this sector – 18th and 126th Infantry Divisions – had lost more than a third of their strength and there was growing concern about the apparent strength of the Soviet units facing them. The division's sector extended for about 24 miles along the

Volkhov River and as had been the case since the Spanish soldiers had first arrived at their training camps in Germany, the Germans around them looked at them with dismay. The march to the front line had reduced their tidiness even further and with no experience of such weapons, the Spanish had not carried out routine maintenance on many of their anti-tank guns and other artillery with the consequence that some of the guns were now useless. Nonetheless, the soldiers performed adequately in the initial German advance across the Volkhov in mid-October and took up new defensive positions to the east of the river. Towards the end of the month, they had their first serious test. In bitterly cold weather, the Red Army made a series of counterattacks and a reinforced Spanish battalion fought a bitter battle to hold on to the village of Posad, guarding the southern flank of the main German forces that had advanced over the Volkhov. Regardless of their often slovenly appearance, the Spaniards fell back on the skills and experiences of the Civil War and defended obstinately. After the war, many Spanish veterans attempted to portray their behaviour on the Eastern Front as different from that of the Germans. In some cases that might have been true, but on other occasions the Spaniards showed little mercy towards captured Red Army soldiers:

> They catch them and we kill them, and it's very unpleasant to see wounded Russian prisoners asking for mercy and we grab a machine-gun and mow them all down, I'd never seen more dead together in that way and it's not a pretty sight.[36]

The relatively ineffective attacks by the Soviet Fifty-Second Army against the southern flank of the Tikhvin salient were paused in mid-November while Lieutenant General Nikolai Kuzmich Klykov, the army commander, reorganised his forces. When he resumed his attacks on 17 November he enjoyed better success, pushing the Germans out of the town of Malaia Vishera. This put the Red Army just 24 miles from the German bridges near Chudovo, creating a serious threat to the German forces in the Tikhvin salient. But the weather conditions that were causing so much difficulty for the Germans were also hindering the Red Army and the advance stopped almost immediately; Halder noted in his diary that the situation was stable and expressed no particular concerns. Indeed, he recorded on 19 November that Hitler was still insisting on the destruction of the Soviet forces in the 'Ladoga Group'.[37] If he was aware of the terrible state of the Wehrmacht units facing the full blast of the Soviet winter, he took little or no account of it. While it struggled to redeploy, 18th Motorised Division reported that its casualties just during November exceeded 5,000 men, reducing its combat strength to less than 1,000. Its 30th Infantry Regiment recorded that 250 men had died, most of them freezing to death.[38] But regardless of Halder's apparent lack of interest in the plight of front-line troops, there were growing signs of the strain that *Barbarossa* had placed upon Germany. On 24 November, Generaloberst Friedrich Fromm, chief of the army's resupply and replacements office, informed Halder that production of military materiel had actually declined, largely because so many factory workers were currently serving in the army. He added that if serious shortfalls in front-line manpower were to be avoided, it might be necessary to draft men born in 1923 a year earlier than would normally have been the case.[39] Such a move would do nothing to reduce the manpower shortages in German industry and would probably exacerbate them. A few days later, Generalmajor Walter Buhle, head of the Operations Department of *OKH*, gave Halder further grim news:

> The eastern army has a shortage of 340,000 men, i.e. 50 per cent of the combat strength of its infantry. Company combat strength is 50 to 60 men.
>
> Current losses and returning convalescents approximately offset each other at this time. Gaps can be filled only by disbanding some divisions …
>
> [The] time needed for the rehabilitation of a panzer division is six months. Units should therefore be returned to Germany for refitting as soon as possible.
>
> We cannot replace even 50 per cent of our motorcycle losses.[40]

On 7 December, the Spanish Blue Division was ordered to pull back over the Volkhov; the battalion in Posad had been reduced to just 38 men. The retreat across the Volkhov seemed to confirm German fears about their allies – many of the Blue Division's guns were abandoned with little or no attempt to render them useless. But if the Germans were disdainful of the Spanish soldiers, the Red Army had a different opinion. Soviet reports highlighted the determined defence of Posad and added that interrogations of Spanish prisoners showed that most were 'fanatical Fascists'.[41] Total Spanish losses in the battles to the east of the Volkhov are difficult to estimate given the periods covered by Wehrmacht reports, but a medical report from the division in mid-January recorded total losses to date of nearly 800 dead, about 1,800 wounded, and over 2,200 sick (including about 900 cases of frostbite). These casualties are similar to those of German divisions in the same sector. Soldiers in the Blue Division received a large number of medals during the winter from the Germans; whilst some of these were undoubtedly deserved, there was also probably a large element of politics involved.

Some German commanders wanted to replace the Spanish soldiers with German infantry but no such replacements were available; in any case, whilst the Germans might criticise the Spaniards for declining combat capability, the same was true of German units that had endured similar conditions.

On 3 December, Fedyuninsky's Fifty-Fourth Army also joined in the offensive operations. The units of *Gruppe Böckmann* were now under the overall control of I Corps, which had felt increasing pressure on its western flank for several days as Fedyuninsky's men drove it back in small-scale attacks. The main blow in early December badly mauled the German 254th Infantry Division and forced General Kuno von Both, the corps commander, to pull back his western flank a short distance, but Fedyuninsky lacked the reserves to exploit his success. After discussions with Khozin, he was assigned two additional rifle divisions, and he set to work deploying these for a resumption of the assault. In the meantime, he noted with amusement that the German radio broadcasts were proclaiming that he had committed suicide in despair at the perilous situation.[42] The freezing weather had another effect that worked very much to the benefit of the Red Army: the Neva was now frozen, permitting men on foot to cross to the Neva bridgehead. On 16 November, engineers started constructing a reinforced ice bridge, strong enough for motorised vehicles, even tanks, to cross.

The Red Army attacks on Tikhvin at first were beaten off by the German garrison but they steadily increased in intensity. On 5 December, the Red Army began its counteroffensive outside Moscow with operations to the north of the Soviet capital. There was little concern in *OKH* at this development, and even the following day Hitler was attempting to play down the significance of German losses – he argued that while the average reduction in the strength of each German division was about 3,000–4,000 men, the Red Army had lost at least ten times as many men. The Wehrmacht's armies had claimed the destruction of more Soviet divisions than Kinzel's *FHO* had told them to expect, so even if the Red Army was still fighting, it must be close to the end of its strength. Orders remained as before for Army Group North: Tikhvin was to be held; firm contact was to be established with the Finns before the end of the winter; and Red Army units of the 'Ladoga Group' – largely Fedyuninsky's Fifty-Fourth Army – were to be destroyed.

The situation on the ground was becoming increasingly difficult for Leeb's army group. The three attack groups around Tikhvin from the Soviet Fourth Army continued to apply pressure, with the southern group working its way towards the rear of the German positions and threatening to cut their supply lines. From the north, Soviet soldiers had reached the outskirts on 8 December, and, aware that the flanks of the salient had almost no protection, Leeb requested permission once more to abandon the town. At first Hitler refused to agree, but then acknowledged reality and Halder informed Leeb that he could withdraw, but had to keep Tikhvin within artillery range. Aware that his troops faced almost certain encirclement and destruction in the town, Leeb had already issued orders for a withdrawal. It was a morale-sapping moment for Stahlberg and his comrades. Suffering from a high fever, he was in a half-track during the retreat:

> Sometimes we were on the move, sometimes at a standstill – I lost all sense of time. I remember a good deal of shooting, shouted orders, cries of pain and calls for the medical orderlies. I lay comatose under my blankets, indifferent to it all.
>
> At some point – and this I remember with dreadful clarity – I pushed aside the blanket over my head for a moment, to see all around me bodies upon bodies, sick and wounded, sitting, lying, squatting; and on the back of our tractor lay the dead, or rather, they did not lie but were stacked, bound on with ropes. Our soldiers would not leave a dead comrade lying in the snow, but would load him up whenever possible. The stack behind us rose from day to day, probably contributing decisively to my survival, because when the Russians fired on us from behind, our dead became a bullet-screen, a protective shield.[43]

Halder's diary entries for these days show an increasingly dysfunctional atmosphere in the German high command. He noted that Brauchitsch, the commander of the army, was increasingly sidelined and reduced to passing on instructions from Hitler; on many occasions, the Führer simply contacted field commanders directly without even the courtesy of informing Brauchitsch, who had suffered a heart attack and was clearly struggling. On the other side of the front line, Stalin was taking steps to improve the performance of his command structures. On 10 December, he summoned several senior officers from the northern sector to Moscow, where he informed them that Fourth, Fifty-Second, Twenty-Sixth, and Fifty-Ninth Armies, currently directly controlled by *Stavka*, were to be grouped together in a new Volkhov Front. Meretskov was named as its commander, a remarkable turnaround for a man who had been arrested on charges of treason and then beaten into signing a confession just a few months before.

Having regrouped his forces, Fedyuninsky made a fresh attack against the western flank of the German I Corps on 15 December, enjoying a rapid success and advancing about 12 miles. At the same time, the northern group of Fourth

Army near Tikhvin had regrouped further west and now threatened the eastern wing of I Corps. Far from attempting to complete the operation to capture Volkhov, the German corps was in serious danger of being enveloped and Both, its commander, had no choice but to order a withdrawal to Kirishi. Two improvised ski battalions had been created by Fedyuninsky and these succeeded in slipping through the German defences and mounted raids in the rear, adding to the atmosphere of dismay and growing confusion.

A bitter German retreat now began, with the Wehrmacht falling back to the Volkhov River from Tikhvin while I Corps pulled back from the city of Volkhov, both German groups leaving a trail of abandoned equipment and frozen corpses behind them – Stahlberg might have been correct that the Germans tried to take their dead with them, but particularly for the infantry it was hard enough for the living to drag themselves through the snow without any additional burden. Fedyuninsky's men were able to reach and cross the railway line from Mga to Kirishi, but as Fifty-Fourth Army came closer to Kirishi its advance slowed rapidly. The Germans were benefiting from withdrawing closer to their supply dumps and were able to mount a far more effective defence; conversely, it was now the Red Army that had to struggle to bring forward supplies.

The sense of desperation that had sometimes gripped *Stavka* during the preceding weeks, as German forces edged closer to Moscow and threatened to isolate Leningrad completely, was replaced by euphoria and a sense of confidence that the worst was past and the Germans faced imminent defeat. This was to result in a series of wasteful, overoptimistic attacks against Army Group Centre, which were defeated in detail by the Wehrmacht. In the north too, as is described below, *Stavka* issued ambitious orders for a major offensive in the second half of December, intended to drive back the Germans from the outskirts of Leningrad and destroy the forces between the city and Lake Ilmen to the south. But even when these attacks, both in the north and elsewhere, failed to deliver all of the expected gains, there was widespread rejoicing in the Red Army. The Germans had been thrown back from Moscow, and their attack over the Volkhov had also been defeated. The counterattacks at Moscow and the defeat of Leeb's thrust to Tikhvin were the first major setbacks experienced by the Wehrmacht since the invasion of Poland in 1939; far from being on its last legs, the Red Army had demonstrated that it was still a formidable opponent and the war in the east was not going to end as quickly as German planners had expected. But the victories in the north came at a high price. In its battles against the German thrust to Tikhvin and the counteroffensive that followed, the Red Army lost 89,000 men, roughly half of all those committed to the fighting. In addition, Fedyuninsky's

Fifty-Fourth Army lost nearly 55,000 men, and there were similar losses in the Neva bridgehead. German casualties came to about 45,000.[44] The weakened state of the German forces can be seen from the example of 12th Panzer Division. It started the campaign against the Soviet Union with a combat strength of 12,338 men and 234 tanks; by the end of the year, despite receiving replacement drafts and – occasionally – new equipment, it could field only 7,243 soldiers in the front line and just 33 tanks. This represented a reduction of 41 per cent of its manpower strength and 86 per cent of its armour.[45]

The failure of the Wehrmacht to achieve total victory over the Soviet Union brought consequences for senior figures in the German Army. The commanders of Army Group Centre's formations suffered a series of dismissals as Hitler vented his wrath on them first for failing to capture Moscow and win the war, and then for retreating without his specific permission. In Army Group North, Leeb – who was now aged 64 – informed Hitler in early January 1942 that he was unable to continue as commander of the army group unless he was given greater freedom to redeploy his forces as he saw fit; this was effectively a criticism of Hitler's insistence that his permission had to be obtained before any territory could be given up, or even for the lateral movement of divisions between corps and armies. In the absence of such permission, Leeb wrote, he would have no choice but to tender his resignation. After a few days, Hitler informed him that he was to be replaced. It was the end of Leeb's career, but Hitler rewarded him with two large country estates. In 1948, he was charged together with other senior officers with responsibility for war crimes that took place within his jurisdiction. His defence was based upon the assertion that he had not passed on any illegal orders, which was patently untrue, and that he had been in no position to overrule such orders. In a closing statement, Leeb spoke on behalf of all the defendants, claiming that he and his colleagues had always followed their soldierly principles, which included the duty to obey orders from their superiors, saying that 'No soldier in all the world has ever yet had to fight under such a load and tragedy.'[46] Because the prosecution was unable to produce any orders signed by him personally, he was found guilty only of permitting the Barbarossa Decree – which permitted military authorities to deal with resistance without any formal legal process – to be passed on to his subordinates. He had been in captivity since the end of the war and was sentenced to time served and was released. He died in 1956. Leeb's replacement in Army Group North was Küchler, who had commanded Eighteenth Army. The post of commander of Eighteenth Army was taken by Generaloberst Georg Lindemann, the commander of L Corps.

After a long series of defeats and setbacks, the Red Army could claim with justification that it ended 1941 in the north with a substantial victory, even though it was gained at a heavy cost. But despite this, Leningrad remained isolated with only the most tenuous connection with the outside world. The German plan to starve the city to death remained a realistic threat, and the resilience of soldiers and civilians alike within the siege perimeter would be stretched to breaking point through the winter.

CHAPTER 7

STARVATION: THE FIRST WINTER

When Zhukov was recalled to Moscow, overall responsibility for Leningrad was passed to Zhdanov, secretary of the Leningrad branch of the Communist Party. Although he had oversight of military matters and played a major role in mobilisation of the city for defence, particularly the raising of militia units, he was also responsible for the civilian administration.

Zhdanov was an early adherent of the Bolsheviks and was a political commissar in the Red Army during the Civil War. He gave the appearance of a cheerful character and rapidly established a reputation as a formidable and hard-working individual; despite little formal education, he diligently and almost obsessively studied anything that was of interest or relevance to his work. He quickly rose through the ranks of the Communist Party and after the assassination of Kirov in 1934 he was appointed as the new Party secretary in the Leningrad region. Immediately, he became involved in Stalin's terrible purges; in 1935 alone, he oversaw the deportation of nearly 12,000 people accused of having aristocratic links or being supporters of Trotsky. He wholeheartedly embraced the purges, seeing them as a means of cleansing Soviet society so that all reactionary traits could be eliminated and he personally signed 176 documents that listed persons to be executed. Amongst those arrested under his orders were senior figures who had themselves been active in the purges, such as Yagoda, the head of the NKVD.[1] When another veteran Bolshevik, Dora Abramovna Lazurkina, complained to him about the arrest of a former mayor of Leningrad, she too was arrested and spent the following 17 years in a prison camp.

Many saw Zhdanov as a likely successor to Stalin and this attracted the enmity of other potential candidates. Once war broke out in June 1941, Malenkov and Beriya ensured that Zhdanov was not made part of the small State Defence

Committee in Moscow; instead, he was left in the increasingly isolated outpost of Leningrad.[2] With characteristic determination, he applied his energies to almost every aspect of the functioning of the city. His office in the Smolny Institute became the centre of painstaking work as he struggled with the task that had been assigned to him, increasingly turning to alcohol as a support as he worked long into the night, reading voraciously on both civil and military matters.

As the war came ever closer to Leningrad, German air activity increased proportionately. At first there had been a few reconnaissance flights and raids, but these were then replaced by heavier attacks as the Luftwaffe began to implement Hitler's plan to bombard the city to rubble – whilst the Luftwaffe lacked the ability to carry out the type of devastating raids that became increasingly common in Germany, it could still do extensive damage by targeting power stations, water pumping facilities, and other key targets. In an attempt to hinder German navigation, many of the prominent buildings in the city had their appearance altered. The great golden dome of St Isaac's Cathedral was painted a dull grey and the statue of Peter the Great on horseback, on the shores of the Neva, was carefully hidden behind wooden panels to protect it from shrapnel. The Smolny Institute, from which Lenin and Trotsky had overseen the October Revolution and which remained the location of much of the Communist Party apparatus, was heavily camouflaged with netting and from the air it resembled parkland – the colour of the camouflage was even altered as the year progressed to simulate the change in foliage. Civilians were employed in large numbers in the manufacture of camouflage netting, including children and even people with poor eyesight. Production facilities were set up in buildings of all sorts, even a disabled railway locomotive and a stranded ship. Some of the nets were also used for fishing in order to supplement the city's food stocks.

In cases where it was impossible to hide the presence of a building, its appearance was often altered by the addition of wooden structures. There was an oval racetrack near the centre of Leningrad that was clearly visible from the air; wooden buildings were erected there to make it look as if the surrounding buildings extended into it seamlessly. In the case of buildings like the Admiralty and the tower of St Nicholas' Cathedral, it was decided that grey paint could not be used to cover the gold leaf as it was too thin and removal of the paint at a later date would inevitably strip off the gold. Instead, tarpaulins were hauled over the gilded roofs. For this task, a special group of 30 people was organised consisting of carefully selected military personnel and civilian volunteers. Five such volunteers, who had been enthusiastic rock-climbers before the war, undertook the most risky tasks. The long, slender spire of the Peter and Paul Fortress was a particularly difficult challenge, with the team of climbers repeatedly ascending it during the hours of darkness, their task made all the more difficult by icy conditions as winter set in. One of the volunteer climbers, Mikhail Boborov, was 18 years old at the time and described the arduous task, worsened by the poor rations that he and everyone else received:

> First we used an inner staircase, carefully moving past the counterweights of the spire's great clock. The steps were encrusted with pigeon shit and above us we could hear the scuttling sounds of the few remaining birds, so weakened by hunger and cold that they could no longer fly. Then we clambered through a hatch on to the outside of the spire and inched upwards, rung by rung, on a small exterior ladder. We were now about 120m above the city.
>
> It was an incredible view. I could see the city below me, engulfed in mounds of uncleared snow, and beyond it the ships of the Baltic Fleet at their moorings, encrusted with ice …
>
> I felt I had used up the last reserves of strength getting up [to the top] and for a few minutes I dangled on the wings of the angel, unable to haul myself any further. Then with a last supreme effort I pushed myself upwards and my hands clasped the cross. I unfastened the ropes behind my back and securely attached myself to the carving …
>
> I paused for a moment, only to hear suddenly the sound of our anti-aircraft guns opening up with their quick, staccato volleys of fire. I turned my head in alarm. Emerging from the clouds was a large formation of German bombers, flying low, and heading straight towards me. The planes were coming in so close I could clearly see the pilots' faces. Then they turned, banked over the city, and began dropping their bombs. The shockwave from the explosions knocked me off the cross but fortunately the knots of my climbing rope held firm and I swung round and round the spire, while all around me shell bursts erupted from our guns. It was a miracle that I stayed unharmed. When the raid ended, another of our climbers managed to haul me to safety.[3]

Two of the volunteer climbers died of starvation during the work on the Peter and Paul fortress; Boborov and the others survived by catching the emaciated pigeons in the spire and eating them.

It was impossible to camouflage all the important buildings, and inevitably many of them attracted the attention of German bombers and artillery. As well as targeting factories, railways, bridges, and other important targets, the bombardment was sometimes less discriminate, intended merely to add to the overall destruction and death toll. The first artillery shells struck the city on 4 September and the intensity of bombardment grew steadily. Even as early as 19 September, city authorities recorded the deaths of 254 civilians from artillery and air attacks, and the wounding of another 1,485.[4] Before long, the German bombers adopted a pattern that was used later in the war by British and American air attacks on German cities: the first wave of bombers dropped high explosives to blow off the roofs of buildings, and the second wave then dropped incendiaries that burned more freely, with the roofless buildings acting as giant chimneys.

The plans that were drawn up before the war for the defence of the Leningrad region included air defence, but like all the plans these were incomplete and in many cases proved impossible to implement – the weapons required were not available. Nevertheless, the anti-aircraft batteries in and around the city steadily increased in number and Zhdanov authorised the creation of *Mestnaia Protivo-Vozduzhnaia Oborona* ('Local Air Defence Forces' or *MPVO*); about a dozen such groups were raised with 700 civilians in each. At first they were given the task of observers both to help detect incoming raids and to report on damage; small groups took up positions on rooftops every night with buckets of sand, ready to try to extinguish any incendiary bombs that the Germans might drop. Later in the siege, many of these groups provided crew for the increased number of anti-aircraft batteries manning both guns and searchlights. The command arrangements of the air defences were improved and barges carrying guns were deployed off the coast to fire on German aircraft approaching from the west. As the intensity of anti-aircraft fire increased, German bombers took to dropping their bombs from higher altitudes. This reduced accuracy, but by this stage the raids were conducted largely to destroy sectors of the city rather than at specific targets, in an attempt to comply with Hitler's orders for the city to be destroyed by bombing and shelling.

Yura Riabinkin was aged 16 when the war with Germany began and kept a diary until early January 1942. He had hoped to be able to join the Naval Academy but he had poor eyesight and had suffered from tuberculosis as a child, so this was always an unlikely ambition. Instead, he was given part-time work escorting patients who were being transferred from one hospital to another whilst also still attending school. It paid a very small amount of money, but it gave him access to the hospital canteens where he could get an occasional meal. Together with a school friend, he also served his turn on the rooftops, watching for incendiaries. In mid-October 1941, he was on watch for incendiary bombs:

The night was generally peaceful and Dodya and I went up on the roof. No sooner had we started to look around when searchlights appeared in the sky and, without any warning whatever, we heard a bomb whistling down, getting louder and louder. In less time than it takes to tell, Dodya and I plunged back into the attic, not caring if we hurt ourselves in the process. We decided that it would be dangerous for us to stay in the attic so we headed down the stairs, and just at that very moment there was a brief whistling sound followed by explosions above our heads. It suddenly became brighter than day. Dodya realised what it meant before me and, grabbing a shovel, hurried to deal with an incendiary bomb. I followed. It became a mad race against time. We worked in thick, choking smoke that irritated our throats and penetrated into our lungs; sweat poured from our faces but we kept on dealing with the bombs. I ran to the first observation post. There was a woman standing there, shouting in a terrified voice, 'A bomb! Put it out!' She scraped up sand in her bare hands and threw it onto the burning fragments of thermite. I grabbed a shovel and in just a few seconds had smothered all the burning fragments with sand.[5]

In order to try to counter artillery fire, long-range guns were formed into counter-battery groups. Voronov, who in addition to being deputy defence minister was also commander-in-chief of the Red Army's artillery, flew into the city in the autumn to oversee such measures. Although these batteries were able to inflict some losses on the Germans they couldn't suppress all the shelling, and other measures were taken to protect civilians. Signs appeared on some of the city streets warning people of the likely direction from which shells would fall. One such sign has been preserved on Nevsky Prospekt. Stencilled on the wall of a building that was at the time a school, its message is simple: 'Citizens: During German shelling, the other side of the road is safer.'

Zhdanov and his party organisation had to work to protect more than just the civilian population: the industrial production of Leningrad was vital for the continuing defence of the city. German artillery concentrated on factories as priority targets, inflicting considerable casualties amongst the workers as well as destroying industrial machinery. Despite this, production of vital equipment continued. The Kirov works, formerly the Putilov factories, managed to complete nearly 500 tanks before the end of 1941; most of these drove straight from the factory to the front line, arriving without having had any time for gunsights to be aligned properly. In addition, over 300 artillery pieces were manufactured together with thousands of mortars and small arms and huge quantities of ammunition.[6] Commencing in August, Zhdanov began the task of moving some of Leningrad's factory equipment east as part of the general redeployment of Soviet industry to regions safe from German advances and even after the advancing Wehrmacht closed land routes, evacuation of both equipment and essential factory workers continued by barges over Lake Ladoga. Such activity finally came to a halt when the Germans captured Shlisselburg; a large quantity of factory equipment, scheduled for evacuation, was left stranded between Leningrad and the shores of Lake Ladoga. Many of the technicians for these factories were evacuated by air and laboured to reassemble their equipment in primitive conditions. Several improvised factories went into production before they were even housed properly, with workers labouring under open skies in roofless buildings through the bitterly cold winter months.

There was also an evacuation of children from Leningrad, which in the first weeks of the war emulated the British policy of removing children from cities that might come under air attack. Several trainloads left but at that time it was still believed that the Germans would be halted a considerable distance from Leningrad and the intention was simply to move the children from being close to potential bombing targets. There were few suitable towns for the evacuees to the east and as a result a large number of children were transferred to the towns to the south of Leningrad, which would become battlegrounds as the Germans threatened the Luga Line and pushed to the east past the southern tip of Lake Ilmen. In the town of Lychkovo, about 30 miles to the southeast of Lake Ilmen, one such train arrived on 18 July carrying children and a group of their schoolteachers who were acting as escorts (some accounts give the date as 18 August, which would probably be more in keeping with the military situation, but the memorial in Lychkovo records the earlier date). As they waited to disembark, the occupants of the train became aware of approaching aircraft. Ivan Fedulov was one of the children and had just stepped onto the railway platform:

> Suddenly I heard a terrible cry. Someone was shouting, 'Bombers! Bombers!' A plane flew right over us – and along the train – dropping bomb after bomb, with terrifying, methodical precision. There was a huge explosion, and when the smoke cleared carriages were scattered everywhere, as if they had been knocked off the tracks by a giant hand …
>
> A plane circled and came back. Then it began machine-gunning the fleeing children. It was flying so low that I could clearly see the pilot's face – totally impassive.[7]

Many believed that the bombing was a deliberate and callous attack on children, saying that the planes were so low that they must have been able to see that their victims were not adults. The aircraft are not identified accurately. If they were

Stuka dive-bombers, they would have commenced their attack from an altitude at which individual people would have been little more than specks on the ground; if they were conventional bombers, they would have passed at a speed that was too great for accurate identification of the ages of the train passengers. Whilst some aircraft may have swept back to machine-gun the survivors of the bombing, it seems unlikely that many of the pilots would have spotted the ages of the few passengers who had succeeded in disembarking before the raid. Nonetheless, even if they had been aware, it is perfectly possible that the pilots would have attacked anyway – they had been told that this was a war of extermination and that they were to show no mercy and Luftwaffe pilots repeatedly machine-gunned columns of civilian refugees in almost every theatre of the Second World War. The mass grave in Lychkovo records that the remains of over 2,000 children and adults are buried there.

As the Germans moved closer to Leningrad, many of the children who had been evacuated to the towns to the south returned to the city. The early evacuations had been haphazard, but more organised attempts were made from mid-August and there was also a plan to remove as many non-essential people as possible from the city. Many of the city's institutions, such as the orchestras and film studios, were granted spaces on trains so that their members and their families could leave and as the German advance severed rail links to the south and east, these trains became far fewer. Shostakovich, his wife and two children were still in the city; the composer had started work on a new symphony and was reluctant to leave, but was pressured by his wife Nina into agreeing to depart for the distant town of Alma Ata, where Shostakovich's sister Mariya had briefly been exiled as a consequence of the purges of earlier years. Unfortunately, they left it too late. A train carrying a large number of children passed through Mga on 25 August, even as German forces attacked the town. When the railway line was cut, further evacuations overland became impossible.

Outside the siege perimeter, the Germans were making fresh arrangements for the continuation of the siege. Reconciled to not crowning the campaign with the physical capture of Leningrad, Leeb looked at the practicalities of how to implement the orders to starve the city to death. One matter that seems to have concerned him was the possible effect on his soldiers of having to deal with starving refugees attempting to escape from the city. Orders passed down to front-line units made clear that if civilians tried to flee, they were to be shot. But in a meeting in late October many division commanders expressed doubts that their soldiers would be willing to fire repeatedly on women and children. One suggestion to deal with such an eventuality was to lay dense minefields in front of German positions, but after a visit to the massed artillery batteries that were drawn up around the southern edge of Leningrad, Leeb chose an additional measure:

> [Leeb] visited several firing positions of heavy and light artillery batteries. After inspecting winter quarters and the newly constructed gun emplacements, he had discussions with unit and battery commanders about the use of artillery to prevent the Russian civilian population breaking out from Leningrad. In accordance with Army Order 2737, such attempts are to be prevented, if necessary by the use of arms. The artillery is required to deal with such a situation as far forward of our front lines as possible, preferably opening fire on civilians at an early state so that the infantry is spared the task of having to shoot the civilians themselves.[8]

The reaction of ordinary German soldiers to the instructions that they received is difficult to assess. Throughout the preparations for *Barbarossa* and as the campaign unfolded, the unique nature of this conflict had repeatedly been stressed, and in early October Generalfeldmarschall Walter von Reichenau, commander of Sixth Army in Ukraine, issued a reminder to his men – Hitler promptly ordered all army commanders to reissue this 'Severity Order' in their own words. The text of the order shows the ongoing demonization of Jews and the Bolsheviks:

> With regard to the conduct of troops towards the Bolshevik system, there is still a lack of clarity in many cases.
>
> The main goal of the campaign against the Jewish-Bolshevik system is the complete destruction of the means of power and eradication of Asiatic influence on European culture.
>
> This also creates tasks for the troops that go beyond traditional soldiering. The soldier on the Eastern Front is not only a fighter according to the rules of the art of war, but also the bearer of an irresistible racial view and the avenger for all the bestialities that were inflicted on German and related people.
>
> Therefore the soldier must have full understanding of the need for harsh but just punishment of Jewish subhumanity. This has the additional purpose of nipping in the bud any uprisings in the rear of the Wehrmacht, which experience has shown were always instigated by Jews.
>
> The fight against the enemy behind the front line is not taken seriously enough. Insidious, cruel partisans and degenerate women are still being made prisoners of war and semi-uniformed or civilian-clad snipers and stragglers are still being treated like decent soldiers and taken to prison camps. Indeed, captured

Russian officers sneeringly state that Soviet agents move through the streets unmolested and often eat at German field kitchens. Such behaviour by the troops can only be explained by complete thoughtlessness. But it is now time for superiors to awaken awareness of the nature of the current struggle.

Feeding local residents and prisoners of war who are not in the service of the Wehrmacht in military kitchens is just as much a misunderstood act of humanity as giving away cigarettes and bread. What the homeland lacks and has renounced, what the high command brings forward with great difficulty, the soldier should not give away to the enemy, not even if it is actually booty …

The soldier has two tasks:

1. The complete annihilation of the Bolshevik heresy, the Soviet state and its armed forces;
2. The merciless extermination of alien malice and cruelty, thus safeguarding the lives of German Wehrmacht personnel in Russia.

Only in this manner can we do justice to our historical task of liberating the German people once and for all from the Asia-Jewish danger.[9]

It should be remembered that the men in the front line were from a generation that had grown up in the 1930s, constantly immersed in the rhetoric of the Nazi Party. In their memoirs written after the war, some like Wilhelm Lubbeck recorded that they were uneasy about what was expected of them:

There was real concern that the Russian authorities might decide to send the city's women and children across the lines to our side. It was not clear what would ensue in such a situation, but everyone agreed that mowing down a crowd of civilians with our weapons was inconceivable. My own inclination was to feed them and then send them further back, once we made certain that the enemy had not exploited such a population transfer to slip military-age males into our rear areas.[10]

It isn't clear how many others shared Lubbeck's views, or how accurately he recalled them – as an artillery observer, he would almost certainly have been aware of the orders relating to shelling any such escaping civilians as far from German lines as possible, and his intention to feed any refugees would have been in direct contravention of the Severity Order. Other gunners recalled a rather different attitude from Lubbeck. They described how they received large quantities of ammunition and that they were aware that they were firing on residential areas rather than at military targets. Some took a particularly callous attitude: 'Our soldiers, who were firing on the city, would say, "Today we are feeding Leningrad again. They should be grateful to us – they have a famine there, after all."[11]

The evacuation of Soviet specialists and casualties from German bombing and shelling had a significant detrimental effect on the ability of the remaining factories to produce materiel for the city's defenders, but another factor had an even greater impact. A total of over 3 million people – soldiers and civilians combined – were trapped within the Leningrad siege perimeter, and food stocks rapidly came under pressure. In the last week of September, it was estimated that warehouses across Leningrad held about 35,000 tons of flour. Daily consumption was about 1,100 tons, which would deplete the stockpile in about a month, and it was essential for more food to be brought in. After the German advance cut land routes to Leningrad, there were only two remaining options: by air or across the waters of Lake Ladoga. The ability of Soviet air units to carry large cargoes was very limited and in the second half of November, the total that was delivered amounted to about a day's requirements in normal conditions.[12] By the end of the year, the total amount of cargo brought into the city by air came to a little under 6,200 tons, of which about 4,300 tons was food. Supplies delivered by boats and barges on Lake Ladoga were rather more significant. The shipments got off to a slow start, with only seven barges carrying goods to the encirclement in the first week of September.

This flow of goods had to be increased. In addition, it was clearly essential to organise a proper rationing system if the population was to survive and Hitler's plan to starve Leningrad to death was to be thwarted. The first rationing coupons were issued in August but the administration of rationing was inefficient, with many different agencies issuing their own coupons, resulting in endless wrangling. Dmitry Vasilyevich Pavlov was a member of the Soviet Food Commissariat and he was dispatched to Leningrad on 8 September to take control. He had to squeeze into a cargo plane that approached the city across Lake Ladoga with a small group of aircraft, discovering that regardless of the challenges of his new post, merely reaching Leningrad was a challenge in itself:

> We settled down among the heavy boxes. Soon all six aircraft were airborne. They were armed with machine-guns and covered each other, flying at a low level just above the water. Such tactics reduced the risk of attack from the Messerschmitts watching for solitary planes over the lake. Groups of aircraft could concentrate their fire and the enemy was less likely to attack them.
>
> The aircraft commander, a senior lieutenant, invited me to the cockpit. From there we could see clearly two other aircraft to right and left a short distance away,

identical to ours. A similar formation was behind us. Each carried a little more than two tons of cargo, the weight limit of the Li-2 aircraft [Lisunov Li-2, a license-built version of the American DC-3].

'How many flights do you make a day?' I asked.

'Two,' replied the pilot.

'Are you tired?'

'Of course, but we're really pleased when we make three flights – our cargo helps the defenders.' ...

Soon, in the haze of a sunny morning, Leningrad appeared. We landed at the main airfield.[13]

Pavlov's first task was to assess the quantity of food in Leningrad, and over the first two days in the city he and party officials carried out a wide-ranging survey and registration. To his relief, he found that stockpiles were a little better than he had first believed – in addition to there being sufficient grain for flour for about a month, there were similar reserves of other cereals and meat, and slightly larger quantities of fats and sugar. Before the siege began, a trainload of food had been sent to Leningrad, but Voroshilov and Zhdanov decided that it wasn't required and diverted it elsewhere and this was later cited as further evidence of Voroshilov's incompetence. Although any such shipment would have been welcome once the siege began, its importance is probably overstated – given the size of the population within the siege perimeter, a single trainload would perhaps have been sufficient for just a day or two of consumption. Similarly, the loss of the food stored in the destruction of the Badayev warehouses had little overall impact on the supply of food.

Aware that replenishment of these stocks was impossible, Pavlov immediately imposed rationing with priority given to industrial workers. Other employees and children received a second level of rations, and dependants were given the smallest quantity. In order to extend stocks, bread would now be made with a blend of wheat, soya, oats, and malt – later, industrial cellulose was also added. Even the modest quantities specified in this set of instructions had to be scaled down several times. By the last week of November, for example, the daily bread ration for children, originally set at 300g, had been reduced to 125g. The quantity was the same for all children, regardless of age – it was therefore quite adequate for younger children, but those on the verge of adolescence were significantly underfed, as were all adults other than those who received the highest ration allocation. The reduced rations amounted to about a quarter of the calories required to avoid weight loss, and the search for extra food became an increasingly time-consuming exercise. And as is almost always the case, there were numerous cases of clearly corrupt practice. It soon became widely known that senior Communist Party figures and their families were able to secure larger supplies than anyone else. Yura Riabinkin, who continued to go to school, helped patients move from hospital to hospital, and watched for incendiary bombs at night, suffered a faster decline than his mother and sister, even though he was pilfering some of their rations to augment his own – it seems likely that his tuberculosis had become active again and contributed to his deterioration. His neighbour, Anfisa Nikolayevna, seemed to have no difficulty procuring as much food as she wished, largely due to her husband's contacts. Riabinkin recorded in his diary at the end of October:

> I have become so weak now that I can hardly make my legs obey me and even climbing the stairs seems like a huge effort for me ... I don't know if I can continue with my studies. A couple of days ago I wanted to do some of my algebra, but I couldn't think of the formulae, my head just had loaves of bread in it ...
>
> But what offends me most of all, what is unquestionably the worst thing for me, is that I am here, living in hunger and cold amongst fleas, and next door there is a room where life is completely different, where there is always bread, porridge, meat, sweets, warmth, a bright Estonian oil lamp, and comfort. What I feel when I think about Anfisa Nikolayevna is called envy, but I can't suppress it.[14]

One officer involved in food distribution later described how he had to organise a small fleet of trucks to transport ten tons of rice, 15 tons of flour, two tons of caviar, five tons of butter, more than 200 smoked hams, and numerous other items from the main airfield to the Smolny Institute, where they were presumably shared by Zhdanov and other senior figures.[15] It wasn't just the elite in the Smolny Institute who had preferential status – it applied to Communist Party members throughout the city. At the end of the siege, figures showed that the death rate amongst Party members had been about 15 per cent, half that of the general population.[16]

The introduction of a rigid rationing system was merely one step: people still had to collect their rations, and waited with varying degrees of patience in long queues in the streets. Cold weather made the wait more of an ordeal, but perhaps a greater problem was German shelling. Taking cover meant losing a place in the queue, but staying in line risked death or injury. At first, the authorities tried to impose a rule that shops closed during shelling, but this was rapidly abandoned. Some parts of Leningrad introduced locally devised schemes whereby everyone in the queue received a ticket with a number and could then go home and return at a later time, but this often resulted in bitter arguments when different agencies tried to implement their own ticket systems. Occasionally, the arguments turned violent, but this was tempered by the growing exhaustion of the population. Those waiting in line chatted about the same few subjects: food; the cold; and their personal tragedies. Nevertheless, police and NKVD records show that there were 325 arrests during January 1942 for violence related to food. Some of those arrested included policemen.[17] In order to try to improve law enforcement in the city, police officers were transferred to Leningrad from Moscow towards the end of the winter. Most thefts were opportunistic and the items stolen showed the growing desperation of people on the edge of death. One man seized a dog from a neighbour, killed it, and skinned it; when his neighbours remonstrated with him, he stubbornly replied that he would not give up his prey, rejecting their argument that nobody else had behaved like this with the words, 'Now, anything is possible.'[18]

As supplies began to run out, Zhdanov and his team were forced into increasingly desperate steps. They discovered a stock of 4,000 tons of cotton and asked their scientific advisers whether these were edible. They were told that cotton contains a phenolic compound, gossypol, which is poisonous to mammals, damaging the immune and reproductive systems, but the chemical was not heat-stable. Reasoning that the high temperature of baking would be sufficient to render the gossypol harmless, Zhdanov authorised the use of the cotton stockpile to make bread supplies last longer.[19] Even the dust in flour-mills and bakeries was swept up on the grounds that it contained quantities of flour, and was added to the mix. Despite these measures and the prioritisation of supplies for essential workers, factories began to report that increasing numbers of workers were absent because they were too weak to continue working.

With the city now dependent largely on food being brought across Lake Ladoga, Pavlov turned his attention to the point where the vessels were being unloaded. The small village of Osinovets was marked by a lighthouse and little else:

There were no piers, and in any case the shore sloped gently and ships couldn't come close to land, and there were some rocky reefs. But there was no better point and I had to manage with what we had. Construction of the port began in early September but was not done with the alacrity that the situation required. To build a port and to unload vessels in the shortest possible time, to protect personnel, cargo, and piers from enemy aircraft – this required an outstanding leader, a strong-willed person of character with good organisational skills. On 19 September the Front Military Council entrusted Admiral [Ivan Stepanovich] Isakov with overall authority over the work at Osinovets ...

Isakov willingly took up the task of port construction. Under his supervision, workers deepened the shoreline of Lake Ladoga and built moorings on the deserted banks ... Thousands of people worked hard to restore decommissioned vessels. Everything that could float was mended and used to transport goods.[20]

A second harbour was created about two miles further north, and finally a third was established at Morye. During October and November, 45,000 tons of food reached the city across the lake despite repeated and worsening storms, together with over 6,000 tons of ammunition and a similar quantity of fuel. In one particularly stormy spell in mid-September, 12 barges were wrecked on the coastline at Osinovets. Air attacks were frequent. One barge was left adrift as a result of stormy weather and then endured repeated German attacks for three days; Valentin Ivanovich Antoshikhin, the captain, ordered the small crew to partially flood the hold so that the barge would be barely afloat and had timber strewn across the deck to make it look as if it had been severely damaged. After deciding that the barge was about to sink, the Germans directed their air attacks elsewhere and Antoshikhin and his crew successfully managed to reach the western shore. Another barge was driven aground by artillery fire; one of its crew, Tatyana Shubina, improvised a raft and managed to reach safety. She returned the following night aboard a tug that was able to recover the barge.[21]

In addition to the official efforts to bring in food, smaller but still useful quantities reached Leningrad from the civilian population of neighbouring areas. Despite the efforts of the Wehrmacht to seal off the city, local people made their way through the frozen swamps and along streams and small rivers, slipping past German patrols and positions. This food was often traded on the burgeoning black market as Leningrad's population used any assets to try to buy extra supplies. The quantity of food smuggled through German lines varied greatly, but in late January 1942 about 300 tons of food managed to reach the city by this route over three days.[22]

Despite all of the endeavours of Pavlov and others, food supplies came under increasing pressure. Aware that civilians were suffering severe shortages, the soldiers of Fifty-Fourth Army passed a resolution that they would donate a proportion of their rations to help out. Whilst this gesture of solidarity was helpful, its value was probably greater in terms of morale and propaganda than nutrition. The morale of both soldiers and civilians was an important concern for the city authorities. Shostakovich had spent much of the period of Stalin's purges in disgrace after the Soviet leader criticised his Fourth Symphony, but when they learned that he was working on a new symphony the authorities asked him to speak about it on Leningrad Radio. On 17 September, he left his home to walk to the radio studios; he was forced to take cover en route when a German air raid struck but managed to reach his destination safely and on time. He then told those listening:

> If I manage to write well, if I manage to finish the third and fourth movements, the work may be called my Seventh Symphony ...
>
> Why am I telling you this? I'm telling you this so that the people of Leningrad listening to me will know that life goes on in our city. All of us now are standing military watch. As a native of Leningrad who has never abandoned the city of my birth, I feel all the tension of this situation most keenly. My life and work are completely bound up with Leningrad ...
>
> At the moment the work is going quickly and easily. My ideas are clear and constructive. The composition is nearing completion. Then I shall come on the air again with my new work and wait anxiously for a fair and kindly appraisal of my efforts.
>
> Leningrad is my country. It is my native city and my home. Many thousands of other people from Leningrad know this same feeling of infinite love for our native town, for its wonderful, spacious streets, its incomparably beautiful squares and buildings. When I walk through our city a feeling of deep conviction grows within me that Leningrad will always stand, grand and beautiful, on the banks of the Neva, that it will always be a bastion of my country, that it will always be there to enrich the fruits of culture.[23]

For those who sat in homes damaged by German bombardment or who faced the universal worry of finding sufficient food, the words of Shostakovich – well known in his native Leningrad, throughout the Soviet Union, and indeed across the world – painted a picture of better times, when their city was not scarred by the craters left by shells and bombs. Whilst Leningrad had always been beautiful, it had also been a place of darkness with the constant fear of arrest or denunciation, but the portrait that Shostakovich painted with his words was what the people needed to give them hope. He returned to the apartment where he and his family lived and continued to work on the symphony, stopping only when air raids took place; the original score that he wrote records these moments, when he wrote the abbreviation 'VT' in the margin: *vozshushnaya trevoga*, or 'air raid'.

Other artists were also contributing to the efforts to boost morale. Olga Berggolts was another native of Leningrad and was one of many 'intellectuals' who were arrested in 1937; in her case, it was because her husband, Boris Kornilov, was detained. Kornilov was sentenced to death and executed in 1938. Berggolts was badly beaten by her interrogators and suffered a miscarriage while being questioned. After seven months in prison she was released, but despite these appalling experiences she joined the Communist Party in 1940 and then joined the team at Leningrad Radio House when the war began. With characteristic fearlessness – she had refused to sign any confessions during her imprisonment or to denounce anyone else – she told listeners about the realities of the siege, reading out some of her poems. One such piece was entitled *The February Diary*:

> It was a day like any other.
> A woman friend of mine called round.
> Without a tear she told me she'd
> Just buried her one true friend.
> We sat in silence till the morning.
> What words were there to say to her?
> I'm a Leningrad widow too …
> We already cannot describe our sufferings,
> No measure, no name, no comparison.
> But we are at the end of the thorny path,
> And we know that the day of liberation is near.[24]

After the death of Kornilov and her release from prison, Berggolts had married Nikolai Molchanov, a journalist and literary critic. He was one of thousands who died from starvation during the first winter of the siege.

Leningrad Radio became a source of solace for many Leningraders during the siege, and its broadcasts were repeated across the Soviet Union. When there were no live broadcasts, the radio played the sound of a metronome, symbolic of the still-beating heart of the city. As the winter progressed, the number of live broadcasts diminished and Zhdanov complained that the few speeches that were being transmitted were uninspiring, and the metronome had become a dull and depressing sound – surely it was possible for music to be played? But by this stage, the few professional musicians left in Leningrad were suffering from starvation.

Olga Fedorovna Khuze, a teacher and librarian in Leningrad, recorded her experiences in her diary and documented the decline in mood of much of the population as hardships worsened. On 29 November, she wrote that an acquaintance had prepared dog soup, but she wasn't desperate enough to sample some. People had started eating cats a week before, and in just a few days this had become unremarkable. She grew increasingly impatient of government broadcasts, and wrote on 20 December:

> The way Leningrad lives now is astonishing ... Of course, we need to hold our heads up, but we should speak the naked, harsh truth ... It is more worthy than hiding behind omissions and evasions. I will never forget how skilfully the wording about the abandonment of Odessa was veiled – outwardly everything seemed to be fine, but then a few days later they made an announcement about a monstrous pogrom against the Jews. Sometimes I think wistfully that the suave radio broadcasts about exploits at the front are created deftly by the professional efforts of literary scholars. They all sound the same and the enemy is depicted in a simplified, vulgar manner, either a beast or stupid Hans ... In our broadcasts, only the Germans freeze – our men are warm. The Germans are starving – our men are full to satiety, the Germans take losses but we have no casualties. But after all, we the listeners are adults and know that our men fall every hour, and we need to talk seriously about it with dignity ... The happiness of future generations will be bought with the blood and death of entire generations now involved in the war. May this never be forgotten.[25]

Lyudmila Andreyevna Kulakova was nine years old when the siege began and lived with her parents and her brother in a large communal apartment in the Petrogradsky district of Leningrad, just to the north of the small island where the Peter and Paul Fortress stands. Her father was in the Baltic Fleet and her mother worked in a factory producing bandages, so she at least received the full ration allotted to an essential worker:

> Our mother divided the entire bread ration equally into three and we ate it twice a day. Everything that could be eaten was used as food. My brother brought frozen sparrows from the street, and there were so few of them. We even ate wood glue.
>
> The Badayev warehouses burned down in the first days [of the siege]. My brother brought sweet earth from there, it was like peat. And we ate it. Once, my dad brought a cat and it never occurred to us to refuse it. We were so hungry that

it seemed very tasty to us. My mother's friend had a cat, Muzha, so my mother went to her and asked her for Muzha for us, the hungry children. We ate it too … Leningraders ate not only cats and dogs, but everything that was more or less edible.[26]

The food stocks in the city declined at an alarming rate, and the first deaths from starvation were recorded at the end of September. The numbers of such deaths climbed in a terrifying manner; the total number of deaths in December from all causes, though primarily from starvation, exceeded the total deaths for all of 1940, with over 4,000 starvation deaths per day. Increasingly desperate to find food, the population resorted to drastic measures. Household pets simply disappeared. Wallpaper glue was found to have slight nutritional value and families peeled their walls and scraped and licked at the dried paste. Similarly, wood glue was derived from boiling bones to extract gelatine, and people dismantled their furniture so that they could scrape off the glue and try to use it to create soup. Amongst those who suffered the worst were individuals who were caught on the cusp between two categories for rations. Teenagers who worked in factories or technical training schools laboured up to 11 hours a day, as much as adult factory workers, but received the same rations as dependants. One report estimated that out of 200,000 such teenage workers, 190,000 died during the siege, the main cause of death being starvation.[27]

Those who were recruited into labour battalions could look forward to marginally better rations, but the price they paid was twofold. Firstly, the act of labour consumed energy, more than offsetting the modest increase in calorific intake. Secondly, they were sometimes exposed to the risk of air raids. Valentina Ilyinishna Bushuyeva worked unloading timber from barges on Lake Ladoga and experienced several air raids. She was aboard a barge when one raid took place:

A bomb hit a motor-launch and a bollard flew at us … Pieces of this bollard and logs were flying at us. There were usually many boats there … and as soon as there was an air raid alert, they would quickly go out onto the lake. This boat for some reason stayed behind. And a log, a two-metre log, broke through the deck and hit a sergeant in the belly. He lived for 40 minutes after that, died when they were carrying him on a stretcher … And then the barge started sinking. We got frightened and rushed up. I don't even know how I did it, but I simply leaped onto the pier … When the air raid was over, we still had 40 minutes to go on our shift. The commander of our battalion, Mankevich, came and ordered: 'Back to work!' We were in such a state … But what could we do? We went back to work.[28]

For Yura Riabinkin, there was a small improvement: it seemed that his well-connected neighbours believed that they would soon be able to secure safe passage out of Leningrad and Anfisa Nikolayevna began to give some of her food to the Riabinkin family. She was to be disappointed – after several occasions when she told everyone that her evacuation was imminent, she found herself stuck in Leningrad for most of the winter. Riabinkin's mother also applied for evacuation, but as she had no specialist skills she would simply have to wait her turn. Later in the winter, she even contemplated trying to walk to safety across Lake Ladoga. Such an attempt would have been extremely difficult for someone who was fit and healthy – for a woman suffering from malnutrition with the 16-year-old Yura and his eight-year-old sister in a similar state, it would have amounted to suicide.

Some of the animals in Leningrad Zoo were slaughtered and eaten. Betty the elephant, a pre-war favourite in the zoo, was killed in a German air raid in early September and other animals died later as a result of both bombardment and starvation. Remarkably, a decision was made at the highest level to continue keeping many of the zoo animals alive; this may have been influenced by the fact that if the zoo closed, its director (a prominent member of the local Communist Party) and his workers would no longer have been classified as essential workers and would have been given reduced rations. Extraordinary steps were taken to feed the animals. There were several tiger cubs and it was increasingly difficult to find meat for them, but the zoo staff found a stock of rabbit skins and stuffed them with a mixture of husk, oilcake, and vegetable oil, flavoured with fish oil. The zoo was also home to a hippopotamus named Krasavitsa ('Beauty'), and to keep her alive the zoo had to provide at least 77 pounds of food every day. Her personal attendant, Yevdokiya Ivanovna, spent much of her time with the hippo, attempting to comfort it during German air attacks. A baby monkey that was born in November was in danger of dying due to hunger but a local maternity hospital agreed to provide half a litre of human milk every day. The uplifting effect of such measures on morale must be set against the cost: the food consumed by the animals, particularly the breast milk donated by the maternity hospital, could have helped keep human beings alive.

During October, many barges had to make the crossing with reduced cargoes to avoid being swamped by the increasingly rough water. After waiting either in the improvised berths or a short distance offshore – the lack of proper dock facilities meant that it took up to a week for a barge to be unloaded after it arrived, during which time it was constantly at risk of air attack – the vessels set off on their journey to the east, taking with them evacuees from the siege perimeter. These were a mixture of technical staff and wounded and sick soldiers and civilians. Again, they risked stormy waters and attracted the attention of the Luftwaffe. A barge carrying 300 evacuees was wrecked by a storm on 17 September resulting in the deaths of over half those aboard. On 4 November, two patrols ships, *Konstruktor* and *Purga*, left Osinovets with a large number of women and children aboard. Shortly after they sailed, they came under air attack. The first attack failed to inflict significant damage but the German aircraft returned for a second strike. A bomb struck *Purga* and blew off part of her bow. Just in time, the gunboat *Dora*, which had been involved in the rescue of the occupants of another stricken barge just a few days earlier, arrived and took *Purga* in tow, pulling the wrecked vessel backwards. Two more ships joined the rescue attempt and *Purga* was brought back to the western shore. The attacks on *Purga* and *Konstruktor* killed about 200 of those aboard, and the survivors found themselves back in the encircled city.[29]

Meanwhile, Pavlov continued his efforts to improve the trickle of supplies reaching the city. To date, aircraft flying food across Lake Ladoga had brought complete animal carcasses, but this meant that they were usually physically full before their cargo limit had been reached. Switching to pre-butchered meat increased the amount of meat carried by each plane by over a quarter.[30] Changes were made to speed up turnaround at each end of the air bridge, permitting planes to make three round trips per day; encouraged to compete against each other, some pilots routinely managed four flights, occasionally more if the weather was favourable. Most of the flights out of Leningrad, like the vessels on the shuttle across Lake Ladoga, took evacuees with them. These refugees might face a long rail journey to their ultimate destinations, but at least they received improved food supplies. Their removal from within the city also meant that there were fewer mouths to feed.

In November, the worsening weather brought even worse storms to Lake Ladoga, exacerbating matters still further, and the plummeting temperatures resulted in the lake beginning to freeze on 10 November. With starvation growing worse and the stockpiles in the city almost exhausted, Pavlov had a meeting with Major General Feofan Nikolayevich Lagunov, the chief of the rear services of Leningrad Front, and Major General Mitrofan Ivanovich Moskalenko, who held a similar post for the Baltic Fleet. With their agreement, the Military Council was asked to release food reserves held by the army and navy. Faced with reducing civilian rations even further if no food was released by the military, Zhdanov approved the suggestion. The impact of this measure was probably modest; there were nearly 53,000 deaths from starvation during December.[31]

The increasing ice and bad weather made it harder for ships and barges to continue ferrying supplies across Lake Ladoga, though such shipments continued in small numbers until early December, but preparations to exploit the ice sheet began even before the lake froze. In early November, *Stavka* issued instructions for preparations to be made for the construction of a road across the ice, and on 19 November Leningrad Front ordered the creation of *Voenno-Avtomobilnaia Doroga 101* ('Military Vehicle Road 101' or *VAD 101*). Colonel Vasily Georgiyevich Monakhov, an engineering officer, was put in charge of the task. The road was to run from Kobona in the east to Vaganovo in the west, across a small section of Lake Ladoga, via a small cluster of islands. This would result in a crossing covering about 18 miles. However, this was a far from ideal solution. Kobona lies to the west of Volkhov, which was threatened by the advance of Eighteenth Army through the late autumn and early winter, and supplies would have to be brought on a railway line that ran through both Tikhvin and Volkhov – at the time, Tikhvin was still in German hands. Accordingly, construction of a second road was ordered – *VAD 102*, running across frozen marshland to the north of Tikhvin and permitting supplies to be transferred until the town was recaptured. A further problem was that the planned route of *VAD 101* would be within range of German guns on the southern shore of Lake Ladoga – the only way to avoid this was to construct a longer road further offshore, but the lake froze from the shore outwards, and the ice was therefore thicker closer to the shore. Moving the route of the road would thus require construction to be delayed.

The Russians had experience of building routes over frozen waterways. From 1892 to 1913, a single-track railway was constructed over the Volga River every winter near the city of Kazan; another railway line was built over the Volga at Saratov during the same era, where the river was rather wider. This experience meant that engineers had an understanding of the thickness of ice required for such activity to be possible. Nonetheless, the Ladoga crossing would be on a completely different scale from anything that had been attempted before. Hastily, data was gathered on ice formation and average thickness on the lake. There were concerns that the heavy ChTZ tractors in widespread use – weighing nearly ten tons – would be unusable. Wooden reinforcement of the ice would be necessary. Several different proposals – alternative routes, or using a mixture of rail and wheeled transport – were considered. Finally, a decision was made: the road would be at least 10m wide, and would be used for motor vehicles and tractor-drawn loads.

The route across Lake Ladoga soon became known, justifiably, as the *Doroga Zhizni* ('Road of Life'). At first, the lake was incompletely frozen and the route had to detour around areas of water. The ice had to be at least eight inches thick to support the weight of a loaded truck. The first attempt to cross took place on 16 November when seven vehicles set off from the east bank of the lake. Cautiously, the column passed the Zelentsy Islands, about a third of the way across the lake, but after travelling most of the way to the west shore they encountered thin ice and had to stop. Eventually, they unloaded their cargo of flour on the ice and turned back, leaving the sacks in a pile to be recovered at a later date.

The following day, teams set off from the west bank to try to find a safe route. One group turned back after reaching a point roughly half way to the east bank after encountering open water, but a second group managed to find a way across, reaching Kobona a day after setting out from the west bank. On 19 November, they retraced their footsteps and returned to their start point. They were disappointed to discover that whilst they had been walking across the lake, a major had succeeded in riding on horseback across the ice, claiming the first crossing.[32] After the reports from the various groups who had ventured onto the lake had been assessed, the decision was made to commence operations to transport supplies from Kobona to the encirclement.

The first attempt to run a substantial convoy was made by a battalion from a horse-drawn transport regiment that had recently been created within the encirclement under the command of Captain Mikhail Sergeyevich Murov. His unit consisted of a number of soldiers from 13th Rifle Division and a larger number of civilian volunteers, many of whom had inadequate winter clothing. The horses assigned to the unit were also in poor physical shape due to the lack of fodder. Murov cautiously led his group onto the lake early on 20 November:

> In front of us, the dark ice cover of the largest lake in Europe stretched away like a polished, dark sheet. The horses were immediately covered with hoarfrost, and the riders began to get frost forming on their legs and stirrups. I had to dismount and lead my horse by the reins.[33]

The sleighs crossed the ice leaving gaps of about 30m between each vehicle and managed to travel about a third of the way without incident. They then encountered a large crack in the ice crossing their path. As they tried to find a way around it, some sleighs fell through thin segments of ice and were lost, but most of the column managed to reach the Zelentsy Islands where they halted for two hours to catch their breath. From there, the rest of the journey to Kobona proved to be relatively simple. Flour was loaded into the sleighs and they set off on the return leg at night, and once again a few sleighs and their crew were lost when they broke through the ice; in some places, it was necessary to unload the flour temporarily to lighten the sleighs. On the morning of 21 November, Murov led his little band into Osinovets, carrying 63 tons of flour.

In terms of the daily requirements of the population of Leningrad, it was a trivial amount, but it was hugely symbolic, even more so because the group that had carried out the crossing had come from within the siege perimeter and included a large number of civilian volunteers. The first truck convoy delivered 70 tons of food on 22 November. The daily quantity of food transferred across the ice in the week that followed averaged a little over 100 tons, but the ice grew thicker and stronger with every day and it was soon possible to step up the operation.

Running vehicles across the frozen lake was a hazardous business. There remained weak areas of ice, worsened by German shelling and bombing. The route was marked with blue lights, which inevitably attracted the attention of German gunners, but despite the dangers many truck drivers preferred to make the run with their headlights burning so that they could avoid broken areas of ice. Some drove with their doors open so that they had a chance of leaping to safety if their truck slid into a gap. One driver described a typical crossing:

The vehicles carefully moved out ... onto the Ladoga ice. The column of GAZ-AA trucks was led by the company's political commissar, Captain Smirnov ... We drove with our headlamps off. We followed the lead truck, which followed the milestones. In some places there was the flickering light of a kerosene lantern. We kept a distance of 100m, it was safer that way ...

The huge frozen lake was a lifeless plain. A sharp wind blew snow at us. The dark areas were worrying – it seemed that these contained thinner ice sheets. It was new ice, not yet strong enough, and it buckled and cracked under the wheels. It was terrifying! Our cabin doors were open, just in case.

We reached the halfway point. It became foggy on the lake. It was getting harder and harder to drive the trucks and our nerves were stretched. The drive wheels slipped frequently due to poor grip on the ice and it became difficult to steer.

The head of the column gave a signal with a pocket flashlight to increase the spacing ... More time passed and the instrument panel showed we had covered 30km.

Here was Kobona – the long-awaited mainland coast. All the drivers were exhausted but nobody showed it. Everyone was anxious to complete our worthy mission.

We loaded eight sacks of flour per truck … The trucks now weighed more, but the ice remained as thin and as fragile as before. Almost in the middle of the lake, the truck of Filip Yemelyanov, an experienced driver, broke through and sank. The driver managed to get out of the hole with difficulty. The trucks driven by Andreichuk, Popov and Tikhomirov got stuck on hummocks. It took a lot of time and effort to get them out. After a series of misadventures, exhausted and frozen, we reached the shore of the long-suffering encirclement on 24 November.[34]

By 29 November, the officers overseeing the road had recorded the loss of 52 vehicles – nine of which broke through the ice and sank, whilst 41 were left stranded, and two were destroyed by German air attacks – and 60 horses. As the relief effort stepped up, losses also rose. A week later, the number of lost and stranded vehicles had more than doubled, partly because towards the end of November there was a new problem: the weather temporarily grew warmer, resulting in thinning of the ice. By this stage, the Road of Life encompassed several parallel routes and some had to be suspended – for one day, it was too risky for motor vehicles to venture onto the ice at all. There was general relief when the unseasonably warm spell passed and was replaced by a renewed freeze.

In order to deal with constant German attempts to interdict traffic with air attacks, Leningrad Front deployed about 350 anti-aircraft guns and 100 searchlights to protect the vehicles that drove back and forth. A variety of units, mainly from Fifty-Fourth Army, monitored the south shore of Lake Ladoga in order to deter any German forays onto the ice and to give early warning of air attacks. The heaviest air raids against the Road of Life took place in March 1942, but the Germans were hindered by frequent spells of low cloud and fog over the lake. The Soviet fighter pilots who escorted transport planes and tried to hold off German air attacks also had to contend with difficult conditions, made worse by the poor standard of many of the aircraft that they used, as one pilot later described:

In open, windswept, and often completely frozen fighter cockpits, without two-way radios, with poor navigation equipment and minimum quantities of fuel, usually flying alone often in unpredictable flying conditions, fighter pilots were their own commanders and commissars, pilots and navigators, engineers and weather forecasters, air fighters and vigilant guardians of the transport aircraft they were protecting.

The very task of flying on the routes of the air bridge didn't allow even for a short moment to think about yourself or your personal safety.[35]

The Soviet engineers were familiar with operating motor vehicles on ice and took care with another factor: the combination of vehicle weight and engine vibration could create resonance, which would cause the ice to crack. This was often worse for smaller vehicles that attempted to cross at a faster rate than trucks, and strict speed limits were imposed. The quantity of supplies brought across the Road of Life each day climbed steadily. By the end of the first week of December, it reached 300 tons; by the end of the month, it was 1,000 tons.[36] Food was not the only item that was transported. The city was also desperately short of fuel, resulting in difficulties in moving cargoes from where they were landed on the west bank to Leningrad itself. As a result, the limited capacity of the Road of Life had to include an allocation for gasoline and diesel.

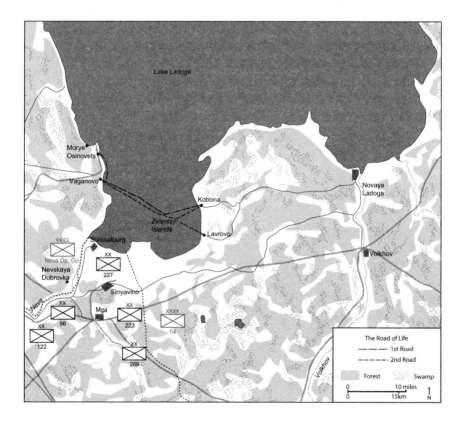

Other fuel was also in short supply in the city. There was almost no coal or firewood available and the starving population had to resort to breaking up items of furniture and hacking down the trees in the city. Attempts to harvest wood from nearby woodland proved to be futile. The limited supplies were soon gone and deaths from freezing exacerbated the ever-climbing toll. Electricity supplies became irregular and then stopped completely for most people. Water froze in pipes, which ruptured, adding to the hardship of the inhabitants. Soon, the ground was too frozen – and people were too weak – for bodies to be buried. Those who died were stacked in the streets and on open ground. In many cases, the survivors didn't report the deaths – this allowed them to continue using the ration cards of their dead relatives. At first, people slept with their spare clothes draped over their blankets; before long, they went to bed wearing everything they possessed.

After the war, Soviet historiography portrayed the people of Leningrad as being united in their determination that their city would stand firm against the Germans, but the reality was much more nuanced. At no point in the war to date had a large city held out against German attack, and some believed that whilst much of the population – in particular, the Jews and Communists – faced a grim future under German occupation, the rest would survive and therefore it was preferable to surrender 'for the greater good'. In an attempt to clamp down on any 'defeatist' undercurrents, there were widespread arrests of those who spoke out or who were suspected of being sympathetic to the Germans. Between August 1941 and September 1942, the total came to almost 130,000 individuals.[37] Even the Communist Party proved to be less than completely reliable. One of Zhdanov's assistants wrote in a report:

> At many factories Communists do not unify or lead the non-party masses, nor give a rebuff to organisers, panickers, and anti-Soviet elements, but frequently lag behind ... Several Communists show themselves to be cowards and panickers, refusing to take part in party mobilisations to the army.[38]

Some of this reluctance was driven by fear amongst lower-ranking Party officials that they would be amongst the first victims if the Germans occupied the city. But whilst the grip of the Communist Party seemed to be less firm than in the years before the war, Leningrad remained generally calm. By contrast, in mid-October, there was rioting and looting in Moscow when it was feared that the Wehrmacht was about to seize the Soviet capital; many government departments were evacuated to Kuibyshev and documents were burned in huge quantities, triggering widespread panic. The minority of the population of Moscow and Leningrad that might have welcomed the arrival of the Germans, even if only because it brought an end to Bolshevik rule, must have been dismayed when Soviet newspapers published details on 31 October of Hitler's intention to kill at least 20 million people in order to make way for German settlers. Some began to worry about another possibility: if the Germans were prepared to starve Leningrad to death, might they consider using chemical weapons to accelerate their programme of extermination?

It seems that there was active consideration of such a step. By 1941, the Wehrmacht had stockpiles of the nerve agent Tabun amounting to 40,000 tons, with lesser amounts of other agents and there was some discussion amongst the German general staff during December about using these weapons against Leningrad – the total tonnage of gas munitions to saturate the Leningrad area was carefully calculated, as was the railway capacity required to transport the shells and bombs.[39] Given the willingness to use poison gas to exterminate Europe's Jewish population – the first experiments with vans that had their exhaust fumes diverted into the back of the vehicle had already taken place by this time, and Zyklon-B, the agent used for mass killings in later years, had been tested on Soviet prisoners of war – it seems remarkable at first glance that Hitler did not give approval for the use of nerve agents to bring the siege to a rapid conclusion. There were probably several factors at work. Firstly, despite the setbacks before Moscow, Hitler still believed that Leningrad would starve to death during the winter, a view reinforced by the constant stream of intelligence from German agents and informers in the city. In such a situation, using gas seemed an unnecessary step. Secondly, although the actual gas attacks could have been carried out over a matter of days, it would have taken time and precious railway capacity to move stockpiles of nerve agent into position at a time when there was insufficient capacity to deliver all of the conventional munitions and food required for the armies in the front line, particularly as the failure to achieve victory against the Soviet Union meant that winter clothing was urgently needed. Thirdly, the experiences of the First World War had shown that the use of gas weapons was not without risk – an unexpected change in wind direction could result in the gas being blown back over German troops. Fourthly, Hitler would have been aware that the Soviet Union also possessed poison gas stockpiles, as did the British. Discussions between Stalin and Churchill would lead to a public declaration by the British in May 1942 that German use of chemical weapons on the Eastern Front would result in the British using gas against German cities; consequently, by the stage of the war when German use of chemical weapons might have had a decisive effect in altering the ultimate outcome, there was a very real threat of massive retaliation against Germany. Finally, Hitler had served in Flanders in the First World War and his personal experiences of the use of gas may have played a part too.

Some civilians in Leningrad lost heart relatively early in the siege, due to personal tragedies. Georgy Alekseyevich Knyazev was a historian who worked in the Academy of Sciences, and he recorded the mixed attitudes of his fellow Leningraders in his diary in late September:

> When I was at work today, a colleague told me that she found it hard to pull herself together and stop straining her ears in the silence after yesterday's bombing raid, and to get to sleep. Many people spend every night in the bomb shelters … Some people are still stoical and determined: some are fatalistic and others are religious believers or people who are just not touched by anything; some are either naturally very extremely calm or temperamentally the opposite but are now completely exhausted. Yesterday, when we were standing on the embankment in the entrance porch of a building opposite St Isaac's Cathedral during an alert, there was one young woman who was unwilling to come in off the street, despite of the repeated orders of a police officer.
>
> 'I longer care whether I live or die,' she said angrily. 'I'm fed up with everything, I loathe it all.' At that moment a coffin was driven past on a lorry, with mourners carrying wreaths sitting around it. 'Now there goes a lucky man,' the woman said.
>
> I couldn't stop myself and I asked her: 'Why are you so despondent, and so downhearted?'
>
> 'I've lost two of my family already and have absolutely no idea of where the third is: he was wounded and was brought to Leningrad, but I have no idea where they have put him.' …
>
> There are others who have more stamina than this young woman, but everywhere there is a mood of utter exhaustion and extreme anxiety.
>
> 'How long can this really go on for?' Petrova, a young mother, asked me. 'And what will happen afterwards? … My husband gave me 500 roubles out of his pay, but the money has stayed unspent because I can't find anything to buy with it. How on earth can we go on living?'[40]

In Leningrad, the only significant unrest in the first half of the winter was in factories where small groups of workers refused to work the newer, longer shifts required for armaments production unless they were given more food. Attempts to put pressure on them by reducing their wages had no effect – like Knyazev's colleague, the workers shrugged and pointed out that there was nothing to buy anyway. To an extent, the preceding years had conditioned the population of Leningrad and other cities to living in a state of constant threat and that stoic instinct for survival now proved to be invaluable. Stalin's purges sometimes had an unpredictable legacy.

Remarkably, many theatres remained open as the siege began to bite. On 7 December, an improvised orchestra, including a group of volunteers from a brass band, performed Tchaikovsky's 1812 Overture in the Great Philharmonic Hall.[41] The Musical Comedy Theatre in Leningrad struggled on, trying to put on shows to raise morale, even though the actors were in no better state than their audience. Tamara Salnikova was an actress in the performance and laboured through the snow on 7 December to reach the theatre, taking shelter from artillery shells when she approached the Kirov Bridge. She had to warm her makeup over a lamp before it was soft enough to apply to her face. Part of the way through the performance, she was waiting for her cue to go onto the stage:

I looked out to see that one of our best actors – Sasha Abramov – had collapsed. He had been standing next to the hot water tank, trying to warm himself, and drinking a little tea. His cup lay shattered beside him. Sasha died during the intermission. At that time, thousands were dying of starvation but the loss of my colleague, lying there, still in his musketeer's costume, left me absolutely stunned. The stage director spoke to us and tried to rally us. He told us that we needed to go on – for the audience's sake – but I felt lost in a fog of disbelief …

[When the performance resumed] I was supposed to sing and dance – but nothing happened. I couldn't find my voice and my feet simply refused to move. Then as I looked out at the full audience, waiting expectantly, I recalled the exhortation of our stage director. 'It is the duty of us – as artists – to continue.' The power of his words awoke something in me and somehow my duet happened after all.[42]

Most of the city's symphony orchestra had been evacuated and others died during the siege. Some managed to put on small performances in the numerous hospitals across the city, but most such activity came to an end as starvation left everyone with no energy. In an attempt to lighten the mood of Leningrad Radio's transmissions, a call went out in late February asking musicians remaining in Leningrad to contact the Radio Committee so that a symphony orchestra could be put together. Kseniya Makianova Matus was an oboist in the city:

When I took up my instrument, I saw that it had turned green. The valves were green; the pads were coming off. It was impossible to play it. I took it to be repaired by someone who lived far away … I arrived and opened the door. There he sat wrapped in a rug, dressed warmly. He recognised me. I told him: 'I'm going to work. I have to get this instrument fixed.' …

In the corner he had an armchair and lying on it were various pelts – like muffs or collars. I was embarrassed to look at them for too long. And when he agreed to fix my instrument and I asked 'What do I owe you?' he replied, 'Bring me a little cat! I have eaten five cats already.' I said, 'Oh, there are no cats, or birds, or dogs left in the city. They've all been eaten. I can only pay with money.' But he repaired my instrument anyway.[43]

On 5 March, there was welcome news from the outside world. Shostakovich, who had been evacuated shortly after his radio broadcast, had finished his Seventh Symphony and it was performed in Kuibyshev that evening. The starving people of Leningrad listened on their radios to a piece of music that would be named after their city. Many interpreted the first movement, with its gradual development of a march into a strident theme, as portraying the approach of the Wehrmacht to the city; others, particularly in later years, interpreted it in a wider context, suggesting that Shostakovich was writing about the destruction of the city's population that had been started by Stalin and was then accelerated by Hitler. Such was the power of the music, and of its symbolic importance, that copies of the manuscript were sent by circuitous routes to London and New York. Within Leningrad, artists began to think about a live performance. But they would need an orchestra of over 100, and most of the surviving musicians were too weak to handle such a task. It would have to wait until conditions had improved.

Lidiya Georgiyevna Okhapina was living in Leningrad with two small children. Her husband, a factory technician, left the city shortly after the war began. His wife believed that he was safe somewhere in the east, but he had been sent to Smolensk where he was caught up in an encirclement, ultimately slipping through German lines and making his way to safety. The conditions that his family had to endure were later described by his wife:

The apartment was terribly cold. There was hoar frost on the walls, just like you see inside barns in the winter. When Ninochka's nappy needed to be changed, I slid my hand under the blanket without lifting it off to put a dry one on her, so that she wouldn't catch cold, and then I threw the wet nappy out onto the floor where it quickly froze … By then I had lost so much weight that there was no flesh on my legs at all. My chest was as flat as a man's chest – just nipples … The children were also very thin and my heart faltered when I saw their bony little arms and legs and their wan little faces and huge eyes … There was no running water in our apartment, so I had to go to the Neva to fetch it. I walked there pulling a small sled with a bucket and a pot on it. We needed a lot of water because the nappies had to be washed too as well as for cooking.[44]

Not long after, Okhapina suffered a potentially fatal blow. She had moved into a different apartment with someone she encountered on the street, but this woman stole her ration cards. The next issue of ration cards was five days away, and she had no means of surviving until then. Desperately, she prayed for salvation:

The next day someone started knocking on the front door … He was a soldier from the front, a messenger from my husband. He handed me a small package with a letter. Vasili had written 'Darling Lidiya' – after reading just those words, I burst into tears and I thought to myself, 'If only he could see his Lidiya now!' Further on in the letter he wrote that he was sending a kilogram of semolina, a kilogram of rice, and two packets of biscuits. For some reason I read this out loud. After the word 'rice', Tolya said piteously, 'Mama, make some porridge, but please make it thicker than usual.' … The soldier, a lieutenant, suddenly began to blow his nose loudly and to wipe away the tears that were running down his cheeks when he looked at us. He said, 'It's dreadful that children are so desperately hungry. We will get you out. Be patient just a little while longer. I will tell your husband about you. And the Nazis – they will pay for it all. For your tears, for the fact that you are starving like this, for everything.'[45]

The reaction of her visitor was typical of the way that soldiers felt about what was happening to civilians. A factory in Leningrad organised a visit to the front line for a group of women workers, where the soldiers might enjoy better rations than the civilians in the city but also had to endure much harder physical labour and the ever-present threat of death. Daniil Aleksandrovich Granin was serving in one of the regiments facing the Germans and recalled that they seldom received any reinforcements and had to work hard to clear snow from their trenches, venturing out occasionally into no-man's land to try to dig for cabbages. When news reached the men of the failure of the German assault on Moscow, and of the initially successful counteroffensive that threw the Wehrmacht back from the city outskirts, they became convinced – perhaps for the first time – that they too would be able to hold out. He described the visit by the three women who came to his company:

> All three of them were wrapped up in shawls and scarves, belted, buttoned and done up. When they had finally removed their outer clothing in our dugout, they were transformed into thin young women – indeed, very bony ones, judging by how their collarbones and cheek bones stood out. The dugout was well heated and we went in and received from them gifts of socks, tobacco pouches and mittens. Their dresses hung limply from their thin, bony shoulders – they were far too big for them – but each of them seemed lovely to us. They arrived at our dugout in the evening when it was already dark. An hour later a sergeant brought in our *kasha*. The pot of *kasha* with some salted meat and a little sugar was our dinner and our supper, and those who could would put a little aside for their breakfast. We also had bread and biscuits. That evening we shared our *kasha* with our visitors, which actually meant that we gave it all to them so each of them had nearly two helpings … then they fell asleep. Actually they had begun to doze off straight after they had eaten. The journey had exhausted them, but mostly they were made sleepy by the food and the warmth. They slept on our wooden beds … It seemed like years since we had seen women in dresses. But what women these were! Emaciated, exhausted, looking neglected. Soldiers crowded in the entrance to the dugout and looked at the sleeping women with expressions in which there was no trace of any masculine thoughts, only compassion.[46]

Back in Leningrad, Lidiya Okhapina managed to get some firewood shortly after receiving the life-saving package of food from her husband, but because the wood was damp she filled the apartment with choking fumes and the family was lucky to survive. Before long, they were once more dependent upon the inadequate rations they received:

> We began to starve again. By then, February 1942 was nearing its end. We had eaten what was in the parcel a long time ago. More than once Tolya suggested to me, 'Mama, let's make fumes again and die. Our heads will ache at first, but then we will fall asleep.' It is unbearable to hear this coming from a child.[47]

As conditions worsened, the hitherto limited unrest began to spread. There were talks of strike action and rumours that 'the bosses' were getting far better rations than the workers. In the last six weeks of 1941, nearly 1,000 workers were arrested by the NKVD; some of them had openly threatened their managers that once the Germans arrived, they would be the ones who were forced to beg for food.[48] Nonetheless, there were few public demonstrations or protests. In November, a small crowd gathered to demonstrate and a political commissar ordered NKVD troops to open fire; the men refused, and he started firing at the crowd himself, but the sudden onset of renewed German shelling drove everyone to shelter.[49]

As the brutal nature of the German attempt to starve a city of several million people to death became clear to everyone, any lingering pro-German sentiment faded away completely, but there was an attempt to organise a mass demonstration for 22 January. The NKVD moved swiftly to identify those calling for a public gathering and arrested them. When the day came, the only gathering at the designated spot was of NKVD personnel – the quest for survival consumed whatever energy people still had. There was no point in wasting strength in futile protests. The combination of cold weather, no heating, and completely inadequate food resulted in increasing listlessness and difficulty in concentrating as well as physical weakness. There were innumerable incidents of small scuffles in ration queues, or of people being robbed of their meagre allotment or their ration cards, but there were also moments of unexpected kindness. Yekaterina Kirillovna Bokareva was nine years old at the time of the siege, living with her mother and two sisters; one was pregnant, having been widowed when her husband died in the war against Finland. Usually, one of the older sisters would collect the family's rations, but occasionally this wasn't possible:

My mother was at work. Maryusa was in the last month of her pregnancy. Nina had a fever. They said that Spanish flu was widespread. Maryusa handed me the wallet of ration cards and I went to exchange them. The shopkeeper said, 'Kid, you need an adult with you.'

'But we don't have anyone to ask – everyone is sick and my mum is at work.'

'I'll be in the shop all day,' he said, and gave me back the wallet. I slipped it in my jacket and trudged home. At the door I reached for the wallet – but it wasn't there. I felt a cold wave over me. It was lost! I'd dropped it! I felt weak with fear. I couldn't see it anywhere and I crossed back over the road. The store had a raised entrance, up ten steps. I climbed up. A man was standing at the door. I can remember him now. He was thin, wearing an autumn coat, with large dark eyes. 'I knew you'd be back, girl.' And he handed me my wallet.

I can't remember much else, it felt like a dream. Did I thank him? I didn't tell anyone at home. I couldn't understand why this man had saved our lives. But despite this, my mother died on 4 March, and Maryusa on 18 March.[50]

The everyday horrors – corpses in the street, the ever-present danger of death – soon became normal for almost everyone in the city. Some Leningraders saw the siege as merely the continuation of the pre-war years. One woman recorded in her diary in September, before the real privations began, that despite the imminent existential threat to Leningrad, the authorities continued to pursue those who had somehow fallen foul of the state:

> The Germans are at the gates, the Izhorsk Works has been partly destroyed, the Germans are just about to enter the city, and we are busy arresting and deporting old women and lonely, defenceless, and harmless people …
>
> We are on death row now; we just don't know who is next. For 23 years we have all been on death row in theory, but now we have reached the epoch's grand finale. An inglorious finale.[51]

People frequently collapsed while queuing for food or trying to reach one of the holes in the ice on the Neva from where they could get water. Yevgeny Moniushko, who had worked with a labour battalion digging anti-tank ditches near Kingisepp, was now back in the city living with his parents and brother. When the water supply to their apartment ceased functioning, the nearest source of water was one of the city's canals, but this was too polluted to be drunk:

> The most common alternative sources of water supply were bomb craters that contained broken water mains. These craters were filled with water that kept coming under low pressure from punctured pipes. The closest of these improvised water fountains to us was located in Turgenev Square, about 1km from our house. Although that seems quite close, we needed no less than one hour to bring back 4–5 litres of water, since we lacked the strength necessary to carry any more.[52]

As the winter progressed, many citizens stopped trying to help those who collapsed. They had no energy to spare and a fatalistic mood set in: why help someone back to their feet in the knowledge that they were almost certain to collapse again? One woman described how she tried to help another woman get back to her home:

> I walked about a hundred paces with her and saw that we couldn't go on like that with only me helping, and I said, 'Now you'll be able to get the rest of the way on your own.' As I moved away I heard the woman fall again but didn't go back to help her up.[53]

Those who died in the streets were rapidly stripped of their clothing. A few trucks passed from time to time and collected some of the dead, but there were too many people dying – and too little fuel to spare – for the process to be anywhere near comprehensive. At first, civilians were ordered to help clear the streets of snow, rubble, and corpses, but this was difficult due to the emaciated condition of the population. Yelena Vladimirovna Mukhina was a teenager in the city who was required to work in one such team:

> I had no strength left in my arms. As a result I couldn't dig at the ice with a crowbar or pick it up and toss it aside with a shovel. So I was used in the manner of a horse. Other people loaded a metal bathtub they had found somewhere with snow and ice and several people (including me) attached themselves to a harness made of ropes and dragged this bathtub to the Fontanka River. The route was long and arduous. We dragged it with the last of our strength … Near the Gorky Theatre, those who were stronger threw the ice onto the Fontanka. On the way back we tried to walk as slowly as possible in order to get a little rest. And when we reached the yard the bath was immediately loaded again, and we – the 'horses' – again made our way to the Fontanka … I remember well that when this torture came to an end, I no longer had the strength to walk like a human on two legs, but had to crawl on all fours.[54]

Before long, nobody had the strength for such tasks.

Georgy Markovich Valshchikov was a young naval cadet who had been in a marine battalion in the front line. With little more than their basic training to help them, the makeshift marines suffered heavy losses and only 98 survived the first few days of action. Valshchikov was wounded and then sent back to Leningrad, where he was assigned guard duties:

> We guarded the Admiralty from looters, not that there was anything there worth plundering, and I remember how once during the shelling a woman entered the lobby and said, 'Sailor, can I warm up?' I led her to a radiator – we had a boiler in the building so it was warm – and placed her on a chair and then actually forgot about her. When I went back to wake her up, she was cold and dead. This happened many times. We wondered why people came to us like that to die. It turned out that the people in the city believed that the sailors wouldn't just leave their corpses but would bury them.[55]

The debilitating consequences of starvation resulted in a condition that became known as alimentary dystrophy. In addition to weight loss, the reduction in production of digestive enzymes meant that even when food was available, it was poorly absorbed. Reduced serum albumin led to swelling of legs, and deterioration of liver function often produced jaundice. Many of the starving became desperate for any food. A nurse described a typical patient:

> It was very difficult to take blood for analysis from a dystrophic patient, as a prick of the finger produced nothing. Both the patient and I were crying ... He spoke without pause and tried to push away anyone if he was prevented from seeking food. He was obsessed with food and talked of nothing else ... He was ready to snatch a piece of bread from the hands of another person and despite screams and abuse, devoured it completely. He was seen rummaging through heaps of rubbish and licking the plates of other people.[56]

During that terrible winter, there was a further macabre development. Quantities of minced meat began to appear in the Haymarket, a large market that had been present in the city almost since its inception. Before long, rumours began to circulate about the provenance of this mince. Those rumours proved to be correct. The authorities became aware of two types of cannibalism. *Trupoyedstvo* or 'corpse-eating' was the more common form; many of the bodies that lay in abandoned buildings or even in the open began to show signs of having fleshy parts hacked off. Even entire limbs disappeared and one man reported finding the severed heads of several people, including a small girl, buried in a snowdrift – presumably, the bodies had already been butchered. A family of three was arrested after being caught stealing corpses from a hospital mortuary, and a nurse was found to be selling the amputated limbs of wounded people.[57] The corpses of children were particularly favoured.

The NKVD investigated as a matter of urgency and arrested nine people in the first ten days of December 1941. The number of arrests rose alarmingly, not least because Zhdanov and his colleagues decided that the development was simply too macabre to be publicised, and as a consequence those who had been eating the flesh of corpses continued to do so, largely unaware that the authorities were attempting to track them down. The arrests highlighted another problem. Most of those who were caught were people who had fled to the city from the south in order to escape the German advance. Many of these refugees lacked the documentation to qualify for ration cards and were thus forced to resort to other measures to feed themselves.

The second form of cannibalism was far more serious: *lyudoyedstvo*, or 'people-eating'. The first cases recorded by the NKVD occurred in late November 1941.

Lyubova Vasilyevna Shaporina, a woman living in Leningrad, described one such incident in her diary. A woman and her daughter planned their attack together, enticing a teenage girl into their apartment with the promise of food. Once she was inside, the mother launched a brutal attack on their intended victim while the daughter played an accordion and sang loudly to drown out the screams. With blood streaming from her wounds, the intended victim fled down the corridor from the apartment, still pursued by the knife-wielding mother in front of the astonished neighbours; the daughter continued to play her accordion throughout the incident.[58]

On 23 December, the men and women who laboured to deliver supplies via the Road of Life achieved an important milestone: for the first time, they brought in marginally more food than was being consumed per day. Two days later, Zhdanov cautiously increased the bread ration in Leningrad by a fraction. The effect on morale was probably far greater than the effect on nutrition, but at least it was a step in the right direction. However, despite this slight increase, another problem became evident: distribution of food was often patchy, meaning that many people in Leningrad didn't receive their allocated rations. Moreover, even if the food situation was improving, the supply of fuel for the frozen city remained far short of what was required and due to the extreme cold the death rate continued to rise inexorably. To make matters worse, the last functioning water pumping station broke down, with the consequence that the city's bakeries were left without water for several days. As a result, they were unable to produce bread and people queued in vain for hours before being turned away. The death rate continued to rise throughout January and into February, as German intelligence reports summarised:

> One of our informers undertook to count for us, one afternoon, passing sledges carrying corpses on one of Leningrad's streets. He saw over a hundred of them in less than an hour. In many cases the corpses are now piled up in yards or fenced in squares ... In the Aleksandrovskaya Hospital there are about 1,200 corpses placed in unheated rooms, corridors and the yard outside.
>
> At the beginning of January the number of victims of starvation was being given as 2–3,000 per day. Now towards the end of the month, the rumour is that at least 15,000 people a day are dying ...
>
> Children are now particularly vulnerable to starvation – and small children, for whom there is no food, can be expected to die quickly.[59]

Steps had already been taken to increase the number of convoys crossing Lake Ladoga and the quantity of supplies rose steadily. Another milestone was passed on 18 January when sufficient quantities of both food and fuel were delivered to exceed daily requirements, and there was a further slight increase in daily rations on 24 January. Nonetheless, this was still far from enough to reverse the slow starvation of the population: the ration for priority workers was 500g of bread per day, with 400g for other factory workers, 300g for non-physical workers, and 250g for dependants and children.[60] Even after these increases, the rations represented barely half the calorific intake to preserve body weight and health; it would be a further two months before supplies were sufficiently reliable and large-scale for rations to reach a level where people could be given enough food to sustain them. The death rate remained appallingly high, alleviated only marginally by the growing provision of fuel for heating. Most of the city's population would end the war not having recovered their former weight.

Evacuation from the city was slow at first but built up as the winter progressed, though Anfisa Nikolayevna, the neighbour of the Riabinkin family, was repeatedly disappointed in her attempts to secure passage. By contrast, the Riabinkins were fortunate and were given permission to leave Leningrad in early January 1942, but by this stage Yura was too weak to accompany them – he could barely stand and move around the apartment. They left him lying on his bed with his face to the wall; they never saw him again. Yura's mother and sister boarded a freight wagon on a train that took them to Lake Ladoga. Eventually, they reached the city of Vologda, far to the east, where they received the first proper meal they had eaten for months. Yura's mother died the following morning on the bench in the railway station where she and her daughter had spent the night. After the war, Yura's sister Irina returned to Leningrad, but was unable to discover the final fate of her brother. For many years, she continued to hope that he had survived, but it is far more likely that he became another of the casualties of that terrible winter.

Lidiya Okhapina and her two small children survived the first months of 1942, always hungry and struggling. In early March, she was visited once more by the lieutenant who had brought her the package of food from her husband; he told her that she should secure travel documents as he had managed to get passage for her out of Leningrad. Merely reaching the assembly point, dragging her sled with her two children placed upon it, was almost too much for her. A truck took the evacuees through a snowstorm to Lake Ladoga and they crossed the ice in a convoy led by a man on skis who reconnoitred the route for breaks in the ice. After numerous stops, the family eventually reached Cherepovets, 231 miles north of Moscow, where she was reunited with her husband.

The people who were evacuated gathered in the Finland Station in Leningrad, where Lenin had arrived from exile in 1917. Although they were meant to be given food to take with them for their journey, this often didn't happen or was provided in inadequate quantities. Many were dead by the time the trains reached Lake Ladoga from the effects of cold or starvation and there were occasional artillery and bombing attacks that resulted in further deaths or wounding. Anyone who was deemed to be seriously ill – a strange designation in a city full of people on the brink of starving to death – was removed from the train and left behind. Many were suffering from dysentery as a consequence of malnutrition or dirty water, or were infested with lice; if either condition was detected, the person was removed.

Inevitably, the usefulness of the Road of Life fell as winter came to an end. By mid-March, open pools of water began to appear and the ice started to crack under the constant load of traffic and movements had to be reduced. By mid-April, heavy vehicles could no longer venture onto the lake; all movements stopped in the last week of the month. But the worst was past. By the narrowest possible margins, Leningrad had been saved from starvation. Hitler's plan to march into a city that had perished from cold and hunger was thwarted. The price was terrible. Estimates of the total deaths in the city vary considerably, not least because fewer people had the strength to report deaths as the winter progressed and there were large numbers of unregistered refugees from the surrounding area. Official recorded civilian deaths totalled just under 200,000. The administrative body responsible for burials in both individual and mass graves kept no records during January and February, but recorded nearly 90,000 burials in March, nearly 102,500 in April, and 53,500 in May.[61] As a result of the deaths and the evacuation of non-essential people, the population of Leningrad fell from about 2.3 million in December 1941 to 1.1 million by the time that the ice on Lake Ladoga broke up; this reduction of over a million takes no account of those who had already died before December. It is estimated that at least 620,000 civilians died during the terrible winter.

These stark figures are dreadful enough; by comparison, British civilian casualties during the Blitz on London in 1940–41 came to about 43,000. But throughout this time, heavy and costly fighting continued outside the city both on the main battle lines and behind them, adding still further to the butcher's bill.

CHAPTER 8

BANDENKRIEG: THE PARTISAN WAR

The German advance across the Soviet Union was, at first, greeted with considerable enthusiasm by civilians in the Baltic States and Ukraine, and to a much lesser extent in the Soviet-occupied parts of Poland and Belarus. When the people of these regions realised that far from coming as liberators, the Germans were intent on imposing just as repressive a regime as the one that they had replaced, this enthusiasm waned rapidly. Many in rural areas had hoped that the hated collectivisation of farms would be abolished and land would be returned to local ownership; instead, they discovered that they faced even greater requisitioning of food than they had endured under Soviet rule. The harshness with which the Germans stamped down on any dissent or resistance further increased resentment. In an area that was littered with military equipment following the retreat of the Red Army, it was inevitable that many local people would take up arms against the new occupiers.

In the most western parts of the Soviet Union, particularly areas that had only come under Soviet control recently, the situation was complex. Many local men served – with varying degrees of willingness – in paramilitary units that were raised by the Germans. These units served as auxiliaries for the occupation forces and were often responsible for the mass slaughter of Jews, Bolsheviks, and others. Some who took up arms against the Germans were equally hostile to Soviet rule, and in regions like the disputed region of eastern Lithuania around Vilnius, there were soon multiple factions hiding in the forests and countryside – Poles who were loyal to the government-in-exile in London; Jewish partisans, some of whom were Zionists and others who were pro-Soviet; and at first relatively small numbers of other pro-Soviet fighters. These bands often clashed with each other as much as they did with the Germans. Once the German advance carried it over the old borders between the Baltic States and the Soviet Union, the willingness of local people in what had always been Russian territory to take up arms and fight for the restoration of Soviet rule increased considerably. Moreover, there were large numbers of Red Army stragglers still hiding in the countryside, and their numbers swelled the ranks of the partisans.

Soviet military planning had considered the use of partisans for many years. As early as 1932, there were exploratory exercises to investigate the use of partisans to disrupt rail traffic using explosives and large quantities of small arms, ammunition and explosives were buried at secret locations across the western parts of the Soviet Union. However, in late 1930s, the mood changed. Talk of fighting against an invader within the Soviet Union was seen increasingly as defeatist and risked arrest in the general atmosphere of paranoia. Stalin was also unenthusiastic about encouraging partisan preparations – after all, any partisan organisation intended to oppose German occupation might form the basis for resistance to his rule. The weapons caches were largely removed and training literature was destroyed.[1] It is a further example of the manner in which Stalin's paranoia and repressions severely damaged the ability of the Soviet Union to defend itself.

Everything changed after the onset of *Barbarossa*. On 29 June, the Central Committee of the Communist Party issued orders to all party and government bodies in the western parts of the Soviet Union, instructing them to take steps to strip the land of any usable assets and to organise partisan groups:

> The Central Committee of the Supreme Soviet oblige all Party, Soviet, trade union and Komsomol organisations to … mobilise all our organisations and all the strength of the people to defeat the enemy …
>
> In the event of a forced withdrawal of Red Army units, all rolling stock is to be seized, not a single steam locomotive or wagon is to be left for the enemy, not a kilogram of bread or a litre of fuel. Collective farms must move their cattle and hand over grain for safekeeping to state bodies for its transportation to the rear. All valuable property including non-ferrous metals, grain and fuel that cannot be evacuated must be completely destroyed. In enemy-held areas, organise partisan detachments and sabotage groups to fight against enemy military units, incite partisan war everywhere, blow up bridges and roads, damage telephone and telegraph communications, set fire to warehouses etc. … Create unbearable conditions for the enemy, pursue and attack them at every turn, and disrupt all their activities.[2]

Local Party heads were to ensure sufficient Party officials remained in the area to oversee the partisan movement. In addition to this Party-based structure, there were also chains of command from the army and the NKVD. Further instructions followed over the next few weeks, adding flesh to the bones of the first announcement. Partisan detachments should consist of no more than 150 fighters, organised into two or three companies, each in turn consisting of two or three platoons.[3] The intention was to create local partisan groups that would operate within a specific district, thus maximising their local knowledge and contacts with the civilian population.

The involvement of the NKVD proved to be detrimental. When a Central Headquarters of the Partisan Movement was created, Lavrenty Beriya – the head of the NKVD – had several members arrested under various pretexts; he wished to have complete personal command of the partisans. His men and women in the field also proved to be less effective than other partisans. Due to a variety of reasons, not least a failure to ensure that they were on good terms with the local population, the partisan groups dominated by NKVD personnel suffered disproportionately high casualties. Many in the German-occupied territories of the Baltic States and Ukraine in particular were hostile to the NKVD, associating it with the conduct of Soviet authorities during the months (and in the case of Ukraine, an entire decade) of repression, and showed little hesitation in denouncing NKVD partisans to the Germans. By the first anniversary of the war, 93 per cent of these groups had been wiped out.[4]

The first task of the new partisan organisations was to organise groups prior to the arrival of the Wehrmacht that would function as 'destruction battalions', responsible for security in the immediate rear area of the Red Army; if the Germans then advanced further, they would transition into true partisan units with tasks that included destroying infrastructure to prevent the Germans from using it. In the opening months of the war, these groups formed the bulk of the partisan movement and although many of their personnel had undergone at least some training in partisan warfare, the early stages of the partisan war were hindered by an error in tactics. Once they were operating behind enemy lines, the partisan units were expected to engage with German troops rather than concentrating on disrupting supply lines, sabotaging railway lines and bridges, etc – those tasks were intended to be carried out by Soviet cavalry, which would slip through the front line and roam in the rear of the German forces. For the lightly armed partisans, combat against anything but the weakest German units was likely to end in disaster.

The Germans anticipated that they would have to deal with possible partisan activity and when he became aware of the new orders emanating from Moscow,

Hitler told his immediate associates on 16 July that as well as being a threat, this was an opportunity: the Germans would have a pretext to stamp out resistance of any sort. At the end of July, this was formulated in a new order. As the troops available for security in the conquered areas would not suffice if proper legal process was followed, it was necessary to ensure that the occupation forces inspired sufficient fear among the population to stop them from any acts of resistance. In other words, the units responsible for security were given a completely free hand without any thought of legal restraint.

Rear area security was the mission of several separate German formations. The rear area behind each German army was nominally under the control of a *Kommandant Rückwärtiges Armeegebiet* ('Commandant of Army Rear Area' or *Korück*); this officer had control of up to three security divisions, made up of a mixture of reservists too old for front-line service and police battalions. These units were intended to provide guard detachments for key installations and also took part in many of the atrocities that took place immediately after the German invasion – 221st Security Division, for example, was involved in a massacre of Jews in the city of Białystok. As the German advance slowed, the security divisions were pressed into service in the front line, where they proved to be fragile in the brutal intensity of combat. The area over which the *Korück* had control varied in depth and as the army pressed into the interior of the Soviet Union, this area was progressively handed over to civilian occupation authorities. There were two such authorities – *Reichskommissariat Ostland* for the Baltic States and Belarus and *Reichskommissariat Ukraine* further south. Within each of these, there were both military and SS hierarchies. The former were responsible for overseeing rear area units such as hospitals and repair workshops; as the war dragged on, a variety of industrial concerns, particularly those repairing or manufacturing uniforms and winter clothing, also came under the control of the military rear area authorities. The SS was responsible for police functions, and each region had a *Höherer SS-und Polizeiführer* ('Higher SS and Police Commander' or *HSSPF*). All ghettos and concentration camps were under the control of the SS, and this proved to be a lucrative opportunity: the SS hired out the inmates as slave labour to other agencies. In addition, there were the formations of the *Einsatzgruppen*, whose responsibilities and areas of operation overlapped with both those of the *Korück* and the civilian authorities. As already described, the *Einsatzgruppen* and their subordinate units were heavily involved in the killing of both real and perceived or suspected enemies of the Reich. High in their priorities was the killing of the Jewish population.

Nikolai Ivanovich Afanasyev was a worker in Leningrad who, like thousands of others, volunteered in July 1941 to join the militia. He expected to be sent to bolster the defences that were hastily being erected to defend the city approaches from the advancing Germans, but instead found himself assigned to a completely different sort of unit: he was to join the newly formed 6th Partisan Regiment as a battalion commander. His experiences are typical of the haste with which fresh partisan units were raised and sent to the front line to augment or replace the stay-behind units that had been created earlier. He and the other volunteers were immediately sent to a nearby school that had been designated a training centre:

> The first order we received upon arrival was to hand over all documents. No Party cards, no Komsomol tickets, no passports or other passes – we should have none of those. In addition, we were warned that no one in the battalion, including commanders like me, had permission to make any kind of record or diary, official or unofficial.
>
> The orders were clear: we were preparing to go behind enemy lines. But I remember that I faced a lot of difficulties – it's not easy to get to know a unit of more than a hundred people, without even a simple list of names! And we needed to get to know each other as soon as possible. Moreover, we didn't know how long we would have for preparations or even what we were preparing for, but it seemed as if we would be sent behind enemy lines at any moment.[5]

The new partisan regiment was sent to Novgorod a few days later, and their experiences in the next few days were typical of those of so many of the ill-prepared partisan units. Afanasyev was given a pistol and a submachine-gun, the only automatic weapon in the entire battalion. After a brief meeting between the partisan officers and Vatutin, chief of staff of Northwest Front, the regiment moved to Staraya Russa and then further west to Volot and Morino. Many of the volunteers had brought backpacks crammed with whatever they thought might be useful – food, extra clothing etc – and they were now ordered to discard anything that they wouldn't need in the next few days. Ammunition and rifles were issued and retreating Red Army units handed over a small number of trucks, sufficient for perhaps half the partisans. The regiment commander, Petrov, set off with half of his command, taking with him the unit's only radio and all of the regiment's baggage.

Afanasyev led the rest of the regiment along the road towards Dno on foot, encountering retreating Red Army units that sometimes mocked them for being so poorly equipped – many of the 'partisans' had loaded not only their baggage but also their weapons onto the trucks. Eventually, after marching for two days, they reached the village where they were meant to link up with Petrov and the rest of the regiment and eventually made contact with some of them. Afanasyev was ordered to proceed to Fedovo, about 35 miles southeast of Pskov. The battalion soon found itself moving through territory with the sounds of German motor traffic almost everywhere. Despite this, the partisan battalion marched with confidence that was often misplaced and reflected the inexperience of the men – when they entered the village of Plotovets, they marched along the main road in a column, singing loudly.

The following day, the group reached the village of Dubye, close to their intended destination. Here, shortly before first light, they were preparing to cross a highway when they ran into German troops for the first time and realised that the partisans couldn't expect support from all the civilians they encountered:

> We were waiting for our scouts to return. It was clear that we couldn't cross the highway before dawn and that we had to hide somewhere for the day until our scouts returned.
>
> 'Listen!' Chudnov [his deputy commander] unexpectedly nudged me. 'Something's coming!'
>
> Several vehicles were actually heading right towards us across the field. Soon we could hear fragments of speech. I gave the command to get ready to fight, realising clearly how pointless it was.
>
> The vehicles passed literally a few metres from my men who were preparing to attack. It was a small detachment and we might have dealt with it in a single rush. But from there, near the highway, they would be able to rush forces against us that we couldn't resist. Fortunately, the Nazis didn't spot us. They drove by, chatting merrily, unaware of how close death was to them in those moments.
>
> After a while, it became impossible to stay near the village. Dawn was approaching. Without waiting for the scouts to return, we moved into the fields along a stream overgrown with willows and then, using the folds of the terrain, to the only nearby cover – a group of bushes. It was now getting quite light. If we were to remain unnoticed, a miracle had to happen.
>
> But it didn't turn out well. An old miller spotted us … But we were lucky. Just at the moment when he saw our battalion, our scouts appeared near the mill. Seeing them, the old man assumed that they were Germans and ran out to meet them, shouting loudly that there were lots of Bolsheviks in those bushes. I don't know what motivated him – maybe he was one of those who disliked the Soviet government, or perhaps he hoped for a reward from the invaders. In any case, if he ran into the Nazis instead of our men, we would inevitably face death.

We locked the old man in the mill. He was told not to leave for two days. His dog was with him and he was ordered to keep it quiet. The frightened miller followed our instructions. In the meantime, unaware of the danger they had just avoided, the men camouflaged themselves in the bushes and took up defensive positions. All we could do was wait.[6]

If their treatment of the miller was genuinely as Afanasyev describes, it was purely because they had little or no experience of partisan warfare. Such behaviour in later months and years would have resulted in the miller being shot out of hand, not least to act as a deterrent to others. German traffic continued to pass by on the highway and Afanasyev's group encountered a young cowherd, who told them of the local German positions. The partisans were then able to cross the highway, slipping between the German convoys, and continue on their way. They were fortunate; the neighbouring battalions ran into German troops and were overwhelmed in clashes with their better-armed opponents. Within days of infiltrating through the front line, most of the regiment had evaporated. Over the following weeks, several fragmented partisan units found their way – with little coordination – to the safety of forests in the southern part of their intended area of operations and were able to regroup. Hard lessons were being learned in the most difficult circumstances, and not just about how and when to fight:

If you were to ask any former Leningrad partisan today about the conditions they regard as the most important for successful military operations behind enemy lines, communication with the local population will certainly be one of the first things they mention. This is the start and end of the science of guerrilla warfare. But we didn't grasp this fact immediately. In the early days of the war, there was a general point of view that our strength lay in absolute secrecy and this was the only way to ensure the success of operations behind enemy lines. Therefore, contact with the local population should be avoided whenever possible. But it was precisely by making contact with the local population ... that [we] created a situation that was favourable for successful military operations, ensured our survival, and allowed us to remain elusive.[7]

In mid-August, a report on the activity of a partisan regiment operating near Kingisepp recorded a mixed picture, with successful attacks coming at a high price. The conclusions of the report highlighted the difficulties faced by the partisans:

The personnel of the regiment, both leadership and rank and file, began combat operations without any experience, not only of partisan warfare but of military operations in general. The personnel knew the rudiments of combat but didn't know how to organise reconnaissance, observation, and movement, and often became disoriented when in contact with the enemy, exaggerating the numbers and firepower of the enemy. As a result of this, the regiment suffered unnecessary losses and low effectiveness. Twenty days of combat operations at the front and behind enemy lines, particularly when defending positions, changed the appearance of the regiment and transformed it into a combat-ready unit as a consequence of the daily experience for officers and other ranks during combat. Due to the emergency situation, the regiment was formed rapidly, hastily armed and equipped, and given the mission of reaching the rear of the enemy en masse. Experience of combat operations behind enemy lines has shown that it is very difficult and ineffective to operate in large detachments behind enemy lines. The enemy set fire to forests alongside roads and burned back large areas of woodland on the roads leading to his rear areas in order to improve visibility for units on the ground and in the air. Food resources in the rear of the enemy are insignificant. There are few people left in the villages. It is impossible to manoeuvre, operate, and especially feed large detachments. Recommendation: it is far more expedient and effective to operate in small detachments of 30–40 people.[8]

Slowly, the surviving partisans began to reorganise themselves. There was a gradual move away from the original concept of partisan groups being tied to a specific district – instead, the partisans would have more freedom to move from one area to another in order to maximise their ability to evade the Germans and to attack tempting targets. The Political Directorate of Northwest Front issued a new directive that was distributed to newly forming partisan groups and eventually reached those that had already been deployed, instructing them to avoid costly clashes with their better-armed opponents. This would be followed by further refinements in the weeks and months that followed and as more lessons were learned. The partisan groups in the field made contact with each other, sometimes encountering formations that had been created by local Communist Party officials before the arrival of the Germans, and with Red Army stragglers. As autumn approached they became more effective, choosing their targets with greater care – isolated small garrisons and road convoys, and the destruction of bridges, railway lines and telegraph poles. The partisans began to reorganise into new brigades for purposes of administration, though they continued to operate in small groups to reduce the risk of detection; by mid-autumn, there were two such brigades operating with about 18,000 combatants.

A recurring problem for the partisans was overall command and control. The numerous agencies – Communist Party, NKVD, local Front – all had their lines of communication and often issued instructions to local partisans without reference to each other. The commanders in the field were then left to try to make sense of these often conflicting orders. Failure to follow instructions might result in arrest under suspicion of deliberately sabotaging the partisan movement – just as commissars in military units were often regarded with fear and suspicion by army officers, known Communist Party officials in partisan groups were also often seen as likely to condemn men who failed to carry out their instructions to the letter. Quite often, the most effective partisan units were those where such multiplicity of competing structures was absent or greatly reduced, or where local commanders took a calculated risk and ignored or overrode some of the orders they received. Such action was only justifiable if the result was a success for the partisan group and the risk of betrayal to higher authorities was low, and it is unsurprising that few commanders were willing to take such risks.

The partisan groups at the southern end of the Leningrad theatre, operating to the east of Pskov, were particularly effective, not least because this was the area where German troops had struggled in the face of strong Red Army resistance and the small number of roads running through the swamps and forests. The commander of 2nd Partisan Brigade was Lieutenant Colonel Nikolai Grigoryevich Vasilyev, who had served as a machine-gunner in the army in peacetime before becoming a junior officer. He then returned to civilian life, though he remained involved in military affairs, acting as head of the garrison club for Red Army personnel in Novgorod. He was then approached by an officer from Northwest Front who suggested that he should join the partisans. Vasilyev willingly agreed and for a man of fairly limited military experience, he showed great skill and energy in organising his fighters. Within a short time, he had established what became known locally as the *Partisanskoi Respubliki* ('Partisan Republic'). Centred on the village of Kruglovo, the 'republic' stretched for up to 75 miles from north to south and 56 miles from east to west. Party officials re-established schools and village councils, and despite repeated German efforts the partisans remained in at least partial control of much of the 'republic' through the winter. As partisan activity throughout the region lessened during the winter months, 2nd Partisan Brigade maintained a relatively high level of activity, including an attack on the German garrison in Kholm. The authorities in the region even tried to help the population trapped in Leningrad, as Yekaterina Mattynovna Petrova, deputy chair of one of the village committees, described:

> The issue was discussed with great enthusiasm among the collective farms (to be honest, we did not anticipate such an outcome). The collective farmers declared one after another: 'I can give a sheep' or 'I can give a cow', etc ... The collection of food aid for the people of Leningrad took place in very difficult conditions. The Germans sent three punitive detachments from different directions ... [which] were defeated by the partisans.[9]

The partisans then organised for the food aid to be taken through the front line into Soviet-held territory. There is no record of whether it was then actually dispatched to Leningrad; it seems more likely that it was simply used by local Red Army units.

The reports sent to Berlin by Stahlecker's *Einsatzgruppe A* during this time are a good indication of the level and effectiveness of partisan activity. Unlike the conquered towns and villages of the Baltic States, the Germans reported that nearly half the population of the towns on the Russian side of the old frontier fled before the arrival of the Wehrmacht.[10] Partisan activity was causing increasing problems throughout the region, as the report of 10 August recorded:

> In the last few days, partisan activity with attacks on troops and ambushes of rear area units has grown considerably. The military authorities give this matter particular attention. They have sought our help in all such cases. Partisan activity in the extensive forests and swamps to the north and east of Pskov is particularly energetic.[11]

It was the widespread policy, in the Soviet Union and other parts of occupied Europe, to take large numbers of hostages whose survival was dependent on the good behaviour of the local population. Almost inevitably, the Germans selected disproportionately large numbers of Jews for such hostage groups in the Soviet Union and used the slightest pretext – even the rumour of attacks on German troops – as an excuse to massacre them. There was no attempt to 'win hearts and minds' – Hitler's ideology of the war being a clash between incompatible cultures, a war of extermination to create limitless space for German resettlement, prevailed widely with few exceptions. Undoubtedly, some local people were sufficiently cowed by the slaughter of hostages to become reluctant to help partisan groups, and even denounced many of them to the Germans; but others were embittered by the German actions and actively sought to help the partisans. To complicate matters further, many partisan groups carried out reprisals of their own against civilians who were believed to have collaborated with the Germans. Many people in the countryside therefore lived in fear of both sides; it is likely that some helped whichever side seemed the most threatening at that particular moment. Nor was it purely the activity of anti-partisan units like the *Einsatzgruppen* that resulted in local people turning against the Germans. The German policy of forcible requisition of agricultural produce took no account of the needs of the farmers themselves, and the result was widespread starvation. The region with the most complex tangle of partisan groups was around Vilnius, in what is now eastern Lithuania. Prior to 1939, the region had been under Polish control despite being claimed by the Lithuanians and was then handed back to Lithuania by the Soviet Union after Poland was overrun in 1939. In this area, there were Polish partisan groups who were loyal to the government-in-exile in London as well as pro-Soviet partisans, and Red Army stragglers. As the war progressed, the widespread killing of Jews resulted in groups of Jewish partisans joining the already volatile mix. Survivors of these Jewish groups later recalled that the Polish *AK*-associated partisans were often fiercely anti-Semitic and actively attempted to destroy the Jewish groups.

A report produced for Northwest Front described the experiences of ordinary Russians in the occupied zone:

In 2nd Pyatpletka Collective Farm (Plyussy district), the Germans carried out executions, herding the collective farmers together. The old men and women who remained in the village were beaten with clubs because they refused to say where the partisans were. In the village of Mlyutino in the same district, the Germans arrested 24 collective farm workers on 18 July, put them in a barn and tried to torture them to extract information about which of them were Communists. Having achieved nothing, the Nazis shot six farmers.

In the village of Zeleny Klin and several other villages, many collective farmers were shot for refusing to hand over Party members and Communists. When they occupy villages and towns, the German troops rob the entire population without exception, taking away bread and other food, stealing livestock, clothing and other property, down to the smallest detail. Anyone who offers any resistance to the marauders is killed on the spot.[12]

The report stressed that Jews were particularly badly treated, being either taken away or executed on the spot.

After the war, many German veterans would seek to place the blame for all atrocities on the SS, particularly units like the *Einsatzgruppen* that were active behind the front line. The reality is that the Wehrmacht played a large role in the operations of units like those commanded by Stahlecker, simply because the *Einsatzgruppen* lacked the personnel to fulfil their tasks without help. However, front-line units were generally unwilling to release significant bodies of men for such tasks if they were likely to be required for a lengthy period. In order to increase the manpower available, steps were taken as early as mid-August to raise new police battalions from Lithuanian, Latvian, and Estonian 'volunteers' for deployment in the occupied parts of Russia, with the expectation that as a consequence of the year of Soviet rule over the Baltic States, there would be plenty of men who were only too willing to carry out brutal reprisals against the Bolsheviks. Some of these police battalions were indeed involved in terrible atrocities in all parts of the Eastern Front. The anti-partisan sweeps that were carried out often degenerated into indiscriminate killing, particularly where they came across large Jewish communities. The Nazi mindset that Jews and Bolsheviks were essentially the same meant that there was rarely any hesitation in slaughtering the Jewish populations of towns and villages if anti-partisan forces came across them.

The close cooperation between *Einsatzgruppe A* and Wehrmacht forces can be seen in the report for 21 August:

> In accordance with the agreement made with Sixteenth Army, part of *Sonderkommando 1b* [a subunit of *Einsatzgruppe A*] was dispatched to Yaski, 20km southeast of Porkhov, in order to conduct security police tasks there with the leading [Wehrmacht] regiment. Investigations revealed that small partisan units were active in the Yaski area. A Soviet telephone exchange that was still fully functional was discovered in the post office in the village of Porevich. The postmaster, two technicians and two female telephonists were taken prisoner. Interrogation revealed that a partisan group numbering 15 men had infiltrated into Porkhov ... Conversations had taken place between the partisans and Soviet military units in Staraya Russa. As the investigation revealed that the postmaster had freely permitted the partisans to use the telephone exchange to make contact, and had been assisted in this by the two technicians and the female telephonists, they were all shot.[13]

The report of the following day described how personnel of *Einsatzgruppe A* worked closely with troops from Fourth Panzer Group to clear and secure the area where the Wehrmacht units were operating. Priority was given to capturing any remaining Communist Party officials and Jews. The report described the difficulties of patrolling an area where there were few good roads, a situation made worse by uncleared minefields. With so many partisans wearing no identifiable uniforms, it was almost impossible to detect small groups or individuals without the assistance of local people, which the report added could only be achieved if civilians were 'addressed and treated in the necessary brusque manner'.[14]

Warfare against partisans is never an easy task, but the Germans made it unnecessarily difficult for themselves. Had they genuinely behaved as liberators, it is likely that many of the local population – particularly in rural areas – would have been supportive. But Hitler's vision of the future was that the area would be settled by Germans and the local population would either work as helots for the Germans or be left to die. Even at this stage of the war, when a German victory seemed at least possible, if not likely, there were some within Germany who doubted the effectiveness of this policy. Alfred Rosenberg, who was technically in charge of the implementation of occupation policies but had to compete with a chaotic level of overlapping responsibilities between different competing agencies, explicitly wanted to set up a series of client states in the occupied areas and then use them to help Germany in its war against the Soviet Union, but Hitler and others unambiguously rejected any such policy. Instead, all German units in the east were expected to deal with any dissent and resistance with brutal reprisals. There were few exceptions; the Germans often gave civilians food or money in return for information relating to partisan activity and whereabouts, but otherwise took whatever food they wanted and left the local population to fend for itself. Although receipts were sometimes given to farmers when livestock and other supplies were requisitioned, the value assigned to the items was trivial, and in any event exchanging the receipts for anything meaningful proved to be difficult if not impossible. As the SS reported, the information acquired from the local population in exchange for payments was often of dubious value, but sufficient numbers of civilians were prepared to cooperate that the Germans were able slowly to build up a network of informers, resulting in significant numbers of partisans and their helpers falling into German hands. They were either executed immediately or after interrogation. The houses of people thought to be aiding the partisans were routinely burned to the ground, but each step taken by one side resulted in countermeasures taken by the other:

> The tactic of using terror against terror worked outstandingly well. Out of fear of reprisals, farmers came from 20km or further afield to the headquarters of *Einsatzgruppe A* subunits on foot or horse to give reports of partisans, which in

most cases proved to be accurate. In total, 48 partisan helpers, including six women, were shot. In this context, one example demonstrates the correctness of this policy. In the village of Yakhnova it was determined from the report of a farmer, Yemelianov, and by carrying out further investigations, that partisans had received food from the house of Anna Prokofievna. The house was burned down at 9pm on 8 August and its occupants taken prisoner. Shortly before midnight, partisans set fire to the house of the informer Yemelianov. When a detachment was sent once more to Yakhnova the following day, it discovered the farmer's wife Ossipova had informed the partisans that Yemelianov had made the report that led to our intervention. Ossipova was shot and her house burned down. In addition, two 16-year-olds from Yakhnova were shot as they had delivered messages for the partisans.[15]

In addition to operations against partisans in the field and conducting 'sharp terror tactics', *Einsatzgruppe A* was responsible for the killing of the personnel of 'destruction battalions' that fell into German hands. A group of about 250 such individuals were captured in central Estonia in the last days of July by the Wehrmacht and handed over to Stahlecker's personnel. All but 40 of them were immediately executed. The report describing this incident went on to describe the personnel of the captured units:

> The members of these destruction battalions are recruited mainly from militia, frontier guards, volunteers and conscripts. The conscripts are from lists that had already been drawn up ... and 90 per cent are members of Communist organisations, as they have to be particularly trustworthy. Amongst the personnel of the destruction battalions there are typically large percentages of Jews ... [Amongst the female personnel] as everywhere in the Soviet Union, the Jews play a major role.[16]

After remaining in Novoselye – about 28 miles to the northeast of Pskov – throughout August, the headquarters of *Einsatzgruppe A* moved forward closer to Leningrad the following month and set up base in Kikerino, just 41 miles from Leningrad. During these weeks, partisan activity increased considerably. The reorganisation of the partisan movement played a large part, particularly as soldiers who had been left behind during the Red Army's retreat – in some cases, this was deliberate, but most were stragglers – were incorporated into the ranks of partisan units, greatly increasing their expertise and competence. There was also a shift in tactics, with deliberate targeting of the weakest elements in the

German rear area rather than military garrisons. Hit-and-run raids on supply dumps or convoys became a major feature, particularly where roads ran through forested regions where there was ample opportunity for the partisans to disappear quickly; according to the daily reports from Stahlecker's headquarters, attacks on railway lines, bridges, and isolated convoys were a growing problem even by mid-August, requiring the immediate deployment of two security divisions and an additional battalion of SS police in the area to the east of Lake Peipus.[17] On the occasions that the partisan groups found themselves in firefights with the anti-partisan forces deployed against them, the Germans almost always came off better, but the disruption of supply and communication lines was clearly more than just a nuisance and the casualties suffered by the Germans from these attacks continued to mount. A report from 2nd Partisan Brigade at the end of September summarised recent actions – numerous solitary vehicles were shot up, the railway lines were attacked repeatedly, and a few road bridges were also destroyed. These successes came at a price. One detachment started August with 44 personnel but by the end of September was reduced to 23.[18]

Nonetheless, the partisans continued to inflict damage on the Germans. Stahlecker's report of 2 September listed some of the encounters in his area in the last two days. A supply truck was shot up in broad daylight resulting in the death of one of the soldiers aboard; partisans set fire to a signal-box on the railway line between Pskov and Luga; the railway line from Pskov to Porkhov was blown up at two locations and a watering station for locomotives destroyed; and a train that halted due to the destroyed tracks was then shot up. In response, *Einsatzgruppe A* conducted a sweep through the area, rounding up and executing several Red Army stragglers and seizing various weapons caches. Several partisans were killed in firefights and some were captured. The report added ominously that they gave away nothing despite 'the severest interrogation'.[19]

Even small groups of partisans were able to mount attacks that caused considerable disruption. An exasperated report from *Einsatzgruppe A* recorded that by the end of August, the railway line from Ostrov to Porkhov, about 53 miles to the northeast, suffered damage almost every night despite the deployment of a battalion from a security division to guard the stretch. This resulted in considerable disruption to the delivery of supplies to units of Sixteenth Army. In order to bring the situation under control, an anti-partisan sweep was carried out in mid-September using men from *Einsatzgruppe A* reinforced by two 20mm anti-aircraft guns and a company of military police, supported by two aircraft. About a dozen partisans were killed or captured, and for the moment the attacks on the railway line died down. The report continued with a list of people who had been executed in the occupied towns in the area – many were identified as members of the NKVD or other Soviet organisations, but the number included several who were shot purely because they were being held as hostages. When a truck of military police came under fire, resulting in the deaths of two soldiers, a nearby village was razed to the ground in revenge with little concrete evidence that the local people had been involved. This local action demonstrates the resources that were tied down by the partisans. In addition to the disruption of rail traffic, this small group of pro-Soviet fighters required the attention of a substantial German force to disrupt their activities. Numerous other actions across the area had a similar effect.[20] But despite claiming that his men were getting on top of the partisan problem, Stahlecker glumly reported two days later that a building being used as accommodation by *Einsatzgruppe A* was bombed and destroyed – although all the SS personnel managed to escape, it was a further indication of the continuing activity of the partisans.

The lack of food as well as German action steadily reduced the efficacy of the partisan bands as 1941 drew to an end. The towns and villages were increasingly suffering from food shortages and there was no longer any thought of sending symbolic gifts of food to Leningrad. A Spanish soldier recorded his impressions when he passed through Krasnogvardeisk:

> There are lots of people on the streets ... old bearded *muzhiks*, dirty and ragged; shabby old women with faces yellowed from many months of hunger. Pretty young women nonetheless poor and dirty; not as thin as the old women as they can work some and are better suited to finding food thanks to their youth. Barefoot urchins with hats on their heads but so horribly thin their legs look like they belong to skeletons ... The hunger among these civilians is honestly frightening. They may not even survive the next winter. I often see men with juvenile features but who look horribly aged, paled by avitaminosis and their legs swollen from hunger. And these half-men are the lucky ones, they are not in the prisoner camp.[21]

Despite suffering losses, the Germans began to grind down the partisan units throughout the region. Afanasyev's partisan group was now in a poor state and he was relieved to receive orders by radio that gave him permission to break out to the east and escape from the German rear area. He led his men across the Lovat River, where they encountered a large group of Red Army stragglers; they too were low on supplies and the combined group made its way southeast through the woodland. After an exhausting march that lasted 11 days, they reached Lake

Sterzh, close to the front line. Afanasyev decided that the easiest way to escape was to cross the lake to the eastern shore, which was still held by the Red Army:

> In the morning, we concentrated near the village of Belka. Here, the lake was at its narrowest, about 350–400m. We sent out a reconnaissance group. When it returned, we learned that there were no Nazis in the village and the local population had several boats – most of the people were fishermen. As it grew dark, we decided to start the crossing.
>
> And then events took an unexpected turn. The least organised part of our group, made up of the stragglers, rushed to the shore and grabbed the boats, and soon the previously empty lake was churned up as a whole flotilla of fishing boats loaded to capacity feverishly paddled for the opposite shore. Nothing could stop the stragglers trying to rush to their goal as it was so close, and more and more boats set out across the lake, completely defenceless.
>
> It seemed as if only the intervention of God could save these people – a miracle was needed. Not only could the Germans fire on them, but our own units might open fire, mistaking them for an enemy attempt to cross. And yet, a miracle did happen. Apparently caught by surprise, the Nazis failed to grasp what was happening – in any case, they opened fire very late when our boats were already approaching the far shore. And it turned out that our units on that shore had outposts on guard in case of a landing attempt but didn't open fire.
>
> But my partisans didn't benefit from this miracle. The indiscipline of the stragglers, bordering on betrayal, left us in danger of having to fight – unexpectedly and completely contrary to what we wanted, in a situation where the enemy would be superior in every respect. Savchenko [one of Afanasyev's subordinate commanders] had to come up with a solution in the most difficult of circumstances. The appearance of the Nazis could be expected at any moment – it was necessary to find the most advantageous position for all-round defence ...
>
> A battle began and lasted for over three hours – in daylight, an open fight of a partisan detachment against a unit of the regular Nazi army. Having learned from the stragglers what was happening, our military units supported the detachment with artillery fire, but our situation remained very difficult.
>
> In the evening we retreated into the forest, covered by the ensuing darkness, and we were safe until the following morning ... Savchenko then made a seemingly desperate decision – to cross the lake at the very place where the stragglers had crossed, starting the following night ...
>
> By this time we had become masters of camouflage. As far as the Germans were concerned, the detachment disappeared without a trace. We sent a small

reconnaissance group across on the first night to contact the commander of our army units, informing them of the timing of the detachment's crossing and arranging for several large boats to be sent to us …

At the appointed time, the units of the partisan group began to move to the crossing point. Here we had another surprise: our scouts had managed to bring back only two boats, the others having been blown away by the wind when the stragglers left them on the lake shore … We started our crossing.

Each boat was able to take up to 20 people, not counting the rowers and helmsman. Consequently, our two boats had to cross the lake more than ten times in both directions in order to transport the entire detachment. The crossing went surprisingly smoothly due to the good preparation of the operation and the organisation and discipline of the partisans. By 5am the entire detachment had reached the advanced outposts of the Red Army units. Not a single shot had been fired.[22]

Afanasyev and his group were fortunate: their brief battle prior to the crossing cost them only seven dead and 25 wounded. The group was now able to feed and rest in safety for the first time for several months. Almost immediately, it was dispatched north to prepare for a new insertion behind German lines.

In mid-October, *Einsatzgruppe A* moved to Krasnogvardeisk, where the business of eliminating those thought to be enemies of Germany was carried out with brutal efficiency: about 260 local people were executed with little or no legal process. The fight against saboteurs and partisans continued; shortly after moving to this area, *Einsatzgruppe A* issued a proclamation to the residents of one small town:

> On 6 October 1941 ten people were shot in Slutskaya as they were about to cut a Wehrmacht telegraph cable in an attempted act of sabotage. Should further acts of sabotage occur in future, 20 people will be shot.[23]

As part of the switch from pushing on to Leningrad and taking up siege positions, Army Group North ordered that all non-essential civilians should be removed from the area immediately behind the front line. These civilians were simply transported to cities and towns further to the rear of the German lines and left there – no provision was made for their housing or food, placing an even greater burden upon the local population, which was in most cases faced with a struggle to survive in war-damaged buildings and was already suffering from food shortages due to the disruption of agriculture and food seizure by the Germans.

The intention was to deprive partisans of any support; in practice, some of those who were forced to leave their homes and ended up being abandoned further to the rear became hostile to the Germans and either gave support to partisans or joined their ranks.

Not all rear areas were hostile to the Germans, not least because the constant food shortages put the civilians in a situation where they came to rely upon the Germans as a source of sustenance. Inevitably, this was often exploited, as Wilhelm Lubbeck described:

> There were ... troops in my regiment who exploited the dire Russian food situation for sexual gratification. Putting a loaf of bread under their arm, these men would head for a certain area a couple of miles behind the front where there were hungry Russian women or girls who would willingly exchange sexual favours for food.
>
> One tale circulated that a particularly heartless soldier had responded to a woman's request for her 'payment' of a loaf by slicing off a couple of slices for her while retaining the remainder for himself. Most German officers and troops disapproved of such behaviour but I knew of no one who was reprimanded or punished for engaging in this type of act.[24]

Generally, the Wehrmacht frowned on liaisons between German soldiers and local women. Leaving aside the racial policies of the Third Reich and the portrayal of Slavs as inferiors, there were serious security issues as it was widely suspected – with good reason in some cases – that partisan groups would use such contacts as a means of obtaining information about which German units were in the front line and which were currently resting in the rear areas. On occasion, partisans were also able to use advance warning of meetings between German soldiers and local women to abduct the soldiers, who were then interrogated. Few survived this experience. Nevertheless, the deployment of so many young men meant that there would always be sexual appetites that would seek an outlet and in some areas military brothels were established. Although many women may have volunteered to work in them in return for pay or food, there was also a great deal of coercion involved. A report for the International Military Tribunal in Nuremburg after the war described one such brothel:

> In the city of Smolensk the German command opened a brothel for officers in one of the hotels into which hundreds of women and girls were driven; they were mercilessly dragged down the street by their arms and hair.[25]

Rape in war is as old as human conflict and was a recurring feature on the Eastern Front, where it was often associated with the most horrific brutality. Predictably, few German memoirs of the Second World War mention such incidents, but reports at Nuremberg made clear just how widespread such incidents were:

> In the Ukrainian village of Borodayevka … the Fascists violated every one of the women and girls.
>
> In the village of Berezovka … drunken German soldiers assaulted and carried off all the women and girls between the ages of 16 and 30.
>
> Near the town of Borissov in Belarus, 75 women and girls … fell into their hands. The Germans first raped and then savagely murdered 36 of their number … The soldiers marched … a 16-year-old girl into the forest, where they raped her … and cut off her breasts.
>
> In the Leningrad region, a 15-year-old girl … was raped by a group of German soldiers and died as a result of the assault.[26]

It is easy – even tempting – to dismiss these descriptions as exaggerations, but there was plenty of corroborative evidence to support the allegations. There were also suggestions that the brutality shown by the Germans towards women increased as the war continued, a sign of the manner in which the ongoing violence of war desensitised the soldiers to what they were doing and normalised such behaviour. Inevitably, these incidents – and even rumours of them – resulted in increasing hatred of the occupying forces, feeding the recruitment of the partisan movement. And when the Red Army moved west from mid-1943 onwards, it too was guilty of widespread rape, even before its units had moved out of Soviet territory. Such behaviour by Red Army personnel was completely absent from accounts of the war that emerged during the Soviet era and even now is rarely acknowledged in Russia.

The attitude of local people towards the occupying forces varied. In the rear area behind the front line of Army Group North, civilians had a more positive attitude towards the Spanish soldiers of the Blue Division than towards German troops. The Spanish were often unpredictable, largely because of inconsistent enforcement of discipline, but they regularly shared their food with local people and unlike the Germans they took few steps to force civilians to labour on roads and snow clearance. Whilst there were undoubtedly cases of sexual assault involving Spanish soldiers, these seem to have been fewer than in German-occupied areas. A few Spanish soldiers were charged with rape, but acquittals were common and even when men were convicted, the punishments were rarely severe. The Spanish authorities issued orders that all liaisons with local women were to be avoided, but the reiteration of these orders on several occasions suggests that they were ineffective. Although – perhaps predictably – few Blue Division veterans admitted involvement in anti-partisan reprisals against local people, the Spanish troops were used from time to time by the Germans, though their efficacy was often poor; on at least one occasion, an anti-partisan operation failed to achieve a great deal and the Germans attributed this to the Spanish soldiers leaking details of the forthcoming operation to local people. On other occasions, Spanish soldiers responded to attacks on their personnel with local reprisals, but it seems that in general the Spanish were less systematic and ruthless than the Germans.

Similarly, the reaction of Jews in the occupied territories towards the Spanish was different from their reaction to the Germans. There were very few Jews in Spain at that time and anti-Semitic attitudes were perhaps more on the basis of religion than race. Although some men in the Blue Division fully embraced the German view of Jews as racial inferiors who were the prime proponents of Bolshevism, this was a minority view. Despite strict orders about avoiding fraternisation with Jews, many Spanish soldiers struck up friendships with Jews, particularly women. There were almost no Jews in the rear area behind Army Group North due to the activities of *Einsatzgruppe A*, but as contingents of Spanish soldiers marched through Belarus and the Baltic region or were sent to hospitals in Latvia and Lithuania, they sometimes encountered Jews in ghettos and work gangs. A Jew in the city of Grodno later wrote:

> As if to illustrate how different the Germans were, one day a Spanish brigade came through the city … They were in Grodno for about two weeks, and while they were there, the atmosphere changed entirely. They associated with the Jewish men without a sign of dislike or hatred. They went out with the Jewish girls. And when they left, it was even harder to face the barbarians who had taken control of our lives.[27]

But whilst the Spanish may have been less harsh on Jews than their German comrades, there were very few occasions when they intervened to save Jews from persecution or slaughter.

Afanasyev and the other officers of his partisan group were debriefed after their escape across Lake Sterzh as the authorities tried to learn lessons from the recent actions. In mid-November, Afanasyev was assigned to a new group of about 60 partisans made up mainly from engineering troops. They were to infiltrate across the front line to mount a series of attacks and almost immediately the group ran into German forces. Quickly, the unit commander – Senior Lieutenant Kuchin – divided his group in two, ordering one group to pull out while the other fought a rearguard action. Afanasyev commanded this second group and was able to disengage successfully after mounting an ambush that drove off the pursuing Germans. After trying in vain to locate Kuchin and the first group, Afanasyev led his men back to Red Army lines after an exhausting march through the frozen marshes. He was then sent to a partisan school in Valdai; even though his formal military training was modest, his experience of partisan warfare was invaluable. When the men he was training were organised into a new regiment in early 1942, Afanasyev was struck by how much had changed since the beginning of the war:

> Compared to the regiment with which I left Leningrad in July 1941, everything had changed for the better. The new regiment was incomparably better equipped: everyone had excellent sheepskin coats, camouflage overalls, skis, and good weapons. In July there was only one automatic weapon in my entire battalion, now we had several. There were also mortars in the regiment. And the morale of the personnel also changed for the better: many were experienced partisans, seasoned in combat, who knew what lay ahead of them and were confident in their abilities.[28]

Meanwhile, Stahlecker continued to wage a war of terror against the partisans. In his report of 21 November, he described recent activity by his men:

> In screening in Krasnoye Selo between 18 and 28 October, 70 suspects were detained and interrogated. Seven were identified as members of partisan groups and members of the Communist Party, and of being involved in acts of sabotage and were executed after confessing. The rest of the detained persons were released. The mayor and some of his helpers who had been appointed by the area commander were found to be politically unsuitable. After agreement with the area commander they were dismissed and in view of their previous activity on behalf of the Communist Party, two were executed. In total between 24 October and 5 November 118 persons were executed, including 31 who were active enemy agents. Further executions took place after a few cases of unrest, refusal to work, and sabotage ... There was a major act of sabotage in Tosno where a sawmill, where construction material for five German divisions was being prepared, was burned down on 25 October ... Investigations revealed that it was due to arson, which was

possible due to inadequate security. As a retaliatory measure, 13 hostages who had previously been specified as being held against acts of sabotage were shot in the presence of community representatives at the scene of the sabotage.[29]

Partisan groups were active in almost every part of the Eastern Front, even in territory that had only recently been seized by German troops. The closer to the front line the partisans operated, the greater the risk that they would encounter regular troops. One partisan detachment under the leadership of the local district Communist Party committee attempted to disrupt German supply lines immediately to the west of Tikhvin during the Soviet counterattacks that eventually recaptured the town. A German infantry battalion carried out a ruthless attack against the partisans, wiping them out completely, a clear illustration of the limits of their combat abilities, but even in this case their activity required the diversion of an infantry battalion that might have been more profitably deployed in trying to hold back the attacking Red Army units.[30]

Throughout this time, the personnel of *Einsatzgruppe A*, aided by police battalions and locally recruited auxiliaries, had been working on exterminating other enemies of the Reich. The numbers killed in this period are horrifying. In a single 'special action' in the suburban areas to the south of Leningrad that had fallen under German control, *Sonderkommando 1b* killed 855 people on 20 November. At the end of January 1942, Stahlecker proudly summarised the activities of his units. Since the beginning of *Barbarossa*, he wrote, his men had been particularly active against the Jewish populations of the occupied areas. They had killed 41,848 Jews in Belarus, 136,421 in Lithuania, 35,238 in Latvia, 963 in Estonia, and 3,600 in the territory between the old Estonian frontier and Leningrad – a total of 218,050 men, women, and children. Just two weeks later, he reported that the total, including Communists, partisans, and others, stood at 240,410. Nearly all of these individuals had been shot. After the war, several SS officers who were prosecuted for war crimes attempted to claim that reports like this routinely exaggerated the number of those killed in order to impress superiors, but there can be no doubt about the bloody trail left by *Einsatzgruppe A* as it moved towards Leningrad in the wake of Army Group North.

Given his constant actions against partisans and their supporters, real or suspected, it was perhaps appropriate that partisan activity was ultimately Stahlecker's nemesis. On 22 March, partisans mounted a sudden raid on the Security Police headquarters in Krasnogvardeisk, machine-gunning the building and then disappearing before German troops could be summoned. Stahlecker was leaving the building at the time and was hit in the thigh. His men took him immediately to a military hospital in the town, where it was confirmed that the bullet had injured his femoral artery. He was flown to Riga where he underwent emergency surgery to save his leg, and after a lengthy operation he was declared fit enough to travel on to the Reich. Once again he was put on an aircraft, this time taking him to Prague where his wife and children lived, but during the flight the injured femoral artery began to bleed once more – either it hadn't been adequately repaired, or the wound started to bleed again as a result of his being moved. He was dead before he reached his destination.

Of all the SS personnel to have been killed on the Eastern Front by that date, Stahlecker was the most senior. He was typical of a generation of senior SS figures: he was highly educated and an early adherent of the Nazi Party, too young to have served in the First World War but old enough to have experienced the trauma of defeat as an angry teenager. He came from an affluent family and like many Germans of a similar socioeconomic class he had a deep-seated hostility towards Bolshevism. Anti-Semitism was commonplace throughout central Europe at the time and the radical influences to which men like Stahlecker were exposed as young men found fertile ground, permitting them effortlessly to equate Jews with Bolshevism. Men like Stahlecker were carefully selected by Heydrich and Himmler for high office. Like so many of his contemporaries in the SS, he wasn't a bloodthirsty fanatic. He was a highly efficient, politically committed man who used his energy and organisational skills to implement the murderous policies that had been assigned to him. It was typical of the Nazi system that men like him were given considerable freedom of action, to encourage them to compete against each other. In the context of the *Einsatzgruppen*, this led to a horrific competition to see which group could slaughter the greatest number of men, women, and children. He was the most prominent figure to fall victim to the partisans. Heydrich, his direct superior, read a eulogy at his funeral and both Hitler and Himmler sent wreaths.

By the end of 1941, many of the original partisan groups had been eliminated through a combination of German anti-partisan activity, food shortages, inappropriate tactics, and poor training. The newer partisan groups were showing better results, but their activity was greatly boosted by the military events of the winter. The German defeat outside Moscow gave many people hope that the tide was about to turn against the invaders and the partisan movement itself became better organised and led, choosing its targets with greater care. Their equipment was enhanced with supplies dropped by air and additional personnel were flown in with radios, allowing the partisans to coordinate their activity better with regular units.

Although the partisans frequently communicated with the Red Army to report German troop movements, the Red Army's intelligence service often avoided contact with the partisans, preferring to operate alone. There were several reasons for this. Part of the motivation was to increase security – the fewer people who knew about intelligence operations, the better. There was also an institutional tendency to restrict information sharing. As the war progressed and command and control of the partisan groups improved, their role in intelligence gathering was steadily increased, particularly in rural areas. Throughout 1942, this role grew in stages, with partisan groups having a designated intelligence officer who would ensure that reconnaissance was carried out as requested by the Red Army and would also gather political intelligence, about the mood and loyalty of the civilian population. As the first anniversary of the start of the war approached, a 'Guerrilla Reconnaissance Manual' was distributed, specifying the sorts of information that should be collected.[31] But even prior to these developments, some of the intelligence that was collected was of considerable value. A report in September 1941 to Northwest Front gave details of German units in the rear area:

> In the area along the line Gryazno–Domishche–Batovo villages, the enemy organised defences. In the village of Domishche in the school, the headquarters of a large unit is located; it is guarded by a reinforced unit armed with tanks and trucks. To the west of Domishche the enemy is concentrating tanks and artillery. In the area of the village of Petkina Gora ... the enemy is moving heavy artillery into position; there are several aircraft at the airfield near Domishche; the airfield is protected by anti-aircraft guns ... Along the Volosovo–Gryazno road, the enemy is bringing up new reserves of tanks, armoured vehicles, and anti-tank guns.[32]

The overall effectiveness of the partisan operations in the Leningrad region – and indeed elsewhere – is a controversial subject. The partisan movement became a key part of post-war Soviet historiography; it was portrayed as a demonstration of the manner in which the ordinary people of the Soviet Union, led by the Communist Party, helped defeat the German invaders. Soviet-era accounts of partisan activity are full of glowing descriptions of men and women, young and old, sacrificing their lives for the great cause, and estimates of the damage that they inflicted are improbably high – one account states that in the Leningrad region alone, partisans killed 104,000 'invaders and their accomplices', attacked over 1,000 rear area units, and destroyed 100 aircraft, 300 tanks, 4,600 other vehicles, 1,380 bridges and 326 supply dumps.[33] This is a staggeringly high figure; whilst there may have been repeated attacks on bridges that approached this total, the other figures must be overstatements, not least because Army Group North possessed very little by way of armoured formations after the withdrawal of Fourth Panzer Group in 1941 and the partisans would therefore not have had the opportunity to destroy 300 tanks. The reference to the 'accomplices' of the Germans is also worth noting. Just as the Germans showed little hesitation in killing those they thought were collaborating with partisans, many partisan groups behaved the same way when they suspected civilians of aiding the Germans. The behaviour of civilians in occupied areas is another area that has been difficult to assess because of orthodox Soviet historiography, which attempted to portray the people of the Soviet Union as being united in their resistance to the Fascist invaders. Undoubtedly, many willingly helped the partisans in every way they could. Others helped because they feared the partisans. In the early months of the war, the Germans portrayed the Russian civilians in occupied areas as being nearly as friendly and cooperative as people in western Ukraine and the Baltic States, but this is difficult to reconcile with accounts from Stahlecker and others about the manner in which every anti-partisan operation seemed to find numerous civilians who were suspected of working against the Germans. In any event, the behaviour of Stahlecker and others ensured that any initial friendliness towards the Germans soon faded away. It seems likely that the majority of civilians tried to maintain a reserved distance from both sides, merely hoping that they would be left with sufficient means to survive.

Even if the achievements of the partisan groups were exaggerated, there can be no doubt that they had a considerable impact, particularly in disrupting rail traffic. The Germans were forced to deploy large numbers of troops in rear areas, but the scale of the landscape was such that these garrisons were often isolated and barely able to fend for themselves, let alone take the war to the partisans. From time to time, front-line divisions were pulled out of line and used in extensive anti-partisan sweeps to try to 'pacify' the rear areas. The regular army was often reluctant to release personnel for such operations – the infantry losses of 1941 left the Wehrmacht permanently short of troops, and the diversion of resources to the rear area was an additional strain, only to be undertaken when partisan activity became so widespread and disruptive that not addressing it would result in even greater difficulties.

Experience across the world has shown that anti-partisan activity is best conducted by relatively small units of well-trained troops who are able to operate in the same territory as the partisans – in the case of the Soviet Union, this meant being able to move swiftly through wooded and swampy terrain. The older personnel of the security divisions and many of the police battalions that were deployed in rear areas lacked the physical fitness and stamina for such operations;

moreover, many German personnel found the vast forests and the sheer size of the terrain very daunting. The most effective anti-partisan units were often made up of Russian, Ukrainian, and Baltic men who took up arms on behalf of the Germans and more widespread use of such units might have proved decisive. At first, Hitler was adamantly opposed to arming and training a population that he regarded as inferior and marked out either for extermination or reduction to slave status other than in police battalions under strict German control. By the time that this mood changed, it was too late.

In addition to their service with *Einsatzgruppe A*, some of the men who followed Stahlecker's bloodstained path through the Baltic States were involved in partisan warfare in ways other than direct fighting behind the German front line. The SS officer Joachim Hamann was a particularly virulent persecutor of the Jews and was responsible for the creation of *Rollkommando Hamann*, a mobile killing team that roamed across rural Lithuania and slaughtered thousands of Jews. In early October 1941, *Rollkommando Hamann* was disbanded; by this date, the rural Jewish population of Lithuania had been almost completely exterminated. Hamann returned to Berlin, proud to have played his part in ridding the German people of their greatest foes – it is estimated that his *Rollkommando* killed about 60,000 Jews, and he personally claimed that the number was as high as 77,000.[34] Either of these numbers is a horrific total for activities that lasted just three months. He was accompanied on his journey to Berlin by Grauer and Kortkampf, two fellow officers in Karl Jäger's *Einsatzkommando 3* who were also no longer required in Lithuania. All three were assigned to the staff of a training unit that would prepare future SS officers for service in the field, but Hamann was found to be unsuitable for this task. Instead he was assigned to an operation codenamed *Zeppelin*, an attempt to use Russian émigrés and deserters, and also volunteers from the hundreds of thousands of Red Army prisoners of war, to create military and paramilitary units. Many – perhaps most – of the volunteers from prison camps were motivated by a desperate desire to escape the appalling conditions in the camps rather than any ideological wish to fight for the Germans. These units were then to be parachuted behind enemy lines to carry out similar activities to those being performed by pro-Soviet partisans behind German lines; in addition, they would attempt to disrupt the preparation of Soviet partisan groups before they crossed the front line, either by direct attacks or by joining such groups with the intention of acting as intelligence sources for the Germans. Hamann had been responsible for the pre-deployment 'militarisation' training of many of the personnel of *Einsatzkommando 3* – he was a paratrooper at the beginning of the war, but was released for SS duties amidst allegations that he had been deeply unpopular with his men because of his casual brutality both to enemies and his subordinates. As part of *Zeppelin*, he returned to Army Group North to train these new units and rapidly demonstrated that his reputation for harshness from his paratrooper days was entirely justified. The regime for the Russians under his command was brutal; men who failed to reach the required standard were either executed or dispatched to concentration camps. When they were deployed, the efficacy of the *Zeppelin* units was almost zero. Most used the German operation as a means to return to Soviet territory and then promptly deserted back to the Soviet side. Some ran away from their training camps to join anti-German partisans even before they were deployed.

As coordination between the Red Army and the partisans improved, the Germans recognised the manner in which partisan activity would often be stepped up prior to a major Soviet assault on the front line in order to disrupt lines of supply. On these occasions, the unwillingness of the Wehrmacht to release significant forces for anti-partisan operations was offset by the need to ensure rear area security. The tactics used in these operations usually consisted of establishing a rough perimeter with infantry and security division personnel while more mobile units, often borrowed from panzer divisions, then swept through the area. On occasion, the forces committed to such operation were considerable – two major anti-partisan operations in Belarus involved most of the combat troops of two army corps. Such operations were usually very effective at disrupting the partisans, but the nature of the terrain where they operated meant that the partisans were often able to slip away, finding a weak point in the encirclement. Even if these sweeps rarely resulted in the complete destruction of partisan groups, they had a significant impact on their organisation and ability to mount raids against German targets. Inevitably, there was a tendency during such operations to inflict widespread damage on the civilian population – entire villages were set ablaze and the civilian population either driven off or shot. If these measures had been taken to their logical and horrifying extreme, with the area being entirely cleared of civilians, the impact on the partisans would have been considerable as they would have been deprived of any support. Instead, the brutal half-measures that were adopted alienated the population and almost ensured that there would be continuing support for the partisans when they returned.

CHAPTER 9

LYUBAN: THE PRICE OF OPTIMISM

The Red Army counterattack outside Moscow struck the Wehrmacht at a critical moment. With their forces deployed in an attacking posture, the Germans had attempted one final push to reach and encircle Moscow, using up the last of their rapidly diminishing offensive power to do so. As this attack came to a halt in the bitter cold, the reserves that Stalin and Zhukov had mustered were unleashed, rapidly driving back the German pincers to the north and south of Moscow. When reports began to reach *Stavka* of widespread successes, there was elation. The Germans had overreached themselves. Their fighting power had been broken and the Red Army would now roll them back in defeat. The pre-war thinking in Soviet circles had been that a war would see a period of time in which the Red Army fought a defensive campaign to bring the invading enemy to a halt, and thereafter transitioned to an offensive war that saw it sweep the foe first from Soviet territory and then deep into the enemy homeland. The defensive phase might have taken far longer than anyone in the Soviet Union had expected, but this was surely the start of the triumphant second phase.

For a few heady days, this belief seemed to be confirmed by events on the ground. In reality, the Wehrmacht was switching to a defensive posture, slowly – and often in the face of Hitler's reluctance – pulling back into positions that could be held against the Red Army. As the end of 1941 approached, Soviet units found it increasingly difficult to overcome German defences. There were still gaps in the German lines through which Red Army formations were able to advance, but wherever they encountered German units the advance usually came to an abrupt halt. The orders from *Stavka* were uncompromising and often inflexible. In similar circumstances, German commanders in the field might have been expected to improvise in order to achieve the same overall objective, but the

Soviet officers were still learning how to fight and how to win, and such flexibility was far beyond their capabilities. Furthermore, the environment that still prevailed in the Red Army – of suspicion and fear, denunciation and arrest – left most officers with little option. Having encountered resistance, they threw their troops at the German defences again and again, suffering huge casualties and giving their enemies the opportunity to use their superior firepower and coordination of forces to maximum effect.

In the case of the northern sector a fresh Soviet offensive was planned to break the German ring around Leningrad, but the new operation was to be far more ambitious than a relatively restricted attack near Shlisselburg. Under the overall title of the 'Leningrad-Novgorod Offensive Operation', the forces of Leningrad Front, Volkhov Front and the northern part of Northwest Front were to mount attacks against the German units facing them. Converging attacks from Leningrad and the Soviet armies along the Volkhov River would lift the siege of the city and would destroy the German forces interposed between Leningrad and Volkhov Fronts. In the south, the attack by Northwest Front was expected to capture Demyansk and Staraya Russa before pushing on to the west – this would put Northwest Front's armies in a position to block the lines of retreat of much of Army Group North. As was the case with the directives sent to other sectors of the Eastern Front, it was a hugely ambitious set of operations, requiring advances on a scale that had not yet been achieved by the Red Army. It also ignored an important consideration. The Red Army's successes outside Moscow and in the north near Tikhvin had occurred when the German forces were overextended in an attack. The new offensives would be directed against German units that were ready to defend their positions against attack.

The truth was that the Red Army had won its victory outside Moscow at a very heavy price. The armies standing in front of the Soviet capital needed reinforcements, new equipment, and rest. Moreover, despite their successes, the Germans were only 42 miles from Moscow, and Zhukov wished to retain as much strength as possible in the immediate area rather than launching widespread attacks against the Germans. However, Stalin's view prevailed and a new directive was sent out by *Stavka* on 10 January:

> Having succeeded in sufficiently weakening the German-Fascist forces, the Red Army will switch to a counteroffensive and will begin to drive the German invaders towards the west.
>
> The Germans are going over to the defence to stop us from advancing and have commenced construction of defensive lines of foxholes, obstacles, and

fortifications. In this manner, the Germans expect on fending off our offensive until the spring when, having once more gathered their strength, they can launch a fresh offensive against the Red Army. Therefore, the Germans wish to gain time to get their breath back.

Our mission is to prevent the Germans from catching their breath and to drive them west without a pause, forcing them to commit their reserves before spring, when we will have large fresh reserves and the Germans will have none available. We will thus be able to ensure the complete destruction of Hitlerite forces in 1942.[1]

Meretskov and Khozin travelled from the headquarters of Volkhov and Leningrad Fronts respectively, accompanied by Zhdanov, to Moscow on 12 December to learn about the new offensive. As the plan was outlined, Meretskov became concerned about the ability of his troops to play their part. His Fifty-Second and Fourth Armies had suffered considerable losses during the battle for Tikhvin and he doubted that they could carry out an assault across the Volkhov River. He was also aware that Fifty-Ninth Army and Second Shock Army would be slow to assemble – there was limited railway capacity in this sector, and much of that was being used to try to move supplies to Lake Ladoga in order to keep Leningrad alive. When he outlined the problems, he was told to proceed with the armies available. The rest could serve as reinforcements as they arrived; acutely aware of the worsening situation in Leningrad, both Khozin and Zhdanov were anxious to avoid any delays. In order to improve the resources available and arguing that it would provide better coordination of the units outside the siege perimeter, Meretskov pressed for Fedyuninsky's Fifty-Fourth Army to be transferred to his Front. Khozin and Zhdanov both objected to this and Meretskov's suggestion was rejected. Given his recent arrest and brutal interrogation, Meretskov didn't press the point. Indeed, it is remarkable that he raised objections in the first place. He returned to his headquarters to commence detailed planning – the offensive was to start no later than 25 December, giving him less than two weeks for preparations. He had been promised an additional army with a significant number of specialised ski battalions, but he would have to start the operation with what was available.[2]

Definitive instructions for the offensive arrived on 17 December, confirming what Meretskov had been told in Moscow. At about the same time, Hitler gave permission for the two remaining armies of Army Group North – Sixteenth Army along the Volkhov and Eighteenth Army further north facing Leningrad – to withdraw from the remaining areas that they held to the east of the Volkhov and to take up defensive positions along the river. These positions, Hitler stressed, were to be held to the last man. Compared to the plight of the German armies facing Moscow, those in the north were in a rather better position. The lines that they currently held had been much the same for several weeks and as a result the infantry had prepared extensive defences, making good use of the terrain.

All along the Eastern Front, German units made hasty improvisations to cope with the changed circumstances – there was no more talk of an imminent victory. In an attempt to produce sufficient units to make a continuous front line, men who had never been intended for combat service were deployed; part of 12th Panzer Division's anti-tank battalion, for example, was assigned to a battlegroup that consisted largely of older men who had originally been sent to Army Group North as a construction battalion responsible for road repairs. When it reached the front line and took over the positions of a regular infantry regiment, the personnel of this battlegroup rapidly realised the scale of the problem that faced the Wehrmacht: the regiment that was being relieved could field no more than 390 men, less than the establishment of a single battalion. When replacement drafts arrived for 12th Panzer Division, they were used almost exclusively as infantry rather than replenishing the ranks of the panzer, artillery and anti-tank battalions. In any case, there was no point in sending the drafts to the heavy weapons formations of the divisions. The recruits lacked the necessary training, and the division lacked the heavy weapons to use the reinforcements in any role other than as infantry.[3]

One of the biggest irritations for the Germans in the northern sector was the continued existence of the Red Army's enclave on the Baltic coast to the west of Petergof, the Oranienbaum bridgehead. Leeb had considered eliminating this as an alternative to mounting his operation towards Tikhvin but had been overruled. In any case, it would have been a costly operation had an attack been launched. The guns of the Soviet Baltic Fleet provided plentiful fire support for the Red Army troops in the bridgehead, who were entrenched in positions that would have been difficult to overrun. Instead, Eighteenth Army was forced to leave four infantry divisions facing the bridgehead, troops that could have been of great value if they had been available for use elsewhere. In addition, the Oranienbaum garrison were able to provide a little early warning of the approach of German bombers from the southwest. Like the defenders of Leningrad, the troops in the bridgehead endured a difficult winter with drastically reduced rations and little or no fuel for heating, but the mixture of regular Red Army soldiers, naval personnel, and militia remained determined to hold out and tie down as many German units as possible. Several large naval guns had been dismounted from warships and deployed in the bridgehead, including a set of 12-inch guns from a battleship. Ammunition for these guns was in short supply; Petr Yegorovich Melnikov, the commander of the small battery, had to request permission from a naval staff officer every time that he wished to fire. Designed for warfare at sea, the guns had impressive range and – within the limits of their ammunition – were able to hit targets far behind the German front line. The direct value of these weapons in combat may have been limited, but their usefulness in harassing German units was considerable, and the thunder of their fire was a welcome morale boost for the Oranienbaum garrison.[4]

During the winter, one of Melnikov's gunners, a sailor called Fedorov, received a message that his family – who lived in Leningrad – were unwell. As there was a lull in the fighting, Melnikov arranged for him to visit the city. When he returned, his account of his trip horrified the men in the battery:

'I went from Oranienbaum to Kronstadt,' Fedorov said in an impassive voice. 'Then from Kronstadt to Lisiy Nos on foot across the ice. Three times along the way I came under fire. From Lisiy Nos a passing car gave me a ride to the city. When I was walking down the street, there was a loudspeaker announcement: "This area is under fire. Traffic must halt and people must take shelter." I stood for a while in a yard and went on. I came across some people – pale, their legs swollen, eyes sunken. Everyone was wrapped up in scarves and blankets. I saw some stumble and fall. And they didn't get up again.

'At home I found a terrible scene. It's difficult to put into words. The plumbing wasn't working. There was no electricity. There was no firewood. The rooms are freezing. I arrived just in time. My wife was still breathing. She lay on the bed, panting. But she couldn't speak any more. She looked at me and then at the children. The children were on the other side of the bed, next to each other. I rushed around to them. My son was already dead. My daughter was breathing. I raised her head. She didn't open her eyes. After a few moments, she too stopped breathing.

'I broke up the last chair and heated the iron stove. There was a big air raid on the city that night. Of course, I stayed there. I sat on the bed with my wife and thought, "If only we were hit [by a bomb], we could both go together." By the morning, my wife was dead.

'I took a sled from the janitor, put everyone on it, tied them on and took them to the cemetery. On the way there, I passed so many corpses. Some were covered in material, while others just lay there. I tried to dig a grave. Just half a metre, no more. And I buried my entire family. And I felt as if I should just lie down there with them.'[5]

Conditions within the Oranienbaum bridgehead were little better than those of the civilian population of Leningrad. Although the soldiers received better rations, these were still far from adequate to prevent weight loss, particularly for men doing physical work in the bitterly cold conditions. The few civilians in the bridgehead were in a desperate situation and most were evacuated as the winter progressed; they were taken to Leningrad, where many perished in the weeks that followed.

Most of the soldiers in the trenches and positions on either side endured the cold with as much stoicism as they could, but there were cases of self-inflicted injuries as men tried to escape. Dmitry Vasilyevich Konstantinov was a lieutenant in a rifle regiment who found himself caught up in a possible case of self-inflicted injury, and his experience sheds an interesting light on how such cases were investigated and, on occasion, manipulated; it also highlights the ongoing climate of fear and the manner in which this could be used to apply leverage. The incident occurred when he was visiting a building where some of his men were living:

As soon as I sat down, there was a sudden shout from the opposite end of the building:

'Down, down, throw it now!' And there was the hiss of a grenade fuse, familiar to everyone. I was stunned. Because of a bunk separating me from what was happening, I didn't see anything. But hearing the familiar sound, I broke out in an instant sweat. The platoon had a number of so-called 'defensive action' grenades, which had a particularly powerful explosive charge and created a great deal of shrapnel ...

Hearing the hissing fuse, most threw themselves on the ground. It only took a moment. There was the crackle of the fuse detonating, a groan, swearing, and a loud shout: 'Medics!'

There was no grenade explosion. Mikhailov, a soldier, sat on a bunk groaning. Two fingers of his right hand were completely torn off and a third was badly damaged. A medical orderly bustled about him. I turned to the sergeant. Stepping aside with me, he told me what had happened. He had been explaining how the fuse worked and had taken it out of the grenade and passed it around for everyone to examine. When it reached Mikhailov, he began to twist it for some reason, pulled out the ring, and triggered the fuse, which then went off. When the sergeant shouted 'Throw it now!' he continued to hold the fuse in his right hand, and then it went off.

The explosion of a fuse without the grenade is insignificant and doesn't pose much danger, but if it occurs in a tightly clenched fist, the consequences are of course not particularly pleasant, as we obviously had in this case. Mikhailov was an old and experienced soldier who had gone through the Finnish campaign; he knew all this very well. Before me was an undoubted case of self-harm, or as they said in the Red Army, a 'crossbow', an attempt to be released from military service. The sergeant who had been conducting the training was of the same opinion.

I realised that if this was confirmed as self-mutilation, Mikhailov would face execution and we would all be in a great deal of trouble. Interrogations by the 'special department' [NKVD] were unavoidable but in any event things would be much simpler if this was treated purely as an accident. The sergeant and I agreed to testify in just such a way ...

Late in the evening, at about 2300, a messenger from regimental headquarters summoned me. I knew what it meant. At headquarters, the duty officer, a good friend of mine, greeted me and then showed me silently to a door with a laconic inscription – 'Special Department'. After knocking, I entered. A small table lamp lit the room, illuminating the table and two people seated there. The rest was in darkness. One of those sitting was the head of the regiment's special department; the other, unknown to me, with a major's insignia, was an investigator from 'higher up'. I was asked to sit down. The usual general questions followed – name, year and place of birth, social status, parents' origins and occupations, pre-war profession and occupation, any previous legal proceedings and, finally, whether I had any relatives abroad and whether I corresponded with them, whether I had been abroad, and whether any relatives had been 'repressed' by the Soviet authorities.

After asking about the circumstances of my recruitment and military training, he went on to the details of the case. He emphasised that quite recently, in my unit, there had already been a case of a grenade explosion, but there was now an almost identical case in my platoon – he assured me that he thought this merely a coincidence, but it seemed rather strange and he therefore advised me to be completely frank, as this would be in my best interests.

Knowing that there would be interrogations, the sergeant who had been in charge of the training, two other witnesses who had seen everything that happened, and I had agreed not to denounce Mikhailov and to say that it was an accident ... I told the investigator the whole incident as it happened. When asked for my assessment of events, I replied that it was an accident caused on the one hand by the soldier's lack of experience and on the other hand due to his ignorance on what to do.

'But you know, Lieutenant,' declared the investigator, 'that as platoon commander you are entirely responsible for what happened?' ...

[The investigator continued:] 'We will look at how you conducted training and generally worked in the unit as its commander, and will draw the necessary conclusions. But, you still insist it was an accident and not a "crossbow"?' He looked straight at me as he asked me the question. 'After all, as far as I am aware, Mikhailov is an experienced soldier, yet you say this happened due to insufficient experience?'

I felt a little confused, but only for a moment. I then gathered my thoughts. Looking straight back at the investigator, I replied, 'Yes, I very much believe that it was an accident, not a "crossbow". The circumstances of the case, as I have described, show this. As for Mikhailov, he is a simple farmer … He first joined the army during the Soviet–Finnish War and served as a driver. It's more than likely that he never held a defensive grenade before in his life. So I see no reason to think otherwise.'

'Yes, but bear in mind that if there are no apparent grounds, it is precisely the task of the NKVD to find them. Anyone who tries to interfere with us or deceive us will be in serious trouble. Do you understand?' …

After reading the statement I signed it and left … I was not called again. The sergeant and two other witnesses unanimously corroborated my testimony. The company and battalion commanders gave positive reports about my handling of the case. There was no meat, as they say. But in this case, someone had to pay. Quite unexpectedly, it turned out to be the company commander. Of course, he wasn't to blame, but the battalion commissar was unhappy with him and wanted to get rid of him – this was the real reason for his dismissal. They criticised him, saying that as an experienced career officer, he failed to check how training was conducted in platoons, particularly my platoon, as I had only just started my military service, had little experience, and shouldn't be left unsupervised.

The absurdity of the decision was obvious, but it was unsurprising in the Red Army. However, as sometimes happens in wartime, this unpleasant incident saved the company commander's life, because he didn't take part in subsequent operations that were disastrous to our regiment. He was removed from his post and assigned to the regiment's reserve. I didn't find out the fate of the soldier Mikhailov.[6]

Meanwhile, Meretskov and his staff raced to draw up plans and orders for the coming offensive. The first assault would be made by Major General Ivan Vasilyevich Galanin's Fifty-Ninth Army; once the German lines had been penetrated, Meretskov intended to send the fresh Second Shock Army, commanded by Lieutenant General Grigory Grigoryevich Sokolov, through the breach. The first objective was Lyuban, about 22 miles to the west of the Volkhov River. The southern flank of Volkhov Front was to cooperate with the northern flank of Northwest Front to defeat and destroy the southern flank of the German Sixteenth Army in and around Novgorod. At the same time, Leningrad Front would attack from the north with Fedyuninsky's Fifty-Fourth Army.

A measure of how badly prepared Meretsokov's forces were can be seen from the air assets available to him: to support all of its armies, Volkhov Front had just 52 aircraft, with many of them unable to fly because of shortages of replacement parts. Furthermore, although Second Shock Army was fresh and made up of newly raised units, these had little or no experience of operating in forested regions, as Meretskov described:

> It should be noted ... that the newly arrived units of Fifty-Ninth Army and Second Shock Army, formed in a short time, had not completed the full course of training. They were sent to the front without solidly established skills in tactics and in handling weapons. In addition, some of the units and subunits were made up from men from the steppe regions, many of whom found themselves in the midst of forests for the first time. Their officers complained – I myself saw it – that the forests and swamps had a depressing effect on the men and even the officers, who were accustomed to the open spaces of their native land. Many were afraid of getting lost and were drawn to each other, confusing their battle formations and resulting in crowding together. Ski battalions were a more appropriate response to the terrain. Unfortunately, their personnel had poor skiing skills. More than once I saw how skiers preferred to move on foot, dragging their skis behind them. And our rear area services did not provide these battalions with everything that was necessary. Clothing was uncomfortable – short fur coats, padded trousers and felt boots restricted movement and quickly became soaked, with the consequence that men couldn't stay outside away from buildings for long periods ...
>
> The headquarters of the new armies also looked weak. Like the troops, they had not had sufficient time to complete the necessary training programmes ... The armies did not have enough communications equipment and the personnel of the units had a very poor understanding of communications technology. We had to train them during the actual fighting.[7]

Many of the soldiers had no experience of using skis and simply strapped them to the tops of their packs, preferring to wade through the deep snow on foot.

To make matters worse, Sokolov had very limited practical experience. He had extensive service in the ranks of the NKVD, but although he had been assigned to roles with border guards, these had been exclusively administrative. On 22 August 1941, he had been appointed chief of staff of Central Front, a post that he held for just three days, and was then sent to take command of Twenty-Sixth Army in Ukraine. When he reached his new unit, he found that it had effectively ceased to exist and he spent the next few weeks organising fresh units into a new Twenty-Sixth Army, which was then renamed Second Shock Army and sent to the north. Fifty-Ninth Army was also a new formation, but unlike Second Shock Army it was made up of men recruited from Siberia and the Ural Mountains. Furthermore, many of its officers had experience of war, having served against the Japanese at Khalkin Gol.

In addition to Fedyuninsky's Fifty-Fourth Army, Leningrad Front would mount an attack out of the Neva bridgehead; the former Neva Operational Group had been renamed Eighth Army, with the staff of this army being withdrawn from the Oranienbaum bridgehead – command of the mixture of units in Oranienbaum, renamed the Primorsky Front Operational Group, now came under Major General Andrei Nikitovich Astanin. The new Eighth Army on the banks of the Neva to the east of Leningrad was under the command of Major General Andrei Leontyevich Bondarev. Together with the neighbouring Forty-Second and Fifty-Fifth Armies, the relatively weak force in the Neva bridgehead – probably no more than 13,000 men – were to attack in support of the main operation. These attacks would tie down German units, and would also serve to exploit any weaknesses that might develop.

Given the manner in which the war had unfolded to date, the plans for the Lyuban Offensive and other attacks at the end of 1941 seem astonishingly ambitious – just a few weeks before, the Red Army had been struggling to halt the Germans from advancing to isolate Leningrad and threaten Moscow, yet now there were proposals for a wide-ranging series of offensives to sweep away the invaders. In the north, the paper strength of the two sides was markedly in favour of the Red Army, which outnumbered the Wehrmacht in terms of men, guns, tanks, and even aircraft, the parlous state of Volkhov Front's air assets notwithstanding. But such an analysis took little account of the reality on the ground. The German forces were all seasoned veterans, whereas many of the Soviet units had yet to go into action, and even where they had a proportion of experienced personnel there had been little or no opportunity for these men to pass on their knowledge and skills to their unskilled comrades. Moreover, the terrain was the same densely forested landscape that had proved so troublesome for the Germans when they were advancing. The marshes might be frozen and much easier to cross than had been the case in the autumn months, but the same shortage of good roads that had hindered the Germans so much would have a major impact on the ability of the Red Army to advance. Indeed, the manner in which the Lyuban Offensive was planned, with little or no regard for the terrain, was typical of many of the operations that unfolded in the weeks that followed. For the Germans to make such mistakes, as they undoubtedly did in the last weeks of 1941, could be explained by a lack of familiarity with the landscape and over-reliance on inaccurate maps; for the Soviet planners to make similar mistakes when planning operations deep within their own country was a remarkable error.

The widespread nature of the offensives, with multiple objectives even within each theatre, created further problems. If the available forces had been concentrated for more limited operations, it is likely that they would have achieved much greater success. Instead, by pursuing so many targets, there was a considerable risk that there would be insufficient strength at any one point to achieve the intended objective. And the logistic factors that forced the Red Army to make a staggered start to their offensives gave the Germans an opportunity to concentrate their limited mechanised resources on each fresh attack as it appeared.

The Germans were, at the very least, off balance; consequently, it was important to exploit this as widely as possible. In his memoirs, Zhukov claimed that he urged caution but was overruled by Stalin who was convinced that an opportunity existed to win the war within the next few months. There is at least some evidence to support Zhukov's claim, and even if his account overstates the energy with which he put forward his views there is no doubt that he did attempt to moderate expectations:

> After Shaposhnikov's presentation about the situation on all fronts and his draft plans, Stalin said, 'The Germans are dismayed by their defeat near Moscow and are poorly prepared for the winter. Now is the best moment to begin a general offensive. The enemy is counting on us delaying our offensive until the spring – by then, having mustered his strength, he will once more resume offensive operations. He wants to buy time to recover.' None of those present, as I recall, raised any objections to this, and Stalin developed his thoughts further. 'Our task,' he mused, walking as usual around the conference room, 'is to not give the Germans this respite, to drive them to the west without a pause, to get them to commit their reserves before the spring.' He emphasised his last words, paused a little, and then continued. 'We have new reserves, and the Germans have none.'

Having outlined his understanding of the possible options for offensives, the Supreme Commander proceeded to practical plans for each front. The *Stavka* plan was as follows. Considering the successful course of the counteroffensive by the troops of the Western Direction [i.e. the Fronts defending Moscow], the aim of the general offensive was to defeat the enemy on all fronts.

The main blow was planned to be delivered against Army Group Centre and its defeat was to be carried out by the left wing of Northwest Front and Kalinin, Western, and Bryansk Fronts, which would conduct a double envelopment and subsequent encirclement and destruction of the main forces in the Rzhev–Vyazma–Smolensk region. The troops of Leningrad and Volkhov Fronts, the right wing of Northwest Front, and the Baltic Fleet were tasked with crushing Army Group North and breaking the Leningrad blockade. The troops of Southwest and Southern Fronts were to defeat Army Group South and liberate the Donbas region, while Caucasian Front and the Black Sea Fleet were to liberate Crimea. The transition to a general offensive was supposed to be carried out in an extremely short time.

After outlining this plan, Stalin invited those present to speak.

'In the Western Direction,' I reported, 'where favourable conditions have been created and the enemy has not yet managed to restore the combat effectiveness of his units, we must continue the offensive. But for a successful outcome, we need to replenish our ranks with men and military equipment and reinforce them with reserves, particularly tank formations. Without this replenishment, our offensive cannot succeed. As for the offensive of our troops near Leningrad and towards the southwest, our troops face substantial enemy defences. Without powerful artillery, they will not be able to break through these defences. They will be exhausted and will suffer heavy, unjustifiable losses. I propose strengthening the Fronts of the Western Direction and conducting a more powerful offensive here.'

[Nikolai Alekseyevich] Voznesensky [First Deputy Chairman of the Council of People's Commissars] supported me. 'We do not yet have the material resources sufficient for a simultaneous offensive on all Fronts.'

'I spoke to Timoshenko [who was now commander of Southwest Front and with overall control of the Southwest Direction],' said Stalin. 'He is in favour of action on the Southwest Direction. We must grind down the Germans faster so that they can't advance in the spring. Who else would like to speak?' There was no response. A proper discussion of his proposals never took place.

As we left the conference room, Shaposhnikov said to me, 'Your arguments were in vain. This issue was decided in advance by the Supreme Commander.'

'Then why did he ask our opinion?'

'I don't know, my dear fellow, I don't know!' replied Boris Mikhailovich, sighing heavily.[8]

To coordinate matters in the north, Stalin dispatched Commissar Lev Zakharovich Mekhlis, the Deputy People's Commissar for Defence, to ensure the activities of the various Fronts were properly aligned. Mekhlis owed his prominence and survival to his unbending support for Stalin, and despite almost no military experience – he had served as a lowly soldier in the First World War – he had huge confidence in his abilities. It was well known in the army that he behaved as if Stalin's orders had to be obeyed to the letter and had ordered the arrest of several officers for failing to show the appropriate amount of commitment. An indication of his character can be gained by an exchange between Yefim Ivanovich Smirnov, a senior medical officer in the Red Army, and Stalin in 1949. Smirnov speculated that perhaps Mekhlis should be appointed as head of one of the government commissions. Stalin's reaction was to laugh uproariously, clutching his stomach and wiping away tears of merriment. He turned to Smirnov and replied: 'Can Mekhlis ever be appointed to a constructive role? If there's something that needs to be destroyed, destroyed, destroyed – for that, he's suitable.'[9]

If this is a true representation of Stalin's opinion of Mekhlis, the fact that he chose Mekhlis as his envoy at this stage of the war gives an insight into the Soviet leader's state of mind. Sergei Matveyevich Shtemenko, who would later rise to the post of chief of the general staff, was a colonel working in the Near East Operations Directorate of the staff at this time. He had encountered Mekhlis during the war against Finland:

> On the instructions of Stalin, Mekhlis was sent to Ninth Army. His messages often passed through my hands and always left a bitter aftertaste in my mind: they were as dark as night. Using the powers assigned to him, Mekhlis dismissed dozens of men from their commands, replacing them immediately with others ...
>
> Later, I had to meet Mekhlis more than once, and that finally convinced me that this man was always inclined to use the most extreme measures.[10]

The reaction of Meretskov, still suffering the physical effects of his recent ordeal at the hands of the NKVD, to the appearance of Mekhlis can only be imagined.

Regardless of Stalin's instructions and any efforts by Mekhlis, the planned start date of late December had to be postponed. *Stavka* continued to demand swift action all along the Eastern Front and Meretskov, who was understandably anxious to impress Stalin and Mekhlis and thus avoid being re-arrested, was equally energetic in his orders. But it proved impossible to get all the units into position in time. Stalin now dispatched Colonel General Nikolai Nikolayevich Voronov, commander-in-chief of Red Army artillery, to the region to investigate and he discovered that Fifty-Ninth Army's artillery lacked gunsights, radio and telephone equipment, and in many cases even gun limbers; all of these items and many more were stranded on railway lines far to the rear, as Meretskov later wrote:

> By the time [Voronov] left, he had arranged the arrival of several wagons of telephone sets, field cabling, and artillery pieces. Voronov stayed at the Front for several days. He familiarised himself with the conditions for warfare here, in particular with the use of artillery in a wooded and swampy area, and attempted to increase the provision of shells for the Front's artillery. However, even with his assistance, we were unable to ensure that the Front had everything it needed, and we remained short of artillery ammunition.
>
> An important reason that prevented the timely start of the offensive was the fact that by the beginning of 1942 the Front basically did not have proper rear area formations. In the short time that the Front had existed, we had not been able physically to assemble rear area units in the right locations, organise supply routes, and build up stockpiles. All supplies were delivered directly from the centre to the armies, bypassing the Front ...
>
> The build-up of ammunition and other supplies was very slow. By the beginning of January the troops had, as I recall, no more than a quarter of the required ammunition and completely inadequate supplies of food and fodder.[11]

The lack of ammunition was part of a problem created by the dislocation of Soviet war industry. The evacuation of so much industrial capacity from the threatened cities in the west to safer locations in the east was an astonishing achievement and the factories were now once more coming into service, often based in buildings without glazed windows or even roofs, but overall production was still below pre-war levels. In time, Soviet production of armaments and munitions would climb to remarkable heights, but at the beginning of 1942 there was a shortage of all weapons and the ammunition that they needed. The reserve armies that Stalin threw into the winter counteroffensives represented the strategic reserves available to the Soviet Union, but they were relatively poorly equipped. Despite this, Stalin expected them to perform as if they were at full strength, fully trained and with their full complement of equipment. Nonetheless, he had to bow to reality for the moment and reluctantly, he agreed to a delay. The main attack would now start in early January, but he sent Meretskov an ominously worded letter:

> The operation that has been entrusted to you is a historic matter. You understand that the liberation of Leningrad is a great task. I wish that the forthcoming offensive of the Volkhov Front should not be a series of small skirmishes, but should be conducted as a single powerful blow against the enemy. I have no doubt that you will try to mount the offensive as a unified assault against the enemy, overwhelming the units of the German invaders. I send you my greetings and wish you success.[12]

Failure to comply with this letter would almost certainly result in severe sanctions, and Meretskov had no choice but to accept the start date. The movement of troops to their starting positions was a slow and painful business, made worse by the bitterly cold weather. One soldier in a rifle division recalled the conditions:

> We moved only at night, hiding in the forest by day. The road was not easy. To move along the road in deep snow, we had to assemble columns of 15 men in a row. Those at the front walked and trampled down the snow, which was waist deep in places. After ten minutes, the leader moved aside and dropped to the tail of the column … In places there were swampy regions that hadn't frozen and small rivers covered in ice. Our boots became wet, then frozen. It was impossible to dry them as we weren't permitted to light fires in our rest areas … The supply horses were exhausted. Fuel ran out and vehicles came to a halt. Ammunition stockpiles, all our equipment and our food had to be carried.[13]

Even with this delay, the first attack that was made by Meretskov's troops on 4 January against the German I Corps near Kirishi struggled forward for perhaps three miles before being brought to an abrupt halt. To make matters worse for the Red Army, the German 12th Panzer Division was available for a counterattack. After heavy fighting in the battles for Tikhvin, the division had been withdrawn to Estonia for a chance to recover but was ordered back to the front line on 1 January; even this brief pause had allowed its repair workshops to return a large number of tanks to service, increasing its tank strength from just 33 in mid-December to 100 vehicles. But it was to be an unhappy return to action for the division; in the coming weeks, Army Group North had little option but to break it into small battlegroups and send them to support different divisions in the front line.

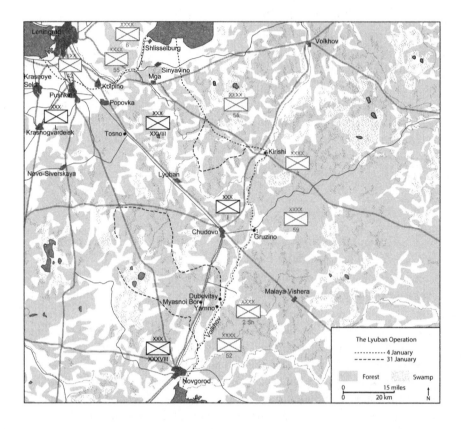

For men of the panzer arm, steeped in the doctrine of *Klotzern, nicht klechern* ('A flood, not a sprinkling') this resulted in the division failing to operate with its full potential. The problem that the Wehrmacht faced was that without the support of these battlegroups from panzer divisions, German infantry formations were weak in anti-tank firepower. This had been less of an issue in the days of German advances, but now that the Wehrmacht was fighting a defensive war – particularly in Army Group North – this weakness was increasingly exposed. The German doctrine of launching counterattacks to restore the front line after any penetration by enemy forces also required the presence of motorised formations, and with so few panzer divisions available – Army Group North had only two, 8th Panzer Division and 12th Panzer Division – there was little choice but to disperse the armoured units, particularly as the road network was so poor that the panzer divisions couldn't be held some distance behind the front line, ready to be dispatched to wherever they might be needed. There were several independent panzer regiments and battalions of assault guns, and the numbers of these would increase as the war progressed, but there were never enough and the Germans were repeatedly forced to disperse the precious panzer divisions along the front line. But when they reached the front line, the small groups of men from the panzer divisions saw for themselves the desperate state of some of the infantry units facing the Red Army. When Stahlberg was sent to the Chudovo sector with five soldiers late one evening, they took up a machine-gun position that was about 50 yards from any other German defences. Stahlberg and his comrades surveyed their surroundings as the moon rose just after midnight:

> The scene revealed to us when its pale light illuminated the landscape was one of horror: we were in the middle of a graveyard, the dead, German and Russian, lay all around us. Here a helmet was visible through the snow, there only an arm freed by the wind, here an entire body, there only – the unspeakable.
>
> We were staring around, appalled, when suddenly a bullet whistled close over our heads and forced us back into cover …
>
> We were there for three weeks … My five comrades suffered so badly from lice that hunting them down became their only leisure activity; but no more than three men at a time could devote themselves to the hunt, since it meant removing all one's clothes.[14]

At least Stahlberg and his comrades could look forward to being rotated out of the front line; they spent three or four weeks enduring deeply unpleasant conditions before returning to their base camp in Estonia. By contrast, the soldiers of most infantry divisions spent long spells in their swampy trenches with few spells of rest in the rear areas. Every rotation to the front line saw rising casualties for the small groups from 12th Panzer Division. Before the end of the winter, Stahlberg – who was officially adjutant to Oberstleutnant Heinrich Becker, commander of the division's anti-tank battalion, but was serving primarily as an improvised infantry commander – realised that he and Becker were the only surviving officers from the original anti-tank battalion out of those who had left their home town of Stettin with such high hopes.

Other elements of 12th Panzer Division were fortunate enough to be deployed in their intended role rather than as infantry. An armoured battlegroup counterattacked against Volkhov Front's penetration and drove the Soviet units back to their start line; at one location, they found that a group of Red Army tanks had broken through to an assembly point for German wounded and had deliberately crushed the tents under their tank tracks. However horrified the men of 12th Panzer Division might have been, they must have known that the Wehrmacht had frequently executed wounded Red Army soldiers, or left them in the most primitive prison compounds without any medical help.

Meretskov pleaded in vain for a delay in further operations of at least three days, which would permit him to build up ammunition stockpiles for his artillery, but Stalin overruled him. The rigidity with which Stalin – and therefore *Stavka* – behaved was a major contributor to the failure of many of the winter offensive operations along the Eastern Front, but this reflects the belief held by Stalin at the time that the Germans were off balance and that any delay in exploiting this would only work to the advantage of the Wehrmacht. There may have been some truth in this in relation to the areas where the Germans had recently been advancing, for example outside Moscow, but in the north it was of far less significance as the Germans were largely holding positions that they had occupied for some considerable time. Even though the German thrust to Tikhvin had been beaten back, the consequence was merely that the Germans were back on their previous fortified start line. If the Red Army had been able to mount an immediate attack following the German withdrawal, there might have been some chance of catching the Germans off balance. Now, the assault would face an enemy who was thoroughly prepared for defensive fighting. In addition, Stalin's constant insistence on officers sticking to his timetable was partly because of his assessment that they had performed poorly in 1941. He therefore had little confidence in field commanders. And his demands that they adhere to rigid and ultimately unachievable timetables merely reinforced this lack of confidence. If he was aware that his purges and the climate of fear that they engendered contributed to the poor performance of his officers, he made no allowance for it.

In the case of Volkhov Front, Stalin wasn't the only person who doubted the abilities of the army commanders. Meretskov visited the headquarters of Second Shock Army on the eve of the offensive and had a lengthy discussion with Sokolov, the army commander. He came away deeply concerned. Sokolov had little idea about the precise locations of his units or their combat strength. He was undoubtedly popular with his men, issuing orders to ensure that they should be properly fed and clothed, and often played a personal part in reconnaissance, but his efforts usually stopped at the point of telling others what should be done – he rarely investigated whether his orders about food, clothing etc. had actually been carried out. Meretskov sent a signal to *Stavka*, requesting that Sokolov be replaced by someone more competent. For the moment though, Sokolov remained in post.

The renewed attack by Fifty-Ninth Army made even less progress than before. The infantry struggled forward through deep snow after an inadequate artillery preparation and crossed the frozen Volkhov only to be brought to a halt by intense defensive fire. More units were fed into the battle largely as they arrived – both Fifty-Ninth Army and Second Shock Army were still in the process of completing their deployment – but throughout 7 January German defensive firepower proved to be decisive. Second Shock Army left 3,000 men dead or wounded on the battlefield after its first half hour in combat for no tangible gain. Despite these losses, the German accounts of the fighting make no mention of any particularly intense fighting, with Halder's diary recording that the fighting in the north was of no significant consequence.

Meretskov ordered his armies to gather their strength and regroup. Voronov had promised further supplies of artillery ammunition and much of this now began to arrive, which would ensure that the next attack could be preceded by a rather better bombardment than had previously been the case, but it remained to be seen whether it would be sufficient to guarantee success. The German defences consisted of at least two lines, the second about three miles behind the main front, and both were made up of hardened bunkers and firing points, carefully positioned to maximise interlocking fields of fire. Minefields and barbed wire entanglements covered much of the space between the two defensive lines, ensuring that even if a Soviet attack succeeded in breaking through the first line of defence, it would not be able to advance quickly to the second line, giving time for the defenders to fall back and to mount the counterattacks that had become such a hallmark of German defensive doctrine. Moreover, the Germans had detected the Soviet build-up, despite the attempts to move troops only at night. On 9 January, Halder wrote in his diary that whilst the attacks to date had not achieved anything, the main attack was clearly yet to come.[15]

With only a proportion of Volkhov Front's troops having actually attacked, Halder's expectations were correct and Meretskov once more persuaded *Stavka* to allow him a further pause. He was granted three days to complete his preparations. Additional reinforcements were promised, particularly artillery, but these promises came with their own problems. At least one of the tank brigades being sent to Volkhov Front was equipped with heavy KV-1 tanks, and the attacking armies would therefore have to ensure that they either captured a substantial bridge over the frozen Volkhov River or that they were able to construct one rapidly. Other forms of help were perhaps well intended but not always received as such. Even if Stalin refused to acknowledge that the purges of the late 1930s followed by the dismissal of several senior officers after the beginning of the

German invasion meant that many army and Front commanders lacked the in-depth experience and skills for their roles, others within the Soviet command structure were trying to remedy matters. The training directorate of the Red Army issued detailed directives on how operations should be conducted, emphasising the need to concentrate resources at key locations in order to inflict a critical blow with four rifle divisions being massed and used as a single shock group. Similar 'advice' was sent to the armies to the west of Moscow, which had initially thrown back the German pincers threatening the city but once the Germans had been able to take up defensive positions, resorted to repeated, stubborn attacks that achieved nothing.

There were several factors that accounted for this failure to concentrate effort where it would be most effective. In 1916, the Russian Army had achieved one of its very few successes in the First World War when it broke through the lines of the armies of the Austro-Hungarian Empire in what became known as the Brusilov Offensive. In this assault, General Aleksei Alekseyevich Brusilov deliberately made multiple attacks on the grounds that he would then reinforce whichever attack showed the greatest likelihood of success. This became a repeated feature of the manner in which Russian and then Soviet forces operated. Secondly, *Stavka* was at least partly to blame for the dispersion of attacking units, because its instructions often stipulated a profusion of divergent objectives, and failure to comply with these might result in arrest and execution for field commanders. Thirdly, Stalin and *Stavka* were guilty at a strategic level of precisely the same errors: they were pursuing far too many objectives across the breadth of the Eastern Front, rather than concentrating their resources at a few key locations.

The reality on the ground for Meretskov was starkly different from what he was being ordered to do. By dawn on 10 January, Fifty-Second Army had only 14,000 infantry and 900 cavalry combatants in the front line, barely enough to equip a single division; far from being concentrated at a single point, this very limited force was organised in three distinct groups over a front of 18 miles.[16] Rather more useful for Meretskov, perhaps, was approval for the replacement of Sokolov as commander of Second Shock Army. Mekhlis undoubtedly played a major role in this change, having sent several messages to Stalin making clear that Sokolov was out of his depth. In Sokolov's place, Lieutenant General Klykov, who had been commander of Fifty-Second Army, would lead Second Shock Army. His place at Fifty-Second Army was taken by Lieutenant General Vsevolod Fedorovich Yakovlev. It was the end of Sokolov's brief time as a front-line commander. He was given the task of overseeing the training of the Moscow militia, and then returned to NKVD duties. Klykov now had the unenviable task of taking over an inexperienced army, with inexperienced officers in its headquarters, just three days before the resumption of the offensive.

Stalin was beginning to show his impatience at Meretskov's failure to deliver results. He now ordered a change of plan: instead of holding back most of Second Shock Army as an exploitation force, it was to be used in the initial assault. This had the benefit of bringing relatively fresh and strong units into the battle, but it meant that the exploitation element was badly weakened. But even if Stalin hadn't made such changes, Meretskov would probably have had little choice – the armies of Volkhov Front that had been in the thick of the fighting through the winter were so weak that they could achieve little, and all would depend on the efforts of the fresher divisions of the new armies. Mekhlis continued to haunt Meretskov's headquarters, an unwelcome reminder of the probable price of failure, but on this occasion he proved to be useful. When he became aware of the problems faced by Volkhov Front's artillery – despite the equipment delivered by Voronov after his visit a few weeks earlier, many regiments still hadn't received all their guns and many of their weapons were effectively useless as gunsights and other essential equipment hadn't arrived – Mekhlis telephoned Stalin to make him aware of the problem. The result was the delivery of a trainload of equipment.[17]

In addition to the regular forces available to the Red Army, the local partisan groups were expected to contribute to the offensive. Volkhov Front had contact with about 25 such groups in its sector, each numbering about 25 fighters, but reports from the partisans weren't encouraging. The German sweeps through the area had been effective at disrupting partisan movements and the 'extreme terror tactics' favoured by Stahlecker and others had resulted – at least for the moment – in making the local population unwilling to help the partisans. Short of radios, weapons, ammunition, and even food, the partisans could not be expected to contribute a great deal.

The efforts of Mekhlis, Voronov and others to improve the state of Volkhov Front's artillery hadn't remedied all of the problems. Ammunition remained in relatively short supply; although stockpiles were sufficient for a one-hour preparatory bombardment, there was little left for further supporting fire or for use against targets deeper to the rear of the German lines. Nevertheless, the bombardment was far more effective than the shelling that preceded earlier attacks and in a pattern that was to be repeated throughout the war, the Red Army concentrated on the seam between two German formations, 126th and 215th Infantry Divisions, on the assumption that if they were forced back, they might retreat on diverging axes, thus creating a gap.

The two sides were separated by an area that the Germans had deliberately cleared of any cover, at least 800 yards deep, and when Meretskov's four armies attacked in mid-morning, the Germans hammered them with machine-guns, mortars, and artillery. The frozen Volkhov River was left strewn with corpses as the desperate infantrymen pressed forward, scrambling up the west bank and trying to get to grips with the Germans. Both Fourth and Fifty-Ninth Armies failed to make any impression, but Fifty-Second Army and Second Shock Army enjoyed at least a degree of success. Colonel Dmitry Ivanovich Barabanshchikov's 305th Rifle Division, part of Fifty-Second Army, had already secured a foothold on the west bank in earlier attacks and the experienced men of the division conducted an energetic reconnaissance in force after the artillery bombardment. Identifying relatively weak positions occupied by the Spanish 'Blue' Division, Barabanshchikov and his infantry worked their way forward through the intense hail of defensive fire, supported on their northern flank by the rest of Fifty-Second Army. Another of the divisions of the army benefited from a lucky artillery hit on a German ammunition dump but still suffered heavy losses getting close to the German defences. An attack late in the day overran several villages, the first concrete gain of the offensive. A little to the north, Second Shock Army's 327th Rifle Division, reinforced by a ski battalion and an additional regiment of artillery, stormed across the Volkhov and fought its way into the village of Dubovitsy, which was held by the German 126th Infantry Division. The commander of its leading regiment was prominent in the attack, and somewhat surprisingly he was wearing a distinctive officer's sword belt and a yellow hat. This inevitably drew the fire of the Germans and he was killed before the day came to an end.[18] One of the neighbouring divisions failed to cross the Volkhov in the face of resolute defensive fire from the German side, and when it requested further artillery support, the shortage of ammunition prevailed: the gunners had nothing left to fire.

At the same time, Fedyuninsky's Fifty-Fourth Army also attacked from the north. Positioned on the seam between Leningrad and Volkhov Fronts, Fedyuninsky was meant to advance southwest to capture Tosno and Lyuban, supported from the east by the badly weakened Fourth Army on the northern wing of Volkhov Front. In addition to ten rifle divisions, Fedyuninsky had two extra brigades of infantry – one an independent rifle brigade and one made up of 'marines', in reality sailors who had been redeployed as foot-soldiers. He also had two tank brigades, but they had just a handful of tanks between them. For the new offensive, Fedyuninsky chose to attack with three rifle divisions. Like the forces of Volkhov Front, he attacked at the end of the first week of January with no significant success, and his troops were left exhausted by their futile efforts:

After several days of constant fighting, the men were very tired. Being in the open for days on end in severe frost, in snow-covered forests, the soldiers had no opportunity for rest. We couldn't withdraw any unit even for a short time to the second echelon – indeed, due to a significant shortfall in personnel, most units could only field a single echelon of combat troops. When I visited the divisions, I met unshaven soldiers blackened by soot, their overcoats scorched by fire. Forage supply [for the horses] was also bad. I remember how in one memo I read: 'The lack of bulk feed and irregular supplies of grain result in the horses often "standing around" all day and they then collapse with exhaustion.' … The lack of fodder made it extremely difficult to transport ammunition and food and to evacuate the wounded, as only horses could move along the narrow forest roads and through deep snow.[19]

When the new offensive began on 13 January, Colonel Teodor-Verner Andreyevich Sviklin's 285th Rifle Division failed to assemble in time for the attack and other units struggled to make any impact – one division commander complained to Fedyuninsky's headquarters that his men were pinned down by heavy fire but couldn't give clear answers when asked about where the fire was coming from. When Fedyuninsky tried to contact Sviklin to find out what was happening, the hapless division commander couldn't be found in his headquarters – apparently he was away in the front line. Brigade Commissar Vasily Andreyevich Sychev, a member of Fifty-Fourth Army's military council, then spoke to Sviklin's commissar, Bragin, showing the manner in which the political hierarchy often intervened in military matters, not always with the best outcome:

'Are you going to follow orders?' Sychev asked him and then continued in the most resolute tone, 'Don't make excuses that you don't have enough forces. You need to organise the battle better. If you do not complete your mission today, then the Army military council will remove you as an inadequate commissar.'

Half an hour later, [Colonel Aleksandr Romanovich] Belov [Fedyuninsky's chief of operations] called 285th Rifle Division again. This time, Sviklin came to the phone. 'Well, how is the destruction of the enemy on the railway embankment proceeding?' Belov asked.

'No news. I haven't seen any information yet. The artillery is destroying [the German] firing points. When I receive more information, I will report immediately.'

I smoked one cigarette after another. It was clear that 285th Rifle Division was just marking time. 'What's happening with 181st Rifle Division?' I asked Belov.

He contacted Korobeinikov [the division commander]. 'Have you broken through past the railway?'

'No, not yet,' answered the division commander. 'We're going around in circles. Nothing has been accomplished yet.'

Disappointing information arrived from other divisions. We didn't succeed anywhere in advancing beyond the railway embankment, which was heavily fortified by the enemy. The next day, despite our best efforts, we again didn't succeed. The troops of the army were still in the same positions from which they began their attacks.

The reasons for our failures were essentially the same as before: lack of clear cooperation between artillery and infantry; poor reconnaissance, especially on the flanks; and disorganisation and lack of coherence in attacks delivered by small groups on a fairly wide frontage in diverging directions. It should also be noted that the enemy resisted stubbornly and had a highly developed system of fire.[20]

Ultimately, the war between Germany and the Soviet Union would be decided by a number of interlocking factors, and dominance in any one factor alone was insufficient to guarantee victory, either in local battles or the war as a whole. Firstly, there was the question of numbers, and from the outset the Red Army had enjoyed a significant advantage. But the Germans had made excellent use of two further factors – the quality of training and experience of the troops, and the quality of their officers – to nullify the Red Army's numerical superiority. The fourth factor was the quality and quantity of equipment – tanks, guns, aircraft, radios – and this would also have a major impact. The widespread use of radios, for example, permitted the panzer divisions – often equipped with tanks that were inferior to those of opposing armies – to function with great flexibility and power, and the adoption of radios was one of the factors that turned the T-34 from a tank with good potential into a war-winning machine. Finally, there was the often-neglected question of logistics. Without adequate supplies, the best armies in the world could achieve nothing. Fedyuninsky's comments highlight the weaknesses of the Red Army in almost every one of these categories in early 1942. Numerical superiority was often wasted by failure to concentrate and by pursuit of too many objectives, both at local and strategic levels; the quality of the troops was far below the standard enjoyed by the Wehrmacht, and the highly professional German officer corps was able to direct the experienced soldiers of German units with great effect in both defensive and offensive fighting; and although some items of equipment, like T-34 tanks, were superior to those possessed by the Germans, their use was often clumsy and ineffectual. Poor provision of logistic support was exacerbated by the dislocating effect of the evacuation of so much Soviet industry to the east and the sheer scale of the landscape, combined with a relatively poor rail and road network, meant that the huge volumes of ammunition, food, and other supplies that were essential simply couldn't be gathered together in time. The Red Army still had a long way to go before it could mount operations with confidence of success, but the only way that it could achieve the required improvements was to continue trying to learn, in the most testing and demanding circumstances imaginable.

Fedyuninsky wanted to stop the attacks in order to regroup. In particular, he wanted to wait for 177th Rifle Division, which had been sent to him by Leningrad Front but was still en route, delayed by a shortage of transport across the ice of Lake Ladoga. Aware of the pressure being applied by Stalin and Mekhlis, Khozin refused permission for a halt and demanded that efforts should be redoubled. Grimly, Fedyuninsky issued the required orders. Once again, his soldiers struggled forward through the snow; once again, the Germans cut them down in droves. The front line didn't move. There were only two small rays of light. One was the capture of the small town of Pogoste after bitter fighting on 17 January. The other was the activity of 311th Rifle Division, which had managed to penetrate the German defences in an earlier attack and was now largely cut off, but was making a nuisance of itself in the German rear. Supplies were dropped by air and a ski battalion managed to infiltrate through to join the rifle division, but although the Germans were forced to divert troops to try to pin down the Soviet group, it proved impossible to sustain it for more than the short term. By the end of January, Fedyuninsky was forced to order 311th Rifle Division to make its way back through the front line.

The constant hammering of the German front line was beginning to have some effect. A small number of tanks – mainly light T-60s, armed with 20mm guns and armour that was no more than 20mm thick at the strongest points – managed to cross the Volkhov and joined the attacking troops as they edged forward to the village of Yamno, one of the German strongpoints close to the Volkhov that continued to hold out. The defences here were manned by 126th Infantry Division, reinforced by elements of 12th Panzer Division, and the light T-60s were rapidly knocked out. Without adequate artillery fire to suppress the German defences, the infantry attacks on the village foundered. But slowly and at great cost, Klykov's Second Shock Army managed to secure a length of the German first defensive line, but the advance to the second German line was slow.

The weather had deteriorated with heavy snowstorms sweeping the region and several German strongpoints in the first defensive line continued to hold out, preventing free movement by the Red Army units. The artillery of Volkhov Front was also now in the wrong position to provide support for further attacks and needed to move forward. Regardless of Stalin's impatience, there would have to be a pause while supplies were brought up and troops had the chance to regroup. As Leeb departed from Army Group North and Küchler took his place, there was a brief respite for the men on both sides of the front line.

Within the siege perimeter, the half-starved forces that had been defending Leningrad were also ordered to mount attacks. Konstantinov, in the front line with his rifle company, described the briefing that he was given:

> We were amazed. It was perfectly clear to everyone that no offensive was possible for our division – firstly because we were talking about men swollen with starvation, fit only at best for rear area duties, and secondly because the morale of the division and in particular our regiment made such an order completely impracticable at that moment. But an order was an order. The battalion commander continued to issue instructions to the company commanders, explaining the situation and setting specific targets for the offensive. When asked if artillery would support our regiment, the battalion commander replied that we had been assigned a mortar battalion and regimental artillery; but we knew that they were completely inactive due to the shortage of ammunition.
>
> The battalion commander specified the instructions for individual platoons. After speaking to the commander of 4th Company, who listened very thoughtfully to the commander and at the end of the discussion muttered indifferently, 'They will chop us up,' the battalion commander moved on to 5th Company and turned to me.
>
> 'Comrade Konstantinov, you have the following task. Your platoon must reach here.' He pointed at the map and the terrain plan, with the lines of defence of our troops and the enemy drawn on it. 'During the offensive,' he continued, 'you must, together with 1st and 2nd platoons, break through the enemy's defence line and then move forward to reach Pesochny farm, here.'
>
> He pointed at a location deep in the rear of the enemy. 'May I ask the distance to Pesochny farm from the front line?'
>
> 'About 7km.' I smiled involuntarily. Others glanced at each other. The commander noticed this. 'What are you laughing at?'
>
> 'Well, why shouldn't we laugh? After all, you can't seriously think that a platoon from a company of half-dead men will break through the line of a very

deep, fortified and completely unexplored German defence, and then these 20 men should perform a specific task of fighting forward 7km and taking a farm. It's just crazy, after all. The truth is, these men will be cut down by machine-guns before they have a chance to cross the 400m to the German trenches. After all, they're barely able to run or crawl!'

The other officers began to speak in my support. The commissar intervened. 'Comrades, it is not our business to discuss the order! We are here to fight and, if necessary, to die for our country. Since there is an order, it means that it was considered and discussed at division headquarters. And they know better about what can or can't be done. We must fulfil it, we must fulfil our honourable duty and break through the German defences. There are no fortresses that the Bolsheviks can't take, Comrade Stalin said. And we, all Bolsheviks, Party members or not, will give our lives for our homeland and the great Stalin, for our dear people who are in the besieged city, waiting for our heroic army to break the blockade. We are not marching alone. Our battalion is only a small link in a general offensive on this sector of the front.'

The meeting was over. We parted, contemplating our grim thoughts.[21]

Fortunately for Konstantinov and his men, their attack was cancelled and instead the division was pulled out of line and dispatched to Lake Ladoga, but it is worth taking note of the manner in which Stalin's name was invoked to justify the orders. Part of this was because of the fear factor – everyone would have known a friend or relative who had been rounded up in preceding years on imagined crimes, and failing to follow an order that emanated from Stalin was certain to result in punishment. But there was also a growing personality cult around Stalin, despite his dire warnings in the early days of Bolshevik rule when he had criticised Trotsky for promoting a similar cult.

After a completely inadequate spell on extra rations to restore their strength, Konstantinov and his comrades were dispatched as reinforcements for Fedyuninsky's Fifty-Fourth Army and immediately thrown into the bloody fighting. His experience epitomises the manner in which the Red Army's strength was squandered all along the Eastern Front in response to Stalin's orders for a general counteroffensive:

For the duration of what was a very short battle, I didn't see a single [friendly] aircraft, not a single explosion of a heavy artillery shell, not a single tank. Everything existed on paper, in staff plans. Some of our regimental artillery was held up in deep snow. For the guns that reached us by a miracle, there were no shells.

Several medium-calibre mortars had a limited quantity of ammunition. It was all we had. The regiment commander personally walked around the regiment before the battle, talking to soldiers and officers. The meaning of his conversation was uncomplicated: 'Unfortunately, the promised support will arrive too late. The artillery is stuck in the snow. But we will fulfil our duty without it and, of course, we will drive the enemy back.'

Why this man tried to throw the regiment into an apparently impossible operation remains incomprehensible to me. It was either sheer stupidity and a misunderstanding of the situation, or out of concerns for his own career.

The fight didn't last long. Thrown into a frontal attack without artillery support, the companies were cut down one by one by enemy machine-gun fire. German mortar batteries literally smothered us with shells. Only one company, having detoured to one side, broke into the enemy defences, but it was destroyed in an unequal battle. Three hours later, a handful of men remained in the regiment. At the beginning of the battle, I was stunned by shellfire and sent to the nearest aid post. I was lucky because the great majority of the wounded died, or rather froze to death, because they couldn't be brought out under continuous enemy fire.

The regiment was destroyed without even partially fulfilling its assigned task. Hundreds and thousands of men died senselessly, paying with their lives for the chaos, confusion, endless stupidity, criminal plans, bureaucratic inertia, and disregard for human lives shown by the commanders of the Red Army.[22]

During the pause between 17 and 21 January, the Red Army units struggled through the snow, laboriously hauling their guns and other equipment closer to the front line. Artillery ammunition remained in short supply, but Meretskov ordered Klykov to attack again as planned. With the attacks by Fourth and Fifty-Ninth Armies showing no signs of success, Meretskov sent a message to *Stavka* on 22 January asking for permission to concentrate all his efforts in the sector where Second Shock Army and Fifty-Second Army were struggling forward. This was in effect a rather belated attempt to reduce the number of attacks, but it was beyond Meretskov's authority to make such decisions without permission. He must have been greatly relieved when he received the reply. The two weak armies to the north were to cease their assaults, permitting valuable artillery ammunition to be sent to the main axis of advance. Fourth Army would take responsibility for a larger sector of the front line, allowing Fifty-Ninth Army to move a little to the south and thus help the main effort being made by Second Shock Army.

Klykov's men were slowly driving forward and had now expanded their foothold across the Volkhov to a breadth of about 15 miles, with a maximum depth of three miles. Units of Fifty-Ninth Army had now crossed into the bridgehead in support of the attack and the village of Myasnoi Bor became a typical focus of fighting on the Eastern Front – an insignificant cluster of buildings that both sides came to regard as vital. The last German strongpoints close to the river were slowly mopped up, and Myasnoi Bor finally fell after several attacks as darkness fell on 22 January. A day later, under continuing pressure from *Stavka* to show results, Meretskov ordered his exploitation force – XIII Cavalry Corps – to advance through what he hoped was an adequate breach in the German lines. If he could get a mobile exploitation group into action, he hoped that the Germans would be forced to divert forces away from their front line in order to deal with it, thus allowing Second Shock Army to make better progress. It needed all the help it could get. The men were suffering from exposure to the bitterly cold weather; they were forbidden from lighting fires that might attract the attention of the Germans and there continued to be great difficulties moving forward supplies and reinforcements.

Major General Nikolai Ivanovich Gusev had been in command of XIII Cavalry Corps for just a few days. He had three cavalry divisions at his disposal and his men moved into the breach on 24 January. Finally, the Soviet advance began to gain momentum with both infantry and cavalry moving forward along a single road through the dense pine forest to the west of Myasnoi Bor. Rather worryingly for Gusev and Meretskov, the advance might be making good progress towards the west, but every attempt to turn northwest towards Lyuban was blocked by determined German units that were able to take advantage of very favourable terrain and few if any roads that might allow the Soviet cavalry to turn towards Lyuban. Halder's note in his diary shows that although this thrust was of concern, he was confident that the Wehrmacht would prevail:

> We are faced with a full-stage offensive. Two enemy 'assault groups' of about a dozen divisions have broken through in this sector and are advancing southward [they were actually moving towards the west]. That is, in any event, better than if they were going north, for now they are driving right towards our reinforcements that are moving up now.[23]

This perhaps shows a difference in what Halder might have attempted if he had been commanding Soviet forces in the area – a powerful thrust from the breakthrough towards Lyuban and Tosno, directly towards Leningrad rather than towards the west and thus into the deep rear positions of Army Group North. A direct attempt to reach the siege perimeter would surely have been more appropriate given the limited resources available, and a deep penetration ran multiple risks. Unless it was supported by penetrations elsewhere – as had actually been the original plan produced by *Stavka* – this thrust was effectively into open space and would achieve little. Secondly, the shoulders of the breakthrough continued to hold firm, and the Germans, always minded to launch counterattacks, began to consider whether the Red Army was about to give them an enticing target. If the two shoulders could be reinforced and could attack towards each other, there was a good likelihood of isolating and destroying the Soviet units that had broken through.

It was a tempting option for the Germans. The breakthrough was barely two miles wide, with Zemtitsky on the southern side and Spasskaya Polist on the northern side, both in German hands. In an attempt to give more coherence to his attack, Meretskov issued new orders on 27 January. Fifty-Ninth Army was to attack a little to the north, in an attempt to outflank the German units on that side of the breakthrough and thus break up the northern shoulder of the penetration. An operational group was to be formed under the command of Major General Ivan Terentyevich Korovnikov to crush the German resistance around Spasskaya Polist, while a second operational group under Colonel Fedor Mikhailovich Zhiltsov attacked the southern shoulder at Zemtitsky. A third group, led by Major General Petr Frolovich Privalov, would advance to the west and northwest in order to exploit the penetration. These operational groups, in Meretskov's words, were substitutes for the rifle corps headquarters that had recently been disbanded, largely because the losses of senior officers made it impossible to keep them in existence. Nonetheless, there was a need for coordination of several formations at a level between divisions and armies.[24]

The German reinforcements that Halder mentioned in his diary were also approaching the Volkhov sector. In order to tighten control of the forces defending the river line, Küchler assigned XXXVIII Corps to oversee operations on the southern side of the breakthrough, under the overall control of Sixteenth Army, while I Corps would be responsible for the northern side, as part of Eighteenth Army. The southern group, commanded by General Friedrich-Wilhelm von Chappuis, had 126th Infantry Division and the Spanish Blue Division, together with two companies of 203rd Panzer Regiment, a unit that had been raised the previous July and equipped with captured French tanks before receiving German vehicles immediately prior to its deployment in the Soviet Union at the end of 1941. To the north, I Corps, commanded by Both, was a much stronger formation with five Wehrmacht infantry divisions and the *SS-Polizei* Division. In addition, 20th Motorised Division had been dispatched as reinforcements for XXXVIII Corps.

Despite a slow and painful start, the Volkhov Offensive had reached a point at which matters were rapidly becoming critical. As January drew to an end, the leading units of Privalov's group were up to 46 miles from the Volkhov River, and the ability of the German units along the northern side of the breakthrough to keep extending their lines to prevent Privalov from turning north had reached its limit. If the shoulders of the penetration could be widened and supplies and reinforcements moved forward, there was a good prospect of the Red Army reaching Lyuban and Tosno from the south, threatening the German forces between them and Fedyuninsky's Fifty-Fourth Army with encirclement and destruction. But the German units holding those shoulders were strong and gaining fresh reinforcements. If they were able to link up and restore the old front line along the Volkhov, Second Shock Army would be encircled. Everything depended upon the battles for Zemtitsky and Spasskaya Polist.

CHAPTER 10

LYUBAN: ATTRITION AND FAILURE

All along the Eastern Front, the Soviet optimism of the first days of 1942 was being replaced by a growing realisation that the Wehrmacht was far from defeated. Despite its losses in the winter battles outside Moscow and elsewhere, it remained a formidable fighting force. Victory for the Red Army would be far from easy. In the north, there was the added strain created by the urgent need to improve the situation in Leningrad. The gap between the leading units of Second Shock Army and the siege perimeter remained substantial, about 60 miles, but with thousands starving to death every day, the pressure – military, political, and moral – on the officers and men of the Red Army was immense.

For the Wehrmacht, the crisis and near-panic of late December was gone, replaced by professional assessments of firepower and defensive strength. The confident predictions of winning the war in 1941 were a forgotten dream and the Red Army clearly had resources that greatly exceeded all German estimates. But nevertheless, huge damage had been inflicted in 1941, and the first month of 1942 saw terrible Soviet losses as stubborn, clumsy assaults all along the Eastern Front foundered in the face of concentrated defensive fire. If these attacks could be weathered, there was every prospect that improved weather would bring with it a further opportunity for Germany to defeat the Soviet Union.

For Meretskov at the headquarters of Volkhov Front, there were two immediate priorities. His logistic problems continued to hamstring every attempt to attack the Germans and it was vital that these problems in moving food and ammunition to the front line were solved. He also expected fresh reinforcements

– at one stage, he was told that he would receive an additional army – and, aware of how long it had taken for Second Shock Army and Fifty-Ninth Army to assemble, he was anxious to see some sign of these fresh troops arriving. The second priority was to widen the breach so that more forces could deploy to exploit the ground that had been gained at such cost.

At the end of January, another senior officer descended on the headquarters of Volkhov Front: Lieutenant General Andrei Vasilyevich Khrulev, a deputy defence minister with responsibility for logistics. Although he had little front-line experience, he had held a series of high-level posts ranging from finance through construction to logistics and was regarded as an expert in logistics. In an era in which the Red Army – and indeed the Wehrmacht – regarded the function of the rear area services as little more than ensuring that the demands of the front line were always met, he strove to deliver the materiel that was required whilst trying to inject an element of reality into the plans of his superiors. His energy and efficiency was widely respected, but occasionally attracted enemies. Immediately after the fighting for Stalingrad, Khrulev arranged for a bridge to be built across the Volga. Nikita Khrushchev, the future ruler of the Soviet Union, was at that time a member of the military council of Southwest Front and sent a report to Moscow claiming credit for the bridge. Stalin preferred to believe Khrulev's account and Khrushchev received a minor reprimand, but it was a slight that he didn't forget. Khrulev died in 1962 when Khrushchev was at the height of his power; despite requests from several senior figures, Khrushchev refused at first to permit the interment of Khrulev's body in the Kremlin Wall, finally conceding permission for his old rival to be buried in Red Square.[1] Having championed rear area services for much of his working life, Khrulev was acutely aware of the manner in which their activity was so often taken for granted. Writing after the war, he recalled:

> There are many who seem to know everything, who are always quick to tell you how to raise difficult children, how to treat incurable diseases, how to build houses, and finally how to control the activity of the rear area services. War is a tough nut to crack, and not everyone can do it. However, everyone considers they have the right to judge and criticise the work of those who labour at it.[2]

Khrulev went to work immediately with the limited resources at his disposal and managed to improve supplies to a level where Meretskov could address his second concern: the narrowness of the breakthrough. Another operational group was created around 11th Rifle Division, reinforced with a tank brigade. This force attacked the northern side of the penetration on 12 February, overrunning two German strongpoints. The breach in the defensive line was now nearly nine miles wide and Meretskov dispatched fresh reinforcements to Second Shock Army in order to accelerate the advance and, he hoped, overcome the German defences to the south of Lyuban. But conditions in the front line remained terrible. The senior medical officer in Volkhov Front, Colonel Aleksandr Aleksandrovich Vishnevsky, described the situation in his diary:

> We reached Bolshoi Vyazmische. Medical Battalion 460 had just arrived. It was a terrible scene: there were no vehicles available, no means of evacuation. There was only a single table in the treatment room. They said they had started work just two days before after walking all the way across the Vologda region [a distance of nearly 300 miles] …
>
> It is bitterly cold. A man was on his knees by the side of the road. He silently bowed and fell over, apparently frozen. A medical battalion was ten minutes' walk away. My driver and I picked up the freezing man by the arms and took him there … The wounded are being brought back from the front line on horseback. The horses sometimes stop on the road and collapse. There are no blankets and the wounded are covered with overcoats, or at best a single blanket. Not only our soldiers are freezing. German snipers (the soldiers call them 'cuckoos') are found frozen to death in trees.[3]

The medical situation improved over the following weeks; dog sleds were deployed to help evacuate the wounded, but German aircraft showed little inclination to respect targets marked with red crosses and Vishnevsky's field hospitals were frequently attacked.

Gennady Iosifovich Gerodnik was a member of a ski battalion raised in the Ural Mountains and was amongst those inserted into the breach as reinforcements for Second Shock Army:

> We passed the villages of Bor, Kostylevo, Arefino, and Yamno. They looked even more wrecked than Paporotno and Selishchenskiy Poselok [where the regiment had previously been in position]. Almost all of the time, high above, we could hear the rumble of German reconnaissance planes. Sometimes groups of 'Messers' or 'Junkers' rushed past, lower. But we weren't attacked. Our 'hawks' appeared far less frequently. We had already learned to distinguish planes not just by silhouettes but also by sound. Ours had a uniform rumble, the Germans had

engines that performed a duet. The lead voice was a measured, deep base. It was accompanied by a painfully vibrating falsetto, more than an octave higher …

We reached Myasnoi Bor before dark … where Second Shock Army pierced the German defence. The station and nearby houses had been wiped from the face of the earth. Among the ruins of the station's water tower, the end of a steel pipe stuck out, connected to an underground tank. A line of soldiers formed by the pipe. Water was taken out using an artillery shell case suspended on telegraph wire …

The Germans still hadn't been driven from the nearby villages and towns. They clung to the Volkhov sector like ticks on a living body. Some villages were completely encircled, others – perhaps a third – were partially occupied by our troops. Transport planes dropped food and ammunition to the encircled villages. The Germans were not going to surrender or break out of the encirclements. They waited for the approach of reinforcements.[4]

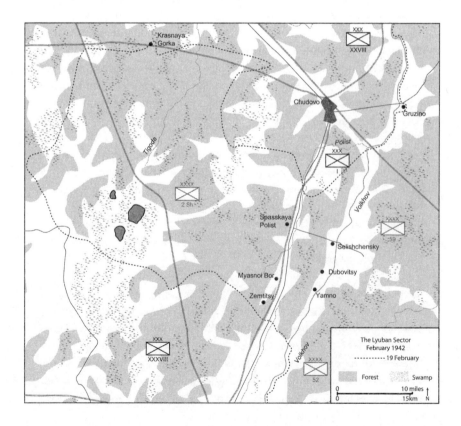

All was far from well in the headquarters of Second Shock Army. Klykov, the commanding officer, was suffering from illness and was often unable to perform his duties; consequently, he was increasingly dependent upon Major General Petr Fedorovich Alferyev, his second-in-command. Meretskov considered replacing Klykov but for the moment permitted him to remain in command and at first this seemed to be the correct decision; using some of the reinforcements that he had received, Klykov threw two rifle divisions, a cavalry division, and two ski battalions at the German defences before Lyuban. None of these units were remotely near full strength but they made a determined attack that captured Krasnaya Gorka late on 19 February, only six miles from the city. If the attack could reach Lyuban – and especially if Fedyuninsky's Fifty-Fourth Army could advance towards the city from the north – there was a possibility that the German I Corps would be cut off and, at long last, the Soviet offensive operation would inflict a sufficiently large defeat on the Germans to make the lifting of the siege of Leningrad a reality. But this advance effectively exhausted the Soviet forces and the drive ground to an abrupt halt. Much of Gusev's cavalry corps was dispersed in fighting all around the perimeter of the breakthrough and there were no local reserves that could be committed to sustain momentum.

Meanwhile, Gerodnik's ski battalion was deployed in the costly attacks to widen the breakthrough, learning quickly about the skilful manner in which the Germans had fortified their positions:

We stormed villages that were half-buried in snow. It looked like nothing significant, just ordinary rural huts which it seemed we would be able to capture without much effort. But the external impression was very deceptive.

In front of the huts there was an absolutely bare strip of snow 200–300m wide. Everything that interfered with the view, the Germans removed. Trees, including fruit trees, were cut down and used for fortifications. Bathhouses, sheds, and other outbuildings were dismantled and burned. They didn't even leave stumps or fences.

And the ground in front of the huts contained minefields, conventional wire fences, and barbed wire entanglements. Behind them were full profile trenches. They were connected by communication trenches to second and third rows of trenches. Between the huts there were pillboxes, bunkers, and machine-gun points. And the huts themselves were serious points of resistance. Many of these had so-called *podyzbitsi*, a bit like a ground floor. Unlike basements, they had low windows above the ground itself. The Germans fortified these *podyzbitsi* and turned the windows into firing points. When it was quiet, they lived in the rooms above. They slept on soft beds and had plenty of time to fry, boil and slice their food. And when they were in danger – some ran to the pillboxes and bunkers, others into the trenches.

It would be necessary to bomb the enemy who had settled into the villages thoroughly, but our planes were rare performers here. We needed to bombard Fritz more heavily with artillery and large-calibre mortars. But because of the terrible terrain and the heavy snowdrifts, artillery and mortar formations were stuck en route. And those that had arrived had a strict ration of ammunition. But we couldn't wait. Orders came from above, urging us on with strict and super-strict instructions: move on, move on, move on! We ourselves understood that any delay threatened to disrupt the entire operation.

The success of the first battle of 172nd Ski Battalion at Myasnoi Bor was very modest: we helped our fellow Slavs drive the Germans from half of the village of Zemtitsy. And we lost 18 killed and twice as many wounded. Sasha Belov, the singer from 3rd Company, was fatally wounded.

Very soon, the harsh reality of the front line forced us to reassess our first battle. We understood that the expensive price for Zemtitsy's huts was justified. The dug-in Fascists had to be driven out of … the villages adjacent to Myasnoi Bor.[5]

The failure to turn the breakthrough across the Volkhov into a decisive success resulted in bitter recriminations. *Stavka* criticised Meretskov for making uncoordinated, piecemeal attacks and for ignoring directives that instructed him to concentrate his resources better. In reply, Meretskov and his staff complained about shortages of tanks and artillery ammunition, lack of air cover, and the poor training of new recruits. Stalin sent an irritated message to Meretskov at the end of February demanding an immediate advance to cross the railway line between Lyuban and Chudovo; in order to try to help this, Fifty-Fourth Army was ordered to renew its attacks to link up with Second Shock Army from the north. At the same time, a new delegation arrived from Moscow. It was led by Voroshilov but also included Georgy Maksimilianovich Malenkov, a prominent member of the State Defence Committee, and an officer who would play a major role in the events that followed: Lieutenant General Andrei Andreyevich Vlasov.

Vlasov had been in the army since the days of the Russian Civil War and had spent a period of time with the Chinese nationalists of Chiang Kai-Shek as a military adviser. He came through the purges of the Red Army unscathed and may have been responsible for a report that criticised the commander of 99th Rifle Division, resulting in the commander's arrest and replacement by Vlasov. At the beginning of the war with Germany he was commander of IV Mechanised

Corps, part of the forces defending Kiev, and during the initial battles between Kiev and the western frontier of the Soviet Union he and his men were repeatedly encircled but managed to break out to safety. After conducting an energetic defence he was given command of Thirty-Seventh Army. When his army was caught in the great encirclement at Kiev, he stayed with his men and succeeded in leading a substantial group to safety. He was then given command of the new Twentieth Army with which he fought with distinction in the Battle of Moscow. Stalin held him in high esteem, trusting him to meet foreign delegations and journalists. He was now appointed deputy commander of Volkhov Front, perhaps because of Stalin's sense of frustration with Meretskov. In his memoirs, Meretskov had nothing positive to say about his new deputy, but this was almost certainly coloured by the role that Vlasov would play later in the war. It should be borne in mind that at this stage, Vlasov was widely respected and regarded as entirely trustworthy. Some later wrote that the success of his Twentieth Army outside Moscow went to his head and left him with an inflated opinion of his abilities, but again, it is difficult to separate these accounts from the manner in which Vlasov was later demonised by the Soviet state.

The new delegation moved swiftly, removing the chief of staff and chief of operations of Second Shock Army from their posts. If Malenkov and Voroshilov recognised that the failings of Volkhov Front were at least in part due to systemic logistic failures, they showed no recognition of this in their actions. Meretskov made a brief tour of the units in the penetration to assess the situation on the ground and found that it largely confirmed his personal views:

> Everywhere we saw the same picture: there was a shortage of units, the men were exhausted, and enemy aircraft dominated the sky. Voroshilov also … visited almost all of the units and spent a long time with XIII Cavalry Corps, talking with soldiers and commanders, encouraging them, making appeals and where necessary demands, and urging them onwards.[6]

When he returned to his headquarters, Meretskov submitted a further request for a pause in operations. He wanted to transfer a cavalry division from Fourth Army as reinforcements for XIII Cavalry Corps and to use the time for the battered divisions attempting to cut the Lyuban–Chudovo rail and road link to regroup and receive further supplies. The situation of the cavalry was particularly desperate. With inadequate fodder reaching the front line, horses either were dying or were too weak to be used, greatly restricting the mobility that was the main weapon of the cavalry divisions. He also needed time for the laborious task of moving forward artillery. The response was uncompromising. The movement of reinforcements was approved, but there was to be no delay in making further attacks, which showed little understanding of the losses suffered by the divisions of Volkhov Front. On 25 February, Fifty-Second Army reported that its six rifle divisions could field just 19,500 combatants between them – insufficient to make two full-strength divisions.[7] Most of the other units of Meretskov's Front were in a similar state or worse.

Meanwhile, the Germans were moving against the penetration at Krasnaya Gorka. With characteristic vigour, Both's I Corps counterattacked. Generalleutnant Siegfried Haenicke formed a group from his 61st Infantry Division, reinforced by elements of the neighbouring 215th Infantry Division, to the east of the Soviet assault group while 291st Infantry Division attacked from the west. The two attacks met in Krasnaya Gorka and retook the town on 27 February.[8] Most of the men of the Soviet 327th Rifle Division and 80th Cavalry Division were cut off; they fought on for five days before their ammunition and food was exhausted, and then slipped through the German lines in the dense forests and were able to reach safety. But even though most of the personnel escaped the encirclement, the Red Army's threat to Lyuban and the road and rail corridor from Lyuban to Chudovo – which was essential for supplies for the German I Corps – had for the moment been eliminated. Gerodnik and his ski battalion were fighting a little to the east, caught up in a seemingly endless cycle of attacks and counterattacks for insignificant objectives:

Rockets flew overhead, swiftly pursuing each other. Sometimes they curled away. The enemy machine-gun: *zatatata*! A second, a third, a fourth joined in. Some bullets ricocheted off the ice with piercing howls. The first shells exploded in the alder forest that we had just left. Our precious artillery and mortar preparation began. Now the sappers needed to get to work, every second was vital. Ahead, very close to our line, there were frequent explosions, and clouds of smoke and snow flew up. A strong north wind blew the smell of gunpowder and explosives to us.

After the artillery preparation commenced, the enemy calmed down. But how suppressed was he? That was another matter. Everything would become clear in our attack. Half-sitting, leaning on his left shoulder against the dead-end wall of the snowy trench, Naumenko glanced forward anxiously and then looked back expectantly. He was worried he would miss the signal flares.

The fiery bursts of our shells moved on into the depths of the German defence and immediately two bright red rockets soared over the alder forest. Crawling out of the trench, our lieutenant waved his hand and shouted something. We didn't hear what it was but we understood clearly: 'Let's go!' We didn't run forward, but followed the commander's example and crawled. Perhaps the lieutenant was right and it was still too risky to stand, a German machine-gun was clattering away mightily on the right flank.

We crawled to the strip that the sappers had cleared. Beyond it was barbed wire. The passage through the wire was marked by two flashlights. The leading men were crawling into it and we followed. On the other side of the wire was a mined strip. Skilful and agile, the sappers managed to clear a passage. It was marked with coloured flags stuck in the snow. The strip stretched along the south-facing slope of a long, low mound. Behind it, on a hillock, there was a rampart of snow and ice. It wasn't difficult to guess: the snow that had fallen on fortifications had been raked away by the Germans from the areas where they laid mines. Loopholes had been made in the rampart, as in a fortress wall.

We crossed the cleared area at a run. When we lay in the snow we had to remain silent – not even a cough. We crawled as quietly as we could … But as soon as we ran forward, everyone involuntarily, synchronously burst into a deep roar: 'Urraaah!'

The machine-gun on the right flank, still extremely dangerous for us, fell silent. Apparently, the enemy gun team had to move. Or perhaps we were out of his field of fire. Bullets whistled, but much less frequently than before our artillery preparation. A few scattered shells fell. Apparently the enemy gunners too had to move to a new firing position further back. It seemed that our artillery, the 'God of war', had given the Germans a hard time for 15 minutes.

At the snowy rampart we caught up with the sappers. There was a lull there, it was a dead zone for bullets. The rampart was about 2m high. Of course, we could climb over with each other's help, but that would be reckless. Up there, anyone that daring would be cut down in no time. And if you survived being shot, who knew what awaited us on the other side? Another mined strip?

The sappers were planting explosives. They waved at us and shouted, 'Step away!' A risky short fuse was lit – every second saved was precious – and they too ran back to us. Ba-ba-boom! Three explosions merged almost into one. There was a lot of noise, but the result was far from impressive. The explosions broke the surface shell of ice but the snow beyond wasn't completely cleared. A high threshold remained in the gap, and climbing over you could easily be hit by a bullet. The sappers and skiers rushed to the gap together, all mixed up. They crawled the last few metres to assess the situation. What smoke! Both the gap and the lowland beyond were covered. But this worked both ways – a smokescreen would protect us.

With trained eyes, the sappers immediately determined that there were no more mines. Again we ran forward, again there was a rolling shout of 'Urrah!' And immediately it faded away. It was difficult to run and we were breathless. Someone fell to the left, another to the right – stumbling? Injured? Killed? We'd find out later. In the meantime – forward, only forward!

The smoke cleared and the parapet of a trench was close by. There were dark spots from the explosions of our shells clearly visible. Behind the parapet, the terrible, unknown trench. What awaited us in it? The flat dagger bayonet of a German rifle? A blast at point-blank range from a machine-pistol? A hefty Bavarian who would stick a hunting knife in you? No, to hell with such fears. We had to beat the Bavarian to it by any means possible.

This enemy trench that promised us death was also our salvation. It would protect us from bullets and to a large extent from shrapnel. Such is the dialectical unity of contradiction! Forward, forward with all your might! The last few metres left. We sprayed the parapet with machine-gun fire on the run. The enemy didn't appear. Several hand grenades flew out from the trench, one after another. They were as long as children's bats and tumbled over us, falling on the line of the second attacking platoon. Musa dropped to one knee, pulled the pin with his teeth and threw a return grenade into the trench ... Then the decisive moment in the mortal soldier's lottery: we rolled over the parapet into the trench. There were no Germans visible, just us in our white overalls. What to do next? Right or left?

On the right, there was some ... machine-gun fire, grenade explosions, and I ran towards those sounds, following Musa. The platoon philosopher was behind me. We stumbled over the body of a dead German. It was half trampled into the snow and mud. Stop! Who or why we were stopped wasn't clear. Then the rather haphazard occupation of the trenches finally became more organised. The voices of Naumenko and Gilev could be heard. They ordered us to spread out along the trench about 5m apart and wait for further orders. Watch the northwest – a counterattack might come from there.[9]

Hastily, the ski battalion organised its defences. Some soldiers searched the dead Germans. Some pocketed valuables, others were more anxious to grab newspaper, which they could use to make cigarettes. All letters and other documents were gathered together and sent back to regimental headquarters. Later in the day, they handed over the trench to another unit and returned to the ruined farm that had been their home for several days. Many men were missing, including a popular company sergeant-major.

Regardless of the urging of *Stavka*, further advances by Second Shock Army were impossible given the weakened state of its units. Similarly, the attempts to widen the neck of the breakthrough continued in the following days with no gains; the number of casualties rose steadily and soldiers continued to complain about shell shortages and a lack of air support. In the north, Fedyuninsky's Fifty-Fourth Army renewed its assault on 28 February; previous attacks had made little impression on the German lines, but the new attack succeeded in creating a V-shaped salient in the German defences extending to a depth of about nine miles, though at great cost. In order to support the attack – and perhaps in tacit recognition of the poor performance of Soviet aircraft to date – *Stavka* issued detailed instructions for air support, including the deployment of reserve air regiments. Regardless of the impact of these air strikes, neither Meretskov nor Fedyuninsky mentioned them in their memoirs, suggesting that they contributed little to the fighting.

Just like the officers and men of Volkhov Front, Fedyuninsky's troops were showing signs of exhaustion:

> The personnel were very tired. Even at army headquarters, officers had no more than two or three hours' rest each day and literally collapsed from fatigue. Colonel Semenov, who replaced Colonel Belov as head of the operations department, was so overworked that he often fell asleep over a map or a report. He used to dictate the operational report to Front Headquarters to the telegraph operator and one day fell silent in mid-sentence. 'What's happened? Why was the transmission interrupted? Where's Semenov?' demanded Front Headquarters.
>
> 'He's asleep,' replied the telegraph operator.
>
> 'Wake him!'
>
> Semenov awoke and continued to dictate, but a few minutes later his head once more fell helplessly onto his chest, and the cycle repeated itself.[10]

However exhausted staff officers like Semenov were, at least they were in warm accommodation with hot food. The soldiers in the field usually had neither. A further push took Fedyuninsky's troops to within six miles of Lyuban, but they could go no further.

While Meretskov and the other Soviet commanders struggled to implement the orders they received from above, the Germans were devising plans to restore their front line. In addition to the penetration achieved by Second Shock Army, the Red Army had cut off the German II Corps south of Lake Ilmen around the city of Demyansk on 8 February; a total of six divisions, including *SS-Totenkopf*, were encircled, and the Germans now intended to break through to this pocket and also to eliminate the penetration achieved by Volkhov Front. The details of the battles around Demyansk are of limited relevance to the fighting closer to Leningrad, but they were of great significance to the huge battle that would be fought around Stalingrad at the end of 1942. Throughout the period of encirclement in Demyansk, II Corps was sustained by an air bridge and this would ultimately form the basis for the German belief that it would be possible to sustain Sixth Army by air when it was encircled in Stalingrad. The air bridge to Demyansk should have shown quite the opposite: the Luftwaffe managed to deliver an average of 250 tons per day to the encirclement, which proved barely enough to sustain six divisions, a total of about 85,000 men. When the Stalingrad encirclement was created in November, a total of over 250,000 Germans and Romanians were trapped, yet the expectation was that they could be sustained by as little as 500 tons of supplies per day and even this figure was never achieved. A true comparison between the two encirclements should have suggested a minimum requirement of at least 50 per cent greater than that figure.

On 2 March, Halder recorded the outcome of a discussion between Hitler and Küchler. An operation would commence on 7 March, lasting for five days, in order to pinch off the Soviet penetration across the Volkhov River. This would be preceded by heavy air attacks on Second Shock Army and was to be carried out as rapidly as possible. Once the salient was converted into an encirclement, Second Shock Army would be contained without any attempt to destroy the trapped units. Instead, they were to be left to starve to death. This would permit the Germans to redeploy the forces used to other sectors.[11] But the strike against Second Shock Army had to be delayed. It wasn't until 9 March that the ground forces were in position, and the advance of the Soviet Third Shock Army on the southern side of the Demyansk encirclement towards Kholm could only be countered by the diversion of substantial German air assets. As a result, it wasn't possible for the extensive aerial bombardment specified by Hitler to commence on time and the operation was put off until 15 March. The Germans had identified two supply routes that ran across the Volkhov and into the narrow neck of Second Army's sector, and had assigned them the codenames *Erika* in the north and *Dora* a little to the south; some accounts describe a third route, *Friedrich*, at the northern side of the corridor, with four major log roads running north to south across the pocket. The entire operation to sever the narrow neck was codenamed *Raubtier* ('Predator').

Even with the short delay, there was insufficient time for the Luftwaffe to carry out the extensive preparation that had been intended. The entire sector was now assigned to the German Eighteenth Army so that Sixteenth Army could deal with the situation further south and make preparations to break through to the Demyansk encirclement. The northern pincer of the German counteroffensive was under the control of I Corps and consisted of *SS-Polizei* and elements of 215th Infantry Division; there was also a small battlegroup from 20th Motorised Division. The southern pincer, under the control of XXXVIII Corps, had 58th and 126th Infantry Divisions. Compared to similar sized operations conducted by either side, the forces assembled had few tanks, but this was a reflection of two factors. Firstly, armoured units were thinly stretched along the front line and most were still struggling to make good the losses they had suffered in preceding months. And secondly, the forested and swampy terrain was far from ideal for armoured operations; there were no roads in either attack axis that could be used by fighting vehicles and their equally important supply columns.

When it began, *Raubtier* encountered the same difficulties that plagued Red Army operations in the area. The terrain was greatly favourable to the defenders and the northern pincer managed to move forward a little less than two miles on the first day; the southern pincer fared even worse, grinding forward barely half a mile. With ongoing heavy air support, the Germans battered their way forwards despite determined resistance. Two days after the attack commenced, Meretskov received a signal from *Stavka* urging him to continue his attacks towards Chudovo and Lyuban, but also to prevent Second Shock Army from being cut off. Meretskov was told that he was personally responsible for the elimination of the two German pincers, and was to submit his proposals for ongoing operations – including an ambitious plan to reach and capture Novgorod – within the next three days.[12] The following day, before Meretskov could respond, the northern German pincer reached and cut the supply route codenamed *Erika*; the southern route, *Dora*, was cut on 19 March and shortly before dawn the following day the two groups linked up. Second Shock Army was surrounded, though contact between the German groups was tenuous at best. With increasing desperation, Meretskov's army commanders committed whatever reserves they had available, but in vain.

There are stark contrasts between the German operation and the Red Army operation that preceded it. The Germans used aerial reconnaissance to guide artillery fire, repeatedly shelling Soviet units as they were assembling for counterattacks. By contrast, Soviet aviation was almost completely absent and provided no reconnaissance support whatever. Although the German attacks struggled through the same difficult terrain as the Soviet attacks, they had a clearer objective, the achievement of which was well within the resources available. The Germans also enjoyed close tactical air support, guided in by *Fliegerverbindungsoffiziere* ('Air Liaison Officers', often abbreviated to *Flivo*) who could direct air attacks. It was something that the Red Army would not routinely be able to do until the last year of the war, and even then without the flexibility and efficiency of the Germans. Supply issues were also continuing to cause problems for the Red Army. Meretskov ordered considerable artillery assets to be brought to bear against the two German groups, each of which currently occupied a narrow strip of territory; crushing artillery fire followed by a swift counterattack held the prospect of destroying one or even both German groups. But although many of the guns were moved into position, artillery ammunition remained in very short supply. Heavy fighting continued, and the northern supply route – *Erika* – became a deadly stretch of land with neither side in complete control, swept by fire from both armies. A junior commissar with the Soviet 65th Rifle Division described the fighting:

> Enemy aviation is unopposed. During the day, it is absolutely impossible to move anywhere, let alone to the front line. The vultures prey on everyone.
>
> There are terrible things happening on the highway [*Erika*]. There is no piece of land where shells and bombs haven't exploded. The enemy attacks without pause. Our thinned, exhausted divisions are still standing.[13]

Wilhelm Lubbeck was also involved in the fighting, directing the fire of his division's artillery batteries:

> I was about half a mile south of the *Dora* route. The primary mission of our heavy weapons company was to support our infantry in a defensive capacity. As a secondary task, we also sought to harass the Red Army forces passing through the corridor as well as prevent them from widening the breach. Meanwhile, the combined fire of approximately 120 150mm artillery pieces located on both sides of the corridor plus air strikes by Stuka dive-bombers relentlessly hammered the grid of roads that ran through the gap.[14]

At the headquarters of the German Eighteenth Army, Lindemann was pleased with the progress of the counterattack but was also aware of the pressure upon his army. With so much resource – both ground troops and aerial support – tied up in the fighting around Myasnoi Bor, his units elsewhere were increasingly stretched and his chief of staff, Generalmajor Kurt Waeger, recorded a few days later: 'It is slowly becoming impossible for the army to prevent the Russians from capturing Lyuban, because we do not have sufficient men to do so.'[15]

The bitterly cold weather of the winter months was gradually giving way to the spring thaw. Although the warmer temperatures were a welcome change from the biting cold, the result was that the ground began to soften, making all movement far more difficult. The few roads in the region slowly transformed into treacherous rivers of mud with the deeper ground still frozen solid, creating further problems for both sides. Intermittently the temperature would plummet again, and vehicles, men and horses that had been trapped in mud would then find themselves frozen in the hard ground; many wounded men on both sides died before they could be dug free. An officer cadet in the Red Army described the conditions as he and his comrades struggled to hold the two German attack groups apart:

> Together with other units, we broke through to create a corridor up to 500m wide. It opened, then closed, then opened again but only narrowly, then widened. It was constantly like that – the corridor would be broken and it was impossible to pass through it because of heavy shelling. The losses in those battles were huge, but much greater on our side as the enemy could carry out continuous artillery, mortar, rifle and machine-gun fire from our front, flanks, and rear, and enemy pilots attacked even individual men on the ground.
>
> There was nowhere to bury the dead – below the surface, the ground was deeply frozen everywhere, or there were trees, or waist-deep snow. All the clearings were littered with corpses. We walked among them, sat on them, lay beside them. When we had to mark a path in the forest, or passages through the snow, the bodies of the dead were used instead of milestones.[16]

Whilst the battle for *Erika* continued, Meretskov reported to *Stavka*. He wrote that Fifty-Second Army could deploy four divisions for the proposed attack towards Novgorod, which would also destroy the southern pincer of the German counterattack, but these divisions required substantial reinforcements as they collectively fielded fewer than 20,000 men. Even if adequate rail capacity could be provided, it would take several days for fresh drafts to be incorporated into the ranks of the depleted regiments and he proposed a start date of 29 March. Once the attack reached the railway line running northwest from Novgorod – an advance of about nine miles from the Volkhov River – he recommended the use of an airborne brigade to cut off the city from the west. However, he added a further note regarding reinforcements:

> Given that Fifty-Second Army lacks any troops in a second echelon, it is essential to plan for the provision of reinforcements during the operation so that the attacking divisions are not completely exhausted and to ensure that they will remain fully capable of combat as they approach Novgorod.[17]

Stavka responded with approval, but the clock was against Meretskov. Lindemann's two attack groups continued to strike against the Soviet forces struggling to keep contact open with Second Shock Army. On 26 March, the Germans once more linked up, but were too exhausted to hold back a Soviet counterattack that opened *Erika* once more. Aware that the units of Second Shock Army were in urgent need of resupply, Meretskov ordered a column of trucks to be prepared and when a further Soviet counterattack widened the corridor temporarily – in the process, 376th Rifle Division was reduced to fewer than 800 combatants – the column was ordered to drive through. The entire area was constantly swept by German fire and only five trucks managed to reach Second Shock Army. The rest joined the litter of wrecked vehicles of both sides, which provided almost the only cover for the exhausted soldiers. Red Army engineers even managed to construct a narrow-gauge railway line through the corridor, and despite constant shelling it was used – mainly at night – to drag supplies into the pocket and to try to bring out wounded men.

Two days before the new attack towards Novgorod was planned to commence, Meretskov sent a further signal to *Stavka*. He still planned to attack towards Chudovo and Lyuban with Second Shock Army, but the attack by Fifty-Second Army would have to be delayed, not least because the promised reinforcements had not arrived. He reported confidently that the corridor to Second Shock Army had been re-established and was secure, but this was not remotely the case. The fighting remained inconclusive, with first one side, then the other achieving successes that rarely lasted more than a day or two. Increasingly impatient with the failure of his units to cut off Second Shock Army and to establish a strong encirclement, Küchler at the headquarters of Army Group North dismissed Chappuis, commander of XXXVIII Corps. Chappuis was bitterly disappointed and argued in vain that he had done everything he could in almost impossible conditions. He returned to his home city of Magdeburg; the following August, he shot himself. His replacement in XXXVIII Corps was Haenicke, the commander of 61st Infantry Division. Hitler demanded further action, criticising

Generalleutnant Karl von Graffen, commander of 58th Infantry Division; for the moment, Graffen remained in post.

The weather was now turning increasingly rainy. Although both *Dora* and *Erika* were now back in the hands of the Red Army, the area remained swept by German fire and movement was only possible at night. By the end of the first week of April, both roads were impassable due to mud and to make matters worse, the river ice on the Volkhov began to break up, meaning that supplies could only be moved via the few bridges, which were under regular air and artillery attack. The attack towards Novgorod barely got off the ground before the ground conditions made it impossible to continue and Second Shock Army remained effectively isolated – although Red Army soldiers remained in their swamped trenches around the fiercely contested corridor, it was almost impossible to move meaningful quantities of men and supplies. An airstrip was established within the pocket but was regularly attacked by German aircraft; although up to 100 tons of supplies reached Second Shock Army by air on some nights, the average was far lower and in any event even this quantity was insufficient to keep such a large force operational. Gusev's cavalry supplemented their diet with meat from horses that had died, but the infantry had no such recourse. Some of XIII Cavalry Corps was able to break out through the tenuous corridor, taking their surviving horses to safety; the animals were transferred to a specially prepared camp and the soldiers returned to the pocket to fight on as infantry. It wasn't just the cavalry that found their mobility reduced. Gerodnik and his ski battalion were also converted to regular infantry, often forced to scour the landscape to salvage supplies from the corpses that littered the battlefield:

We entered a large clearing in the forest. Strawberries grew there profusely. There was already little snow, but due to the dense forest around the clearing, it was only half melted. As it disappeared, it gradually revealed the secrets it had kept through the winter ...

Throughout the forest – traces of a fierce battle. Dozens of unrecovered corpses frozen in the snow. To the south of the clearing, our men, to the north, German soldiers. In deep silence we walked through this cemetery of the unburied, starting from the south. We took identity discs from the pockets of tunics. Each of the dead had his own posture, but the great majority lay with their heads to the north. So, they were advancing in that direction, towards Chudovo. Here lay a sergeant with his arms outstretched. His triangular buttons were homemade – cut from a tin can. Empty machine-gun belts were scattered around the sergeant. Of course, there was no machine-gun – those who were still alive

319

took it with them and continued the advance. Canvas boots stuck out of a snowdrift. Whose were they? We would find out perhaps a week later, or even earlier when the spring warmth set in properly in this forest. A soldier with his helmet pierced by a bullet died just as he was clambering over a tree felled in a storm. I found an identity disc and a rolled up piece of paper. He was a Bashkir from Belebey, born in 1920.

We found well-preserved items in the pouches of the dead: tins of food, biscuit, concentrates, dried fish. Even lumps of sugar had survived in tightly closed boxes. There were flasks of alcohol, pouches of tobacco. In short, so many items that the commissar ordered, 'Hand them over to the NCOs. We can share them all equally.' We saw that every dead man had a gas mask. We had abandoned ours, using the canvas bags for other items and the authorities turned a blind eye to it.

The German side of the 'panorama' had its own characteristics. Gas masks in cylindrical metal cases, leather satchels like our high school students once had, cloth caps with headphones attached to them. The German identity disc was an aluminium plate, either a rectangle or an ellipse. Along its major axis was a row of holes punched in a dotted line – the rectangle or ellipse could easily be broken into two equal halves along this …

It wasn't difficult to imagine, in general terms, the drama played out here in the 'strawberry meadow'. It seemed that this took place two months ago in the first days after the breakthrough of Second Shock Army at Myasnoi Bor. Our infantry unit moved north, expanding the breakthrough. There was a short fight here. There was no time to bury the dead … But a strong February blizzard arrived here before the burial detail. It buried the fallen, sang their requiem. And then there were more blizzards and heavy snowfalls. Finally, spring opened the cover that hid the 'Volkhov panorama' during February and March. Here we saw another grimace of the terrible face of war.[18]

As the winter weather relaxed its grip, the city of Leningrad – the object of all the bitter fighting – began to come back to life. Leaves appeared on the trees and grass began to grow; the starved population frequently ate both, desperate for whatever tiny nutrient value they might contain. The thawing snow and ice revealed the full scale of the horror of the siege: thousands of corpses everywhere, most stripped of their clothing, some bearing the unmistakable signs of cannibalism. Work parties were rapidly organised to start the long business of clearing the streets. Wagons took the dead to the Piskarevskoye Cemetery and a few other sites where they were interred in mass graves. Rations were now at a level where body weight was sustainable and the death rate from starvation fell steadily; the German guns and planes that had added to the death toll in the first part of the winter remained silent, their munitions needed for the heavy fighting along the Volkhov River. On 5 April, the musicians who had been asked to register at Leningrad Radio held their first rehearsal. Most were still in a very poor state of health, as Kseniya Matus, the oboist, described:

> We had no strength at all, and the rehearsals were quite short – 40 minutes. But the first concert was in the Pushkin Theatre … the theatre was cold, 8°C. At that first concert we played the Glazunov Overture, then we played the *Waltz-Chardash*, then something from The Nutcracker … And when we had finished the last piece the audience began to applaud … [but it seemed] there were only the ghosts of listeners, and on the stage the ghosts of performers. Because the men who played the brass instruments couldn't hold them in their hands – they were beginning to freeze.[19]

The piece of music that captured the imagination of everyone in Leningrad – and indeed across much of the planet – was the symphony that Shostakovich had written whilst enduring the winter siege. This, his Seventh Symphony, received its premier on 5 March in the distant city of Kuibyshev. It is a long piece and requires a substantial orchestra, and given the official criticism that he had endured before the war, Shostakovich was understandably anxious on the day of the performance. He addressed the audience before the symphony began, and it is hard to know how much his fear of Stalin shaped the words he used:

> My music is my weapon. We are struggling for the highest human ideals in history. We are battling for our culture, for science, for art, for everything we have created and built … I dedicate my Seventh Symphony to our struggle with Fascism, to our coming victory over the enemy, and to my native city, Leningrad.[20]

Performing such a long piece in Leningrad itself was, for the moment, an insurmountable challenge – there simply weren't enough musicians and such a performance was beyond their strength. Nevertheless, preparations began. Several musicians who had left Leningrad were permitted to return to the city and there were short rehearsals of different parts of the symphony, their duration carefully calculated not to tax the fragile performers.

On the Volkhov River, two pontoon bridges were constructed to ferry supplies across to the tiny corridor that was the lifeline of Second Shock Army. Two ferries were also established, but traffic was constantly disrupted by bombing, artillery attacks, and floating mines that the Germans released upstream. Conditions for the soldiers on both sides were terrible. The accelerating thaw turned trenches and dugouts into water-filled morasses of mud, and the stench of decomposing bodies was everywhere. Concerned about both the health effects and the impact on morale of so many unburied corpses, Meretskov's headquarters issued orders that burial teams were to be established, but this proved to be a dangerous exercise with large parts of the pocket constantly swept by German fire. In any case, there was nowhere within the pocket where the ground was firm enough for burial to take place.

There were changes in command as a result of the recent fighting. The failure of the last attempt to reach Lyuban – inevitable, given the weakened state of both Fifty-Fourth Army in the north and Second Shock Army in the south – resulted in a commission being sent by Volkhov Front's military council to investigate. The reasons for the failure were of course abundantly clear to all concerned, but someone had to be blamed. Georgy Yermolayevich Degtyarev, who held the rank of colonel at the time and was commander of Second Shock Army's artillery, later recalled that the commission questioned men within the pocket for three days.[21] Despite receiving abundant testimony that the operation had been doomed from the outset, the commission made its report to the military council and shortly afterwards, Klykov learned that he was being dismissed from command of Second Shock Army. He had still not fully recovered his health, and the decision to remove him may have been partly motivated by his infirmity, but it was undoubtedly a convenient way for Meretskov to ensure that someone else would take the blame for the setback.

Klykov's replacement as commander of Second Shock Army was the subject of discussions between Meretskov, Army Commissar Aleksandr Ivanovich Zaporozhets, a senior member of the Volkhov Front military council, and Division Commissar Ivan Vasilyevich Zuyev, a member of Second Shock Army's military council. The result was that the post was assigned to Vlasov, currently working as Meretskov's deputy. In many respect, this seemed an obvious choice. Vlasov had successfully led Red Army units out of encirclement battles in Ukraine and his reputation was riding high after his successes outside Moscow during the winter. Meretskov's memoirs paint an unflattering picture of Vlasov, describing him as sullen and not contributing very much to discussions at Front headquarters, and it seems that Meretskov was very happy to have Klykov and Vlasov swap roles.

The battles further south around Demyansk are beyond the scope of this work, but their outcome was that the German forces that had been surrounded earlier in the year – the only occasion when the Red Army's winter offensives succeeded in pinching off a large group of German soldiers – ended when a powerful German group commanded by Generalleutnant Walther von Seydlitz-Kurzbach attacked from the west on 21 March. At the same time, the troops within the encirclement attacked towards the east, resulting in the two forces linking up with each other after four weeks of heavy fighting. Rather than evacuating the pocket, Hitler insisted that it be held and reinforcements were brought in, gradually stabilising the front. It would be the basis for Hitler's decisions in late 1942 around Stalingrad: the encircled troops were ordered to hold out, while they received supplies by air, and an attempt was made to break through to them from the outside. Even if the attack by Fourth Panzer Army had reached the Stalingrad encirclement, Hitler had no intention of permitting the trapped Sixth Army to withdraw. He fully intended to follow the same plan as had been imposed at Demyansk, with the positions in the city on the Volga continuing to be held. Those decisions lay in the future; but the one major success of the Red Army in the rolling offensives of early 1942 was gone.

The huge number of Soviet offensive operations that took place in January, February, and March 1942 shows the degree of over-optimism and misjudgement on the part of Stalin in particular and *Stavka* in general. On several occasions – in the context of the fighting in the north, at Lyuban, but also on several occasions to the west of Moscow – the Red Army came close to encircling large German formations but the offensives faltered because of inadequate reserves, heavy losses, and poor logistics. All of these operations were predicated upon a belief that the Wehrmacht had overstretched its resources to such an extent that attacks had a high likelihood of success, and were perhaps also influenced by the memory of the manner in which multiple attacks had been made on the German and Austro-Hungarian forces in the First World War; in that earlier conflict, this had been a deliberate policy to exhaust the reserves of the Central Powers so that ultimately, a weakness would arise somewhere along the front that would result in a breakthrough. Indeed, the grand strategy of the Entente Powers repeated this policy on a continental scale, with offensives in the west and east intended to stretch German resources beyond breaking point. The Wehrmacht demonstrated in the first months of 1942 that it was far from beaten and although there were some difficult moments – some of the defenders of Lyuban felt that their survival owed as much to pure luck as to German military prowess – the Red Army failed to land a major blow on its opponent. Many German divisions were badly mauled, but Red Army losses were consistently greater. Had Stalin concentrated resources on fewer operations, it seems highly that these would have delivered greater results.

There were numerous analyses of the failures in the weeks and months that followed. Many of the problems that had prevented success – shortage of artillery ammunition, poor logistics, a failure to concentrate combat resources at key locations at strategic, operational, and tactical levels – were correctly identified. Communications failures between infantry and artillery resulted in the Red Army's guns having to operate to strict fire plans that were inflexible and took no account of changing circumstances, and when they met resistance Soviet commanders repeatedly resorted to frontal attacks in futile attempts to bludgeon their way to victory rather than attempting any outflanking manoeuvres. There were many reasons for this last failing. Partly, it reflected the poor level of training of Soviet officers; partly, it was due to ongoing fear that failing to adhere strictly to every order from above might result in sudden arrest.

The swapping of roles by Klykov and Vlasov wasn't the only change in command arrangements in the north. Khozin, the commander of Leningrad Front, travelled to *Stavka* in late April. Here he held discussions with senior commanders, and Vasilevsky described the discussions:

> [Khozin] reported that the Lyuban setback had occurred through the lack of joint command over troops defending Leningrad. He suggested combining Leningrad and Volkhov Fronts and giving him command of the combined Front. I am sure he had faith in the correctness and expediency of his plan.
>
> Shaposhnikov immediately opposed the suggestion. But Stalin took Khozin's side and a decision was taken to do away with Volkhov Front, transfer its troops to Leningrad Front, and assign Volkhov Front commander Meretskov first as deputy commander of Western Front and then, at his request, commander of Thirty-Third Army of that Front. The Leningrad Front commander Khozin was now able to combine actions in lifting the Leningrad siege. It was soon evident, however, that it was both difficult and well nigh impossible to command nine armies, three separate corps and two groups that were split by the enemy-occupied zone. The *Stavka* decision to disband the Volkhov Front thus turned out to be a mistake.[22]

Khozin later claimed that this was not his idea, but originated with Stalin and Shaposhnikov.[23] In some respects, this seems a more likely description of events, given that Khozin hadn't been keen on taking command of Leningrad Front in the first place. Regardless of who proposed the new arrangements, Khozin now faced a difficult problem: how to extract Second Shock Army from the swamps where it was slowly being strangled to death. He flew directly to the former headquarters of Volkhov Front, where he was briefed on the situation. Inside the encirclement were 11 rifle divisions, three cavalry divisions, and five independent rifle brigades. The corridor to the Volkhov River was little more than a mile wide, and the entire area was dominated by German aircraft. Khozin immediately submitted a report to *Stavka*: if Second Shock Army remained in position, it faced certain destruction. It would be better to extract its battered divisions from the encirclement and bring them back to strength so that they could be used in a new offensive later in the year. Stalin had already concluded that the north would be a secondary sector in the coming campaign season – he fully expected a renewed German effort in the central sector towards Moscow, and wanted to concentrate reserves in that area. Hitler meanwhile had decided that the best option available to him was to strike in the south, advancing to the Don and Volga before sending strong forces into the Caucasus. Both sides wanted to avoid expensive commitments in the north for the moment, and aware that further offensives in this area were impossible given these constraints, Stalin agreed with Khozin's suggestion.

During the bloody and indecisive battles along the Volkhov River, the Germans mounted two operations against Leningrad itself. As it became clear that the intended plan – to starve the city to death during the winter months – was not going to succeed, there was a reassessment. The reasons for treating Leningrad as a priority target were threefold. Firstly, the city was a centre of armaments production; the elimination of this had largely been achieved, either by the damage inflicted on the city or as a consequence of Stalin's evacuation of industry to the east. Secondly, Leningrad clearly had a symbolic value to the Soviet Union as the cradle of the revolution and its capture would, it was hoped, have a major impact on morale throughout the Soviet system. But the Germans were now realising that although that might have been the case, the survival of Leningrad, particularly in such terrible circumstances, was a source of considerable moral strength. Thirdly, Leningrad – or more accurately Kronstadt – was the home of the Soviet Baltic Fleet. Whilst it may have been considerably constrained by German minefields in the Gulf of Finland and the threat of German air attacks, the surface ships and submarines of the fleet remained a threat, and their guns continued to provide considerable support to the defenders of the Oranienbaum bridgehead. The destruction of the Baltic Fleet was therefore a potential way in which one of the strategic objectives of the advance to Leningrad could be achieved, and at the same time a successful operation against this fleet would, it was hoped, be some compensation for Leningrad continuing to defy the Wehrmacht.

With the army both unable and unwilling to move closer to Leningrad, the Germans opted for a major air attack on Kronstadt. This would be carried out by *Fliegerkorps I*, commanded by Luftwaffe General Helmuth Förster. With nine *Kampfgeschwader* and four *Jagdgeschwader*, it was a powerful force. Each *Jagdgeschwader* (fighter wing) had between two and four *Gruppen*, which were further made up of *Staffeln*, with an overall strength of up to 124 aircraft per *Jagdgeschwader*. The *Kampfgeschwader* (bomber wings) were similarly structured. None of these units were at full strength in early 1942; losses had not been replaced, and large numbers of aircraft were unavailable due to shortages of spare parts and the difficulties of operating in such cold conditions. Furthermore, there were constant demands for air support by almost every sector of the front line, meaning that the Luftwaffe was rarely able to concentrate its resources for a single operation on a sustained basis.

The first operation against the Baltic Fleet was codenamed *Eis Stoss* ('Breaking Ice'). The intention was that German artillery would bombard known and likely positions of anti-aircraft defences immediately before the bombers attacked. Such suppression would be sorely needed, as the Baltic Fleet had been strengthening its air defences. Additional anti-aircraft weapons had been deployed on all its ships and there were eight anti-aircraft regiments defending Leningrad. Whilst the Soviet fighter regiments – five belonging to the air force and two to the Baltic Fleet itself – were far from full strength, the Germans intended to deploy a considerable part of the fighter forces of *Fliegerkorps I* to prevent the Soviet fighter planes from intervening.

In preparation for *Eis Stoss*, the Germans set up silhouettes of several Baltic Fleet ships on a frozen lake. Unfortunately for the Germans, one of the few Soviet reconnaissance flights over the area spotted the silhouettes and an additional anti-aircraft regiment was deployed to protect the ships. On 4 April, the operation began with a force of 132 German bombers, escorted by 59 fighters, deployed in three waves. Few if any Soviet fighters appeared, and the defence consisted entirely of anti-aircraft fire. Despite the preliminary German artillery bombardment, the barrage from the defences was sufficiently strong to prevent the Germans from making precision attacks. The only notable success was when the cruiser *Kirov* suffered several hits, knocking out most of her anti-aircraft guns and killing or wounding about 130 sailors.[24] Although the anti-aircraft gunners submitted claims that they had destroyed up to 24 German aircraft, all the German fighters and bombers returned safely to their bases; four Soviet fighters, which appeared late in the day, were shot down.[25]

That night, the bombers returned for a second attack. About 30 planes attacked the battleship *Oktyabrskaya Revoliutsya*. The ship had been bombed before, suffering heavy damage in a raid in September, and was now hit by three medium bombs and one heavy bomb; no major damage resulted.[26] On 5 April, the Luftwaffe mounted the third and last attack of *Eis Stoss*. On this occasion, no significant hits were scored. With growing pressure to divert resources to support German forces fighting along the Volkhov River and in the battles for the Demyansk encirclement, *Fliegerkorps I* called a halt to attacks.

As April drew to a close and the Germans succeeded in reaching and rescuing the troops surrounded around Demyansk, there was a further opportunity for *Fliegerkorps I* to direct its strength against the Baltic Fleet. The new operation was codenamed *Götz von Berlichingen*, the name of a German mercenary commander of the Thirty Years War who famously invited the Bishop of Bamberg to kiss his posterior when the latter called upon the mercenary to surrender. On 24 April, there was a further artillery bombardment followed by a raid by 62 bombers and 28 fighter escorts over a period of about three hours. Unlike the first attack, this was made by small groups of planes attacking from multiple directions and it succeeded in confusing the air defence. A Soviet submarine had already been hit by artillery fire during the bombardment and there was further damage with several casualties aboard *Oktyabrskaya Revoliutsya* from shrapnel. Again, the anti-aircraft gunners claimed to have destroyed several German aircraft; only one German plane failed to return to its base. Further raids took place on 25, 27, and 30 April with a few ships suffering damage, but the overall intention of the mission – to eliminate the Baltic Fleet as a fighting force – was unsuccessful. A total of three small vessels were sunk, and the only major damage was to the cruiser *Kirov*.

There are differing accounts of *Eis Stoss* and *Götz von Berlichingen*, with some disagreements on which ships were hit in which operation, but the end result was disappointing for the Luftwaffe. The Baltic Fleet remained in existence. The ships might be effectively bottled up in the eastern part of the Gulf of Finland, but their guns remained a constant threat to German land forces.

Within the pocket held by Second Shock Army, Gerodnik and his ski battalion – now fighting as regular infantry – continued to suffer losses. They were in woodland when they came under mortar fire, and as they attempted to escape they found themselves in a German minefield. After evacuating a wounded comrade, Gerodnik was running back when he triggered a mine, which blew away part of his right foot. He became one of about 5,000 wounded who couldn't be evacuated. After three days lying in a barn, he received surgical treatment and was put on a peasant cart with two other men. An emaciated pony pulled the cart to another field hospital where he underwent further surgery before a night-time transfer through the narrow neck of the pocket, now known widely to Soviet troops as the 'Valley of Death'. In the village of Selishchensky, on the Volkhov River, there was a pause and the men endured a new enemy: the appearance of swarms of mosquitoes. Finally, they were able to cross to safety. Several of the wounded men being evacuated with Gerodnik died at various points of the journey.[27] The ordeal of the wounded men of the ski battalion was typical of the suffering of so many wounded men, on either side of the front line.

The Germans too were plagued by mosquitoes as the weather grew warmer. Lubbeck described the conditions in which he and his comrades lived and fought:

The standing water around us generated swarms of mosquitoes from which there was no escape. Even with netting around our tents, they still ceaselessly hounded us. This compounded the persistent irritation from the lice on our bodies, making restful sleep almost impossible. With hot soup a rare luxury, our rations consisted mostly of crackers and canned fish and sausage. Though our morale remained high, inadequate sleep and a poor diet, and the stress of combat left us physically weakened and mentally exhausted.[28]

Having inherited command of the situation – either at his own instigation or at that of senior figures in *Stavka* – Khozin drew up orders to try to extract Second Shock Army. In addition to Vlasov's army, there were elements of Fifty-Ninth and Fifty-Second Armies in the pocket, and the combined force was to pull back in stages, maintaining a continuous front line throughout. At the last moment, *Stavka* issued further instructions, requiring the Volkhov Group of Forces – as the old armies of Volkhov Front were now known – to destroy the northern pincer of the German counterattack, in order to shorten the front line. Once the withdrawal was complete, this new group was to be further subdivided into a Ladoga Group in the north and a Volkhov Group in the south.

By creating the Volkhov Group of Forces, *Stavka* was effectively recognising that there were now too many disparate formations under the command of Leningrad Front, over too wide an area. On 24 May, Second Shock Army began to pull back towards the east. Khozin's plan had explicitly called for Fifty-Second and Fifty-Ninth Armies to make new attacks towards Second Shock Army in order to facilitate the latter's withdrawal, and had specified the need for reinforcements for the two depleted armies. No such reinforcements appeared and the only additional strength came in the form of a depleted tank brigade with very limited ammunition. Remarkably, sappers had succeeded in creating a log road through the Valley of Death despite constant German shelling and machine-gun fire and the first units to be withdrawn were the last formations of XIII Cavalry Corps, followed by a heavy artillery column accompanied by many of the wounded.

Inevitably, the Red Army's movements were detected by the constant Luftwaffe reconnaissance flights. Küchler and Lindemann discussed the situation and ordered the units on either side of the Valley of Death to renew their efforts to pinch off the pocket. In the northern pincer, the German I Corps had been fending off attacks by the Soviet Fifty-Ninth Army from the east and Second Shock Army from the west since the end of April, but the reality was that Fifty-Ninth Army was simply too weak to accomplish anything. Bock began to group his men for another attack towards the south.

At first, it seemed as if Khozin's plan for a phased withdrawal was proceeding smoothly. After abandoning the most westerly parts of the pocket and falling back to the first withdrawal line, Second Shock Army then pulled back across the Tigoda River, south of Lyuban, on 28 May. Here, there was a pause while a large part of Second Shock Army moved into the northern part of the pocket with the intention of breaking through the northern German pincer in order to link up with Fifty-Ninth Army. Even as these troops were forming up – the planned start date for this final phase of the operation was 5 June – the Germans struck against the Valley of Death. I Corps in the north and XXXVIII Corps in the south renewed their assaults, with heavy air support. The fighting was bitter, with XXXVIII Corps' 58th Infantry Division, 20th Motorised Division, and 2nd SS Infantry Brigade taking heavy losses, but the two pincers met on 30 May, once more isolating Second Shock Army. A desperate attempt to re-establish the corridor using the newly arrived, full-strength 165th Rifle Division on 3 June ended in disaster after half of the division's men became casualties as its attack foundered in the face of heavy German air attacks and artillery bombardment.

The only hope for the Red Army soldiers remaining in the pocket was a successful breakout through the northern German pincer. As planned, the operation began before dawn on 5 June and, somewhat surprisingly, the weakened Fifty-Ninth Army succeeded in reaching its initial objectives on the Polist River, near the village of Spasskaya Polist. But the attack from within the pocket was poorly organised, and in any event ran into a German attack heading in the opposite direction. Unable to move closer to the men of Fifty-Ninth Army, the soldiers of Second Shock Army were driven back deeper into the pocket. Increasingly desperate orders from Khozin for Vlasov to concentrate his men better and to fight his way to freedom were in vain, as the German I Corps continued to drive Second Shock Army back towards the west. Further German attacks near the Valley of Death widened the German link between I Corps in the north and XXXVIII Corps in the south, effectively ending any lingering hope that the Red Army might be able to re-establish its original corridor.

On 8 June, a further delegation from *Stavka* led by Vasilevsky arrived in the north. Khozin was told that he was being dismissed for the failure to withdraw Second Shock Army from the encirclement. Volkhov Front was to be re-established, and would once more be commanded by Meretskov, who accompanied Vasilevsky. Khozin was now sent to take command of Thirty-Third Army in Meretskov's place. The criticism of Khozin was justified insofar as he threw units into action without pausing to concentrate them, but this ignores the manner in which Stalin rarely accepted any excuse for delay. Ultimately, Khozin's undoubted failure was the result of Stalin's pernicious influence that continued to inhibit field commanders from taking prudent measures to increase their chances of success.

Leningrad Front also received a new commander: Lieutenant General Leonid Aleksandrovich Govorov. He had fought in the ranks of Admiral Aleksandr Vasilyevich Kolchak's army on the side of the White Russians during the Civil War before defecting to the Bolsheviks, and despite exemplary service in the rest of the Civil War it was inevitable that his past would bring him under severe scrutiny during Stalin's purges. He was accused of sabotaging artillery production and of having links with several other senior officers who had already been charged and convicted, but somehow he escaped arrest and punishment. As an artillery expert, he served as chief of artillery of Western Front during the first phase of the Battle of Moscow before being given command of Fifth Army in mid-October, leading it with great skill. He was now to oversee preparations for another attempt to break the siege ring around Leningrad.

Within the encirclement to the west of the Volkhov River, the plight of Second Shock Army worsened steadily. Supply by air proved to be impossible – nearly 300 flights were attempted in June, but many were forced to turn back and most merely dropped their cargo as they flew past and the Germans steadily pushed in from almost every side. Given the shortages of ammunition and food, it is unsurprising that Vlasov couldn't organise the troops to mount a more robust defence, let alone fight his way to freedom; after escaping several encirclements in the previous year, his luck had now run out. On 21 June, one of the members of Second Shock Army's military council reported to the council of Front headquarters: 'Army troops receive 50g of biscuit [per day]. For the last three days there has been absolutely no food [delivered by air] … People are completely exhausted … We are almost out of ammunition.'[29]

The fighting around the perimeter was intense as desperate Red Army troops attempted to break through the German lines. Wilhelm Lubbeck was in the front line in his role as an artillery observer. Near his position was a machine-gun team armed with the new MG-42, a significant improvement on the older MG-34, with a far higher rate of fire and better reliability. The rate of fire was so high that it produced a distinctive tearing sound when fired, rather than a series of distinct shots; to the soldiers of the Red Army, it became known as the *Gitler Pila* ('Hitler saw'). The position soon came under attack from Soviet infantry attempting to escape the encirclement:

Calling back a fire mission, I requested our 75mm guns to drop shells in a curtain roughly 25m in front of our position, as close as I dared risk.

With the Red Army troops still closing on our location, I added my own MP-40 submachine-gun's fire to the torrent of bullets spilling from my comrade's machine-gun. Despite the absence of any return fire and the lack of any clearly visible targets in the thick foliage, the gunner and I raked our weapons over the entire field in front of us as shells from our heavy guns began to slam down in support.

When the barrel of the MG-42 finally overheated from the relentless firing, the soldier yanked it off and tossed it into a puddle next to us, producing a cloud of steam. Locking a fresh barrel into the machine-gun, he started blazing away again. Already, the gunner stood in a mound of empty shell casings.

Perhaps half an hour passed with no let-up in our fire. Upon emptying my third or fourth 32-round clip, I again ducked down behind the wooden walls in order to avoid exposing myself as a target … At that moment I became aware that the machine-gun had grown silent, but assumed the gunner was also reloading or again switching the barrel of his weapon.

A glance to my right revealed the gunner crumpled on the ground beside me. A second later, I spotted blood running from a hole in his temple just under the rim of his helmet. The shot that killed him had not been audible in the din of combat, but its precision made it instantly obvious to me that it came from a sniper's rifle.

There is not much time to contemplate one's life in the middle of a battle, but the thought flashed through my mind that it could have been me lying there with a bullet through my head, if I had not ducked down or my submachine-gun's magazine had run out a few seconds later.[30]

On 22 June, a further attempt was made to rescue the trapped soldiers – by this stage, Second Shock Army consisted of a little over 23,000 men, many of them wounded, and nearly 5,000 local civilians who wanted to escape alongside the soldiers. The rest of Vlasov's army was dead, prisoner, or had already left the encirclement either singly or in small groups, attempting to escape. A tenuous breakthrough was made in the German encirclement over the Polist River; the ground was almost carpeted with the dead as exhausted, hungry men from Second Shock Army attempted to escape under constant German fire. Some came out as the remnants of the army units that had entered the pocket, while others streamed through in small groups or as individuals, many of them wounded. Within hours, there were determined German attempts to cut off the pocket once more; although the southern side of the tenuous corridor beat off the German attempts, the northern side was driven back, but by the end of the day perhaps a quarter of the Soviet soldiers and civilians within the encirclement had made it to safety.

Throughout the period of the encirclement, German aircraft dropped leaflets on the trapped Soviet soldiers, urging them to surrender. Inevitably, these leaflets contained assurances that all soldiers who laid down their arms would be treated with mercy, and many Red Army personnel would have been highly sceptical of any such words. But perhaps in an attempt to encourage surrender, orders were issued to the German units attempting to destroy Second Shock Army: the immediate execution of suspected commissars was now forbidden.[31]

After further bitter fighting with heavy losses on both sides, the Germans closed the encirclement again on 24 June. With the last of its strength, Fifty-Ninth Army attacked again the following night and succeeded once more in establishing the most precarious contact with the encirclement. By now, with the entire area under constant German fire, there was little or no coordination of the surviving soldiers of Second Shock Army. One of the very last groups to attempt the corridor to the Volkhov River was a medical unit. A nurse later described the episode:

> The escape began. People began to fall, the wounded joined us – at first they were carried, but then we got into such hell that it is difficult to put into words. There was thunder all around and everything was ablaze, and tracer rounds whistled past like tiny torches. Everything seemed to be collapsing, [it was like] the end of the world ... It was impossible to raise our heads; we crawled up to our necks in the mud like lizards, and from the [German] positions in the bushes on the left

there was a constant monotonous shout of 'Rus, surrender, Rus, surrender.' Before our eyes, those with whom we had endured all the horror of the situation were dying. The living crawled, trying to survive, perhaps because they had only lived for 18 or 19 years.

I can't describe in detail everything that I had to endure that night, from 11pm on 24 June to 5am on 25 June, when finally, exhausted – completely exhausted – we crawled out in ones and twos.[32]

The pocket began to break up under constant pressure from the encircling Germans. As the sun rose on 25 June, the Germans renewed their attacks and closed the encirclement for the last time. Fighting continued for several more days as groups of Soviet soldiers encountered German units sweeping the area. Some survivors managed to reach the lines of Fifty-Ninth Army; most of those that remained in the swamps and forests died or were taken prisoner.

By now, communications between Vlasov and outside bodies had ceased. A last plane was sent to the encirclement to fly Vlasov and other senior officers to safety, but the general who had stayed with his men in previous encirclements chose once again not to leave his soldiers. With a group of officers and men, Vlasov moved north through the swamps, encountering the remnants of 92nd Rifle Division under the command of Colonel Andrei Nikolayevich Larichev. Perhaps on the assumption that his men were more likely to succeed in a breakout on their own, Larichev chose not to join Vlasov's group of about 50 survivors and turned east, where he ran into German infantry moving in the opposite direction. Larichev suffered injuries to both legs and was last seen manning a machine-gun. Only one officer and 91 men from the division managed to escape; the officer crawled nearly seven miles through the swamps and forests with several wounds including a broken jaw.[33] Meanwhile, Vlasov encountered a second group of soldiers who warned him that he was heading for a German minefield. After further attempts to move east, the group turned south again.

The accounts of the following days are varied. Several partisan groups attempted in vain to locate Vlasov, who dispersed his remaining command into smaller groups. Either hiding in a bunker or wandering through the dense woodland, Vlasov avoided capture until 13 July. Accompanied by a nurse, he attempted to get food from a village but was locked in a barn by a local official who then contacted the Germans, who took him prisoner; in return for his cooperation, the headman of the village received a gift of a cow, a quantity of tobacco, two bottles of vodka and a certificate of good conduct.[34]

It seems that Meretskov issued an order in the last days of June for Vlasov to be placed under arrest and it is possible that Vlasov was aware of this when he refused to board the last plane out of the encirclement. Meretskov's motive for such an act are obvious: he was still living under the shadow of his arrest the previous year, and would have been desperate to ensure that, if at all possible, blame for the disaster that engulfed Second Shock Army fell on someone other than himself.

The rest of Vlasov's life played a huge part in the manner in which he has been remembered. He was taken to the prison camp near Vinnitsa in Ukraine, where the Germans held several senior officers who had fallen into their hands. The reasons for what followed will never be known for certain. He may have been embittered by what he saw as the failure of Volkhov Front to rescue his trapped army; Meretskov's attempt to arrest him may also have played a part. Before the end of 1942, he had agreed to work with the *Komitet Osvobozhdeniya Narodov Rossii* ('Committee for the Liberation of the People of Russia' or KONR), an anti-Bolshevik group that saw itself as the inheritor of the mantle of the White Russian forces of the Russian Civil War. At first, the Germans did little to take advantage of this group other than helping circulate its documents, including the *Smolenskaya Deklaratsiya* ('Smolensk Declaration'), which called on support for the overthrow of Stalin and the Bolsheviks and the creation of a new Russian state that would make an honourable peace with Germany. In 1943, Vlasov and other senior figures in the KONR began to organise Red Army prisoners of war into units of the *Russkaya Osvobodyitelnaya Armya* ('Russian Liberation Army' or *ROA*), which were used at first for anti-partisan and security operations. Whilst many of the men who joined its ranks may have been motivated by a desire to oppose the Bolsheviks, others – probably most – of the recruits of the *ROA* joined because it was an opportunity to escape the harsh conditions of the prison camps. The *ROA* was organised into a proper field force in the last months of the war, seeing its first proper action against the Red Army as late as February 1945, but some of the anti-partisan bodies may have encountered Red Army units earlier in the war. It became routine for Red Army personnel to refer to any former Red Army soldiers who fought against them as 'Vlasovites', though most of those they encountered had little or nothing to do with Vlasov and the *ROA*. By the end of the war, the *ROA* had grown to three divisions. About 20,000 fell into the hands of the Red Army near Linz in Austria in 1945; most were executed within days of capture. Others surrendered to the Americans but were then handed over to the Soviet Union, where their officers were executed and the men sent to labour camps.

As the Red Army closed in during mid-April 1945, Vlasov was offered an escape route by Franco, the Fascist ruler of Spain; Franco was prepared to fly him to safety, but characteristically, Vlasov refused and remained with his men. He was captured by soldiers of the Soviet 1st Ukrainian Front and taken to Moscow where he was put on trial. It seems that he attempted to take full personal responsibility for the *ROA*, perhaps in an attempt to spare other figures from the wrath of Stalin. If that was his intention, he was unsuccessful; together with all the other senior figures of the *ROA*, he was found guilty of treason and was executed on 1 August 1946. In the years that followed, he was universally portrayed in Soviet accounts as a self-serving traitor. Even Vasilevsky, who was almost always kind in his assessment of others, was harsh in his judgement of Vlasov:

> The plight of Second Shock Army was made even worse by Vlasov betraying his country; he voluntarily went over to the enemy and, in an attempt to wheedle himself into Nazi service fast and deftly – already considering the Nazis the victors – he declared his intention of taking up the fight against the Soviet Union …
>
> Soviet and progressive foreign literature have a long established incontestable opinion of Vlasov as a time-server, a self-seeker, a careerist and traitor.[35]

This is a distortion of events. Vlasov did not join the ranks of those opposed to the Bolsheviks until after he had been captured. Nor are the attempts by Meretskov and others to blame the failure of the Lyuban operation on Vlasov justified. By the time that he took command of Second Shock Army, it was already almost completely isolated and it was impossible for its troops to concentrate sufficiently to break out to the east. It is difficult to see how any other commander could have done any better in such circumstances.

Attempts have been made in recent years to secure some form of rehabilitation for Vlasov; in 2001, a campaign mounted by the movement *Za Veru I Otechestvo* ('For Faith and Fatherland'), which styles itself as a 'traditionalist organisation that sees as its goal the formation of a Russian national-monarchical state', applied to the Chief Military Prosecutor's Office and to the Military Collegium of the Supreme Court of the Russian Federation for a review of the case. Both applications were unsuccessful. Whilst the judgement of Soviet and later Russian history has been overwhelmingly damning of Vlasov, there have also been suggestions that the manner in which the Soviet system treated former Red Army personnel who became prisoners of war – they were all suspected of having betrayed the Soviet Union by surrendering, and of having been exposed to anti-Bolshevik influences – and the purges carried out by Stalin during the pre-war years are at least mitigating factors.[36] Inevitably, there have been numerous comparisons between his conduct and that of other senior officers who found themselves cut off. General Mikhail Grigoryevich Yefremov, the commander of Thirty-Third Army, was left stranded behind German lines by a counterattack that isolated a large part of his army; when he was unable to break through to safety, he shot himself. In the First World War, General Aleksandr Vasilyevich Samsonov's Second Army was surrounded during the Battle of Tannenberg in East Prussia in 1914, and he too took his own life rather than surrender. However, many other senior Soviet commanders chose surrender over death; for example, Vlasov's partner in the foundation of the formation of the KONR was Major General Vasily Fedorovich Malyshkin, formerly the chief of staff of Nineteenth Army, who became a prisoner in October 1941. The performance of senior German officers who found themselves surrounded was also varied. Hitler deliberately promoted Friedrich Paulus to Generalfeldmarschall in January 1943 when he was already surrounded in Stalingrad with his Sixth Army, on the expectation that no German officer of such high rank would surrender to the enemy, but Paulus went into captivity at the end of January and then joined the *Nationalkomitee Freies Deutschland* ('National Committee for a Free Germany') and sent letters to old comrades urging them to lay down their weapons rather than continue the war. By contrast, Generalfeldmarschall Walter Model shot himself in 1945 when encircled in the Ruhr area rather than surrendering to the Western Allies.

The fighting along the Volkhov River died down once more and the Red Army counted the cost. The losses were as dreadful as those in other battles on the Eastern Front, as the Red Army tried to substitute sheer weight of numbers for tactical expertise. Official Soviet sources recorded the loss of over 308,000 men killed or wounded up to the end of April in the attempts to break through to Chudovo and Lyuban, with a further 94,000 casualties in May and June.[37] Of these, the loss of Second Shock Army amounted to at least 66,000 men. German casualties, though heavy, were a fraction of this, but even those who were not killed or wounded were left drained by their experience. Lubbeck described how his weight fell from 185 pounds to 161 pounds, though he felt that compared to many, he was fortunate.

After their winter defensive fighting in the area immediately to the north and northeast of Novgorod, the soldiers of the Spanish Blue Division were involved both in *Raubtier* and in the subsequent reduction of the encircled Soviet troops. Once again, German officers were unimpressed – the Spanish troops showed great urgency in their initial attacks, they reported, but didn't have sufficient experienced NCOs and officers to deal effectively with changing circumstances. However, it should be noted that they made similar criticisms of the fresh drafts of German replacements that arrived at the front in the first half of 1942, but the problems of the Spanish troops were compounded by the manner in which officers and NCOs were regularly sent back to Spain and replaced with inexperienced men. For the Spanish soldiers who remained in the front line, their experiences left a deep mark. One wrote in his diary:

> The change of mentality that we have all suffered and that will mark us if we survive … The terrible hours on the front, and the disappearance of good friends and comrades has this positive aspect … We kill, and we die simply because. It is a hidden instinct in humankind that we like to dress up with pretty words … The more we disregard life and the less we desire it, the more intensely we live it.[38]

Others recorded how the intensity of combat left its mark on their comrades. The words of one Spanish veteran could have been written by any of the men of whatever nationality who fought on the Eastern Front:

> Those two and all the others who 'have been there' now look like sleepwalkers. Their conversation is incoherent and missing half the words. They have a sunken, lost look, without vigour, with a feverish sheen and veiled. They have become horribly thin and are black from gunpowder … One might say the shadow of death, which was so close to them and has repeated its deed so many times before them, still hangs over them.[39]

As it struggled to learn how to fight and win, the Red Army attempted to analyse the reasons for its failure both here and elsewhere in the first half of 1942. Whilst it was convenient to heap as much blame as possible on Vlasov, there were unquestionably other factors involved. There were errors in planning at every level. Stalin and *Stavka* showed strategic greed in attempting so many operations all along the Eastern Front. At Front and army level, similar errors were made with the pursuit of too many objectives, though in defence of Front and army commanders this was often because of rigid instructions from above that effectively dictated that such policies were followed. At a tactical level, the Red Army was still paying a huge price for the purges of the pre-war years that stripped it of so many experienced officers, but unlike the Wehrmacht and the armies of the Western Allies, the Soviet forces were also badly hamstrung by having no tradition of experienced and highly skilful NCOs who were able both to lead in battle and to help new recruits learn how to survive in as short a time as possible. The structure of forces was also scrutinised. In particular, artillery – the Red Army's 'god of war' – had insufficient ammunition, targets were not reconnoitred effectively, there was little ability to correct bombardment once fighting began, and it was impossible to move the guns forward in a timely manner to sustain any advance.

In 1942, it was almost impossible to direct criticism at *Stavka* and Stalin, and their contributions to the disaster were barely acknowledged until long after the war – it was in 1966 that Khozin wrote about the battles and acknowledged failures of command at every level.[40] Many Soviet-era accounts played down the costly failed offensive, and if it was mentioned at all it was in the context of the Siege of Leningrad: by making such a huge sacrifice on the Volkhov River, it was argued, the Red Army saved Leningrad by preventing the Germans from mounting a fresh assault on the city at a time when its defenders and population were still terribly weakened by the winter of starvation. But such interpretations ignore the simple fact that the Germans had no plans for an offensive to capture Leningrad in early 1942.

A more balanced view emerged in 1989, finally acknowledging properly how Stalin's stubbornness played a huge part in the disastrous campaign both on the Volkhov River and to the west of Moscow:

> The facts and eyewitness accounts showed clearly that the greater share of blame for the tragedy of Second Shock Army should be laid at the door of *Stavka* headed by Stalin and his closest associates. They are to blame for the incorrect assessment of the military-strategic situation at the end of 1941 and for setting the Fronts unrealistic objectives. They are to blame for the poor organisation of the offensive and unsatisfactory logistic supply of troops, particularly those of Volkhov Front. They are to blame for restricting the initiative of commanders and the frequent reshuffling of senior cadres … It was due to their stubbornness that Second Shock Army was not withdrawn in good time from the killing ground, which resulted in unjustifiable death and capture of tens of thousands of our men.[41]

Many of the bodies of those who fell in the battles of the Volkhov sector were never recovered. Their remains still lie in the forests and swampy fields of the region and more are uncovered almost every year; in a two-week search operation near Myasnoi Bor in 1994, about 3,500 bodies were found. The families of the fallen received little information about what had occurred; their loved ones simply disappeared into the conflict, their fate unknown and unacknowledged by the Soviet state.

But long before the tragedy of Second Shock Army had fully run its course, it was surely clear even to Stalin that regardless of its defeat outside Moscow, the Wehrmacht was far from defeated. Despite their mauling in the winter battles, the Germans were clearly full of confidence in their superiority over the Red Army. But despite this clear superiority, Leningrad continued to survive the siege throughout the fighting near Lyuban and Chudovo. It was inevitable that the Red Army would once more gather its strength and try to reach the encircled city.

CHAPTER 11

SUMMER 1942

The winter fighting of 1941–42 was a severe test for the Wehrmacht. Had Stalin and *Stavka* been more prudent in their strategic plans, and had their subordinates made better use of the resources they had available, the outcome might have been disastrous for Germany. Instead, as the spring thaw progressed and the ground steadily grew firmer, it was the Wehrmacht rather than the Red Army that looked forward to a resumption of offensive operations with growing confidence.

The main emphasis in the summer would be in the south, with a major drive to the Volga and into the Caucasus region. Stalin feared a resumption of German attacks towards Moscow and the Germans did their best to reinforce this fear, issuing maps of Moscow to troops in Army Group Centre and simulating other planning measures with considerable success. A German liaison aircraft was shot down behind Soviet lines and full plans for the coming attack towards Stalingrad and the oilfields of the Caucasus region were recovered from the corpse of the staff officer on the plane, but such was the strength of his belief in a resumption of German attacks on Moscow that Stalin dismissed this as an attempt by the Germans to mislead him. The consequence was that when the Germans struck in the south, the great bulk of Soviet reserves remained in the Moscow area.

Partly as a result of Red Army reserves being poorly positioned to respond to the German offensive, the Wehrmacht surged forward with great speed once the new campaign began. Its initial success hid several major changes that had taken place during the preceding months. The huge losses of soldiers, particularly in the ranks of the infantry divisions, meant that many formations were now far from full strength – in the infantry, this state would persist in most units until the end of the war. The Germans paid a heavy price just in the winter battles – Halder recorded in his diary on 21 April that the battles along the Eastern Front had cost 900,000 men, and only half of these had been replaced. Losses of equipment were also heavy – the Wehrmacht lost over 74,000 wheeled vehicles and 2,300 tracked vehicles in the winter battles, and replacements fell far short of what was required. Only 10 per cent of the motorised losses had been replaced, though the figure for the tracked replacements was rather better, coming to 80 per cent of those lost.[1] It should be remembered that these figures account only for losses and replacements since the beginning of October 1941 – most of the losses incurred before that date had also not been entirely replaced. Halder estimated that the Eastern Front was about 625,000 men short of what was needed to bring its units up to full strength, and estimated that on 1 May the northern divisions were at about 50 per cent of their strength and the southern divisions were even worse, at only 35 per cent of their infantry strength. In order to make good these losses, priority was given to the southern divisions. Infantry divisions in the central sector were reduced from nine battalions to just six, but were usually left to hold the same length of front line. The only way that this was possible was by removing the reserves that were normally held behind the front line, ready for counterattacks to restore the line, or by reducing the number of divisions pulled out of the front line for rest and recuperation. For the moment, the forces that remained were adequate to the task, but their capacity to absorb additional pressure – their resilience, in many respects – was greatly reduced.

The casualty numbers hide another important factor. The men who had been lost were often the experienced NCOs and junior officers whose skills had given the Wehrmacht a considerable tactical advantage in the first year of the war in the east. The replacements were qualitatively inferior, and although the full impact of this would take another year to be felt, the trend would continue to grow. At the same time, the overall skill of the Red Army was heading in the opposite direction. Although Soviet losses remained staggeringly high, the Red Army was slowly and painfully evolving into a more effective force. The factories that had been relocated further east were now producing large quantities of materiel and the men in the front line were learning how to survive and win – the heaviest casualties, as in so many wars, were amongst the newest recruits.

Although the panzer divisions that led the Wehrmacht towards the Don River were restored to something approaching their establishment, this was partly due to the fact that their structure had been changed. The divisions had been reduced to a single panzer regiment of two battalions, though still retaining two infantry regiments. The result was that the panzer divisions of 1942 fielded fewer tanks per division than they had a year before. Many of the tanks of the 1941 divisions had in any case been obsolescent or completely obsolete at the commencement of *Barbarossa* and the newly restored divisions were generally equipped with newer vehicles, but even this was of questionable quality. Although there were more Pz.IV tanks than before, many were fitted with short-barrelled 75mm guns that were inferior to the long-barrelled 75mm L/43 gun that had been ordered in late 1941. As the year progressed, more of these more effective guns would appear, but in the meantime the panzer divisions would engage their Soviet opponents with a weapon that was ineffective at long range. But even though the newer Pz.IVs had the longer gun, most of the panzer divisions' tanks were Pz.IIIs, armed with 50mm guns. Soviet T-34s were impervious to these guns at anything beyond short range.

Nonetheless, the shock of the winter setbacks rapidly became a fading nightmare in German circles as the advance progressed swiftly. Crimea was overrun and German units seemed to be advancing into eastern Ukraine meeting very little resistance; far to the south, Rommel won a victory at Tobruk, resulting in his elevation to the rank of Generalfeldmarschall. A recurring theme on the Eastern Front was the manner in which both sides often drew premature conclusions about the state of the war, and the summer of 1942 was no different. A year before, the initial successes of the Wehrmacht had resulted in over-optimistic assumptions that the Red Army was broken beyond repair, leading to discussions about how many German divisions could safely be demobilised after the fighting was over, and during the winter the German setbacks had led to Stalin's belief that the tide had turned decisively in favour of the Soviet Union and therefore the Red Army could mount offensive operations almost wherever it wished. Now, the initial German success left Hitler believing that the objectives of the campaign in the south would be achieved with little difficulty, and therefore it was time to consider operations elsewhere. Attention turned once more to the north and to Leningrad.

The initial German drive towards Leningrad was brought to an end more by the need to move panzer forces to the Moscow axis than it was due to the resistance of the Red Army, and with the benefit of hindsight this was almost certainly a mistake. Had the panzer divisions of Fourth Panzer Group remained in the north for a further month, it is highly likely that the Wehrmacht would have succeeded in cutting off Leningrad from Lake Ladoga and would have established contact with the Finnish forces to the northwest. Had that happened, there would have been no miraculous Road of Life and Leningrad would have been starved into defeat during the winter months, much as the Germans had intended. Instead, by the thinnest of margins, the city and its defenders survived in terrible conditions and as the days grew longer in 1942, both soldiers and civilians in and around Leningrad began to recover their strength. The Germans now began to consider how they could tighten the siege in order to achieve their desired outcome. On 30 June, Küchler visited Hitler's headquarters and was promoted to Generalfeldmarschall; he also discussed his plans for the coming weeks. Under the codename of *Nordlicht* ('Northern Light'), he planned an operation that would essentially achieve what had not been completed the previous year: after a powerful artillery bombardment and heavy air attacks, Army Group North would attack to cut off Leningrad from Lake Ladoga.

Additionally, Küchler proposed four further operations. The Soviet Fifty-Fourth Army remained in its salient to the west of Kirishi and an attack codenamed *Moorbrand* ('Moorland Fire') was intended to eliminate this; Hitler promised reinforcements in the shape of the first battalion of Germany's new weapon, the Tiger tank, in support of this attack. The second operation was codenamed *Bettelstab* ('Beggar's Staff'), intended to eliminate the Oranienbaum bridgehead. The other two operations sought to expand the German positions at Demyansk, in cooperation with Army Group Centre.

The Tiger tanks promised for the attack against Fifty-Fourth Army weren't the only reinforcements for Army Group North. Küchler estimated that he would need an additional four divisions and as the German conquest of Crimea reached its conclusion, units of the successful Eleventh Army were ordered to move to the other end of the Eastern Front. In particular, the heavy siege guns that had helped reduce the Soviet fortress of Sevastopol were sent north; these, it was hoped, would permit an accurate and heavy bombardment of Kronstadt, finally removing the irritant threat of the Baltic Fleet.

As part of the preparations for *Bettelstab*, the German 58th Infantry Division was moved from the Volkhov River to the Oranienbaum bridgehead where it took over a 15-mile length of front line. Both sides conducted raids to capture prisoners for interrogation; some of the men caught by the Germans told their captors that they had been ordered to try to capture MG-42s so that they could be examined and assessed. For the men of 58th Infantry Division, it was a welcome opportunity for rest after the long weeks of fighting on the Volkhov. Even though the division's weakened state meant that most of its men remained in the front line, the sector was generally quiet and the bunkers and trenches were dry and well constructed. There was even the opportunity for some men to go home on leave, and Lubbeck and a small group of lucky comrades caught a train back to East Prussia at the beginning of the month. Lubbeck's family ran a small farm, and like many such farms it was now reliant upon prisoners of war. Rules within Germany about how such prisoners were to be treated were strict, but many – perhaps most – farmers paid little notice to what they saw as needless interference. Although prisoners were meant to have their meals separately from Germans, Lubbeck's mother fed the farm's workers – a mixture of French, Belgian, and Polish prisoners – at the same table as her family.[2]

In the meantime, the Red Army also began to make plans for its summer operations in the northern sector. Govorov was given approval to create a new Second Shock Army; this was built around the divisions of XIII Cavalry Corps, one of the few major elements of the original Second Shock Army to survive relatively intact. The new army commander was Klykov, who had been replaced by Vlasov just a few weeks before. Further units would be added to Klykov's command in the following weeks but the Red Army rapidly became aware of Küchler's preparations for a resumption of offensive operations. On 20 July, in an attempt to disrupt this, Forty-Second Army attacked at Staro-Panovo, on the southwest approaches to Leningrad. The small village was captured, triggering inevitable German counterattacks that continued for several days. A similar attack was made by Fifty-Fifth Army to the southeast of Leningrad, again resulting in several days of hard fighting. There was little overall change in the front line, but the fighting served to tie down German forces; battles continued until early August and drew in three German infantry divisions and elements of 12th Panzer Division. It was also an opportunity for the Soviet front-line units to reassess their strength and capabilities after the long, hard winter.

For the Soviet commanders in the north consideration of how they might break the siege ring around Leningrad was far more important than mounting disruptive spoiling attacks. After discussions between *Stavka*, Volkhov Front, and Leningrad Front, there was agreement that given the limited resources available and the difficulties of mounting major, wide-reaching operations in such difficult terrain, it would be best to concentrate on the shortest possible route by which the Red Army could lift the siege. There would be a further attack in the Shlisselburg–Mga–Sinyavino sector involving converging attacks from both within and outside the siege ring. The attack, it was hoped, would serve three major purposes. Firstly, by re-establishing land contact with Leningrad, the Red Army would be able to prevent another winter of starvation. Secondly, the attack would forestall any renewed German offensive in the region to tighten the siege perimeter. And thirdly, an operation in the north would prevent the Germans from transferring forces elsewhere, in particular to the southern sector where the Wehrmacht was advancing steadily towards Stalingrad and the Caucasus. This latter objective might, of course, be achieved even if the siege ring was not broken.

Although an attack in this sector would be directed at the narrowest part of the siege perimeter – the distance between the Red Army forces either side of the German corridor to Shlisselburg was no more than eight miles at the narrowest point – the attack would face formidable problems, not least because it was such an obvious point of attack, and accordingly the Germans had established strong defences, as Meretskov later recalled:

A space of only 13–16km, occupied and fortified by the enemy, separated the troops of Volkhov and Leningrad Fronts. It seemed that one strong blow was enough, and the attempts of the two Fronts to unite would succeed. But it only seemed so. I have seldom seen terrain less suitable for attack. I will always remember the endless forests, soft swamps, flooded fields of peat, and degraded roads. A difficult struggle with the enemy was matched by a difficult struggle with nature. In order to fight and survive, the troops were forced to build wood and earth ramparts instead of trenches and to use open areas instead of fortified firing points, and to lay logs for many kilometres [to make roads] and to build wooden platforms for artillery and mortars.[3]

The area selected for the offensive had, in Meretskov's opinion, only two benefits. The first was that it represented the shortest route to the Leningrad encirclement. The second was that given the difficult terrain, he hoped that it was an unlikely point at which to attack, and perhaps the Germans wouldn't be expecting a major assault here. As he glumly pointed out, there was in any event no better option: the terrain everywhere in the region was similarly unsuitable for major operations and any alternative route would involve a longer advance.

The German defences were partly under the control of the German XXVI Corps under the command of General Albert Wodrig. The main strength of the corps consisted of the veteran 223rd and 227th Infantry Divisions, with the latter in the northern part of the salient. Facing the Leningrad side of the salient were elements of Böckmann's L Corps: *SS-Polizei*; 5th Mountain Division; and 322nd Infantry Regiment, originally part of 207th Infantry Division before being sent to the Eastern Front, where it was intended to form the nucleus of 285th Security Division. During the invasion of the Baltic States, it functioned as an independent regiment and in October took part in the protracted fighting against partisans in the Luga sector. The winter campaign saw the regiment suffer heavy losses in the Tikhvin battles, with its battalions reduced to the strength of companies. By the summer of 1942 it had recovered some of its strength and its battalions, which had been assigned to different parent units during the winter, were once more united as a single formation. Supporting these infantry forces was a battlegroup of 12th Panzer Division, and almost the entire salient consisted of defensive lines and strongpoints. The only significant high ground was the Sinyavino Heights, rising no more than 150m above the surrounding terrain, and the widespread swampy areas precluded the use of armoured formations en masse. Breaking through these defensive positions would be a tough task for the Red Army, as Govorov and Meretskov were well aware.

In addition to these operations, there was further heavy fighting around the town of Kirishi on the Volkhov River. The town lies partly on the east bank of the river and the Germans had retained a small bridgehead here after the winter fighting that saw the Wehrmacht advance to Tikhvin. This bridgehead was at the tip of a larger salient, which had been created by the advance of Fedyuninsky's Fifty-Fourth Army from the north towards Lyuban. The winter fighting that finally culminated with the encirclement and destruction of the Soviet Second Shock Army included several attempts by Volkhov Front to reduce and destroy this German bridgehead; as a result of these, the Red Army was left with its own small bridgehead over the river, while the German enclave in Kirishi shrank to just part of the ruined town. To the Germans, the entire pocket in the northeast corner of the front line became known as the *Sekt Pfropfen* ('champagne cork') because of its distinctive shape on maps.

As part of the preparations for the summer fighting, Khozin – prior to the arrival of Govorov at Leningrad Front headquarters – proposed a series of attacks to destroy the German bridgehead at Kirishi as a precursor to a renewed attempt to push on to Lyuban. Deeming this to be overly ambitious, *Stavka* issued him with instructions to limit his operation purely to recapturing Kirishi. Few troops could be allocated to the task as most Red Army resources were fighting to try to save Second Shock Army at the time, but when it began on 5 June the assault by the Soviet Fourth Army made encouraging progress at first. But as was often the case with Red Army operations at this stage of the war, a lack of reserves prevented these early gains from being exploited properly; German counterattacks then followed, restoring the original front line. As a result, Major General Petr Ivanovich Lyapin, commander of Fourth Army, was the subject of sharp criticism. A telegram from Volkhov Front to *Stavka* placed the blame entirely upon him:

> The exceptional carelessness and dishonest attitude of General Lyapin to his duties led to the fact that German reconnaissance groups penetrated deep into the battle formations of the army and inflicted great damage on the troops ...

The towns of Kirishi and Plavnitsa, recaptured at the cost of heavy losses, were conceded to the Germans within a few hours.[4]

This was an exaggeration, implying that Kirishi had actually been captured by the Red Army before the German counterattack; in reality, only part of the town had been seized. As a consequence of the failed operation, Lyapin was dismissed and replaced by Gusev, the erstwhile commander of XIII Cavalry Corps, but without any change in fortunes; additional attacks supported by Fifty-Fourth Army failed to make a significant impression upon the German positions. This attack might have been all that was possible given the limited resources that could be spared, but to continue costly assaults on a well-fortified German position with little likelihood of success was an indication of the continuing lack of flexibility in senior Red Army circles. The bridgehead was dependent upon a railway bridge across the Volkhov River, and throughout the fighting the Soviet forces were unable to interdict or destroy this supply route with either artillery or air attacks; it is difficult to imagine the Wehrmacht failing to take advantage of such an opportunity.

On 23 July, Hitler issued his Directive No. 45. Much of this dealt with the ongoing operations in the southern sector; Army Group South was divided into Army Group A and Army Group B, with the former turning south into the Caucasus region and the latter pushing on to Stalingrad and the Volga. The reference to Army Group North was minimal:

> The local operations currently being prepared in the central and northern army group areas should be conducted as far as possible in quick succession. Their result must be the maximum possible disruption and disintegration of enemy commands and forces.
>
> Army Group North is preparing to capture Leningrad by the beginning of September. Codename is *Feuerzauber* ['Fire Magic'; a week later, it reverted to its previous name of *Nordlicht*].
>
> For this operation, it will be reinforced by five divisions from Eleventh Army, by heavy and super-heavy artillery, and other such army troops as may be required.[5]

Manstein, who had led Eleventh Army in its successful conquest of Crimea, had been on leave in Romania after the fall of Sevastopol and was now sent north to take part in the coming campaign. His memoirs suggest that he felt that his army might have been better employed in strengthening the German offensive in the south, as this was clearly the main area of operations for the Wehrmacht on the Eastern Front in 1942:

> When I broke my flight north to call at Hitler's headquarters and talk over my new commitments, I discussed this problem with the Chief of the General Staff, Halder. He made it quite clear that he completely disagreed with Hitler's proposal to try to take Leningrad in addition to conducting an offensive in the south, but said that Hitler had insisted on this and refused to relinquish the idea. However, when I asked if he thought it practicable to dispense entirely with Eleventh Army in the south he told me that he did.[6]

Like most memoirs, those of Manstein seek to portray him in the best possible light. Just how strongly opposed Halder was to an operation against Leningrad is not clear – there is no mention of major reservations in his diary, though the increasingly difficult relationship between Halder and Hitler is clearly described. Most of the problems faced by the Wehrmacht in the southern sector in July and early August seemed to owe more to logistic problems than Soviet resistance; ignoring advice from Halder, Hitler had ordered several panzer units to cross the lower Don near Rostov, resulting in major traffic jams that left several panzer divisions stranded, and there were frequent occasions when the divisions that were pushing on towards Stalingrad had to halt while food, ammunition, and fuel was brought forward. At this time, there was only one major permanent railway bridge over the Dnepr River, and all of the supplies needed for Army Groups A and B had to be channelled over this bridge. The result was that the railway lines either side of the bridge were repeatedly attacked by the partisan movement in Ukraine. Whilst the Ukrainian partisans weren't as active as those in Belarus or around Pskov, they could hardly fail to take advantage of the profusion of opportunities to disrupt the vital railway line. If Manstein's wishes for Eleventh Army to remain in the southern sector – and perhaps to attack across the Kerch Straits – had been followed, it seems unlikely that the stretched logistic services would have been able to cope. As Army Group A finally made its way across the lower Don and thrust far to the south and Army Group B's Sixth Army found itself caught up in increasingly bitter fighting for the ruins of Stalingrad, another problem arose. The Luftwaffe had sufficient aircraft in the region – and sufficient supplies for those aircraft – to support either the drive towards the Caucasus Mountains, or to support operations in Stalingrad. It couldn't do both. The limited air support capacity was switched from one theatre to the other, always to the detriment of whichever theatre was losing support.

Had Manstein's Eleventh Army remained in the area, an already strained logistic and support situation would have worsened both for ground and air forces, and it is possible – perhaps probable – that Manstein's men would have been able to contribute comparatively little to the fighting.

There had been tensions in the Führer's headquarters from the early days of *Barbarossa* and these had worsened significantly with each German setback. Even though the Wehrmacht was advancing once more, these tensions continued to grow. Halder was increasingly exasperated by Hitler's refusal to follow his advice and placed the blame for the traffic problems at the Don crossings entirely on Hitler. On 23 July, he wrote:

> It is becoming obvious even to the layman that the Rostov area is crammed with armour which has nothing to do, while the critical outer wing ... is starving for it. I warned emphatically against both these developments.
>
> Now that the result is so palpable, he explodes in a fit of insane rage and hurls the gravest reproaches against the General Staff.
>
> This chronic tendency to underrate enemy capabilities is gradually assuming grotesque proportions and develops into a positive danger. The situation is getting more and more intolerable. There is no room for any serious work. This so-called leadership is characterised by a pathological reacting to the impressions of the moment and a total lack of any understanding of the command machinery and its possibilities.[7]

It was against this background that preparations continued in the northern sector. To an extent, the coming battle became a competition of which side would complete its preparations first. By concentrating on such a narrow front, Meretskov hoped to avoid some of the problems experienced earlier in the year, with Eighth Army initiating the attack and IV Guards Rifle Corps available as a second echelon. Second Shock Army would form a third wave, and in this manner Meretskov hoped that he would be able to maintain momentum and avoid giving the Germans time to reorganise their defences. The start date for the operation was 19 August for Leningrad Front, which would have to secure substantial bridgeheads across the Neva; nine days later, the two Fronts would make their main convergent attacks.

Inside Leningrad, the terrible suffering of the winter months was slowly easing. As the ice on Lake Ladoga broke up, ships of varying sizes resumed traffic across the lake, bringing much-needed supplies into the city. German artillery and air attacks disrupted shipping from time to time, but it seems that fog and other weather problems had a greater effect. Despite the steady improvement of rations, most people remained desperately weak and far from their pre-siege weight, but civilians turned out in large numbers to try to restore order to their battered city. Almost every patch of available ground was dug up and used for planting crops and the corpses were steadily cleared from the streets and the rubble of destroyed buildings. Everyone bore the scars of the terrible winter, but in some respects it was the young who were affected the most. Many children became very withdrawn and seemed to have forgotten how to play or socialise. Nearly all had lost members of their families, and some were left as orphans. When asked why he sat silently for hours at a time, one child said: 'I remember how mama died at home. When she came in she fell down on the floor … I put her on the bed, she was very heavy, and then the neighbours said she was dead.'[8]

Purely surviving the horrors of the winter wasn't enough. Zhdanov and other senior Party officials felt the need to demonstrate – to the Germans, to the rest of the Soviet Union, to the inhabitants of Leningrad, and to the entire world – that the city was still alive. One way of doing this was to show that despite everything, sporting life continued within Leningrad. Prior to the war, the city had three football clubs – Dynamo, Spartak, and Zenit, the latter being made up originally of workers at the Nevsky Zavod industrial plant. In 1940, Zenit was taken over by *LOMO* (an optical-mechanical manufacturer) and most of the team was evacuated to Kazan during the siege, but Zhdanov now asked for both Zenit and Dynamo to field teams in a match.

Organising a football match in a city that was still recovering from starvation and remained under constant threat of bombardment wasn't simple. Players had to be brought back to Leningrad, in some cases from the front line. Many of the Dynamo team were serving either in the police or the army and therefore were in better physical condition than the Zenit players, drafted mainly from workers at Nevsky Zavod. Despite receiving additional rations during preparation for the match, none of the players were anywhere near the level of fitness required for a serious sporting event. There were other problems too. The Dynamo stadium had been heavily damaged during an air raid and the match would have to take place on the reserve training pitch; even here, the terraces for spectators had been removed and broken up for firewood. The neighbouring football pitch had been dug up for vegetable planting and the players were warned not to kick the ball onto the plants growing there.

Inevitably, the match that ensued has become the stuff of legend with numerous conflicting accounts – there is even disagreement on the date on which it took place, but it is likely to have been 31 May that the two sides faced each other. Fresh, clean kit was provided and the players were carefully shaved and groomed but their physical state couldn't be hidden. It was impossible for the match to last the full time and instead there were two truncated halves – again, there are different accounts varying between 20 and 30 minutes per half. Anatoly Mishchuk was a forward who had played for Zenit before the war and was one of those diagnosed with post-starvation dystrophy, but still took part. Early in the game he attempted to head the ball into the Dynamo net but collapsed on the ground and had to be helped back to his feet by the other players as he lacked the strength to rise unaided. At half-time, most of the players remained standing, fearing that if they sat down they would struggle to get to their feet again. Although Soviet propaganda claimed that several thousand Leningraders turned out to watch, it is more likely that the number present was far smaller, largely the workers in a nearby factory and the residents of a hospital. One account even describes the players having to seek shelter during the match due to German shelling, but the outcome of the game is undisputed: Dynamo won 6–0. But the score was almost irrelevant. The real purpose of the match had been achieved: to demonstrate that despite everything, Leningrad was still able to stage sporting events.

The musicians who had answered the call from Leningrad Radio began rehearsals for a performance that would be one of the most symbolic moments of the Siege of Leningrad: the first performance of Dmitry Shostakovich's Leningrad Symphony in the city to which it was dedicated. The score for the symphony was delivered to the city by plane and when Karl Ilyich Eliasberg, the conductor of the Leningrad Radio Orchestra, first saw the sheer size of the score – it ran to four substantial volumes – his initial reaction was despair. His poor musicians could barely manage 15 minutes of practice, yet here was a piece that would last for a little over an hour and required more than 100 performers. Eliasberg himself was desperately weak after the winter months; he was unable to walk from the room that he shared with his wife in the Astoria Hotel to the radio studios and for several weeks he had to be dragged in a sled. At that stage, Eliasberg had only 15 players in his orchestra; he made his way to the Smolny Institute where he met Govorov and explained that despite instructions from the local Communist Party to perform the piece, he lacked the means to do so. Govorov promised to help and over the following weeks groups of musicians who were serving in the army units defending Leningrad were released for rehearsals with Eliasberg. However, they still had to serve in the front line. A trombonist in 45th Rifle Division described his routine:

'Rehearsals in the morning, then straight to the front for concerts, then our military duties. One day we went from rehearsal to the Piskarevskoye Cemetery to bury piles of corpses in mass graves ... we were back to rehearse the music next day.'[9]

The preparations for the performance were a monumental task. Eliasberg concentrated on simpler, briefer pieces for his musicians, slowly building up their stamina, skill, and importantly their confidence. At the beginning of May, the Radio Orchestra performed their longest piece to date, Tchaikovsky's Sixth Symphony. People listening to their radio sets could clearly hear German shells landing near the radio station during the performance.[10] As rehearsals for Shostakovich's symphony began in July, Eliasberg broke the score into smaller, more manageable fragments. Even with these measures, Eliasberg frequently had to explain his instructions several times before the musicians could understand. As there was only one copy of Shostakovich's score, the musicians personally copied out their parts. At no stage prior to the performance did they actually play the entire symphony, and perhaps this contributed to their general apathy to the project. Despite improving rations, musicians regularly collapsed during rehearsals and three musicians died due to their wrecked health before the performance took place. Ultimately, the project was held together by Eliasberg and his iron determination. Kseniya Matus, the oboist who had been asked to pay for the repairs to her musical instrument with a cat, remembered his determination:

Of course, without Karl Ilyich there undoubtedly would have been no symphony. He stood on the podium and conducted the orchestra. And there sat the first trumpeter – he had a solo. But the trumpet was down on his knees.

Karl Ilyich demanded: 'Why aren't you playing?'

'Karl Ilyich, I don't have the strength.'

'What do you mean you don't have the strength? And do you think we have the strength? Let's get to work!'

That's how demanding he was of everyone.[11]

But even if the musicians themselves had misgivings, these were not shared by the citizens of Leningrad. For them, this was a piece of music that had been dedicated to their city, to them. The symbolism was unquestionable and it would be a great act of defiance against the Germans. In the midst of the cruellest of sieges, in which the Germans deliberately attempted to starve to death a city of several million people, they would respond by producing a great piece of musical art. For some, the symbolism was even greater. The terrible suffering of the siege was merely the end of a prolonged period of terror and oppression and on behalf of 'Piter', the symphony would stand out as a defiant declaration of endurance against all the city's oppressors.

As the Wehrmacht carried out its offensives across Ukraine, Hitler boasted to some of his entourage that he would drink champagne in the Astoria Hotel in Leningrad on 9 August after the capture of the city, and the Soviet authorities deliberately chose this as the date of the performance of the Leningrad Symphony. Tickets were put on sale and it is a measure of the importance of the moment that many Leningraders exchanged some of their still-meagre rations for these tickets. Inevitably, the Germans were aware of the plans and there were fears that their siege artillery would bombard the concert hall. In anticipation of this, Govorov drew up plans for an operation codenamed *Shkval* ('Squall'). On the evening of the performance, the gunners of Leningrad Front commenced a heavy bombardment of German positions, targeting artillery emplacements and their lines of communication. The shelling then switched to German headquarters locations and was sustained for the duration of the performance. Whilst damage to the German positions was limited, the bombardment served its purpose: there was no German shelling of the Grand Philharmonia Hall.

The performance began at 7pm. Kseniya Matus remembered seeing Govorov in the audience:

> When we entered the hall and went out on stage, a floodlight shone from the balcony onto the stage ... Karl Ilyich came out and everyone stood up and applauded. He had us stand up, and this all went on for a long time ... [In previous performances by the orchestra] as soon as we would start to play – u-u-u – the air raid signal sounded. And the conductor would put down his baton, and everyone would go to the bomb shelter. And sometimes concerts would end that way. But this time there were no sirens, no air-raid alarm ... So we finished the symphony and they applauded for a long time. Of course we were all inspired, because we knew we had done something great ... We proved that even in such hunger and cold, in such living conditions, Leningrad could perform this symphony.[12]

The army trombonist who had described having to combine his rehearsals with military duties remembered the performance:

> It had been an everyday job until now. But we were stunned by the number of people, that there could be so many people starving for food but also starving

for music. Some had come in suits, some from the front. Most were thin and dystrophic.[13]

At the end of the performance, Govorov made his way to the podium and congratulated Eliasberg. When the conductor thanked him for attending, Govorov replied that he should also thank him for the artillery bombardment that had prevented German interference. Zhdanov invited the orchestra to a grand reception where the exhausted musicians were given a feast the like of which they hadn't seen since the beginning of the war. Most ate so much that they promptly vomited.

Fifty years later, the 14 surviving musicians from that night gathered once more. Kseniya Matus reflected:

So many years have passed since that day and memory is a funny thing, like drying paint. It changes colour as it dries. But that symphony has stayed with me the way it was that night. Afterwards, it was still a city under siege, but I knew it would live. Music is life, after all. What is life without music? This was the music that proved our city had come back to life after death.[14]

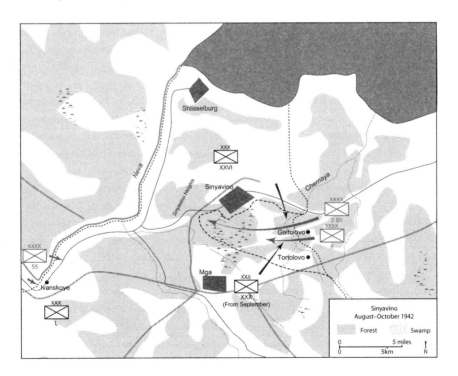

Outside Leningrad, the fighting continued. The latest Red Army operation to break through the siege ring in the Shlisselburg–Mga–Sinyavino sector is referred to in Soviet-era accounts as the Third Sinyavino Offensive, whereas many western accounts make no distinction between the first two offensives in this sector and describe the battles of August 1942 as the Second Sinyavino Offensive. Leningrad Front's Fifty-Fifth Army, commanded by Major General Vladimir Petrovich Sviridov, duly attacked on 19 August. At the same time, two rifle divisions attacked south of the Neva near Ivanovskoye. Its opponent was *SS-Polizei* and although the first assault succeeded in securing two bridgeheads across the Neva, expanding them proved almost impossible. *SS-Polizei* rapidly recovered from its initial setback and resolutely prevented any further Soviet advance and matters were worsened by a repetition of an earlier problem with Red Army operations: although the initial artillery bombardment had on this occasion been fairly effective, there was insufficient coordination with the advancing troops once they had secured their bridgeheads and the advancing infantry was unable to call for artillery support to destroy German positions that held them up. The attack on Ivanskoye made almost no headway. Sviridov doggedly fed more troops into the two bridgeheads, but the Germans were also reinforcing their formations. A regiment from 61st Infantry Division and a panzergrenadier regiment from 12th Panzer Division arrived on 23 August and were used to block further Soviet advances. The best that Sviridov could claim was that the Germans had not destroyed his bridgeheads with counterattacks; the two leading formations in his attack, 136th and 268th Rifle Divisions, had lost over 7,000 men for little gain. Despite the original plans for Leningrad Front to attack first in order to secure bridgeheads and then tie down as many German reserves as possible prior to Volkhov Front's attack, Govorov ordered a pause. He decided that his part of the operation would be more likely to enjoy success if he waited until Volkhov Front began its attacks.

On the German side, Küchler at the headquarters of Army Group North had successfully persuaded Hitler that he couldn't commence the planned operations immediately – his divisions were still far from establishment strength and he wanted to wait until Eleventh Army arrived. Whilst Hitler agreed to this delay, there was a price that Küchler paid: Eleventh Army would not be part of Army Group North, but would instead be directly under the control of *OKH*. According to some sources, Hitler gave explicit instructions to Manstein that Leningrad was to be completely flattened – he had always intended for the city to be destroyed, and its defiance of the Wehrmacht over the preceding year had hardened his opinion.[15] Manstein makes no mention of this instruction in his memoirs. He arrived in the north with his staff on 27 August as the Red Army was renewing its offensive to find that the original German intentions were already looking unworkable. He reached his headquarters on the same day that 12th Panzer Division, which was still dispersed into separate battlegroups, received orders that it was to take part in *Nordlicht*. For the soldiers who had come so close to reaching Leningrad in late 1941, there were mixed feelings. On the one hand, there was a sense that a victory that might have come easily the previous November would now be a much tougher proposition; on the other hand, there seemed to be a prospect that the long, painful stalemate of 1942 might come to an end.

Meretskov's preparations for the new offensive saw the development of practices that would become increasingly common in the Red Army in operations in the rest of the war. The air cover available to Volkhov Front was insufficient to prevent German reconnaissance aircraft from surveying much of the Red Army's rear area, but Major General Grigory Davydovich Stelmakh, the chief of staff at Volkhov Front, and Colonel Vladimir Yakovlevich Semenov, the chief of operations, did all they could to prevent the Germans from recognising preparations for an offensive. A fake concentration of Soviet forces was created near Novgorod and all troop movements were in railcars that were labelled as carrying food or fodder. Tanks on flatcars were extensively camouflaged too, and wherever possible instructions were passed verbally rather than in written orders or even by radio and telephone – the Red Army was increasingly aware of the effectiveness with which the Germans monitored radio traffic and tapped into Red Army telephone cables. Despite this, the preparations couldn't be hidden entirely and German aircraft began to pay particular attention to the area from 25 August. The following day, Meretskov decided that rather than wait until the concentration of forces was fully completed, he would attack as soon as possible to prevent the Germans from taking countermeasures.

Amongst the units preparing for the new offensive was 19th Guards Rifle Division. It had been formed a year earlier in Siberia as 366th Rifle Division but was raised to 'Guards' status after its bloody involvement in the Lyuban offensive. In order to strengthen its depleted ranks, it received troops from other formations that were being disbanded but was still only at about 60 per cent of its establishment strength at the beginning of the offensive. Despite still being far from full strength, the division's personnel were confident of success; Petr Ivanovich Sotnik was a commissar in the division's 56th Guards Rifle Regiment and later wrote that he and his comrades believed it would take them no more than four or five days to link up with Leningrad Front.[16] Before dawn on 27 August, Volkhov Front began a series of attacks intended to break through the German lines and to push forward to the Sinyavino Heights. Careful reconnaissance – something that was often absent in the fighting the previous winter – had identified the seam between the German 227th and 223rd Infantry Divisions and this point was the deliberate target of the Soviet Eighth Army. A further difference was better concentration of the attacking units, with a main shock group of four rifle divisions leading the way. Despite suffering heavy casualties, the group forced its way into the German positions between the two infantry divisions, capturing the village of Tortolovo and securing a penetration of a little over three miles. It was an encouraging start: the soldiers of Eighth Army had covered nearly half the distance to the lines of Leningrad Front. For Meretskov's Front, the priority was to reinforce this success and widen the penetration. For the Germans, the shoulders of the penetration had to be held while all available reserves were committed to drive back or destroy Eighth Army's shock group.

Another of the Red Army units that was sent into battle was 98th Tank Brigade, which had been badly mauled in the fighting of the Lyuban offensive. Thereafter, it recovered its strength through the supply of new equipment and on the eve of the new assault it fielded 3 KV-1s, two companies each with ten T-34s, and about 20 T-60 light tanks. As Sergeant Rodion Mikhailovich Mokhov, a mechanic in the brigade, later recalled, this constituted a strong tank brigade at that time. When the brigade moved up to the front line, it experienced typical problems that plagued the armoured forces of both sides, with alarming numbers of vehicles breaking down before they even entered combat:

> One tank stalled, another shed a track, and a third slipped into a ditch and was stranded on its belly. We pulled the tank back onto the road with a cable, but usually one vehicle wasn't enough for this – we had to hook two together.
>
> On the way [to the front], tracks began to break, perhaps due to poor quality metal. I replaced one track link, and then had to repair more. One roller had a broken bearing. Another had a sluggish starter motor but by adjusting the relay switch, I got it working.[17]

Problems with tracks were a recurring feature with T-34s. Mokhov's suspicions were correct: the metal used for track pins was prone to breaking, and this was not addressed adequately at any stage of the war. It became common practice for T-34 drivers to slow drastically before driving around corners in order to reduce the strain on track pins; inevitably, it was only a matter of time before German anti-tank gunners became aware of this and took to covering bends and corners where they knew that their targets would proceed with caution. Tank repair teams were essential to prevent breakdowns from adding to unit attrition, and this was an area where the German panzer divisions enjoyed a substantial advantage over the Soviet armoured units – the panzer divisions included engineering and vehicle recovery teams in their establishment, and although there were mechanics like Mokhov in Red Army tank units, they were far fewer and not as well equipped. Throughout the war, the Red Army increased the efficacy of these repair teams by augmenting their numbers.

The soldiers of 19th Guards Rifle Division had been part of this attack and despite their losses they remained confident of victory. Moving into ground that was far more swampy than the area they had taken on the first day of the attack, the division made slower progress on 28 August and then the advance effectively ground to a halt in this sector with attack followed by counterattack. Sotnik, who had been so confident of being able to reach Leningrad Front in just four or five days, described a typical episode in the bitter fighting:

> During the attacks by 56th Guards Regiment, a camouflaged enemy battery of four guns with stocks of ammunition was discovered. Yaroshevich, the regiment commander, attacked the battery with his reserve group and captured it. After checking the condition of the guns, our gunners opened fire on a German battery in Sinyavino. By the end of the day, all ammunition was used up. The crews took out the breeches of the guns and buried them in the ground. The enemy brought a company of submachine-gunners into battle and forced our fighters out of the battery location, and a report was sent to the divisional commander. At 1800 Colonel [David Markovich] Barinov ordered Yaroshevich by telegraph to counterattack the enemy. All those who were in the front line rose to their full height and shouted 'Urrah!' and charged forward in the attack. The Germans met us with fierce machine-gun fire. An artillery officer, Lieutenant Buryak, and I were wounded. The counterattack faltered.[18]

Yevgeny Yefremovich Palkin was a medic with 22nd Rifle Brigade. This unit was one of those extracted from the encirclement of Second Shock Army earlier in the year, and the survivors were given extra rations during their period of recuperation before being sent back into battle. The conditions in which they fought were terrible:

> Before we could finish digging trenches and building bunkers – in fact, we had only just begun – we saw they were filling quickly with water, streaming in from

the high water table of the marshy lowlands. We had no choice but to sit in trenches that were knee deep with dirty mud.

Early in the morning the soldiers and men in our battalion prepared for another attack. However, its start had to be postponed due to a big raid by enemy aircraft. Despite the unfavourable conditions we faced, the battalions and companies of our brigade tried twice that day [28 August] to break through the defences of the enemy in their newly entrenched line. However, the attacks faded away one after the other; men died or were put out of action by wounding, and we couldn't move forward. Under destructive machine-gun fire and mortar and artillery bombardment, our platoons were driven to ground and after each attack they returned to our start line with heavy losses. The enemy aircraft dominated the sky. Bombs exploded close to our trenches and the earth shook. With the help of Olga Karpenko, a medical officer, I treated the wounded without interruption, my forearms soaked in blood – we applied countless bandages, tourniquets, and splints. During the first ten days of fighting, we lost most of our personnel killed or wounded. From our battalion, which initially numbered 318 combatants, there were only 12 left. Things were no better in neighbouring battalions.[19]

Throughout this period, the stubborn attacks by Gusev's Fourth Army against the Kirishi bridgehead continued. Losses mounted on both sides; the German garrison was composed mainly of 11th Infantry Division but as losses piled up, the division was replaced by 21st Infantry Division. The bridgehead had contracted to the point where a single German regiment was able to hold all of the positions, but resistance came at a price. The first unit from 21st Infantry Division to deploy in Kirishi – 3rd Infantry Regiment – lost its commander, Oberst Herrmann, within days of arriving. From their commanding positions in the ruins of Kirishi, the Germans dominated all of the lines of approach and subjected every Soviet attack to heavy fire even as the Red Army troops were preparing for their assault. Throughout the rest of the summer season, the bridgehead remained intact, defying every Soviet attempt to eliminate it.

Even before he arrived, Manstein had been considering how best to mount the attack required for *Nordlicht*. He was clearly still irked that Leningrad had not fallen to German forces the previous year:

We were aware that the success of the operation was somewhat problematical, and the fact that it need not have been necessary at all hardly made it any more palatable to us. In the summer of 1941 there had probably been a very good chance of taking Leningrad by a *coup de main* … As Schiller once said: 'What we omit from a single hour is lost to all eternity.'[20]

Over the following days, the fighting around the Soviet penetration intensified. Several German counterattacks were made from all directions with little success, and despite their constantly rising casualties the four divisions of Eighth Army continued to grind forward towards Sinyavino. By the end of August, the Red Army had reached the outskirts of the town, but even if the German counterattacks failed to make progress, the attempts by the units on the flanks of Eighth Army to widen the penetration also failed. As a result, moving supplies and reinforcements to the tip of the penetration continued to be difficult, with the entire wedge that the Red Army had secured being constantly swept by German artillery and air attacks.

In addition to local reserves, Küchler moved additional forces into the sector. Two divisions – 5th Mountain Division and 28th Jäger Division – that had been earmarked for *Nordlicht* were deployed to strengthen the German positions; the former was ordered to take up position along the southern side of the Soviet penetration while the latter was positioned to prevent any further advances towards the siege perimeter. Reinforcements were also en route from elsewhere: 3rd Mountain Division had been on garrison duty in Norway but was now transferred via Finland to Tallinn before boarding trains for the Leningrad sector. Additional units were shuffled within Army Group North to mount counterattacks; one such counterattack against the tip of the penetration saw the debut of the Wehrmacht's newest tank.

Germany had been considering the development of a new heavy tank since before the outbreak of the Second World War; this was at least partly in response to the existence of tanks in Britain and France that were heavier and better armoured than German tanks of that era. The original specification was for a tank weighing about 27–30 tons with 50mm armour, but initial trials of prototypes led to progressively heavier designs and in May 1941 the Henschel company received an order to design and build a new chassis. Krupp would be responsible for the turret. The result of the project was the 57-ton Pz.VI, better known as the Tiger tank, and the first production variants began to reach the Wehrmacht in the summer of 1942. The first unit to receive them was *Schwere Panzer Abteilung 502* ('Heavy Tank Battalion 502'), which began to assemble in May 1942.

Otto Carius was one of the tank commanders of the new heavy tank battalion, and he and his comrades examined their new vehicles with interest. The outward appearance wasn't encouraging – the armour of the Tigers was made up of perpendicular slabs rather than the sloping armour that made the T-34s of the Red Army difficult to kill – and Carius' first impression was that the tank looked 'plump'. Although it could achieve a speed of 27 miles per hour on roads and 12 miles per hour across country, the crews rapidly discovered that the engine would overheat at such speeds and it was usual to drive at about half these speeds unless in an emergency. The fuel tanks held 117 gallons of gasoline, which gave the Tiger a cross-country range of only 48 miles; for an army that was perpetually short of fuel, this would add to the supply problems that bedevilled all Wehrmacht operations. The Maybach engine was a 4.6-gallon V12 configuration, and the tank needed prodigious quantities of lubricant – 6.2 gallons for the engine, 6.6 gallons for the gearbox and transmission, 1.1 gallons for the turret, and 1.5 gallons for the ventilation fans. The huge tanks had to be fitted with narrow transportation tracks before they could be loaded onto railway flatcars to prevent them from extending beyond the sides of the train. Compared to the Pz.IV, the latest model of which weighed 24 tons, these were monstrous vehicles, and a company equipped with 14 Tigers was a formidable formation.[21] For the moment, fully equipping a battalion was beyond the resources of German industry; in their first deployments, the troops of *Schwere Panzer Abteilung 502* had just a few Tiger tanks, with the rest of their strength made up of older Pz.III and Pz.IV models.

Hitler was anxious for the new tanks to be tested in combat as soon as possible and ordered the first company to be dispatched to the Leningrad sector. Carius and the other tank crews arrived by train at Krasnogvardeisk, where they got off to an inauspicious start: as they detrained, one of the Tigers slipped off the flatcar and ended up on its side. They were actually the second company to reach the area – the first company had been earmarked to play a leading part in *Nordlicht*, but instead it was pitched into the counterattack against the Soviet Eighth Army's penetration on 29 August. This company also suffered several mishaps prior to coming into battle, as Stahlberg later recorded. He had been reassigned to the division headquarters, as the adjutant of Major Hellmut Bergengruen:

> I seized the opportunity to ask him whether and where I could see the new Tiger tanks – one should at least know them from the outside, if we were to take Leningrad with them. But he put me off. One of the monsters had a technical fault and was not usable [and] the other three had proved too heavy for the log roads and bridges of northern Russia, Bergengruen told me, his face expressionless.[22]

Much of the long Eastern Front ran through terrain that was unsuitable for the deployment of heavy tanks – even though its wide tracks gave it good mobility, the sheer bulk of the Tiger meant that it required firm ground and ideally reasonable roads. Neither of these two conditions existed in the Shlisselburg–Mga–Sinyavino sector, and the dense woodland also reduced the efficacy of the Tiger's 88mm gun; in better conditions, the Tiger crews would have been able to engage Soviet armour at a range where the 76mm guns of the T-34s and KV-1s were ineffective. However, despite their huge size, the Tigers had some advantages over their predecessors. An important factor that influences cross-country mobility of tanks is ground pressure. Although the Tigers were more than double the weight of Pz.IVs, their exceptionally wide tracks meant that this weight was distributed over a larger area, giving a ground pressure of 0.76kg/cm^2. By comparison, the Pz.IV had a ground pressure of nearly 20 per cent more due to its narrow tracks. But a vehicle that weighed 57 tons would still be very limited by bridges; at a time when almost no other vehicles were remotely as heavy as that, most bridges couldn't support anything approaching that weight. It was even necessary for the Wehrmacht to create new bridging companies that could construct bridges capable of carrying such a load.

The first company equipped with the new vehicles went into action as ordered by Hitler and immediately ran into trouble. Despite its fairly long gestation, the Tiger was still not fully ready for battle and of the four vehicles that were deployed for the first attack, two tanks soon broke down with transmission problems, followed by a third that stopped with engine failure. The personnel of the Tiger company had been ordered to ensure that none of their vehicles fell into enemy hands and strenuous efforts were made that night to recover the stranded tanks; due to the weight of the Tigers, it took three towing vehicles to pull each tank from the battlefield. Worse was to follow. In a later counterattack across soft ground, four Tigers were knocked out by Soviet anti-tank guns. The frontal and side armour of the new tanks was formidable and it was almost impossible for any but the most powerful Soviet anti-tank guns to penetrate, but the decks were vulnerable to fire from higher positions or to plunging artillery fire; the tracks were also vulnerable and were no more immune to anti-tank fire than the tracks of any vehicle. With commendable swiftness, Red Army gunners learned to concentrate their fire on the tracks in order to leave the Tigers stranded in the mud, where heavy artillery fire could then be directed against them.

It was possible to recover three of the wrecks, but the fourth was stuck firmly in deep mud and had to be abandoned. Although demolition charges were set off to destroy it, the wreck fell into the hands of the Red Army and it was examined in great detail. This would influence both the tactics used by the Red Army against Tiger formations in later battles and the design and weaponry of future Soviet tanks. Although the Tiger remained a formidable weapon of war throughout the conflict, its initial impact might have been greater if it had been used in more favourable ground – when it was deployed in the open plains of eastern Ukraine in the following winter, the Red Army was already aware of its existence and had distributed information to tank and anti-tank units on the strengths and weaknesses of the vehicle that had been recovered from the swamps of Sinyavino. The battlefield impact of these deployments in the northern sector was almost negligible, and the experience of the fighting was not a happy one for the Tiger crews. Carius described a typical operation, and the anxieties experienced by the men of *Schwere Panzer Abteilung 502*:

> Once, we were employed with the company against 'Bunker Village'. I moved from the southeast. After reaching the village, I was supposed to be relieved by an attack from a patch of woods southwest of me.
>
> After reaching our objective, however, we waited in vain for the second group of Tigers ... We had to slug it out by ourselves with the [Soviet] anti-tank positions.
>
> We also got a glimpse of a few tanks, but soon we didn't even know ourselves where the front and rear were. With a lot of luck, we got out of there but without having shook up the Russians at all. I was as happy as could be to have all my Tigers collected together again. Who would have had time in such a mess to follow orders and ensure that no damaged Tiger was left behind!
>
> Someone had 'thoughtfully' provided every Tiger tank commander a demolition charge. It was fastened upright in a holder next to the tank commander's right side beside the seat in the turret ... I could gladly have done without them ... I finally used the holder to secure a bottle of schnapps. For my five-man crew, it was more soothing than any demolition charge.[23]

On the other side of the front line, soldiers were also struggling with breakdowns. Mokhov, the mechanic with 98th Tank Brigade, was told that one of the brigade's precious KV-1s had broken down in the front line. Together with an officer and two other mechanics, he was to investigate the problem – tank crews risked court martial if they simply abandoned a tank, and aware that the Germans monitored radio traffic, details of breakdowns and particularly the locations of stranded vehicles were rarely transmitted to the rear. Carrying what spare parts they thought they might need, the small team made its way forward in darkness. Just before dawn, Mokhov – now separated from his comrades – came across tank tracks amidst the trees of a clump of heavily shelled woodland and followed them to the stranded tank. Hastily, he set to work:

> My guess turned out to be correct: the starter motor had broken. I replaced it and reinstalled the starter. 'Start the engine!' I shouted to the driver. There was the characteristic sound of gear cogs, the engine snorted and fired up, and I was surrounded by familiar exhaust smells …
>
> Matters were complicated by the fact that during shelling a shell had struck the top of the turret but didn't detonate. The crew were hiding under the tank and were uninjured but the turret was jammed by the impact and stopped rotating with the gun to one side.[24]

The tank brigade had already been ordered to pull back and the crew wasted little time, clearing sufficient ground to turn the tank, and after sheltering under the hull during another German air attack, they headed for safety.

The slow, costly advance of Volkhov Front towards the Neva River took a heavy toll on Meretskov's troops: in five days of fighting, Eighth Army had lost over 16,000 men, perhaps a little over half its combat strength – this in itself is an indication of how comparatively weak the Soviet armies were, and how they had still not recovered their numerical strength after the battles earlier in the year. As a result of the demands for reinforcements, the forces held back for exploitation of initial successes were now fed into the battle, but the narrowness of the penetration meant that this was in a piecemeal fashion. The use of artillery – Volkhov Front had started with a substantial advantage – was also a cause for concern, as Meretskov later admitted:

> It is appropriate to ask: how could it be that the strong artillery grouping of Eighth Army, which before the start of the offensive outnumbered the enemy artillery 2:1, could not pave the way for the infantry? In answer, Major General [Georgy Yermolayevich] Degtyarev, who commanded the artillery of the Front and took part in the offensive, subsequently studied the artillery support of the operation. In his opinion, the artillery commanders at Army and Front level at that time had not yet learned the correct manner of using artillery and made several mistakes. The main error was the violation of the principle of the massive use of artillery on the main axis. All additional artillery was distributed almost evenly among the divisions …

A serious shortcoming was the absence of the Front artillery commander and his staff from the planning of local operations: we left everything in the control of Eighth Army and the artillery command of the army was not up to standard. Major General [Semen Fedorovich] Bezruk, Eighth Army's artillery commander, and his staff drew up plans for the preparation for the attack. As it later transpired, his plan only provided support for the advancing infantry and tanks up to the capture of strongpoints in the front line and not to the depth of the entire mission of the first echelon of rifle divisions.[25]

It was a measure of how the Red Army continued to be hamstrung by the consequences of the pre-war purges. Whilst Meretskov can be criticised for failing to ensure proper concentration of forces, and he was undoubtedly correct in criticising the artillery preparations of Eighth Army – which perhaps he should have scrutinised more closely – he and his staff were still learning how to fight and win and how to plan operations in the current war, as were his subordinates at army and division level. Such a learning curve would have been less arduous if so many senior officers hadn't been removed from the Red Army immediately prior to its desperate fight for survival. The cost of this learning process was the ongoing slaughter both in the north, but also elsewhere – throughout this period, the Red Army tried in vain to batter the German defences of the Rzhev salient to the west of Moscow into submission, at a staggering cost.

Nonetheless, the incremental advance of the Soviet Eighth Army continued, albeit at a painful price. A lieutenant in a Red Army rifle regiment described a typical day:

[It was] 4 September 1942. The previous day there was a combat order: a breakthrough to the highway to Dubrovka and Leningrad [immediately to the northwest of Mga]. We were now in the start line. The outcome for the division was that on a width of 2km, we advanced 3.5km, thereby creating a salient. Further advance without a breakthrough would be imprudent. Despite this, on the instructions of the corps commander our regiment, which had been attacking all day, held its positions. By 6pm we had lost two thirds of the rank and file and all of our officers.[26]

A neighbouring formation experienced the consequences of the poor organisation of Soviet artillery and logistics:

We advanced from the Chernaya stream and Kolkolovo without artillery support. The shells sent for the division's guns did not fit our 76mm guns. We had no grenades. The machine-guns of the German bunkers remained intact and were not suppressed, and the infantry suffered huge losses.[27]

One of the units of the second echelon that was thrown into the battle was 140th Rifle Brigade, an independent infantry formation under the command of Colonel Boris Aleksandrovich Vladimirov. His unit was part of the rifle corps that formed the second wave of Soviet troops:

On the [approach] march, 11 enemy dive-bombers attacked parts of my brigade. As a result of this raid, we lost about 20 men and a similar number of horses. The relatively small losses were because in order to camouflage ourselves against air attack, the brigade moved forward in dispersed formation along several tracks. We managed to shoot down one plane with a PTR [*Protivo Tankovoe Ruzhe*, or anti-tank rifle] and heavy machine-guns. The next day, we approached the Chernaya River and received fresh orders: to advance on the left flank of the corps towards Hill 38.3.

The banks of the Chernaya River are very swampy, a quagmire that literally sucked men in over their heads. At night, with great difficulty, we finally crossed the swamp, and in the morning we came under bombardment that persisted all day with short breaks, from dawn to dusk. There were also air attacks and this time the losses were more significant.

On the morning of 2 September we continued the advance, pushing back the enemy infantry, and reached a country road to the Torfyanik–Kelkolovo state farm. German planes didn't give us a moment's rest and attacked incessantly while it was light.

The next day I brought the second echelon of the brigade – 3rd Rifle Battalion – into action to exert more decisive pressure on the enemy. Aircraft continued to bomb and fire at us. Soon, fresh enemy forces appeared and the fire of their artillery, especially mortars, increased significantly. From the Sinyavino Heights, our battle formations could be observed perfectly, and the enemy could conduct aimed artillery and mortar fire, crippling our units and limiting our actions. At times it was impossible to raise one's head, let alone advance. Shrapnel from shells and bombs roared over us. We felt as if we were in hell.[28]

On the northern side of the salient tip, 19th Guards Rifle Division was also making repeated attempts to drive the Germans out of Sinyavino. Commissar Sotnik later recalled that every attack foundered in the face of well-organised German defensive fire and constant German air attacks. One of the division's regiments reported the deaths of a battalion commander, and two company commanders were wounded and unable to continue; Sotnik's regiment lost a battalion commander, a company commander, and two platoon commanders. It is worth noting that one of the battalion commanders killed in this fighting held the rank of lieutenant, another indication of the manner in which the Red Army had been forced to put relatively junior men in positions of responsibility one or two levels above their training. Two days later, the Germans launched their inevitable counterattack with tanks and infantry from 12th Panzer Division and 19th Guards Rifle Division was able to beat it off, albeit at the cost of further heavy casualties. Using their mortars and machine-guns to good effect, the Soviet units were able to drive the German infantry to ground and separate them from the tanks, and then deal with the small number of German tanks at close quarters – slowly and painfully, the Red Army was learning how to fight effectively.

The independent 33rd Rifle Brigade was a Red Army unit that was created in the summer of 1942 in the city of Semipalatinsk in Kazakhstan. When it reached Volkhov Front, it numbered 3,700 men and was sent into action at the end of August in an abortive attack to the north of the main assault, in an attempt either to tie down German forces to prevent their transfer to the battlefields to the south or to probe for any weaknesses that might have arisen due to earlier troop transfers. As the new recruits moved forward, following a line of white poles that had been stuck into the swampy ground in the forest to guide them, they came under heavy artillery fire. Sergei Sergeyevich Seitenov was a machine-gunner in the brigade who became separated from his comrades during the night march, and the following morning he witnessed the German use of reconnaissance aircraft to direct artillery fire:

> At dawn there were two vehicles to the left of me in a small hollow, with some sort of cage structure on them. Planes with Fascist markings were overhead. They didn't drop bombs or open fire. And there was no fire at the planes. This surprised and frightened me. Suddenly, there were some explosions and the cars burst into flames. The German planes flew away. There was a terrible, deeply troubling, lifeless silence.
>
> By noon, several Red Army soldiers who didn't know each other and who had got lost gathered together. We didn't know where we were or in which direction we should go. We were in the middle of a half-burned, heavily shelled forest. Ahead of our column was an open field, 550m long and about 300m wide. There were dense forests on three sides. The soldiers asked each other – are there any of our men over there? At this difficult moment for us, as green soldiers, five or six

Red Army officers crawled up to us. One of them said that our men were over there, beyond the clearing in the forest, but the Germans were on either side. We needed to cross the field. The command was given: 'Get ready! Short dashes! Follow me!'

When we reached the middle of the clearing, enemy planes suddenly appeared. There were a lot of them. There was a shout: 'Get down!' We threw ourselves to the ground. The grass was tall and green and the earth was soft. Bombs rained down from above, falling next to us. Luckily, no bombs exploded on the surface, sinking into the swampy ground. The planes were very low, flying over ceaselessly. One of the officers shouted, 'Back, run to the trench!' When we gathered in the trench, we were all unrecognisably black from the swamp mud.

We sat in the trench until evening and at sundown we found the battalion kitchen in the middle of the half-burned forest. I was one of the last to go up to the cook. He asked in surprise, 'Where are you from?'

'Kazakhstan,' I replied.

'Yesterday morning, you and 14 others got breakfast from me,' he said sadly. And then I realised that this was real war, not a tactical exercise on the sands of Semipalatinsk.[29]

At the end of the month, Seitenov and what remained of his brigade were pulled out of the front line. Of 22 men in his platoon at the beginning of the attack, only six were still alive.

The attacks to widen the penetration also failed in the face of well-positioned and resolute defences. On the northern flank, 3rd Guards Rifle Division was bled to death in repeated futile assaults; by the second week of September, its combat strength was less than 400 men. On the German side of the line, Oberst Maximilian Wengler, commander of 227th Infantry Division's 366th Infantry Regiment, stubbornly held a small salient that became known as the 'Wengler nose', defying every attempt by the Red Army to drive him back. Losses continued to accumulate to the south too. The Soviet 11th Rifle Division had been almost wiped out in heavy fighting earlier in the year – by 15 February, it could field only 107 combatants. In the months that followed, it was slowly rebuilt, absorbing fresh drafts as well as survivors of other units that were being disbanded, and it went into action as part of Eighth Army's attack to break up the stubborn German defences that continued to restrict the width of the Red Army's advance, by attempting to drive back the German 132nd Infantry Division. In just nine days of fighting, the division lost over 500 dead and 3,000 wounded. Men were transferred from the division's limited rear area units to the front line, but whilst this may have augmented the combat strength for a short time, the price was that the already modest support services were reduced still further in capability.[30]

Nonetheless, the Red Army remained tantalisingly close to breaking through the German lines and linking up with the besieged units in the Leningrad sector. To add to German concerns, Leningrad Front now resumed its attacks from the west, but like so many Red Army operations of 1942 these suffered from poor planning, coordination between artillery and infantry, and failure to respond quickly to changes on the battlefield. This last factor was an area where the Germans retained a significant advantage, with experienced junior officers and even NCOs able to show initiative in order to deal with changing circumstances. By contrast, the poor training of their equivalents in the Red Army resulted in repeated, costly attacks at the same points. Although a fresh bridgehead was seized, it was impossible for Leningrad Front to make any significant progress and the lines of *SS-Polizei* remained firm. As casualties continued to mount for no gain, *Stavka* gave permission for the remnants of the Soviet attack groups to pull back across the Neva.

Gradually, German reserves were arriving as the divisions of Eleventh Army completed their redeployment from Crimea. For the Germans, the situation was serious but not critical. The narrowness of the Soviet penetration meant that like the advance towards Lyuban earlier in the year, it was vulnerable to a German counterattack, even if it managed to edge further to the west – indeed, any such advance merely made it more vulnerable if the penetration wasn't widened. For the Red Army, the strength that had been gathered over the summer was rapidly dwindling in costly attacks. Was there sufficient strength remaining to force the issue?

CHAPTER 12

A BLOODSTAINED AUTUMN

It was clear to everyone in positions of command on both sides of the front line that the soldiers of Volkhov Front were suffering huge losses for very little gain. But despite the continuing strength of the German defensive effort, there was growing concern in Hitler's headquarters – much of the strength intended for *Nordlicht* seemed to be frittered away on defensive operations and counterattacks, without succeeding in eliminating the worrying advance of Volkhov Front towards the siege perimeter. Moreover, despite these counterattacks, the battered divisions of Volkhov Front were still gnawing their way closer to Leningrad, even if it was at a terrible cost. On 4 September, the Führer telephoned Manstein and ordered him to take control of the German forces trying to stop Meretskov's advance, which had now reached an area just over a mile to the northeast of Mga. This instruction was, intentionally or otherwise, a rebuke to Lindemann at the headquarters of Eighteenth Army, and Manstein wrote that he did his best to be diplomatic about taking control of a large sector of Lindemann's front line. Having reinforced the units blocking further Soviet advances towards the west, Manstein began to build up forces to the north and south of the salient in preparation for a counterattack to destroy it.

The first counterattack of note took place on 6 September, with a thrust into the northern part of Meretskov's salient. In the meantime, Manstein gathered 24th and 170th Infantry Divisions, reinforced by most of 12th Panzer Division, on the southern side of the salient under the aegis of XXX Corps, commanded by General Maximilian Fretter-Pico; prior to the redeployment of Eleventh Army from Crimea to the Leningrad sector, XXX Corps had been one of the leading units in Manstein's drive towards Sevastopol. Fretter-Pico had a good working relationship with Manstein, and he and his officers were full of confidence that they would be able to sweep away the Red Army units in their path, particularly as the two infantry divisions, though weakened by their involvement in the storming of Sevastopol, were veteran units.

Their confidence was not entirely justified. The counterattack began on 10 September but immediately ran into trouble. The Red Army units had anticipated a major German counterattack almost from the beginning of the operation and had laid extensive minefields on the relatively few areas of firm ground where tanks could operate and these were covered by anti-tank guns; this combination, used with increasing frequency as the war progressed, rapidly brought 12th Panzer Division to an abrupt halt. The Soviet gunners were also emulating a tactic that the Germans had employed in the closing months of 1941. Prior to this, German anti-tank guns operated under the command of each gun commander, but the use of massed tanks by the Red Army resulted in the adoption of the *Pakfront*, in which the anti-tank guns (known in the Wehrmacht as *Pak*, an abbreviation for 'Panzer Abwehr Kanone' or 'anti-tank gun') would coordinate their fire on the orders of a single officer. The Red Army rapidly adopted the same practice, adding further nuances; teams of sappers were regularly attached to anti-tank units to lay mines so that German tanks would be funnelled into the field of fire of the guns, and the size of these anti-tank units increased steadily. Such was the inevitability of German counterattacks that it became increasingly commonplace for the Red Army to deploy these defensive units in expectation of these attacks, and in combination with the growing size of the anti-tank units this became an increasingly effective tactic.

Attempts by the German infantry to pick their way forward foundered under heavy artillery and mortar fire and Manstein was forced to call a halt while aerial reconnaissance identified the Soviet defensive positions and artillery locations. Only 170th Infantry Division was able to make significant headway, but pressure from the west and north continued to compress Meretskov's forces into an increasingly perilous position. The use of German air power continued to give the Wehrmacht a decisive advantage, as Vladimirov, commander of 140th Rifle Brigade, described; his men were still under orders to try to break through the German lines:

> According to our orders, we still had to move towards the Neva to link up with units of Leningrad Front.
>
> Our position was extremely difficult. Having been ordered to attack, it was impossible to go onto the defensive in our current positions and regroup. The Nazis were around us like wolves, constantly bringing fresh troops into battle.

We didn't know precisely where the troops of Leningrad Front were. We had to execute our orders – to attack despite the fierce resistance of the enemy. Our battalions fought heroically but with every step they melted away like spring snow. We were especially plagued by enemy aircraft, which dived with howling sirens, bombing and firing with heavy machine-guns. They circled overhead constantly, trying to stop us at all costs. We had no anti-aircraft weapons and we were helpless …

The Germans began their counterattack. After a long unequal battle against numerically superior enemy forces, our depleted battalions were encircled. The fighting continued for a day. Several groups of soldiers managed to break out. We attacked to rescue the encircled troops many times but could achieve nothing. We lost many officers and men, including the brigade commissar Trefilov and the intelligence chief Lieutenant Chernov. Four soldiers and the head of the NKVD detachment, Major Kot, were blown apart by a direct hit of a 250kg bomb …

Encountering no resistance from our aviation and anti-aircraft weapons, the Nazis ruled the sky as if they were on home ground. Men moving up to reinforce us were subjected to such heavy bombardment that it was difficult to assemble units. Many soldiers were scattered by air attacks and wandered around the rear area in small groups, searching for their units. With Lopolov, a battalion commissar, I gathered stragglers and replenished our units with them.[1]

Another of the German units that came north from Crimea was 132nd Infantry Division. Gottlob Bidermann was an infantryman who had served with the division throughout the war with the Soviet Union and after the capture of Sevastopol on 4 July he and his comrades were sent to the Kerch Peninsula in eastern Crimea. The men recuperated in the warm sunshine on the coast, with groups being sent in rotation to Yalta where a recreation area had been established, Some of the division's men were fortunate enough to be granted home leave. At the end of August, 132nd Infantry Division began its transfer to the Leningrad sector where the men expected to take part in the forthcoming attack on the city itself, only to discover that they were going to be used against the salient held by Volkhov Front; at first the division was held in reserve, but it was then transferred to Fretter-Pico's XXX Corps. Bidermann recalled the deployment of the division in very different conditions from those they had known in the balmy south:

On barely passable roads the regiments slogged toward their objectives throughout the period of 17–19 September. Every movement required extraordinary effort. The bunkers and defensive positions were situated in swamps with little or no shelter available, and the troops were constantly exposed to the saturated earth and the clammy, cool air. Winter supplies were still lacking, and the troops suffered in the cold temperatures that descended on the shivering *Landsers* with every nightfall.[2]

The weather was now beginning to deteriorate towards winter, with night frosts often freezing the surface water in the marshes; on many days, there was torrential rain, adding to already difficult conditions for troop movements. Manstein wanted to resume his attack against the southern side of the salient in the middle of the month but had to grant a delay in the face of roads turning to mud, preventing any build-up of men and supplies. On 21 September, after laborious work over the preceding days, XXX Corps reported that it had been able to concentrate its units and a new strike began, coinciding with 121st Infantry Division attacking the neck of the salient from the north. Bidermann and the soldiers of 132nd Infantry Division were part of the assault:

> The distance from the bivouac area to the point of attack had been only 2km, but due to the poor roads and terrain conditions the transit required in excess of two hours. The attack was planned to be launched at 1200, and 436th and 437th Infantry Regiments were immediately aware that the timetable could not be met and that the attack would not be possible before 1400. The staff adjusted the schedule to the greatest extent possible, delaying the attack to 1300. Despite all efforts, the soldiers could not keep to the time schedule, and the attack was again delayed. The fact that the attack ... was eventually launched at all remained a tribute to the individual efforts of the *Landsers*, and the inevitable failure of the troops to push further to the north and win more ground could only be attributed to the lack of time available for assault preparations.[3]

Just as the Red Army had found it at first difficult, and then impossible, to advance through the same territory, the Germans too struggled and the cost of the advance was high; 132nd Infantry Division recorded 510 killed and many more wounded in just the first day of combat. On 23 September, after trying to regroup, the division attacked once more; on this occasion the infantrymen were accompanied by tanks and assault guns but most of these failed to reach the start line, becoming stranded in the mud. The attack gained perhaps 100 yards before foundering and repeated efforts to renew the advance failed despite extensive artillery support. Finally, on 25 September, 132nd Infantry Division reached and captured the village of Gaitolovo. The northern pincer was also grinding forward and the leading elements of both German attack groups made contact towards the end of the day. Most of the Soviet Eighth Army and Second Shock Army were isolated in a new pocket. However, in the difficult terrain, there was little by way of a coherent front line and the leading regiment of the German 132nd Infantry Division found itself almost isolated and out of contact with neighbouring formations. It wasn't until 30 September that 3rd Mountain Division managed to move up alongside the regiment and restored contact.

Palkin, the medic with 22nd Rifle Brigade, was wounded in the fighting at the beginning of September. He and the survivors of the brigade were amongst those who were cut off:

> Attempts to break out were unsuccessful. I was given a machine-gun and grenades, which I used more often than bandages and iodine. I was wounded for a second time, in the left leg. After applying a dressing I hurried to the aid of my comrades. In an attempt to persuade us to surrender, the Germans dropped masses of leaflets from aircraft. I remember one of them. On one side of the paper ... there were several rows of shells, bombs, and mortar rounds. The drawing was accompanied by the laconic inscription in Russian, '*U Vas*' ['You have these'], from which we understood that we would receive the deadly 'gifts' depicted in the drawings if we continued to resist. On the reverse side of the leaflet were sausages, hams, and other foodstuffs that were promised to us if we surrendered. Under this picture was a similar laconic inscription as on the first: '*U nas*' ['We have these']. Below was a pass printed in German to permit passage through the forward German positions.
>
> I don't recall any in our group using these notes from the enemy, but there were lots of jokes about them.[4]

The confidence with which the veterans of the German Eleventh Army had come to the northern sector was gone. Bidermann's 132nd Infantry Division was a shadow of its former self:

> The losses suffered during these days were exceedingly high, to the extreme that the regiment [that had been effectively isolated] was only strong enough to remain on the defensive, lacking the strength to break even minimal Russian resistance. From 5 October the division was officially on the defensive, and on 11 October came the order for it to be replaced on the line by 24th Infantry Division. The shocked and weakened troops turned the positions over to their relief columns

and made their way to the rest positions in the area of Viritsa [about nine miles southeast of Krasnogvardeisk and some distance behind the front line].

During the fighting at Gaitolovo our division's Catholic priest had earned the nickname 'the rucksack priest'. He was constantly on the move with his worn field pack strapped to his back, from which he consistently provided the troops on the foremost lines with simple food items that had come to be regarded by the *Landsers* as luxuries. He was always willing to assist the wounded, and on one occasion he personally located and rescued a badly wounded soldier who had fallen to a sniper's bullet in an exposed position on the line. His constant exposure to the front and physical risks for the benefit of the soldiers came to an untimely end when he received a severe shrapnel wound to his arm. Inflicted by a Russian mortar fired from the dense forest several hundred metres distant, the wound was severe enough to require amputation of the limb; thus the division lost a valuable soldier and friend. The division commander did attempt officially to recognise his numerous acts of bravery and dedication by recommending him for a high award; however, this recommendation was disapproved in light of the typical National Socialist philosophy, which was to refuse to grant such an esteemed decoration unless the priest agreed to surrender his cloth and collar.

During the weeks between 22 September and 7 October our battalion suffered a total of 62 killed, 280 wounded, and 30 missing. Some 20 or 30 lightly wounded and sick remained with the battalion, leaving us with an effective strength of 50 combatants within the battalion.[5]

Bidermann and his comrades remained in the rest area for the remainder of 1942. In order to try to bring the combat elements of the division back to strength as quickly as possible, all rear area units were 'combed out' to release men for the front line. Few if any replacements arrived from Germany until December, and it was only after this date that the division began to recover its former combat strength, at least in numerical terms – it would take several more months before the new drafts and the rear area men pressed into front-line service acquired the skills and experience necessary for survival in the brutal combat conditions of the Eastern Front.

Throughout the period of the German attempts to restore the old front line, Meretskov continued to be under pressure to deliver results. Even as Manstein began his pincer attack, the commander of Volkhov Front submitted fresh plans for the approval of *Stavka*. These new plans once more pursued earlier objectives – an advance to Sinyavino and widening of the penetration. In order to achieve this, Meretskov wrote, he would need more resources, and he requested further reinforcements of aircraft, tanks, and two more rifle divisions. Some of the reinforcements were promised, but events were rapidly overtaking both Meretskov and *Stavka*. As the German pincers met, Meretskov struggled to keep abreast of events with his attention divided between preparing for fresh offensive operations and salvaging the rapidly worsening situation on the battlefield. He later described the confusion that prevailed:

> A difficult situation had arisen in the area contested by the enemy and our troops. Our formations and their subunits were mixed up with each other and control broke down regularly. Contradictory reports were received from Second Shock Army. As a result, *Stavka* reproached us for not knowing what was happening on the ground and for insufficiently firm leadership in combat operations. In order to intervene directly in the organisation of the withdrawal of our men, I went to the command post of IV Guards Rifle Corps to meet its commander, Major General [Sergei Vasilyevich] Roginsky, who in early September had replaced Major General [Nikolai Aleksandrovich] Gagen, whose performance had been unsatisfactory in this role. The location was in the zone being shelled by artillery. Rounds were exploding all around the dugout of the corps commander. Shortly after I arrived, I was told that my car had been damaged. The same fate befell the second car sent from the Front headquarters. While I was at the corps headquarters there were several calls for me from *Stavka* via the direct telephone line. On 30 September when I [returned to Volkhov Front headquarters and] began my report to *Stavka* on the withdrawal of my men, Stalin immediately asked: 'Why didn't you come to the phone?'
>
> 'Two cars were wrecked,' I replied. 'And most importantly, I was afraid that if I left the command post, the staff would just follow me [and not stay in their headquarters].' From the rest of the conversation, it became clear to me that *Stavka* was as concerned as we were about the stability of the front line along the Chernaya River.[6]

As had been the case throughout the year, Meretskov would have been acutely aware that further failures might result in him being placed under arrest once more, and he was therefore anxious to show that he was not personally avoiding danger and was doing all he could to hold his units together. Leningrad Front was given permission to make a fresh attack from the west on 25 September and did so a day later, triggering a further series of bloody engagements. Reinforced by battlegroups of 12th Panzer Division, the German lines held firm and even eliminated some of the earlier gains of the Red Army. Had these attacks by

Leningrad Front been better coordinated with Meretskov's efforts, they might at least have diverted German reserves and thus made the task of Volkhov Front easier; instead, they merely added to the already terrible total of dead and wounded.

The German encirclement of Meretskov's forces was tenuous and it was still possible for some units to escape. A Red Army platoon commander later described his experiences, demonstrating how even in such desperate circumstances, Soviet officials were inclined to be suspicious of anyone who appeared to be acting without direct orders:

> We were given verbal orders to withdraw. We retreated at night, taking cover in small groups. Then [our pursuers] would catch up with us and we moved on once more. On the Chernaya River, my platoon was left to cover the retreat. In the end, there were three of us left alive.
>
> On our own initiative, we crossed the Chernaya River. It wasn't wide, but the banks were marshy and the bottom was just silt. We plunged in up to our waists. Supporting each other, we somehow got to the far bank. The gunfire was terrible. It was good that many shells didn't detonate when they landed in the mud.
>
> In the afternoon, an officer with two men gathered the scattered groups into a line and said, 'If you want to live, you need to break through before the Germans have time to strengthen their lines properly.'
>
> We got ready and at his command we rushed forward with loud shouts of 'Urra!' Many fell, and some turned back to the forest. At night, we tried to crawl through the German defences. Automatic bursts rang out ahead – they sounded like ours! We could tell by the sound, as the German machine-guns had a higher rate of fire. I was crawling past a trench when I suddenly heard, 'Ach, mein Gott!' A German peered fearfully from his trench and threw a grenade over the parapet. I should have grabbed it and thrown it back into the trench but I didn't react in time and it exploded, injuring my right thigh and hand. When I came to, there was nobody around. I crawled forward, dragging an arm and a leg. How long I crawled, I don't know.
>
> It began to get light. I hid between two hillocks. I lay there all day, often drifting off into oblivion. My whole body ached. I started crawling again at dusk. Two soldiers joined me. One crawled ahead, I followed him, and the third was behind me. We continued until dawn. In the morning, the leading man's head dropped to the ground and he stopped moving. Shortly after, the one following me groaned and lay still. It was a German 'cuckoo' sniper who killed them. For the first time in my 20 years of life, I prayed to God to keep me alive. I lay there again all day, hardly moving. I crawled on later, holding a pistol in my left hand.

I was dragged into a trench. I don't know who gave me a cigarette, who gave me water, or bread ... A nurse ran up, cut open my padded jacket and trousers, and applied dressings. Suddenly, pushing everyone aside, an officer from *Smersh* [the Soviet counter-espionage service – this officer was more likely just from a unit of the NKVD] appeared and started interrogating me, asking who I was, how I escaped, which unit I belonged to, why I was alone.

The soldiers were indignant, shouting, 'Leave him! Can't you see he's wounded? He needs help urgently!'

But he didn't listen and shouted back, 'Where did you get that gun?'

The junior commander [of the trench] couldn't stand it and exclaimed: 'So what do you think? A wounded man crawled out on his own, and you're going to arrest him?' He fired a burst from his machine-gun at the officer. Nobody betrayed him. They reported that a 'cuckoo' hit him when he stood up in the trench.[7]

Such interrogation of soldiers who managed to return to the Soviet lines was widespread, even in a situation like this where it was almost impossible for normal systems of orders and instructions to prevail. It isn't possible to assess how often the front-line soldiers took matters into their own hands as described here, but it is likely that such incidents were rare as there was the ever-present danger of soldiers denouncing their officers to commissars or senior commanders – only a man who knew he had the complete loyalty of his men would dare to act in such a manner. The Soviet authorities were constantly on guard against the Germans using such stragglers as a means of sending spies across the front line, and after interrogation many of these men would be reduced in rank or sent to penal battalions if their questioners concluded that they had failed to follow strict rules about adherence to orders. Soldiers who had become prisoners of the Germans and then subsequently escaped were treated with even greater suspicion. It was regarded as unacceptable that a Red Army soldier should surrender unless he was wounded or incapacitated; moreover, there was strong suspicion that if they had been held by the Germans, their ideological purity might have been corrupted and as the war continued, both sides tried to recruit prisoners of war who could then be released to return to their own side where they were meant to try to persuade other soldiers to become deserters. In practice, men recruited in this manner often used this route as an opportunity to return to their own side, but then faced suspicion, interrogation, and possible punishment.

The remnants of Palkin's 22nd Rifle Brigade received orders at the end of September to break out of the pocket by whatever means possible. The exhausted men began their attempt early on 30 September:

There seemed little hope of getting out of the encirclement: on our own, as our experience in earlier battles had shown, we could achieve little and we could hardly hope for help, knowing the situation of the Front. No help could reach us as the troops of the Front were only with difficulty holding back the onslaught of the enemy, especially after he had brought into battle the reserves he had intended for the assault on Leningrad – but we didn't know these details at that time.

Attempts by small groups to break out continued intermittently throughout the day. Our numbers were dwindling rapidly. Ammunition stocks fell even faster. We couldn't expect more of either. On the last attack of the day – perhaps the sixth or seventh consecutive attempt – when only a few combat-ready soldiers and commanders remained in our companies and platoons, we attacked with determination to fulfil our duty to the Motherland to the end, relying mainly on bayonets because each of us had no more than four or five rounds left. There was no artillery ammunition at all and the soldiers disabled the guns so that the enemy couldn't use them. A bullet hit the butt of my machine-gun, smashing it into smithereens, and fragments slashed into my hand. Over 20 splinters remain in my hand to this day.

Darkness fell and in the dark we had a respite, which we used to help the wounded. There were far more of them than those who remained unscathed in the ranks. Those who no longer needed our help were buried in a trench. Indeed, it became a grave for unknown soldiers, as we simply hadn't had the time to learn the names of the soldiers who had gathered together for the last time …

Late on 30 September we made another attempt to get out of the encirclement stealthily, under cover of darkness. This was our last chance! We distributed the wounded amongst us – two lightly wounded men or one seriously wounded man per soldier. In total darkness, we managed to crawl undetected almost to the end of no-man's land. Here our movement was spotted and a flurry of mortar bombs, artillery shells, and machine-gun fire swept over us. Although it was night, it was suddenly as bright as a fine sunny day – the Germans fired more and more parachute flares into the sky.

I was wounded again and probably stunned at the same time, as I lost consciousness. I awoke at dawn. There was silence all around, and I could hear the sound of artillery fire, but only in the distance. When it was completely light, some unfamiliar orderlies approached me, put me on a stretcher and carried me away. To my horror, they took me to a prisoner-of-war camp.[8]

Survival in German prison camps was a challenge in itself, particularly in the first year of the war – confident of a victory that would be followed by the full implementation of Germany's racial policies, the Germans left prisoners to starve or succumb to their wounds by the tens of thousands, and death rates rose steadily as colder weather set in; there was little or no provision for warm accommodation. In return for a meagre increase in rations, prisoners were encouraged to denounce other prisoners who were Jewish or Communists, For men who had escaped such treatment, interrogation and suspicion from their own side must have seemed an appalling further abuse. Nikolai Ivanovich Moskvin was a political commissar in an artillery regiment that was cut off to the west of Vitebsk during the initial German advance in 1941. He remained in the area working with partisans, and encountered several Soviet soldiers who had escaped from German captivity:

> They say there's no shelter, no water, that people are dying from hunger and disease, that many are without proper clothes or shoes. They are treated like slaves, shot for the slightest misdemeanour, or just from mischief, for a kind of fun …
>
> I realise how naïve our army training was. We excluded the idea of becoming prisoners entirely from our view of what was acceptable in war, but what we told the soldiers and ourselves was that the enemy would use prisoners to extract secrets, that he would torture people to persuade them to betray.[9]

Reports reached the Soviet authorities in a steady stream. One such report reached the NKVD from partisans in the central region of the Eastern Front:

> There is a concentration camp near the city of Rzhev with 15,000 captured Red Army soldiers and 5,000 civilians. They are held in unheated huts and they are fed one or two frozen potatoes each a day. The Germans throw rotten meat and bones through the barbed wire to the prisoners. This has led to widespread illness. About 20–30 people die every day. Those who are too ill to work are shot.[10]

Zygmunt Klukowski, a Polish physician, watched in horror as a column of Soviet prisoners marched past in the city of Zamość:

> They all looked like skeletons, just shadows of human beings, barely moving. I have never in my life seen anything like this. Men were falling in the street; the stronger ones were carrying others, holding them up by their arms. They looked like starved animals, not like people. They were fighting for scraps of apples in the gutter, not paying any attention to the Germans who would beat them with

rubber truncheons. Some crossed themselves and knelt, begging for food. Soldiers from the convoy beat them without mercy. They beat not only prisoners but also people who stood by and tried to pass them food. After the macabre unit passed by, several horse-drawn wagons carried prisoners who were unable to walk. This unbelievable treatment of human beings is only possible under German ethics.[11]

The death rate amongst prisoners was terrible. A Wehrmacht report written in December 1941 recorded that up to 70 per cent of prisoners died between being captured and reaching prison camps, where they continued to perish in huge numbers – one large camp in Poland held 80,000 prisoners when it was first created, but by February 1942 only 3,000 were still alive. In all, it is estimated that over 300,000 Soviet prisoners died after reaching prison camps during 1941.[12] Over the course of the war, the Germans captured about 5.7 million Soviet soldiers; of these, German records suggest that 3.3 million did not survive, a death toll of 58 per cent. Whilst the treatment of German prisoners of war in Soviet hands was also often brutal, it was by comparison far less lethal – about 2 million German soldiers were captured by the Red Army, and about 257,000 died in captivity, a death rate of 18 per cent. Neither of these figures takes account of the large numbers of civilians who were used as forced labour, both near the front line and in factories far away; the death rates in such groups in German captivity was terrible, and German civilians who were taken away as forced labour by the Soviet forces at the end of the war fared little better.

By early 1942, with the war looking increasingly likely to drag on for months if not years, many within the Wehrmacht were openly questioning the mistreatment of prisoners, but mainly on grounds of pragmatism rather than out of any humanitarian concern. A report written by an intelligence officer in February stated:

> Our treatment of prisoners of war cannot continue without consequences. It is no longer because of lectures from the *politruks*, but from his own personal convictions that the Soviet soldier has come to expect an agonising life or death if he falls captive.[13]

Inevitably, the ordeal of Jewish Red Army soldiers was the worst – they were swiftly segregated from other prisoners and summarily executed. Gabriel Temkin was a Polish Jew, aged 18 when the Germans invaded Poland in 1939. Aware of the widespread abuses suffered by Jews in Germany, he fled from the western city of Łódź to the Soviet-occupied eastern sector before the Germans arrived.

When *Barbarossa* began, he was conscripted into the Red Army but as a Polish Jew he was treated with suspicion and put in a labour battalion that dug fortifications for the combat troops. He became a prisoner of the Wehrmacht in the summer of 1942 but his Aryan appearance protected him from German suspicion; at one stage, he feared that a fellow prisoner who knew he was a Jew would betray him, but whilst this prisoner had no love of Jews, his hatred of the Germans was even greater. Temkin was put in a camp run by the Hungarians, whose mistreatment of Soviet prisoners seemed to be every bit as bad as that of the Germans, with guards inventing sadistic and humiliating activities largely for their personal entertainment. Eventually, he escaped as the Red Army began its advance into eastern Ukraine in early 1943 and managed to reach Soviet lines, where he was promptly dispatched to a 'verification camp' run by the NKVD. Conditions here proved to be little better than those in German and Hungarian prison camps:

> The NKVD 'verification camp' was located on a guarded poultry farm ... Inmates, housed in chicken coops, were all from the recently liberated territories – policemen, *starosti* (village headmen), priests, draft dodgers, deserters, escapee POWs – all alike under suspicion of collaboration with the enemy. The chicken coops were extremely overcrowded. We slept on floors covered sparsely with straw. At night people were stepping over the bodies of snoring men. Even in daytime, moving from place to place, one would inevitably tread on someone's legs. Only lice had complete freedom of movement; the place was crawling with them and they were creeping into all our private parts. There were no washing facilities of any kind inside the chicken houses. As the doors were kept closed ... the air inside was foul and full of smoke; at times the stench was overwhelming. Going out to the latrines where, while relieving ourselves, one could get a breath of fresh air, was strictly regulated. Worst of all, however, was hunger. The food was meagre, about a pound of claylike bread and tea-like hot water in the evening, and two *balandas* (watery soups), one for breakfast, the other for lunch.[14]

Like many other former prisoners of war, Temkin found himself being treated under a presumption of guilt and realised that he was expected to have to prove his innocence – he and his fellow prisoners described this using the Russian phrase *Dokazhi chto ty ne verblud* ('Prove you are not a camel'). Proof could come in several forms, but usually required corroborating statements from other prisoners – in the circumstances of individual escapees, this was an almost impossible requirement. The pressing need for soldiers, however, resulted in

Temkin being returned to active service. He was fortunate not to be sent to a penal battalion.

Palkin was taken to a temporary prison compound near Sinyavino where he and other prisoners were held in an enclosed area with no shelter from the elements. He had time to contemplate the various fates that awaited soldiers in wartime:

> Military fate is an astonishing thing. It seems that all soldiers and officers are bound by the same conditions, but it is absolutely impossible to predict in advance whom fate, like a rope thrown across an abyss, will bring to safety in the difficult conditions of war and, in addition, will reward with laurels; who will get the same laurels at the cost of their lives; and who will lay down his head in an unequal battle with the enemy on a nameless hill and will, along with others, lie in the tomb of the unknown soldier.
>
> But there are those for whom fate has prepared the most difficult trials. They were not only ignored by the leaves of the noble laurel, but their very names remained only in the memories of their friends and relatives, who still search for them, publishing advertisements in newspapers from time to time under the heading 'Can anyone help?' But even the fates of those who were missing varied. For those who, for various reasons, ended up in the hands of the enemy and couldn't break free, their fate was often a slow painful death in the prisons of the Fascists. These 'unknown soldiers' have no graves. There is nothing worse in the entire world than this fate …
>
> We spent only a few hours in a temporary camp in Sinyavino, and I remember that different armbands were tied to the wounded: yellow for seriously wounded, red for lightly wounded. A medic gave me a yellow armband. On the same day – 1 October – the Germans loaded the wounded prisoners of war into railcars and transported them through Mga to Krasnogvardeisk. Here, on the northern outskirts, there was a camp for prisoners of war.
>
> Before putting us in barracks, the Germans selected us according to nationality – Russians, Ukrainians, Balts, and so on, all separated. Only at the end of this were we led or carried to the barracks by our orderlies.[15]

Some of the German guards tormented the prisoners by staging mock executions, and shortly after the Communist Party members were singled out and taken away. The remaining prisoners expected that they would never see them again, and were surprised when the group of Party men returned a few hours later; the Germans had merely showed them a newsreel extolling the successes of the Wehrmacht and predicting the imminent defeat of the Soviet Union. After a week in which they received little or no medical care, the prisoners were taken to Lithuania. Several men died during the brief stay near Krasnogvardeisk, and others succumbed to their wounds en route and in the new camp. In the months that followed, there were more deaths from disease, malnutrition, and punishments – anyone who attempted to escape was severely beaten or shot immediately.

After enduring many months of imprisonment, Palkin and about 60 other prisoners leaped from a railcar that was taking them from Lithuania to Germany; they had heard rumours that they were to be transferred to Dachau, where they would all be killed. The guards on the train opened fire but the train continued on its way and most of the men managed to reach the cover of some nearby woodland. Accompanied by two others, Palkin came across a small Lithuanian farm, where the escapees were given food and civilian clothing – their prison garb bore the letters 'SU' on their backs, clearly visible from a distance. The three men were later able to join a local partisan group and took part in several operations against the Germans. When Soviet forces moved into Lithuania in the late summer of 1944, Palkin and the others were finally able to return to the Red Army, and by this stage of the war the pressing need for men to replace the losses that had been suffered during the Soviet advance meant that their 'interrogation' by the NKVD was perhaps less rigorous than that inflicted on former prisoners in earlier years. They were soon back in the front line as regular soldiers.

In order to ensure that the latest attack by Leningrad Front failed to reach the pocket of Eighth Army and Second Shock Army, Manstein was forced to dispatch much of 28th Jäger Division as reinforcements for *SS-Polizei* and the other units facing Govorov's forces, delaying his reduction of the trapped Red Army units. Early on 29 September, *Stavka* finally seemed to have realised that it had been basing its decisions on information that was at best incomplete, and at worst misleading. Meretskov was probably relieved that most of the criticism for 'criminal carelessness and false complacent information' was directed at the commanders of the two armies rather than at him, though the latest instructions from Vasilevsky added:

> It is clear that neither the Front nor Second Shock Army headquarters wish to acknowledge the real situation that exists west of the Chernaya River and to the southwest of Gaitolovo with appropriate seriousness. They are managing to issue orders regarding a possible withdrawal of Second Shock Army to an area east of Gaitolovo that bear no resemblance to the true situation.

Stavka therefore orders:

1. Provide a fully honest report about the real situation of the units west of the Chernaya and about the corridor southwest of Gaitolovo by 1000, 29 September.
2. You and your staff will take over control of the withdrawal of Second Shock Army to the area east of Gaitolovo immediately.[16]

The encircled troops continued to filter through the German lines for several days – despite Vasilevsky's further instructions, there was no organised breakout, and in any case communications were so poor that such coordination would have been impossible. The German divisions encircling the isolated units began their attacks to eliminate the pocket on 30 September and fighting continued for two weeks as the weather steadily deteriorated. As was consistently the case in this sector, the army fighting a defensive battle had a considerable advantage and German losses were severe. Estimates vary, not least because the two sides defined battles or operations with different start-dates and end-dates, making direct comparison difficult, but the most conservative estimate would be nearly 27,000 German officers and men killed or wounded both in defending against the attacks of Leningrad and Volkhov Fronts and then in the counterattack to restore the old front line.[17] A higher figure of a little over 41,000 is reached by considering the total losses of Eleventh and Eighteenth Armies during this period.[18] At the very least, this meant that the divisions intended for *Nordlicht* were now far too weak to mount a serious attack and the operation was cancelled. The price paid by the Red Army was, almost inevitably, far higher. Estimates vary between about 113,000 dead or wounded and a higher – and perhaps more accurate – figure of between 130,000 and 160,000 casualties.[19] Both armies were back where they had been before the Red Army's attacks commenced in August.

Second Shock Army, which had effectively been destroyed earlier in the year at the end of the Lyuban offensive, was badly mauled once more; in a report to *Stavka*, Meretskov estimated that by early October it was reduced to a little under 4,700 men. Klykov remained in command for the moment, but he was replaced in early December by Lieutenant General Vladimir Zakharovich Romanovsky, who had been in command of First Shock Army a little further south. He was removed from that particular post after his perceived failure to destroy the German forces around Demyansk, but like Meretskov he was deemed to be worth a further chance. But unlike Meretskov, he didn't have to endure a period of imprisonment, interrogation, and mistreatment. Klykov now became deputy commander of Volkhov Front.

Given the losses that the Wehrmacht suffered, Hitler had no choice but to abandon plans for an autumn start date for *Nordlicht*, though at first the operation remained as a probable option for a later date. Within days, fresh orders arrived from Hitler's headquarters. There would be no such operation in the foreseeable future, and the artillery of Army Group North was to resume its reduction of Leningrad by heavy bombardment. Even this plan was then abandoned as developments around Stalingrad in late November created a crisis with the potential to change the course of the war.

Despite Vasilevsky's chastening message of 29 September, Meretskov continued to send upbeat reports to *Stavka*, claiming that his men had inflicted nearly 52,000 German casualties and had destroyed an improbable 260 German aircraft and 197 tanks. Even though he acknowledged that his divisions were exhausted and had suffered heavy losses both in terms of personnel and equipment, he wished to continue local active operations to tie down German forces around Mga, if only to prevent any new German concentration against Leningrad.[20] Vasilevsky's response was blunt: Leningrad Front was given permission to abandon its hard-won bridgeheads, which would in any event have been difficult to supply and hold through the winter. All further offensive operations by both Leningrad and Volkhov Fronts were put on hold.

At that time, Meretskov couldn't know that Vasilevsky was heavily involved in plans for an operation codenamed *Uranus*, the great encirclement of Sixth Army at Stalingrad; nor would he have been aware of Zhukov overseeing preparations for *Mars*, another bloody attempt to destroy the German-held Rzhev salient to the west of Moscow. Both would place a huge burden on the resources of the Soviet Union, and there was little to spare for further operations in the north. After several months that saw repeated setbacks for the Red Army due to over-optimism and too many operations being launched with too little concentration of effort, *Stavka* was learning that concentrating effort on fewer operations was a policy that had to be remembered at all levels – if army and Front commanders were criticised for trying to pursue too many objectives, the same criticism could be applied to the highest commands. Perhaps Vasilevsky and Stalin had access to information via the channel of political officers in the north that gave them a more realistic view of the situation than Meretskov's reports – even if the Front commander remained optimistic that further attacks were possible, they knew that a respite was needed, not least if they were going to ensure adequate supplies for the attacks planned for the centre and the south.

As the Red Army units pulled back into defensive positions, there was a new development on the battlefield. Until now, the heavy KV-1 tanks of the Red

Army had proved almost impervious to German tank guns and most anti-tank guns – only the famed 88mm guns could penetrate their tough armour. But in October, Mokhov, the tank mechanic, saw the results of the continuing evolution of German weapons:

> In October ... new German sub-calibre shells penetrated the armour of the KV for the first time. They had a lightweight aluminium head around a steel core. As the round was smaller, the same amount of propellant could give it greater acceleration ... After penetrating the armour, the projectile remained intact. Several senior officers from Moscow came to inspect the damage: until now it was thought that the KVs were impenetrable.
>
> During the Finnish war of 1939–40, the KV tank demonstrated the superiority of its armour: not a single regimental artillery piece could penetrate its 100mm armour. This led to the decision to increase the production of heavy tanks, with an increase in weight to 50 tons, making the propulsion systems and engines more complex ...
>
> Now the KV tanks had lost their main quality: reliable armour protection. This clearly caused a stir in command circles.[21]

Coming after the advent of the Tiger tank, this new development was a reminder to the Red Army that just as it was steadily improving its equipment, the Germans too were making fresh developments. The gun of the KV-1 was the same as that of the T-34, a much lighter and more mobile tank. The only advantage that the KV-1 had enjoyed over the T-34 was its superior armour – it was a more expensive tank, and its greater weight meant that it often chewed up roads or destroyed bridges, making movement by units following behind much more difficult. The year of 1942 saw production of the KV-1 peak, with a total of over 2,500 being built, but thereafter it was decided that there was little further benefit in building such a heavy tank with the same weapon as the T-34, especially given that it could no longer rely on superior armour.[22] A few modified versions with the more powerful 85mm gun appeared in 1943, but this too could be fitted to the T-34, albeit with an enlarged turret; thereafter, production of the KV-1 ceased, at least in the form of a tank. But the fighting of late 1942, particularly around Stalingrad, demonstrated the requirement for a mobile weapon capable of destroying field fortifications; emulating the highly successful German assault guns, Soviet designers fitted a powerful 152mm gun to the KV chassis, creating the SU-152, which entered service in 1943.

As was almost always the case, the Red Army attempted to analyse the battles to see why the operation had failed to break through and advance over the relatively short distance to the Leningrad siege perimeter. Even before the fighting had died down completely, some factors were already obvious. Many units had entered the battle with inadequate supplies of munitions, particularly shells, mortar bombs, and hand grenades, all of which were essential for storming prepared defences. At every level, command and control problems were identified: division commanders sometimes lost contact with their regiments and were unable to coordinate their actions; army commanders failed to maintain tight command of their divisions; and Meretskov's reports to *Stavka* were often misleadingly inaccurate. Tanks were often deployed piecemeal, though the terrain was such that neither side could really send armoured units into action en masse; there was poor coordination between tanks and infantry, and once the tanks became separated from the infantry they became easy prey for German anti-tank guns, particularly as the boggy terrain often left the tanks struggling to move. And there was criticism of the manner in which Meretskov brought forward his exploitation forces, throwing them into the battle as individual divisions rather than as a coherent whole.[23]

These findings missed several points, perhaps the most important of which was that there was little or no coordination between the forces of Volkhov Front and those of Leningrad Front. Had they timed their attacks better, they would at least have had the chance of creating increased pressure on German resources; instead, there was almost no occasion when both Fronts were attacking at the same time, allowing the Germans to concentrate first on one side, then the other. Nor were all the issues that were identified entirely due to Meretskov's errors. The terrain was unsuitable for armoured warfare and both sides suffered considerable tank losses due to vehicles becoming stranded in deep mud. The criticism about the deployment of second and third echelon forces piecemeal rather than en masse was to an extent irrelevant, as the manner in which Meretskov used his reserves was largely dictated by the manner in which the battle unfolded, and deploying the forces as originally intended was impossible given the narrow salient created by Eighth Army's initial attack. Nonetheless, a scapegoat was found. Gagen, the former commander of IV Guards Rifle Corps, was caught up in the encirclement but resolutely led a small group of men to safety. Regardless of this, he found himself shouldering the blame for the ineffective use of reserves, even though his deployment of his troops was in accordance with the instructions that he received from Meretskov. But by this stage of the war, Stalin knew that he could no longer apply ruthless discipline to those who he regarded as having failed.

The Red Army was going to have to learn how to fight and win with the personnel available. Gagen was given command of a rifle division, but within weeks was once more in command of IV Guards Rifle Corps.

It was one thing to study the operations and draw up a list, however incomplete, of the problems that had arisen. The greater challenge was ensuring that those errors were not repeated in future, and this was an area where the Red Army constantly struggled, particularly in 1941 and 1942. The basic training of combat troops had been truncated due to the demands of war and most of the recruits who reached the front line had low levels of skill – this was one of the reasons why the heavy losses suffered by Soviet units included a disproportionately large number of the newest arrivals. To an extent, the Wehrmacht would also start to suffer from such shortcomings as the war continued, and in an attempt to remedy this many German armies and army groups established 'war schools' close to the front and sent as many new recruits as possible on crash courses where they learned the skills essential for survival on the Eastern Front. The Red Army had no such arrangement, and ongoing training once recruits reached the front line was almost always on an ad hoc basis. Reliance on sheer weight of artillery would gradually be augmented by better use of reconnaissance to identify German positions and to crush them before the infantry attacked. Implementation of this concept should have been straightforward, but ensuring tight cooperation between artillery and attacking units as the battle progressed was a different matter. Furthermore, even if better reconnaissance was put in place, it wasn't always easy to identify all the strongpoints that the Germans would hold if they were driven out of their front-line positions, and in order to smash these with artillery fire there would have to be a great improvement in communication and coordination between the gun batteries and the advancing troops they were supporting.

The sheer scale of the Red Army created its own problems. There was no tradition of experienced NCOs, as was the case in the Wehrmacht and the armies of the Western Powers – a hard core of older soldiers who had learned over the years how to get the best performance out of equipment, and the importance of the simple things that prevented degradation of performance over time, such as proper cleaning of weapons and personal equipment and paying attention to personal hygiene. These were also the men who in other armies ensured that the new recruits learned the vital skills of warcraft as quickly as possible. Without such 'role models' in the front line, these lessons frequently had to be learned again and again, often at great cost. Nor was there any rigorous attempt to alter basic training in order to try to remedy the problems that were identified. Although the criticism about lack of coordination between artillery, tanks, and armour was something that recurred in almost every Red Army operation of 1941 and 1942, few practical steps were taken to avoid repetition in future, either in the training of ordinary soldiers or their officers. As a result of the heavy losses that the Red Army continued to experience throughout the war, any progress made in these areas was often lost before the following battle or operation.

Slowly, Stalin was beginning to trust a small group of senior military figures around him – Zhukov and Vasilevsky more than most, but also men that these generals regarded as praiseworthy, such as Vatutin and Govorov. As his confidence in his generals grew, they learned that they could operate with a greater degree of freedom than had been the case in the dark years of the purges and the opening months of the war, but even then they were aware that their freedom to do so depended very much on results: too many failures would result in their removal. As the war progressed, though, Stalin's freedom to remove and punish officers who failed to deliver became constrained by reality. Even by late 1942, it was clear that the Red Army would have to fight the war with the senior officers it had. There simply wasn't the time or opportunity to replace them with men who might perform better. To an extent, this explains the continued survival of Meretskov. His performance after his rehabilitation was lacklustre and Vasilevsky and others clearly knew that his reports were deliberately misleading, but by sticking closely to the orders that he had been given he was able to avoid much of the criticism directed at others. He also became increasingly adept in transferring blame as rapidly as possible to his subordinates.

For the Germans too, there were lessons to be learned. Even while the Wehrmacht's divisions in Ukraine were pouring east towards and ultimately beyond the Don River, there were increasing signs that the Red Army's resources remained huge. There were bitter battles in the central sector for much of the year and the sheer scale of Soviet losses around the Rzhev salient showed just how much the optimistic pre-war assessments of Soviet military strength had been off the mark. Both in the central sector and in the north, German defensive fighting was highly effective, but in both cases this was on terrain that was very favourable to the defending side – the combination of dense woodland and swampy ground ensured that an attacker had limited axes on which to advance, and it was therefore possible to concentrate defensive fire on those axes to maximum effect. The weakness of the anti-tank weaponry of German infantry units was therefore not exposed as completely as it might have been – along the Volkhov front and in the central sector, many of the engagements with Soviet armour took place at close range due to the opportunities for defences to remain hidden until advancing Soviet units were very close. At such ranges, the German anti-tank guns could still be fairly effective and soldiers rapidly learned to use demolition charges to disable and destroy tanks that were not supported by infantry. When the Red Army moved forward against the German positions over difficult terrain, there was ample time for German artillery and mortar fire to drive any infantry accompanying the tanks to cover. To an extent, this led to over-confidence in the ability of German infantry to fight defensive battles. During the winter of 1942–43, the Red Army would mount a series of offensives that tore away the long German front line along the Don River where there was far less cover and the terrain was less ideally suited to defensive warfare, smashing the Romanian, Italian, and Hungarian armies – but also brushing aside German divisions further north with just as much ease. However, such was the belief in German circles about their defensive abilities that the failures of Germany's allies were the subject of sharp criticism and disdain, while the collapse of German infantry when the German Second Army came under attack was largely ignored.

The weakness of German forces in a defensive role was twofold. Firstly, as already mentioned, their anti-tank firepower was limited, placing a great strain on supporting panzer divisions, which often had to 'loan' their assets to infantry units to prevent collapse. Secondly, there was a problem of mobility, which led to a brittleness in the German infantry. Despite the much-vaunted ability of German mechanised units to wage mobile warfare in a revolutionary manner, the infantry divisions that made up the bulk of the army remained heavily dependent upon horses to move their artillery and heavy equipment. By the summer of 1942, the shortage of fodder for horses meant that many of the divisions deployed around Leningrad had sent many or most of their heavy draft horses far to the rear, even to Estonia, where supplies were more easily obtained. As a consequence, German artillery became increasingly immobile. During the fighting outside Moscow in the winter of 1941–42, losses of horses due to fodder shortages, casualties, and the weather meant that large numbers of guns had to be abandoned; in the months and years that followed, the horse shortage remained a persistent problem, meaning that if German infantry units were driven out of their positions, even at great cost to the Red Army, the fighting power of the German units fell rapidly as they were forced to withdraw and abandon much of their artillery. The attacks of Meretskov's armies (and of the Soviet armies deployed against the Rzhev salient throughout 1942) repeatedly failed to achieve a sufficiently deep advance to force the Germans to abandon their artillery, thus failing to expose a critical weakness.

One of the issues about the attempt to break the siege ring in the late summer of 1942 – and the German response to it – is the deployment of the German Eleventh Army. As already described, Manstein claimed in his memoirs that he would have preferred his troops to remain in the south, but it is important to separate hindsight from what was known and believed at the time. When the decision to send Eleventh Army to the Leningrad sector was made, it seemed that Army Groups A and B had adequate strength to complete their missions to capture Stalingrad and the Caucasus; between them, they consisted of two panzer armies, two other German armies, two Romanian armies, an Italian army, and a Hungarian army. Although the supplies for most of these allied troops came from their home nations, they still had to be transported to the East on an inadequate railway system and there were frequent pauses in operations due to supply shortages. Had Eleventh Army been added to the logistic burden – particularly when there didn't seem to be a need for its troops in that sector – the strain would have been even worse. As events turned out, the presence of Manstein's veteran divisions in the southern sector would have had a major impact on the battles that developed there in November and December, but the decision to send them north was made when there was no apparent threat of a major Soviet counteroffensive and seemed like correct judgement at that time. The consequence was that the long flanks of the German salient stretching to the Volga at Stalingrad would be defended by the relatively weak armies of Germany's allies. Even this risk would have been reasonable if Hitler's assessment – often with the support of those around him in his headquarters – that the Red Army was a spent force had been correct. At one point during the summer of 1942, Hitler exulted: 'The Russian is finished, I'm sure of it', and Halder happily agreed, even though within days he was changing his mind. Just as over-optimism led to the German setback at Moscow in 1941 and repeatedly undermined the Red Army's operations, it played a huge part in the decision to send Eleventh Army north.

CHAPTER 13

TOWARDS THE SECOND WINTER

The German plans for *Nordlicht* – a renewed attack against Leningrad – were repeatedly postponed through the late summer and early autumn of 1942. Even before the onset of the Third Sinyavino Operation and the arrival of Manstein's Eleventh Army, it was increasingly clear to Küchler at the headquarters of Army Group North that any renewed attack would involve a radical redistribution of troops; Lindemann, the commander of Eighteenth Army, advised him that he would have to abandon the Kirishi and Gruzino bridgeheads in order to release sufficient men for *Nordlicht*, and such a step would weaken the east-facing positions of his army. When the fighting to the east of Sinyavino began, almost everyone in the German chain of command realised that there could be no question of resuming operations against Leningrad itself until the threat from Meretskov's Volkhov Front had been eliminated, and a combination of the heavy casualties suffered by the Germans in their counterattack and the increasingly inclement weather meant that there was now no prospect of attacking Leningrad. But even if time and numbers had permitted *Nordlicht* to go ahead, it is highly questionable whether it would have succeeded.

As Leningrad began to recover from almost starving to death, the city authorities took several steps to improve the defences in case the Germans should attack again. The improvised defensive lines that had developed as the Wehrmacht moved ever close to Leningrad in late 1941 were turned into a formidable series of fortifications. When the siege began, the positions of each battalion – and often each company – consisted of isolated trenches and bunkers, and throughout the winter and the spring of 1942 the soldiers – most of whom were almost as hungry as the civilians in Leningrad – worked to link up these positions into a continuous belt. The officers in each location redesigned their trenches and bunkers as required to ensure that there were better fields of fire, and repositioned weapons in order to provide mutual support. As had been the case in the frantic months of building the Luga Line, civilian battalions helped with the work – they received a small increase in rations, but probably not even enough to cover the additional energy expenditure of such work – and even as Küchler was drawing up his plans for *Nordlicht*, the reality was that the Soviet positions were now a far more formidable prospect than before. Concrete bunkers and firing points had been constructed in the old improvised positions and there were secondary lines all along the front, carefully designed to ensure that if the Germans overran the first defensive line they would be exposed to heavy fire from the secondary positions. As the autumn weather turned progressively colder, Leningrad Front reported to Moscow with considerable satisfaction that its main defensive line protecting the city now consisted of 93 miles of anti-tank ditches and other barriers, 125 miles of barbed wire entanglements, over 7,000 trenches, and hundreds of miles of communications trenches that would allow troops to move from the main line to the secondary line and vice versa. There were more than 600 bunkers and firing points reinforced with concrete and a further 1,400 bunkers built with earth and timber.[1] By the time that the Germans abandoned *Nordlicht*, there were three distinct defensive belts with further fortifications between them so that troops falling back from one line to the next would be able to hold off any pursuers.

Most of these fortifications were visible to the German reconnaissance aircraft that were constantly overhead and in the late summer of 1942 Küchler drew the attention of *OKH* to the formidable obstacles that faced any renewed attack on Leningrad. Whilst Hitler expressed dismay at the defences, he assured Küchler that close support by the Luftwaffe would overcome all such problems. His confidence was almost certainly misplaced. Even if the Wehrmacht had succeeded in battering its way through these multiple lines, it would then have faced the task of fighting in Leningrad itself. The most determined resistance to the German offensive in the southern sector during 1942 came in urban areas – first in Voronezh, then in Stalingrad – and any attempt to penetrate into Leningrad would have resulted in similar fighting. Despite the transfer of several militia units to the regular army, the number of civilians enrolled into 'workers' battalions' increased during 1942. By the end of the year, there were 52 such battalions, fielding nearly 27,000 personnel; a little over a third were women. Many of these continued to work at least part-time in Leningrad's factories, but if the Germans had succeeded in breaking the formidable defensive lines to the south of the city, these battalions would have manned the defences in the southern fringe of Leningrad itself. Any attack into Leningrad by Eleventh Army would have been hugely costly. It is unsurprising that despite the orders to make preparations for *Nordlicht*, the senior officers of the Wehrmacht – Manstein, Lindemann, and Küchler – had little enthusiasm for such an operation.

Even if Army Group North had followed its previous intention of advancing between Leningrad and Lake Ladoga to link up with the Finns, this could only be achieved by forcing the line of the Neva River and then driving north in an area where the only good roads running in the desired direction were close to Leningrad itself. Such an advance might have been possible in late 1941 when the Red Army was still in disarray after its defeats and retreats, but was almost certainly beyond the capabilities of the Wehrmacht forces available in late 1942.

Many of the Soviet volunteer militia formations that had been raised in 1941 were now gone; some had been destroyed entirely in the battles between the Luga Line and Leningrad, but others were transformed into regular army units. After fighting in the Oranienbaum bridgehead, the men of 2nd Militia Division were redesignated 85th Rifle Division and in the spring of 1942 the unit was evacuated by sea back to Leningrad. The division was brought up to strength through a mixture of fresh drafts – many raised from the workers of Leningrad's factories – and the incorporation of disbanded units, and was then thrown into the attempts by Leningrad Front to advance towards the approaching units of Volkhov Front in August; as had been the case in the fighting of 1941, it suffered terrible casualties and had to be pulled out of the front line.

As they emerged from the grip of the terrible winter of 1941–42, Leningraders began the slow recovery from starvation. Slowly, the city was tidied up, rubble and corpses removed from the streets. The profusion of bodies and sewage that gradually thawed in the warmer weather resulted in a surge in the city's rat population as well as increasing illness, and the exhausted and weakened population was urged to join in the efforts to improve conditions. There were worrying rises in transmissible diseases such as dysentery, typhoid, and spotted typhus in the spring months, not helped by the widespread prevalence of lice infestations. Lieutenant General Sergei Ivanovich Kabanov, the commander of the Leningrad garrison, wrote to Zhdanov on 11 May to warn that the lack of washing facilities made it difficult to deal with this problem, with the result that there was a serious danger of the spread of infectious disease to the city garrison.[2] Efforts were made to repair and restore the city's water and sanitation systems but despite the best efforts of the city authorities with the limited resources available to them, infectious disease remained a major killer throughout the year.

During the spring months, the city's trams began to function again and many of the factories that had ceased work began to operate once more. Yevgeny Moniushko, who celebrated his 17th birthday in the summer of 1942, was working with his brother in a factory that had originally been involved in shipbuilding. It now produced a variety of items, including shell casings for the city's defenders and simple 'pontoons' or 'tenders' that could ferry supplies and people across Lake Ladoga. Ration coupons could be used in the factory canteens, meaning that workers didn't have to spend precious time hunting for shops that might have food. In any event, the supply of food, while still restricted, was far better than in the winter months:

By the spring of 1942, the rations far exceeded the meagre rations of the past winter, and if we had not been so extremely emaciated, they would have been more than sufficient to sustain both life and limb, and work. However, the rations were not sufficient for us to restore our normal body mass and physical strength and to overcome the constant feeling of hunger, which did not go away even after a rather filling dinner. Finally, the rations were not adequate enough for us to fight off our natural thoughts about the possibility of a renewed starvation.[3]

With a view to avoiding a second famine, Zhdanov and other senior figures in the Leningrad administration began a sustained programme of evacuation over Lake Ladoga. In order not to impair industrial activity in the city, everyone had to undergo a medical examination, and the elderly, infirm, and children were then selected for evacuation. As he had lost so much weight, Moniushko was one of those selected, together with his family. They left the city in August 1942, shortly before the Third Sinyavino Operation began. They made the crossing in one of the flat-bottomed tenders built in the factory where Moniushko had worked; despite good weather, the lack of a keel meant that the small craft rolled about in the water and the evacuees were relieved to reach Kobona. Here, they were put on trains that took them east to Siberia. A total of 300,000 civilians were brought out of the city in a first wave of evacuation; only those regarded as essential for industrial production, manning the city's defensive perimeter, or other vital tasks were to stay. But even with this strict requirement, about 800,000 civilians would remain in Leningrad.[4]

Inevitably, the starved population of Leningrad was at serious risk of illness due to their malnutrition as well as from infections. Many showed signs of scurvy, caused by deficiency of Vitamin C, and there was a need to find a plentiful source of the vitamin. Fortunately, there was a precedent. In the winter of 1536–37, a French expedition that was exploring the region of North America that is now Quebec was suffering from scurvy and was saved by local Iroquois people who gave them a special tincture made from pine needles and bark from a particular tree. This became known throughout Europe in the centuries that followed and the Leningrad authorities put this knowledge to good use. Pine needles were collected in the forests between the city and the Finnish front line and over 16 million doses of an unpleasant-tasting liquid were consumed by civilians and soldiers, resulting in a great reduction in the incidence of scurvy. However, care had to be taken, as there was a detrimental effect if too large a dose was administered.[5]

It wasn't enough to recover from the ordeal of the preceding winter – it was also necessary to make preparations for the winter to come, especially as the attempts to break the siege ring had failed. There were several key areas that had to be addressed, and Zhdanov turned to these problems with his usual energy. It proved to be possible to address two issues at the same time: the shortage of fuel and the dilapidated state of many of the city's buildings. Structures that were too badly damaged were torn down and any timber stockpiled as fuel, or used to repair other buildings in order to make them warmer and more weatherproof. Large quantities of firewood and peat were gathered during the summer months, but whilst this might allow people to warm their apartments by using their stoves, it did little to solve the problems of the factories and other large buildings that needed coal or fuel oil. Coal was therefore shipped across Lake Ladoga and stockpiled, and in order to address fuel oil shortages, engineers created a pipeline that was laid across the floor of Lake Ladoga, running for 22 miles. From mid-June onwards, this supplied Leningrad with an impressive 300 tons of fuel per day. Electrical cables were also run under the lake, allowing the power station at Volkhov – heavily damaged by German air and artillery attacks, but still functioning – to transmit electrical power to the city.[6]

The scale of repairs needed to curb the spread of disease and to ensure the continuing survival of the population – particularly into another winter – was immense. Nearly half a million yards of water and sewage pipes were repaired, and over 6,000 wrecked buildings were restored at least to a standard at which they could be inhabited. Combined with the evacuation of tens of thousands of civilians, the result was that the city would be in a far better position to survive another winter than it had been in late 1941.

As the ice of Lake Ladoga thawed in the spring of 1942, the ships of the Lake Ladoga Flotilla made preparations to resume convoys. The facilities at the western shore, near Osinovets, needed to be upgraded, particularly with respect to ship repair capabilities. The workforce of the new repair teams was drawn partly from Leningrad itself, and partly from personnel brought in over the lake. At first, the work capacity of these teams was limited as much by the semi-starved state of many of the workers as the lack of facilities, but matters improved steadily throughout 1942.

In addition to providing food and fuel for Leningrad itself, the transport units of the Lake Ladoga Flotilla had to convey huge quantities of military materiel into the siege perimeter. As the ice broke up on the lake in April 1942, temporarily disrupting all movement across its surface, plans were drawn up for the coming year. The daily shipment of 2,500 tons of food and 100 tons of coal would be sufficient to feed and warm both the civilian and military population of the besieged city, but in addition to this targets were set for other categories. At least 300 tons of ammunition were to be transported into Leningrad every day over Lake Ladoga, together with reinforcements for the divisions of Leningrad Front. The returning vessels would take with them up to 3,000 evacuees per day. In order to cope with this anticipated traffic, work teams expanded the wharfs that had been constructed the previous winter while they waited for the ice to thaw completely, and through a combination of ship repair and new construction, the transport capacity of the Lake Ladoga Flotilla was increased steadily. As the last week of May 1942 began, it was possible to start movement across the lake. Captain Viktor Sergeyevich Cherokov was the commander of the flotilla at the time, and was in Kobona on the eastern shore of Lake Ladoga when the first attempt to make a crossing after the ice broke up took place:

> On 22 May, with a group of officers from the headquarters of the flotilla and members of the Northwest River Shipping Agency, I arrived at the new wharfs in Kobona to inspect the icebreaker tug *Gidrotekhnik*, which was going to make the first voyage by the most direct route. It was commanded by an experienced captain … Breaking through the ice, sometimes creating a channel with dynamite and pickaxes, the tugboat crew had taken almost a day to travel from the western shore of the lake to the east (in clear water, a ship could cover the distance of about 30km in less than two hours) … We greeted the arrival of the ship with great joy.
>
> A few days later, the gunboats *Selemdzha*, *Burya*, and *Nora*, five minesweepers and the small freighter *Vilsand* arrived in Kobona, forcing their way through large chunks of broken ice … There was heavy fog across the lake and one by one, the ships departed from the moorings. They carried hundreds of tons of food. Their decks were crowded with soldiers and officers being sent

to the west coast – replenishments for Leningrad Front and the Baltic Fleet. On 28 May, the first convoy of ships, many of them towed, reached Osinovets with cargo for Leningrad.[7]

The fog kept German aircraft from interfering, but three days later the weather changed and clearer conditions prevailed. Throughout the preceding months, the Red Army had been building up its anti-aircraft defences around Leningrad and the docks on Lake Ladoga, and these now came into action. Cherokov witnessed the first German air attack of the season:

> We were in the control room in Kobona when 70 enemy bombers and 24 fighters appeared overhead … Anti-aircraft gunners in the port and on the ships engaged them with heavy fire. Their well-directed barrage forced many aircraft to turn away from their attack runs. Some of the ships on the lake avoided bombs by fast manoeuvres. But nevertheless the enemy managed to destroy two piers and some barges and tugboats were damaged. Captain-Lieutenant Zhukov, an artilleryman aboard the gunboat *Nora*, was killed. *Bureya* suffered particularly badly due to a direct hit and several of the crew were killed. The ship's commander, Captain-Lieutenant Dudnik, an outstanding and courageous officer, was seriously wounded. The gunboat division commander, Captain 2nd Class Ozarovsky, was also wounded.[8]

Nikolai Yurevich Ozarovsky had been appointed commander of the gunboat flotilla at the beginning of the war. *Bureya* was built in Germany before the conflict as a dredger with a displacement of 1,000 tons, but was then converted to her war role. Although she lacked the clean lines of a fast gunboat, her intended role as a dredger meant that she was solidly built and her twin diesel engines gave her considerable power and endurance. Ozarovsky and his fellow officers oversaw the conversion from dredger to gunboat and their first experience of combat came in August 1941 when they were escorting a group of vessels carrying troops to Leningrad and they came under air attack. On occasion, the ship's powerful engines meant that she could tow barges as well as provide armed security. Ozarovsky later described the attack that damaged the ship:

> I had gone to the pier to confirm the start time of loading. Unexpectedly, enemy planes flew over and began to bomb the port. The ships opened fire. The first bombs fell to the right of the gunboat *Nora*. One bomb fell on the pier. *Nora* pulled away in reverse, retreating quickly to the roadstead. She was surrounded by

columns of water and smoke from the explosions. Rushing to the gunboat *Bureya* to hasten her departure from the pier, I ran into the dockworkers who had fled to the bomb shelter. There was a howling from the stabilising fins of falling bombs.

Something hit me in the leg. The pier was blocked with wreckage from an explosion, I had to find a way through on the remaining intact logs and boards. At that moment a bomb hit *Bureya* on the port side amidships, in front of the bridge. I gave up trying to find an intact route and, balancing on a swaying, burning timber, I ran up to *Bureya* and jumped aboard with the help of one of the crew.

There were light anti-aircraft guns on the forecastle. The commander of the anti-aircraft battery, Lieutenant Popov, bellowed commands energetically, his face covered in blood. A week ago I had scolded him for his sluggish orders – now his voice rose above the noise of battle.

The Nazi Ju-88 planes made a fresh attack on the ships, piers, and warehouses along the coast. They dropped bombs from shallow dives or level flight at an altitude of 200–300m. One plane, diving at *Bureya*, was at the bottom of its curve when it came under concentrated fire from the gunboat's defences. Several shells exploded along the fuselage of the bomber. The bomber plunged into the shallows at an angle of 70°. Its tail with the black and white swastika remained above water.

To get to the bridge, I went to the starboard poop. The radio operator Moseikov was lying by the rickety ladder to the bridge, his eyes closed and looking as if he were asleep, but his sleep was eternal. The bridge and adjacent radio room were wrecked. The smell of black powder wafted from the bridge doors as cartridges in the flares box were alight. The steel sheet on the front of the bridge had been thrown forward. Steam belched from several broken pipes. There was a constant whistling … The First Officer, Lieutenant Tomigas, appeared in a burnt padded jacket. He told me of the damage to the ship and our losses, and that a repair team was working on extinguishing the fires.

'Where's the ship's commander? What's wrong with him?' I asked.

'He's badly wounded.'

We went down below decks. Lieutenant Commander Dudnik, the commander of *Bureya*, was lying on a sheepskin coat that had been spread out on steel bars laid on the main engine. He tried to raise himself to make his report.

'No report is needed, Anatoly Ivanovich,' I said, 'Please, lie back.'[9]

Bureya settled in the shallow waters, and the crew repaired the holes in her hull before the Germans could take advantage of the ship's immobility and destroy her. On 29 March, *Bureya* was refloated and towed to safety.

The generally improved anti-aircraft positions both on the shores of Lake Ladoga and in Leningrad itself were more than merely an irritation for the Luftwaffe; the density of fire from the defences was such that Leningrad was soon ranked by Luftwaffe crews alongside three other unpopular targets – London, Moscow, and Malta – which collectively became known to Luftwaffe personnel as the 'two Ls and two Ms'. Bombing raids against these were increasingly associated with a high risk of being hit. Mass raids began to prove counterproductive – Soviet ground observers established a network of aircraft spotting posts, which would report large German formations as soon as they were detected crossing the front line, thus alerting anti-aircraft defences further to the rear.

But as was the case with tank warfare, the Soviet fighter units were hampered by pre-war thinking and doctrine that prevented them from making the best use of their resources, including a problem that was almost unique to the Soviet Air Force, as Petr Lvovich Roitberg, a fighter pilot, later recalled:

> The lack of two-way radio equipment made control of aircraft very difficult. The pilots could hear ground controllers but could not reply and were powerless to report the situation or to ask for support. This problem was partly remedied by the organisation of remote control stations. These were placed immediately in the location that was to be protected, or aboard one of the warships of the Ladoga Flotilla if cooperation with shipping was required. This made it possible to observe the actions of our aircraft, to see the situation in the air, and call up aircraft from airfields in a timely manner to help the air patrols.[10]

From their small strip of the coast of Lake Ladoga near Shlisselburg, the Germans operated a small group of vessels. These included the Italian *XII Squadriglia Motoscafi Armati Siluranti* ('12th Torpedo Armed Motorboat Squadron'). This Italian force had four small vessels of 20 tons, equipped with powerful 2,000hp engines, giving them high performance and speed. Their armament of two torpedo launchers and a 20mm gun made them formidable opponents, but they were light with little or no armour and struggled in rough water. In addition, the Germans had several other vessels, many of a much larger size – some consisted of two barge or boat hulls laid in catamaran fashion with a deck built on top, bearing heavy weapons including 88mm guns, 105mm howitzers and mortars, and light armour. However, the naval forces of the Germans and their Italian ally were limited by the ability to transfer such vessels to Lake Ladoga – all boats had to be brought to Shlisselburg overland and launched from there, and many of the German vessels were either improvised, or were little more than military ferries.

The *Marinefährpram* ('naval ferry barge') was a flat-bottomed boat of about 220 tons, originally designed for the invasion of Britain in 1940 and intended to transport small groups of men or limited equipment, but some were converted into *Artilleriefähre* ('artillery carriers') with two 88mm guns and several smaller calibre anti-aircraft cannon. As a result of the presence of this threat, most Soviet traffic on the lake was escorted by armed vessels, but single boats often risked a crossing without protection, particularly at night.

The German and Italian vessels operated out of Shlisselburg, their coming and going closely monitored by the Red Army – a small garrison was stationed in the Oreshek Fortress, on a small island immediately off the coast where the Neva flows out of Lake Ladoga. From May 1942, Finnish vessels operated from ports further north. There were frequent attempts by both the Germans and the Finns to lay mines in the lake, either by boat or from the air, but Soviet traffic continued to flow across the lake in both directions with few interruptions.

As plans for *Nordlicht* were repeatedly postponed, an alternative solution to tightening the siege was proposed. There were several islands in Lake Ladoga and if a German presence could be established on at least one island, it could have a severely disruptive effect on Soviet traffic across the lake – a German force on an island could monitor shipping more effectively, and the Germans would then be able to mount attacks on the ships or could anticipate the moment of their arrival in port and could thus carry out bombing raids that would seek to destroy the Soviet vessels and their cargoes while they were stationary. After considering several options, the Germans decided to make an attempt to land troops on the small island of Sukho, a tiny body of land just 50 yards across. This was ideally situated close to the main convoy route, its lighthouse serving as a useful navigation aid for Soviet shipping even if it was no longer lit. The operation was codenamed *Brasil*, and would involve the use of a substantial part of the German and Italian shipping available.

The original date for the operation was 9 October, but dense fog banks made Luftwaffe cooperation impossible and the ships were ordered to turn back; they then ran into a small group of Soviet vessels and there was a brief but fierce exchange of fire, as a result of which each side suffered the loss of one boat. After further delays due to persistent fog, a second attempt was made 12 days later. As it grew dark on 21 October, Korvettenkapitän Hans Joachim von Ramm led the force out once more, a small fleet consisting of his headquarters barge, a military ferry carrying command elements for the landing party, a medical ferry, three supply ferries, and seven ferries carrying infantry. There were also 11 *Artilleriefähre*, seven equipped with heavy weapons and four with lighter guns; in addition, one of the Italian torpedo boats accompanied the group, while two more Italian boats patrolled the waters of Lake Ladoga to the south, between Sukho and the southern shore.

Moving cautiously – the military ferries could only achieve a speed of 10 knots when empty, and were slower when carrying a full load – Ramm's group moved north during the evening and night, approaching Sukho the following morning. The weather had deteriorated during the night and visibility was poor, resulting in the fleet not being detected until it was just a short distance offshore. Ivan Konstantinovich Gusev was a platoon commander in the coastal battery on Sukho and he described the beginning of the German attack, shortly after dawn:

> I went down to the shore of the bay to wash. At that moment, the watch signalman reported that a convoy of ships was visible to the south, in the direction of Novaya Ladoga. Suddenly, quite unexpectedly, a shell exploded a few metres from the shore. What a shock! I immediately shouted orders to the radio operator to inform the flotilla headquarters that the enemy was shelling the island …
>
> At 0720 we started a battle with the enemy ships, whose firepower was many times superior to our battery. At first we fired only with our second and third guns, as there were no targets in the arc covered by the first gun. The Nazi ships opened a rapid fire trying to suppress the battery. Exploding shells smashed boulders and fragments rained down on us, together with the enemy's bullets … Two tall wooden poles supporting the battery radio antenna were swept away by shellfire in the first minutes of the battle. Involuntarily, I thought, 'Did the radio operators manage to transmit a report about the enemy attack to the flotilla headquarters?' As it turned out, they didn't have enough time.[11]

Fortunately for Gusev and his little garrison, a vessel of the Soviet Lake Ladoga Flotilla was nearby. Built in Estonia in 1900, the diminutive *Aunus* was a vessel of just 1000 tons, with a coal-fired boiler. After Finland gained independence in the wake of the First World War, *Aunus* fell into Finnish hands and was converted into a gunboat and deployed on Lake Ladoga, where she became a Soviet possession after the Winter War between Finland and the Soviet Union and was renamed *TShch-100* and used as a minesweeper. The captain of the minesweeper was Petr Konstantinovich Nargin; he had been in command since the beginning of the war, and in the summer of 1941 he engaged Finnish shore batteries on the northern coast of Lake Ladoga. In one such action, his vessel took several hits, resulting in heavy casualties amongst the crew. After this engagement, *TShch-100* was rebuilt with somewhat improved weaponry, but she remained without any meaningful armour.

Early on 22 October, *TShch-100* was drifting silently on Lake Ladoga to the south of Sukho; the vessel and its crew were listening for the sound of approaching aircraft or surface ships. One of the men on watch caught the distinctive sound of diesel engines. The alarm was raised a few minutes before Gusev's guns opened fire on the German vessels and Nargin promptly informed higher commands in an uncoded transmission, judging that the delay spent in encrypting the message was too long. Immediately, shells began to land in the water around the minesweeper, which continued to transmit updates.

It was fortunate that the minesweeper raised the alarm. Four German aircraft joined the attack and many of the Soviet defenders on the island were killed or wounded by the combination of shellfire, bombs, and machine-gun attacks by the aircraft; Gusev was injured by glass splinters that lacerated his face. The fire of the shore batteries was, however, effective at first, and two German ships were hit and left ablaze, but half of Gusev's men were dead or wounded in a relatively short time and the first assault craft soon approached the shore. This landing attempt was repulsed, but a second landing was more successful, with about 70 German soldiers coming ashore, and Sukho's rapidly diminishing garrison pulled back to the lighthouse at the centre of the little island.

Still exchanging fire with German vessels, the minesweeper *TShch-100* edged closer to Sukho, attempting to prevent further landings. An assault craft was hit as it approached the shore, but Nargin and his crew were now under heavy fire. Fortunately for them, reinforcements arrived in the shape of a smaller vessel, which succeeded in laying down a smokescreen. On the island, Gusev was wounded a second time, this time in the stomach, but Soviet fighter aircraft suddenly intervened, driving off the German planes overhead. As more Soviet patrol craft began to appear, the Germans abandoned their landing attempt and evacuated the troops that had been put ashore. The result of the landing attempt was an unqualified defeat for the Germans with heavy losses, as a report later described:

> Sandbanks that were not marked on maps resulted in one light [artillery] ferry running aground. Two ferries that were summoned to pull it free were also run aground by large waves, as was an infantry ferry, which it was possible to refloat later. After removing and throwing overboard the breechblocks of the guns and the evacuation of their crews, two light ferries and a heavy ferry were destroyed with demolition charges and gunfire.

During the landing of the raiding party, a light ferry took a direct hit, resulting in heavy losses. Until the commencement of the withdrawal, losses were as follows: 18 dead; 22 severely wounded; 21 lightly wounded. In addition, during the withdrawal a heavy ferry that could no longer be kept afloat as a result of enemy fire from ships and aircraft was abandoned and destroyed. The crew was evacuated. Similarly, an infantry boat had to be abandoned after its personnel were taken off.

The flotilla was in constant combat with enemy land, sea, and air units from 0614 to about 1500. From our observations and those of our aircraft, two significant hits were recorded on [enemy] gunboats. Judging by the explosions, the enemy fired ... with guns of 100–130mm calibre. As a result of their greater speed, the enemy was largely able to surround our force and bring it under concentrated fire from long range.

The flotilla and our fighter aircraft sustained a total of 20 hits, of which four were on Finnish fighters, 11 on German fighters, and five on the ferry flotilla. The deployed fighter aircraft gave the flotilla no significant support against the superior enemy guns.

The weather forecast was completely different from the actual weather conditions during the operation. Instead of the expected favourable conditions, the reality was an unfavourable situation.[12]

The entire operation seems to have been poorly conceived and handled from a German perspective. It was certainly within the resources of the local German forces to organise better air support and it should therefore have been possible to overcome the defenders on the island. But if the attack had been successful, the Germans would have faced difficulties in ensuring that any garrison they established was then adequately supplied through the winter. Eleven of the German and Finnish aircraft that sustained damage were destroyed. In addition, the Soviet forces captured 61 Germans, a mixture of men left behind on Sukho and a few rescued from sinking vessels. It was the last significant operation by German and Italian shipping on Lake Ladoga. The surviving vessels were soon withdrawn; the four Italian boats were deployed in the Gulf of Finland to the north of Estonia, and after the collapse of Mussolini's government were handed over to the Finns.

The Soviet transport programme over Lake Ladoga during 1942 after the spring thaw proved to be highly effective, shipping nearly 800,000 tons of cargo and about 310,000 military personnel from starting points at Gostinopol and Kobona to Osinovets. Timber was usually transported by making huge rafts of logs, which were then towed; this slowed the towing vessels considerably and wasn't possible in rough weather. The ships also carried livestock – about 15,000 horses, cattle, and sheep were delivered to Leningrad during 1942. In order to facilitate movement of people and goods between Leningrad and the growing port facilities on the west coast of the lake, railway lines were improved considerably – an additional mile of railway was constructed over swampy ground at Osinovets using a special narrow gauge, built mainly during the interval between the ice road becoming unusable in the spring of 1942 and the resumption of shipping. The first major transfer of civilians from Leningrad to the port area using the new railway facilities took place on 28 May, with a fraction under 400 people reaching Lake Ladoga, and as ships began to move people from Osinovets to the eastern shore, the numbers increased rapidly. By 3 June, the daily total was in excess of 2,500, rising to nearly 8,000 per day in July. But as is often the case, the improvement of one part of an overall process highlighted bottlenecks elsewhere. The narrow gauge railway was the best option given the soft ground and the limited resources available, but there were few railway wagons of an appropriate gauge and until more were built, the new line was not used to full capacity. The limited facilities for loading civilians aboard ships returning to the eastern shore and poor coordination between the number of berths available and the transfer of civilians from Leningrad to Osinovets often resulted in large numbers of people being left waiting in and around Osinovets, and German air raids of the area resulted in considerable civilian casualties. Special services had to be created to deal with children who became separated from parents, under the control of Aleksei Nikolayevich Kosygin, the future Cold War statesman; he urged officials to ensure better nutrition for children, and to try to provide them with sweets. A makeshift medical centre was established so that refugees who were too weak to travel could be brought back to a sufficient level of health for the crossing. Over 500,000 evacuees were ultimately brought to the east bank of Lake Ladoga, together with nearly 300,000 tons of factory equipment that was sent to the new industrial centres near the Ural Mountains.[13]

Unlike the first winter of the siege, the lake remained navigable right to the end of the year, even if ships had to dodge ice floes for much of the crossing; a little to the south of the convoy route, the ice was thick and continuous enough for a road to be created for truck traffic. Unable to complete their plans for *Nordlicht* and lacking the resources to destroy Leningrad by air and artillery attacks – particularly as the growing crisis in and around Stalingrad meant that the northern sector was assigned a far lower priority in terms of supplies – the Germans could do no more than sit back and continue their attempts to starve the city and its defenders, but this was now a much harder task. The civilian population of Leningrad was reduced to 700,000; combined with an estimated garrison of 420,000, this was a far more manageable number of people to feed, particularly as the careful cultivation of every available square metre of land in Leningrad meant that vegetable supplies lasted well into the autumn, thus allowing shipments to concentrate on building up stockpiles for the winter. The first winter of the siege had been a terrible ordeal, not least because even by the standards of these northern latitudes, it had been particularly severe; by contrast, the winter of 1942–43 was far milder. Combined with a smaller population, this meant that less fuel was needed for heating. And the experiences of the previous year meant that all aspects of the Soviet operation to sustain Leningrad progressed far more efficiently. People continued to die, but it was more due to illness and the residual effects of the previous year's starvation than a new surge caused by hunger.

In the area behind the German front line, the partisans of the Leningrad region continued their operations. The extensive anti-partisan sweeps of late 1941, combined with winter conditions, resulted in a considerable reduction in partisan activity. There were sporadic attacks against German supply lines and rear area units, but either these were not coordinated with Red Army attacks or they were too weak to have much of an impact; an exception was the Soviet attacks to the south of Novgorod around Demyansk. But the reduced partisan activity also resulted in a slackening in German repression with units being sent back to the front line to defend against Volkhov Front's assaults. The partisans used this opportunity to reorganise their groups. In order to reduce the risk of detection, the partisans now often functioned in smaller groups, usually fewer than a dozen men, only forming larger formations when an operation required such strength. There was better, more centralised control, with the Communist Party and the Red Army both playing a role and cooperating far more than they had in 1941. Just how effective these partisans were is debatable – Soviet sources claimed that during 1942, the partisans killed or wounded 15,000 German soldiers and destroyed over 100 bridges, 26 supply dumps, and large numbers of tanks, aircraft and trucks.[14] One particularly effective attack took place at Dedovichi in February 1942; the partisans claimed to have killed 650 Germans and destroyed a railway bridge and large stockpiles of ammunition, in return for the loss of 58 partisans killed and 72 wounded.[15]

On occasion, the Germans were successful in subverting partisan groups and a few units operated ostensibly as partisans but actually helping the German occupiers, and fearing such infiltration, the new command structures for the partisan movement often treated many of those under their control with suspicion. Afanasyev, who had been acting as a partisan officer for several months, encountered a partisan group led by 'Senior Sergeant Buchnev'. The group seemed to be made up entirely of Red Army personnel who had been left behind and were well armed with automatic weapons – most partisans either lacked these guns, or were cautious about using them because of their high rate of ammunition consumption. Buchnev and his group departed the village where Afanasyev was currently staying:

At noon [the same day], I was brought a radio message from brigade headquarters signed by Vasilyev [commander of 2nd Partisan Brigade]. It was addressed to all commanders and commissars of partisan detachments and other units operating independently in the region. It was an order that in the event of encountering Buchnev's detachment, we should disarm the entire group and arrest Buchnev together with his commissar ... and deliver both under escort to brigade headquarters.

A lot of questions swirled in my head. Buchnev hadn't aroused any suspicions in me, but on the other hand, arrest orders were not given out indiscriminately, which meant – what, exactly? Why did the squad need to be disarmed? If this group was dangerous, how dangerous was it? If we were to encounter them again by chance, would it be necessary to turn our weapons against them? But the radio message didn't answer any of these questions. To an extent, the only reassurance was that there was no talk of arresting the fighters of the detachment – they were only to be disarmed. Much was still obscure. But we immediately radioed headquarters to tell them about the recent meeting with Buchnev and our readiness to follow orders strictly in the event of his reappearance.

A few days later, Buchnev's detachment again entered the territory controlled by our regiment. It was necessary to act.

Intelligence reported that the detachment had settled down to rest in the village of Maryni, about 15km from us. I ordered Aleksei Ivanovich Pushkin, who was from the special department [i.e. NKVD] to go to Buchnev and order him to come to regiment headquarters. Soon, Buchnev and his commissar joined me, with his detachment in the street outside our headquarters, not really knowing what was happening but clearly suspecting something was wrong. Buchnev was also alarmed but tried to remain calm.

When I prepared for this meeting, I particularly feared a clash of arms – who knew what crimes had resulted in the order to arrest Buchnev, perhaps he had nothing to lose! Of course, despite its armament, this group stood no chance against the entire regiment, but there would be casualties. We had to try to solve the problem without resort to weapons, and I took every precaution.

I decided to talk to Buchnev and his commissar personally. Before they arrived, I deliberately placed my weapons, as if by chance, in plain sight, but away from the table where he was sitting. I ordered Tsvetkov to stand outside the door with a machine-gun and to shoot at their left if complications arose. And now there were the three of us in the room, with Buchnev's detachment chatting under the windows.

I was sitting at the table while Buchnev and his commissar stood about five paces from me, since I didn't invite them to sit down. Calmly, as if talking about some everyday triviality, I said, 'I received an order from brigade headquarters for your arrest.' I saw how Buchnev tensed up and put his hand on his gun. Turning my head to the window, I stood slowly, looking out onto the street, pausing, and only then turned to look at the pair standing in front of me. I wanted them to see that I was unarmed. I saw Buchnev glance at my submachine-gun, which was propped in the far corner, and belt lying next to him on the bench with the pistol handle sticking from its holster. Buchnev calmed a little and I continued, 'Your detachment has been ordered to disarm. As a military man, you understand of course that this order will be obeyed. I suggest you surrender your weapons first.'

Silence hung in the air, broken only by the clock on the wall, its pendulum clicking regularly. Buchnev suddenly burst out, 'For what?' He was almost shouting. 'Why are we being arrested? Do you know why?'

'I don't know,' I interrupted him. 'There is nothing about that in the order. There's no need to raise your voice.'

At this point, the commissar spoke up. 'There must be some kind of mistake, Comrade Commander,' he boomed. 'We've just come from battle. We hit the Fritzes! Maybe it's not about us?'

He spoke confidently enough, yet I felt that both of the men standing before me knew of some guilt behind them, though I couldn't imagine what it was. I replied, 'There is no mistake. It clearly said Buchnev's detachment.'[16]

After a tense few moments, Buchnev's detachment was disarmed. He and his commissar were dispatched under escort to higher headquarters, but were later returned to their detachment; Afanasyev was informed that the incident had arisen because Buchnev had previously refused to place his men under the command of another group. In circumstances of mutual suspicion and fear, the incident might have ended far more violently. A few weeks later, Afanasyev's partisans encountered more suspicious characters:

Two men were brought to regimental headquarters from one of our checkpoints – according to their statements, they were looking for partisans so that they could join our ranks. They were aged about 20, and God had given them good health and strength and they both made a good impression. But there was one detail in their story that made us wary. According to them, they came from distant villages – it was likely that we wouldn't know them. But as it happened, our regiment had been in that area at the end of March and according to the information we had gathered at the time, both named villages were real hornets' nests of traitors. This often happened – entire villages, like individual people, could suffer from serious vices. But it is difficult to explain the shameful mark of betrayal.

With regard to these two individuals who came to us, one could be mistaken. After all, even if it was known that nine out of ten inhabitants of a village were traitors, who would raise a hand to hang a label on the tenth on the sole basis that the others were criminals? We couldn't do that, but nor did we suffer from excessive gullibility …

Several days passed and Aleksei Ivanovich Pushkin, using his authority in the special department, placed a photograph before me: our two new acquaintances were in a group of laughing young adults. And they were all wearing Hitler's uniforms. It was of course foolish to take such a 'visiting card' with you to the partisans, but it was hardly my position to answer for the errors of our enemies.

Their task was to penetrate the ranks of the regiment and to supply the Nazis with information about our forces, weapons, plans, and operations. Later, Pushkin tried to use the mailbox they revealed to misinform the enemy, but I can't recall if this was successful. And the ultimate goal of these two bastards was the physical destruction of the regiment command post, then the brigade command post.

In those days, betrayal was stopped in one way: by a bullet.[17]

Afanasyev's memoirs portray him acting with caution and prudence, but on many occasions, people were executed – by either side – purely on suspicion, without any firm evidence of their allegiance to the opposing forces. It seems unlikely that these men would have carried such an incriminating photograph with them, and this little embellishment may have been added by Afanasyev as justification for acting against them.

In May, German forces moved to suppress the partisans in the region to the southwest of Lake Ilmen, where Afanasyev was operating. Several villages in the area were under partisan control and the Germans made several attacks with mixed results, and when they encountered more determined resistance, they adopted tactics that were becoming all too familiar:

As a rule, our persecutors adopted offensive tactics of a barbarously simple design ... They approached to about a kilometre from the village under attack, and then brought up their guns for direct fire and shelled the roofs of the houses. At that time, houses in the Pskov region were usually roofed with straw and it was very easy to set them on fire. The village started to burn. It was impossible to remain in it and the defences that had been previously prepared were now unusable. At this point, [enemy] tanks moved into action, accompanied by several groups of infantry.

The attackers weren't interested in the villages themselves: they sought to clear the territory of partisans and what remained afterwards was of no concern to them. They often didn't capture villages, rather the ashes and ruins that had been abandoned by the population, in which stoves and chimneys rose like monuments in graveyards, and heaps of ash and wreckage and the remains of destroyed possessions were like grave mounds. What could we do to oppose the enemy, when our regiment's entire artillery consisted of one small-calibre gun without gunsights and a single unreliable anti-tank rifle?[18]

Instead of fighting an unequal battle, Afanasyev's partisans withdrew and waited for the Germans to move on before attacking them from behind. When the Germans turned to drive them off, the partisans pulled back once more, and the pursuing German vehicles then found themselves in a minefield that the partisans had hastily laid. Such actions did little to alter the outcome of the big battles raging to the east, but they tied down large numbers of German troops in inconclusive fighting in a vast landscape.

As the weather improved in the summer of 1942, partisan activity grew more troublesome for the Germans all along the Eastern Front. Following the well-established pattern of Soviet industry before the war, high commands set the partisans targets of numbers of German soldiers, vehicles, trains etc. that were to be destroyed each month, encouraging each group to try to out-perform other groups. Like other partisan units, Afanasyev's regiment submitted monthly reports listing the achievements of each of its subordinate groups, ranking them according to their 'scores'. The activities of individual partisans were also recorded in a competitive manner. Such reports were almost certainly exaggerated – after all, there was little or no chance of them being checked with any accuracy – and the partisan commanders who received the reports probably added further exaggerations when they sent summaries to higher commands. The result was the improbably large numbers of soldiers killed and bridges, trains, and ammunition dumps destroyed that were circulated after the war to show just how effective the partisan movement had been. But the movement was portrayed as an important demonstration of the will of the ordinary people of the Soviet Union to oppose the Fascist invaders and critical consideration of the claims of its effectiveness remains controversial even today.

The rising tide of partisan activity resulted in a new order from Hitler in mid-August, urging greater energy in dealing with the 'bandits' in the occupied territories. The directive stated that partisan activity was increasing to an unacceptable level and it was essential to suppress it prior to the onset of winter. To that end, military forces were to coordinate their efforts more effectively. Hitler stressed the importance of anti-partisan warfare, showing unusual awareness of the need to avoid alienating local people and perhaps recognising the counterproductive outcomes of operations like the one described by Afanasyev:

> The fight against banditry is as much a matter of strategy as the fight against the enemy at the front. It is therefore to be organised and conducted by the same staff groups.
>
> The destruction of the bandits requires active operations and the most severe measures against all members of their groups or those guilty of supporting them ...
>
> The confidence of the local population in German authority is to be gained by strict but just conduct.
>
> The destruction of bandit groups requires the local population to be assured of the minimum needs for life. If this fails or – particularly importantly – available supplies are not distributed fairly, the consequence will be more recruits for the bandits.
>
> The cooperation of the local population is indispensable in the fight against the bandits. Persons who deserve recognition should not be treated cheaply; rewards should be as attractive as possible. On the other hand, reprisals for those who act in support of the bandits must be even more severe [than before].
>
> Misplaced confidence in the local population, particularly in individuals working for the German authorities, must be strictly avoided. Even though the majority of the population is opposed to the bandits, there will always be spies who are active, and whose task is to inform the bandits of all plans of operations against them.[19]

The directive continued with instructions for the deployment of security divisions and the recruitment of local groups, though Hitler stressed that these local groups were not to be deployed in the front line and care had to be taken to prevent 'members of the former intelligentsia' from joining the ranks of armed groups – the last thing that the Germans wanted was for these groups to become potential sources of resistance. Non-military German personnel – members of the railway services, agricultural staff, men working in the *Reichsarbeitsdienst* ('Reich Labour Service') – were to be armed as effectively as possible.

In response to this directive, Army Group North organised several operations to try to stamp down on the partisans. In the late summer of 1942, large parts of 218th Infantry Division were deployed to the southwest of Lake Ilmen in an operation that involved about 6,000 troops. Fighting lasted for several weeks, often taking the form of battles to recapture territory that had been overrun the previous year – on the opening day of the operation, the German units moved forward on a broad front, capturing about five miles of ground. Regardless of Hitler's instructions about the 'indispensable' nature of local cooperation, farms and villages were left ablaze across the entire region. Afanasyev was summoned back to his brigade headquarters in the midst of the fighting and tasked with constructing a formal defensive line, but the weight of German attacks was too heavy and the partisans were forced to commence a full evacuation in order to escape complete destruction. Over the weeks that followed, the remnants of Afanasyev's regiment moved slowly to the west, continuing to carry out attacks on railway lines and other targets when opportunities arose.

When fighting died down in September, much of the local area had been depopulated. As a result, the partisans were driven from the area, moving either northeast towards Novgorod or west towards Ostrov. Much as Hitler had warned, the indiscriminate destruction of villages and the killing of thousands of civilians proved to be counterproductive and most of the surviving population either became supporters of the partisans, or actually took up arms against the Germans. The growing intensity of fighting in the front line and the constantly rising death toll meant that it became almost impossible for the Wehrmacht to conduct anti-partisan operations on this scale in the months that followed, resulting in the partisan movement growing in strength and confidence. After finally escaping across the front line to safety, Afanasyev's unit was replenished and sent back into action in December 1942. The territory in which it had been active earlier in the year now had a very different and desolate appearance, not purely because of winter:

We walked through forests, through swamps, through villages in which every house was known to us. It was a sad march.

Almost all the villages in our path were abandoned. And what remained of them? Ashes, charred chimneys sticking up here and there, trees blackened by fire. In some places there were dogs that couldn't comprehend that all the people had gone and continued to wait for them, trying to keep up their usual tasks of guarding. But what could they guard? And from whom?[20]

The year was drawing to an end; here in the northern sector, it marked the close of an inconclusive period. Little had changed on the battlefield, but both sides had suffered heavy losses and seen their plans fail. The German plans to starve Leningrad to death failed in the face of desperate improvisation and stubborn determination to survive; subsequent plans to renew offensive operations and create a tighter siege perimeter – something that could have been achieved with comparatively little additional effort or delay in late 1941 – were abandoned in the face of rising casualties and the great crisis that developed in and around Stalingrad. For the Red Army, the year had been one of frustration, with repeated attempts to break the siege ring failing in the face of tough German defences, terrain that was hugely unfavourable for offensive operations, and the great mismatch in expertise between the two sides. The likely direction of any Soviet attack was easily anticipated by the defenders, who were then able to concentrate their forces both to blunt any initial attack and to launch counterattacks to restore the front line. The Red Army still had a long distance to travel before it could hope to show the level of tactical and operational expertise that was essential in the era of mechanised warfare, but here in the north the limitations of the battlefield ensured that further operations to break through to Leningrad would be repetitions of the slow, bloody grinding battles of 1942.

CHAPTER 14

A BITTER STALEMATE

The year of 1942 saw terrible battles along the entire length of the Eastern Front. The campaign that has dominated most accounts of the conflict in that year unfolded in eastern Ukraine and the Caucasus region, where the German Army Group South – later divided into Army Group A and Army Group B – first defeated an ultimately disastrous Red Army counteroffensive under the command of Timoshenko near Kharkov and then moved on to strike across the Donets River, reaching the Don River at Voronezh before turning to the southeast. After crossing the Don near the town of Kalach the Germans pushed on to their objective at Stalingrad, but this city was originally intended purely as an interim goal. It was to form a bastion to protect the northern flank of the Wehrmacht's drive to the south into the Caucasus, an attempt to capture the oilfields that Hitler regarded as the main objective of the campaign. Denying the Soviet Union access to these fields, he told his generals, would be an irreparable blow to the ability of the Soviet Union to continue the war; at the same time, securing the oilfields would solve the Reich's abiding fuel shortages. Neither of these statements was correct. The Soviet Union was able to use oil from Iran and by the end of the war, the United States had delivered nearly 3 million tons of oil, petroleum, and other oil-based products as part of its huge aid effort – this amounted to nearly 60 per cent of the fuel consumption of Soviet aviation during the conflict.[1] Nor would seizure of Maikop and Grozny have provided the Germans with unlimited oil resources. The former city was captured by the troops of First Panzer Army, but the retreating Soviet forces wrecked the oil facilities before they left and the only oil products that the Germans were able to use were small quantities of fuel left in the storage tanks in the city. Restoring the oil wells to meaningful levels of production would have taken several years.

The southern campaign eventually ground to a halt in the ruins of Stalingrad and the Caucasus Mountains. Arguably, the Wehrmacht had sufficient resources to secure one or other of these objectives, but the pursuit of both at the same time doomed the campaign to failure. For example, the Luftwaffe was able to provide considerable support on either axis, but only at the cost of effectively leaving the other axis unsupported.[2] The fuel shortages that were intended to be solved by the campaign plagued the advance, ultimately contributing indirectly to the disaster that overtook the German Sixth Army at Stalingrad. In an attempt to provide support for the Romanian armies protecting the long northern flank of the German positions in Stalingrad, 22nd Panzer Division was positioned some distance behind the front line, but due to the constant fuel shortages the panzer crews dug in many of their vehicles, lining the compartments with straw to prevent cold and damp penetrating into the interior. Unfortunately, the straw attracted mice, and the rodents chewed through electrical insulation and cables. When the division attempted to move forward to intercept the Soviet assault that would result in the encirclement of Sixth Army, more than half of the division's tanks either couldn't be started or broke down almost as soon as they moved off.

But whilst the great German advances to and over the Don were the most striking phases of the fighting on the Eastern Front in 1942, bitter fighting raged elsewhere. Throughout the year, the Red Army attempted – and failed – to destroy the Rzhev salient to the west of Moscow at a terrible cost. The assaults were made across terrain that was similar to that around the Volkhov River – dominated by swamps and dense forests – with the added disadvantage of numerous hills and ravines. Displaying a degree of stubbornness that is hard to comprehend, Soviet forces were pitched repeatedly into action against strong, well-prepared German defences that had been established and then strengthened over several months. Hundreds of thousands of men perished for no gain. After the war, Soviet accounts either ignored these battles or attempted to portray them as an essential part of the process that weakened the Wehrmacht, and the final battles of the autumn and winter of 1942 around the Rzhev salient – a wide-ranging operation codenamed *Mars* – were later interpreted as an integral part of *Uranus*, the encirclement of the German Sixth Army at Stalingrad. Zhukov (the creator and overseer of *Mars*) claimed that it was a deliberate attempt to tie down large numbers of German troops in the central sector, thus preventing them from intervening further south.[3] But in reality, *Mars* was little more than a manifestation of Zhukov's obsession with destroying a salient that appeared to threaten Moscow, and – on maps at least – looked vulnerable and an easy target for a Soviet offensive. At best, it could be argued that *Uranus* and *Mars* were conceived as two attacks that might potentially lead to important victories, with the intention being to reinforce whichever succeeded.

In the north, the repeated attempts by the Red Army to break the siege ring around Leningrad were defeated in battles that raged along the line of the Volkhov River and at Sinyavino. These battles were every bit as bloody for both sides as the fighting around the Rzhev salient and in the Stalingrad campaign. The newly formed Second Shock Army was encircled and effectively destroyed twice and other formations suffered huge casualties; but the German successes in stopping these relief attempts came at a considerable price. Losses in the Wehrmacht infantry divisions that endured terrible conditions in the swamps and forests were heavy, contributing to the permanent degradation of German capabilities; and the Germans had to abandon any lingering plans for a renewed advance to achieve a closer encirclement of Leningrad or to attempt the capture of the city. By the end of 1942, even without the huge holes torn in the Eastern Front in and around Stalingrad, the Wehrmacht struggled to field sufficient men to maintain a continuous front line.

Both sides could look back at the period since the commencement of the German invasion with mixed feelings. For the Wehrmacht, the capture of Leningrad had seemed tantalisingly close in late 1941, but Hitler's decision to avoid costly urban fighting stopped the German armies almost at the gates of the city. Had the advance continued, it is highly likely that German divisions would have been drawn into just the sort of bitter streetfighting that Hitler attempted to shun, but it would surely have been within the strength of the Wehrmacht to break through the Soviet lines along the Neva, link up with the Finns to the north, and thus isolate Leningrad from Lake Ladoga. Had such an advance been carried out – perhaps in preference to the attack towards Tikhvin – it seems certain that the Soviet forces that had withdrawn into the siege ring would not have been strong enough to stop such a German advance, and Leningrad would have been starved into submission during the winter of 1941–42. But this is with the benefit of hindsight. At the time, it seemed as if there was sufficient time for an attack to capture Moscow, which surely would inflict a fatal blow upon the Soviet Union. Even when the Germans were defeated in the frozen battlefields around the Soviet capital, the survival of Leningrad through a bitterly cold winter, with few supplies reaching the city from the outside, was an unlikely prospect. Nobody in German circles could have anticipated the extraordinary achievements of the Road of Life and the indomitable spirit of ordinary Leningraders. Even with the supplies that were brought across Lake Ladoga, the city came close to collapse at several stages of the winter. The defiance of the city known to its residents as 'Piter' justly became a symbol of the will of ordinary people to hold out against the Germans.

The German attempt to reach Tikhvin was of limited value unless it was combined with an attack by the Finns from the north. The strategic failure to secure detailed agreement with the Finnish government resulted in the panzer divisions that laboured forward across the snow and ice of northern Russia having to abandon their hard-won gains, and the operation was reduced to little more than a disruptive raid. But despite this failure to coordinate properly with Finnish forces, the Germans continued to expect more from the Finns than was actually being offered. During the planning of *Nordlicht*, there was an assumption both in Army Group North and *OKH* that the Finnish Army would launch complementary attacks to link up with the Wehrmacht to the east of Leningrad, between the city and Lake Ladoga. Such beliefs persisted even though Mannerheim informed Berlin that the Finns would attack with only limited forces, and with the intention of securing only modest gains – this was far short of the level of commitment that the Germans expected and assumed would be provided.[4]

Even if the battlefield barely changed during 1942, the strategic situation for Army Group North worsened considerably. There was a possibility – perhaps a probability – in late 1941 that the physical capture of Leningrad was unnecessary, and that the city would be starved and frozen into submission; a year later, this could no longer be expected. The civilian population of Leningrad had been reduced to a far more manageable total as a result of the deaths of the first winter and the evacuations that took place in the following year, and the stockpiling measures taken during 1942 ensured that whilst there would still be food shortages in the siege perimeter, there was no longer any risk of mass starvation. At the end of 1941, the Red Army's defences facing the Wehrmacht were manned by exhausted troops, demoralised by constant retreats and defeats. The 12 months that followed saw those men recover their strength and resilience. Defensive lines were systematically improved and strengthened resulting in a formidable array of positions that would have to be overrun one by one, and a steady stream of reinforcements further ensured that any German attack towards Leningrad would be a costly and difficult undertaking. Victory via a number of possible routes seemed likely in December 1941 – it was only the diversion of German forces to the central region that brought the advance on Leningrad to a halt, and the plan to starve the city and its defenders to death looked highly likely to succeed. In December 1942, by contrast, there was little or no prospect of decisive victory without major developments elsewhere. Army Group North had suffered heavy losses in its successful defence against Soviet attacks and was too weak to win a decisive victory without reinforcements. The best that the Germans could do was improve their defences in anticipation of further Soviet attacks. Each attack cost the Red Army huge losses, but it must have seemed to the German soldiers that the resources of their enemies were infinite, whereas their own numbers dwindled steadily. Sooner or later, one of these Soviet assaults would break through.

The Red Army that faced the Wehrmacht in late 1942 across the front line in the northern sector was very different from the force that had stood there a year earlier. The huge damage inflicted upon the Soviet military by Stalin's purges continued to have a negative effect, but large numbers of officers and soldiers at every level had spent a tough year learning how to fight. Despite this, many of the mistakes that occurred during 1942 would be repeated in the years that followed. There was growing awareness of the importance of proper preparation, particularly in stockpiling sufficient ammunition and other supplies to maintain an offensive after its initial phase, and the ability of the Soviet war industry to provide those resources improved steadily through the year. However, having better resources was merely the first step. Using those resources effectively was something that would have to improve further if the Red Army was to defeat the Wehrmacht. Although the weight of preparatory artillery bombardments increased steadily throughout 1942, both in the northern sector and elsewhere, a constant criticism in the reports produced after these battles was that much of the fire was poorly targeted. In particular, there was insufficient attention paid to identifying and destroying German positions that could be used to create secondary lines of defence. As a result, even if the Red Army managed to break through the front line, attacks often came to a standstill shortly after.

The remedy for this particular issue was better reconnaissance and intelligence. Since the beginning of the war, the Germans had enjoyed a big advantage in aerial reconnaissance capabilities; the memoirs of Red Army soldiers make frequent mention of German reconnaissance planes appearing with depressing regularity, and their presence was often followed by German shelling. Such close cooperation between air assets and ground troops was beyond the capabilities of Soviet forces in 1942. Many aircraft were equipped with radio receivers but could not transmit information, and the quality of Soviet photo reconnaissance fell far short of the standard routinely achieved by the Luftwaffe. The optical equipment used by German reconnaissance planes was probably superior to that used by any other nation at the time, and by contrast the Soviet forces placed far more emphasis on visual reconnaissance and reports from the aircrews after their return.

As the war progressed, increasing numbers of Soviet aircraft were equipped with radio transmitters as well as receivers, allowing two-way communication, but coordination of ground and air formations continued to lag behind the capabilities of other nations.

Throughout the war, the Red Army made frequent use of raids on opposing positions to capture 'tongues' – enemy soldiers who were taken back to the Soviet lines for interrogation. The information thus acquired was of varying usefulness, often limited to identifying the unit that was occupying the German defences, but occasionally a prisoner had valuable information about positions and fortifications. Reconnaissance missions were mounted with increasing frequency, attempting to infiltrate through the depths of the German positions, and there was also extensive use of the concept of 'reconnaissance in force'. Colonel Maksim Afanasyevich Voloshin, chief of intelligence of the Soviet Thirty-Ninth Army, fighting in the central sector of the Eastern Front, defined this as follows:

> Reconnaissance in force, generally speaking, is active action aimed at fully discovering the enemy's fire system, and clarifying the characteristics of his defences ...
>
> The task was to force the enemy to believe that [the reconnaissance in force] was really an offensive operation, making them use all their firepower and perhaps to bring forward reserves. Having done this, the unit conducting the reconnaissance in force withdrew to its previously occupied positions.[5]

Other armies also used the concept of reconnaissance in force, but although Voloshin went on to describe the special training of the men who would carry out such a reconnaissance, more often than not a front-line battalion was simply ordered to conduct the operation with little or no preparation. Frequently, this resulted in the reconnaissance in force suffering heavy losses without succeeding in gaining very much by way of information. Boris Semenovich Gorbachevsky, an ordinary soldier in the central sector, had a far less favourable – and perhaps more realistic – view of reconnaissance in force than Voloshin:

> How many tragic stories I have heard about reconnaissance in force: How the generals believed in it and valued it highly, and with what horror the soldiers spoke those words – few survived them and it was considered good fortune if they were wounded and dragged back from the battlefield by their comrades ...
>
> The most it could do was clarify the position of the leading edge. With defence in depth and the constant movement of firing points, even this couldn't

be achieved. Counting on the complete suppression of the enemy's firing points during an attack was just stupidity: like us, the Germans quickly figured out such tricks. Like a monster, reconnaissance in force devoured lives and when the attack took place, the enemy's weapons usually opened fire and the infantry bled to death when they reached the enemy's positions.[6]

A recurrent feature of the failed Soviet offensives of 1942 was the failure to achieve a wide penetration of the German defensive lines, and more specifically to widen such penetrations once they were created. As a consequence, nearly every Soviet penetration left a very narrow neck through which all supplies and reinforcements had to move forward. This practically invited counterattacks that would envelop and destroy any Red Army units that attempted to advance further to exploit the initial success. To an extent, this was a manifestation of the limited resources available to Soviet commanders. In order to improve the chances of success, they had to concentrate their efforts on a narrow front, but once they had broken the first line of defence, they repeatedly failed to push back the shoulders of the breach. This was largely due to a combination of two factors. The initial penetration usually came at a great cost, meaning that the remaining forces weren't strong enough both to advance further and widen the neck of the penetration; and the supply of artillery ammunition remained too poor to permit guns to batter the German positions around the neck of the breakthrough with sufficient intensity. The German doctrine of aggressive counterattacks was a feature of German operations in both world wars, but the Red Army's attempts to anticipate and defeat these counterattacks often failed. But even in the midst of these failures, there were signs of change. When Manstein's Eleventh Army attempted to pinch off the Red Army salient projecting towards Sinyavino, the attacking German units suffered heavy losses as a result of a combination of difficult terrain conditions and the growing skill of Soviet defenders. In particular, the rapid deployment of anti-tank units with supporting engineers and infantry would become an increasingly important feature of Soviet operations, and the successful encirclements of Second Shock Army in both the summer and autumn of 1942 owed more to dogged determination on the part of German infantry than the swift use of armoured forces. Even if Army Group North had possessed such armour, the terrain made its use almost impossible.

Despite many of the veterans in the ranks of the Red Army becoming more skilled in warfare at every level, the casualty rates of Soviet units remained catastrophically high. As is so often the case in war, new recruits suffered disproportionately high losses, and the failure of the Red Army to prepare these recruits properly for battle played a major part. The failure of the Soviet military – and to a large extent the Russian military in more recent years – to appreciate the value of having an experienced core of veteran NCOs, the men who represented the 'institutional memory' of the army and could be expected to bring recruits up to standard in the shortest possible time, is striking. To an extent, Soviet authorities were uneasy about permitting the creation of such a large group of experienced soldiers who would have the knowledge and skill to think independently and flexibly – such independence of thought and decision-making might easily overflow from purely military matters into the far more dangerous sphere of political action. The established doctrine of the Red Army was for rigid vertical control, with junior officers and NCOs expected to deliver results by strict adherence to orders from above. Without training and encouragement in showing initiative and in constant fear of being arrested for failure to deliver results exactly as ordered, these junior leaders could do little but pass on instructions that they probably knew were doomed to failure. As a result, units were thrown repeatedly and stubbornly at the same objectives in attacks that left the Germans baffled at the blind perseverance of their enemy.

The terrible history of Second Shock Army during 1942 demonstrates another major weakness of the Red Army. The Wehrmacht succeeded in encircling and effectively destroying Second Shock Army twice in just a few months, and although the Red Army rebuilt Second Shock Army on both occasions, there was little or no systematic attention to ensuring that the rebuilt army would perform any better in future. In recent years, the US Army has studied the reconstitution of formations after heavy losses and drawn up detailed guidelines on experiences stretching back to the Second World War. In addition to providing replacement personnel and equipment, it is necessary to ensure that there is adequate provision of support services so that both personnel and equipment can perform at a high level of capability, and changes need to be made in training to address the reasons for earlier losses and failures. The quality of leadership is also stressed, and a clear distinction is made between reorganisation and regeneration. The former is defined as the redistribution of surviving personnel in order to ensure that all components of the unit have a similar proportion of veteran survivors; the latter is the overall rebuilding of a unit, including the absorption of fresh drafts and equipment.[7] The current US guidelines state:

> There is a misconception that reconstitution is only the replacement of personnel and equipment … Reconstitution operations require more than just requesting replacement personnel and equipment [and] include retrograding units from

combat [i.e. withdrawing them completely from the front line], assessing their combat effectiveness, re-establishing chain of command, training for future operations, and re-establishing unit cohesion.[8]

The Red Army rebuilt its battered units with fresh drafts, but there was little or no change to their training prior to their arrival in the front line. Nor was there any consistent policy of reorganising survivors to ensure that when these new drafts arrived, they would be deployed alongside seasoned veterans who might be able to accelerate their learning. The units were then often thrown back into battle even before they had been fully replenished; the result was a constant cycle of units being generated, pitched into combat without proper preparation, huge losses, and an inadequate period of rest and replenishment before the next operation.

The difficulties experienced by both sides in attempting to conduct offensive operations in the northern sector in 1942 were in stark contrast to the German advance of 1941; a similar pattern can be seen in the central sector around the Rzhev salient. The underlying reasons were the same in both sectors. The Wehrmacht was able to drive swiftly through the swamps and forests in the northern and central sectors in late 1941 because the Red Army was too weak to put up organised resistance. As a result, the unsuitability of the terrain for offensive operations was of less importance, though German accounts of that era repeatedly comment on difficulties caused by poor roads and the unfavourable terrain. Throughout 1942, both sides had sufficient strength to make the most of the terrain and to exploit it fully for defensive purposes. The result was that neither side could achieve anything approaching the swift advances of 1941. The failure of the Red Army in particular to recognise this – after all, it was fighting on home ground and should therefore have been more aware of the limitations imposed by the ground conditions than the Wehrmacht – resulted in over-ambitious objectives being set for almost every operation that was attempted. The abiding fear of the consequences of failure meant that few were prepared to question such over-ambition, particularly in the case of men like Meretskov who had recent and painful memories of Stalin's wrath.

The consequences of the Red Army's losses during its failed offensives on so many fronts throughout 1942 are worth considering. If the forces that were destroyed around the Rzhev salient had instead been deployed in the north to try to lift the siege of Leningrad, would Volkhov Front's operations have had better success? Such assessments are difficult. Meretskov repeatedly demanded further reinforcements, and had he been given some of the resources that were used elsewhere with so little effect it is arguable that he might have been able to break through to Leningrad. Conversely, the Germans might have been able to move resources from elsewhere to counter such a policy, but at the very least the Red Army would have been in a better position to widen initial breakthroughs and thus avoid many of the problems that arose from attempting to channel its advance through too narrow a corridor. Perhaps the only conclusion that can be drawn from the widespread failures of the Red Army is that these costly battles were an essential part of the price that the Soviet Union had to pay for final victory. It was through these battles that the soldiers and officers of the army – and those at the highest levels of command – learned how to fight and win, and it was as a result of these battles that the Wehrmacht was steadily degraded to the point at which it could no longer expect to impose itself on its opponent.

The attempts by the Red Army to study its operations in order to understand better why they had failed to deliver the expected results continued throughout the war, but whilst this structured approach was highly commendable, its value was reduced by several factors. Firstly, there was often too much emphasis on one or two issues, such as artillery preparation. Fixing these without considering wider weaknesses did little to improve combat effectiveness. Secondly, the solutions that were adopted – the increasing use of reconnaissance in force is a case in point – repeatedly failed to produce better results. Thirdly, whilst these lessons were disseminated at Front and army command level, and may have percolated down to division commanders, the analysis of failings at a lower, tactical level was far less thorough. In some areas, there was considerable and systematic progress. For example, the German use of anti-tank guns organised into *Pakfronts* with a coordinated command was copied and improved with the provision of sappers to lay mines that helped channel German tanks into killing zones, and there was growing recognition for better assets for armoured formations to recover and repair vehicles without having to evacuate them to the rear areas. But basic infantry tactics – where most of the casualties of the Red Army occurred – barely changed during the Second World War. Indeed, by the end of 1944, the training of the newest recruits, often pressed into service from the population of recently liberated parts of the Soviet Union, was so poor that there was increasing use of 'human wave' attacks to swamp and overwhelm German defences.

The legacy of Stalin's purges was terrible, but in many respects they were a manifestation of a recurrent theme in Russian (and later Soviet) history. As has been described above, Peter the Great and his successors showed little hesitation in resorting to brutal repression, and the behaviour of Stalin was little different.

Russian literature is full of descriptions of ordinary Russians as people with a strong sense of fatalism and stoic endurance, and if these descriptions are indicative of underlying cultural traits in Russia, they help explain the manner in which the population both endured and enabled such repression by the rulers of the state. In the case of Leningrad, this stoicism and ability to endure suffering was tested to the very limit in the bitterly cold winter of 1941–42.

Leningrad was one of three Soviet cities to endure siege warfare during 1941–42. The other two – Odessa and Sevastopol – both fell to the besieging forces, but Leningrad held out. It was of course much larger than either of the other cities, but Sevastopol benefited from extensive fortifications and difficult mountainous terrain over which attackers had to advance in order to capture the city. In many respects, Leningrad had a unique mixture of advantages that allowed it to survive. It had considerable industrial resources that could help arm the defenders; unlike many Soviet cities of that era, most of its urban area consisted of stone and concrete buildings rather than timber constructions, making urban warfare a far more difficult prospect; and the presence of the naval base in Kronstadt ensured the supply of high-quality military personnel, artillery support, and even fuel oil.

But there were other factors at work too, which influenced the character of the men and women – military and civilian – who found themselves trapped in Leningrad. A large element of popular history is the manner in which the past becomes mythologised. Prior to the Russian Revolution, the way in which Peter the Great had created his new capital and Catherine the Great later embellished it resulted in a strong belief that this modern city was a far more advanced, sophisticated place than other Russian cities like Moscow, but this somewhat mythical version of the past was largely restricted to the aristocracy and middle classes. Nonetheless, the belief that the city had been intended from its creation to be a window to the west was widespread amongst the intelligentsia who believed that they lived in the most enlightened and forward-looking part of the Russian Empire. This led to a strong tradition of independence of thought, with many of Russia's great thinkers and writers living in St Petersburg. However, not all saw the city as a positive influence. Arkady Ivanovich Svidrigailov, an unsavoury character in Dostoyevsky's *Crime and Punishment*, reflected on one particular aspect of this character: 'There are few places where there are so many gloomy, strong and queer influences on the soul of man as in Petersburg.'[9]

Such views were widespread in an era in which cities all across the world were struggling with rapid population growth and industrialisation. It is arguable that the combination of the tensions created by the urban squalor in which ordinary residents lived and died, the pressures of the First World War, and the radical intellectual atmosphere of the city contributed to the revolutions of 1917, but regardless of the causes, the revolutions themselves added to the city's mythology. Many of those who suffered and died in Leningrad in the first winter of the siege were relative newcomers to the city, but everyone saw the city as something special: the cradle of the Revolution, the city named after Lenin, a glittering array of magnificent buildings and monuments that showed Russia's past in a more positive light than places like Moscow.

Just as the stoic, stubborn character of ordinary Russians is a recurring theme in Russian literature, so too is the special character of the city on the banks of the Neva. The poet Joseph Brodsky, who was expelled from the Soviet Union in 1972, was born in Leningrad a year before the war with Germany commenced. He once told a journalist that there was something curious about St Petersburg: in some manner that was impossible to define, the city affected the souls of those who lived there and anyone from the city – whether they had been born there or had lived there for a few years – was easily distinguishable from other Russians. Others too have shared this view. Leningraders saw themselves as different from other citizens of the Soviet Union, and this contributed to their defiance of death and the German invaders.

Far to the south, the decisive battles of the war were raging in late 1942. The German Sixth Army was trapped in the ruins of Stalingrad, enduring starvation in a siege that was in many respects just as terrible as that of Leningrad the previous winter. On the vast open steppe, Soviet armoured formations moved with increasing confidence, attempting to turn a major success into a war-winning one; if the Red Army could reach Rostov, or the coastline of the Sea of Azov, there was potential for the entrapment and destruction of large parts of the German forces that had advanced into the Caucasus, or that were struggling to rebuild the front line after the Soviet encirclement of Stalingrad. All along the line of the Don River, the defences held by German, Hungarian, Italian, and Romanian troops collapsed like a line of dominoes, and for a few heady weeks it seemed possible that the Soviet forces would achieve complete success. But such was the scale of the landscape that by trading space for time, Manstein – now commanding Army Group B and fighting simultaneously against the Red Army and against Hitler's unwillingness to concede ground – was ultimately able to restore the front line along the line of the Northern Donets River. In the central region, the last attempt by the Red Army to destroy the infamous Rzhev salient to the west of Moscow was dying away, ending like every previous attempt in huge casualty lists for no significant gain. And in the north, despite the bloodshed along the Volkhov River and at Sinyavino, the front line had barely moved all year.

Most countries entered the Second World War and discovered that their military forces were poorly prepared for the realities of the new conflict in terms of training, doctrine, equipment, or combinations of all three. In the case of the Soviet Union, all of these factors applied. But the 'unique sadness' in Tolstoy's terms suffered by the Soviet Union came about because of the vandalism wreaked by Stalin's paranoia, making the impact of the weaknesses in training, doctrine, and equipment far more serious. This brought the nation to the brink of defeat in 1941 and in a conflict of terrible suffering, the citizens of Leningrad paid a particularly severe price. The siege of the city continued into 1943, but the similarity in positions compared to the previous winter was misleading. The Red Army was in a position to dictate the course and pace of events. The best chance for the German Army Group North to achieve a decisive success was long gone, and both sides looked forward to the resumption of Soviet attempts to break the siege ring – the Germans with foreboding, their opponents with a mixture of apprehension, confidence, and hope. The long, drawn-out suffering of the city created by Peter the Great in the swamps of the north was, surely, coming to an end. Before that could be achieved, the butcher's bill would rise still further.

NOTES

To Besiege a City

1   L. Tolstoy, *Anna Karenina* (trans. A. Maude, Everyman, London 1977), p.1.

Chapter 1

1   R. Massie, *Peter the Great: His Life and Work* (Random House, London, 1992), p.167

2   Ibid., p.195

3   V. Kliuchevsky, *Sochineniia v Vosmi Tomakh* (Izdanie Politicheskoy Literaturi Puis Socialno-Ekonomicheskoya Literaturi, Moscow, 1956–59, 8 volumes), Vol. IV, p.125

4   W.B. Lincoln, *Sunlight at Midnight: St Petersburg and the Rise of Modern Russia* (Basic, New York, 2002), p.29

5   I. Georgi, *Opisanie Rossiyisko-Imperatorskogo Stolichnogo Goroda Sankt-Peterburga I Dostopamiatnostei v Okrestnostiakh Onogo, c Planom* (Liga, St Petersburg, 1996), pp.148–49

6   T. Hasegawa, *The February Revolution: Petrograd 1917* (University of Washington Press, Seattle WA, 1981), p.210

7   I. Gordienko, *Iz Boevogo Proshlogo 1914–1918gg* (Gos Isd-Vo Polit Lit-Ry, Moscow, 1957), p.57

8   E. Burdzhalov, *Vtoraia Russkaia Revoliutsiia* (Nauka, Moscow, 1967, 2 volumes), Vol. I, p.179

9   W.B. Lincoln, *Passage Through Armageddon: The Russians in War and Revolution* (Oxford University Press, Oxford, 1994), pp.334–35

10 I. Mints, *Istoriia Velikogo Oktiabria* (Nauka, Moscow, 1967, 2 volumes), Vol. I, p.534

11 For a fuller account of the events of 1917 in Russia, see P. Buttar, *The Splintered Empires: The Eastern Front 1917–1921* (Osprey, Oxford, 2017), pp.138–247

12 A. Rabinovich, *The Bolshevkis Come to Power: The Revolution of 1917 in Petrograd* (Vintage, New York, 2004), pp.300–04

13 L. Trotsky, *History of the Russian Revolution* (trans. M. Eastmann, 1922, republished Haymarket, London, 2008), pp.1414–15

14   A. Knox, *With the Russian Army 1914–1917* (Hutchison, London, 1921), pp.709–11

15   V. Antonov-Ovseyenko, *V Semnadtsatom Godu* (Gosudarstvennoe Izd-vo Khudozhestvennoi Lit-ry, Moscow, 1933), p.319

16   M. Hoffmann and K. Nowak, *Die Aufzeichnungen des Generalmajors Max Hoffmann* (Verlag für Kulturpolitik, Berlin, 1929), p.187

17   Lincoln, *Sunlight at Midnight*, p.243

18   D. Volgokonov, *Lenin: Life and Legacy* (Harper Collins, London, 1994), p.482

19   S. Naida and S. Budennyi, *Istoriia Grazhdanskoi Voiny v SSSR* (Izd-vo Politicheskoi Litry, Moscow, 1957–1959, 4 volumes), Vol. II, p.155

20   Quoted in W.B. Lincoln, *Red Victory: A History of the Russian Civil War* (Simon & Schuster, London, 1990), p.288

21   M. Margulies, *God Intervencii* (Izd. Z I Gržebina, Berlin, 1923, 2 volumes), Vol. II, p.120

22   O. Figes, *A People's Tragedy: The Russian Revolution 1891–1924* (Bodley Head, London, 2014), p.672

23   L. Trotsky, *Kak Vooruzhalas Revoliutsiia (Na Voyennie Rabote)* (Vysshii Voennyi Redaktsionnyi Sovet, Leningrad, 1923–25, 5 volumes), Vol. II, pp.383–86

24   G. Zinovyev, *Borba za Petrograd, 15 Oktiabria–6 Noiabria 1919 Goda* (Gos. Izd-vo, Moscow, 1923), pp.52–53

25   Quoted in Figes, *A People's Tragedy*, p.674

26   Trotsky, *Kak Vooruzhalas Revoliutsiia*, Vol. II, pp.441–42

27   Quoted in Lincoln, *Red Victory*, p.299

28   P. Avrich, *Kronstadt, 1921* (Princeton University Press, Princeton NJ, 2014), p.67

29   B. Ruble, *Leningrad: Shaping a Soviet City* (University of California Press, Berkeley CA, 1990), p.27

CHAPTER 2

1   A. Vaksberg, 'Kak Zhivoi c Zhivymi' in *Literaturnaia Gazeta* (Moscow, 1988), 29 June, p.13

2   A. Solzhenitsyn, *The Gulag Archipelago* (Vintage, London, 2018), pp.8–9

3   N. Werth, 'The NKVD Mass Secret National Operations (August 1937–November 1938), Mass Violence & Resistance' in *Mass Violence and Resistance – Research Network* (Academie Sciences-Politiques, Paris, 2010) published online, www.sciencespo.fr/mass-violence-war-massacre-resistance/en/document/nkvd-mass-secret-national-operations-august-1937-november-1938.html

4   R. Conquest, *The Great Terror: A Reassessment* (Oxford University Press, Oxford, 2008), p.352

5   P. Aptekar, 'Chimchistka po-Tambovski' in *Rodina* (FGBU Redaktsiya Rossiyskoy Gazety, Moscow, 1994), No. 5, p.2

6   W. Widder, 'Auftragstaktik and Innere Führung: Trademark of German Leadership' in *Military Review* (Army University Press, Fort Leavenworth KS, 2002), 82/5, p.4

7   K. Simonov, *Glazami Cheloveka Moyego Pokeleniya: Razmyshleniya o Staline* (Novosti, Moscow, 1988), p.478

8   Conquest, *The Great Terror*, p.211; S. Courtois, *The Black Book of Communism: Crimes, Terror, Repression* (Harvard University Press, Cambridge MA, 1999), p.198

9   O. Suvenirov, *Tragediya RKKA 1937–1938* (Terra, Moscow, 1998), p.137

10   M. Anderson, *Symphony for the City of the Dead: Dmitri Shostakovich and the Siege of Leningrad* (Candlewick, Somerville MA, 2017), pp.126–27

11   B. Spence, *Trust No One: The Secret World of Sidney Reilly* (Feral House, Port Townsend WA, 2002), p.392

Chapter 3

1   *Izvestiia Tsentralnogo Komiteta KPSS* (Izvestiia, Moscow, 1990), No. 1, p.211

2   M. Clemmesen and M. Faulkner (eds), *Northern European Overture to War, 1939–1941: From Memel to Barbarossa* (Brill, Leiden, 2013), p.76; E. Kulkov, O. Rsheshevskii, and H. Shukman (eds), *Stalin and the Soviet–Finnish War, 1939–1940* (Frank Cass, London, 2002), p.16

3   J. Leskinen and A. Juutilainen, *Jatkosodan Pikkujättiläinen* (Werner Söderström, Helsinki, 2005), p.152

4   B. Sokolov, *Taiyni Finskoi Voiny* (Veche, Moscow, 2000), p.340; G. Krivosheyev, *Soviet Casualties and Combat Losses in the Twentieth Century* (Greenhill, London, 1997), pp.77–78

5   Y. Kilin, 'Soviet–Finnish War 1939–1940 and Red Army's Losses' in *Proceedings of Petrozavodsk State University, Social Sciences and Humanities* (Petrozavodsk, 2012), No. 5 (126), pp.21–24

6   S. Zaloga and J. Grandsen, *Soviet Tanks and Combat Vehicles of World War II* (Arms & Armour, London, 1984), p.130

7   D. Glantz, *Stumbling Colossus: The Red Army on the Eve of World War* (University Press of Kansas, Lawrence KS, 1998), p.161

8   *Sbornik Boevykh Dokumentov Velikoi, Otechestvennoi* (Voenizdat, Moscow, 1958) 36, p.99

9   Quoted in D. Glantz, *The Battle for Leningrad 1941–1944* (University Press of Kansas, Lawrence KS, 2002), p.17

10   For an account of the annexation of the Baltic States, see P. Buttar, *Between Giants: The Battle for the Baltics in World War II* (Osprey, Oxford, 2013), pp.27–74

11   Y. Gorkov and Y. Semin, 'Konets Globalnoi Izhi: Na Sovetskom Severozapade – Operativnye Plany Zapadnykh Prigranichnykh Okrugov 1941 Goda Svidetelstvuiut: SSSR ne Gotovilsia k Napadeniiu na Germaniiu' in *Voenno-*

Istoricheskii Zhurnal (Russian Ministry of Defence, Moscow), 6 (Nov–Dec 1996), pp.3–4

12 Glantz, *The Battle for Leningrad*, p.552

13 Tsentral'nyy Arkhiv Ministerstva Oborony, Moscow, F.16 op.29500, D.406, I., pp.104–19

14 *Bundesarchiv-Militärarchiv Freiburg*, N 372/29, Bl.3

15 C. Burdick and H.-A. Jacobsen (eds), *The Halder War Diary 1939–1942* (Greenhill, London, 1988), pp.293–94, 297–98

16 *Akten zur Deutschen Auswärtigen Politik 1918–1945 Serie D* (Hermes KG, Bonn, 1964), Vol. XI, Document 532, pp.750–853

17 For an overview of *FHO*, see D. Thomas, 'Foreign Armies East and German Military Intelligence in Russia 1941–45' in *Journal of Contemporary History* 22, No. 2 (1987), pp. 261–301

18 G. Buchheit, *Der Deutsche Geheimdienst. Geschichte der Militärischen Abwehr* (Paul List Verlag, Munich, 1966), p.25; H. Höhne, J. Brownjohn (trans.), *Canaris* (New York, 1979), p.441

19 Quoted in Thomas, 'Foreign Armies', p.277

20 T. Diedrich, *Paulus: Das Trauma von Stalingrad. Eine Biographie* (Brill Schöningh, Paderborn, 2008), p.166

21 Burdick and Jacobsen, *The Halder War Diary*, p.315

22 G. Megargee, *Inside Hitler's High Command* (University Press of Kansas, Lawrence KS, 2000), pp.122–23

23 Burdick and Jacobsen, *The Halder War Diary*, p.315

24 Megargee, *Inside Hitler's High Command*, p.349

25 Quoted in M. Jones, *Leningrad: State of Siege* (John Murray, London, 2008), pp.17–18

26 Burdick and Jacobsen, *The Halder War Diary*, p.343

27 Glantz, *Stumbling Colossus*, p.107

28 Burdick and Jacobsen, *The Halder War Diary*, p.346

29 W. von Leeb, G. Meyer (ed.), *Generalfeldmarschall Wilhelm Ritter von Leeb: Tagebuchaufzeichnungen und Lagebeurteilungen aus Zwei Weltkriegen* (Deutsche Verlags-Anstalt, Stuttgart, 1976), p.172

30 E. Klee, *Das Personenlexikon zum Dritten Reich. Wer war Was vor und nach 1945* (Fischer, Frankfurt-am-Main, 2007), p.347

31 S. Neitzel, *Deutsche Krieger: Vom Kaiserreich zur Berliner Republik – eine Militärgeschichte* (Propyläen, Berlin, 2020), p.217

32 G. Ueberschar and W. Wette (eds), *Unternehmen Barbarossa: Der Deutsche Überfall auf die Sowjetunion 1941* (Schöningh, Paderborn, 1984), p.305

33 Burdick and Jacobsen, *The Halder War Diary*, p.383

34 G. Zhukov, *Vospomimaniya I Razmyshleniya* (Olma, Moscow, 2002, 2 volumes), Vol. I, pp.249–50

35 Ibid., p.250

36 Ibid.

37   G. Gorodetsky, *Grand Delusion: Stalin and the German Invasion of Russia* (Yale University Press, New Haven CT, 1999), p.212

38   O. Matthews, *An Impeccable Spy: Richard Sorge, Stalin's Master Agent* (Bloomsbury, London, 2019), p.121

39   Quoted in S. Sebag Montefiore, *Stalin: In the Court of the Red Tsar* (Weidenfeld & Nicholson, London, 2003), p.361

40   Quoted in ibid., p.365

41   Quoted in A. Clark, *Barbarossa: The Russian-German Conflict 1941–45* (Hutchinson, London, 1965), p.27

CHAPTER 4

1   C. Clasen, *Generaloberst Georg-Hans Reinhardt 1887–1963* (Zeitungsverlag RM, Stuttgart, 1976), p.228

2   R. Stolfi, *German Panzers on the Offensive* (Schiffer, Atglen PA, 2003), p.150

3   Zhukov, *Vospomimaniya I Razmyshleniya*, Vol. I, pp.263–64

4   Ibid., p.264

5   V. Zolotarev (ed.), *Velikaia Otechestvennaia Voina 1941–1945* (Nauka, Moscow, 1998, 2 volumes), Vol. I, p.148

6   Glantz, *The Battle for Leningrad*, p.32

7   Quoted in ibid., p.33

8   W. Paul, *Brennpunkte: Die Geschichte der 6. Panzerdivision 1937–1945* (Biblio, Osnabrück, 1984), p.107

9   Quoted in ibid., pp.108–09

10   *Sbornik Boevykh Dokumentov Velikoi, Otechestvennoi* (Voenizdat, Moscow), Vol. 34, p.323

11   A. Vetrov, *Tak I Bylo* (Voenizdat, Moscow, 1982), pp.117–18

12   Bundesarchiv-Militärarchiv Freiburg, *Kriegstagebuch 3. Leichte Division/8 Panzer-Division, 26/6/41*, RH27-8

13   D. Lelyushenko, *Moskva-Stalingrad-Berlin-Praga. Zapiski Komandarma* (Nauka, Moscow, 1987), p.7

14   Ibid., p.8

15   *Sbornik Boevykh Dokumentov Velikoi, Otechestvennoi* (Voenizdat, Moscow), Vol. 33, pp.40–41

16   National Archives and Records Administration, College Park MD, *Kriegstagebuch LVI AK (Mot)*, T314 Roll 1839

17   E. von Manstein, A. Powell (trans. and ed.), *Lost Victories* (Presidio, Novato CA, 1982), p.185

18   Burdick and Jacobsen, *The Halder War Diary*, pp.446–47

19   W. Haupt, *Die 8. Panzer-Division im Zweiten Weltkrieg* (Podzun-Pallas, Friedberg, 1987), p.154

20   Burdick and Jacobsen, *The Halder War Diary*, p.457

21 W. Lubbeck and D. Hurt, *At Leningrad's Gates* (Casemate, Newbury, 2006), pp.85–86

22 E. Klee, V. Riess, and W. Dressen, *Schöne Zeiten: Judenmord aus der Sicht der Täter und Gaffer* (Fischer, Frankfurt am Main, 1998), pp.39–40

23 Ibid., p.38

24 A. Dzeniskevich, V. Kovalchuk, G. Sobolev, A. Tsamutali, and V. Shishkin, *Nepokorennyy Leningrad* (Nauka, Leningrad, 1970), p.16–17

25 E. Moniushenko, O. Sheremet (trans.), *From Leningrad to Hungary: Notes of a Red Army Soldier, 1941–1946* (Cass, Abingdon, 2005), p.5

26 S. Platonov, *Bitva za Leningrad 1941–1944* (Voenizdat, Moscow, 1964), pp.27–30

27 Tsentralnyy Gosudarstvennyy Arkhiv Istoriko-Politicheskikh Dokumentov (TsGAIPD), *Oborona Leningrada 1941–1944, Vospominaniya I Dnevniki Uchastnikov* (Nauka, Leningrad, 1968), Fond 2281, I, 194

28 S. Bardin, *I Shtatskiye Nadeli Shineli* (Sovetskaya Rossiya, Moscow, 1974), p.12

29 Bundesarchiv-Militärarchiv Freiburg, *Kriegstagebuch 3. Leichte Division/8 Panzer-Division, 14/07/41*, RH27-8

30 Platonov, *Bitva za Leningrad 1941–1944*, p.49

31 Burdick and Jacobsen, *The Halder War Diary*, p.487

CHAPTER 5

1 *Jäger-Bericht* in W. Wette, *Karl Jäger: Mörder der Litauischen Juden* (Fischer, Frankfurt-am-Main, 2011), Appendix

2 K.-M. Mallmann, A. Angrick, J. Matthus, and M. Cüppers (eds), *Die Ereignismeldungen UdSSR 1941: Dokumente der Einsatzgruppen in der Sowjetunion* (WGB, Darmstadt, 2011), p.139

3 Ibid., p.178

4 *Sbornik Voenno-Istoricheskikh Materialov Velikoi Otechstvennoi Voiny* (Voenizdat, Moscow, 1960), 18, pp.231–37

5 Glantz, *Stumbling Colossus*, p.15

6 V. Zolotarev, 'Stavka VGK: Dokumenty I Materialy 1941 god' in *Russkii Arkhiv: Velikaia Otechestvennaia* (Terra, Moscow, 1996, 16 volumes), Vol. XVI, No. 5, pp.111–12

7 Bardin, *I Shtatskiye Nadeli Shineli*, p.47

8 Interview with G. Kudryavtsev, available at https://iremember.ru/memoirs/razvedchiki/kudryavtsev-grigoriy-konstantinovich/

9 R. Stoves, *Die 1. Panzer-Division 1935–1945* (Podzun, Bad Neuheim, 1961), pp.233–36

10 Bardin, *I Shtatskiye Nadeli Shineli*, pp.55–56

11 Mallmann et al., *Die Ereignismeldungen UdSSR 1941*, p.272

12 Paul, *Brennpunkte*, p.127

13   Lubbeck and Hurt, *At Leningrad's Gates*, p.99

14   A. Stahlberg, P. Crampton (trans.), *Bounden Duty: The Memoirs of a German Officer 1932–45* (Brassey, London, 1990), p.173

15   Burdick and Jacobsen, *The Halder War Diary*, p.514

16   Budesarchiv-Militärarchiv Freiburg, N 510/48

17   *Der Prozess Gegen die Hauptkriegsverbrecher vor dem Internationalen Militärgerichtshof* (Komet MA, Frechen, 2001, 42 volumes), Vol. 31, p.84

18   A. Kay, *Exploitation, Resettlement, Mass Murder: Political and Economic Planning for German Occupation Policy in the Soviet Union, 1940–1941* (Berghahn, New York, 2006), p.134

19   C. Streit, *Keine Kameraden: Die Wehrmacht und die Sowjetischen Kriegsgefangenen* (Dietz, Bonn, 1997), p.128

20   Burdick and Jacobsen, *The Halder War Diary*, p.515

21   Manstein, *Lost Victories*, p.202

22   J. Erickson, *The Road to Stalingrad* (Cassell, London, 2003), p.187

23   Stahlberg, *Bounden Duty*, p.174

24   Haupt, *Die 8. Panzer-Division im Zweiten Weltkrieg*, pp.169–71

25   A. Hermann and E. Fröhlich (eds), *Die Tagebücher von Joseph Goebbels: Teil II Diktate 1941–1945* (Saur, Munich, 1996, 15 volumes), Vol. I, p.378

26   Anderson, *Symphony*, p.122

27   D. Pavlov, *Leningrad v Blokade* (Voenizdat, Moscow, 1958), p.121

28   Hermann and Fröhlich, *Die Tagebücher von Joseph Goebbels*, Vol. I, p.442

29   Bundesarchiv-Militärarchiv Freiburg, *Vortragsnotiz Leningrad*, RW 4/578

30   Burdick and Jacobsen, *The Halder War Diary*, p.524

31   Interview with N. Karpenko, available at https://iremember.ru/memoirs/svyazisti/karpenko-nikolay-matveevich/

32   H. Rudel, *Stuka Pilot* (Black House, London, 2013), p.31

33   S. McLaughlin, *Russian & Soviet Battleships* (Naval Institute Press, Annapolis MD, 2003), pp.402–14

34   N. Khrushchev, *Vremya, Lyudi, Vlast: Vospominaniya* (Novosti, Moscow, 1999), p.122

35   Interview with Y. Smirnov, available at https://iremember.ru/memoirs/pulemetchiki/smirnov-yuriy-konstantinovich/

36   Ibid.

37   Stoves, *Die 1. Panzer-Division 1935–1945*, p.244

38   Quoted in G. Roberts, *Stalin's General: The Life of Georgy Zhukov* (Icon, London, 2013), p.171

39   I. Fediuninsky, *Podnyatyye po Trevoge* (Voenizdat, Moscow, 1961), pp.42–43

40   Ibid., pp.45–46

41   Bardin, *I Shtatskiye Nadeli Shineli*, pp.81–82

42   Bundesarchiv-Militrarchiv Freiburg, *Kriegstagebuch XLI Armeekorps (mot) / XLI Panzerkorps 17/9/41*, RH 24-41

CHAPTER 6

1   D. Schleglov, *V Opelchenii* (Voenizdat, Moscow, 1960), pp.68–69

2   Quoted in A. Pechenkin, 'I Vydvizhenets, I Zhertvya Stalina' in *Nezavisimoye Voyennoye Obozreniye* (Moscow, 16/6/2006), No. 119 (3799)

3   N. Volkovsky (ed.), *Blokada Leningrada v Dokumentakh Rassekrechennykh Arkhivov* (Polygon, St Petersburg, 2005), p.38

4   I. Ivanova, *Sinyavino: Osenniye Boi 1941–1942 godov: Sbornik Vospominaniy Uchastnikov Sinyavinskikh Srazheniy* (Vesti, St Petersburg, 2012), p.7

5   Ibid., p.18

6   Ibid., p.80

7   Zhukov, *Vospomimaniya I Razmyshleniya*, Vol. I, pp.395–96

8   Quoted in Jones, *Leningrad: State of Siege*, p.119

9   V. Konkov, *Vremya Dalekoye I Blizkoye* (Voenizdat, Moscow, 1985), pp.104–06

10   Ibid., p.121

11   Schleglov, *V Opelchenii*, p.116

12   V. Mosunov, *Bitva za Sinyavinskiye Vysoty. Mginskaya Duga 1941–1942 gg* (Yauza, Moscow, 2015), p.234

13   Burdick and Jacobsen, *The Halder War Diary*, p.543

14   Stahlberg, *Bounden Duty*, pp.175–76

15   Quoted in Haupt, *Die 8. Panzer-Division im Zweiten Weltkrieg*, p.185

16   Stahlberg, *Bounden Duty*, p.176

17   A. Andreev, *Ot Pervogo Mgnoveniya – Do Poslednego* (Voyenizdat, Moscow, 1984), p.39

18   Fediuninsky, *Podnyatyye po Trevoge*, p.65

19   Bundesarchiv-Militärarchiv Freiburg, *Kriegstagebuch 3. Leichte Division/8 Panzer-Division, 21/10/41, 23/10/41*, RH27-8

20   D. Zherebov (ed.), *Tikhvin, god. 1941* (Lenizdat, Moscow, 1974), pp.214–15

21   Stahlberg, *Bounden Duty*, p.178

22   Suvenirov, *Tragediya RKKA 1937–1938*, p.336

23   Zhukov, *Vospomimaniya I Razmyshleniya*, Vol. I, p.169

24   Interview with S. Spitsin, available at https://iremember.ru/memoirs/svyazisti/spitsin-sergey-nikolaevich

25   Ibid.

26   V. Zolotarev, 'Stavka VGK' in *Russkii Arkhiv* (Terra, Moscow, 1999), Vol. 20, p.277

27   Ivanova, *Sinyavino*, p.112

28   Fediuninsky, *Podnyatyye po Trevoge*, p.73

29   Bundesarchiv-Militärarchiv Freiburg, *Kriegstagebuch 3. Leichte Division/8 Panzer-Division, 18/11/41*, RH27-8

30   Quoted in Haupt, *Die 8. Panzer-Division im Zweiten Weltkrieg*, p.197

31   Quoted in X. Núñez Seixas, *The Spanish Blue Division on the Eastern Front 1941–1945* (University of Toronto Press, Toronto, 2022), p.45

32 For more information about the Blue Division, see G. Kleinfeld, *Hitler's Spanish Legion: The Blue Division in Russia in WWII* (Stackpole, Mechanicsburg PA, 2014); Juliá Xavier Moreno, *La División Azul: Sangre Española en Rusia 1941–1945* (Critica, Barcelona, 2005)

33 Quoted in Núñez Seixas, *The Spanish Blue Division*, p.93

34 Quoted in ibid., p.80

35 Quoted in ibid., p.160

36 Quoted in ibid., pp.154–55

37 Burdick and Jacobsen, *The Halder War Diary*, p.558

38 P. Carrell, *Hitler Moves East 1941–1943* (Little & Brown, Boston MS, 1963) pp.269–70

39 Burdick and Jacobsen, *The Halder War Diary*, pp.564–65

40 Ibid., pp.571–72

41 B. Kovalev, *Dobrovolci na Cyzoi Voyne. Ocerki Istorii Goluboi Divizii* (Novgorodskiy Gosudarstveneyi Universitet, Novgorod, 2014) pp.224–31

42 Fediuninsky, *Podnyatyye po Trevoge*, pp.84–87

43 Stahlberg, *Bounden Duty*, p.182

44 Quoted in Glantz, *The Battle for Leningrad*, p.116

45 G. Niepold, *Ursprung und Lebenslauf der Pommerschen 12. Panzerdivision* (Pechlerberg, Koblenz, 1988), p.40

46 V. Hébert, *Hitler's Generals on Trial: The Last War Crimes Tribunal at Nuremberg* (University of Kansas Press, Lawrence KS, 2010), p.126

CHAPTER 7

1 J. Getty, O. Naumov, and B. Sher, *The Road to Terror: Stalin and the Self-Destruction of the Bolsheviks, 1932–1939* (Yale University Press, New Haven CT, 2010), p.425

2 A. Antonov-Ovseyenko, *The Time of Stalin: Portrait of a Tyranny* (Harper, New York, 1983), p.267

3 Quoted in Jones, *Leningrad: State of Siege*, pp.155–56

4 A. Burov, *Blokada Den' za Den'* (Lenizdat, Leningrad, 1979), p.61

5 A. Adamovich and D. Granin, *Blokadnaia Kniga* (Azbuka, St Petersburg, 2020), p.185

6 Platonov, *Bitva za Leningrad 1941–1944*, p.194

7 Jones, *Leningrad: State of Siege*, p.99

8 Bundesarchiv-Militärarchiv Freiburg, *Kriegstagebuch Oberkommando der Heeresgruppe Nord, 31/10/41*, RH19-II

9 J. Mendelson, *The Holocaust: Selected Documents in Eighteen Volumes* (Garland, New York, 1982), Vol. X, pp.7–8

10 Lubbeck and Hurt, *At Leningrad's Gates*, p.112

11 Quoted in Jones, *Leningrad: State of Siege*, p.131

12 Platonov, *Bitva za Leningrad 1941–1944*, p.201

13 D. Pavlov, *Stoykost* (Politisdat, Moscow, 1983), pp.49–50

14 Adamovich and Granin, *Blokadnaia Kniga*, pp.277–78

15 R. Thurston and B. Bonwetsch (eds), *The People's War: Responses to World War II in the Soviet Union* (University of Illinois Press, Champaign IL, 2000), p.96

16 V. Kovalchuk (ed.), *Ocherki Istorii Leningrada: Period Velikoi Otechestvennoi Voiny Sovetskogo Soiuza, 1941–1945 gg.* (Nauka, Leningrad, 1967), p.202

17 S. Yarov, *Povsednevnaya Zhizn Blokadnogo Leningrada* (Molodaya Gvardiya, Moscow, 2013), p.153

18 Diary of D. Zelenskaya, quoted in ibid., p.161

19 Pavlov, *Stoykost*, p.67

20 Ibid., pp.66–67

21 V. Kovalchuk, *Leningrad I Bolshaya Zemlya* (Nauka, Leningrad, 1975), p.74

22 Platonov, *Bitva za Leningrad 1941–1944*, p.203

23 Anderson, *Symphony*, pp.6, 230–32

24 O. Berggolts, *Stikhotvoreniya– Rodina Moya* (Khudozhestvennaya Literatura, Moscow, 1967) p.55

25 'Blakadnyy Dnevnik Olgi Fedorovny Khuze', available at www.militera.lib.ru/huze_of01/huze_of01.html

26 I. Volkova (ed.), *900 Blokadyi Dnei* (Nash Gorodok, Novosibirsk, 2004), p.78

27 R. Bidlack, 'The Political Mood in Leningrad During the First Year of the Soviet-German War' in *Russian Review* (Wiley, Hoboken NJ, 2000), Vol. LIX, No.1, p.105

28 C. Simmons and N. Perlina, *Writing the Siege of Leningrad: Women's Diaries, Memoirs and Documentary Prose* (University of Pittsburgh Press, Pittsburgh PA, 2002), p.138

29 Kovalchuk, *Leningrad I Bolshaya Zemlya*, pp.76–77

30 Pavlov, *Stoykost*, p.83

31 Ibid., pp.90–91

32 Kovalchuk, *Leningrad I Bolshaya Zemlya*, p.100

33 M. Murov, 'Na Sanyakh Cherez Ladogu' in *Zvezda* (Leningrad, 1965), No. 5, p.9

34 Quoted in Kovalchuk, *Leningrad I Bolshaya Zemlya*, p.122

35 Quoted in V. Michelson and M. Yalygin, *Vozdushnyy Most* (Politizdat, Moscow, 1982), p.57

36 Kovalchuk, *Leningrad I Bolshaya Zemlya*, pp.126, 133

37 A. Dzeniskevich (ed.), *Leningrad v Osade: Sbornik Dokumentov o Geroicheskoi Oborone Leningrada v gody Velikoi Otechestvennoi Voiny 1941–1944* (Liki Rossii, St Petersburg, 1995), p.442

38 *Tsentralnyi Gosudarstvennyi Arkhiv Istoriko-Politicheskikh Dokumentov Sankt-Peterburga (TsGAIPD) SPb*, f.24, op.2v, d.4189, 1.3

39 H. Boog, J. Förster, J. Hoffman, E. Klink, R.-D. Müller, R. Ueberschär, E. Osers, *Germany and the Second World War* (Clarendon Press, Oxford 1998), Vol. IV, p.763

40 Adamovich and Granin, *Blokadnaia Kniga*, pp.244–45

41 Burov, *Blokada Den' za Den'*, p.101

42 Quoted in Jones, *Leningrad: State of Siege*, pp.178–79; also Burov, *Blokada Den' za Den'*, p.101

43 Simmons and Perlina, *Writing the Siege of Leningrad*, p.148

44 Adamovich and Granin, *Blokadnaia Kniga*, pp.117–18

45 Ibid., pp.123–26

46 Ibid., pp.402–03

47 Ibid., pp.126–27

48 V. Kovalchuk, N. Lomagin, and V. Shishkin, *Leningradskaia Epopeia: Organizatsiia Oborony I Naselenie Goroda* (Sankt-Peterburgskii Filial In-ta Rossiiskoi Istorii Rossiskoi Akademii Nauk, St Petersburg, 1995), pp.224–25

49 Thurston and Bonwetsch, *The People's War*, p.121

50 Volkova, *900 Blokadyi Dnei*, p.54

51 Simmons and Perlina, *Writing the Siege of Leningrad*, p.22

52 E. Moniushko and O. Sheremet (trans.), *From Leningrad to Hungary: Notes of a Red Army Soldier, 1941-1946* (Cass, Abingdon 2005), p.24

53 Quoted in Yarov, *Povsednevnaya Zhizn Blokadnogo Leningrad*, p.37

54 E. Mukhina, *Sokhrani Moiu Pechalnuiu Istoriu* (Azbuka, St Petersburg, 2011), p.338

55 Volkova, *900 Blokadyi Dnei*, p.61

56 Quoted in Yarov, *Povsednevnaya Zhizn Blokadnogo Leningrad*, p.118

57 A. Reid, *Leningrad: Tragedy of a City Under Siege 1941–1944* (Bloomsbury, New York, 2012), p.289

58 L. Shaporina, *Dnevnik* (Novoe Literaturnoe Obozrenie, Moscow, 2017), p.308

59 Quoted in Jones, *Leningrad: State of Siege*, p.199

60 Platonov, *Bitva za Leningrad 1941–1944*, p.207

61 H. Salisbury, *The 900 Days: The Siege of Leningrad* (Da Capo, Cambridge MS, 2003), pp.491–515

Chapter 8

1 V. Kvachkov, *Spetsnaz Rossii* (Russkaya Panorama, Moscow, 2007), p.206

2 Quoted in V. Kovalchuk (ed.), *V Tylu Vraga Borba Partizan I Podpolshchivkov na Okkupirovannoy Territorii Oblasti* (Lenizdat, Leningrad, 1979), pp.27–28

3 For an overview of these instructions, see J. Armstrong, *Soviet Partisans in World War II* (University of Wisconsin Press, Madison WI, 1964), pp.655–61

4 A. Popov, *NKVD I Partizanskoye Dvizheniye* (Olma, Moscow, 2003), pp.47–53

5 N. Afanasyev, *Front Bez Tyla. Zapiski Partizanskogo Komandira* (Lenizdat, Leningrad, 1983), p.26

6 Ibid., pp.41–42

7 Ibid., p.48

8 Kovalchuk, *V Tylu Vraga*, pp.88–89

9   I. Almukhamedov, *Nepokorennaia Zemlia Pskovskaia, 1941–1944: Dokumenty I Materialy iz Istorii Partizanskogo Dviskheniia i Part.-Komsomolskogo Podpolia v Gody Velikoi Otechestvennoi Voiny* (Lenizdat, Leningrad, 1969), p.115

10 Mallmann et al., *Die Ereignismeldungen UdSSR 1941*, p.216

11 Ibid., p.272

12 Kovalchuk, *V Tylu Vraga*, pp.99–100

13 Mallmann et al., *Die Ereignismeldungen UdSSR 1941*, p.324

14 Ibid., p.334

15 Ibid., p.334–35

16 Ibid., p.283

17 Ibid., p.293

18 Kovalchuk, *V Tylu Vraga*, p.123

19 Mallmann et al., *Die Ereignismeldungen UdSSR 1941*, pp.390–91

20 Ibid., pp.473–74

21 Quoted in Núñez Seixas, *The Spanish Blue Division*, p.176

22 Afanasyev, *Front Bez Tyla*, pp.55–57

23 Mallmann et al., *Die Ereignismeldungen UdSSR 1941*, p.690

24 Lubbeck and Hurt, *At Leningrad's Gates*, p.114

25 K. Askin, *War Crimes Against Women: Prosecution in International War Crimes Tribunals* (Martinus Nijhoff, Dortrecht, 1997), p.72

26 Quoted in ibid., pp.57–58

27 Quoted in Núñez Seixas, *The Spanish Blue Division*, p.198

28 Afanasyev, *Front Bez Tyla*, p.122

29 Mallmann et al., *Die Ereignismeldungen UdSSR 1941*, pp.822–23

30 K. Meretskov, *Na Sluzhbe Narodu* (Politizdat, Moscow, 1968), p.238

31 Armstrong, *Soviet Partisans*, pp.484–86

32 Ibid., p.488

33 P. Ponomarenko and A. Samsonov, *Vsenarodnaya Borba Nemetsko-Fashistskikh Zakhvatchikov 1941–1944* (Nauka, Moscow), pp.229–30

34 K. Stang, *Kollaboration und Massenmord: die Litauische Hilfspolizei, das Rollkommando Hamann und die Ermordung der Litausichen Juden* (Lang, Frankfurt am Main, 1996), pp.170–71

CHAPTER 9

1   Zolotarev, *Velikaia Otechestvennaia* (1996), Vol. XVI, p.33

2   Meretskov, *Na Sluzhbe Narodu*, pp.255–56

3   Stahlberg, *Bounden Duty*, p.184

4   P. Melnikov, *Zalpy s Berega* (Voyenizdat, Moscow, 1971), pp.101–05

5   Ibid., pp.116–17

6   D. Konstantinov, *Ya Srazhalsya v Krasnoy Armii* (Novoe Slovo, Buenos Aires, 1952), pp.40–44

7   Meretskov, *Na Sluzhbe Narodu*, pp.263–64

8   Zhukov, *Vospomimaniya I Razmyshleniya*, Vol. II, pp.43–44

9   K. Zalesskiy, *Imperiya Stalina. Biograficheskiy Entsiklopedicheskiy Slovar* (Veche, Moscow, 2000), p.18

10   Ibid., p.20

11   Meretskov, *Na Sluzhbe Narodu*, p.258

12   B. Gavrilov, *Dolina Smerti. Tragediya I Podvig 2-y Udarnoy Armii* (Institut Sossiyskoy Istorii RAN, Moscow, 1999), p.14

13   Quoted in Zalesskiy, *Imperiya Stalina*, p.22

14   Stahlberg, *Bounden Duty*, pp.186–87

15   Burdick and Jacobsen, *The Halder War Diary*, p.600

16   Zalesskiy, *Imperiya Stalina*, p.24

17   Glantz, *The Battle for Leningrad*, p.161

18   Zalesskiy, *Imperiya Stalina*, p.26

19   Fediuninsky, *Podnyatyye po Trevoge*, p.93

20   Ibid., pp.96–97

21   Konstantinov, *Ya Srazhalsya v Krasnoy Armii*, pp.45–47

22   Ibid., pp.51–52

23   Burdick and Jacobsen, *The Halder War Diary*, p.606

24   Meretskov, *Na Sluzhbe Narodu*, p.270

CHAPTER 10

1   M. Smirtukov, *Sovetskii Gosudarstvennyi Apparat Upravleniya: Voprosy Organiza Tsii I Deyatelnosti Tsentralnykh Organov* (Politizdat, Moscow, 1982), p.255

2   A. Khrulev, 'Stanovleniye Strategicheskogo Tyla v Velikoy Otechestvennoy Voyne' in *Voyenno-Istoricheskii Zhurnal* (1961), No. 6, p.71

3   Gavrilov, *Dolina Smerti*, p.42

4   G. Gerodnik, *Moya Frontovaya Iyzhnya* (Srednya Ural, Sverdlovsk, 1987), pp.116–17

5   Ibid., pp.129–30

6   Meretskov, *Na Sluzhbe Narodu*, p.272

7   Gavrilov, *Dolina Smerti*, p.56

8   Burov, *Blokada Den' za Den'*, pp.148–49

9   Gerodnik, *Moya Frontovaya Iyzhnya*, pp.155–56

10   Fediuninsky, *Podnyatyye po Trevoge*, pp.105–06

11   Burdick and Jacobsen, *The Halder War Diary*, p.608

12   Zolotarev, *Velikaia Otechestvennaia* (1996), Vol. XVI, p.133

13   T. Andreyevich, *Srazhalis na Volkhove* (Lenizdat, Leningrad, 1986), p.113

14   Lubbeck, and Hurt, *At Leningrad's Gates*, p.123

15   Quoted in E. Ziemke and M. Bauer, *Moscow to Stalingrad: Decision in the East* (Center of Military History, Washington DC, 1987), p.194

16 Quoted in Gavrilov, *Dolina Smerti*, p.88

17 Zolotarev, *Velikaia Otechestvennaia* (1996), Vol. XVI, p.507

18 Gerodnik, *Moya Frontovaya Iyzhnya*, pp.212–14

19 Simmons and Perlina, *Writing the Siege of Leningrad*, pp.148–49

20 Quoted in Anderson, *Symphony*, p.309

21 Gavrilov, *Dolina Smerti*, p.102

22 A. Vasilevsky, *A Lifelong Cause* (Progress, Moscow, 1981), p.140

23 Gavrilov, *Dolina Smerti*, p.112

24 J. Jordan (ed.), *Warship 2009* (Conway, London, 2009), p.91

25 A. Smirnov and A. Usov, 'O Vzaimodeystvii sil I Sredstv PVO v Period Blokady Leningrada' in *Voyenno-Istoricheski Zhurnal* (1978), No. 11, pp.32–39

26 J. Rohwer, *Chronology of the War at Sea 1939–1945 The Naval History of World War Two* (Naval Institute Press, Annapolis MD, 2005), p.157

27 Gerodnik, *Moya Frontovaya Iyzhnya*, pp.277–90

28 Lubbeck and Hurt, *At Leningrad's Gates*, p.125

29 S. Gagarin, 'Pravda I Legendy o Voyny' in *Vosprosy Literatury* (Academy of Sciences, Moscow, 1989), No. 9, p.136

30 Lubbeck and Hurt, *At Leningrad's Gates*, pp.126–27

31 Núñez Seixas, *The Spanish Blue Division*, p.148

32 Quoted in Gavrilov, *Dolina Smerti*, pp.143–44

33 Meretskov, *Na Sluzhbe Narodu*, p.283

34 K. Aleksandrov, 'Predatel ili Poryadochnyy Soldat? Novyye Facty o Generale A A Vlasove' in *Istoriya* (Pevroye Sentyabrya, Moscow, 2005), Vol. 32, No. 3, p.33

35 Vasilevsky, *A Lifelong Cause*, pp.140–41

36 C. Andreyev, *Vlasov and the Russian Liberation Movement: Soviet Reality and Émigré Theories* (Cambridge University Press, Cambridge, 1987), p.370

37 G. Krivosheev, *Grif Sekretnosti Sniat: Poteri Vooruzhennykh Sil SSSR v Voinakh, Boevykh Deistviiakh I Voennykh Konfliktakh* (Voyenizdat, Moscow, 1993), pp.224–25

38 Quoted in Núñez Seixas, *The Spanish Blue Division*, p.140

39 Ibid.

40 M. Khozin, 'Ob Odnboi Maloissledovannoi Operatsii' in *Voenno-Istoricheskii Zhurnal* (Russian Ministry of Defence, Moscow, 1966), No. 2, pp.35–36

41 E. Klimchuk, 'Vtoraia Udarnaia I Vlasov ili Pochemu Odin Predal, a v Predateli Popala Vsia Armiia' in *Sovetskii Voin* (Voyennoi Izdatelstvo NKO SSSR, Moscow, 1989), No. 20, p.81

CHAPTER 11

1 Burdick and Jacobsen, *The Halder War Diary*, p.613

2 Lubbeck and Hurt, *At Leningrad's Gates*, pp.129–31

3 Meretskov, *Na Sluzhbe Narodu*, p.299

4   M. Vozhakin (ed.), *Velikaya Otechestvennaya. Komandkory: Voennyi Biogafichesky Slovar* (Kuchkovo Pole, Moscow, 2006), p.138

5   H. Trevor-Roper, *Hitler's War Directives 1939–1945* (Pan, London, 1966), p.144

6   Manstein, *Lost Victories*, p.261

7   Burdick and Jacobsen, *The Halder War Diary*, p.646

8   A. Fadeev, *Leningrad in the Days of the Blockade* (Greenwood, Westport CT, 1977), pp.43–44

9   Quoted in Anderson, *Symphony*, pp.338–39

10 B. Schwartz, *Music and Musical Life in Soviet Russia 1917–1970* (Norton, New York, 1973), p.177

11 Simmons and Perlina, *Writing the Siege of Leningrad*, p.150

12 Ibid., pp.150–151

13 Quoted in Anderson, *Symphony*, p.344

14 Quoted in ibid., p.349

15 See for example, Glantz, *The Battle for Leningrad*, p.213

16 Ivanova, *Sinyavino*, p.236

17 Ibid., p.314

18 Ibid., p.240

19 E. Palkin, 'S Veroy v Pobedu' in *Veteran* (Lenizdat, Moscow, 1988), No. 4, pp.54–55

20 Manstein, *Lost Victories*, p.263

21 O. Carius, R. Edwards (trans.), *Tigers in the Mud: The Combat Career of German Panzer Commander Otto Carius* (Stackpole, Mechanicsburg PA, 2003), pp.2–27; P. Chamberlain and H. Doyle, *Encyclopaedia of German Tanks of World War Two* (Arms & Armour, London, 1999), pp.134–36; J. Restayn, *Tiger I on the Eastern Front* (Histoire & Collections, Paris, 2001), p.14

22 Stahlberg, *Bounden Duty*, p.195

23 Carius, *Tigers in the Mud*, pp.28–29

24 Ivanova, *Sinyavino*, p.319

25 Meretskov, *Na Sluzhbe Narodu*, pp.309–10

26 Ivanova, *Sinyavino*, p.130

27 Ibid.

28 B. Vladimirov, *Komdiv: Ot Siniavinskikh Vysot do Elby* (Eksmo, Moscow, 2010), pp.92–93

29 Ivanova, *Sinyavino*, pp.263–64

30 Ibid., p.434

Chapter 12

1   Vladimirov, *Komdiv*, pp.94–95

2   G. Bidermann, D. Zumbro (ed. and trans.), *In Deadly Combat: A German Soldier's Memoir of the Eastern Front* (University Press of Kansas, Lawrence KS, 2000), p.145

3   Ibid., p.146

4   Palkin, 'S Veroy v Pobedu', p.57

5   Bidermann, *In Deadly Combat*, pp.148–49

6   Meretskov, *Na Sluzhbe Narodu*, pp.313–14

7   Ivanova, *Sinyavino*, pp.221–22

8   Palkin, 'S Veroy v Pobedu', pp.58–59

9   Gosudarstvennyi Arkhiv Smolensko Oblasti, Smolensk,1/1/1500, p.15

10 Tsentr Dokumentatsii Noveishei Istorii Smokenskoi Oblastii Smolensk, 8/2/82, p.50

11 Z. Klukowski, *Dziennik z lat Okupacji Zamojęczczyzny* (Lubelska Społdzielnia Wydawn, Lublin, 1959), p.109

12 R. Evans, *The Third Reich at War* (Penguin, Harmondsworth 2008), p.302

13 *Bundesarchiv-Militärarchiv* Freiburg, RH2-124, p.22

14 G. Temkin, *My Just War: The Memoir of a Jewish Red Army Soldier in World War II* (Presidio, Novato CA, 1998), p.87

15 Palkin, 'S Veroy v Pobedu', pp.59–60

16 Volkovsky, *Blokada Leningrada*, p.118

17 Y. Syakov,'Chislennosti Poteri Germanskoy Gruppy Armiy 'Sever' v Khode Bitvy za Leningrad (1941–1944 gg)' in *Voprosy Istorii* (Rossiyskaya Akademiya Nauk, Moscow, 2008), No. 1, pp.133–36

18 *Bundesarchiv-Militärarchiv Freiburg*, RW 6/556, 6/558

19 G. Krivosheyev, *Soviet Casualties and Combat Losses*, p.312; Mosunov, *Bitva za Sinyavinskiye Vysoty*, pp.287–92

20 Glantz, *The Battle for Leningrad*, pp.227–28

21 Ivanova, *Sinyavino*, p.323

22 N. Stokes, *KV Technical History and Variants* (Air Connection, Mississauga ON, 2010), pp.30–33

23 Zolotarev, *Velikaia Otechestvennaia* (1996), Vol. V, p.350

CHAPTER 13

1   Platonov, *Bitva za Leningrad 1941–1944*, p.99

2   Dzeniskevich, *Leningrad v Osade*, pp.307–08

3   Moniushko, *From Leningrad to Hungary*, p.37

4   Dzeniskevich, *Leningrad v Osade*, pp.88–89

5   A. Raal, K. Nisuma, and A. Meos, 'Pinus Sylvestris L. and other Conifers as Natural Sources of Ascorbic Acid' in *Journal of Pharmacy and Pharmacognosy Research* (Departamento de Ciencias Farmacéuticas, Antofagasta 2018), 6[2], p.90

6   Platonov, *Bitva za Leningrad 1941–1944*, p.216

7   S. Rusagov, *Ladoga Rodnaya: Vospominaniya Veteranov Nrasnoznamennoy Ladoshsnoy Flotilii* (Lenizdat, 1969), pp.44–45

8   Ibid., p.45

9 Ibid., pp.74–77

10 Ibid., p.275

11 Ibid., pp.357–58

12 *Laatokan Rannikkoprikaatin Esikunta. Sotapäiväkirja. 1.3. – 31.3.42, Tiedosto 2* (available at www.ariksto.fi), pp.630–31

13 Platonov, *Bitva za Leningrad 1941–1944*, p.218

14 Ibid., p.155

15 Afanasyev, *Front Bez Tyla*, p.142

16 Ibid., pp.144–46

17 Ibid., p.151

18 Ibid., p.148

19 W. Hubatsch (ed.), *Hitlers Weisungen für die Kriegsführung 1939–1945* (Bernard & Graefe, Koblenz, 1983), pp.275–76

20 Afanasyev, *Front Bez Tyla*, p.172

CHAPTER 14

1 A. Weeks, *Russia's Life-Saver: Lend-Lease Aid to the USSR in World War II* (Lexington, Lanham MD, 2004), p.9

2 J. Hayward, *Stopped at Stalingrad: The Luftwaffe and Hitler's Defeat in the East 1942–1943* (University Press of Kansas, Lawrence KS, 1998), pp.152–60

3 For a comprehensive account of the fighting in the central sector in 1942, see P. Buttar, *Meat Grinder: The Battles for the Rzhev Salient, 1942–1943* (Osprey, Oxford, 2022)

4 I. Moshchanskiy, *Proryv Blokady Leningrada. Epizody Velikoy Osady 19 Avgusta 1942–30 Yanvarya 1843 goda* (Veche, Moscow, 2010), p.6

5 M. Voloshin, *Razvedchiki Vsegda Vperedi* (Voyenizdat, Moscow, 1977), pp.43–44

6 B. Gorbachevsky, *Rzhevskaya Myasorubka. Vremya Otvagi. Zadacha – Vyzhit'!* (Eksmo, Moscow, 2007), pp.135–36

7 See J. Cullen, R. Walck and J. Young, *Corps and Division Planner's Guide to Reconstitution Operations* (Center for Army Lessons Learned, Fort Leavenworth KS, 2020)

8 Ibid., pp.7–8

9 F. Dostoyevsky, *Crime and Punishment* (Penguin, Harmondsworth, 2002), p.610

BIBLIOGRAPHY

Bundesarchiv-Militärarchiv Freiburg
Gosudarstvennyi Arkhiv Smolensko Oblasti Smolensk
National Archives and Records Administration, College Park MD
Russkii Arkhiv: Velikaia Otechestvennaia (Terra, Moscow)
Tsentr Dokumentatsii Noveishei Istorii Smokenskoi Oblastii Smolensk
Tsentral'nyy Arkhiv Ministerstva Oborony, Moscow
Tsentralnyi Gosudarstvennyi Arkhiv Istoriko-Politicheskikh Dokumentov Sankt-Peterburga
    St Petersburg

Istoriya (Pevroye Sentyabrya, Moscow)
Izvestiia Tsentralnogo Komiteta KPSS (Izvestiia, Moscow)
Journal of Contemporary History (Sage, London)
Journal of Pharmacy and Pharmacognosy Research (Departamento de Ciencias
    Farmacéuticas, Antofagasta)
Literaturnaia Gazeta (Moscow)
Mass Violence and Resistance – Research Network (Academie Sciences-Politiques, Paris)
Military Review (Army University Press, Fort Leavenworth KS)
Nezavisimoye Voyennoye Obozreniye (Moscow)
Proceedings of Petrozavodsk State University, Social Sciences and Humanities (Petrozavodsk)
Rodina (FGBU Redaktsiya Rossiyskoy Gazety, Moscow)
Russian Review (Wiley, Hoboken NJ)
Sbornik Boevykh Dokumentov Velikoi, Otechestvennoi (Voenizdat, Moscow)
Sovetskii Voin (Voyennoi Izdatelstvo NKO SSSR, Moscow)
Veteran (Lenizdat, Moscow)
Voenno-Istoricheskii Zhurnal (Russian Ministry of Defence, Moscow)
Voprosy Istorii (Rossiyskaya Akademiya Nauk, Moscow)
Vosprosy Literatury (Rossiyskaya Akademiya Nauk, Moscow)
Zvezda (Leningrad)

https://iremember.ru/

447

Adamovich, A. and Granin, D. *Blokadnaia Kniga* (Azbuka, St Petersburg, 2020)

Afanasyev, N., *Front Bez Tyla. Zapiski Partizanskogo Komandira* (Lenizdat, Leningrad, 1983)

Akten zur Deutschen Auswärtigen Politik 1918–1945 Serie D (Hermes KG, Bonn, 1964)

Almukhamedov, I., *Nepokorennaia Zemlia Pskovskaia, 1941–1944: Dokumenty I Materialy iz Istorii Partizanskogo Dviskheniia i Part.-Komsomolskogo Podpolia v Gody Velikoi Otechestvennoi Voiny* (Lenizdat, Leningrad, 1969)

Anderson, M., *Symphony for the City of the Dead: Dmitri Shostakovich and the Siege of Leningrad* (Candlewick, Somerville MA, 2017)

Andreev, A., *Ot Pervogo Mgnoveniya – Do Poslednego* (Voyenizdat, Moscow, 1984)

Andreeva, E., *Vlasov and the Russian Liberation Movement: Soviet Reality and Émigré Theories* (Cambridge University Press, Cambridge, 1987)

Andreyevich, T., *Srazhalis na Volkhove* (Lenizdat, Leningrad, 1986)

Antonov-Ovseyenko, A., *The Time of Stalin: Portrait of a Tyranny* (Harper, New York, 1983)

Antonov-Ovseyenko, V., *V Semnadtsatom Godu* (Gosudarstvennoe Izd-vo Khudozhestvennoi Lit-ry, Moscow, 1933)

Armstrong, J., *Soviet Partisans in World War II* (University of Wisconsin Press, Madison WI, 1964)

Askin, K., *War Crimes Against Women: Prosecution in International War Crimes Tribunals* (Martinus Nijhoff, Dortrecht, 1997)

Avrich, P., *Kronstadt, 1921* (Princeton University Press, Princeton NJ, 2014)

Bardin, S., *I Shtatskiye Nadeli Shineli* (Sovetskaya Rossiya, Moscow, 1974)

Berggolts, O., *Stikhotvoreniya – Rodina Moya* (Khudozhestvennaya Literatura, Moscow, 1967)

Bidermann, G., Zumbro, D. (ed. and trans.), *In Deadly Combat: A German Soldier's Memoir of the Eastern Front* (University Press of Kansas, Lawrence KS, 2000)

Buchheit, G., *Der Deutsche Geheimdienst. Geschichte der Militärischen Abwehr* (Paul List Verlag, Munich, 1966)

Burdick, C., Jacobsen, H.-A. (eds), *The Halder War Diary 1939–1942* (Greenhill, London, 1988)

Burdzhalov, E., *Vtoraia Russkaia Revoliutsiia* (Nauka, Moscow, 1967, 2 volumes)

Burov, A., *Blokada Den' za Den'* (Lenizdat, Leningrad, 1979)

Buttar, P., *Between Giants; The Battle for the Baltics in World War II* (Osprey, Oxford, 2013)

Buttar, P., *The Splintered Empires: The Eastern Front 1917–21* (Osprey, Oxford, 2017)

Buttar, P., *Meat Grinder: The Battles for the Rzhev Salient, 1942–43* (Osprey, Oxford, 2022)

Carius, O., Edwards, R. (trans.), *Tigers in the Mud: The Combat Career of German Panzer Commander Otto Carius* (Stackpole, Mechanicsburg PA, 2003)

Carrell, P., *Hitler Moves East 1941–1943* (Little & Brown, Boston MA, 1963)

Chamberlain, P. and Doyle, H., *Encyclopaedia of German Tanks of World War Two* (Arms & Armour, London, 1999)

Clark, A., *Barbarossa: The Russian-German Conflict 1941–45* (Hutchinson, London, 1965)

Clasen, C., *Generaloberst Georg-Hans Reinhardt 1887–1963* (Zeitungsverlag RM, Stuttgart, 1976)

Clemmesen, M. and Faulkner, M. (eds), *Northern European Overture to War, 1939–1941: From Memel to Barbarossa* (Brill, Leiden, 2013)

Conquest, R., *The Great Terror: A Reassessment* (Oxford University Press, Oxford, 2008)

Courtois, S., *The Black Book of Communism: Crimes, Terror, Repression* (Harvard University Press, Cambridge MA, 1999)

Cullen, J., Walck, R. and Young, J., *Corps and Division Planner's Guide to Reconstitution Operations* (Center for Army Lessons Learned, Fort Leavenworth KS, 2020)

Der Prozess Gegen die Hauptkriegsverbrecher vor dem Internationalen Militärgerichtshof (Komet MA, Frechen, 2001, 42 volumes)

Diedrich, T., *Paulus: Das Trauma von Stalingrad. Eine Biographie* (Brill Schöningh, Paderborn, 2008)

Dostoyevsky, F., *Crime and Punishment* (Penguin, Harmondsworth, 2002)

Dzeniskevich, A. (ed.), *Leningrad v Osade: Sbornik Dokumentov o Geroicheskoi Oborone Leningrada v gody Velikoi Otechestvennoi Voiny 1941–1944* (Liki Rossii, St Petersburg, 1995)

Dzeniskevich, A., Kovalchuk, V., Sobolev, G., Tsamutali, A. and Shishkin, V. (eds), *Nepokorennyy Leningrad* (Nauka, Leningrad, 1970)

Erickson, J., *The Road to Stalingrad* (Cassell, London, 2003)

Evans, R., *The Third Reich at War* (Penguin, Harmondsworth, 2008)

Fadeev, A., *Leningrad in the Days of the Blockade* (Greenwood, Westport CT, 1977)

Fediuninsky, I., *Podnyatyye po Trevoge* (Voenizdat, Moscow, 1961)

Figes, O., *A People's Tragedy: The Russian Revolution 1891–1924* (Bodley Head, London, 2014)

Gavrilov, B., *Dolina Smerti. Tragediya I Podvig 2-y Udarnoy Armii* (Institut Sossiyskoy Istorii RAN, Moscow, 1999)

Georgi, I., *Opisanie Rossiyisko-Imperatorskogo Stolichnogo Goroda Sankt-Peterburga I Dostopamiatnostei v Okrestnostiakh Onogo, c Planom* (Liga, St Petersburg, 1996)

Gerodnik, G., *Moya Frontovaya Iyzhnya* (Srednya Ural, Sverdlovsk, 1987)

Getty, J., Naumov, O., Sher, B. (eds), *The Road to Terror: Stalin and the Self-Destruction of the Bolsheviks, 1932–1939* (Yale University Press, New Haven CT, 2010)

Glantz, D., *Stumbling Colossus: The Red Army on the Eve of World War* (University Press of Kansas, Lawrence KS, 1998)

Glantz, D., *The Battle for Leningrad 1941–1944* (University Press of Kansas, Lawrence KS, 2002)

Gorbachevsky, B., *Rzhevskaya Myasorubka. Vremya Otvagi. Zadacha – Vyzhit'!* (Eksmo, Moscow, 2007)

Gordienko, I., *Iz Boevogo Proshlogo 1914–1918gg* (Gos Isd-Vo Polit Lit-Ry, Moscow, 1957)

Gorodetsky, G., *Grand Delusion: Stalin and the German Invasion of Russia* (Yale University Press, New Haven CT, 1999)

Hasegawa, T., *The February Revolution: Petrograd 1917* (University of Washington Press, Seattle WA, 1981)

Haupt, W., *Die 8. Panzer-Division im Zweiten Weltkrieg* (Podzun-Pallas, Friedberg, 1987)

Hayward, J., *Stopped at Stalingrad: The Luftwaffe and Hitler's Defeat in the East 1942–1943* (University Press of Kansas, Lawrence KS, 1998)

Hermann, A. and Fröhlich, E. (eds), *Die Tagebücher von Joseph Goebbels: Teil II Diktate 1941–1945* (Saur, Munich, 1996, 15 volumes)

Hébert, V., *Hitler's Generals on Trial: The Last War Crimes Tribunal at Nuremburg* (University of Kansas Press, Lawrence KS, 2010)

Hoffmann, M. and Nowak, K., *Die Aufzeichnungen des Generalmajors Max Hoffmann* (Verlag für Kulturpolitik, Berlin, 1929)

Höhne, H. and Brownjohn, J. (trans.), *Canaris* (New York, 1979)

Hubatsch, W. (ed.), *Hitlers Weisungen für die Kriegsführung 1939–1945* (Bernard & Graefe, Koblenz, 1983)

Ivanova, I., *Sinyavino: Osenniye Boi 1941–1942 godov: Sbornik Vospominaniy Uchastnikov Sinyavinskikh Srazheniy* (Vesti, St Petersburg, 2012)

Jones, M., *Leningrad: State of Siege* (John Murray, London, 2008)

Jordan, J. (ed.), *Warship 2009* (Conway, London, 2009)

Kay, A., *Exploitation, Resettlement, Mass Murder: Political and Economic Planning for German Occupation Policy in the Soviet Union, 1940–1941* (Berghahn, New York, 2006)

Khrushchev, N., *Vremya, Lyudi, Vlast: Vospominaniya* (Novosti, Moscow, 1999)

Khuze, O., 'Blakadnyy Dnevnik Olgi Fedorovny Khuze', available at www.militera.lib.ru /huze_of01/huze_of01.html

Klee, E., Riess, V. and Dressen, W. (eds), *Schöne Zeiten: Judenmord aus der Sicht der Täter und Gaffer* (Fischer, Frankfurt am Main, 1998)

Klee, E., *Das Personenlexikon zum Dritten Reich. Wer war Was vor und nach 1945* (Fischer, Frankfurt-am-Main, 2007)

Kleinfeld, G., *Hitler's Spanish Legion: The Blue Division in Russia in WWII* (Stackpole, Mechanicsburg PA, 2014)

Kliuchevsky, V., *Sochineniia v Vosmi Tomakh* (Izdanie Politicheskoy Literatury Puis Socialno-Ekonomicheskoya Literaturi, Moscow, 1956–59, 8 volumes)

Klukowski, Z., *Dziennik z lat Okupacji Zamojçzczyzny* (Lubelska Społdzielnia Wydawn, Lublin, 1959)

Knox, A., *With the Russian Army 1914–1917* (Hutchison, London, 1921)

Konkov, V., *Vremya Dalekoye I Blizkoye* (Voenizdat, Moscow, 1985)

Konstantinov, D., *Ya Srazhalsya v Krasnoy Armii* (Novoe Slovo, Buenos Aires, 1952)

Kovalchuk, V. (ed.), *Ocherki Istorii Leningrada: Period Velikoi Otechestvennoi Voiny Sovetskogo Soiuza, 1941–1945 gg* (Nauka, Leningrad, 1967)

Kovalchuk, V., *Leningrad I Bolshaya Zemlya* (Nauka, Leningrad, 1975)

Kovalchuk, V. (ed.), *V Tylu Vraga Borba Partizan I Podpolshchivkov na Okkupirovannoy Territorii Oblasti* (Lenizdat, Leningrad, 1979)

Kovalchuk, V., Lomagin, N., Shishkin, V., *Leningradskaia Epopeia: Organizatsiia Oborony I Naselenie Goroda* (Sankt-Peterburgskii Filial In-ta Rossiiskoi Istorii Rossiskoi Akademii Nauk, St Petersburg, 1995)

Kovalev, B., *Dobrovolci na Cyzoi Voyne. Ocerki Istorii Goluboi Divizii* (Novgorodskiy Gosudarstveneyi Universitet, Novgorod, 2014)

Krivosheyev, G., *Soviet Casualties and Combat Losses in the Twentieth Century* (Greenhill, London, 1997)

Kulkov, E., Rsheshevskii, O., Shukman, H. (eds), *Stalin and the Soviet–Finnish War, 1939–1940* (Frank Cass, London, 2002)

Kvachkov, V., *Spetsnaz Rossii* (Russkaya Panorama, Moscow, 2007)

Laatokan Rannikkoprikaatin Esikunta. Sotapäiväkirja. 1.3. – 31.3.42, Tiedosto 2, available at www.ariksto.fi

Leeb, W. von and Meyer, G. (ed.), *Generalfeldmarschall Wilhelm Ritter von Leeb: Tagebuchaufzeichnungen und Lagebeurteilungen aus Zwei Weltkriegen* (Deutsche Verlags-Anstalt, Stuttgart, 1976)

Lelyushenko, D., *Moskva-Stalingrad-Berlin-Praga. Zapiski Komandarma* (Nauka, Moscow, 1987)

Leskinen, J., Juutilainen, A., *Jatkosodan Pikkujättiläinen* (Werner Söderström, Helsinki, 2005)

Lincoln, W.B., *Red Victory: A History of the Russian Civil War* (Simon & Schuster, London, 1990)

Lincoln, W.B., *Passage Through Armageddon: The Russians in War and Revolution* (Oxford University Press, Oxford, 1994)

Lincoln, W.B., *Sunlight at Midnight: St Petersburg and the Rise of Modern Russia* (Basic, New York, 2002)

Lubbeck, W., Hurt, D., *At Leningrad's Gates* (Casemate, Newbury, 2006)

McLaughlin, S., *Russian & Soviet Battleships* (Naval Institute Press, Annapolis MD, 2003)

Mallmann, K.-M., Angrick, A., Matthus, J. and Cüppers, M. (eds), *Die Ereignismeldungen UdSSR 1941: Dokumente der Einsatzgruppen in der Sowjetunion* (WGB, Darmstadt, 2011)

Manstein, E. von and Powell, A. (trans. and ed.), *Lost Victories* (Presidio, Novato CA, 1982)

Margulies, M., *God Intervencii* (Izd. Z I Grżebina, Berlin, 1923, 2 volumes)

Massie, R., *Peter the Great: His Life and Work* (Random House, London, 1992)

Matthews, O., *An Impeccable Spy: Richard Sorge, Stalin's Master Agent* (Bloomsbury, London, 2019)

Megargee, G., *Inside Hitler's High Command* (University Press of Kansas, Lawrence KS, 2000)

Mendelson, J. (ed.), *The Holocaust: Selected Documents in Eighteen Volumes* (Garland, New York, 1982)

Melnikov, P., *Zalpy s Berega* (Voyenizdat, Moscow, 1971)

Meretskov, K., *Na Sluzhbe Narodu* (Politizdat, Moscow, 1968)

Michelson, V., Yalygin, M., *Vozdushnyy Most* (Politizdat, Moscow, 1982)

Mints, I., *Istoriia Velikogo Oktiabria* (Nauka, Moscow, 1967, 2 volumes)

Moniushko, E., Sheremet, O. (trans.), *From Leningrad to Hungary: Notes of a Red Army Soldier, 1941–1946* (Cass, Abingdon, 2005)

Moreno Juliá, X., *La División Azul: Sangre Española en Rusia 1941–1945* (Critica, Barcelona, 2005)

Moshchanskiy, I., *Proryv Blokady Leningrada. Epizody Velikoy Osady 19 Avgusta 1942–30 Yanvarya 1843 goda* (Veche, Moscow, 2010)

Mosunov, V., *Bitva za Sinyavinskiye Vysoty. Mginskaya Duga 1941–1942 gg* (Yauza, Moscow, 2015)

Mukhina, E., *Sokhrani Moiu Pechalnuiu Istoriu* (Azbuka, St Petersburg, 2011)

Müller, R.-D., *Germany and the Second World War* (Oxford University Press, Oxford, 2003)

Naida, S., Budennyi, S., *Istoriia Grazhdanskoi Voiny v SSSR* (Izd-vo Politicheskoi Litry, Moscow, 1957–1959, 4 volumes)

Neitzel, S., *Deutsche Krieger: Vom Kaiserreich zur Berliner Republik – eine Militärgeschichte* (Propyläen, Berlin, 2020)

Niepold, G., *Ursprung und Lebenslauf der Pommerschen 12. Panzerdivision* (Pechlerberg, Koblenz, 1988)

Núñez Seixas, X., *The Spanish Blue Division on the Eastern Front 1941–1945* (University of Toronto Press, Toronto, 2022)

Paul, W., *Brennpunkte: Die Geschichte der 6. Panzerdivision 1937–1945* (Biblio, Osnabrück, 1984)

Pavlov, D., *Leningrad v Blokade* (Voenizdat, Moscow, 1958)

Pavlov, D., *Stoykost* (Politisdat, Moscow, 1983)

Platonov, S., *Bitva za Leningrad 1941–1944* (Voenizdat, Moscow, 1964)

Ponomarenko, P., Samsonov, A., *Vsenarodnaya Borba Nemetsko-Fashistskikh Zakhvatchikov 1941–1944* (Nauka, Moscow)

Popov, A., *NKVD I Partizanskoye Dvizheniye* (Olma, Moscow, 2003)

Rabinovich, A., *The Bolsheviks Come To Power: The Revolution of 1917 in Petrograd* (Vintage, New York, 2004)

Reid, A., *Leningrad: Tragedy of a City Under Siege 1941–44* (Bloomsbury, New York, 2012)

Restayn, J., *Tiger I on the Eastern Front* (Histoire & Collections, Paris, 2001)

Roberts, G., *Stalin's General: The Life of Georgy Zhukov* (Icon, London, 2013)

Rohwer, J., *Chronology of the War at Sea 1939–1945 The Naval History of World War Two* (Naval Institute Press, Annapolis MD, 2005)

Ruble, B., *Leningrad: Shaping a Soviet City* (University of California Press, Berkeley CA, 1990)

Rudel, H., *Stuka Pilot* (Black House, London, 2013)

Rusagov, S., *Ladoga Rodnaya: Vospominaniya Veteranov Nrasnoznamennoy Ladoshsnoy Flotilii* (Lenizdat, 1969)

Salisbury, H., *The 900 Days: The Siege of Leningrad* (Da Capo, Cambridge MS, 2003)

Sbornik Voenno-Istoricheskikh Materialov Velikoi Otechstvennoi Voiny (Voenizdat, Moscow, 1960)

Schleglov, D., *V Opelchenii* (Voenizdat, Moscow, 1960)

Schwartz, B., *Music and Musical Life in Soviet Russia 1917–1970* (Norton, New York, 1973)

Sebag Montefiore, S., *Stalin: In the Court of the Red Tsar* (Weidenfeld & Nicholson, London, 2003)

Shaporina, L., *Dnevnik* (Novoe Literaturnoe Obozrenie, Moscow, 2017)

Simmons, C., Perlina, N., *Writing the Siege of Leningrad: Women's Diaries, Memoirs and Documentary Prose* (University of Pittsburgh Press, Pittsburgh PA, 2002)

Simonov, K., *Glazami Cheloveka Moyego Pokeleniya: Razmyshleniya o Staline* (Novosti, Moscow, 1988)

Smirtukov, M., *Sovetskii Gosudarstvennyi Apparat Upravleniya: Voprosy Organiza Tsii I Deyatelnosti Tsentralnykh Organov* (Politizdat, Moscow, 1982)

Sokolov, B., *Taiyni Finskoi Voiny* (Veche, Moscow, 2000)

Solzhenitsyn, A., *The Gulag Archipelago* (Vintage, London, 2018)

Spence, B., *Trust No One: The Secret World of Sidney Reilly* (Feral House, Port Townsend WA, 2002)

Stahlberg, A., Crampton, P. (trans.), *Bounden Duty: The Memoirs of a German Officer 1932–45* (Brassey, London, 1990)

Stang, K., *Kollaboration und Massenmord: die Litauische Hilfspolizei, das Rollkommando Hamann und die Ermordung der Litausichen Juden* (Lang, Frankfurt am Main, 1996)

Stokes, N., *KV Technical History and Variants* (Air Connection, Mississauga ON, 2010)

Stolfi, R., *German Panzers on the Offensive* (Schiffer, Atglen PA, 2003)

Stoves, R., *Die 1. Panzer-Division 1935–1945* (Podzun, Bad Neuheim, 1961)

Streit, C., *Keine Kameraden: Die Wehrmacht und die Sowjetischen Kriegsgefangenen* (Dietz, Bonn, 1997)

Suvenirov, O., *Tragediya RKKA 1937–1938* (Terra, Moscow, 1998)

Temkin, G., *My Just War: The Memoir of a Jewish Red Army Soldier in World War II* (Presidio, Novato CA, 1998)

Thurston, R., Bonwetsch, B. (eds), *The People's War: Responses to World War II in the Soviet Union* (University of Illinois Press, Champaign IL, 2000)

Tolstoy, L. and Maude, A. (trans.), *Anna Karenina* (Everyman, London, 1977)

Trevor-Roper, H., *Hitler's War Directives 1939–1945* (Pan, London, 1966)

Trotsky, L., *History of the Russian Revolution* (trans. Eastmann, M., 1922, republished Haymarket, London, 2008)

Ueberschar, G., Wette, W. (eds), *Unternehmen Barbarossa: Der Deutsche Überfall auf die Sowjetunion 1941* (Schöningh, Paderborn, 1984)

Vasilevsky, A., *A Lifelong Cause* (Progress, Moscow, 1981)

Vetrov, A., *Tak I Bylo* (Voenizdat, Moscow, 1982)

Vladimirov, B., *Komdiv: Ot Siniavinskikh Vysot do Elby* (Eksmo, Moscow, 2010)

Volgokonov, D., *Lenin: Life and Legacy* (Harper Collins, London, 1994)

Volkova, I. (ed.), *900 Blokadyi Dnei* (Nash Gorodok, Novosibirsk, 2004)

Volkovsky, N. (ed.), *Blokada Leningrada v Dokumentakh Rassekrechennykh Arkhivov* (Polygon, St Petersburg, 2005)

Voloshin, M., *Razvedchiki Vsegda Vperedi* (Voyenizdat, Moscow, 1977)

Vozhakin, M. (ed.), *Velikaia Otechstvennaia: Komandarmy: Voennyi Biograficheskii Slovar* (Kuchkovo Pole, Moscow, 2005)

Weeks, A., *Russia's Life-Saver: Lend-Lease Aid to the USSR in World War II* (Lexington, Lanham MD, 2004)

Wette, W., *Karl Jäger: Mörder der Litauischen Juden* (Fischer, Frankfurt-am-Main, 2011)

Yarov, S., *Povsednevnaya Zhizn Blokadnogo Leningrada* (Molodaya Gvardiya, Moscow, 2013)

Zalesskiy, K., *Imperiya Stalina. Biograficheskiy Entsiklopedicheskiy Slovar* (Veche, Moscow, 2000)

Zaloga, S. and Grandsen, J., *Soviet Tanks and Combat Vehicles of World War II* (Arms & Armour, London, 1984)

Zherebov, D. (ed.), *Tikhvin, god. 1941* (Lenizdat, Moscow, 1974)

Zhukov, G., *Vospomimaniya I Razmyshleniya* (Olma, Moscow, 2002, 2 volumes)

Ziemke, E. and Bauer, M., *Moscow to Stalingrad: Decision in the East* (Center of Military History, Washington DC, 1987)

Zinovyev, G., *Borba za Petrograd, 15 Oktiabria-6 Noiabria 1919 Goda* (Gos. Izd-vo, Moscow, 1923)

Zolotarev, V., *Velikaia Otechestvennaia* (Terra, Moscow, 1996–2005, 25 volumes)

INDEX